ELECTRONICS OF SOLIDS

McGraw-Hill Physical and Quantum Electronics Series

Related Books from McGraw-Hill Electrical and Electronic Engineering Series

Frederic Emmons Terman, Consulting Editor
W. W. Harman and J. G. Truxal, Associate Consulting Editors

Atwater: Introduction to Microwave Theory
Ghose: Microwave Circuit Theory and Analysis
Greiner: Semiconductor Devices and Applications
Harman: Fundamentals of Electronic Motion
Harrington: Introduction to Electromagnetic Engineering
Harrington: Time-harmonic Electromagnetic Fields
Hayt: Engineering Electromagnetics
Javid and Brown: Field Analysis and Electromagnetics
Rogers: Introduction to Electric Fields
Siegman: Microwave Solid-state Masers
Spangenberg: Fundamentals of Electron Devices
Valdes: The Physical Theory of Transistors
Van Bladel: Electromagnetic Fields

Other Related McGraw-Hill Books

Chodorow and Susskind: Fundamentals of Microwave Electronics
Collin: Field Theory of Guided Waves
Plonsey and Collin: Principles and Applications of Electromagnetic Fields
Uman: Introduction to Plasma Physics

ELECTRONICS OF SOLIDS

Walter R. Beam

Professor of Electrical Engineering, Rensselaer Polytechnic Institute

McGraw-Hill Book Company

New York   St. Louis   San Francisco   Toronto   London   Sydney

Electronics of Solids

To
George F. Corcoran

1900–1964

Preface

Most devices and materials of electrical engineering are based on one or more solid-state phenomena. While some of these phenomena may be treated by such simple relations as Ohm's law, others such as semiconduction require some understanding of the physical foundations of electron band theory and conduction theory. With the increasing importance of transistors, masers, ferrites, and other solid-state applications, more electronic engineers must have the background necessary to understand and to develop them further. The fundamental research carried out initially by physicists and chemists gives way to development, refinement, and exploitation by engineers. It is mainly to these solid-state engineers that this text is addressed. With a deeper understanding of fundamentals, the engineer is better enabled to work creatively in the use of new materials and phenomena. Only by understanding the physical bases of devices is he able to exploit new materials and technology described in the scientific literature.

Academic instruction in solid-state theory is possible to only a limited extent in the usual undergraduate engineering curriculum. Unfortunately, in the traditional curricula, there is little time available for a broadening of subject matter. While the fields of applied physics have expanded tremendously in the past twenty years, the applied mathematics of system and communication theory has experienced similar expansion. These subjects in a more traditional realm of engineering have expanded in the undergraduate curriculum, leaving little opportunity in most schools for applied physics study in undergraduate years.   This text is designed for use in either fourth-year or graduate engineering courses.   Prerequisite course material is therefore limited to differential equations and vector analysis, as well as the customary two-year undergraduate physics sequence and electromagnetic principles.   Other necessary material on modern physics is included in the three final chapters.

Arrangement of the material is in five more or less distinct parts: general background (Appendixes A to C), solid-state fundamentals (Chapters 1 and 2), conduction (Chapters 3 to 6), polarization (Chapters 7 to 9), and electronic transition processes (Chapter 10).   This order is suggested by the greater importance of conduction processes in devices.   The material in each area is given coverage in proportion to device significance or potential.   Treatment of quantum-electronic phenomena at the end is necessitated by their dependence on both magnetic and conduction processes.

Each chapter includes problems numbered to correspond with the section they are intended to illustrate.   While this correspondence restricts to a minor extent the scope of problems, it should be valuable to the reader who intends to accent or to eliminate parts of the material.   Problems are of three basic types: those intended to illustrate application of formulas, those intended to develop skill in deriving new but simple formulas, and those in which the reader is expected to discuss intelligently some philosophical aspects of the text which permit simple extrapolation.

The mathematical level of the text is approximately uniform, limited in the case of geometry-dependent phenomena to one-dimensional solutions where possible.   Phenomena which involve either highly advanced or lengthy theoretical descriptions are in general treated qualitatively, and the appropriate physical models discussed in detail.   Material customarily extends from physical theory to the description of electronic devices, but goes beyond this point in those few instances where only circuit arrangements can demonstrate usefulness of a phenomenon.   The arrangement of material in each area, however, is based not on specific devices, but on the basic physical phenomena themselves.   By this means it is meant to suggest that the devices described represent only special applications of broader principles.

The considerable length of the text makes it more than adequate as the formal basis of a two-semester three-lecture-hour course sequence. The author has used the material in a three-semester program plan, of which the introductory material of the Appendixes A to C and Chapters 1 and 2 form the first semester. Chapters 3 to 6 are used in a second semester on conduction processes, and Chapters 7 to 10 in a third semester. The first semester is preparatory for either of the others, which are offered alternatively. A procedure better suited to the usual two-semester terminal sequence would begin with the first chapter, employing Appendix material as required for the development of concepts in later chapters. A two-semester sequence could cover, for example, needed parts of the introductory material, conduction and semiconduction (Chapters 3 to 5), and those parts of the remaining material adjudged most important by the instructor. The material of Chapters 7 to 9 does not require conduction theory as a background, but statistical physics and quantum-theoretical background is employed in all chapters, to varying degrees.

The "do-it-yourself" reader has been given careful consideration in the preparation of the text material. While the Appendixes do not form a complete short course in modern physics, the background required for an understanding of quantum aspects of solid-state electronics is developed from the essentials, as is statistical mechanics. The quantity and arrangement of problems should also be of value to the serious self-study reader. The book should not be considered a substitute for study in electrical engineering and applied physics technical journals, but rather as preparation therefore.

The author would like to express his appreciation to Rensselaer Polytechnic Institute for the opportunity to prepare this material and present it in trial form to several classes of students. Appreciation is also felt for the efforts of the secretarial staff of the Electrical Engineering Department, in particular Mrs. Betty Mattimore and Miss Sandra Elliott. Were it not for the cooperation of the author's wife and the patience of his two sons, time could not have been found to carry through this project.

Walter R. Beam

Contents

chapter 3.   Electronic Conduction

chapter 4.   Semiconductors

chapter 5.   Semiconductor Junctions and Devices

chapter 6.   Superconductivity

chapter 7.   Dielectrics

chapter 8.   Magnetism

chapter 9.   Domain Magnetics

chapter 10.   Quantum Electronics

appendix A.   Elastic Properties of Solids

appendix B.   Quantum Theory

appendix C.   Statistical Physics

1

Crystals

1.1 Simple Atomic Packing in Solids

Atoms and molecules in a gas move with almost complete independence, with occasional collisions taking place. In liquids, they are in essentially constant contact but retain freedom to move past one another. In the solid state of matter, this freedom is greatly restricted. Some materials usually classed as solids are merely liquids of great viscosity, such as glasses. Many organic solids consist of giant interwoven molecules which cannot flow as liquids because of this irregular interconnection. Both glasses and most plastics are termed *amorphous* solids (solids having no regular structure), to distinguish them from *crystalline* solids. In a crystal, atoms or molecules arrange themselves in regular, three-dimensional structures which are characteristic of the material. Some of the most important electronic properties of solids are influenced profoundly by this crystal structure. In this chapter, we define the elements of arrangement which characterize the structure of crystals, how these arrangements are determined by the atoms comprising the crystal, and how the symmetry of the structure influences the electrical and mechanical properties.

The simplest crystals are formed by elements whose atoms behave as though they were spherical balls. The wave functions of some simple-metal atoms (e.g., copper) are almost spherical, and even for transition metals this is a fair approximation. This apparent sphericity, plus the preference of

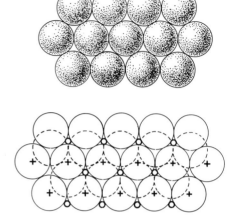

Figure 1.1 (Top) A view from above, of a plane of spheres in contact; (bottom) a third plane may be placed on the second (dashed) in one of two ways. Symbols + mark one set, symbols o the other set.

metals for extremely dense atomic packing, leads to crystal structures which are identical, in symmetry, to arrangements of densely packed spheres.

It is natural, as well as economical, to pack spheres in planar layers. Such layers can be assembled in only one way to achieve minimum area per sphere (Fig. 1.1). Each sphere is in contact with six others surrounding it, in the plane. In packing a second layer atop the first we might place each sphere in the second layer directly above one in the first layer, but the second layer will then rise higher than if the spheres of the second layer are placed over the pockets (called *voids*) *between* spheres of the first layer. Using spheres of diameter d, the additional height required for the second layer is only $\sqrt{\frac{2}{3}}d$. A third layer may be added in the same way; the figure reveals that there are now *two* ways of locating spheres of the third layer, both requiring the same volume. The spheres may be placed either directly over spheres of the *first* layer or, alternatively, in a third set of locations. Each successive layer may again be placed in one of two ways. Proceeding in this way, many layers can be added, each with the same planar area per sphere and the same added height. If we indicate by the letters A, B, C the three distinct sets of locations possible for the first three layers, any set of planar layers can be described by a set of letters, such as $ABABAB$ . . . , or $ABCABCABC$ . . . , describing the location of each layer in the set. The alphabetical symbolism here is not unique, for $ABABAB$ is completely equivalent to $BCBCBC$

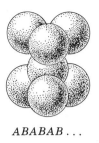

ABABAB . . .   ABCABCABC . . .

Figure 1.2

or $CACACA$. Maximum-density packing requires only that successive layers assume different positions.

A crystal in which all atoms are identical requires identical atomic *environments*. This limits the important close-packed arrangements to only two, the $ABABAB$ . . . and the $ABCABCABC$ . . . patterns. The environment of an atom in the $ABABAB$ packing is depicted in Fig. 1.2. Above it are three atoms at the corners of a triangle, around it are six atoms at the corners of a hexagon, and below it are another three atoms in a triangle. This *particular* packing, with its many 60 and 120° angles, is termed by crystallographers the *hexagonal close-packed structure*, abbreviated hcp.

The environment of an atom in the $ABCABC$ . . . arrangement is slightly but significantly different. The array of three atoms above the central atom is rotated 60° from the three-atom group in the lower plane. Atoms in each plane have similar environments, however, for any plane has adjacent neighboring planes of different types. Although in the form shown in the figure it is difficult to detect much difference between this and $ABABAB$ packing, 14 spheres in the $ABCABC$ array form a *cube* (Fig. 1.3). Since the cubic figure is outlined by only eight of the spheres, while the others appear centered in each of the six square faces of the cube, this is termed a *face-centered cubic structure*, abbreviated fcc. It may be difficult to visualize this without actually making a three-dimensional model; for example, ping-pong balls attached to one another with cellulose cement make a convenient model. A characteristic *symmetry* of cubic forms may be observed by holding any cube so that one corner lies directly behind a diagonally opposite corner (e.g., points A and H in Fig. 1.3c). With this line as an axis, a cube may be rotated 120° to three consecutive positions (the corners B, C, D

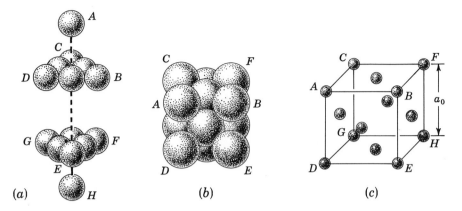

Figure 1.3 (a) Parts from four adjacent close-packed planes, exploded view; (b) combined to form a cubic arrangement; (c) the conventional representation, face-centered cubic structure.

may be interchanged), at each of which it will look the same. Cubic forms are said to have *threefold rotational symmetry* about this diagonal axis, which is the *body diagonal* of the cube. A line such as AE is called a *face diagonal*. Many other symmetry properties of crystals, as well as notation defining major faces and directions, are defined later in this chapter.

These relatively simple close-packed structures are characteristic of a wide range of metallic crystals (Table 1.1). Other elements favor arrangements which are not closest packings of spheres. In some *nonmetallic* elements, the crystal structures are defined in large measure by the valence of the atoms, each atom having as many others adjacent to it as it has valence electrons. This clearly does not apply to close-packed metals, which have 12 adjacent atoms. Many other metals assume a nearly close-packed structure, having only 8 adjacent atoms, the *body-centered cubic* structure.

The environs of an atom in bcc are depicted in Fig. 1.4. If the atoms are still imagined to be spherical in shape, this arrangement will not occupy minimum volume. One may make a simple comparison between the efficiency of packing in the body-centered and close-packed arrangements if each atom is considered to be a sphere of diameter d. In any *closest* packing, the planar spacing (height) is $\sqrt{\frac{2}{3}}\, d$, the spacing per row in the plane is $\sqrt{\frac{3}{4}}\, d$, and the spacing of atoms in the row is d. The volume per atom in any closest packing is

Table 1.1 Crystal structure of the elements

Elements not listed have less common and in general more complex structures. As and Bi share a trigonal structure, Se and Te another trigonal structure. The graphite form of carbon has a hexagonal structure. None of the three possible structures of Mn is close-packed, but they have cubic or tetragonal symmetry. S and Se have a variety of structures. Structure data from R. W. G. Wyckoff, "Crystal Structures," Interscience Publishers, Inc., New York, 1948–1960; specific-density values, for room temperature, from "Periodic Table of the Elements," Central Scientific Co., Chicago, 1962.

Face-centered cubic structure

Element	Name	Cube edge a_0, angstroms	Specific density, g/cm^3
Ag	Silver	4.0862	10.5
Al	Aluminum	4.04934 (25°C)	2.71
Ar	Argon	5.43 (-253°C)	
Au	Gold	4.07864 (25°C)	19.3
Ca	Calcium	5.576	1.55
Ce	Cerium	5.150	6.9
β-Co	Cobalt	3.548^a	8.75
Cu	Copper	3.61496 (18°C)	8.9
γ-Fe	Iron	3.5910 (22°C)	8.02
Ir	Iridium	3.8394 (26°C)	22.4
Kr	Krypton	5.705	
La	Lanthanum	5.296	6.15
Li	Lithium	4.404 (-195°C)	0.53
		4.379 (-194°C)	
Ne	Neon	4.52 (-253°C)	
Ni	Nickel	3.52387 (25°C)	8.9
Pb	Lead	4.9505	11.34
Pd	Palladium	3.8898 (25°C)	12.0
Pr	Praseodymium	5.161	6.5
Pt	Platinum	3.9231 (25°C)	21.45
δ-Pu	Plutonium	4.6370 (320°C)	19
Rh	Rhodium	3.8031 (25°C)	12.5
Sc	Scandium	4.541	3.1
Sr	Strontium	6.0847 (25°C)	2.6
Th	Thorium	5.05	11.7
Xe	Xenon	6.25	
Yb	Ytterbium	5.460	7.01

Table 1.1   Crystal structure of the elements (continued)

Hexagonal close-packed structure

Element	Name	Planar spacing a_0, angstroms	c_0, angstroms[e]	Specific density, g/cm^3
Be	Beryllium	2.2860	3.5843	1.86
Ca	Calcium	3.98	6.52 (450°C)	1.55
Cd	Cadmium	2.97887	5.61765 (26°C)	8.6
Ce	Cerium	3.65	5.96	6.9
α-Co	Cobalt	2.501	4.066[b]	8.9
Cr	Chromium	2.722	4.427	7.1
Dy	Dysprosium	3.584	5.668 (49°K)	8.56
		3.596	5.649 (300°K)	
Er	Erbium	3.558	5.590 (43°K)	9.16
		3.562	5.602 (301°K)	
Gd	Gadolinium	3.629	5.796 (106°K)	
		3.639	5.777 (349°K)	7.95
He	Helium	3.57	5.83 (−271°C)	
Hf	Hafnium	3.1967	5.0578 (26°C)	13.3
Ho	Holmium	3.564	5.630	8.76
La	Lanthanum	3.75	6.07	6.15
Li	Lithium	3.09	4.83 (−195°C)	0.53
Lu	Lutecium	3.516	3.566	
Mg	Magnesium	3.20927	5.21033 (25°C)	1.74
Nd	Neodymium	3.657	5.902	7.0
Ni	Nickel	2.65	4.33	8.9
Os	Osmium	2.7352	4.3190 (20°C)	22.5
Pr	Praseodymium	3.669	5.920	6.5
Rh	Rhenium	2.7608	4.4582 (25°C)	21.0
Ru	Ruthenium	2.70389	4.28168 (20°C)	12.4
Sc	Scandium	3.309	5.255	3.1
β-Sr	Strontium	4.32	7.06 (248°C)	2.6
Tb	Terbium	3.592	5.673	8.33
Ti	Titanium	2.950	4.686 (25°C)	4.5
Tl	Thallium	3.456	5.525	11.8
Tu	Thulium	3.530	5.575	9.35
Y	Yttrium	3.636	5.761	4.34
Zn	Zinc	2.6648	4.9467 (25°C)	7.14
α-Zr	Zirconium	3.232	5.147 (25°C)	6.4

Body-centered cubic structure

Element	Name	Cube edge a_0, angstroms	Specific density, g/cm^3
Ba	Barium	5.025 (26°C)	3.59
Cr	Chromium	2.8839 (25°C)	7.1
Cs	Cesium	6.05 (−185°C)	1.9

Table 1.1 Crystal structure of the elements (continued)

Body-centered cubic structure

Element	Name	Cube edge a_0, angstroms	Specific density, g/cm³
α-Fe	Iron	2.8665 (25°C)	7.86
β-Fe	Iron	2.91 (800°C)	
δ-Fe	Iron	2.94 (1425°C)	
K	Potassium	5.21 (−150°C)	0.86
Li	Lithium	3.5093 (20°C)[c]	0.53
Mo	Molybdenum	3.1473 (25°C)	10.2
Na	Sodium	4.2906 (20°C)	0.97
Nb	Niobium (columbium)	3.3004 (18°C)	8.4
γ-Np	Neptunium	3.52 (ca. 600°C)	19.5
ϵ-Pu	Plutonium	3.638 (500°C)	
Rb	Rubidium	5.63 (−185°C)	1.53
γ-Sr	Strontium	4.85 (614°C)	
Ta	Tantalum	3.3058 (25°C)	16.6
β-Ti	Titanium	3.3065 (900°C)	
Tl	Thallium	3.882	11.85
γ-U	Uranium	3.474	19.05
V	Vanadium	3.040	5.96
W	Tungsten (wolfram)	3.16469 (25°C)	19.3
Zr	Zirconium	3.62 (850°C)	

Diamond structure

Element	Name	Cube edge a_0, angstroms	Specific density, g/cm³
C	Carbon (diamond)	3.56679 (20°C)	3.51
Ge	Germanium	5.65748 (20°C)	5.36
Si	Silicon	5.43086[d] (20°C)	2.33
α-Sn	Tin	6.4912	5.75

[a] In liquid N_2, $a_0 = 3.550$ A; in H_2, $a_0 = 3.557$ A.

[b] Above values *in vacuo*. In N_2, $a_0 = 2.508$ A, $c_0 = 4.068$ A; in H_2, $a_0 = 2.512$ A, $c_0 = 4.072$ A.

[c] At −183°C, $a_0 = 3.4832$ A.

[d] At 1300°C, $a_0 = 5.445$ A.

[e] In an ideal hcp structure, $c_0 = 2\sqrt{\frac{2}{3}}\,a_0$, but atomic asymmetry often alters this dimension. See Fig. 1.8 for definitions.

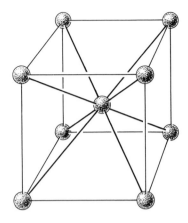

Figure 1.4 The body-centered cube. (The atoms on the sides of the cube form sides of adjacent cubes.)

therefore $d^3/\sqrt{2}$; since the volume of a sphere of diameter d is $\pi d^3/6$, 74 per cent of the space is filled with the spheres. In the body-centered cubic structure, on the other hand, spheres are spaced a distance $(\frac{4}{3})^{\frac{1}{2}}d$ apart in each direction in each plane, and the planes spaced by half that distance, so that the volume per atom is $\frac{4}{3}(1/\sqrt{3})d^3$. This allows only 68 per cent of the space to be filled by spheres.

Since atoms are not truly spherical in shape, it is unwise to extrapolate this spherical-packing treatment. It is qualitatively valuable, however, when comparing the volume of spaces (interstices) between atoms in various structures. Those structures for which large spaces exist between atoms can more readily accommodate other atoms as impurities than can those which are closely packed.

1.2 Crystal Lattices

The forms which actual crystals may assume are many and varied, depending mainly on the composition and the valency of the atom(s) involved. Some crystals have relatively simple structures, such as those just discussed. Others are so complex that only actual three-dimensional models serve to describe them adequately; in some cases, in fact, they are not even understood well enough to build a model. *Every* crystal, despite detailed complexity, has, however, a basic three-dimensional *periodicity* by which it may be classified into one of only 14 groups.

To be described as a crystal, an arrangement of atoms must repeat itself at regular intervals in space, just as a

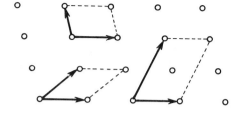

Figure 1.5 Primitive vectors in a two-dimensional lattice. Both choices on the left lead to smallest enclosed areas, closing the figure as shown. The figure on the right does not represent correct primitive vectors.

periodic electrical signal repeats in time. To be periodic, a function of time having period τ must satisfy the *translation operation*

$$f(t + \tau) = f(t) \tag{1.1}$$

The function, when translated (shifted) along the time axis by a distance τ, appears the same as before translation. The period is defined as the *shortest* time interval which translates the function "into itself."

In three dimensions, periodicity requires a *vectorial* definition. This is best supplied through a set of three *translation vectors*, analogous to τ in (1.1). There is a variety of choice of vectors along which one can translate a crystal by a certain distance to translate it into itself (Fig. 1.5), but in a given crystal there are always at least three vectors which, by analogy with the two-dimensional Fig. 1.5, define a minimum enclosed *volume*. Any three of these will serve to define periodicity. These directions will not, in general, be mutually perpendicular; they must not all be coplanar, nor any two parallel; otherwise they will not be capable of describing three-dimensional translations. These minimal translations are termed *primitive translations*, and are defined in direction and length by primitive translation vectors **a**, **b**, and **c**. The periodicity condition on a crystal is then

$$F(\mathbf{r}) = F(\mathbf{r} + m\mathbf{a} + n\mathbf{b} + p\mathbf{c}) \tag{1.2}$$

where m, n, p are integers. The function F may be any unique function of the atomic positions; for example, it might be the electrostatic potential at each point in the solid.

At this point it is desirable to make the distinction between a structure and a lattice. The term *structure* is used to denote an actual atomic arrangement which exists for a real material. For example, the *diamond structure* (Fig. 1.6) denotes a particular atomic arrangement which also serves germanium, silicon, and the "gray" phase of tin,

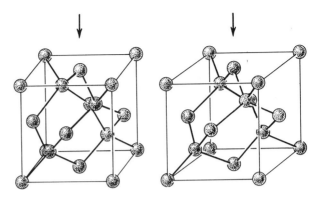

Figure 1.6 The diamond structure.   This is a stereo pair.
Hold the figures about 10 in. from your eyes, using a card to
allow each eye to see only one of the figures.   After some
practice (typically 5 min of frustration), the two images can
be made to merge and a three-dimensional figure is seen.
It is helpful to first merge the two arrows, then look down
at the figure.

as well as carbon.   A *lattice*, on the other hand, denotes only a
particular form of periodicity described as by (1.2).   It
happens that the simple bcc and fcc packings described in the
previous section qualify as structures of particular metals.
At the same time, they define two possible periodic lattices,
to which are given the same titles.   Figure 1.7*a* and *b* illustrate sets of primitive translation vectors for fcc and bcc
lattices.   The diamond structure, however, does not define
a different lattice, for it is equivalent to a *pair* of face-centered
cubic structures shifted by a distance of one-fourth the body
diagonal.   The hexagonal-close-packed structure, as shown in
Fig. 1.7*c*, is not identical with a lattice, since three shortest
translation vectors connecting atoms in adjacent planes do not
satisfy the necessary translation rules.   The true primitive
vector connects *alternate* planes.

Connecting a lattice point O to others by the primitive
translation vectors **a**, **b**, **c**, then joining these points to additional points **a** + **b**, **a** + **c**, **b** + **c**, and **a** + **b** + **c**, makes the
enclosed figure an eight-cornered, six-sided volume (Fig. 1.8).
By the definition of **a**, **b**, and **c** this volume is the smallest
repetitive building block, or "cell," of the lattice; others like it,
placed adjacent in like orientation, would fill out the complete
volume.   There are by definition *no* lattice points in the interior of the cell.   The eight corner points are each shared by

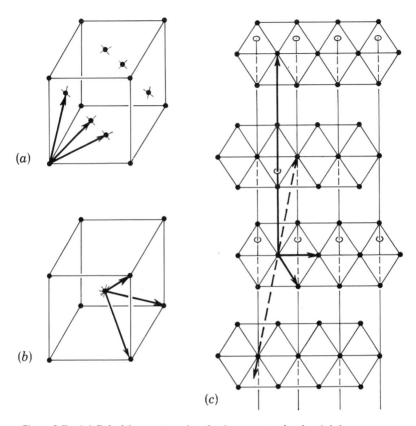

Figure 1.7 (*a*) Primitive vectors for the face-centered cube, joining a corner with three face-centered points; (*b*) primitive vectors for the body-centered cube; (*c*) primitive vectors for a hexagonal close-packed crystal, shown in dark lines.   The dashed line joining the central plane with the one above it is unacceptable as a primitive translation, since the same vector extended down to the plane below *does not* intersect an atom.   The hcp structure is thus more complex than the basic hexagonal lattice (see Fig. 1.8).

seven other cells.   There is precisely one lattice point per lattice cell.   These cells are termed *primitive cells*.   The primitive cells associated with fcc and bcc, though unique in their combinations of vectors **a**, **b**, **c**, are of little use in visualization.   Cubic cells, which enclose the volume of two primitive cells in the case of bcc and four in the case of fcc, are more useful.   They are also repetitive elements, from which the lattice may be constructed, as are primitive cells.   These larger cells are termed *unit cells*.

To define completely a three-dimensional lattice, we need

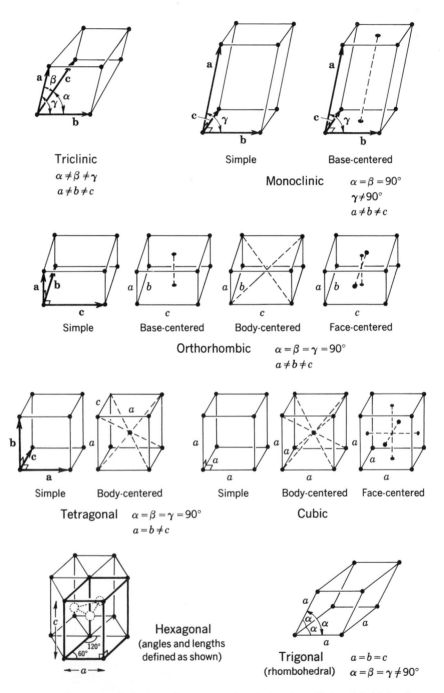

Figure 1.8 The conventional Bravais-lattice unit cells for all 14 distinguishable lattices, together with the conventional lattice constants. The heavy lines outline the conventional primitive (unit) cell of the hexagonal lattice; the spheres indicate the location of atoms in the central plane, for hcp.

only a set of vectors **a**, **b**, and **c**.   If their lengths are arbitrary
and angles not simply defined, the resulting lattice has only
minimal symmetry.   Where the primitive vectors are related
simply, the lattice may have a high degree of symmetry, as
do the cubic lattice forms bcc and fcc.   One can distinguish
only 14 combinations of primitive vectors, which may be
grouped into seven larger *classes*, yielding lattices distinguishable by their symmetry.   These, with the unit (not necessarily
primitive) cell by which they are most easily recognized, are
illustrated in Fig. 1.8.   The a, b, c, α, β, γ values of the unit
cells are quantities by which dimensions of actual crystals
are catalogued.   The nomenclature is such that α is the angle
between b and c, etc., in sensible order.   The letter c is reserved
for a dimension different from the other two, as in tetragonal
lattices.   The letter a is used if all dimensions are equal, as in
cubic lattices.

The number of these *lattice constants* required to define
fully the periodicity of a crystal depends on symmetry, ranging from all six in the triclinic to only one in the cubic class.

The reader may be puzzled as to why the monoclinic
class includes a base-centered lattice, while this does not appear
in tetragonal or cubic classes.   A base-centered tetragonal
lattice could alternatively be described as simple tetragonal, as
one can show by a simple sketch of several adjacent unit cells.
A base-centered cubic is also the equivalent of simple tetragonal.   Placing a face-centered lattice in the tetragonal class
would be incorrect, because the face-centered points could not
qualify as lattice points through primitive translations.

Because of its complete generality, the triclinic lattice
might at first appear very important.   Practically, however,
it is the least important, for there are few materials which
so completely lack symmetry as to require this very lopsided
arrangement.   The main candidates for this are complex
molecules which retain their molecular shape even in crystalline form (for example, $FeSO_4 \cdot 5H_2O$).

The 14 *Bravais lattices*, as they are termed for their dis-
coverer, should be viewed as the "backbones" of actual
crystal structures.   While many elements have one atom
placed at each lattice point, compounds contain several atoms
in each primitive cell.   Where a structure has the periodicity
of a particular lattice, but more than one atom or molecule
occupies each primitive cell, the lattice type is referred to as
the *basis*, and the atoms associated with each lattice point

are enumerated and located. Diamond (Fig. 1.6) is described in detail by an fcc basis with $a = 3.56$ A, with one C atom at each basis point and one at a point $(\frac{1}{4},\frac{1}{4},\frac{1}{4})$. The locations of additional atoms in the unit cell are usually described in this fashion, i.e., in terms of *unit-cell coordinates*. In any case, sketches are useful in defining atomic locations precisely. Although in general the lattice dimensions and structural symmetry can be exactly defined for any crystalline material, exact location of atoms is not straightforward except where other elements of crystal symmetry make it clear. In crystals of pure elements, atomic locations are such as to make all atomic sites equivalent; in diamond, for instance, the four neighbors lie at the corners of a tetragon, with the given atom at center. In crystals composed of complex molecules, however, detailed study may be necessary to define the arrangement of atoms within the unit cell.

1.3 Point-group Symmetries of Crystal Structures

Any crystal structure can be identified with one of the seven crystal classes, and more narrowly with one of the Bravais-lattice groupings according to its translational properties, or periodicity. Structures may be classified in even greater detail, in terms of the symmetry exhibited *about a lattice point.* This means of distinction permits all crystals to be classified into 32 *point groups.* Let us consider the simple body-centered cubic structure as an example. The crystal can be rotated about many possible axes passing through the body-centered position, for example. About axes parallel to the cube sides, the crystal can be rotated any multiple of 90°, and after rotation will appear as before. Rotation about any body diagonal through 120° angles likewise produces equivalent arrangement of atoms, as does 180° rotation about axes parallel to face diagonals. While some of these same operations can be applied to the diamond structure, about axes parallel to cube edges only 180° rotations are possible, to rotate the structure into itself. Many rotations, as well as other operations, are possible. In order to be able to distinguish the 32 point groups, it is necessary to define the nature of meaningful operations about a point. That is, we must define *elements of symmetry:*

 Rotational axes of symmetry were illustrated by the example above. If a crystal rotates into itself by angular motion of $360°/n$ about an axis, the axis is said to have n-fold rotational symmetry. n can have only the values 2 (diad axis), 3 (triad), 4 (tetrad), or 6 (hexad). (Of course, *any* axis might be termed a singlefold axis, but this makes no useful distinctions.)

Inversion axes (again specified as n-fold, with the same limits) define a combined operation: rotation by $360°/n$ about the axis, followed by *inversion* of atoms through some origin O on the axis. Inversion carries an atom described by a radius vector **r** to the point $-$**r**. A crystal may be said to have a singlefold inversion axis if it has *all* atoms in pairs located at **r**, $-$**r** about a properly selected origin. This condition may also be described as a *center of symmetry*.

Mirror planes, also called planes of symmetry, are imaginary planes bisecting the crystal so that the two halves are exact mirror images. Some point groups have many sets of such planes.

Where a crystal has a major axis (as in hexagonal, tetragonal, etc.), this is generally the most important symmetry element. Structures having a single n-fold rotational axis but no other symmetry are described by the symbol n. If the axis is an inversion axis, the symbol $\bar{n}$ is used. A complete symbolic notation has been developed to describe symmetry of each of the 32 groups. Since, however, internationally accepted abbreviations of this symbolism are in even wider use, these will be used without elaboration of the symbolism itself.

The literal description of point-group symmetries, the abbreviated group symbol, an older symbolism (Schoenflies's) still in common use, and simple drawings (*stereograms*) illustrating the symmetry are given in Fig. 1.9, for each of the 32 point groups. A stereogram is an attempt to convey the symmetry in terms of what should be looked on as a simple object of that symmetry. Several schemes are used. The simplest is most useful for groups having a major axis: a series of open and filled circles represent objects below and above (respectively) a plane normal to the principal axis, viewed from along the axis (Fig. 1.10a). In rotation, mirroring, and inversion operations, these figures are invariant. This does not, however, imply that the atoms occupy the positions of the dots, merely positions of like *symmetry*. Straight lines represent mirror planes, viewed parallel to the plane.

A second scheme (Fig. 1.10b) requires one to imagine the

Figure 1.9

International symbol	Schoenflies symbol	Elements of symmetry	Pictorial representation
		Triclinic	
1	C_1	None (every axis a single-fold axis).	
$\bar{1}$	$S_2 = C_i$	An inversion axis, equivalent to a center of symmetry.	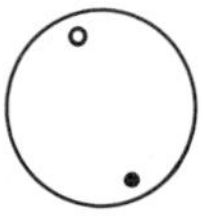
		Monoclinic	
2	C_2	A single diad axis.	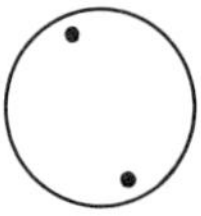
m	C_{1h}	A diad inversion axis, equivalent to a mirror plane.	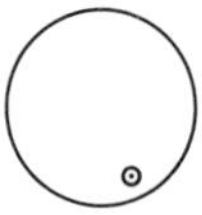
$\dfrac{2}{m}$	C_{2h}	A single diad axis normal to a plane of symmetry, which introduces a center of symmetry.	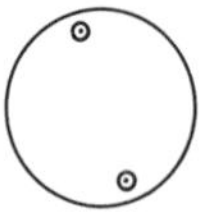
		Orthorhombic	
mm	C_{2v}	Two planes of symmetry at right angles, through a diad axis.	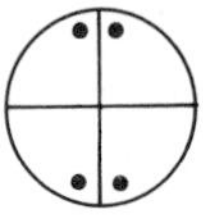
222	$V = D_2$	Three mutually perpendicular diad axes.	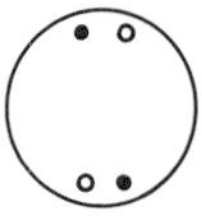
mmm	$V_h = D_{2h}$	Three planes of symmetry intersecting three mutually perpendicular diad axes, which involves a center of symmetry.	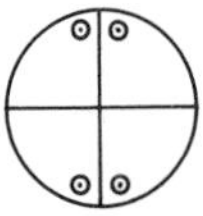

Figure 1.9 *(continued)*

		Tetragonal	
4	C_4	A single tetrad axis.	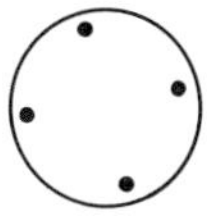
$\overline{4}$	S_4	A single inversion tetrad axis.	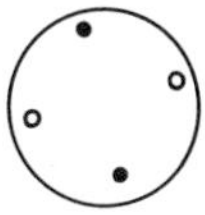
$\dfrac{4}{m}$	C_{4h}	A tetrad axis normal to a plane of symmetry, which involves a center of symmetry.	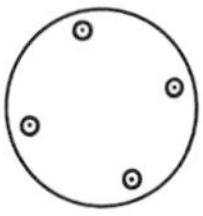
4mm	C_{4v}	Four planes of symmetry at 45° angles, intersecting a tetrad axis.	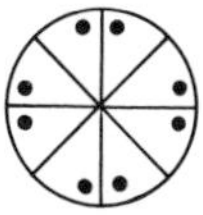
$\overline{4}2m$	$V_d = D_{2d}$	Two planes of symmetry at right angles intersecting in a inversion tetrad axis, and two diad axes at 45° to the planes (but normal to the tetrad axis).	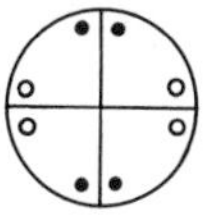
42	D_4	A tetrad axis normal to four diad axes at 45°	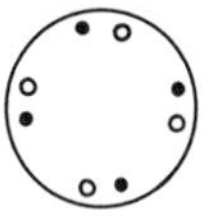
$\dfrac{4}{mmm}$	D_{4h}	A tetrad axis having four planes of symmetry through it at 45°, a diad axis normal to the tetrad axis and through each of the four planes of symmetry, and a plane of symmetry normal to the tetrad axis. Has a center of symmetry.	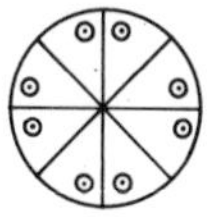
		Cubic	
23	T	Four triad axes and three mutually perpendicular diad axes.	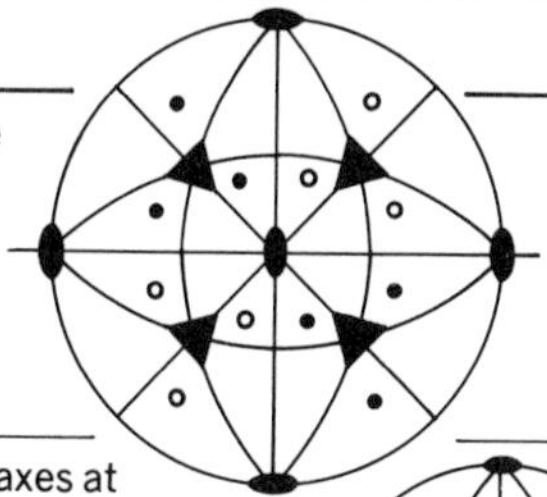
m3	T_h	Four triad axes, three diad axes at the intersections of three mutually perpendicular planes of symmetry, involving a center of symmetry.	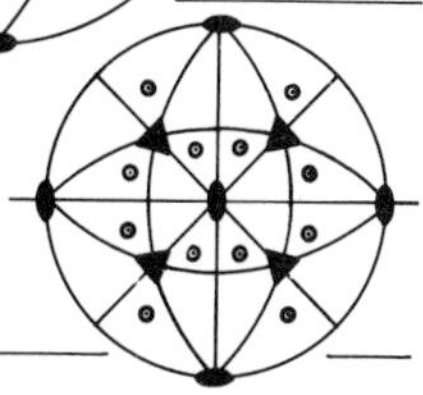

Figure 1.9 (*continued*)

$\overline{4}3m$	T_d	Three inversion tetrad axes, six planes of symmetry, and the usual four triad axes. 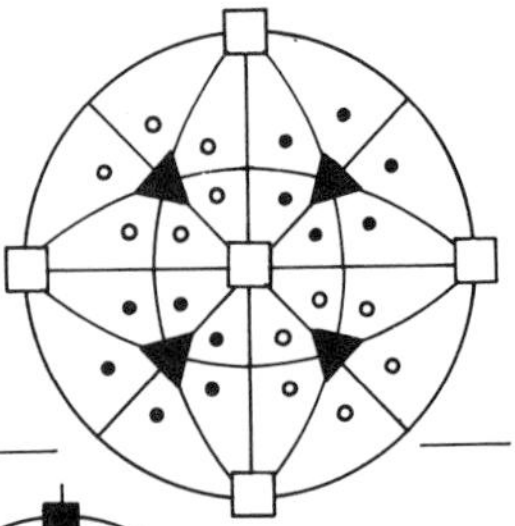

43	O	Four triad axes, three tetrad axes, and six diad axes (the latter along [110] directions). 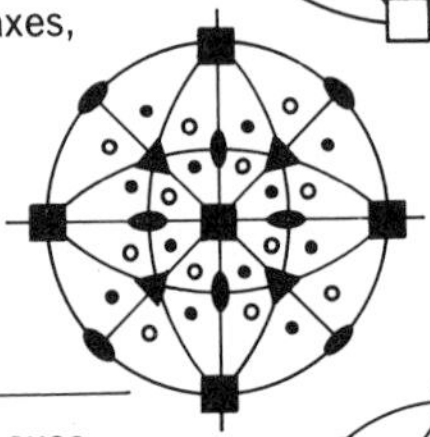

$m3m$	O_h	Four triad axes, three tetrad axes, six diad axes, three planes of symmetry normal to the cubic axes and six planes of symmetry of (110) type and equivalent. 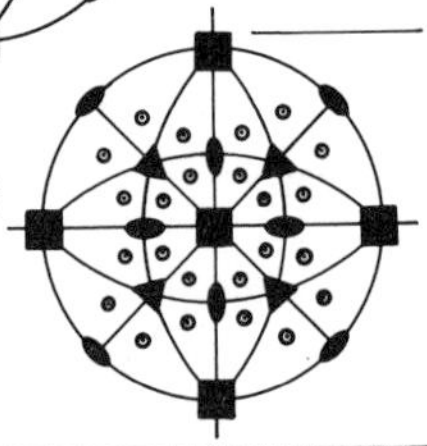

Hexagonal

6	C_6	A single hexad axis. 

$\overline{6}$	C_{3h}	An inversion hexad axis, equivalent to a triad axis normal to a plane of symmetry. 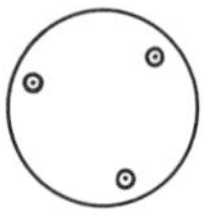

6mm	C_{6v}	A hexad axis intersecting six planes of symmetry, 30° apart. 

$\dfrac{6}{m}$	C_{6h}	A hexad axis normal to a plane of symmetry. Involves a center of symmetry. 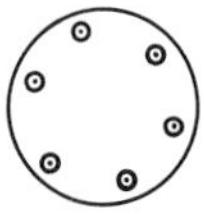

$\overline{6}m2$	D_{3h}	An inversion hexad axis at the intersection of three planes of symmetry. 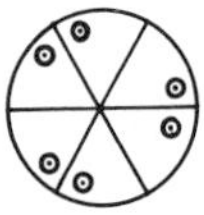

Figure 1.9 (continued)

622	D_6	A hexad axis normal to six diad axes oriented 30° apart.	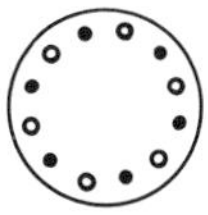

$\dfrac{6}{mmm}$	D_{6h}	A hexad axis at the intersection of six planes of symmetry oriented 30° apart; a diad axis normal to the hexad axis through each of these planes, a plane of symmetry normal to the hexad axis. Has a center of symmetry.	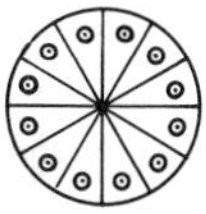

Trigonal (rhombohedral)

3	C_3	A single triad axis.	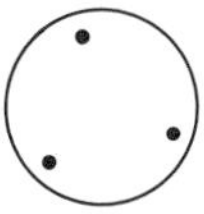
$\bar{3}$	$C_{3i}=S_6$	An inversion triad axis. Has a center of symmetry.	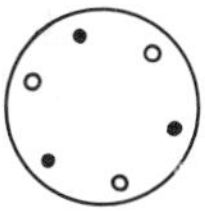
$3m$	C_{3v}	A triad axis with three intersecting planes of symmetry passing through it.	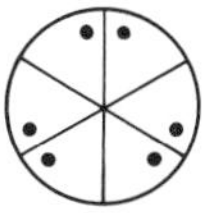
$\bar{3}m$	D_{3d}	Three planes of symmetry passing through an inversion triad axis. Has accordingly three diad axes normal to the triad axis and lying at 30° to the mirror planes.	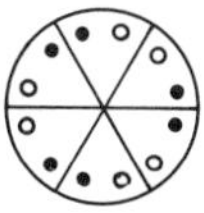
32	D_3	A triad axis normal to three diad axes.	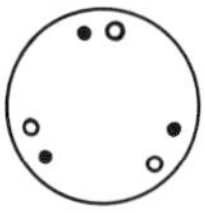

actual axes of symmetry intersecting a large sphere, with the symmetry of the axis represented by an n-sided figure at the projected intersection with the sphere. The figure is solid for rotational axes, hollow for inversion axes. We use these symbols for cubic groups where they are easier to understand than those of the first type. Again, planes of symmetry viewed edge on are represented by lines.

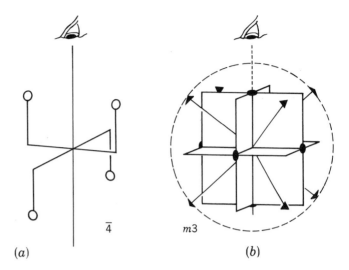

Figure 1.10   (a) The meaning of the stereogram for group $\bar{4}$ (four-bar).   Hollow balls are the ones below the central plane, solid ones above.   (b) The figure represented by cubic-group stereogram ($m3$).   The triad axes intersect 45° great circles on the imaginary sphere (cf. Fig. 1.9).

It is unlikely that the student will find much value in this classification until he studies particular crystal properties influenced by symmetry.   It is desirable at least to understand the principles involved, however.   The practice afforded by exercises such as Prob. 1.3a quickly develops understanding.

A further classification of crystal structures may be made via the so-called "space groups."   Whereas point-group operations relate to symmetry about a lattice point, space-group symmetry goes further to define combined operations whereby the crystal may be both rotated *and* translated into itself. There are a great many (230) such symmetry operations; any structure fits only one such grouping.   Since the electronic and elastic properties (point relations) are limited by point-group symmetry, as discussed in the following section, it will not be necessary to elaborate on space-group properties.

The final and most detailed description of crystal structure is that of the particular structure itself, to wit, the definition of locations of all atoms in a primitive, or unit, cell.   If this information is available, it is always possible to define lattice, point, and space group.   Even where a detailed structural description is not available, however, knowledge of the point group to which a crystal belongs can convey essential information as to its electrical and mechanical behavior. It should be observed that for a given lattice type, the highest point-group (and space-group) symmetries are associated with a structure which is formed by one atom at each *lattice* point. For example, face-centered and body-centered cubic metal structures have $m3m$ point-group symmetry. Complexity in the structure of other cubic crystals reduces the degree of symmetry.

1.4 Linear Properties and Point-group Symmetry

Linear electrical and mechanical properties of materials are defined by relations between vector forces and flows or displacements (for example, **J** versus $\mathcal{E}$, **B** versus $\mathcal{K}$, **D** versus $\mathcal{E}$) or between tensor forces and displacements (**T** versus **S**; see Sec. A.5). The coefficients in these linear relations satisfy the mathematical requirements for *tensors*. The conductivity tensor, for example, comprises the nine components appearing in the equations

$$\begin{aligned}
J_x &= \sigma_{11}\mathcal{E}_x + \sigma_{12}\mathcal{E}_y + \sigma_{13}\mathcal{E}_z \\
J_y &= \sigma_{21}\mathcal{E}_x + \sigma_{22}\mathcal{E}_y + \sigma_{23}\mathcal{E}_z \\
J_z &= \sigma_{31}\mathcal{E}_x + \sigma_{32}\mathcal{E}_y + \sigma_{33}\mathcal{E}_z
\end{aligned} \qquad (1.3)$$

Whenever possible, the z axis of the coordinate system is aligned with the major axis of the crystal; in the case of orthorhombic, tetragonal, and cubic crystals, all three sets of axes are aligned with the crystal axes. This is convenient in simplifying the σ_{ij} and similar components.

The electrical and mechanical variables ($\mathcal{E}$, $\mathcal{K}$, **J**, **T**, **S**, etc.) describing phenomena in a material are *point functions;* i.e., each is a function of the coordinates. Relations such as (1.3) apply *at a point* and depend on the symmetry of the structure about the point. Accordingly, certain limitations on the σ_{ij} are determined by point-group symmetry.

It is shown in Sec. A.1 how compliance coefficients $c_{ij} = c_{ji}$, that is, form a symmetrical tensor. This same property, which in electrical circuits is termed *reciprocity*, may also be shown (independent of crystalline symmetry) for conduction (σ_{ij}) and permittivity (ϵ_{ij}) coefficients. For the former, imagine a cube of unit dimensions with independent electrical contacts on all six sides. Neglecting geometrical fringing effects, the voltage and current across each pair of plates equal

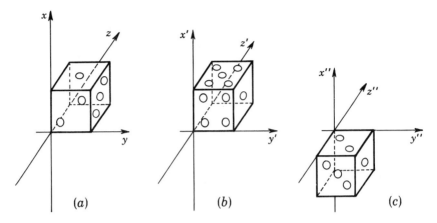

Figure 1.11 Rotations of a cubic crystal about body diagonals, to demonstrate the form of the tensor components. Dots represent the rotation of a die representing the crystal.

$\mathcal{E}_x$ and, respectively, J_x, etc. If *only* $\mathcal{E}_x$ is applied, $J_y = \sigma_{21}\mathcal{E}_x$, while if $\mathcal{E}_y$ only is applied, $J_x = \sigma_{12}\mathcal{E}_y$. The cube must be representable, like any other conductive circuit, by an equivalent resistance network. Applying the *reciprocity theorem* of circuit analysis, a voltage generator and ammeter are placed across x and y plates, respectively, and the converse; with $\mathcal{E}_x = 1$, $J_y = \sigma_{21}$. With $\mathcal{E}_y = 1$, $J_x = \sigma_{12}$. The theorem demands that these currents be equal; hence $\sigma_{12} = \sigma_{21}$. By the same argument with regard to other pairs of plates, $\sigma_{ij} = \sigma_{ji}$ for all i, j. The same may also be shown for the coefficients of permittivity, ϵ_{ij}, by an arrangement based on capacitive-energy storage. It cannot be shown in general for magnetic properties (Sec. 8.9).

In addition, the point-group symmetry of a crystal imposes other restrictions on the components of these tensor properties. As a definitive example we consider the effect of the rotational symmetry of cubic crystals on conductivity. If the cube of Fig. 1.11a is rotated about its body diagonal, through 120°, the new coordinates (Fig. 1.11b) are related to the old by $y' = x$, $x' = z$, $z' = y$. Accordingly, the components of vectors are likewise related by $J_y' = J_x$, $\mathcal{E}_y' = \mathcal{E}_x$, etc. The relations (1.3) may be expressed solely in terms of the primed functions. When rearranged, these are

$$J_x' = \sigma_{33}\mathcal{E}_x' + \sigma_{31}\mathcal{E}_y' + \sigma_{32}\mathcal{E}_z'$$
$$J_y' = \sigma_{13}\mathcal{E}_x' + \sigma_{11}\mathcal{E}_y' + \sigma_{12}\mathcal{E}_z'$$
$$J_z' = \sigma_{23}\mathcal{E}_x' + \sigma_{21}\mathcal{E}_y' + \sigma_{22}\mathcal{E}_z'$$

(1.4)

Since the crystal must be physically identical in both coordinate systems, corresponding coefficients can be equated: $\sigma_{33} = \sigma_{22} = \sigma_{11}$; $\sigma_{31} = \sigma_{12}$; $\sigma_{13} = \sigma_{21}$; $\sigma_{23} = \sigma_{31}$; $\sigma_{32} = \sigma_{13}$; $\sigma_{12} = \sigma_{23}$; $\sigma_{21} = \sigma_{32}$. The last group can be combined: $\sigma_{31} = \sigma_{12} = \sigma_{23}$; $\sigma_{13} = \sigma_{21} = \sigma_{32}$. If, instead, the rotation is about another such body-diagonal axis, as shown in Fig. 1.11c, the new coordinates would satisfy $x'' = -z$, $y'' = x$, $z'' = -y$. By substitution, this leads to

$$
\begin{aligned}
J_x'' &= \sigma_{33}\mathcal{E}_x'' + \sigma_{31}\mathcal{E}_y'' + \sigma_{32}\mathcal{E}_z'' \\
J_y'' &= -\sigma_{13}\mathcal{E}_x'' + \sigma_{11}\mathcal{E}_y'' - \sigma_{12}\mathcal{E}_z'' \\
J_z'' &= \sigma_{23}\mathcal{E}_x'' + \sigma_{21}\mathcal{E}_y'' + \sigma_{22}\mathcal{E}_z''
\end{aligned}
\tag{1.5}
$$

Since these must again be equal to corresponding relations in (1.3), we have in addition the relations $\sigma_{31} = -\sigma_{12} = \sigma_{23}$; $\sigma_{21} = -\sigma_{32} = \sigma_{13}$. Combining these with the previous results gives $\sigma_{31} = -\sigma_{31}$, $\sigma_{21} = -\sigma_{21}$, etc. All terms except $\sigma_{11} = \sigma_{22} = \sigma_{33}$ therefore vanish, and we have, for a cubic lattice, only

$$
J_x = \sigma_{11}\mathcal{E}_x \qquad J_y = \sigma_{11}\mathcal{E}_y \qquad J_z = \sigma_{11}\mathcal{E}_z
$$

or

$$
\mathbf{J} = \sigma_{11}\mathbf{\mathcal{E}}
\tag{1.6}
$$

The conductivity in cubic crystals is therefore the same for all field vectors; hence $\mathbf{J}$ and $\mathbf{\mathcal{E}}$ are always parallel. The conductivity is said to be *isotropic*. This applies to any similar linear relation of two vectors: $\mathbf{D} = \epsilon\mathbf{\mathcal{E}}$, $\mathbf{B} = \mu\mathbf{\mathcal{H}}$, etc., since (1.3) is a linear relation of complete generality between two vector quantities.

The degree of symmetry of other crystal point groups is less than that of cubic. Tetragonal groups, for example, are distinguished by having either a single fourfold (called *tetrad*) axis or a fourfold inversion axis. In the first instance, we could rotate the coordinates $90°$ about the c axis (which we shall make the z axis) to obtain $x' = y$, $y' = -x$, $z' = z$. This leads to $\sigma_{11} = \sigma_{22}$; $\sigma_{12} = -\sigma_{21} = -\sigma_{12} \equiv 0$; $\sigma_{31} = -\sigma_{32} = -\sigma_{31} \equiv 0$, which leaves

$$
J_x = \sigma_{11}\mathcal{E}_x \qquad J_y = \sigma_{11}\mathcal{E}_y \qquad J_z = \sigma_{33}\mathcal{E}_z
\tag{1.7}
$$

The matrix form of such relations is useful, particularly when coordinate transformations must be made. Equation (1.7) can be expressed as

$$
|J| \equiv \begin{vmatrix} J_x \\ J_y \\ J_z \end{vmatrix} = \begin{vmatrix} \sigma_{11} & 0 & 0 \\ 0 & \sigma_{11} & 0 \\ 0 & 0 & \sigma_{33} \end{vmatrix} \cdot \begin{vmatrix} \mathcal{E}_x \\ \mathcal{E}_y \\ \mathcal{E}_z \end{vmatrix}
\tag{1.8}
$$

Table 1.2 Second-rank tensor properties for all classes

| | Tetragonal, | |
| Cubic | hexagonal, trigonal | Orthorhombic |

$$\begin{vmatrix} e_{11} & 0 & 0 \\ 0 & e_{11} & 0 \\ 0 & 0 & e_{11} \end{vmatrix} \qquad \begin{vmatrix} e_{11} & 0 & 0 \\ 0 & e_{11} & 0 \\ 0 & 0 & e_{33} \end{vmatrix} \qquad \begin{vmatrix} e_{11} & 0 & 0 \\ 0 & e_{22} & 0 \\ 0 & 0 & e_{33} \end{vmatrix}$$

Monoclinic, triclinic

$$\begin{vmatrix} e_{11} & e_{12} & e_{13} \\ e_{12} & e_{22} & e_{23} \\ e_{13} & e_{23} & e_{33} \end{vmatrix}$$

The coefficients e_{ij} represent permittivity, conductivity, dielectric susceptibility, etc. The coordinate system is arranged parallel to major crystalline axes.

The other tetragonal symmetry, a fourfold inversion axis ($x' = -y$, $y' = x$, $z' = -z$), leads to this same form. *Two* conductivity (or permittivity, etc.) constants serve to define tetragonal properties, whereas only one is required for cubic crystals. Table 1.2 gives the forms of these *second-rank tensor* properties of crystals, for all classes. In the monoclinic and triclinic classes, one may, by rotation of the crystal, reduce the form to that of orthorhombic.

More complex tensor properties such as elasticity and compliance (Appendix A) are likewise dependent on point-group symmetry. Their forms can be determined in similar fashion. Consider the rotation of Fig. 1.11b: $x' = z$, $y' = x$, $z' = y$. In the new coordinate system, the stress tensor T will have new components $T_{x'x'} = T_{zz}$, $T_{y'y'} = T_{xx}$, $T_{z'z'} = T_{yy}$, $T_{x'y'} = T_{zx}$, $T_{y'z'} = T_{xy}$, $T_{z'x'} = T_{yz}$. In terms of the six independent stress components: $T'_1 = T_3$, $T'_2 = T_1$, $T'_3 = T_2$, $T'_4 = T_6$, $T'_5 = T_4$, $T'_6 = T_5$. The new and old strain components are similarly related. Setting these into (A.10), one finds a number of relations such as $c_{11} = c_{22} = c_{33}$, $c_{44} = c_{55} = c_{66}$, etc. By the application of other rotations, as before, one can show that, for the cubic class, the compliance (or elastance) coefficients[1] have the arrangement

$$|c_{ij}| = \begin{vmatrix} c_{11} & c_{12} & c_{12} & 0 & 0 & 0 \\ c_{12} & c_{11} & c_{12} & 0 & 0 & 0 \\ c_{12} & c_{12} & c_{11} & 0 & 0 & 0 \\ 0 & 0 & 0 & c_{44} & 0 & 0 \\ 0 & 0 & 0 & 0 & c_{44} & 0 \\ 0 & 0 & 0 & 0 & 0 & c_{44} \end{vmatrix} \tag{1.9}$$

[1] Tabulations of coefficients required for compliance or elastance, for all groups, are presented, for example, in W. G. Cady, "Piezoelectricity," p. 54, McGraw-Hill Book Company, New York, 1946.

Although all cubic groups have this symmetry, all tetragonal groups are not the same; i.e.,

Groups $\bar{4}$, $\bar{4}2m$, 42, $4/mmm$

$$|c_{ij}| = \begin{vmatrix} c_{11} & c_{12} & c_{13} & 0 & 0 & 0 \\ c_{12} & c_{11} & c_{13} & 0 & 0 & 0 \\ c_{13} & c_{13} & c_{33} & 0 & 0 & 0 \\ 0 & 0 & 0 & c_{44} & 0 & 0 \\ 0 & 0 & 0 & 0 & c_{44} & 0 \\ 0 & 0 & 0 & 0 & 0 & c_{66} \end{vmatrix}$$

Groups 4, $4/m$, $4mm$ (1.10)

$$|c_{ij}| = \begin{vmatrix} c_{11} & c_{12} & c_{13} & 0 & 0 & c_{16} \\ c_{12} & c_{11} & c_{13} & 0 & 0 & -c_{16} \\ c_{13} & c_{13} & c_{33} & 0 & 0 & 0 \\ 0 & 0 & 0 & c_{44} & 0 & 0 \\ 0 & 0 & 0 & 0 & c_{44} & 0 \\ c_{16} & -c_{16} & 0 & 0 & 0 & c_{66} \end{vmatrix}$$

While symmetry defines which components of permittivity, compliance, etc., are absent and which equal others, this phenomenological theory gives no indication of their physical values in a given material. This information must generally be obtained experimentally.

1.5   Directional Notation

It is often important to define the direction in a crystal across which a field is applied, or a face prepared for studying some surface effect. One way to define directions is simply to measure cosines of the angles they make with respect to pre-defined reference axes. These *direction cosines* are discussed in Chap. 9. A less flexible and quite incomplete notation is via reference to directions such as the body diagonal, face diagonals, etc. A better scheme for *cubic* crystals is that of *Miller indices*, which permit the description of the important directions and planes in a crystal in an abbreviated notation.

In a *cubic* lattice, let us take some lattice point as an origin, with the axes x, y, z parallel to the crystalline axes (Fig. 1.12a). Since the length of one side of the unit cell is a, there will be lattice points at all locations in the complete crystal given by $x = ia$, $y = ja$, $z = ka$, where i, j, k are integers. (There may be others, as in face-centered and body-centered lattices.) Let a plane pass through the crystal, inter-

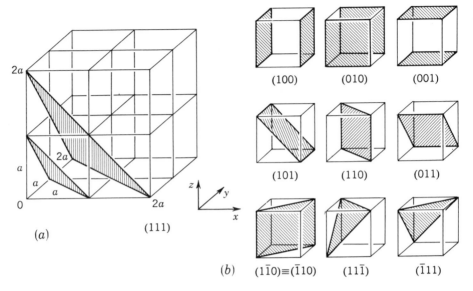

(a)

(111)

(b)   (1$\bar{1}$0)≡($\bar{1}$10)   (11$\bar{1}$)   ($\bar{1}$11)

(100)   (010)   (001)

(101)   (110)   (011)

Figure 1.12

cepting the x axis at some particular point $x = i_0a$, the y axis at $y = j_0a$, and the z axis at $z = k_0a$. The three points uniquely define the plane. The Miller indices defining the plane may be written $(1/i_0, 1/j_0, 1/k_0)$. By convention, how-ever, each index $(1/i_0$, etc.) is multiplied by the least common multiplier, making all indices integers. The Miller indices of a particular plane intersecting at $i_0 = j_0 = k_0 = 2$ are written not as $(\frac{1}{2},\frac{1}{2},\frac{1}{2})$, but as $(1,1,1)$, more simply (111). In the Miller-index notation, the plane intercepting at (a,a,a) and that intercepting at $(2a,2a,2a)$ are both described by the notation (111). As the figure shows, these planes are parallel to one another. The same symbol applies to all planes paral-lel to these and, accordingly, defines not one plane, but all planes of given orientation.

When a plane lies, for example, normal to the z axis, it intersects the x and y axes only at infinity. Such a plane which intersects the z axis at $z = k_0a$ would have indices $(1/\infty, 1/\infty, 1/k_0)$; this is expressed (001). Similarly, a plane normal to the y axis is (010), etc. When the intercept on an axis is negative, as it may be, the corresponding symbol is expressed by a bar over the numeral; a plane intersecting at $(2a,a,-a)$ would be expressed as $(12\bar{2})$. The operation of altering all symbols to the barred symbols and the converse

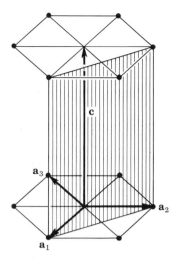

Figure 1.13 Notation describing plane indices in the base plane of a hexagonal crystal. The plane shown is (11, 0).

produces equivalent planes, that is, $(\overline{1}\overline{1}\overline{1}) = (111)$, $(\overline{1}1\overline{1}) = (1\overline{1}1)$, etc.

In any cubic lattice, because of symmetry, the planes (100), (010), (001), $(\overline{1}00)$, $(0\overline{1}0)$, and $(00\overline{1})$ are all equivalent, since x, y, z axes are indistinguishable. Likewise, (011), (101), $(10\overline{1})$, etc., are equivalent, as are (111), $(\overline{1}11)$, etc. It is necessary only to distinguish between these sets when two planes must be distinguished *relative to one another*. The three sets of planes (100), (110), and (111) and their equivalents (Fig. 1.12*b*) are the most significant in terms of electronic phenomena in cubic crystals.

In a tetragonal or an orthorhombic crystal the Miller notation may be used in the same form; since x, y, and z axes are no longer equivalent, it is essential to define which crystal axes correspond to x, y, z.

A somewhat similar notation is applied to hexagonal crystals, but the natural 60 and 120° angles in the base plane must be represented in the indicial notation. The intersection of some plane on the base plane may be described in terms of two unit vectors $\mathbf{a}_1$, $\mathbf{a}_2$ (Fig. 1.13); a convention has been developed, however, whereby all three base plane vectors $(\mathbf{a}_1, \mathbf{a}_2, \mathbf{a}_3)$ are represented. With intercepts from some origin, at coordinates $h\mathbf{a}_1$, $i\mathbf{a}_2$, $j\mathbf{a}_3$, kc, the hexagonal notation is $(hijk)$. Because this is redundant, it is usually written (hi, k). A plane intersecting as shown in the figure could be described as having an intercept $-\frac{1}{2}a_3$ on the $\mathbf{a}_3$ axis; if parallel to the c axis, it could be described by the four-index notation $(1\ 1\ \overline{2}\ 0)$ or by $(11,\ 0)$. In either case the form of the symbolism identifies it as related to hexagonal crystals. The value of the third index in the complete description is always such that the *sum* of the first three indices is zero $(1 + 1 - 2 = 0)$.

Directions may also be described in Miller-index notation; a direction *normal* to a plane (rst) is described using square brackets: $[rst]$. Indices define *only* direction, however, and *not* a coordinate system or origin.

1.6 Crystal Bonding

The crystal structure assumed by a given element, alloy, or compound is determined mainly by the number, arrangement, and binding energies of electrons in the valence states of the various atoms. At a given temperature, a given material will assume a structure having the lowest free energy,[1] unless the preparation of the material has precluded the attainment of equilibrium. In most solids one expects to find that crystalline phase which is in equilibrium just below the melting point, since solid-solid phase transitions occur very slowly at lower temperatures.

Just as in simple molecules, the valence electrons of atoms in crystals interact with one another to *bond* together the entire mass. Various types of bonding can be recognized, in different crystals. In some crystals the valence electrons are freed to wander at will through the crystal. In others, electrons from an electropositive atom (e.g., a metal) become attached tightly to incomplete shells of electronegative atoms. Another possibility is the formation of a *covalent* bond involving a pair of electrons (the same type of bond responsible for the strong attachment of hydrogen atoms in the H_2 molecule). Crystals may even be formed by molecules which retain their electrons in substantially the same configurations as in the free molecules. Each type of bonding, in crystals, produces characteristic electronic and mechanical properties. We may distinguish four major crystal types:

1. Metals (valence electrons essentially free)
2. Ionic crystals (valence electrons taken into atoms having incomplete shells)

---

[1] See Appendix C for a discussion of free-energy, equilibrium, and phase transitions.

3. Covalent crystals (electron-pair bonds)

4. Molecular crystals (electrons remain associated with original molecules)

Although many important crystals have bonding characteristics intermediate between those of the archetypes, many others show distinctly the properties associated with a particular type of bonding. These properties are discussed below for each of the basic types.

Metals

Metals are characterized chemically by outer (valence) electronic shells which are sparsely populated. They fall naturally into monovalent, divalent, and trivalent categories; a further distinction is made between simple metals (closed inner shells) and transition metals (incomplete inner shells). The majority of elements are metals, because of the tendency for $4s$, $5s$, etc., shells to fill before the $3d$, $4f$, etc., shells are completed (Sec. B.11).

When two metal atoms are brought as close as they would be in a metallic crystal, the valence electrons interact so strongly that they move around both ion cores. When a crystal is formed, the valence electrons of the metal atoms also move in paths which cannot be associated with any one nucleus. The result is a high electrical and thermal conductivity, compared with other crystal types. The cohesion (i.e., the ability to remain a solid) of the metallic crystal results from a combination of forces: (1) the attraction of the electron cloud for the ion cores, (2) the mutual repulsion of the electrons, and (3) the mutual repulsion of the ion cores. Figure 1.14 is a sketch of a reasonable form for the potential (free) energy contribution, as a function of nuclear spacing, from each of these charge interactions. This *configuration-coordinate* graph is a convenient way of describing equilibrium situations, although there is no physical way to form a crystal having lattice spacing markedly different from the equilibrium value. The energy of the first two interactions varies slowly with nuclear spacing; that due to ion-core repulsion varies more rapidly. The total energy is a minimum for some equilibrium lattice spacing. The *cohesion* of the lattice depends on the depth of this minimum below the asymptotic energy for large atomic spacing. While one may expect the melting point of the metal to depend on this difference, the relationship is fairly subtle because melting does not imply complete separation of the atoms.

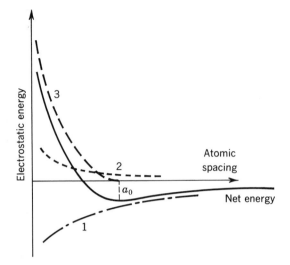

Figure 1.14 The electrostatic contributions to the energy of a metallic crystal (1 and 2), plus the ion-repulsion term (3), have a combined minimum defining the equilibrium lattice constant, a_0.

The structures of most metals are close-packed, or nearly so, as shown in Table 1.1. Nearest-neighbor spacings are of the order of the theoretical diameter of the outer electronic shell of the ion core, so that lattice constants are typically of the order of 2 to 3 A. While simple metals usually prefer a given close-packed structure at all temperatures below the melting point, transition metals frequently assume different structures at different temperatures, because of the influence of incomplete inner electronic shells.

The high mechanical *ductility* characteristic of metals is due to the ease with which close-packed lattice planes can slip over one another. Cohesion is not destroyed in this process because it does not depend on precise alignment of electron bonds of adjacent atoms. The characteristic "shiny" appearance of metal surfaces is caused by free-valence electrons; even at visible-light wavelengths these electrons impart a high electrical conductivity which gives strong reflection of light.

Ionic Crystals

In the usual chemical valence principle, whereby most inorganic compounds are explained, valence electrons freed from

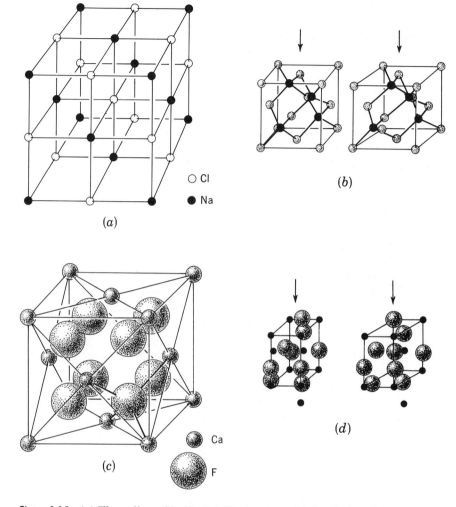

Figure 1.15 (*a*) The sodium chloride (NaCl) structure; (*b*) the zincblende (ZnS) structure (stereo pair); (*c*) the fluorite structure (CaF₂); (*d*) the wurtzite (ZnS) or zincite (ZnO) structure (stereo pair), with its hexagonal unit cell outlined.

a metallic atom are captured by electronegative atoms; the ions thus formed are attracted to one another to form a stable molecule. The same electron-transfer process explains cohesion of ionic crystals. The best-known ionic crystal is sodium chloride (Fig. 1.15*a*). The structure has a face-centered cubic basis, at each point of which is placed one sodium ion at $(0,0,0)$ and one chlorine ion at $(\frac{1}{2},0,0)$. Because attraction between the positive and negative ions provides the necessary cohesion, each positive sodium ion lies equidistant between six negative chlorine ions, and conversely. The regular structure, typically, *does not* distinguish separate *molecules* of sodium chloride. Many of the alkali halide compounds (KCl, NaBr, etc.) form crystals of the NaCl (rock salt) structure.

The zincblende (ZnS) structure (Fig. 1.15b) is also typical of many ionic compounds of chemical form RX, where R represents a metal atom and X a nonmetal, usually of valence 2. It has a face-centered cubic basis, each lattice point containing a zinc ion at $(0,0,0)$ and a sulfur ion at $(\frac{1}{4},\frac{1}{4},\frac{1}{4})$. It is identical in symmetry with the diamond structure, but contains equal numbers of atoms of two types, instead of only a single element.

Several other structures are characteristic of large numbers of simple ionic crystals, such as the wurtzite (another form of ZnS) and fluorite (CaF_2) structures (Fig. 1.15c and d). Valency completely determines the arrangement in ionic structures, and ions of one type are more or less surrounded by those of the opposite type. Materials such as sapphire (Al_2O_3), because of more complicated valency and ratio of atoms of each type, form more complex structures. Most metal oxides and sulfides fall into the classification of ionic crystals, although there are many in which the nature of bonding is in part covalent. Those compounds formed from valence-2 metals and valence-6 atoms (ZnS, ZnO, etc.) which play roles as semiconductors, or as luminescent materials, are probably more nearly covalently than ionically bonded.

Because ions of like polarity repel, crystal planes in ionic solids do not readily slide past one another and the materials are brittle. They may, however, have very high melting points. Many ionic crystals are water-soluble; in water the crystal dissolves to yield not free atoms, but free *ions*. The dissolved ionic solids exhibit high electrical conductivity because of the ability of the free ions to respond to electric fields in the solution. The conductivity in pure ionic *crystals* is due largely to motion of ions, rather than electrons. It is relatively poor, because of the limited freedom of the ions in the crystal. Some ionic materials are excellent insulators, but none are good electrical conductors.

Covalent Crystals

In a covalent bond, two atoms *share* two electrons, which spend most of their time in the region between the two atoms.

This contrasts with the ionic bond, in which valence electrons from metal atoms become affixed to the electronegative atoms. The archetype of covalent crystals is diamond (Fig. 1.6). Each atom has four nearest neighbors, with which it shares its four valence electrons. As in organic chemistry, covalent electronic bonds are often represented schematically by pairs of lines joining atom pairs.

The diamond structure is manifested by the important *semiconductors* silicon and germanium, which as tetravalent elements lie directly below carbon in the periodic chart. Materials such as InSb, GaAs, etc., formed from elements from locations in the periodic chart on either side of the elemental semiconductors, have the similar zincblende (ZnS) structure. These compounds, formed from valence-3 and valence-5 atoms (and called III-V compounds), are electrically and mechanically similar to elemental semiconductors.

Covalent crystals are characterized by hardness, as well as brittleness. They are brittle because adjacent atoms must remain in accurate alignment to share electrons, hard because of the great strength of the paired-electron bond. Diamond, the lightest covalent crystal, is also hardest, with heavier elements (Si, Ge, Sn, Pb) successively softer. In pure form, covalent crystals have all valence electrons paired tightly in covalent bonds. They lack free electrons and are therefore poor conductors of both heat and electricity. When electrons are introduced via impurities, however, they become reasonably good conductors, and are termed semiconductors (Chaps. 4 and 5).

Molecular Crystals

In the crystal bonding described heretofore, atoms are not arranged in such a way that one can define distinct molecules. In *molecular crystals*, however, each molecule may retain its integrity. Bonding is established, not by sharing of electrons or ionization, but rather by weak forces termed *van der Waals forces*. Electrons of one molecule couple weakly to the ions of an adjacent molecule, without materially affecting atomic arrangements inside the molecules. These same forces are required to explain cohesion in liquids.

Physical properties of molecular crystals can cover a wider range than those of other crystal types. In general, they have low melting points. An ideal molecular crystal is nonconducting, since most electrons remain attached to their respective molecules. There may be some conduction due to loosely

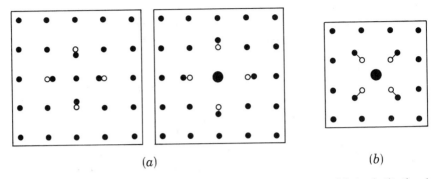

Figure 1.16   (a) Schematic of the effect of a small (left) and large (right) substitutional impurity in a crystal structure. The hollow circles represent the positions of the neighbors in a perfect crystal. (b) Effect of an interstitial impurity.

attached ions. The main application of molecular materials is as insulators or dielectrics. These applications are not dependent on crystalline structure; hence the majority of dielectrics in practical use are amorphous solids or even liquids.

Amorphous Materials

Amorphous materials lack a regular structure; liquids are therefore by definition amorphous. While in many liquids only the relatively weak van der Waals forces hold the atoms or molecules together, in molten solids electronic and ionic bonding processes may still be effective, though less so than in a regularly arranged structure. Mechanically strong but amorphous ("glassy") substances often result when materials of strongly ionic or covalent character (metal oxides, carbides, etc.) are formed, or allowed to cool too rapidly, below their normal crystallization temperatures. They have approximately the same densities as in the complex crystal structures which they would form if equilibrium could be attained.

1.7   Imperfections in Crystals

A *perfect* crystal is a completely regular structure with no atom out of place at any time. Most crystalline materials, even synthetically produced single crystals, are far from perfect. Imperfections fall into two categories: those involving additional or missing atoms and those in which atoms are merely disarranged. The latter include even the thermally

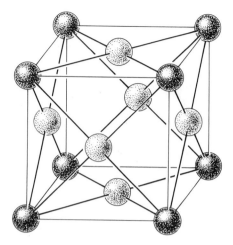

Figure 1.17   The structure of the ordered alloy Cu₃Au. Copper atoms occupy the face-centered sites, gold atoms the corner sites of the face-centered cubic unit cell.

produced acoustical vibrations which exist at any temperature above absolute zero.

Impurity Atoms

Small numbers of foreign atoms in a crystal which is otherwise pure may fit into the structure in one of two ways.   If one of the original atoms is replaced by the impurity atom, it is said to be a *substitutional impurity* (Fig. 1.16*a*).   If the impurity lies in a normally unfilled volume, termed an *interstice*, or *void*, it is said to be an *interstitial* impurity (Fig. 1.16*b*).   Impurity atoms having roughly the same size and valency as the original atoms fit substitutionally with only a slight distortion of the structure.   Large numbers of these well-fitting atoms can fit substitutionally into the host crystal, and *alloys* form over a wide range of temperatures.   An alloy is a crystalline "solid solution" in which metal atoms are intimately mixed.   Most alloys are *disordered*, with any atom likely in any site; *ordered alloys*, where atoms of each type fill one type of site, are really crystalline compounds having only a slight preference for the ordered state.   One such example is copper-gold alloy, which near 75 per cent (atomic) copper forms the ordered structure described by Fig. 1.17.

A *phase diagram* (Fig. 1.18) shows how well two atoms may accommodate to form alloys.   Iron and nickel form alloys in any proportion.   Nickel, with a face-centered cubic structure, dominates its side of the phase diagram, while the body-centered cubic (room temperature) structure of iron

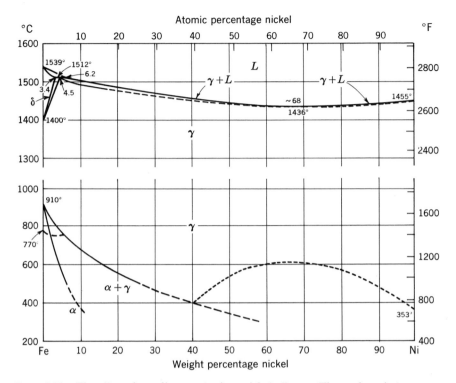

Figure 1.18 The alloy phase diagram for iron-nickel alloys.   The γ phase is face-centered cubic, characteristic of nickel at all temperatures.   Pure iron has two body-centered cubic phases, α and δ, with a face-centered phase stable at intermediate temperatures.   Note the broad range of composition over which the γ phase is stable, indicating the atomic compatibility of the two metals.   (*From American Society for Metals,* *"Metals Handbook," p.* 1211, 1948.)

dominates for large proportions of iron.   An ordered alloy may be formed at 75 per cent nickel.   The lattice constant of the alloy varies uniformly with composition, indicating that the structure averages the differences in dimensions of the two kinds of ions.

The system aluminum-silicon (Fig. C.1) has quite different properties.   The silicon (diamond) structure requires four nearest neighbors.   Pure aluminum has only three valence electrons, one fewer than silicon.   A small percentage of aluminum may be substituted for silicon atoms, despite the incorrect valency.   In so doing they share electrons covalently with only three of the surrounding germanium atoms.   This results in an increase in conductivity, as taken up in detail in

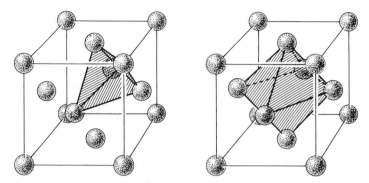

Figure 1.19 Showing the two types of voids in the face-centered cube. A tetrahedral void occurs at each corner of the unit cell, an octahedral void at the center (there are of course parts of other octahedral voids also in the cell).

Chap. 4. When more than a few per cent of Al atoms are added, they find it more desirable to have one another as neighbors than the silicon; a second crystalline phase, consisting of almost pure aluminum, may then appear.

Interstitial impurities can be accommodated in large densities only when the host crystal has relatively large interatomic voids. Such voids should clearly not exist in close-packed lattices, but appear in many ionic and covalent crystals. Interstitial impurity atoms naturally seek out those voids which best suit their valency and "shape." As an example, the face-centered cubic structure has two different sets of voids (Fig. 1.19). One set, termed *tetrahedral* voids, has four "nearest-neighbor" atoms. The larger voids, formed by six "next-nearest" neighbors, are termed *octahedral* voids, from the eight-sided volume formed by surrounding atoms. Impurity atoms in this structure often prefer one type of void to the other. Similar considerations apply to location of metal ions in ferrite structures (Sec. 8.7).

The properties of the substitutional or interstitial atoms or ions themselves may be markedly affected by their environment. While the energy levels of their deep-lying electrons are little affected, the valence electrons will be more or less strongly perturbed by the surrounding atoms. The impurity may, accordingly, give up electrons to its neighbors or accept electrons from them. Strong perturbations of electronic energy levels in the free atom may be observed in the crystalline impurity site.   These effects are fundamental in semi-conductors and luminescent solids.

Lattice Defects

The term *lattice defects* describes variations from perfection *not* involving foreign bodies.   While it is possible to remove foreign atoms from some crystalline materials, so that less than one impurity atom of undesired elements is present per billion host atoms, it is not so easy to prevent defects.   These usually occur in large numbers because of thermal or other agitation of the crystal during its formation.

The least complicated of lattice defects, termed *point defects*, affect only the small volume of the crystal surrounding the defect.   One point defect is a *vacancy*, i.e., the absence of an atom in the otherwise regular crystal.   An *interstitial defect* is the presence, in a void, of one of the atoms native to the crystal.   High-energy radiation may knock atoms out of their normal positions in the lattice, creating simultaneously vacancies and interstitial defects.   This not uncommon combination of a vacancy and an interstitial is termed a *Frenkel defect*.   (There is no implication that the two defects are adjacent, however.)   The presence of vacancies or interstitials distorts the lattice regularity for distances of several lattice spacings from the defect.   As in the case of impurity atoms, the incomplete electronic bonding associated with vacancies and higher-order defects can have important effects on conductivity and on emission-absorption of radiation in ionic and covalent crystals.

Higher-order defects include some which influence entire *lines* of atoms.   These are called *dislocations*.   One type of dislocation, termed an *edge dislocation*, is best visualized by imagining part of an entire plane of atoms removed (Fig. 1.20).   Atoms far from the region of the discontinuity accommodate to the defect, but the influence may extend, in the direction normal to the drawing, to the boundaries of the crystal.   These occur in crystal growth, as well as during inelastic deformations.   The dislocation may (as shown) move from one edge of the crystal to the other; this results in a relative displacement of the two regions.   A *screw dislocation* is typified in Fig. 1.21.   The displacement of the material is *parallel* to the line of the dislocation, rather than perpendicular as in an edge dislocation.   The most pertinent parameter of a dislocation is the direction and distance through which material

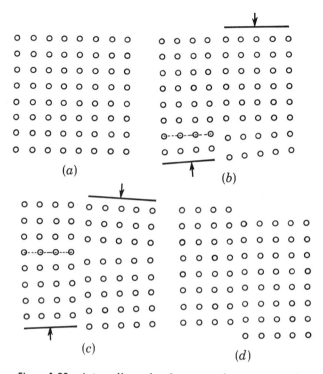

Figure 1.20 A two-dimensional cross-section representation of the deformation of a crystal by motion of an edge dislocation. (*a*) The undeformed crystal. (*b*) Forces are applied as shown by the arrows. The dashed line represents a half-plane of atoms, which, because of the deformation, is terminated at its right-hand edge. (*c*) The dislocation has progressed farther; the *dislocation line* is defined by the highly deformed region at the right-hand edge of the dashed plane (the line is normal to the paper). (*d*) The deformation is complete, and all planes are again continuous.

is displaced to produce it (indicated by the vector **b** in Fig. 1.21). A dislocation produced without actually removing material from a crystal must have the same displacement throughout the path of the disturbed region through the crystal. With the same displacement, however, the dislocation line may change direction. Where the displacement is parallel to the line, the dislocation is best described as a screw dislocation; where perpendicular to the line, it is a simple edge dislocation. In fact, the disturbed region can follow a curved path, so that a *dislocation loop* represents a closed dis-

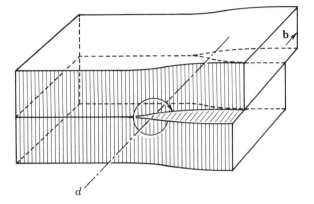

Figure 1.21   A schematic representation of a screw dislocation. Only the material near the dislocation line (d) is
appreciably deformed. The local changes in position of
atoms surrounding the dislocation line follow a helical pattern, as suggested by the curve joining two points which
were coincident before dislocation. The Burgers vector **b**
shows the displacement of the material by the dislocation.
(*From H. G. Van Beuren, "Imperfections in Crystals," p.*
49, *North Holland Publishing Company, Amsterdam,*
1960.)

location line; in this instance deformation is confined to the
interior of a crystal. Dislocations not closed in this manner
terminate at surfaces of the crystal or at other gross defects.
While small defects such as vacancies cannot be observed
directly, electron microscopy permits observation of dislocations. Their terminations at crystal surfaces may also be
detected by the use of corrosive etching solutions, which
attack most strongly those regions of the crystal surface
which are imperfect. Small *etch pits* found after such a
treatment permit an estimation of dislocation densities.

Even more serious defects influence entire *planes* in a
crystal. The most common of these are *stacking faults*. In
stacking of close-packed planes to form a face-centered cubic
structure, for example, it is possible under rapid-growth
conditions for the correct pattern ($ABCABCABC$) to be
interrupted at one point, so that a pattern ($ABC\underline{AC}ABC$)
results. Here, all atoms in the planes underlined have the
environment characteristic of a hexagonal close-packed
structure. The crystal may be expected to behave differently
in this region. While a crystal incorporating such defects is
usually considered to be a single crystal, it could alternatively

be viewed as a pair of crystals fastened together at a plane across which almost perfect atomic alignment is possible. This can also occur at some planes oriented *obliquely* to the major axes. The effect then is that of a pair of crystals oriented differently but meeting at a common plane in which each mirrors the other. A crystal having this defect is said to be *twinned*.

In actual crystals, these point, line, and planar defects occur in all combinations. The relatively simple defects described are merely straightforward examples. In polycrystalline material, where adjacent crystallites are almost randomly oriented with respect to one another, *grain boundaries* separating the crystallites may be described as rows of adjacent dislocations. These permit a large fraction of the atoms at a boundary to be but little perturbed. This helps explain the considerable strength of metals even when in polycrystalline form. Actual *crystal surfaces* form the most serious defects, since all atoms in the surface are in perturbed environments.

The degree of perfection attained in a crystal depends on the process by which it is grown. Most natural gem crystals, while appearing "perfect" to the naked eye, are very highly defected by modern synthetic-crystal standards. It is informative to make a crude calculation of the density of impurities which may be expected in a "perfect" crystal at thermal equilibrium. Frenkel defects are easiest to treat, for there is no addition or removal of atoms and the extent of the defects (unlike that of dislocations, etc.) is well defined.

The generation of a Frenkel defect may be treated as a chemical reaction:

$$(\text{Energy}) \Leftrightarrow \text{vacancy} + \text{interstitial} \tag{1.11}$$

The assumption that there are relatively few of these defects permits the use of Boltzmann statistics.[1] The energy required to introduce an interstitial atom, E_{int}, will be the same for each atom if there are relatively few, as will the energy E_{vac} required to produce a vacancy by removing an atom. Approximately, applying Boltzmann statistics [Eq. (C. 33)],

$$m_{vac} = n_{atoms} e \frac{\mu_{vac}}{kT} e^{-E_{vac}/kT} \tag{1.12a}$$

$$m_{int} = n_{voids} e \frac{\mu_{int}}{kT} e^{-E_{int}/kT} \tag{1.12b}$$

[1] See Sec. C.5.

The number of "available states" for the defects is just the number of atoms in the case of vacancies, of voids in the case of interstitials. The μ's (chemical potentials) for the two defects are related. *At equilibrium*, at constant temperature and pressure the free energy G is a minimum, and any natural reaction must not alter G (Sec. C.1). Thus

$$dG = 0 = \mu_{vac}\,dm_{vac} + \mu_{int}\,dm_{int}$$

We have $dm_{vac} = dm_{int}$, since in forming Frenkel defects no atoms are added. It follows that $\mu_{vac} = -\mu_{int}$. Equating (1.12a) and (1.12b) with the related μ values gives

$$n_{atoms}e^{\mu_{vac}/kT}e^{-E_{vac}/kT} = n_{voids}e^{-\mu_{vac}/kT}e^{-E_{int}/kT}$$

$$e^{\mu_{vac}/kT} = \left(\frac{n_{voids}}{n_{atoms}}\right)^{\frac{1}{2}} e^{-(E_{int}-E_{vac})/2kT}$$

Substituting into (1.12a),

$$\frac{m_{vac}}{n_{atoms}} = \left(\frac{n_{voids}}{n_{atoms}}\right)^{\frac{1}{2}} e^{-(E_{vac}+E_{int})/2kT} \qquad (1.13)$$

If the crystal has energy U when perfect, a combination of a vacancy and an interstitial added to the perfect crystal changes its energy to $U + (E_{vac} + E_{int}) = U + E_{FD}$. The energy $E_{vac} + E_{int} = E_{FD}$ must be positive, since a crystal at absolute zero temperature does not spontaneously generate Frenkel defects. We may estimate the equilibrium density of Frenkel defects at room temperature (300°K), assuming that the energy required to create one defect is ($E_{FD} =$) 1 ev. Neglecting the small square-root factor,

$$\frac{m_{vac}}{n_{atom}} \cong e^{-E_{FD}/2kT} \cong 5 \times 10^{-9}$$

This indicates a density of the order of 10^{13} cm^{-3} in typical solids. In other words, Frenkel defects might be found at equilibrium, separated by spacings of the order of 1,000 lattice constants. While the calculation is admittedly quite crude, it illustrates how far from perfection actual crystals must be.

Since the energy of a dislocation is much larger than that of a Frenkel defect, there will generally be substantially fewer dislocations. The actual number of defects in a crystal depends mainly on details of its growth process. Crystals formed at high temperatures and cooled rapidly may retain indefinitely most defects introduced during solidification. Even though equilibrium calculations may indicate low densities, the energy barrier (activation energy) which must be surmounted to enable a defect to disappear may be many times the available thermal energy (of the order of kT).

1.8   Crystal Growth

When a material having preference for a crystalline form is cooled below its melting point slowly, crystal growth takes place. In most natural situations, unregulated growth results in many crystallites of various sizes, in random orientations. At the precise temperature at which thermal agitation becomes just sufficient to maintain either the solid or the liquid state, crystallization will not occur unless there are atoms sufficiently static to act as *nucleation centers,* to which additional atoms can attach. Pure water can be cooled well below 0°C without freezing; if, however, the walls of the container, or perhaps some large impurities (e.g., dust particles), have a surface sufficiently like that of a growing crystal, crystallites will begin to grow on these nucleation centers. Crystal growth here, or in a metal casting in a mold, begins almost simultaneously at many nucleation centers. Each crystallite unfortunately has in general a different orientation of its crystalline axes. Crystallites from the many nucleation centers grow until they join, forming grain boundaries and halting growth.

Most synthetic single-crystal technology is based upon growth from a *single* nucleation region. If even a small single crystal of the material is available, it may be used as a "seed" to which additional atoms can attach. If such crystals are not available, almost any rough surface will nucleate crystallites. An experiment performed readily in the home demonstrates this principle. A saturated solution of table sugar in water is prepared at a temperature just above room temperature, in a clean glass container. A cotton string is suspended in the center of the liquid, which is allowed to cool slowly. Glucose crystals ("rock candy") will form on the string. Some may be fairly large. The smaller crystallites are removed from the string, and the process is repeated, using a few larger crystallites as seeds. A slow cooling rate is essential for growth of large crystals.

Many crystalline compounds produce large single crystals from low-temperature solutions. Growth from a liquid solution at high temperature is applicable even to some highly refractory metal oxides; the solvent is a molten metal or salt which does not react chemically with the desired materials, and segregates itself from the desired material at the growth surface. A great advantage of growing crystals from solutions is that growth is often possible at temperatures *far below the melting point* of the material. Many materials, in fact, cannot be melted, for they rapidly dissociate into gaseous plus liquid or solid phases. A lower crystal-growth temperature leads to a lower number of defects. Contamination of the desired material, as, for example, by oxidation, is also reduced at the reduced temperatures characteristic of growth from solution.

A major disadvantage of growing crystals from dilute solutions is that small percentages of impurities in the solvent may produce high concentrations in the crystal. Atoms or molecules of the solvent itself may become entrapped within the rapidly growing crystal. Materials such as semiconductors, which must be of highest possible purity and of precisely known composition, are grown directly from the molten material. In the most common technique, attributed to *Czochralski*, a refractory crucible contains the pure material, usually heated by magnetic induction (Fig. 1.22). A seed crystal is fastened to a rod, in the desired orientation. The seed is lowered into the surface of the molten material, and the temperature of the melt adjusted to permit atoms to attach to the seed at a rate determined by the temperature and the cooling effect of the rod and seed. At first, the seed is slightly melted to expose pure and relatively undefected material. The rod is rotated about its axis, and at the same time drawn slowly upward at the rate at which crystal growth increases the length of the crystal. If the rod is pulled up slowly, the diameter increases because build-up occurs on the sides as well as on the end of the crystal. Most germanium or silicon crystals are grown to a diameter of about 1 in. While crystals many inches in diameter are possible, larger diameters involve serious problems in temperature uniformity, and therefore growth rate, over the growing surface; more defects and stresses are introduced.

Some materials, such as diamond and quartz (SiO_2), grow in the desired crystalline form only at very high pressures. The growth of large quartz crystals suitable for piezoelectric resonators was made possible by the development of techniques wherein the material fills a heavy-metal "bomb" and

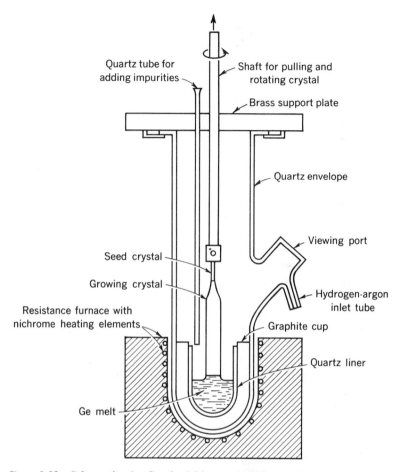

Figure 1.22 Schematic of a Czochralski crystal-pulling equipment. (*From W. C. Dunlap, "An Introduction to Semiconductors," John Wiley & Sons, Inc., New York, 1957.*)

builds up tremendous hydrostatic pressures. Small diamond crystals have been grown in a hydraulic press capable of thousands of atmospheres of pressure.

Crystals of materials containing volatile constituents can be grown by the *Bridgeman* technique, in which a small quartz or glass tube is almost completely filled with poly-crystalline or amorphous material. A heating-cooling temperature gradient is passed from end to end of the material, first melting, then freezing it.   If the end of the tube cooled first is tapered to a point, growth may favor a single crystal of

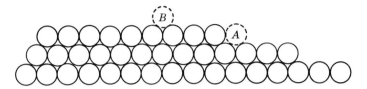

Figure 1.23 Planar growth of a crystal. An arriving atom will find it more attractive to locate at point A than at B, since its energy will be lower at A. This leads to steplike growth patterns.

orientation established by nucleation from the pointed end; this trick is useful when a seed crystal is not available. The Bridgeman method is useful for tellurium and telluride crystals, for example, as well as for many organic crystals. It is extremely valuable for research studies of crystals having unknown growth properties or structure.

In crystal growing, a major requirement is that atoms have sufficient mobility to settle into a proper site on the structure. There is experimental evidence that crystal growth mainly takes place plane by plane, as shown in Fig. 1.23. The bonding of an atom to a site such as A is much stronger than to a site such as B, having fewer nearest neighbors. On large crystal surfaces the planes are initiated at dislocations or other defects. Agitation of the liquid provides sufficient mobility for crystals grown from a melt or a solution. Other growth techniques supply the material in the form of a vapor, and the temperatures of arriving atoms and growing crystal may accordingly differ. The *Verneuil* technique utilizes an extremely hot flame (e.g., hydrogen and oxygen), or an electric arc, into which powders of the desired crystalline material are thrown. Intense heat causes the powder to atomize. A seed crystal is placed just below the hottest region. The surface of the growing crystal is brought somewhere near the melting point, so that the arriving atoms or molecules will have sufficiently high mobility on the growing surface. The Verneuil technique is standard for crystals such as synthetic rubies and sapphires (Al_2O_3, with impurities for coloration).

Growth processes might be likened to attempting to pack spheres in a box by dropping them in. If the spheres are all dropped into the box at once, it is unlikely that they will seek a closest-packed arrangement. If, however, the box is *gently* shaken while adding a few spheres at a time *and* one begins with a close-packed plane of spheres at the bottom, the

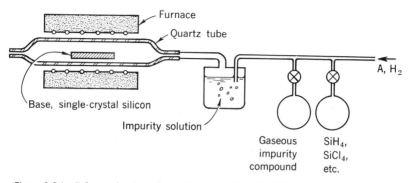

Figure 1.24 Schematic of equipment used to deposit thin layers of single-crystal silicon material on single-crystal substrates of silicon.

incoming spheres will likely arrange in a perfect or near-perfect close packing. If the box is shaken too roughly, the spheres in the box will be tumbled about (equivalent to melting the entire seed crystal); if not shaken enough, a good "crystal" will not result. If the spheres hit with excessive energy, they will disturb previously packed spheres. Crystal growth consequently requires careful control of temperatures.

Vapor decomposition is a vapor-phase growth process used, for example, to produce thin deposits of silicon on a planar single-crystal silicon surface (Fig. 1.24). A readily dissociated gaseous compound, commonly the hydride (SiH_4) or a halide ($SiCl_4$), dissociates well below the melting point of the semiconductor, in an atmosphere consisting largely of hydrogen or argon. Silicon atoms deposit over all surfaces of the container, including the seed wafer. The halogen or hydrogen departs as gas. Atoms desired as impurities in the crystal may be introduced by mixing them, as dissociable compounds, with the other gaseous components. The rate of decomposition is low enough so that there is negligible trapping of unwanted gas atoms in the crystalline layer. The temperature must be high enough so that the arriving atoms will arrange themselves properly on the crystal surface; it is typically in the range 1100 to 1200°C. This growth technique is too costly for depositing large volumes of material. The process of obtaining single-crystal deposits on a single crystal is termed *epitaxy*.

Polycrystalline deposits can be grown on an amorphous surface such as polished glass, by this or other vapor-phase techniques. Thin-film conductors (e.g., gold, copper, aluminum), magnetic alloys (nickel-iron), resistors (nickel-chromium, tantalum, etc.), superconductors (tin, lead), and insulators (silicon monoxide) can be produced. The deposits obtained in this way consist of small abutting crystallites, which are in general larger if the surface is hotter during deposition. The most common vapor-phase deposition technique is the *evaporation* of the source material by heating in a high-vacuum environment.

Many important electronic materials are used in poly-crystalline forms. Structure-dependent properties may be altered after casting of the material, and after mechanical drawing or rolling operations, by heat-treatment (annealing). Even at temperatures well below the melting point, lattice defects will begin to work their way out of the crystallites if there is sufficient thermal agitation. Equilibrium defect density will be approached, and to a limited degree small crystallites will form larger ones. Heat-treatment operations to control mechanical properties of metals are the major concern of metallurgists. Such structure-altering procedure may also profoundly influence electrical properties. Resistivity in metals may change by 2:1 or more, while dielectric properties (of ceramics) and properties of magnetic materials may change by orders of magnitude.

1.9 Segregation of Impurities; Crystal Purification

When a crystal is grown from a melt or solution containing impurities, some impurity atoms become entrapped as interstitial or substitutional impurities. If impurity atoms are much larger than the desired atoms, or have a different valency, they are not so likely to lodge in the solid as are small atoms or ones almost identical with the desired atoms. If one were to attempt to produce single crystals of iron from a melt containing iron, with nickel as an impurity, the nickel would appear in the solid in nearly the same concentration as in the melt. On the other hand, nickel impurity atoms in a melt of germanium or silicon would result in crystals of much lower nickel concentration. This process is known as *segregation*. It is of great value in introducing or removing impurities from semiconductor crystals.

Segregation occurs whenever an impurity has a different solubility in the liquid phase than in the solid. Higher solubility in the liquid is the rule, since the random-ordered liquid state is less sensitive to the "fit" of impurity atoms.   A liquid containing a ratio of impurity atoms to host atoms M_l/N_l is brought into contact with a host crystal (seed).   The temperature is adjusted so that an extremely slow rate of crystal growth occurs.   For small impurity concentrations, there is a constant probability S that a given impurity atom will be entrapped in the growing crystal.   In a very small amount of crystalline material grown from this liquid, then, the ratio of impurity to host atoms will be

$$C = \frac{dM_s}{dN_s} = \frac{SM_l}{N_l} \tag{1.14}$$

S is therefore the equilibrium ratio of concentrations of impurity in the solid and in the liquid.   The relation does not apply when it predicts a concentration of impurities in the solid exceeding the actual solid solubility; that is, SM_l/N_l must be much less than the actual solubility in the solid.   Rearranging, $dM_l/M_l = S(dN_l/N_l)$.   Integrating,

$$M_l = N_l{}^S \times \text{const} \tag{1.15}$$

If the initial melt composition is M, N for impurity and host, respectively, when the crystal is begun, $M_l = M$ and $N_l = N$; hence the constant may be determined:

$$M_l = N_l{}^S \times \frac{M}{N^S} \tag{1.16}$$

We desire to know the composition in the solid vs. the depletion of the melt:

$$C = S\frac{M_l}{N_l} = \frac{SN^{S-1}M}{N^S} = S\frac{(N - N_s)^{S-1}}{N^{S-1}}\frac{M}{N}$$
$$C = SC_0\left(1 - \frac{N_s}{N}\right)^{S-1} \tag{1.17}$$

where $C_0 = M/N$ is the original melt composition.   Figure 1.25 shows the universal curves, for several values of S.   The degree of exhaustion of the melt, x $(= N_S/N)$, may be related directly to position along the actual crystal.

Most of the important impurities in semiconductors have a limit of solid solubility of several per cent, but it is usually desired to eliminate them to the order of 1 part in 10^9.   The data of Table 1.3 show that the segregation coefficient S for most semiconductor impurities is well below unity.   If, for

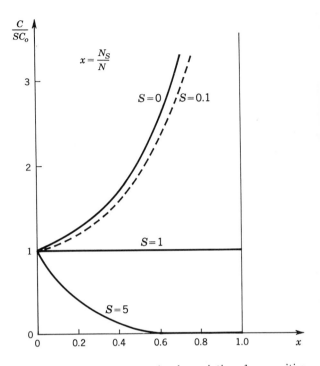

Figure 1.25 Universal curves for the variation of composition due to segregation as a crystal is pulled from an impure melt. Since the curves for $S = 0$ and $S = 0.1$ are so close together, the approximation $C/SC_0 = (1 - x)^{-1}$ is often made for small S.

example, there were 1 per cent of aluminum in a germanium melt, since $S \approx 0.1$, the very first part of the crystal drawn from this melt would contain only one-tenth of 1 per cent aluminum. Segregation of impurities into the melt increases their density in the melt remaining; hence impurity concentration in the crystal increases [according to (1.17)] as it depletes the melt. Most of the impurity is confined to a short region near the end of the crystal or may be discarded in the melt. The resulting crystal may still be insufficiently pure. Several procedures may be used to remove most of the remaining impurities; all are based on the same segregation technique. One of the most attractive of these is the *floating-zone* technique (Fig. 1.26), where only a thin section of the crystal is melted, by induction heating. No contaminants are introduced since the molten material is self-supported by surface

Table 1.3 Segregation coefficients of
semiconductor impurities†

Element	Segregation (distribution) coefficient	
	In Ge	In Si
Boron	~20	0.9
Aluminum	0.10	0.004
Gallium	0.10	0.01
Indium	0.001	0.0004
Phosphorus	0.12	0.35
Arsenic	0.03	0.3
Antimony	0.003	0.04
Tin		0.02
Gold	3×10^{-5}	3×10^{-5}

† After W. C. Dunlap, in L. P. Hunter (ed.),
"Handbook of Semiconductor Electronics," pp.
7-4, 7-5, McGraw-Hill Book Company, New
York, 1962.

tension.   As the molten zone is moved along the crystal by
moving of the heating coil, new material continuously melts,
and previously molten material solidifies into a single crystal.
Impurities concentrate in the molten zone, by segregation.   A
molten zone may be passed along the crystal from end to end
in the same direction several times, leaving most of the
impurities in a small region near the end, where the molten
zone is finally permitted to solidify.   The same floating-zone
procedures are also useful where, as in semiconductors, one
desires to introduce known and uniform quantities of impurity
atoms.   The impurity can be introduced into a molten zone
at one end of the crystal, the molten zone moved nearly to
the opposite end, and returned.   It will leave quantities of
the impurity throughout the crystal.   A molten zone moved
slowly back and forth along a fixed length of the crystal
eventually reaches a constant composition, and leaves as
much impurity material in the crystal which freezes as that in
the material which it melts.   This scheme is known as *zone
leveling*.

The segregation coefficient S is meaningful only at rates
of crystal growth so slow that the impurity concentration in
the liquid *at the growing face* is the same as in the rest of the
melt.   At high growth rates, many atoms of an impurity

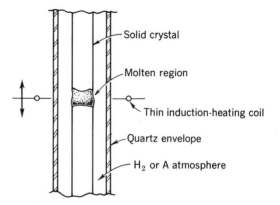

Figure 1.26 Configuration used in vertical zone-melting apparatus. The molten region is kept to a thin region by use of a shaped induction-heating coil, which can be raised and lowered to move the molten zone. Surface tension prevents the molten material from falling; the solid ends must be well supported.

with $S < 1$ must be rejected at the growing face. If they cannot diffuse rapidly into the liquid, their concentration at the growing face will be higher than elsewhere in the melt, and the impurity content will reflect this higher concentration rather than the average of the melt. A material such as boron, which has $S > 1$ in Ge and Si (indicating that it prefers the solid to the liquid), will accordingly produce greater concentration at *slow* than at fast growth rates, while most impurities will be enhanced by rapid growth. These rate-dependent properties are used in the preparation of some semiconductor devices (Sec. 5.13).

PROBLEMS

1.1(*a*) For the fcc, hcp, and bcc structures, determine the number and distances of nearest-neighbor atoms and next-nearest neighbors of any atom. (SUGGESTION: Express the position of a neighbor in terms of its cartesian components.)

1.1(*b*) If a compound $R_m X_n$ containing two types of atoms (R and X) were to form a close-packed layer structure of the form $ABABACABABAC \ldots$, determine values of m and n, presuming of course that each atom always chooses the same crystalline environment.

1.1(*c*) Construct a planar array or circles so that each has (1) three neighbors at 120°; (2) four neighbors at 90°. (3) Show by graphical or analytical means that it is not possible to make a connected array of circles with two or five neighbors or more than six. (4) For cases (1) and (2), determine the efficiency of planar packing as compared with a closest packing.

1.2(a) Determine the number of primitive cells in the conventional unit cell of each of the 14 lattices of Fig. 1.8.

1.2(b) In order to define correctly the triclinic lattice, what combinations of a, b, c and α, β, γ are *not* allowed if a crystal is actually to be triclinic?

1.2(c) When crystals are strained, their lattice is distorted slightly. What lattice type does an initially cubic crystal assume when it is strained (1) along one of the cube edges (e.g., a stress T_1); (2) along two perpendicular cube edges, by different amounts; (3) along a body diagonal; (4) along a face diagonal?

1.2(d) Show that the hexagonal close-packed *structure* is completely described, in terms of two 120°-separated a vectors in the base plane (as in Fig. 1.7b) and the c vector, as having one atom at $(0,0,0)$ and a second at $(\frac{1}{3}, -\frac{1}{3}, \frac{1}{2})$.

1.3(a) What point-group symmetry (state the appropriate symbol) does each of the following *structures* possess: (1) body-centered cubic; (2) face-centered cubic; (3) hexagonal close-packed; (4) diamond?

1.3(b) In studying a crystal of a given class, where the atomic arrangement is known, what elements of point-group symmetry would you look for first, and which later, in attempting to arrive logically at the point group to which the crystal belongs?

1.3(c) A body-centered cubic metal crystal is elongated along the body diagonal by application of stress, making it trigonal. (1) To what point group does it now belong? (2) What symmetry would a similarly strained face-centered crystal assume?

1.4(a) Prove that the conductivity tensor form given in Table 1.2 is correct for all orthorhombic groups, using the method of the text.

1.4(b) Prove that the form of (1.10) is correct for group 4. (HINT: letting $x' = y$, $y' = -x$, $z' = z$, then $T_1 \equiv T_{xx}$ becomes $T_{y'y'} \equiv T_2'$; but $T_5 = T_{xz}$ becomes $-T_{y'z'} \equiv T_4'$, etc.)

1.4(c) All orthorhombic groups have the same form of compliance tensor. Find this form.

1.4(d) Using a two-dimensional model of a structure, where

$$J_x = \sigma_{11}\mathcal{E}_x + \sigma_{12}\mathcal{E}_y \qquad J_y = \sigma_{12}\mathcal{E}_x + \sigma_{22}\mathcal{E}_y$$

and taking a unit square so that, with contacts on the edges, $J_x \equiv I_x$, $\mathcal{E}_x \equiv V_x$ (voltage), etc., form the products $V_x I_x$ and $V_y I_y$, the sum of which is the power dissipated in the conductive area. Show that in order for the power to be positive for all voltages V_x, V_y, it is necessary that $\sigma_{12}{}^2/(\sigma_{11}\sigma_{22}) < 1$.

1.5(*a*) Determine, for a face-centered cubic structure, the spacings between closest planes of atoms, of the following orientations:

(001), (011), (111)

1.5(*b*) Determine the number of atoms *per unit area of plane* for planes of each of the types specified in the previous problem, in terms of *a*.

1.5(*c*) For a hexagonal structure, sketch the planes (11, 0) and (11, 1). In terms of *a* and *c*, calculate the number of atoms per unit area in each type of plane, if the structure is hcp.

1.5(*d*) Show that the set of planes described by indices (*rst*) are completely equivalent to the planes described by ($\overline{rst}$).

1.6(*a*) Assume that the ions of an NaCl lattice are singly charged and that the lattice constant (fcc) is 5.63 A. Estimate the electrostatic potential at the position of a sodium ion by considering only the fields due to nearest, next-nearest, and next-next-nearest neighbor ions.

1.6(*b*) From a standpoint of crystalline bonding, how would each of the following materials be categorized: (1) argon, (2) sodium, (3) dry ice (CO_2), (4) KBr, (5) $CaCO_3$, (6) ice, (7) InSb, (8) CdTe, (9) AgI?

1.6(*c*) It is desired to know whether a crystal is ionically or covalently bonded. The material is unknown, but all manner of electrical and mechanical tests may be made. Indicate what tests you would make and the interpretation of results.

1.7(*a*) In the fcc structure of nickel (*a* = 3.52 A), estimate the diameter of the largest spherical ions which could fit into the octahedral and the tetrahedral voids. Assume that the nickel ions are spheres in contact.

1.7(*b*) When a crystal is heated, excess defects tend to be removed. (1) In the case of a vacancy, describe the processes which must take place. (2) Explain why a crystalline compound (two or more different atoms) is more likely to be defected, other things being equal, than an elemental crystal.

1.7(*c*) (1) Determine the change in the energy of neighboring sodium ions in an NaCl lattice when there is a vacancy of a chlorine ion. Neglect ion movement in the calculation. (2) Will the ions tend to move toward or away from the vacancy? (3) List all the energy contributions which must be considered in estimating the energy associated with a vacancy.

1.7(*d*) Show by sketches and explanation that a dislocation which is entirely contained within a crystal must assume the character of an edge dislocation at some points and a screw dislocation at other points.

1.8(*a*) The rate at which a high-quality crystal may be grown depends on the ease with which it may fit itself into a possible site. Ionic crystals are in general easier to grow than are ordered alloys of metals, because the ions cannot readily assume sites surrounded by like-charged neighbors. Compare on this basis the relative ease of growing single crystals of high-quality (1) copper on a (111) face versus a (100) face; (2) NaCl versus ZnO; (3) Ge versus GaAs.

1.8(b) Would you estimate that the growth of good single crystals, as by the Czochralski technique, would be easier with a material having a low heat of fusion or with a material having a high heat of fusion? Explain. In controlled crystal growth, what happens to the heat of fusion released in the growth process?

1.8(c) When a liquid capable of etching the surface of a crystal (e.g., an acid, in the case of metals) is applied to a polished crystal surface, a phenomenon known as an *etch pit* appears. This is a small terraced depression, deepest at its center, and generally in some simple geometrical shape. (1) Explain the terraced form in terms of the reverse of the process of planar growth described in the text. (2) Why should etch pits on the semiconductors silicon and germanium, on (111) polished faces, be triangular in form? (3) On high-quality crystals, etch pits are associated with dislocations extending to the surface, so that a count of etch pits is related to crystalline perfection. Why should etch pits be associated with dislocations?

1.9(a) A crystal of silicon 200 g in weight known to contain 1 part in 10^4 of arsenic is melted into a crucible and repulled on a small seed. The resulting crystal is to have an *average* arsenic content of 5 parts in 10^5. What fraction of the melt may be used, and what part must be discarded, so that the crystal will have the desired average arsenic content?

1.9(b) A crystal is known to contain an impurity distribution given by $C(x)$, the composition vs. position. Near one end of the crystal, at which $C(x)$ is smallest, the composition is nearly uniform. A molten zone is produced in this region, then moved along toward the higher-impurity end of the crystal. At the other end, without allowing it to refreeze, it is moved back toward the original end. (1) Draw a sketch representing a likely original distribution, the distribution after the molten zone is moved to the high-impurity end, and that after it has been returned to its original position. Assume that the segregation coefficient $S < 1$. (2) What is the effect of increasing the width of the molten zone, in terms of the resulting composition variation?

GENERAL REFERENCES

Azaroff, L. V.: "Introduction to Solids," McGraw-Hill Book Company, New York, 1960. (An excellent introductory treatment of structure and defects.)

Buerger, M. J.: "Crystal-structure Analysis," John Wiley & Sons, Inc., New York, 1960.

Doremus, R. H., et al. (eds.): "Growth and Perfection of Crystals," John Wiley & Sons, Inc., New York, 1958. (A symposium.)

Lawson, W. D., and S. Nielsen: "Preparation of Single Crystals," Butterworth & Co. (Publishers), Ltd., London, 1958. (Deals mainly with semiconductor crystals.)

Nye, J. F.: "Physical Properties of Crystals: Their Representation by Tensors and Matrices," Clarendon Press, Oxford, 1957.

Phillips, F. C.: "An Introduction to Crystallography," 2d ed., John Wiley & Sons, Inc., New York, 1956. (A short description of groups and crystals, from an experimentalist's viewpoint.)

Shockley, W., et al. (eds.): "Imperfections in Nearly-perfect Crystals," National Research Council, Washington, D.C., and John Wiley & Sons, Inc., New York, 1952. (Excellent introductory treatments included.)

Wyckoff, R. W. G.: "Crystal Structures," Interscience Publishers, Inc., New York, 1948–1960. (A collection of structural data on a vast number of materials, including some interesting discussions on structure.)

2

Waves in crystals

2.1 One-dimensional Periodic Structures

Electron waves are influenced strongly by the periodic potentials, the dimensions and symmetries of a crystalline environment. Fortunately, the same mathematical foundations underlie all kinds of waves, acoustical and electromagnetic waves as well as electron waves. Actual wave solutions in crystal structures, however, are generally not simple enough to use as examples. Since lumped-constant one-dimensional electrical and mechanical periodic networks are valuable analogs, particularly in regard to acoustical waves in solid, they are used in this section to introduce the subject of waves in periodic structures.

The electrical tuned circuit of Fig. 2.1 is a very simple form of *harmonic oscillator*. Its steady-state sinusoidal operation is described completely in terms of its terminal voltage. With an *applied* voltage represented in the familiar complex (a-c) notation as $Ve^{j\omega t}$, the current which passes between the terminals is

$$i = Ve^{j\omega t}\left(j\omega L - \frac{j}{\omega L}\right) = Ve^{j\omega t}j\left(\omega C - \frac{1}{\omega L}\right) \qquad (2.1)$$

The frequency of *resonance*, ω_0, is indicated by the vanishing of the current in the circuit; hence $\omega_0 = (LC)^{-\frac{1}{2}}$. If this circuit is now *coupled* to another like it by a capacitor C', as in the

It is suggested that the reader familiarize himself with the material in Appendix B, in preparation for the subject matter in Chap. 2 related to quantum-mechanical solutions of electron motion.

57

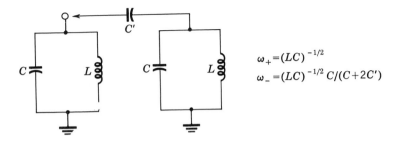

$$\omega_+ = (LC)^{-1/2}$$
$$\omega_- = (LC)^{-1/2}\, C/(C+2C')$$

Figure 2.1   A simple tuned circuit, coupled through a capacitor C' to a second identical circuit.   The two resonances of the combination are shown.

figure, the coupled circuits will be characterized by a pair of resonant frequencies, separated by an amount depending on the value of C'. The larger C', the larger the coupling of the two resonators, and the larger the splitting of the originally degenerate resonances. Figure 2.2 depicts the variation of the two resonances as a function of the ratio of the coupling to resonator capacitances. In the coupled electrical circuits the voltages on the two coupled resonators are 180° out of phase for the lower-frequency resonance and in phase for the higher-frequency resonance (which in this case equals the original resonant frequency). *When circuits are coupled, it is no longer possible to associate a particular resonance with a particular circuit.*

Even at this point, we can draw an analogy with electron-wave phenomena. As discussed in Sec. B.9, if we bring together two atomic nuclei, the wave function of an electron orbiting the pair will to first order be given by the sum or difference of the wave functions characteristic of the electron orbiting a single nucleus. Then, just as in the electrical circuit, one wave will have identical time phase at the two nuclei, while the other will have opposite signs at the two nuclei.

If we now add a third tuned circuit, connected to the second to form a "chain," a third resonant frequency appears, the three resonances being distributed over nearly the same frequency range as were the two resonances of the two-resonator coupled circuit. Additional resonators may be added in the same way; for this particular configuration, the *highest* resonant frequency is always ω_0. This is easily understood, for at this resonance all resonator voltages are exactly in time phase; there is no voltage across the

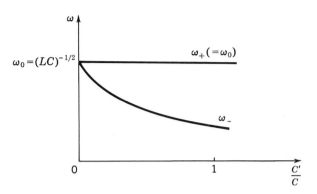

Figure 2.2   The variation of the resonances of the two coupled circuits of Fig. 2.1, as a function of C'.

capacitors C', and *in effect* the resonators are not coupled.
The lowest resonant frequency, on the other hand, always
corresponds to a situation in which each resonator voltage is
180° out of phase with those adjacent to it, since at resonance
all resonators must have voltages in phase or opposed.   At
the lowest resonance frequency, the coupling capacitances
have the largest possible voltage across them (for a given
energy in the system), carry the largest current, and thus
have the largest influence.

Extending this chain of resonators to infinity on both
ends is possible in a formal sense; polynomial solutions to
determine the resonant frequencies would obviously become
intractable.   For an infinite chain of this type, which is a
periodic structure, solutions based on *recurrence relations* permit simplification of analysis.

A one-dimensional periodic structure has characteristic
solutions, for voltage or similar quantities, which have the
form of *traveling waves*.   Considering for the present only
linear systems, any general time function can be represented
as a Fourier series or integral of sinusoidal time functions.
At a single frequency, a traveling wave can be expected to
differ from point to point along a periodic structure by an
exponential factor not dependent on choice of origin.   That
is, if we represent an arbitrarily chosen element in an infinitely
long chain by the subscript n (Fig. 2.3), the voltage at n is
related by a simple exponential factor to that at terminal
$n - 1$.

$$V_n = e^{-j\theta}V_{n-1} \tag{2.2}$$

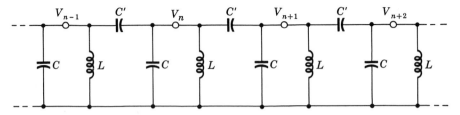

Figure 2.3 An infinite chain of tuned circuits like those of Fig. 2.1.

The parameter θ may be complex, allowing the exponential factor to represent phase shift and/or attenuation. With this stipulation on the terminal voltages, a relation can be written for the sum of the currents leaving terminal n, which must be zero by Kirchhoff's current law; for Fig. 2.3,

$$0 = V_n\left(j\omega C - \frac{j}{\omega L}\right) + (V_n - V_{n-1})j\omega C'$$
$$+ (V_n - V_{n+1})j\omega C'$$

Substituting the recurrence relation (2.2),

$$V_n\left[\left(j\omega C - \frac{j}{\omega L} + 2j\omega C'\right) - j\omega C'(e^{j\theta} + e^{-j\theta})\right] = 0$$

Neglecting the trivial solution $V_n = 0$, this leaves a relation involving ω and θ:

$$\cos\theta = \frac{1}{2}\left(\frac{C}{C'} + 2 - \frac{1}{\omega^2 L C'}\right) \tag{2.3}$$

For particular fixed values of the parameters L, C, and C', $\cos\theta$ may lie between the limits $+1$ and -1 only for certain values of ω, specifically the limits $\omega_1 < \omega < \omega_h$:

$$\omega_h = (LC)^{-\frac{1}{2}}$$
$$\omega_l = (LC)^{-\frac{1}{2}}\left(1 + \frac{4C'}{C}\right)^{-\frac{1}{2}} \tag{2.4}$$

In the range $\omega_l < \omega < \omega_h$, therefore, θ is real. For values of ω below ω_l, or above ω_h, $|\cos\theta| > 1$. In these regions, θ must have a purely imaginary value. This corresponds to recurrence factors of the form $e^{\pm\alpha}$, with α a real number. This is an *attenuative* solution, in which the voltage wave is attenuated without energy loss.

In the region $\omega_l < \omega < \omega_h$, only the phase, and not the amplitude, of the voltage differs from terminal to terminal.

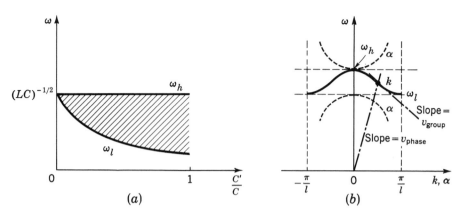

Figure 2.4 (a) The range of frequencies propagated by the chain of Fig. 2.3, as a function of C'. Note the resemblance to Fig. 2.2. (b) The ω-k plot of the chain of Fig. 2.3, for a certain small value of C'. The attenuation α, in this case per unit length, is also shown near the edges of the passband.

A plot of ω_h and ω_l versus C' (Fig. 2.4a) follows in form the variation of resonant frequencies for the two-resonator chain. The limits ω_l and ω_h form an envelope enclosing the infinity of resonances in a chain of infinite length. The ω_l limit is that frequency at which alternate resonators are exactly opposed in phase.

The chain just described is known in electrical engineering as a *bandpass filter*. The propagating region $\omega_l < \omega < \omega_h$ is known as a *passband*, and the adjacent regions ($\omega < \omega_l$, $\omega > \omega_h$) in which the wave is attenuated, *stop bands*. The limit frequencies, or *band-edge* frequencies, are important parameters of such a structure. Also important is the phase shift θ per period; in the stop bands, the attenuation α, or $e^{-\alpha}$, may also be of practical importance. Since only $\cos\theta$ appears in (2.3), for a given frequency, both θ and $-\theta$ are solutions. If we include the time variation,

$$V_n e^{j\omega t} = V_{n-1} e^{j(\omega t - \theta)}$$

or

$$V_{n-1} e^{j(\omega t + \theta)}$$

The first represents a wave traveling to the right, the second a wave traveling to the left.

If the *physical distance* between adjacent terminals is l, then we denote $\theta/l = k$, the phase shift per unit length, or *propagation constant*.[1] The voltage, with respect to some

---

[1] This parameter is most commonly represented by the symbol β in treatises on electromagnetic waveguiding structures.

terminal labeled as the origin, may be written

$$V_n e^{j\omega t} = V_0 e^{j(\omega t \pm k n l)}$$

If we understand that the voltage is measurable only at points $z = nl$, it is permissible to express it as

$$V_h e^{j\omega t} = V_0 e^{j(\omega t \pm k z)} \qquad (2.5)$$

This is the general form of a traveling wave; the concepts of phase velocity and group velocity[1] may be applied. We have, therefore, for any wave of the form (2.5),

$$v_{\text{phase}} = \frac{\omega}{k} \quad \text{and} \quad v_{\text{group}} = \left(\frac{\partial k}{\partial \omega}\right)^{-1} \qquad (2.6)$$

In a plot of ω versus k ($= \theta/l$), phase velocity is therefore the ratio of vertical to horizontal projections of a point on the curve; group velocity is the slope of the curve. Figure 2.4b, showing these constructions, is an ω-k plot for a structure of the type described in Fig. 2.3. Two important general properties are apparent in the curve:

1. The group velocity of the wave propagating along a chain of this type is zero at both frequency limits of the passband, $\omega = \omega_h$ and $\omega = \omega_l$. (This is explained by the fact that each element of the chain is in resonance at these frequencies, and energy oscillates back and forth in the L and C elements, rather than traveling along the line.)

2. The propagation constant k is zero at one limit of the passband and $\pm\pi/l$ at the other. The *range* of k represented by the passband is therefore $2\pi/l$.

Several other simple types of electrical filters, along with their characteristic ω-k variations, are shown in Fig. 2.5. The low-pass structure has a low-frequency limit of zero; the ω-k plot shows a finite group velocity at the lower limit. This situation can occur only at the limit of zero or infinite frequency. This low-pass structure is very useful in describing acoustical waves in solids (Sec. 2.7.)

The structures shown in Fig. 2.5b and c propagate waves in *two passbands* of frequencies. *Each element* of the chain has *two* distinct resonant frequencies, when uncoupled. Each of these, when perturbed by coupling to the adjacent resona-

[1] The phase velocity is that at which points of constant wave amplitude move; group velocity, that at which energy (mass, in the case of quantum mechanics) propagates (see Appendix B).

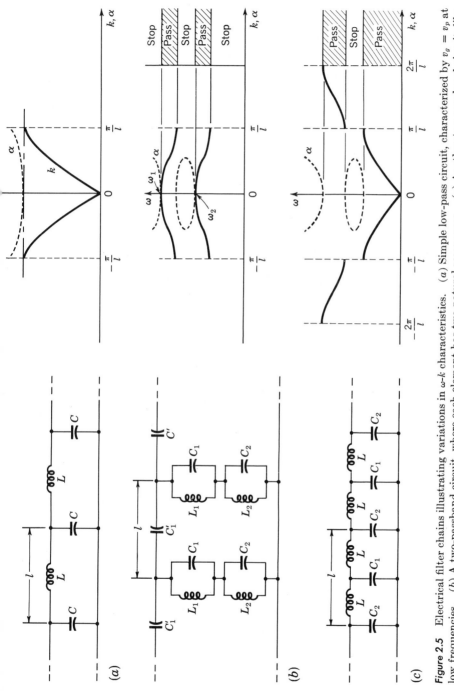

Figure 2.5 Electrical filter chains illustrating variations in ω–k characteristics. (a) Simple low-pass circuit, characterized by $v_g = v_p$ at low frequencies. (b) A two-passband circuit, where each element has two natural resonances. (c) Another two-passband circuit, like (a), but with two alternating values of C. In addition to k, the characteristics show attenuation in the stop band, α.

tors, produces a passband. The two passbands (in this one-dimensional case) are separated by a stop band. The circuit of Fig. 2.5c has the additional distinction that in the upper passband the phase shift per section varies from $\pm\pi$ to $\pm 2\pi$, since the two resonant elements making up each period are connected so that their phase shifts add.

Imagine that an unknown length of either type of structure were placed in a "black box." Through external measurements using only signal sources of frequency in the upper passband, one is asked to tell whether the circuit has the form of Fig. 2.5b or of Fig. 2.5c. A pulse-delay measurement would yield only group velocity, which would not serve to distinguish the two. We might make actual phase-shift measurements, but here we should need to set some arbitrary reference of zero phase (since we have precluded measuring from zero frequency). We can now no longer discern the difference between phase shifts of $3\pi/2$ and $-\pi/2$. Accordingly, without the ability to make detailed measurements *within* the period, or to start from zero frequency, the two cannot be distinguished. As we shall see, this same ambiguity extends to electron waves in crystals, where we are prohibited from investigating the lower-*energy* electronic "passbands."

The region $-\pi/l < k < \pi/l$ is known as the *first Brillouin zone* of the one-dimensional structure; the combined regions $-2\pi/l < k < -\pi/l$ and $\pi/l < k < 2\pi/l$ are known as the second Brillouin zone, etc. A Brillouin zone is merely a region of k in which the ω-k properties of a passband may be defined. The zone must encompass a range of $2\pi/l$ in "k space."

2.2   Waves in One-dimensional, Distributed-constant Systems

The electrical networks used above to introduce band theory have the merit of simplicity. Each periodic element is capable of only one or of several resonances, and the coupled elements have the same number of passbands. The systems dealt with in crystalline solids, except for acoustical waves, are not describable in terms of such *lumped-constant* models, but require a distributed-constant analog. In crystals, electron-wave equations, for example, may have the approximate form

$$-\frac{\hbar^2}{2m}\nabla^2\psi + V(x,y,z)\psi = E\psi \tag{2.7}$$

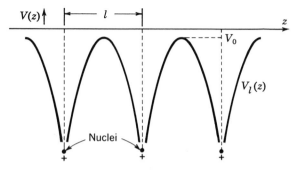

Figure 2.6 An approximation to the potential experienced by an electron in passing through a one-dimensional array of atoms.

where the potential $V(x,y,z)$ has the periodicity of the lattice (1.2). Of course, the true energy of the electron has time-varying terms due to the motion of all the other electrons and the nuclei. The assumption in (2.7) that it may be approximated as time-independent is termed the *one-electron* approximation.

Continuing with the one-electron approximation, in one dimension for clarity, the wave equation takes the form

$$-\frac{\hbar^2}{2m}\frac{d^2\psi}{dx^2} + [V_l(z) - E]\psi = 0 \tag{2.8}$$

where the potential energy $V_l(z)$ is periodic with period l. For example, the potential along a line of nuclei might be schematized by a function such as that described by Fig. 2.6. The potential V_l satisfies

$$V_l(z + l) = V_l(z) \tag{2.9}$$

Equation (2.8) is almost identical in form with the equation for electromagnetic propagation in a simple transmission line with dielectric constant varying periodically along the line:

$$\frac{d^2\phi}{dx^2} + \omega^2\mu\epsilon_l(z)\phi = 0 \tag{2.10}$$

(The symbol ϕ represents voltage or some field quantity.) In this equation, frequency ω is the parameter determining the nature of the solutions. In (2.8), however, electron energy E assumes a comparable position. The frequency bands of electrical circuits are analogous to *energy bands* in electron-wave solutions.

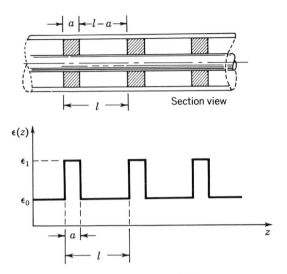

Figure 2.7 An electromagnetic periodic structure, consisting of a coaxial transmission line with periodically placed dielectric supports. The variation of permittivity ϵ with distance is also given.

Let us examine the band structure of the periodic-dielectric transmission line depicted in Fig. 2.7. Each period l of the circuit contains a region a filled with dielectric, plus an air-filled region $l - a$. The equation and solution in this case are analogous to a simple electron-wave solution attributed to Kronig and Penney.[1] As in lumped-constant structures, the band properties of the distributed-constant transmission line may be developed from the resonances of a single period. A period of the transmission line is the equivalent of an electromagnetic cavity resonator; such a resonator will have resonances in which its length contains 1, 2, . . . nodes of voltage (Fig. 2.8). Since *each* period of the transmission line has, therefore, an infinite number of *resonances* extending to infinite frequency, the periodic line must have infinitely many passbands. Figure 2.9 shows the ω-k plot for this type of transmission line, for several values of dielectric length a. At zero length, the diagram is that of a uniform structure whose phase and group velocities equal the velocity of light in free space. The passband is continuous. With the addi-

[1] Cf. C. F. Kittel, "Introduction to Solid-state Physics," pp. 280ff., John Wiley & Sons, Inc., New York, 1956.

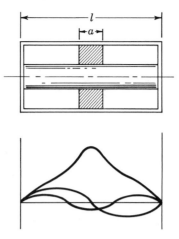

Figure 2.8   A single section of the line of Fig. 2.7, in this case short-circuited, showing also some of the voltage variations of the infinitely many resonances possible in the single period.

tion of *very thin* dielectric spacers, however, narrow stop bands appear at frequencies at which the basic period is an integral number of free-space half-wavelengths. The entire curve is also shifted slightly, to lower asymptotic velocities, because of the average effect of the dielectric loading. The width of the stop bands is a function of the length of dielectric, the

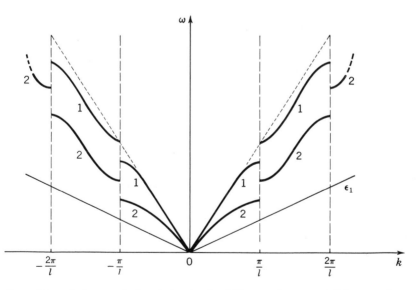

Figure 2.9 ω-k characteristics of the circuit of Fig. 2.7, for several different values of a, the dielectric length.   The dashed line is for $a = 0$, curves 1 and 2 for, respectively, increasing a, and the line marked ϵ_1 is the constant-velocity characteristic of a line filled with dielectric of constant ϵ_1.

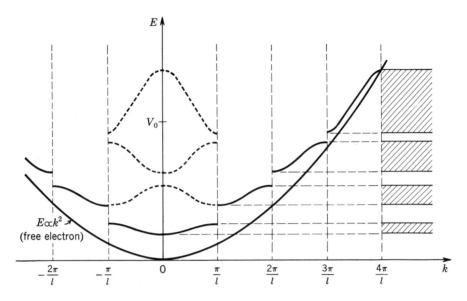

Figure 2.10 E-k characteristics of a particle in an atomic potential-well chain (one-dimensional) like that of Fig. 2.6.   The dashed segments are correctly translated into the first Brillouin zone, $-\pi/l < k < +\pi/l$.

curve falling to the asymptotic constant-velocity characteristic of the dielectric, for 100 per cent dielectric filling.

The ω-k plot of a *uniform* transmission structure, such as a coaxial transmission line without periodic dielectrics, is simply a straight line (Fig. 2.9) of slope v_p ($= c$).   The E-k plot of a uniform "particle transmission line" (that is, $V_1 = 0$ —free space) represents waves of the form $e^{-jEt/\hbar + jpz/\hbar}$. The propagation constant k equals $p/\hbar$, for a free-particle wave (Sec. B.1).   Such a free particle satisfies the relation

$$E = \frac{p^2}{2m} \equiv \frac{k^2\hbar^2}{2m} \tag{2.11}$$

An E-k curve for *free* particles is thus a *parabola* (Fig. 2.10). The E-k plot for waves in an atomic periodic potential (represented by Fig. 2.6) approaches the free-particle relation only at energies well above V_0 where the ionic potentials represent only a small perturbation.

The passbands, where electron waves move unattenuated, are termed *allowed bands* in solid-state theory.   In the other bands, the so-called *forbidden bands*, electron waves are prohibited in a perfect crystal.   Electron waves can be set up in the forbidden bands only if established at the surface of the crystal or at a defect or impurity (Sec. 2.6).

Let us now investigate in more detail the nature of solutions to these distributed-constant wave equations. Whereas in the lumped-constant solutions it was not possible to define the wave except at discrete terminals, here it can be defined anywhere within a period. Because of the periodicity, it should not be surprising that the solution within one period must have a simple relationship with that in the next succeeding period. Solutions to linear wave equations with periodic parameters, such as (2.8) and (2.10), can, by *Floquet's theorem*, be expressed in the completely general form

$$\phi_k(z) = U_k(z)e^{jkz} \tag{2.12}$$

where

$$U_k(z + l) = U_k(z) \tag{2.13}$$

The factor $U(z)$ describes the behavior of the solution within each period.

This solution satisfies a recurrence relation, like (2.2):

$$\phi_k(z + l) = e^{\pm jkl}\phi_k(z) \tag{2.14}$$

Substituting (2.12) into (2.14), we obtain the recurrence relation

$$\phi_k(z + l) = U_k(z + l)e^{jk(z+l)} = U_k(z)e^{jkz}e^{jkl} = e^{jkl}\phi_k(z) \tag{2.15}$$

Functions of the form (2.12) were first used in quantum theory by Bloch,[1] and are termed *Bloch functions*.

We have already shown, in connection with lumped-constant filters, that the assignment of a particular passband to a particular Brillouin zone (i.e., a particular range or ranges of k) may not always be possible from external measurement. This is especially true for electron waves in crystals, where one cannot measure detailed phase variations in the wave functions. Since only electron-wave group velocity (the actual mass velocity) is meaningful, one can regard the plotting of particular bands in particular zones as largely arbitrary. A given wave function written in the Bloch form *does not uniquely define* k. We can write the function equally well as

$$\phi(z) = e^{jk'z}U_{k'}(z) \tag{2.16}$$

[1] Felix Bloch, *Z. Phys.*, **52**:555 (1928).

where k and k' are related by a simple translation

$$k = k' + K \qquad (2.17)$$

With this translation

$$U_k(z)e^{jkz} = U_k(z)e^{jk'z}e^{jKz} \qquad (2.18)$$

Again using the Bloch-function form,

$$U_{k'}(z)e^{jk'z} \equiv U_k(z)e^{jk'z}e^{jKz}$$

Hence

$$U_{k'}(z) = U_k(z)e^{jKz} \qquad (2.19)$$

This function $U_{k'}(z)$ must, however, be periodic in l:

$$\begin{aligned}
U_{k'}(z + l) &= U_k(z + l)e^{jK(z+l)} \\
&= U_k(z)e^{jKz}e^{jKl} \\
&= U_{k'}(z)e^{jKl}
\end{aligned}$$

Periodicity of $U_{k'}(z)$ requires $Kl = 2\pi n$ ($n = 0, \pm 1, \pm 2, \ldots$), or $K = 2\pi n/l$. The plot may be shifted to left or right by an integral multiple of $2\pi/l$. Figure 2.10 shows higher-energy bands plotted in the first Brillouin zone. Observe that the variation of group velocity with energy is unchanged in this translation.

At the band edges which coincide at $k = 0$ after a shift, the wave functions must be the same; otherwise there would be an ambiguous wave function at that point. We can show in fact that *both* limits of the half-bands have *identical* wave functions, so that not only the joined edges but the two remaining limits are *completely equivalent*. That is, for any *given band*,

$$\phi_{n\pi/l}(z) \equiv \phi_{-n\pi/l}(z) \qquad n = 0, 1, 2, \ldots \qquad (2.20)$$

To prove this, write a general wave equation for a one-dimensional periodic structure:

$$\frac{d^2\phi}{dz^2} = P_l(z)\phi \qquad (2.21)$$

where $P_l(z) \equiv P_l(z + l)$. Writing ϕ in the Bloch form $e^{jkz}U_k(z)$, substituting into (2.21), and factoring the exponential,

$$-k^2 U_k(z) + 2jk U_k'(z) + U_k''(z) = P_l(z)U_k(z) \qquad (2.22)$$

The differential equation obtained by alteration of (2.22) to represent $U_{-k}(z)$ is identical with that obtained by conjugating (2.22) (except of course for the different symbol representing the unknown function in the two instances). Since the boundary conditions are the same,

$$U_k^*(z) \equiv U_{-k}(z) \tag{2.23}$$

At the band limits,

$$\phi_{-n\pi/l}(z) = e^{-jn\pi z/l} U_{-n\pi/l}$$
$$\phi_{n\pi/l} = e^{jn\pi z/l} U_{n\pi/l}(z)$$

Hence

$$\phi_{n\pi/l}^*(z) = e^{-jn\pi z/l} U_{n\pi/l}^*(z) = \phi_{-n\pi/l}(z) \tag{2.24}$$

At these band limits, however, the group velocity is zero; the waves are everywhere either in phase or 180° out of phase. They must therefore be *real* functions, so $\phi^* = \phi$ at the band limits. This demonstrates the property (2.20). It applies *only* to waves belonging to the same band, for two functions belonging to different bands have different time-dependent exponential factors $e^{j\omega t}$ (or $e^{jEt/\hbar}$) and could not be equal. In a given band, then, we cannot distinguish between band-limit solutions having the same energy.

The solution of wave equations for periodic systems which are assumed to be infinite in extent leads, as we have shown, to infinite traveling-wave solutions, analogous to the uniform plane-wave solutions which occur naturally in uniform transmission systems. As in the case of uniform waveguiding systems, however, these infinite traveling-wave solutions describe poorly the finite media in which the actual waves propagate. It is desirable to incorporate the influence of boundaries of the periodic system. This can be done in a variety of ways, each best suited for particular problems. The boundary conditions most familiar in acoustical and electromagnetic problems are (1) wave function zero at boundaries or (2) derivative of wave function zero at boundaries. In one-dimensional problems such as organ pipes, vibrating rods, etc., these lead to sets of resonances, i.e., to *standing waves* with sinusoidal spatial dependence (in rectangular systems). Neither of these boundary conditions is really pertinent to electron, electromagnetic, or acoustical waves in a crystal, since the surfaces of a crystal do not represent so idealized a boundary. It must, however, be recognized that the number of wave solutions in a given frequency or energy range is not arbitrary. For this purpose, any boundary conditions are as good as any other. Physicists often make use of *periodic boundary conditions*, the requirement that a wave function at one point in a solid be the same as at a point s periods removed:

$$\phi_k(z + sl) \equiv \phi_k(z) \tag{2.25}$$

Representing the wave by a Bloch function,

$$U_k(z)e^{jkz} = U_k(z + sl)e^{jkz}e^{jksl} \tag{2.26}$$

Since $U_k(z) = U_k(z + sl)$,

$$e^{jksl} = 1 \qquad k = \frac{2\pi m}{sl} \qquad m = 0, \pm 1, \pm 2, \pm \frac{s}{2} \tag{2.27}$$

Since $k = \pi/l$ and $k = -\pi/l$ are equivalent, there are s different solutions, each a traveling wave. Application of any type of boundary conditions to a periodic system of s periods results in a number of "resonances" *equal to the number of periods*.

The type of mathematical wave functions best suited to the description of waves in a crystalline medium depends mainly on the ratio of the dimensions of the crystal to the wavelength of the waves in question. (The wavelength, in a one-dimensional case, is given by $\lambda = 2\pi/k$.) If the dimensions are only a few wavelengths, the wave may best be described in terms of resonant modes. If, on the other hand, the wavelength is much smaller than the crystal dimensions, any such resonances would be closely spaced in energy and frequency and it becomes more appropriate to think in terms of *wave packets* (Secs. B.4 and B.5), which extend over only a fraction of the volume of the entire crystal. While the latter concept is intuitively desirable for electrons, it is even pertinent for acoustical and electromagnetic waves at frequencies well above those at which the crystal has simple acoustical or electromagnetic resonances.

2.3 Brillouin Zones for Three-dimensional Periodic Structures

A three-dimensional Bloch function, by extension of (2.12), may be written as a function of a position vector $\mathbf{r}$ and a *vector* propagation constant $\mathbf{k}$:

$$\phi_\mathbf{k}(\mathbf{r}) = U_\mathbf{k}(\mathbf{r})e^{j\mathbf{k}\cdot\mathbf{r}} \left[\equiv U_\mathbf{k}(x,y,z)e^{j(k_x x + k_y y + k_z z)} \right] \tag{2.28}$$

This is the general form of solutions to linear electronic, acoustical, or electromagnetic wave equations in a homo-

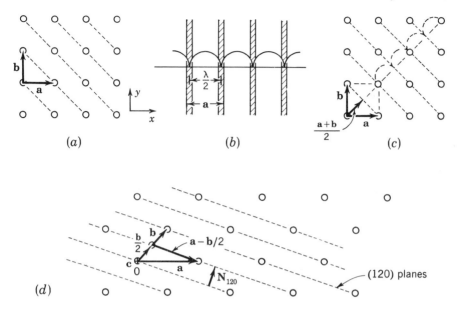

Figure 2.11 (a) A simple square lattice showing small dielectric spheres placed at the lattice points. (b) The spheres imagined arranged into planes normal to the x axis. The curves suggest standing waves in the regions between planes. (c) Conditions for interference of waves by planes formed at 45° to x and y axes. (d) Construction (here in two dimensions) establishing the length and direction of a normal between adjacent lattice planes. The dashed lines represent (120) planes, for lattice vectors **a**, **b**.

geneous crystal. The exponential factor here, along with the (omitted) time factor, represents a plane wave. The length of the propagation vector **k** equals the phase shift of the wave per unit length of travel; the waves travel in the direction **k**, so that planes of constant phase lie normal to **k**. The wavelength is just $\lambda = 2\pi/|\mathbf{k}|$. The periodic factor $U_\mathbf{k}(\mathbf{r})$ has the periodicity of the *lattice*, and is therefore described by

$$U_\mathbf{k}(\mathbf{r} + m\mathbf{a} + n\mathbf{b} + p\mathbf{c}) = U_\mathbf{k}(\mathbf{r}) \tag{2.29}$$

The *limits* of Brillouin zones are dependent only on the periodicity of the system, and not on the particular equation to be solved. We may accordingly use a simple model to derive the Brillouin-zone boundaries. Electromagnetic waves (i.e., x rays) will be assumed to travel through the crystal. We represent the *lattice points* by dielectric spheres, much smaller than their spacing. Figure 2.11 shows a simple cubic lattice of this type, of which we show an xy section. The spheres are grouped into sets of parallel planes. A wave traveling in the

x direction encounters successive (100) planes of dielectric spheres a distance a apart. These produce a cumulative reflection in nearly the same way as would a set of thin plane-parallel dielectric sheets. At frequencies for which a is an integral number of half-wavelengths, interference will result in the entire wave function becoming a *standing wave*, in which the wave function differs only by a factor $e^{\pm jn\pi}$ ($n = 1$, 2, . . .), as we move from a point r to a point $r + a$. Since the $U_k(r)$ factor is already periodic, this condition requires that

$$e^{jk \cdot (r+a)} = e^{jk \cdot r} e^{\pm jn\pi}$$

which is equivalent to the criterion

$$k \cdot a = \pm n\pi$$

This arrangement of the lattice points into planes normal to the x axis is not unique, for from these same points we can also construct other sets of planes. Consider planes arranged at 45° to the x (or y) direction (Fig. 2.11c); the spacing of the planes is $|a + b|/2$. The critical condition for these planes to set up standing waves in the periodic lattice is $k \cdot (a + b)/2 = \pm n\pi$. Likewise, if planes normal to the y direction are considered, a critical condition $k \cdot b = \pm n\pi$ is found.

Each possible set of planes produces a critical condition on k. If $|k|$ is large, many such conditions will be encountered. None of the critical conditions can apply, however, for small values of k, in the range

$$-\frac{\pi}{a} < k_x < \frac{\pi}{a} \qquad -\frac{\pi}{a} < k_y < \frac{\pi}{a} \qquad -\frac{\pi}{a} < k_z < \frac{\pi}{a}$$

This cubic region in k space forms the *first Brillouin zone* of a simple cubic lattice.

Finding all the boundaries of all Brillouin zones demands a more sophisticated approach, aided by the use of the so-called *reciprocal lattice*. Every lattice has a unique reciprocal lattice, which, like the original lattice, is a set of lattice points defined by primitive vectors. The primitive vectors of the reciprocal lattice, represented by a^*, b^*, c^*, are found from a, b, c by the relations

$$
\begin{aligned}
a^* \cdot a &= 1 & a^* \cdot b &= a^* \cdot c = 0 \\
b^* \cdot b &= 1 & b^* \cdot a &= b^* \cdot c = 0 \\
c^* \cdot c &= 1 & c^* \cdot a &= c^* \cdot b = 0
\end{aligned}
$$

(2.30)

Each primitive vector of the reciprocal lattice is *perpendicular* to two vectors of the original lattice. Thus, $\mathbf{a}^*$ is perpendicular to $\mathbf{b}$ and $\mathbf{c}$, etc. It is not difficult to prove that the reciprocal lattice vectors are given by

$$\mathbf{a}^* = \frac{\mathbf{b} \times \mathbf{c}}{\mathbf{a} \cdot \mathbf{b} \times \mathbf{c}} \qquad \mathbf{b}^* = \frac{\mathbf{c} \times \mathbf{a}}{\mathbf{b} \cdot \mathbf{c} \times \mathbf{a}} \qquad \mathbf{c}^* = \frac{\mathbf{a} \times \mathbf{b}}{\mathbf{c} \cdot \mathbf{a} \times \mathbf{b}} \qquad (2.31)$$

The denominators are all equal, merely the *volume* of the primitive cell in the original lattice. For a simple cubic lattice (with lattice constant a), $\mathbf{a}$, $\mathbf{b}$, and $\mathbf{c}$ are equal in length and mutually perpendicular; $\mathbf{a}^*$, $\mathbf{b}^*$, and $\mathbf{c}^*$ will also be perpendicular and equal in length. They form a reciprocal lattice of the same simple cubic form, having a lattice constant $1/a$. *Only* for the simple cubic, however, is the reciprocal lattice the same as the original. The face-centered cubic lattice, for example, has a body-centered reciprocal lattice. Since the basic definitions (2.30) are symmetrical in the original and reciprocal vectors, it follows that the body-centered cubic lattice has a face-centered reciprocal lattice. Reciprocal lattices for all the Bravais lattices, as would be expected, have the same *symmetry* as the original lattices.

To find all Brillouin-zone boundaries for a given lattice, we must form *all possible sets of reflecting planes* from the lattice points. Any lattice plane can be described by its intercepts on the primitive-vector axes. Let these intercepts be $m\mathbf{a}/h$, $m\mathbf{b}/k$, and $m\mathbf{c}/l$, where m, h, k, and l are all integers. (This procedure is similar to that of Miller-index notation, except that $\mathbf{a}$, $\mathbf{b}$, and $\mathbf{c}$ are the *primitive vectors*.) By defining all possible combinations of the indices h, k, l, we define all possible sets of parallel planes. As in Fig. 2.11d, the *closest* (h,k,l) plane to the origin not passing through the origin intercepts $\mathbf{a}$, $\mathbf{b}$, and $\mathbf{c}$ at distances $|\mathbf{a}|/h$, $|\mathbf{b}|/k$, and $|\mathbf{c}|/l$ from the origin, respectively. There is also a parallel plane *through* the origin, since any lattice point must be included in one of such a set of parallel planes. If now we can find a vector $\mathbf{N}_{hkl}$ *normal* to the planes (hkl) whose length is equal to the planar spacing, the conditions on $\mathbf{k}$ describing the Brillouin-zone limits due to hkl planes will be

$$\mathbf{k} \cdot \mathbf{N}_{hkl} = \pm n\pi \qquad (2.32)$$

We shall show that the desired normal vector $\mathbf{N}_{hkl}$ is parallel to and simply related to the vector $\mathbf{R}_{hkl}$ joining an origin in the reciprocal lattice to a point (h,k,l) periods away along the three primitive axes:

$$\mathbf{R}_{hkl} = h\mathbf{a}^* + k\mathbf{b}^* + l\mathbf{c}^* \tag{2.33}$$

The points $\mathbf{a}/h$, $\mathbf{b}/k$, and $\mathbf{c}/l$, measured from the origin, are known to lie *in* the plane nearest to, but not through, the origin. It follows that the vectors $\mathbf{a}/h - \mathbf{b}/k$, $\mathbf{b}/k - \mathbf{c}/l$, and $\mathbf{c}/l - \mathbf{a}/h$ must be parallel to this plane. The desired vector $\mathbf{N}_{hkl}$ must therefore satisfy

$$\mathbf{N}_{hkl} \cdot \left(\frac{\mathbf{a}}{h} - \frac{\mathbf{b}}{k}\right) = \mathbf{N}_{hkl} \cdot \left(\frac{\mathbf{b}}{k} - \frac{\mathbf{c}}{l}\right) = \mathbf{N}_{hkl} \cdot \left(\frac{\mathbf{c}}{l} - \frac{\mathbf{a}}{k}\right) = 0 \tag{2.34}$$

If $\mathbf{N}_{hkl}$ is parallel to $\mathbf{R}_{hkl}$, the required conditions are met, as can be shown by substituting (2.33) into (2.34). Any other choice of $\mathbf{N}$'s direction could not simultaneously satisfy all three relations. The length of $\mathbf{N}$ can also be found, since we know three vectors joining the origin to the plane in question, $\mathbf{a}/h$, $\mathbf{b}/k$, and $\mathbf{c}/l$.

$$|\mathbf{N}_{hkl}| = \frac{\mathbf{a}}{h} \cdot [(\text{unit vector}) \parallel \text{to } \mathbf{N}_{hkl}] = \frac{\mathbf{a}}{h} \cdot \frac{\mathbf{N}_{hkl}}{|\mathbf{N}_{hkl}|} \equiv \frac{\mathbf{a}}{h} \cdot \frac{\mathbf{R}_{hkl}}{|\mathbf{R}_{hkl}|} \tag{2.35}$$

The construction is illustrated in Fig. 2.11*d*. Since $\mathbf{R}_{hkl}$ is defined above,

$$|\mathbf{N}_{hkl}| = \frac{\mathbf{a}}{h} \cdot \frac{h\mathbf{a}^* + k\mathbf{b}^* + l\mathbf{c}^*}{|\mathbf{R}_{hkl}|} \equiv \frac{1}{|\mathbf{R}_{hkl}|} \tag{2.36}$$

$$\therefore \mathbf{N}_{hkl} = \frac{\mathbf{R}_{hkl}}{R_{hkl}^2} \tag{2.37}$$

The required condition on $\mathbf{k}$, at the zone boundary defined by the set of parallel planes hkl, is therefore

$$\frac{\mathbf{k} \cdot \mathbf{R}_{hkl}}{R_{hkl}^2} = \pm n\pi \tag{2.38}$$

This can be put into more convenient form if we use the vectors $\mathbf{G}_{hkl} = 2\pi\mathbf{R}_{hkl}$, which form a reciprocal lattice of dimensions 2π times as great as those of the reciprocal lattice defined by $\mathbf{a}^*$, $\mathbf{b}^*$, $\mathbf{c}^*$. Condition (2.38) then reduces to

$$\mathbf{k} \cdot \mathbf{G}_{hkl} = \frac{n}{2} G_{hkl}^2 \tag{2.39}$$

Since each $\mathbf{G}$ is a constant vector, the limits on $\mathbf{k}$ take the form $C_1k_x + C_2k_y + C_3k_z = \text{const}$, and are thus *planes* in $\mathbf{k}$ space. Since a relation $\mathbf{k} \cdot \mathbf{F} = \text{const}$ defines planes *normal to* the vector **F**, the zone-boundary planes are normal to the vectors $\mathbf{G}_{hkl}$. For $n = 1$, the zone-boundary planes perpendicularly bisect the $\mathbf{G}_{hkl}$ vectors.

Since $\mathbf{G}_{nh,nk,nl} \equiv n\mathbf{G}_{hkl}$, the set of vectors $\mathbf{G}_{hkl}$ already includes all values of $n > 1$. *All* possible zone boundaries are thus defined by

$$\mathbf{k} \cdot \mathbf{G}_{hkl} = \tfrac{1}{2}G_{hkl}^2 \qquad h, k, l = \pm 1, \pm 2, \ldots \tag{2.40}$$

In Fig. 2.12a, the normalized reciprocal lattice **G** of a two-dimensional square lattice is plotted, together with a few of the limits (in this case straight lines) defined by perpendicular bisection of each lattice vector. The first Brillouin zone is the central square; as in the one-dimensional case, higher zones are fragmented, and far from the origin the pieces become very small and sliverlike. We may draw from the one-dimensional case to define the higher Brillouin zones. It was shown that the second Brillouin zone of a one-dimensional representation is in two parts, which can be shifted together properly by translations through a distance $2\pi/a$ (in one dimension). In this two-dimensional problem, the second Brillouin zone comprises the *four* largest triangular regions. These can be shifted to the center by four different translations of distance $2\pi/a$, as shown in Fig. 2.12b. The transformations which shift the second Brillouin zone into the first permit the propagation constant of any band to vary only over the limits $-\pi/a < k_x < \pi/a$, $-\pi/a < k_y < \pi/a$. This process may be carried out for any zone. In each case the parts of the zone are translated into the center by **k**-translations, which are multiples of $2\pi/a$ in the k_x and/or k_y directions. In general, these translations must be vectors $\mathbf{G}_{hkl}$.

Using the construction described, first forming the **k**-space lattice from $\mathbf{G}_{hkl}$, then perpendicularly bisecting each lattice vector $\mathbf{G}_{hkl}$ by a plane, all Brillouin-zone boundaries may be derived, for any lattice. We are generally interested only in the central zone, since the outer ones can be translated into this one. Figure 2.13 illustrates the form of the first Brillouin zones for body-centered and face-centered cubic lattices and for the hexagonal lattice.

In three dimensions, the effect of finite crystal size is to limit to discrete values the propagation vector **k**. Applying periodic boundary conditions to a unit cube of the material, the wave functions must satisfy for a Bloch function

$$U_\mathbf{k}(x,y,z)e^{j(k_x x + k_y y + k_z z)}$$

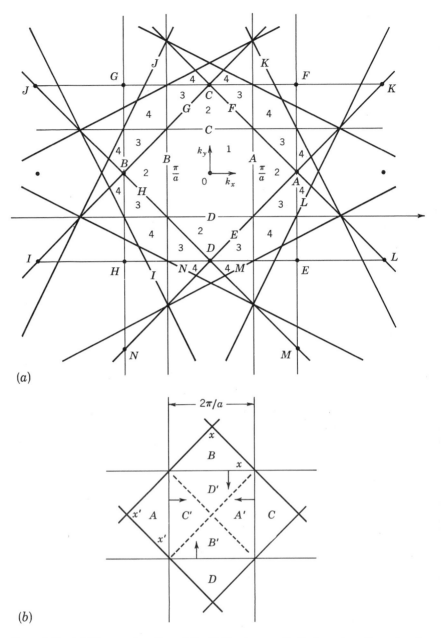

Figure 2.12 (*a*) The construction of the Brillouin-zone limits for a two-dimensional square lattice; lattice points are shown. The same letters are used to indicate the reciprocal lattice points G_{hkl} and the perpendicular-bisecting lines, which are the zone boundaries. The numerals distinguish the parts of the first to fourth zones. (*b*) The second Brillouin zone of a square lattice, translated correctly into the first zone. Note that the line xx after translation lies along $x'x'$, so that the wave function along xx must be identical with that along $x'x'$.

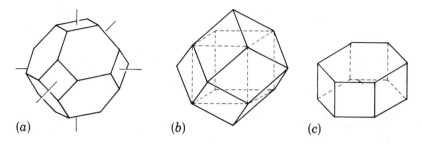

Figure 2.13 First Brillouin zones for (a) face-centered cubic, (b) body-centered cubic, and (c) hexagonal *lattices*. The volume of that for bcc is just twice that of a simple cubic lattice of the same constant, as indicated by the dashed lines.

the following simultaneous conditions on opposite faces of the crystal:

$$U_{\mathbf{k}}(0,y,z)e^{j(k_y y + k_z z)} = U_{\mathbf{k}}(1,y,z)e^{j(k_x + k_y y + k_z z)} \tag{2.41}$$

etc., for other faces. This leads to the discrete states

$$k_x = \pm 2m\pi \qquad k_y = \pm 2n\pi \qquad k_z = \pm 2p\pi \cdot$$
$$m,\, n,\, p = 0,\, 1,\, 2,\, 3,\, \ldots \tag{2.42}$$

The limits of the Brillouin zone, which define all possible $\mathbf{k}$ values, are not usually cubic. We may, however, attribute to each possible state (or mode), in $\mathbf{k}$ space, the volume separating it from its neighbors, which equals $8\pi^3$ (for a unit volume of material). The volume of a Brillouin zone then determines the numbers of states possible *in a single band*.

The first Brillouin zone, in $\mathbf{k}$ space, is defined by perpendicularly bisecting the lines joining the reciprocal lattice point at the origin with all surrounding points. The zone therefore has a volume equal to the volume per lattice point of the reciprocal $\mathbf{G}$ lattice. In the true reciprocal lattice (points $\mathbf{R}$), the volume per lattice point is $\mathbf{a^*} \cdot \mathbf{b^*} \times \mathbf{c^*}$. From (2.31),

$$\mathbf{a^*} \cdot \mathbf{b^*} \times \mathbf{c^*} = \frac{(\mathbf{b} \times \mathbf{c}) \cdot (\mathbf{b^*} \times \mathbf{c^*})}{\mathbf{a} \cdot \mathbf{b} \times \mathbf{c}} = \frac{1}{\mathbf{a} \cdot \mathbf{b} \times \mathbf{c}}$$
$$= \frac{1}{\text{volume of primitive cell}} \tag{2.43}$$

The $\mathbf{k}$-space volume of the Brillouin zone, since $\mathbf{G} \equiv 2\pi\mathbf{R}$, is

$$V_{\text{zone}} = \frac{8\pi^3}{\text{volume of primitive cell}}$$

Accordingly, since each state requires a volume $8\pi^3$, the number of modes in the Brillouin zone is

$$\frac{V_{\text{zone}}}{8\pi^3} = \frac{1}{\text{volume of primitive cell}}$$
$$= \text{primitive cells per unit volume} \qquad (2.44)$$

The number of states therefore equals the number of periodic elements (primitive cells) as in the one-dimensional case.

If, however, the crystal contains more than a single atom per primitive cell (e.g., diamond or hexagonal close-packed structures), there should be additional states, numbering *per band* the number of atoms in the crystal. This is indeed the case. Consider the hexagonal close-packed structure, as a simple example. Whereas we counted as reflecting planes parallel to the c axis only those planes associated with the lattice points, in the structure (Fig. 1.7) there are additional atoms *not* at lattice points, in planes halfway between the planes of lattice points. These atoms act just as effectively to form planes as do those at the lattice points. Since the true interplanar spacing in the c direction is not c, but $c/2$, there is in reality no reflection of waves having k vectors at the supposed zone boundary, and the true zone boundary extends beyond the boundaries of the lattice zone shown in Fig. 1.13. Since an energy band derived from an atomic electronic state must contain as many states as there are atoms in the crystal, the energy band must occupy a region in **k** space having *twice* the volume of the lattice zone. These larger zones are sometimes termed *Jones zones.*[1]

2.4 Electronic Energy Bands in Crystals

The electronic band theory of solids, on which most of modern conduction theory is based, uses Bloch functions to describe electrons in a crystal. Wave functions for a system containing many electrons are written formally in terms of products of one-electron solutions. These *one-electron approximation* solutions take into account only the average electrostatic coupling of one electron to the others. The influence of spin, short-range electron-electron interaction, and interaction of an electron with individual nuclei is generally neglected, when the one-electron approximation is applied to electrons in crystals.

[1] H. Jones, "The Theory of Brillouin Zones and Electronic States in Crystals," North Holland Publishing Company, Amsterdam, 1960.

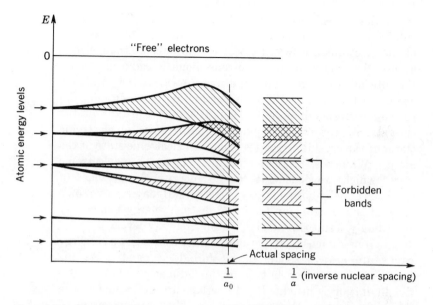

Figure 2.14   The electronic energy levels of the free atoms (arrows) are spread when the atoms are brought close together.   Overlap of electronic bands and splitting of originally degenerate electronic levels as schematized here are characteristic of many solids.

The solution of the quantum-mechanical wave equation of a single electron in a potential field representing the average space charge of the remaining ion cores and electrons of the crystal is found by various approximations, usually involving iteration procedures.   This is not adequate to describe some electronic phenomena, however.   Superconductivity, for example, is due to strong coupling between *pairs* of electrons, involving interactions neglected in the one-electron approximation. Nor can the exchange forces underlying magnetic phenomena be considered in this approximation.   Nevertheless, the one-electron-band theory has been highly successful in explaining metals, semiconductors, and insulators.

In analogy to the coupling of tuned electric circuits, let us extend the concept introduced by Fig. 2.1 to the perturbation of electronic states when a number of atoms are brought into close proximity.   An energy diagram (Fig. 2.14) as a function of the internuclear spacing shows each of the electronic energy levels spread into a band.   Electrons in states nearer the nuclei interact with the fields of neighboring nuclei to a lesser extent; hence the bands they produce will be nar-

rower than those formed by valence electrons. These bands
will lie near the original atomic energy levels. Because most
of the electrons are forced closer to the nucleus than in free
atoms, the energy of the electrons alone is reduced. Since
the internuclear forces are repulsive, however, the total free
energy of the system will have a minimum at an equilibrium
spacing corresponding to the actual lattice constant of the
crystal. As the figure implies, an entire *band* of electronic
states of the crystal originates from *each* electronic state of the
atom. While the original atom may have many electronic
states which are degenerate (same energy), the presence of
the fields of neighboring atoms in the crystal may remove some
or all of this degeneracy. Several distinct energy bands may
accordingly result from a single atomic energy level.

In one-dimensional periodic structures, allowed energy
bands are always separated by forbidden bands. As the
figure shows, however, in two- or three-dimensional structures
this limitation is lifted. Band overlaps are quite common in
the higher-energy electronic bands. They are required, to
explain conductivity of many metallic crystals. In any case,
however, the numbers of states of the crystal must equal the
numbers of states of the individual atoms. In a k-space
(Brillouin-zone) plot, the states derived from each original
electronic state of *each* free atom in the primitive cell must
cover an entire Brillouin zone. This is merely a restatement of
the principle that rearrangement of parts of a system does not
alter the number of degrees of freedom of the system.

An energy diagram like Fig. 2.14 gives no information
about the relation of electron energy and wave vector **k**.
This must be obtained from a map of the Brillouin zone, for
the energy band in question. Since energy is a unique function of **k** in any given band, it is customary to describe the
E-**k** relation by constructing *surfaces of constant electron
energy* in the zone. In the free-electron limit energy is given
in terms of **k** by $E = p^2/2m = \mathbf{k}^2 \hbar^2/2m$. Accordingly, the
constant-energy surfaces are *spheres* about the origin of **k** space
(Fig. 2.15). In the periodic electric fields of a crystal, these
spherical free-electron constant-energy surfaces are perturbed,
as illustrated in Fig. 2.16. Since the **k** components are transformed by point-group operations, in the same way as the
coordinates themselves, the *constant-energy surfaces have the
full point-group symmetry of the crystal they describe.*

Constant-energy surfaces approach normal to some of

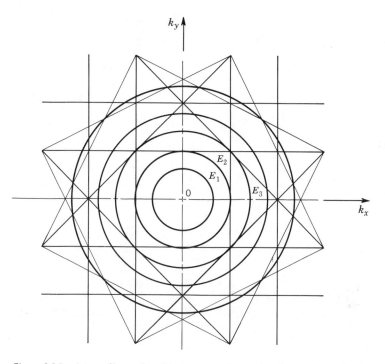

Figure 2.15   A two-dimensional **k** space, or the section $k_z = 0$ for a simple cubic lattice.   The circles (spherical sections) represent constant-energy surfaces of free electrons.

the Brillouin-zone boundaries, corresponding to the zero slope of the one-dimensional ω-k or E-k plots at the zone limits. We shall show that this implies that the (group) velocity of electrons at these boundaries is parallel to the boundaries. This property is limited to those zone boundaries which lie parallel to mirror planes of the structure.   While it applies to all boundaries of the simple cubic first Brillouin zone, it does not, for example, apply to the hexagonal faces of the face-centered cubic first Brillouin zone.   This principle may be appreciated in the two-dimensional square lattice.   Those zone boundaries that lie along 90 and 45° lines, in Fig. 2.16, have the constant-energy surfaces approaching normally, while other oblique boundaries do not.

As in the one-dimensional case, zone-boundary points which differ in position by a reciprocal lattice vector $\mathbf{G}_{hkl}$ correspond to identical electron waves.   Thus points A and A' in Fig. 2.16 are completely equivalent, as are also points

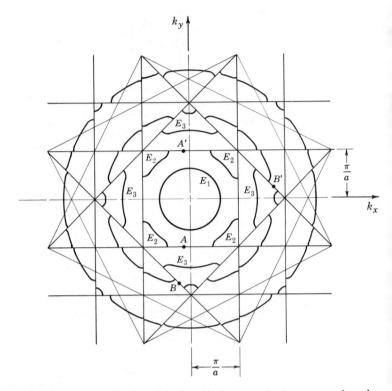

Figure 2.16 Perturbation of the free-electron constant-energy surfaces by periodicity of the lattice.

B and B'. This is the multidimensional equivalent to (2.20).

In the discussions which follow, we shall frequently make use of the simple cubic Brillouin zone to describe electronic phenomena in conductors. Often we shall use only a two-dimensional zone (E versus k_x, k_y) which may be thought to be a $k_z = 0$ cross section of the cubic zone. While the detailed shape of constant-energy surfaces is pertinent in determining the anisotropy of conduction properties, simple spherical or near-spherical surfaces are useful in describing most conduction phenomena.

Although the general nature of electronic energy bands and constant-energy surfaces in **k** space can be described in simple terms, actual solution in even highly simplified approximations becomes a matter for large-scale digital computers.[1] Such computations are still largely in an experimental stage, in

[1] Cf. F. Herman, *Rev. Mod. Phys.*, **30**:102 (1956).

which the chief aim is finding analytical techniques yielding results comparable with experimental findings.

The electronic band theory of solids has been amazingly successful at explaining conduction phenomena qualitatively, as described in the following chapters. These phenomena involve only electrons in crystalline states related to outer shells in free atoms. Polarization phenomena (dielectrics and magnetic materials) may be described most simply by associating electrons with particular atomic nuclei, as described in Chaps. 7 and 8. It appears that the deeper-lying electrons may better be described by *bound*-electron wave functions than by the Bloch functions of band theory. While it has become clear to physicists that low-energy electrons behave much like those in free atoms, and electrons in or near valence states can be described by band theory, the middle ground is poorly defined.

2.5   Electron Wave Packets and Group Velocity in Crystals

The plane-wave solutions arising naturally from the solution of a wave equation in an infinite perfectly periodic structure are simply one possible orthogonal function set. If the structure is limited in size but remains perfectly periodic, the "natural" solutions are fixed-energy standing-wave modes. Experimentally, however, it is possible to "inject" electrons at one end of a crystal and detect their arrival at the other end after a time delay. This suggests that it is more appropriate to think of the electrons as "wave packets," just as in free-space electron motion. As in Sec. B.4, suitable wave-packet wave functions can be defined by Fourier integrals over the wavelength parameter $\mathbf{k}$, using Bloch functions rather than simple plane waves as the generating functions. The approximate range of k_x required to construct a wave function extending over a region Δx of space is again given approximately by the uncertainty principle

$$\Delta x \cdot \Delta(k_x h) \approx h \qquad \Delta x \cdot \Delta k_x \approx 2\pi \tag{2.45}$$

This is in keeping with (2.27), which showed that waves limited to a region $sl\ (= \Delta x) = 1$ were spaced by $\Delta k = 2\pi$.

To determine the electron group velocity—the velocity at which the electronic mass and charge are transported—we may form a simple Gaussian wave packet (Sec. B.4) centered about some average value of $\mathbf{k}$, which we shall call $\mathbf{k}_0$. This wave packet is representable by a Fourier integral expansion of Bloch functions with a Gaussian weighting factor:

$$\psi = \int_{\text{all } \mathbf{k} \text{ in band}} U_\mathbf{k}(\mathbf{r}) e^{-\alpha(\mathbf{k}-\mathbf{k}_0)^2} e^{-jE(\mathbf{k})t/\hbar} e^{+j\mathbf{k}\cdot\mathbf{r}} \, d\mathbf{k} \qquad (2.46)$$

The parameter α may be made as large as desired, to restrict the range of $\mathbf{k}$ considered. The larger α is, however, the larger will be the spatial dimensions of the electron wave.

About $\mathbf{k}_0$, $E(\mathbf{k})$ may be expanded by the series

$$E(\mathbf{k}) = E(\mathbf{k}_0) + (\boldsymbol{\nabla}E)_{\mathbf{k}_0} \cdot (\mathbf{k} - \mathbf{k}_0) + \cdots \qquad (2.47)$$

The second term is a form of the sum

$$\left(\frac{\partial E}{\partial k_x}\right)_{k_{x0}} (k_x - k_{x0}) + \left(\frac{\partial E}{\partial k_y}\right)_{k_{y0}} (k_y - k_{y0}) + \cdots$$

The term $\mathbf{k}\cdot\mathbf{r}$ may be written as $\mathbf{k}_0\cdot\mathbf{r} + (\mathbf{k} - \mathbf{k}_0)\cdot\mathbf{r}$, which permits the wave function as a whole to be written

$$\psi = e^{-jE(\mathbf{k}_0)t/\hbar} e^{j\mathbf{k}_0\cdot\mathbf{r}} \int_{\text{all } \mathbf{k}} U_\mathbf{k}(\mathbf{r}) e^{-\alpha(\mathbf{k}-\mathbf{k}_0)^2}$$
$$\times \exp\left\{ j(\mathbf{k} - \mathbf{k}_0) \cdot \left[\mathbf{r} - (\boldsymbol{\nabla}E)_{\mathbf{k}_0} \frac{t}{\hbar}\right] \right\} d\mathbf{k} \qquad (2.48)$$

The term outside of the integral is a simple plane wave, of propagation constant $\mathbf{k}_0$, and its associated value of E. The integral represents the envelope of the wave. The vector $(\boldsymbol{\nabla}E)_{\mathbf{k}_0}$ which appears in the integrand is a constant in the integration. Since α can be made as large as desired, the significant range of integration in $\mathbf{k}$ space can be made very small.

The detailed result of the integration is not of value to us. Since the vector $[\mathbf{r} - (\boldsymbol{\nabla}E)_{\mathbf{k}_0}t/\hbar]$ does not involve the variables of integration (k_x, k_y, k_z), it should appear unmodified in the final result. This function, however, is a three-dimensional equivalent to the $(z - vt)$ function appearing in simple plane waves. The group velocity of the envelope must therefore be

$$\mathbf{v}_g = \frac{\boldsymbol{\nabla}_\mathbf{k} E}{\hbar} \qquad (2.49)$$

The group velocity of a wave packet in three dimensions is directed in the direction of maximum variation of E (versus $\mathbf{k}$). It is always *perpendicular to the constant-energy surfaces* in k space.   (In Fig. 2.15, for the free electron, v_g will always be directed radially.)

When, as in Fig. 2.16, the presence of periodic potentials causes the energy surfaces to approach normally the boundaries of the Brillouin zones, the group velocity at a boundary must be directed *parallel* to the boundary.   In the situation depicted in Fig. 2.16, the group velocity is zero at the *corners* of the first zone, which correspond also to *energy extrema* in the band.   In general, at both energy limits in electronic bands, the electron (group) velocity is zero, while it reaches maximum values near the center of the energy range.

Because the electron-wave group velocity corresponds to the measurable velocity, while kh assumes the role played by momentum in free-electron motion, it is convenient to use the term "velocity" to denote v_g and "momentum," or "crystal momentum," to denote kh.

2.6 Localized and Surface States

In the electronic band theory, each electron is thought of as traveling through the crystal, so that it cannot be associated with a particular atomic nucleus.   When an electron is removed from the crystal, as in the process of photoemission, one cannot define the particular point from which it originates.

If a crystal is *imperfect*, so that, for example, one atom is different from the others, this atom may have electron-wave solutions which can truly be localized and which have different energies from those in the perfect parts of the crystal.   This can be understood qualitatively using a model similar to Fig. 2.3, but with constants of one section different from the others (Fig. 2.17).   Let us establish heuristically the effect of making the resonant frequency of one element of an infinite periodic circuit different from the others.   When the line is completely periodic, waves travel along it uniformly.   As one element is altered, as, for example, by increasing its inductance, the first effect is that of a localized reflection of waves on the structure. In the analogous electron-wave situation, this corresponds to the reflection (scattering) of electrons from fixed imperfections in a crystal—an effect which lowers the conductivity of an imperfect crystal.   As the local discontinuity is further altered, it finally reaches a value at which the local resonance established lies *outside* the passband of the structure.   At the same time, waves *within* the passband are even more strongly

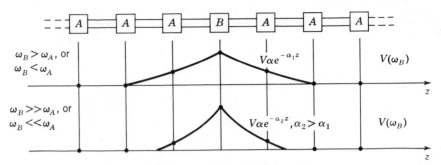

Figure 2.17   A defected periodic structure, for example, an electrical filter as in Fig. 2.3. A represents a normal section, B a section different from A.   The two curves show possible terminal voltages at the resonance of B.   The resonance of B in the lower curve is more remote from the resonance of A.   Hence the frequency is farther from the passband, and attenuation of the local signal is greater.

reflected.   Any periodic structure, in a stop band, shows wave attenuation $e^{-\alpha z}$ which increases rapidly from the edge of the passband, as in Fig. 2.5a.   When the resonance frequency of the defected period is farther from the edge of the passband, the wave associated with the defect is attenuated to a greater degree.   Such a localized wave, once excited on a lossless electrical circuit, will retain its amplitude for all time.   Where the local resonance lies outside the passband of the rest of the filter, this defect produces a state of discrete frequency, localized in both energy and position.

In a crystal, any defects or impurities establish *localized electronic wave functions,* where the energy levels of the imperfections may lie in the forbidden energy bands of the host crystal.   Again, the depth inside the forbidden band determines the space over which the wave spreads, those states of energy nearest the center of the forbidden bands having generally the greatest seclusion.   In three dimensions, compactness in such a localized wave function gives it a low cross section for collisions by traveling electrons or other propagating waves; electrons in such deep-lying states are not so likely to be removed by collision processes as they are in "shallower" imperfection states.

The presence of adjacent host atoms causes substantial perturbations of the energy levels of electrons in a defect or impurity, so that it is not in general possible to predict from free-atom energy levels just what the energy levels may be. Figure 2.18 is a configuration-coordinate plot showing how the energy levels of, for example, an impurity may be per-

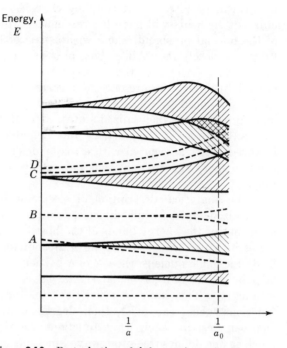

Figure 2.18 Perturbation of defect or impurity levels.
Levels A and B lie in the forbidden regions of the host
crystal, and B's original degeneracy has been split.
Levels C and D are shifted into an allowed band of the
host.

turbed, while the energy levels of the host atoms are spread into
continuous bands.   When an impurity energy level lies *within*
an allowed band of the host crystal, its wave function will
not be localized; it will not be possible to distinguish the
impurity state from the others in the band.   Isolated electronic states of impurity atoms play an important role in
semiconduction and in photon radiation and absorption processes.   States associated with simple *defects* (vacancies or
interstitials) play comparable roles, which are relatively well
understood in alkali halide compounds.   The effect of, for
example, a vacancy may be envisioned also using a model
similar to that of Fig. 2.17, with one of the resonant elements
(but not its coupling elements) removed from the circuit.
In this case it is not the resonance of the defect which is
important, but those of the two elements adjacent to it.
Because of the vacant site, conditions on the adjacent ele-

ments will be altered. If coupling changes sufficiently, the adjacent elements will have *two* resonances which are outside of the normal passband, along with a pair of localized wave functions closely resembling those of a simple pair of coupled resonators. Extending this concept to a three-dimensional crystal structure, the presence of a vacancy will alter potentials experienced by all adjacent electrons, and may accordingly produce sets of localized states, each of which contains as many states as the vacancy has neighbor atoms. The localized states associated with a major defect such as a dislocation are even more numerous and can cover a broad energy range.

The analytical description of electronic wave functions of localized states, while difficult, can be somewhat simpler than that of the energy bands of the host crystal. While the forces in which the electrons move are not quite the central field of a single nucleus, the *site* of a particular impurity atom or point defect in a particular crystal has known point-group symmetry. This imposes restrictions on the possible wave functions which can exist, their degree of degeneracy, etc. One can describe such wave functions via their symmetry, much as one defines free-atom wave functions in terms of their angular momentum and other quantum numbers. While this does not imply that one can readily calculate the energies of the states, this knowledge is helpful in determining if and in what manner electric and magnetic fields applied to the crystal can perturb the energy of the state.

When only a low density of localized imperfections is present, and they are far apart from one another, the wave functions do not appreciably overlap, and all states associated with particular electrons of a particular imperfection will have the same frequency (energy). When the density of imperfections becomes so high that their localized wave functions appreciably overlap one another, the imperfection-state energies will be spread to form a *band* of imperfection states. Were the imperfections uniformly spaced in the crystal, this band would have a regularity like those of the host crystal itself. This is not the case, however, for nature does not space imperfections uniformly. The presence of overlapping wave functions of the imperfection states also permits the possibility of electron *exchange* between the states. It is possible to transfer electrons from one point in a crystal to another, even though the host crystal itself may be an insulator. This so-called *impurity conduction* is not well understood.

Localized electronic states are also produced at crystal *surfaces*, where entire planes of atoms have environments unlike those in the bulk material. Those surface-state electronic wave functions whose energy levels lie in a forbidden band are confined to a few monolayers from the surface. Unlike isolated electronic states of impurity atoms internal to the crystal, however, surface states exist for each of the atoms in any (two-dimensional) surface. There is coupling of these states over the surface. The states can therefore form a band with two-dimensional symmetry—that of the particular crystal face involved. In actual crystals, however, surface layers are so uneven that regular bands of surface states are not observed. Even so, these bands in semiconductors may permit substantial conductivity across the surface of the material, producing current leakage between electrodes. Most of this can be eliminated by special treatment of the surface, for example, by producing a thin electrically insulating oxide of the host crystal on its surface. A surface monolayer of water vapor on an untreated semiconductor surface can materially influence the energy levels of surface electrons and result in high surface conduction.

2.7 Acoustical Waves in Crystals

Acoustical (vibrational) waves in crystals not only represent a part of the thermal (heat) capacity of the solid but are responsible for energy exchanges with electrons which control conduction, magnetic, and quantum-electronic properties. In Sec. A.1 the elastic properties of "homogeneous" solids are considered. It is assumed that, for small deformation, the relations between static stress and strain are linear. This linearization agrees with an atomic description, as we can show from a configurational-coordinate plot (Fig. 2.19) giving the free energy of the crystal as a function of lattice spacing. Near the minimum energy (equilibrium lattice spacing) such a function may be expressed in a series

$$F = F_0 + F_1(a - a_0)^2 + \cdots \tag{2.50}$$

Let us imagine an isotropic compressive stress (pressure) p applied to the entire crystal which causes equal strains along all three axes of the crystal. The relative change in volume of

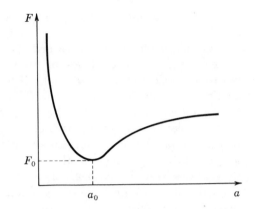

Figure 2.19 Free energy F of a hypothetical crystal, as a function of lattice spacing (cf. Fig. 1.14).

the crystal is then related to the change in lattice spacing a by

$$\frac{dv}{v} = \frac{3da}{a} \tag{2.51}$$

Differentiating (2.50) and substituting (2.51),

$$dF = 2(a - a_0)F_1 \frac{a}{3v} dv + \cdots$$

Equation (C.5) indicates that

$$\left(\frac{\partial F}{\partial v}\right)_{T=\text{const}} = p$$

$$p = \frac{2a}{3v} F_1 (a - a_0) \tag{2.52}$$

The change in lattice constant, $a - a_0$, is accordingly proportional to the applied pressure p.   This second-order free-energy relation leads to *linear* elastic properties.

The continuum theory of elastic media, while correct for static or near-static stresses, neglects completely the fact that crystalline solids are composed of discrete atoms.   Actual vibrations require relative motions of atomic nuclei, with their associated electrons.   In a solid containing N atoms there are $3N$ vibrational degrees of freedom.   While in independent atoms each degree of freedom is associated with one component of translational motion, in the solid one may only define $3N$ modes of vibration of the crystal *as a whole*.

The vibrational modes of a solid are illustrated in one-dimensional form by the mechanical analog of Fig. 2.20, which is an analog of the low-pass electric filter of Fig. 2.5a; the

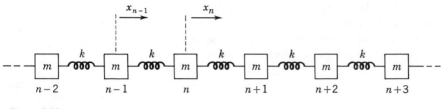

Figure 2.20

corresponding ω-k diagram also applies. The vibration frequencies of a finite crystal, or the allowed frequency band of an infinite one, therefore extend only up to a frequency at which adjacent atoms vibrate 180° out of phase. At low vibration frequencies, acoustical wave velocities approach a limit. This is just the (constant) velocity of the continuum theory. The number of vibrational modes of our one-dimensional model equals the number of sections in the chain, so long as we consider only longitudinal vibrations. If, however, we allow the mass-spring system to have transverse deflections of the masses, there will be $2N$ additional vibrations, corresponding to the shear modes of Fig. A.4.

The extension to two or three dimensions is straightforward. The properties in two or three dimensions can be described by constant-*frequency* surfaces in a Brillouin zone of **k** space. This zone is the same as is used to describe electron waves in the same crystal. If the crystal of N atoms has, for example, only one atom per primitive cell, then *each N* vibrational modes will fill a Brillouin zone. The set of 3 N modes must accordingly occupy three independent Brillouin zones. They constitute three overlapping frequency bands.

In a one-dimensional "crystal" composed of identical atoms, the entire vibrational spectrum extends from zero frequency to some upper-limit frequency, without a band gap. If, however, the "crystal" contains two different atoms, the acoustical spectrum may be divided by a forbidden band. The electrical filter circuit of Fig. 2.5c illustrates this point. In actual crystals, lower-frequency and higher-frequency bands are termed the *acoustical* and *optical branches*, respectively, of the vibrational spectrum.

The low-pass electrical analog (Fig. 2.5a) may be used to obtain a rough estimate of the range of frequencies of the acoustical spectrum of a simple solid. This has an upper cut-off frequency of $\omega_0 = (2/LC)^{\frac{1}{2}}$, which may readily be determined by the method used for (2.4). The low-frequency phase shift per period is $\theta = \omega(LC)^{\frac{1}{2}}$. The low-frequency *wave velocity* of a structure of length a per section is $v_a = \omega a/\theta = a(LC)^{-\frac{1}{2}}$. This gives for the cutoff frequency

$$\omega_0 = \frac{\sqrt{2}\, v_a}{a} \tag{2.53}$$

A typical dense solid such as a metal has an acoustical velocity near 4×10^5 cm/sec and a typical interatomic spacing of 2.5 A. By (2.53), the upper cutoff frequency of the acoustical spectrum should be in the vicinity of $\omega_0 = 2 \times 10^{13}$ rad/sec, which lies in the infrared region.

Since each acoustical mode of a crystal can be represented, for small vibration amplitudes, as a harmonic oscillator,[1] quantum theory requires a zero-point energy of $\hbar\omega/2$ in a particular acoustical mode of frequency ω. The mode amplitude may have only values for which the total acoustical energy is $(n + \frac{1}{2})\hbar\omega$. A quantum of acoustical energy $\hbar\omega$ is called a *phonon*, in analogy to the photon. Using the parameters of the previous rough calculation, the phonon energy of an acoustical wave at the given cutoff frequency ω_0 would be only about $\frac{1}{80}$ ev, or approximately one-half of kT at room temperature.

As in the case of photons, the energy and momentum of phonons are related by $E = pv_a$, in the low-frequency region of the acoustical band, where phase and group velocities of vibrational waves are both $\simeq v_a$. More generally, however, the acoustical group velocity is given by $\mathbf{v}_g = \nabla_k(\omega)$, in complete analogy to (2.49) if $E = \hbar\omega$.

In a solid, a large part of the thermal energy is carried by phonons—in the absence of free electrons, virtually all of it. The equilibrium distribution of phonon energies at a given temperature is given by the Bose-Einstein function (C.48). Unlike the photon spectrum, which extends to unlimited energies, the phonon spectrum is cut off at energies $\hbar\omega_0$ of the order of ~ 0.01 to 0.1 ev. At low temperatures, thermal energy excites the lowest-frequency phonons only. As temperature is increased, the entire phonon spectrum is excited. When temperature reaches a value where kT is well in excess of the highest allowed phonon energy $\hbar\omega_0$, the solid approximates a classical (Boltzmann) system of $3N$ oscillators; the internal energy approaches $3NkT$, and the specific heat approaches an upper limit of $3Nk$ (Fig. 2.21). This situation

[1] Cf. Sec. B.2.

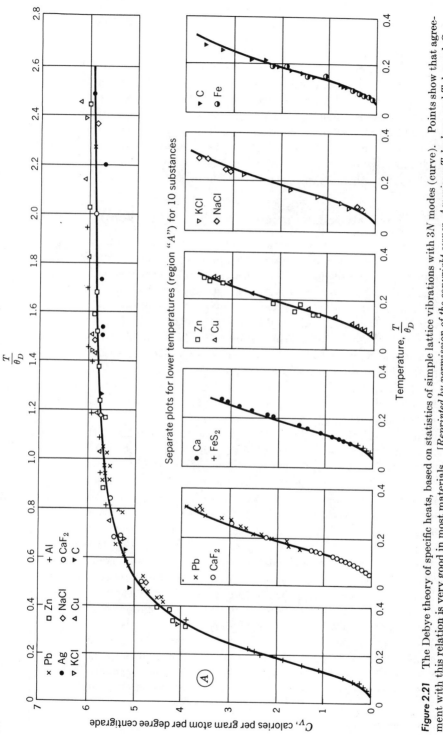

Figure 2.21 The Debye theory of specific heats, based on statistics of simple lattice vibrations with $3N$ modes (curve). Points show that agreement with this relation is very good in most materials. [*Reprinted by permission of the copyright owner, American Telephone and Telegraph Company, and the author W. Shockley. This figure originally appeared in the Bell System Tech. J.*, **18**:645–723 (1939).]

is approached at lower temperatures for materials having a lower-frequency cutoff of their acoustical spectrum. The characteristic temperature in Debye's theory of specific heats of solids, Θ_D ($= \hbar\omega_0/k$), is called the *Debye temperature*.[1] Many solids, particularly insulators, have a specific-heat variation closely following this model, with Debye temperature of a few hundred degrees. Conduction electrons give an additional specific-heat contribution, which is quite different from that of phonons, because Fermi-Dirac statistics apply.

2.8   Wave Interaction Processes in Crystals (Collisions)

The interactions between electrons and wave entities (photons, phonons) control many electronic processes. Three very important types of interaction are those of (1) electrons with massless waves, (2) massless waves with others of their own kind, and (3) massless waves with other types of massless waves. Electron-electron "collisions" appear to be "screened" by space charge, in normal conductors. Collisions of electrons or massless waves with *fixed* imperfections are also significant in conduction processes and elsewhere.

Interaction of electrons and massless waves is generally thought of as a collision process, since here as elsewhere a conservation of energy and momentum is required. A more precise description would be that an electron interacts with such a wave so that a single quantum of energy is absorbed or given off by the electron to the wave. In a perfect crystal structure, a free electron would move without apparent hindrance. The presence of acoustical vibrations (phonons) disturbs the regularity of the lattice, however. The vibration of the nuclei produces changes in the charge distribution surrounding them. To the perfect periodic potential of the crystal at rest is added a perturbation with the phase and group velocity of the acoustical wave. It is this traveling-wave electric field variation which interacts with the electron to permit it to give off or absorb energy. The presence of electromagnetic-wave energy in the crystal, while producing little motion of the nuclei, disturbs their surrounding electrons (as described in Chap. 7) to produce electric fields having the characteristic phase and group velocity of electromagnetic energy propagation. In both cases, it is mainly the time-

[1] J. E. Mayer and M. G. Mayer, "Statistical Mechanics," p. 251, John Wiley & Sons, Inc., New York, 1940.

varying *electric fields* of the wave phenomena which cause perturbation of the electron motion and permit energy release or absorption.

We are accustomed to thinking of collisions in terms of elastic balls colliding; in these collisions, we learn that energy and momentum are conserved. Energy and momentum *transfer* from one colliding object to another, however, depend on the relative *masses* of the two classical objects. If masses are comparable, large energy and momentum exchange can occur. If one is much smaller in mass than the other, little energy transfer will occur, but the momentum of the lighter object will be altered considerably as it "bounces" off the heavier one. This sort of analogy is of some value in dealing with electron-photon and electron-phonon interaction, but it must be remembered that the photon or phonon involved exists only before (or after, if the electron gives up energy) the collision.

The relative efficiencies (in terms of momentum and energy transfer) of these collisions differ widely, depending upon the particular type of material. In a metallic conductor the electrons of most interest are those of energy near the Fermi energy—about 10 ev. The phonons of interest are those which are thermally excited. Since in a simple crystal such as a close-packed metal the range of acoustical vibration frequencies is limited, the phonon energies are unlikely to exceed 10^{-1} ev. The phonon *momenta*, however, include all values in the Brillouin zone, including some which are larger than those of the electrons. Accordingly, in electron-phonon collisions, the electron momentum changes by as much as, or more than, its absolute value, while the electron energy changes by only a small fraction of its initial value. The typical collision changes the *direction* of electron motion substantially, but changes electron *velocity* to a minor degree.

The interaction of electrons and *photons* at low frequencies is best described in terms of interaction of the electric fields with electronic charge, as discussed in Chap. 3. In this case it is of little value to describe the process in quantum terms. At photon energies approximating electron energy-band widths, momentum transfer must be considered in photon absorption and emission by electrons. Since, as indicated in Sec. B.1, the ratio of energy to momentum of photons equals the velocity of light (in the crystal), even photons of energy comparable to electronic Fermi energy have relatively small associated momentum. This characteristic is dominant in processes in which an electron makes a transfer from one energy band to another, where a large energy gap must be bridged but little change in momentum is demanded. This is discussed in Secs. 4.6 and 10.8.

Quantum principles of electron-wave interaction can be understood through perturbation theory, applying to an electron wave the time-dependent perturbation due to the massless photon or phonon wave. The results of such a perturbation calculation[1] are much the same as if the original electron wave is multiplied by the perturbation wave to obtain the final electron wave:

$$
\overset{\text{electron, final}}{\exp\left[j\left(\frac{E_2 t}{\hbar} - \mathbf{k}_2 \cdot \mathbf{r}\right)\right]} = \overset{\text{electron, initial}}{\exp\left[j\left(\frac{E_1 t}{\hbar} - \mathbf{k}_1 \cdot \mathbf{r}\right)\right]}
$$

$$
\overset{\text{phonon (or photon)}}{\times \exp\left[j\left(\frac{E_p t}{\hbar} - \mathbf{k}_p \cdot \mathbf{r}\right)\right]}
$$

(This is merely the final mathematical form, and is not supposed to suggest a method of analysis.) The result is the expected conservation principles

$$
E_2 = E_1 + E_p \qquad \mathbf{k}_2 = \mathbf{k}_1 + \mathbf{k}_p \tag{2.54}
$$

The crystal momentum $\mathbf{k}$, in complete vector form, replaces the classical momentum. There is a further degree of freedom, however, for the Bloch functions representing electrons or massless waves have an ambiguity in the definition of the momentum $\mathbf{k}$; to $\mathbf{k}_1$, $\mathbf{k}_2$, $\mathbf{k}_p$, any or all, we may add any reciprocal lattice vector $\mathbf{G}_{hkl}$ without changing the meaning of the wave function. Accordingly, a more complete statement of momentum conservation in such a collision is

$$
\mathbf{k}_2 + \mathbf{G} = \mathbf{k}_1 + \mathbf{k}_p \tag{2.55}
$$

where $\mathbf{G}$ represents any of the $\mathbf{G}_{hkl}$. This means, for example, that an electron in a state in one energy band can be elevated into a state in a higher energy band by a low-momentum photon if the two $\mathbf{k}$ values, transposed (by shift of $\mathbf{k}$) to the

[1] Cf. J. M. Ziman, "Electrons and Photons," chap. 5, Clarendon Press, Oxford, 1960.

first Brillouin zone, differ only by the amount of momentum carried by a photon of correct energy.

Interaction between massless waves of like form is typified by the common process of the division of a high-energy phonon into two lower-energy phonons whose energy totals that of the original. This process is quite different from electron-phonon collision processes, and its principles may readily be understood classically. In simple terms, waves of one frequency, in a medium, interact to produce waves of another frequency. This process requires only that the medium be *nonlinear* to the waves. Nonlinear *photon* processes occur strongly only at extremely strong electromagnetic field strengths, as might be produced by laser irradiation of a solid. Nonlinear acoustical processes, however, occur even at the lower vibrational amplitudes associated with thermally excited vibrations. These phonon-phonon collision processes are needed to explain how quickly energy introduced into a solid by mechanical or electrical means is reduced to a thermal (Bose-Einstein) distribution of phonon energies, or, in other words, produces heating.

The basic nonlinearity in the interatomic forces binding together solids is indicated in Fig. 2.19. It is apparent in the fact that solids expand upon being heated; it is the greater *extension* of interatomic motion than *contraction* (due to the asymmetry of the energy curve) that produces this macroscopic expansion. Nonlinear phonon-interaction processes can be explained classically, using electrical or mechanical filter analogs, by introduction of nonlinearity into the parameters of the structure. In the mechanical transmission structure of Fig. 2.20, therefore, we might allow the spring to have a nonlinear relation of restoring force to displacement. Using an electrical analog, we may employ a nonlinear capacitor in an electrical periodic structure. This capacitor, placed for the present in the electrical circuit of Fig. 2.22a, has a capacitance which depends on its terminal voltage:

$$C = C(V) = C_0 + C_1 V \qquad (2.56)$$

Let us assume that the capacitor voltage (representing internuclear displacement in the crystal) is the sum of two sinusoidal voltages, the frequency of one double that of the other:

$$V = V_1 \sin \omega t + V_2 \sin 2\omega t \qquad (2.57)$$

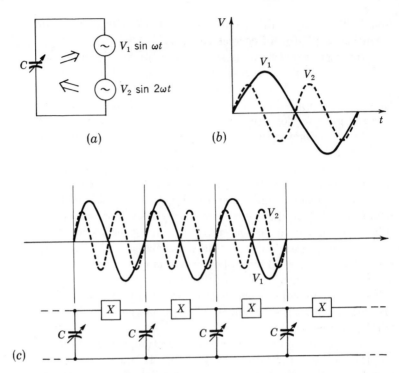

Figure 2.22 (a) A voltage-dependent capacitor C, connected to two sources of frequencies ω and 2ω, respectively, will, under the proper relationship between voltage phases [shown in (b)], accept power from one source and return it to the other. (c) A series of nonlinear elements in a propagating periodic structure will also convert energy from one frequency to another if a proper phase relationship [as in (b)] is maintained for all elements at all times.

The current and voltage in a capacitor are related through

$$i = \frac{dq}{dt} = \frac{d(CV)}{dt} \tag{2.58}$$

$$i = C_0(\omega V_1 \cos \omega t + \omega V_2 \cos 2\omega t)$$
$$+ C_1\left(\frac{\omega V_1{}^2}{2} \sin 2\omega t + \omega V_2{}^2 \sin 4\omega t - \frac{\omega V_1 V_2}{2} \sin \omega t \right.$$
$$\left. + \frac{3\omega V_1 V_2}{2} \sin 3\omega t\right) \tag{2.59}$$

The term containing C_0 is the current which would flow through a simple capacitor C_0. The first of the C_1 terms is a current of frequency 2ω, *in phase with* the $\sin 2\omega t$ voltage, which represents power at frequency 2ω, of average value $C_1\omega V_1{}^2 V_2/2$, passing *into* the capacitor. The third term is a current of frequency ω, exactly $180°$ out of time phase with the sin ωt voltage, representing, therefore, an equal average power passing *from the capacitor* into the external circuit, at frequency ω. These currents represent *lossless* conversion of the energy from one frequency to another. (This, by the way, is the basic principle employed in the *parametric amplifier*.)

We may now imagine a series of these capacitors built into an electrical circuit like those in Fig. 2.22c. A wave of frequency 2ω is fed into one end of the circuit. A wave of frequency ω in the circuit can obtain energy from the higher-frequency wave, because of the action of the nonlinear capacitors. If this is to happen continuously, however, the *relative phases* of the two voltages (ω and 2ω) must be the same at *each* nonlinear element; otherwise some elements will transfer energy from high to low frequency while others will convert in the opposite direction, with no net energy conversion. Figure 2.22c shows a proper conversion condition. At a particular instant of time, the lower-frequency signal is passing through zero in the positive direction and the higher-frequency signal is a maximum, at each nonlinear element. This requires that the phase shift per section (or per unit length) be twice as great at twice the frequency (that is, $k_{2\omega} = 2k_\omega$). This condition is automatically satisfied in a system having constant *phase velocity* vs. frequency. This is not true of actual acoustical wave propagation in crystals, because of the bending of the ω-k relation toward the high-frequency limit of the phonon spectrum (Fig. 2.5a and Prob. 2.8a).

Division of a single high-frequency phonon into two phonons of one-half its frequency is by no means the only type of process that can occur. It is possible for the opposite process to occur; more generally, processes in either direction may involve phonons of two different energies which add to produce one of higher energy (or the opposite). The conservation relations for this interaction are very much like those for electron-phonon collisions:

$$(\mathbf{G}+)\mathbf{k}_3 = \mathbf{k}_1 + \mathbf{k}_2 \qquad E_3 = E_1 + E_2 \tag{2.60}$$

Since $E = \hbar\omega$, it follows that the frequency of the higher-energy resultant phonon is the sum of those of the contributory phonons.

While the same principles apply for photons as for phonons, the actual energy and momentum exchange which occurs in this way is much less because the *degree* of nonlinear-

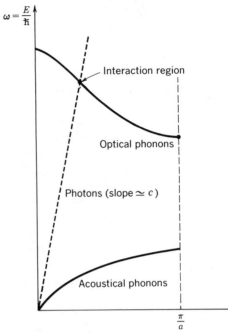

Figure 2.23

ity [analogous to C_1 in Eq. (2.56)] is much smaller in dielectric than in acoustical properties.

Direct interaction can occur between photons and phonons only under conditions where both the energy and the momentum **k** of the quantum transferred are *equal*. Figure 2.23 shows how this can happen only with an optical-band phonon, and not with an acoustical-band phonon. The figure shows the ω-k (which is equivalent to E-k) relations for acoustical propagation and electromagnetic propagation (much higher velocity) superposed. The energy and momentum are both the same (i.e., the curves intersect) only at a frequency near the upper limit of the optical phonon spectrum. This interaction is observable, in crystals such as sodium chloride and other alkali halides, by the presence of a strong absorption of infrared radiation in a narrow frequency range corresponding to the upper limit of the phonon spectrum. This frequency also marks the upper limit of a region of high dielectric constant in such an ionic solid (Sec. 7.4).

Fixed imperfections in crystals afford an even greater

range of collision possibilities than wave-wave interactions. If the energy of the wave colliding with such a defect is low, there may be no other effect than the elastic scattering of the wave. Particularly at low temperatures, where the number of phonons is lower, fixed-imperfection scattering of electrons is a limit to electronic conduction. If the imperfection is ionizable, a phonon (or more likely a photon) of the correct energy can often produce ionization and release an electron of the appropriate momentum for momentum conservation. Imperfections can also have excited electronic states, below the ionization energy. Electrons in these states can relax to lower-energy states in many instances through release of phonons. Here, in order to conserve momentum, it will usually be necessary for two phonons of opposite momenta to be released simultaneously. Processes of these types are highly important in both semiconduction and quantum-electronic applications.

2.9   Diffraction of High-energy Waves and Particles in Crystals

High-energy (short-wavelength) particle or electromagnetic waves impressed upon a crystal must satisfy the same band limitations as do waves more native to the equilibrium crystal. Waves whose wavelengths are related critically to the interplanar spacings will experience constructive-interference effects known as *diffraction*. We used these critical wavelengths in Sec. 2.3 to define the Brillouin-zone limits. When a short-wavelength x ray irradiates a crystal, electrons deep inside each atom have their motion perturbed. This superposed motion reradiates some of the incident wave energy, each electron radiating in a nearly isotropic (dipole) radiation pattern. When arrangement of atoms into planes places the planes in proper relation to an incident wave, the reradiated energy from each plane of atoms combines with that of the others to produce strong reinforcement of this scattered energy in a particular direction. Figure 2.24 is the conventional description of this diffraction, first used by Bragg to define conditions for diffraction maxima. If the planar spacing is d, and the angle of incidence with respect to the plane normal is θ, the condition for maximum diffraction is the *Bragg law*

$$2d \cos \theta = n\lambda \qquad n = 1, 2, 3, \ldots \qquad (2.61)$$

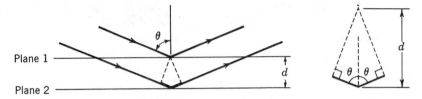

Figure 2.24 Construction showing the maximum-diffraction condition for electromagnetic wave reflections from parallel planes. The heavy segment of the lower path must equal a full wavelength. Detail at right.

This condition may be expressed somewhat more elegantly in terms of the reciprocal lattice vector R_{hkl} defined in Sec. 2.3. The spacings between the set of planes described by the indices h, k, l are given in terms of the reciprocal lattice vector by [(2.37)] a vector $N_{hkl} = R_{hkl}/R_{hkl}^2$, where N is normal to the planes in question. In (2.61), then, $d = 1/|R_{hkl}|$. Describing the *incident* radiation by its propagation constant k, the angle θ is that between k and R_{hkl}:

$$\cos \theta = \frac{k \cdot R}{|k| \, |R|}$$

Bragg's law, then, may be written

$$\frac{2k \cdot R}{|k|R^2} = n\lambda$$

Since the absolute value of k is $2\pi/\lambda$,

$$2k \cdot R = 2\pi n R_{hkl}^2 \qquad k \cdot 2\pi R_{hkl} = \frac{n}{2}(2\pi R_{hkl})^2 \qquad (2.62)$$

This is the same as the condition on k for Brillouin-zone limits, (2.38); it should not be surprising, because we defined the zone boundaries from an interference condition on waves in the crystal. The construction, in k space, requires that the tip of the k vector for the incident beam contact a zone boundary. Since the Brillouin-zone limits in k space are planes lying parallel to the lattice planes they represent, the direction of the diffracted wave is found by reflecting the incident wave vector off the zone boundary plane. Figure 2.25 shows how radiation of fixed wavelength (given length of k) is diffracted by a crystal. If the direction of incident radiation is fixed with respect to the crystalline axes, no diffraction may be possible. If, however, the crystal is physically *rotated* about

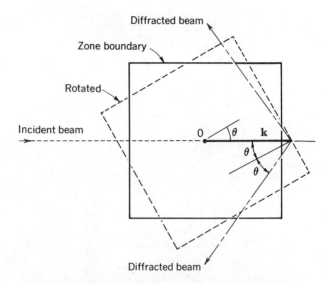

Figure 2.25 Construction for rotation diffraction. The square represents the Brillouin-zone limit, for the first zone. At an orientation for which the k vector touches the limits of the zone, the direction of diffraction is given by simple reflection off the boundary.

an axis normal to the incident radiation, the **k** space will be rotated in the same way. Various diffracting planes will come into proper orientation at particular angles. At each such crystal orientation, incident waves will be strongly diffracted, in a characteristic direction with respect to the incident beam. If the crystal is surrounded by a recording film placed on the inside of a circular drum whose axis coincides with the axis of rotation (Fig. 2.26a), a diffraction pattern is produced. Such a *rotation pattern*, for single-crystal NaCl (rock salt), is shown in Fig. 2.26b. The wavelength of the radiation must be *less than* a critical value (one-half the lattice constant in a simple cubic lattice); otherwise the tip of the **k** vector could not contact the zone limit at any orientation. The pattern obtained from a given crystal thus depends on the wavelength of the radiation. Since there are relatively few types of x-ray sources in use, it is not difficult to standardize on radiation wavelength.

Another common diffraction technique makes use of broad-spectrum radiation which is also obtained from x-ray sources. The incident **k** vector (Fig. 2.27a) extends over a

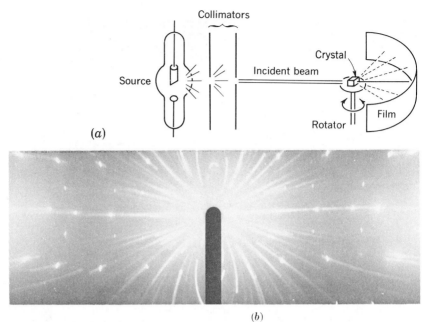

Figure 2.26   (a) Equipment for rotation x-ray diffraction.   (b) A typical rotation pattern, for NaCl (rock salt).   The central part of the film is covered, because the direct-transmitted beam would impinge on it.   Incident beam in a [100] direction.   (*Supplied by N. Stemple, IBM Thos. J. Watson Research Center, Yorktown Heights, N.Y.*)

range of values.   Part of the incident energy will be diffracted by each zone limit lying in this range.   This method, due to Laue, does not require rotation of the crystal; it produces the *Laue pattern* for rock salt shown in Fig. 2.27*b*.   Each dot again corresponds to a particular set of reflecting planes.   The dot positions on the film are no longer a function of source wavelength, but do depend on the distance from the crystal to the film.   Pattern symmetry is the point-group symmetry (if any) about the incident-beam direction as axis.

A third procedure is commonly employed in obtaining structural information on polycrystalline materials.   The so-called "powder pattern," or "Debye-Scherrer" pattern, is obtained by directing a nearly monochromatic x-ray beam at the polycrystalline sample.   If the crystallites are in truly random orientations, there will be crystallites at all orientations required to produce a rotation pattern.   In addition,

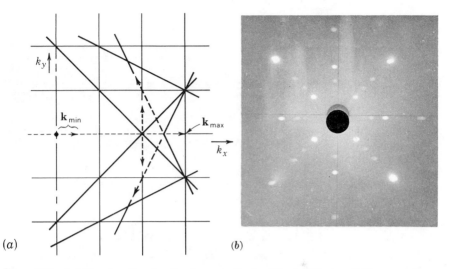

Figure 2.27 (*a*) Construction for the Laue method. The incident radiation contains a range of wavelengths from k_{min} to k_{max}. Each oblique zone boundary produces a diffracted beam (directions shown dashed). (*b*) A Laue pattern for NaCl, [100] axis. (*Supplied by N. Stemple, IBM Thos. J. Watson Research Center, Yorktown Heights, N.Y.*)

however, orientations are random about the axis of the incident beam, so that each individual "dot" is broadened into a circular ring whose center is the beam axis (Fig. 2.28). Each ring represents a set of diffracting planes. The construction of Fig. 2.28*b* illustrates the relationship between ring diameter and plane separation. The diffracted beam makes an angle of $180° - 2\theta$ with the incident-beam axis. If the wavelength of the radiation is short compared with the lattice constants, many rings will appear having small diffraction angles as suggested. Then in terms of the distance from sample to film plane,

$$\frac{r}{L} = \tan (180° - 2\theta) \cong 2 \tan (90° - \theta)$$

But by Bragg's law [(2.61)], $\lambda = 2d \cos \theta = 2d \sin (90° - \theta)$ $\cong rd/L$, since for small angles $\sin \cong \tan$. In cubic crystals, for example, $d = |\mathbf{R}_{hkl}|^{-1} = |h\mathbf{a}^* + k\mathbf{b}^* + l\mathbf{c}^*|^{-1} = a(h^2 + k^2 + l^2)^{-\frac{1}{2}}$. Accordingly, the ring radius is given by

$$r = \frac{L\lambda}{a} (h^2 + k^2 + l^2)^{\frac{1}{2}} \tag{2.63}$$

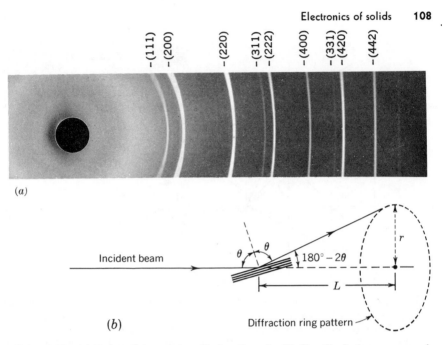

Figure 2.28 (a) Debye-Scherrer (powder) pattern for NaCl. Each ring corresponds to a set of dots in Fig. 2.26b. The numbers indicate the lattice planes producing each ring. (*This figure supplied by N. Stemple, IBM Thos. J. Watson Research Center, Yorktown Heights, N.Y.*) (b) Construction for Debye-Scherrer pattern.

We have thus far discussed only the influence of lattice periodicity on diffraction and disregarded the detailed structure. When the unit cell contains more than a single atom of a given element, some of the Brillouin-zone boundaries applicable to the basic Bravais lattice are no longer pertinent. This, as mentioned before, gives rise to the larger zones. It also means that certain sets of diffraction planes which would produce diffraction patterns in a crystal having a structure identical with the lattice will no longer produce patterns. We can infer which planes will no longer diffract by investigating the general nature of the wave functions in the crystal. The function $U_k(\mathbf{r})$ in the Bloch function (2.28) can certainly be expanded in a Fourier series having the complete periodicity of the *lattice* ($\mathbf{a},\mathbf{b},\mathbf{c}$). Appropriate periodic functions for this expansion are the exponential functions $\exp(j\mathbf{G}_{hkl}\cdot\mathbf{r})$, where $\mathbf{G}_{hkl}$ are the reciprocal lattice vectors defined earlier. A complete expansion of $U_k(\mathbf{r})$ therefore takes the form

$$U_k(\mathbf{r}) = \sum_{h,k,l} A_{hkl}e^{j\mathbf{G}_{hkl}\cdot\mathbf{r}} \tag{2.64}$$

The coefficients A_{hkl} to describe a given periodic function can be found by the usual methods of Fourier analysis. If any coefficient A_{hkl} were identically zero, it would imply that this component of a wave would not occur. For simplicity, let us describe a wave function which is in the form of a Dirac "delta" function at *each* identical atom site in the period (i.e., in the primitive cell) and zero elsewhere. The coefficient A_{hkl} is found, as in the case of one-dimensional Fourier series coefficients, by

$$A_{hkl} = (\mathbf{a} \times \mathbf{b} \cdot \mathbf{c})^{-1} \int U_k(\mathbf{r})e^{j\mathbf{G}_{hkl}\cdot\mathbf{r}} \, dv \tag{2.65}$$

Since $U_k(\mathbf{r})$ is zero except at atom sites, if the atom sites in the primitive cell are designated by radius vectors $\mathbf{r}_i$, then the particular $U_k(\mathbf{r})$ we are using can be written $\sum_i \delta(\mathbf{r}_i)$, where $\delta(\mathbf{r})$ s the three-dimensional delta function. Introducing this into the integral, since $\int \delta(\mathbf{r}_i)f(\mathbf{r}) \, dv \equiv f(\mathbf{r}_i)$, we have

$$A_{hkl} = \sum_i e^{j\mathbf{G}_{hkl}\cdot\mathbf{r}_i} \times \text{const} \tag{2.66}$$

The sum is over all identical atoms in the primitive cell. Since, in a structure, any wave function must behave similarly at each identical atom, if A_{hkl} as defined in (2.66) vanishes, we may expect to find no diffraction from (hkl) planes. The sum of (2.66) is conventionally termed the *structure factor* for a given crystal structure. As an example of its use, we may consider the body-centered cubic structure to be based on the simple cube, with an atom at $\mathbf{r}_1 = 0$ and a second at $\mathbf{r}_2 = (a/2)(1_x + 1_y + 1_z)$. The general reciprocal lattice vector is given by $\mathbf{G}_{hkl} = (2\pi/a)(h1_x + k1_y + l1_z)$. Accordingly, the structure factor is

$$e^0 + e^{j\pi(h+k+l)} \qquad \text{(body-centered cube)}$$

This is zero for any combination $h + k + l$ which is an odd integer. Accordingly, the (100) planes of the simple cube no longer produce diffraction patterns. Examination of the structure shows that the planes formed by body-centered atoms lie midway between planes formed by corner atoms. The (200) diffraction of the simple cube, for which the structure factor is nonzero, does appear in the diffraction pattern of the body-centered cube.

The diffraction pattern produced by a complex crystal

having two or more different elements may most simply be viewed as the composite of the patterns produced by each group of identical atoms in the unit cell. For example, in the NaCl structure, the sodium ions form a face-centered cubic structure, as do the chlorine ions. Each produces its own diffraction pattern, which is that of a face-centered cube; both have the same lattice constant; hence the two patterns are superimposed on one another. If the two types of ions were identical, however, the structure would be equivalent to a simple cube. Since diffraction intensities from the ions are different from those of the chlorine ions, however, the full face-centered pattern appears.

The same general procedures, with limitations, are used in diffraction by high-energy particles. While electron diffraction is the most common, high-energy neutrons have the advantage that they are scattered, not by the electrons of the crystal, but by the nuclei. Their use is limited, however, since one must have a high-energy neutron source such as a nuclear reactor. Electrons of energies in the tens of thousands of volts have wavelengths (given according to the free-electron formula by $\lambda = h/p$) comparable with the lattice spacings of crystals. These electrons are so far above the energy levels of electrons native to the solid that they experience the fields of the ions and electrons of the solids only as slight perturbations. They are therefore diffracted, like radiation, according to the Bragg law.

Electron-diffraction instruments are more complex than x-ray equipment, since they operate in a vacuum. Most electron microscopes are now equipped so that electron diffraction may be carried out by slight alteration of their operation. The chief disadvantage of electron diffraction, as compared with x rays, is the limited penetration of electrons into solids. Only materials of the order of 1,000 A in thickness or less may be studied. Since electron-microscopy specimens must be of this thickness in any event, the combined procedure is an excellent one for detailed investigation of very small areas on thin layers of polycrystalline material. The powder-pattern technique must be used, and the electron beam can be maintained highly monochromatic simply by proper power-supply-voltage regulation. In a common technique, *bulk* material is irradiated by electrons at a glancing angle to the surface. This avoids the necessity for deep penetration, but permits study of only the surface layers of the crystal.

Skilled crystallographers can learn a great deal about crystals from diffraction studies. An unknown single crystal can be *oriented* by rotation in a diffraction apparatus until the pattern which appears has symmetry. The symmetry will correspond to the rotational symmetry of the crystal about the axis of the diffraction system; hence major axes can be readily located. More detailed diffraction studies, after analysis, can lead to a complete structural description, and even to plots showing electron density within a unit cell.

PROBLEMS

2.1(*a*) The electrical *reactance* $X(\omega)$ of a general two-terminal network containing only lossless elements (capacitances and inductances) is a function of frequency which is monotonic and has successive zeros and poles (infinities), as shown in Fig. 2.29*a*. If such reactance elements are arranged into an electrical filter by use of coupling capacitors as shown in Fig. 2.29*b*, show that there will be one passband of the filter for *each* pole of the reactance X. Use the technique employed in deriving (2.3). Show also that the width of the passbands is greater for larger C', by a graphical argument.

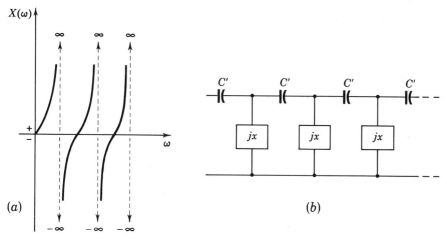

Figure 2.29

2.1(*b*) For the filter of Prob. 2.1*a*, show that $\partial\omega/\partial\theta$ at the band edges must always be zero, regardless of how $X(\omega)$ varies.

2.1(*c*) Calculate, for the circuit of Fig. 2.5*c*, the attenuation constant α per unit length, in the central stop band, showing that it has a maximum near the center of the band. Assume $L = 1$, $C_1 = 1$, $C_2 = 2$ for simplicity of calculation.

2.2 Show that the group velocity of a wave of the form $u_k(z)e^{i\omega t - jkz}$ is given correctly by $v_g = \partial\omega/\partial k$, by the following procedure: (1) Define a composite wave of two frequencies slightly different from ω, $\omega \pm \Delta\omega$, and wave constants $k_0 \pm \Delta k$.

$$\phi_c = u_{k_0+\Delta k}(z)e^{j(\omega+\Delta\omega)t}e^{-j(k_0+\Delta k)z} + u_{k_0-\Delta k}(z)e^{j(\omega-\Delta\omega)t}e^{-j(k_0-\Delta k)z}$$

where

$$\Delta\omega = \frac{\partial\omega}{\partial k}\Delta k$$

(2) Show that $|\phi|^2$ $(z = 0)$ and $|\phi|^2$ $(z = 1)$ differ by a time delay $l/v_g = l(\partial\omega/\partial k)^{-1}$.

NOTE: This proof does not show that the envelope of the wave travels at constant velocity *within* a period, only that the velocity over a *complete* period is given by $\partial\omega/\partial k$.

2.3(a) (1) Sketch the reciprocal lattice for the *two*-dimensional hexagonal lattice (as characteristic of a close-packed plane of spheres). (2) Draw zone boundaries and identify the three lowest Brillouin zones. (3) Show how the parts of the second and third zones may be translated into the first.

2.3(b) Show that the reciprocal lattice must belong to the same class as the original lattice, for each of the seven crystal classes. (You may do this using the primitive vectors.)

2.3(c) Beginning with a simple square lattice, show that the "structure" associated with placing a second "atom" at the center of each square has a Brillouin zone which encompasses precisely the first *two* zones of the original lattice.

2.4 For a two-dimensional hexagonal lattice like that of Prob. 2.3a, draw slightly perturbed free-particle energy surfaces, as in Fig. 2.16. Shift successively the second and third zones into the first, to show the symmetry of surfaces in these bands. Assume full sixfold rotational symmetry.

2.5(a) Show that a wide energy band may have higher electron velocities than a narrower band, from two-dimensional arguments.

2.5(b) Show that when constant-energy surfaces are of the ellipsoidal form

$$\frac{k_x^2}{a^2} + \frac{k_y^2}{b^2} + \frac{k_z^2}{c^2} = E \qquad a \neq b, a \neq c, b \neq c$$

the phase and group velocities of the waves are parallel only in the x, y, and z axes.

2.6(a) (1) Looking from the terminals of a capacitor on the structure of Fig. 2.5a, determine the impedance of an infinite line, as a function of ω in the stop band, with $L = 1$, $C = 1$. (Impedance is that looking into two semi-infinite filters in parallel.) (2) What capacitance is required to resonate with this (reactance) at a frequency 10 per cent above the cutoff frequency? (This will be a resonance in the stop band.) NOTE: This problem requires an understanding of the *characteristic impedance* of a periodic network. Cf. L. A. Ware and H. R. Reed, "Communication Circuits," p. 40, John Wiley & Sons, Inc., New York, 1944.

2.6(b) For the circuit of Fig. 2.5a, within how many periods does a resonance voltage 10 per cent above the cutoff frequency reduce to less than 10 per cent of its amplitude at the localized resonator (cf. Fig. 2.17)?

2.6(c) Explain why conductivity due to *surface* states on a face parallel to the c axis of a hexagonal crystal could (at least ideally) be anisotropic.

2.6(d) In a one-dimensional lattice with a localized impurity, the reflection of waves in the passband is highest when the energy (frequency) of the localized state is farthest from a passband. Explain why this might not be expected in two- or three-dimensional lattices.

2.7(a) A hypothetical one-dimensional "crystal" has variation of energy with lattice spacing like that of Fig. 2.19. Interpreting this as the energy of a nonlinear spring between masses, as in Fig. 2.20: (1) Show that vibrations set up by thermal energy will produce *thermal expansion*, an increase of the average length of the "crystal." (2) What lowest term is required in (2.50) to produce thermal expansion?

2.7(b) In the circuit of Fig. 2.5c: (1) Find, as a function of C_2/C_1, the low-frequency wave velocity. (2) Find the upper frequency limit of the upper band. (3) Use the results to explain how the optical branch of the phonon spectrum of some diatomic materials can extend much higher than the phonon spectrum of simple metals, while the acoustical velocities are not greatly different.

2.8(a) (1) Explain why a high-energy longitudinal-vibration phonon of the acoustical branch, when dividing into two phonons, separates into a pair of shear-vibration phonons or a shear and a longitudinal phonon. (2) Why must the two resultant phonons, in a simple crystal structure, be directed in nearly the same direction as the initial phonon?

2.8(b) An electron in a localized state is hit by a photon and caused to make a transition into an energy band *beginning* 2 ev above the localized state. (1) Approximately *where* will the electron arrive, in the Brillouin zone of the band? (2) If the acoustical velocity of phonons in the crystal is 4×10^5 cm/sec, approximately how much phonon energy is released if the electron then drops into a state at $\mathbf{k} = 0$ by emission of a phonon?

2.9(a) Determine, for a simple cubic lattice of spacing 3 A, (1) the lowest energy of x rays which will give a diffraction pattern, (2) the lowest energy of electrons, (3) the lowest energy of neutrons.

2.9(b) Construct a simple square reciprocal lattice with $a = 2$ A.

(1) What is the longest wavelength which may be used in a Laue pattern to obtain "dots" within 10° of the direction of the incident beam? (2) What set of planes hk produces this diffraction, and at what diffraction angle does it occur?

2.9(c) What sets of diffraction patterns hkl will be missing from a face-centered cubic pattern, as compared with a simple cubic? (Remember that there are four atoms in the unit cell.)

GENERAL REFERENCES

Bijvoet, J. M., et al.: "X-ray Analysis of Crystals," Butterworth & Co. (Publishers), Ltd., London, 1951. (Description of methods and analysis.)

Brillouin, L.: "Wave Propagation in Periodic Structures," 2d ed., Dover Publications, Inc., New York, 1953. (A classic, easy to read, written with extensive use of electrical analogs.)

Buerger, M. J.: "Elementary Crystallography," John Wiley & Sons, Inc., New York, 1956.

Callaway, J.: Electron Energy Bands in Solids, *Solid State Phys.*, vol. 7, 1957. (Theoretical treatise with an introduction.)

Herman, F.: Theoretical Investigation of the Electronic Energy Band Structure of Solids, *Rev. Mod. Phys.*, **30**:102 (1956). (Describes solutions undertaken to that time, and results.)

Jones, H.: "The Theory of Brillouin Zones and Electronic States in Crystals," North Holland Publishing Company, Amsterdam, 1960. (Approached from a general viewpoint, advanced level.)

Lax, B.: Experimental Investigations of the Electronic Band Structure of Solids, *Rev. Mod. Phys.*, **30**:122 (1958). (Explains how experiments demonstrate band structure.)

Mott, N. F., and H. Jones: "The Theory of the Properties of Metals and Alloys," Clarendon Press, London, 1936. (Dover Publications, Inc., 1958.) ((Excellent and readable.)

Ziman, J. M.: "Electrons and Phonons," Clarendon Press, Oxford, 1960. (General description of electron and acoustical waves; much material on wave collisions.)

3

Electronic conduction

3.1 Phenomenological Description

Free electrons in a vacuum are accelerated continuously by electric fields, leading to nonlinear voltage-current relations in vacuum-electronic devices. In plasmas and in solid conductors, however, motion is interrupted very frequently by collisions with fixed or moving bodies or waves; the average velocity of electrons in moderate electric fields is linearly proportional to the field, and since electron density is constant, conductivity is ohmic. The description of electronic conduction in metals using classical mechanics leads, with suitable assumptions, to meaningful results. Even if we neglect for the most part the statistical nature of the electron motion, approximate results may be obtained in some cases which agree with the results of more rigorous statistical theories.

We take as a model for a conductor a confining container filled by an electron gas of density N_0, plus a uniformly distributed and *immobile* positive charge, which does not enter the conduction process. The positive charge cancels space-charge fields, unless the electron density is increased at one point in the conductor and reduced in another. The electron motion, even with applied fields, is still largely due to thermal energy; motion of an electron is exemplified in Fig. 3.1a. An electron in a solid conductor collides very frequently, most often with phonons, less frequently with lattice defects,

The material in Appendix Secs. C.3–C.6 is a prerequisite for a full appreciation of the material in this chapter.

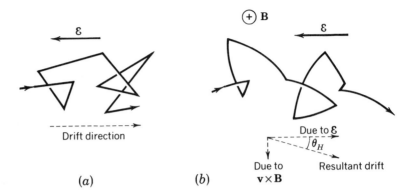

Figure 3.1 (*a*) Motion typical of an electron in a metal, under the influence of an electric field. (*b*) Motion in combined electric and magnetic fields.

and to no significant extent with other electrons. An electron will to a great extent lose all evidence of its initial velocity after a collision, although little energy change takes place in most collisions.

Let us assume that some electron has velocity $\mathbf{v}_1$ immediately after a collision. If an electric field is present, the electron will come under its influence immediately after collision, until at a time t sec after the collision the velocity is

$$\mathbf{v}(t) = \mathbf{v}_1 - \frac{e\mathcal{E}}{m}\, t \qquad (3.1)$$

While we cannot predict the actual length of time during which a particular electron will move between collisions, an average time *between* collisions, or so-called *mean free time*, τ, can be found. The electron in question will in time τ have attained a velocity $\mathbf{v}(\tau)$. We are, however, interested not in one particular electron, but in the average of *all* electrons. In the conductor at any time, some electrons will have just experienced collision, others will be just about to collide, and still others will be near the middle of their free motion. The average "time *after* collision" for all electrons will be about τ, since at any time we observe more of the long-lived electrons than of the shorter-lived ones. The *average* velocity of all electrons at a particular instant, termed the *drift velocity*, is

$$\langle \mathbf{v} \rangle = \langle \mathbf{v}_1 \rangle - \frac{e\mathcal{E}}{m} \langle t \rangle \simeq - \frac{e\mathcal{E}\tau}{m} \qquad (3.2)$$

The average value $\langle v_1 \rangle$ may be assumed to be zero if the collisions effectively destroy memory of previous velocities. The small amount of energy normally acquired from fields between collisions is readily exchanged even in phonon collisions.

Since the drift velocity is a linear function of the applied field, the ratio of drift velocity to field, μ_n (the subscript n refers to negative charges), should be a constant of the material:

$$\mu_n = \frac{e\tau}{m} \tag{3.3}$$

This is termed the *electron mobility*. A space charge of density ρ_n, traveling at velocity v, represents an electric-current density $J = \rho_n v$. In the conductor, the charge density of moving charges is $-eN_0$ and average velocity is given by (3.2); hence

$$J = \frac{e^2 N_0 \tau}{m} \mathcal{E} = \mu_n e N_0 \mathcal{E} \tag{3.4}$$

With the usual definition of (isotropic) conductivity σ_n,

$$\sigma_n = \frac{e^2 N_0 \tau}{m} = \mu_n e N_0 \tag{3.5}$$

This same result is derived from detailed statistical considerations in Sec. 3.5.

In a simple metal such as copper, μ_n is a strong function of the metallurgical condition of the sample. Resistivity tables usually show various values for hard-drawn, annealed, etc., samples of metals. A high-conductivity metal (e.g., copper) may have room-temperature conductivity $\sigma_n \approx 6 \times 10^5$ mhos/cm. The density of conduction electrons, N_0, is of the order of 10^{23}/cm^3, counting one valence electron per atom. From the equations, $\tau \approx 2 \times 10^{-14}$ sec, and $\mu_n \approx 40$ cm^2/volt-sec. If we calculate a *mean free path* $l_0 = \tau(v_{\text{thermal}})$, using for the thermal velocity the Boltzmann value $mv_{\text{th}}^2/2 = 3kT/2$, we find $l_0 \cong 25$ A. This agrees very poorly with a classical theory in which an electron could be deflected by *each* atom in its path. If, instead, we recognize the true energy distribution to be Fermi-Dirac and use for the thermal velocity a value corresponding to the Fermi energy, $E \cong 10$ ev, we find $l_0 \cong 400$ A. In truth, however, the electron collides only with crystal imperfections, mainly phonons. Atoms in a perfect lattice do not impede electron motion.

When applied magnetic fields are present in a conducting solid, electrons are deflected during their free paths (Fig. 3.1b). No observable conduction effects are produced by a steady magnetic field alone, for such a field cannot transfer energy to the electrons. The velocity of electrons after a ($t = 0$) collision with both electric and magnetic fields is

$$\mathbf{v}(t) = \mathbf{v}_1 - \frac{e}{m} \int_0^t (\mathcal{E} + \mathbf{v} \times \mathbf{B}) \, dt \tag{3.6}$$

We now assume that $\mathbf{v}_1$ is very much greater than the average velocity increment, $e\mathcal{E}\tau/m$, given the electron by the electric field. The electron has then a nearly constant velocity between collisions. It experiences a force $-e(\mathbf{v} \times \mathbf{B})$ and travels in a circular path of radius such that magnetic force equals centrifugal force. This radius is, accordingly,

$$r = \frac{mv}{Be} \tag{3.7}$$

The *angular velocity* of the electron in this circular trajectory is always $Be/m = \omega_m$ (the cyclotron frequency). In time τ, the electron will traverse an arc of angle $Be\tau/m$. In our simple model, an "average" electron will have changed its direction from that of $\mathbf{v}_1$ through an angle

$$\theta_H = \frac{Be\tau}{m} \tag{3.8}$$

In the absence of a magnetic field, an electric field produces an electric current in its own direction. The magnetic field alters the direction of the current. With the magnetic field exactly *perpendicular* to the electric field, the magnetic deflection of the current direction will be a maximum and equal to θ_H. If electric and magnetic fields are *parallel*, there will be no change in the current direction, for the average value of the $\mathbf{v} \times \mathbf{B}$ term then vanishes. The change in current direction for an arbitrary magnetic field is proportional to the component of the magnetic field normal to the electric field.

Observation of this phenomenon is made through the *Hall effect*. A thin conductor may for convenience be cut into the form shown in Fig. 3.2. An electric field $\mathcal{E}_x$ is applied through end terminals; a normal magnetic field B_z is applied. Electrons will crowd toward the upper (negative y) side of the conductor. Since they cannot flow out this side, they produce

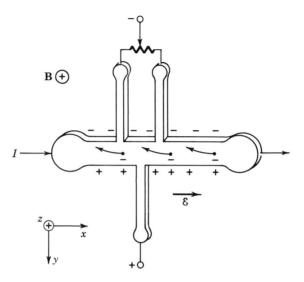

Figure 3.2 A conductor of the form often used for Hall-effect measurements. Two electrode connections are required on one side, to balance the Hall-voltage circuit in the absence of magnetic field.

a slight imbalance from electric-charge neutrality in the conductor, setting up an electric field $\mathcal{E}_y$ along the y axis. The field adjusts itself so that the *average* magnetic force in the y direction will be counterbalanced. This average force is

$$f_{yH} = e\langle v_x \rangle B_z = -e\mathcal{E}_{yH} \tag{3.9}$$

Since the drift velocity is

$$\langle v_x \rangle = \frac{e\tau\mathcal{E}_x}{m} \tag{3.10}$$

the *Hall field* is given by

$$\mathcal{E}_{yH} = \frac{B_z e\tau}{m}\,\mathcal{E}_x = \mu_n B_z \mathcal{E}_x = \theta_H \mathcal{E}_x \tag{3.11}$$

The ratio of the fields, independent of current or N_0, equals θ_H, the so-called *Hall angle*.

In the usual measurement of Hall effect, a given *current density* J_x is passed through the conductor in a field B_z; the Hall field $\mathcal{E}_{yH}$ is the measured voltage across the width of the conductor, divided by the width. It is therefore convenient

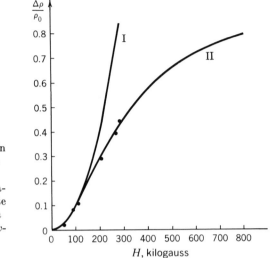

Figure 3.3 Fractional resistance change due to magnetoresistance in copper, as a function of magnetic field. Points are experimental; curve I is the parabolic approximation, curve II from a more accurate theory. (*After F. Seitz, "Modern Theory of Solids," p.* 185, *McGraw-Hill Book Company, New York,* 1940.)

to use a normalized parameter, the *Hall constant*

$$R_n = \frac{\mathcal{E}_y}{J_x B_z} \tag{3.12}$$

Substituting (3.4) and (3.11),

$$R_n = (eN_0)^{-1} \tag{3.13}$$

The Hall constant thus indicates the effective density of electrons. Mobility may be calculated from conductivity and Hall-effect measurements:

$$\mu_{n(\text{Hall})} = \sigma_n R_n \tag{3.14}$$

A more rigorous treatment of Hall effect leads to identical results.[1] The more rigorous theory also demonstrates a second-order magnetic effect, *magnetoresistance*. The conductivity $J_x/\mathcal{E}_x$ in a specimen such as that described by Fig. 3.2 is found to decrease slightly upon application of a magnetic field B_z. The change is proportional to B_z^2, to fields of many thousand gauss. A typical magnetoresistance curve is shown in Fig. 3.3. The curve "saturates" when the field reaches a value at which many of the electrons travel through free circular trajectories which are significant fractions of a full circle. A simplified explanation: Let an electron in fields $\mathcal{E}_x$

[1] Cf. F. Seitz, "Modern Theory of Solids," pp. 137ff., McGraw-Hill Book Company, New York, 1940.

and B_z, after collision, have velocity $\mathbf{v}_1$ in the $-x$ direction. With no magnetic field this electron would make a contribution $v_1 e$ to the current J_x. In the magnetic field, however, the electron has an approximately circular trajectory; its x velocity as a function of time is $\sim v_1 \cos (Bet/m)$. The velocity at the end of a mean free time is therefore $v(\tau) \simeq v_1 \cos (Be\tau/m)$; for small mean free time and/or field,

$$v(\tau) \approx v_1 \left[1 - \frac{1}{2} \left(\frac{Be\tau}{m} \right)^2 \right]$$

(3.15)

The ratio of the conductivity due to this electron, with and without magnetic field B_z, is

$$\frac{\sigma_n(B_z)}{\sigma_n(0)} \cong 1 - \frac{1}{2} \left(\frac{Be\tau}{m} \right)^2$$

(3.16)

A statistical theory gives results of the same general form. With fields of, say, 100 kilogauss, $Be/m \approx 1.75 \times 10^{11}$. If τ were 10^{-12} sec, we should anticipate from (3.16) a magnetoresistive change of the order of $\frac{1}{2}(0.175)^2 \simeq 1.5$ per cent, in order-of-magnitude agreement with Fig. 3.3. In ordinary conductors this effect is so small as to preclude device application, other than in magnetic field measurements. Bismuth, however, has relatively large magnetoresistance; changes of resistance of 1 to 2 per cent are possible in some ferromagnetic metals (nickel, iron, alloys) at low applied fields, because of high internal magnetic fields.

3.2 Momentum-space Representation of Electrical Conduction

In this section we again employ a model consisting of an electron-gas container but will consider the statistical distribution of electron momenta. An electron in uniform motion in field-free space has constant momentum $(\mathbf{p})$. Its representation in momentum space (coordinates p_x, p_y, p_z) is by a single fixed point. A group of electrons is represented by a group of such points. We may therefore describe electron momentum distributions by distributions of points in momentum space ($\mathbf{p}$ space).

While in classical mechanics electrons may take on any momentum value, electrons confined to a conductor of limited volume may assume by quantum theory only one of a discrete

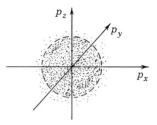

Figure 3.4   The momentum-space electron "swarm" representing free electrons, at a temperature above zero. Each electron is represented by a point at the appropriate momentum value.

set of values. These values are spaced uniformly through values of $\mathbf{k}$, as shown in (2.42). In a unit volume of electron gas, one obtains $(2\pi)^{-3}$ discrete states per unit volume of $\mathbf{k}$ space. Since, for the freely moving electrons in our gas, the classical momentum $\mathbf{p}$ and the electron wave vector $\mathbf{k}$ are related directly by $\mathbf{p} = \mathbf{k}\hbar$, the density of allowed momentum values in $\mathbf{p}$ space is just h^{-3}; this density is $2/h^3$, when we count both possible electron spin values.

Fermi-Dirac theory (cf. Sec. C.6) permits us to define the average *occupancy* of these states under equilibrium conditions. The average density of occupied electronic states, for an electron gas of unit volume, is

$$f_0(\mathbf{p}) = \frac{2}{h^3} \left(e^{(E-E_f)/kT} + 1 \right)^{-1} \tag{3.17}$$

The Fermi energy μ is described by the symbol E_f, in conduction theory, to avoid confusion with the mobility μ_n.

Graphical representations in $\mathbf{p}$ space permit simple visualization of many conduction processes. The equilibrium picture of the Fermi-Dirac electron gas in $\mathbf{p}$ space is much like that of a swarm of bees, even as to temperature dependence. At zero temperature the "swarm" (Fig. 3.4) is motionless, occupying a minimum volume (all electronic states out to $E = E_f$ occupied). As temperature is increased, some electrons on the fringes of the swarm begin to travel away from the original surface, producing a diffuse fringe. At all temperatures, the energy at which the density is half its maximum value of $2/h^3$ is the Fermi energy, which may be a function of temperature. For the semifree electrons under discussion, energy and momentum are related through $E = \mathbf{p}^2/2m$. The surface $E = E_f$ therefore defines a sphere, and as a matter of fact at equilibrium the entire swarm has spherical symmetry. The surface $E = E_f$ is termed the *Fermi surface*, even in crystalline theory, where it is not spherical.

Above zero temperature the Fermi swarm is in constant motion, with electrons shifting from one momentum to another through collisions. The average density is unchanged by these slight fluctuations. The swarm is very compact even at high temperatures. Fermi-Dirac theory indicates that the region of partial occupancy of electronic states extends sensibly only a few kT either side of the Fermi energy. With a typical Fermi energy for a metal of 10 ev, this region (at room temperature, $4kT \approx \frac{1}{10}$ ev) may represent only about $\frac{1}{2}$ per cent of the diameter of the Fermi sphere.

Having defined the Fermi distribution of electrons, we can describe their motion in electric and magnetic fields. The pertinent classical force equation is

$$\frac{d\mathbf{p}}{dt} = -e(\mathbf{\varepsilon} + \mathbf{v} \times \mathbf{B}) \tag{3.18}$$

It will be shown, in Sec. 3.3, that this is also pertinent, with proper consideration for the meaning of $\mathbf{p}$ and $\mathbf{v}$, in quantum theory. Application of a constant electric field therefore causes *each* electron in $\mathbf{p}$ space to move in the direction opposite to the field, *at a constant rate*. Let us idealize for the moment by imagining that the electrons all collide simultaneously, at periodic time intervals τ. Upon application at $t = 0$ of an electric field, the momentum of each electron begins shifting, until, at $t = \tau$, the *entire* $\mathbf{p}$-space electron distribution is shifted by an amount

$$\Delta \mathbf{p} = -e\mathbf{\varepsilon}\tau \tag{3.19}$$

After collision, the distribution returns to its original (centered) position in $\mathbf{p}$ space. With the more realistic assumption that individual collisions occur randomly, some electrons are at any instant being bounced back into a centered distribution while others have reached the shifted position. On the average, the *entire* distribution is therefore shifted by a momentum $\Delta \mathbf{p}$ the order of (3.19). We shall denote by $f(\mathbf{p},\mathbf{\varepsilon})$ the average density of this shifted distribution. Since current conduction is known to result from this shift, the difference $f_1 = f - f_0$ between the shifted and equilibrium distributions describes the effects of the field. Each state in $\mathbf{p}$ space has a given momen-

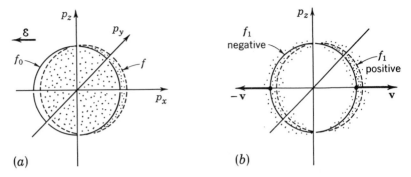

Figure 3.5   (*a*) Application of a field $\mathcal{E}$ shifts the p-space swarm in the direction opposite to the field.   (*b*) The differential density function $f(\mathbf{p}) - f_0(\mathbf{p}) = f_1(\mathbf{p})$ is appreciable only near the surface of the equilibrium distribution, being positive on the side away from the field and negative on the side toward the field.

tum and corresponding velocity $\mathbf{v}$.   When an electron occupies that state, it produces an electric current $\mathbf{I} = -e\mathbf{v}$.   The *net current density* is found by summing $-e\mathbf{v}$ of all *occupied* states.   Thus

$$\mathbf{J} = -e \sum_{\substack{\text{all} \\ \text{occupied} \\ \text{states}}} \mathbf{v} = -e \sum_{\substack{\text{all} \\ \text{states}}} f\mathbf{v} \rightarrow -e \iiint_{-\infty}^{\infty} f\mathbf{v}\, dp_x\, dp_y\, dp_z \qquad (3.20)$$

Since no current flows, in the equilibrium distribution f_0, then

$$\iiint_{-\infty}^{\infty} f_0 \mathbf{v}\, dp_x\, dp_y\, dp_z = 0 \qquad (3.21)$$

and

$$\mathbf{J} = -e \int_{\text{all } \mathbf{p}} (f - f_0)\mathbf{v}\, d\mathbf{p} \equiv \int_{\text{all } \mathbf{p}} f_1 \mathbf{v}\, d\mathbf{p} \qquad (3.22)$$

(Observe the customary abbreviation in the integral notation.)

In the absence of an electric field, every state of a given $\mathbf{v}$ which is on the average occupied by an electron will be matched by a state of $-\mathbf{v}$, and as a result no net direct current will flow.   Because of fluctuations in occupancy of states near the Fermi surface, a *noise current* can flow which has zero average (d-c) value and whose rms value is a function of

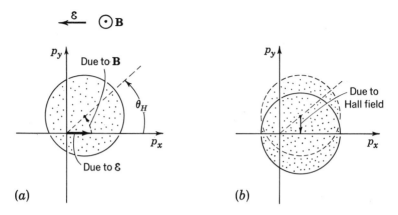

Figure 3.6 (*a*) The field $\mathcal{E}$ shifts the distribution to the right; field **B** rotates it counterclockwise. (*b*) The Hall field must shift the distribution back to the p_x axis since no current component J_y is permitted to flow.

temperature.[1] An applied electric field shifts the electron p-space distribution and destroys the precise cancellation of average current (Fig. 3.5), and steady current flows. This current is always in the direction of the applied field. (This is a limitation of the free-electron theory, but must also be the result in cubic crystals.) The momentum shift shown in the figure is exaggerated for clarity; in actuality the shift in modest fields (for example, 100 volts/cm) is only of the order of 10^{-9} the diameter of the Fermi surface.

A *magnetic* field alone changes each electron's momentum steadily, in a direction *normal* to the electron velocity; the circular trajectory in real space has a corresponding circular trajectory in momentum space. Each point of the distribution will revolve about the origin until a collision throws it elsewhere. The distribution appears to rotate about the magnetic field axis. This rotation produces no net current flow, however, since states of $-\mathbf{v}$ and $\mathbf{v}$ still cancel in **J**.

[1] Thermal noise current in conductors may be shown by thermodynamic arguments to have the mean-square value, over a frequency interval $f \to f + \Delta f$,

$$\langle i^2 \rangle = \frac{4\Delta f}{R} \frac{hf}{e^{hf/kT} - 1} \tag{3.23}$$

This is often used in the approximation $\langle i^2 \rangle = 4kT\,\Delta f/R$, which clearly breaks down at high frequencies where $hf \gtrsim kT$. Here R is the electric resistance of the conductor, and Δf the frequency region over which the noise current is measured.

The effects of combined electric and magnetic fields may be appreciated by imagining the fields applied in sequence. The electric field shifts the distribution, while the subsequently applied magnetic field rotates the shifted distribution through the θ_H angle (Fig. 3.6). The internal Hall field finally shifts the distribution back to the electric field axis, where no J_y is produced. The second-order *distortion* of the originally spherical distribution, in the combined fields, is the source of magnetoresistance.

3.3 Quantum-mechanical Description of Electron Motion in Fields

The preceding description makes use of two basically classical concepts: the free-electron relationship between electron energy and momentum $E = \mathbf{p}^2/2m$, and the Lorentz force equation (3.18). In treating conduction quantum-mechanically, one must not only use correct energy-momentum relations for electrons *in a crystal*, but must also find a suitable form of force equation.

Electron waves in a crystal may be described by Bloch functions:

$$\psi = U_{\mathbf{k}}(\mathbf{r})e^{-jEt/\hbar}e^{j\mathbf{k}\cdot\mathbf{r}} \tag{3.24}$$

Crystalline waves are commonly displayed in a $\mathbf{k}$-*space* plot describing energy versus $\mathbf{k}$ (e.g., Fig. 2.15). We have in crystalline $\mathbf{k}$ space almost the same situation we have been plotting in $\mathbf{p}$ space for free electrons. In what follows, it will accordingly be understood that the symbol $\mathbf{p}$ is always used to represent $\mathbf{k}h$. We shall term $\mathbf{k}h$ the *crystal momentum*, or simply momentum, and use $\mathbf{p}$ or $\mathbf{k}h$ interchangeably. With this understanding, most expressions are the same in the quantum-mechanical description as in the classical approximation. When $\mathbf{v}$ appears, however, as in expressions for current density [(3.20), etc.], it must always be interpreted as the electron-wave *group* velocity. This is because current flow requires actual transport of the electron charge and mass, defined by the group velocity.

Constant-energy surfaces describing electronic states in the valence-electron band of many simple cubic-lattice monovalent metals are spherical, like those of classical free electrons. This does not imply, however, that the electrons behave exactly as if free, for the relation between E and $\mathbf{p}$ may differ from the classical relation $E = \mathbf{p}^2/2m$. These differences can be surmounted, as we shall now show, by introducing the concept of an *effective mass* which need not be equal to the free-electron mass and need not even be constant.

From (2.49) the electron (group) velocity $\mathbf{v}$, as a function of energy, is

$$\mathbf{v} = \frac{1}{\hbar} \nabla_k E \equiv \nabla_p E \tag{3.25}$$

Classically, $\mathbf{F} = d\mathbf{p}/dt$; i.e., the momentum $\mathbf{p}$ has a constant rate of change in a constant electric field. This can also be expressed $\mathbf{F} = m(dv/dt)$; in quantum theory only the first form is meaningful since the mass is no longer a constant. The following is often used as a "proof": The force on the electron is $\mathbf{F}$, given by the Lorentz equation. $\mathbf{v}$ being the (group) velocity of the electron wave, the time rate of change of the electron *energy* is

$$\mathbf{v} \cdot \mathbf{F} = \frac{dE}{dt} \tag{3.26}$$

The energy is, by energy-band theory, a unique function of $\mathbf{k}$; hence its total time derivative is

$$\frac{dE}{dt} = \frac{\partial E}{\partial k_x}\frac{dk_x}{dt} + \frac{\partial E}{\partial k_y}\frac{dk_y}{dt} + \frac{\partial E}{\partial k_z}\frac{dk_z}{dt} = \nabla_k E \cdot \frac{d\mathbf{k}}{dt} \tag{3.27}$$

Combining with (3.25),

$$\mathbf{v} \cdot \mathbf{F} = \hbar\mathbf{v} \cdot \frac{d\mathbf{k}}{dt} \tag{3.28}$$

It is simple (if not rigorous!) to conclude that

$$\mathbf{F} = \hbar\frac{\partial \mathbf{k}}{\partial t} \tag{3.29}$$

It is pointed out by Shockley[1] that a magnetic field produces no such energy interchange with the electrons. Using a *finite* wave packet assembled from Bloch waves like (3.24), he shows, nonetheless, that the proper expression for the change of momentum with field is indeed the same as the classical expression:

$$\frac{d\mathbf{p}}{dt} = \hbar\frac{d\mathbf{k}}{dt} = -e(\boldsymbol{\varepsilon} + \mathbf{v} \times \mathbf{B}) \tag{3.30}$$

[1] W. Shockley, "Electrons and Holes in Semiconductors," pp. 424ff., D. Van Nostrand Company, Inc., Princeton, N.J., 1950.

The velocity in the magnetic-force term is of course group velocity. A clue to remembering the correct relation is that nowhere in (3.30) does mass appear explicitly. It is, however, convenient to define *effective mass* m^* relating the *differentials* of **p** and **v** by

$$\left(\frac{1}{m^*}\right) d\mathbf{p} = d\mathbf{v} \tag{3.31}$$

Writing **v** in terms of E,

$$
\begin{aligned}
d\mathbf{v} &= \frac{1}{\hbar} d\left(1_x \frac{\partial E}{\partial k_x} + 1_y \frac{\partial E}{\partial k_y} + 1_z \frac{\partial E}{\partial k_z}\right) \\
&= \frac{1}{\hbar} 1_x \left(\frac{\partial^2 E}{\partial k_x{}^2} dk_x + \frac{\partial^2 E}{\partial k_x\, \partial k_y} dk_y + \frac{\partial^2 E}{\partial k_x\, \partial k_z} dk_z\right) \\
&\quad + \frac{1}{\hbar} 1_y \left(\frac{\partial^2 E}{\partial k_y\, \partial k_x} dk_x + \frac{\partial^2 E}{\partial k_y{}^2} dk_y + \cdots\right) + \cdots \\
&= \hbar \left(\frac{1}{m^*}\right)(1_x\, dk_x + 1_y\, dk_y + 1_z\, dk_z)
\end{aligned}
$$

The vectors 1_x, 1_y, and 1_z are unit vectors in the x, y, z directions, respectively. This can be satisfied for independent dk_x, dk_y, dk_z only if $1/m^*$ is a *tensor* having components

$$\frac{1}{m^*} = \frac{1}{\hbar^2} \begin{vmatrix} \dfrac{\partial^2 E}{\partial k_x{}^2} & \dfrac{\partial^2 E}{\partial k_x\, \partial k_y} & \dfrac{\partial^2 E}{\partial k_x\, \partial k_z} \\[2mm] \dfrac{\partial^2 E}{\partial k_y\, \partial k_x} & \dfrac{\partial^2 E}{\partial k_y{}^2} & \dfrac{\partial^2 E}{\partial k_y\, \partial k_z} \\[2mm] \dfrac{\partial^2 E}{\partial k_z\, \partial k_x} & \dfrac{\partial^2 E}{\partial k_z\, \partial k_y} & \dfrac{\partial^2 E}{\partial k_z{}^2} \end{vmatrix} \tag{3.32}$$

This complication need not introduce confusion into visualizing electron dynamics in **p** space. Figure 3.7 is a representative E-**k** variation (in two dimensions for simplicity), with **v** for various values of **k** represented by vectors. At the upper and lower energy limits of the band the velocity is zero. At the Brillouin-zone boundaries, **v** is tangent to the boundary. Along the dashed path, while momentum (**k**) increases as one moves away from the origin, the velocity first increases and then decreases. There is *negative effective mass* in regions where change in velocity opposes the change in **p**. Off-diagonal terms appear in (3.32) to explain situations where the direction of **v** is different from that of **p**.

If the constant-energy surfaces of a crystal in the vicinity of $E = E_f$ are *spheres* ($E = \mathbf{p}^2/2m^*$), as is approximately true

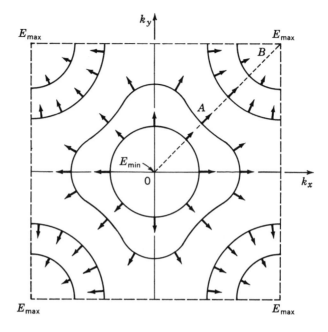

Figure 3.7   A two-dimensional **k**-space plot of constant-
energy surfaces as might apply to a square lattice.   The
electron (group) velocity (shown by vectors) is proportional
to the gradient of E.   Effective mass is largest in regions
where the vector velocity changes little with **k**.

in many simple metals, the effective mass is scalar.   Although
it may be different from the free-electron mass, free-electron
theories are applicable in this case, merely by replacing m by
m^*.

When an electric field is applied, the point representing
each electron will move at a uniform rate in momentum space;
so long as no collisions occur, this motion will continue.   In
the free-electron solution, the electron velocity then increases
without limit.   What then occurs in the crystalline **k** space,
when the electron momentum reaches a boundary of the
Brillouin zone at which the energy E is discontinuous?   An
electron cannot hurdle an energy gap without an abrupt energy
change.   All the electric field can do, however, is alter the
electron's energy slowly.   Since the wave functions on opposite
sides of the Brillouin zone are identical, point A (Fig. 3.8) is
completely equivalent to point A'.   Instead of moving into
another band, the electron merely reenters on the opposite

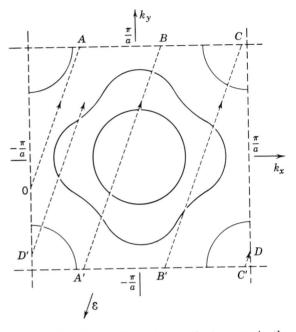

Figure 3.8 Motion of an electron in **k** space, in the unlikely event that collisions do not occur for a long time interval. Electron waves are identical at A and A', at B and B', etc.

side of the zone.   This is quite compatible with effective-mass variation: As the electron approaches the zone boundary, its (group) velocity normal to the boundary slows to zero.   On the opposite side of the zone its velocity normal to the boundary is also zero; the component parallel to the boundary does not change.   As the electron crosses and recrosses the zone, it must accordingly oscillate back and forth in the actual crystal. This quantum effect has no equivalent in classical theory.   In practical fields, however, an electron will suffer a collision long before it can make a complete excursion through the zone. There thus appears to be no direct way to observe this cyclic behavior, although experiments have distinguished negative-effective-mass states.[1]

The conduction properties of metals having Fermi surfaces which approximate the spherical form of the free-electron model are described with reasonable accuracy by the simple results of Sec. 3.1, where mass m is replaced by effective mass

[1] G. C. Dousmanis et al., *Phys. Rev. Letters*, **1**:55, 404 (1958).

m^*. No further discussion of the graphical arguments of this section is needed. We defer discussion of crystalline deviations in conductivity behavior to Sec. 3.7.

3.4 Statistical Conduction Theory; the Boltzmann Transport Equation [1]

The derivations which follow are based on theory developed by Boltzmann and applied later by Drude, Lorentz, Sommerfeld, and others to conduction in metals. It is also a major mathematical tool for treating gaseous discharges. Only strictly applicable where the electron mean free path is small compared with dimensions of the conductor, the assumption is implicit that collisions occur with sufficient frequency so that the *perturbed* **p**-space distribution of electrons, f, differs only very slightly from the unperturbed distribution, f_0. There is an implicit assumption that at each collision an electron is restored to the effective temperature of its environment (the lattice), losing all evidence of its former state. Through this type of theoretical development, it is possible to appreciate the electrical and thermal properties of conductors.

The system of electrons is described completely by the density function $f(p_x, p_y, p_z, x, y, z)$ representing the density of the "Fermi swarm" in a given range of momentum $(dp_x \, dp_y \, dp_z)$ and a given region in space $(dx \, dy \, dz)$. With f a function of coordinates as well as momenta, thermal gradients may be introduced. The density function is assumed to be *time-independent;* the theory is therefore applicable only to processes in which electric fields, etc., change relatively slowly in time. This is seldom a limitation in metals, however, for since electronic processes revert to steady state typically in a few τ, this theory may be applied (at room temperature) even at frequencies of 10^{11} or higher.

The *total* electron density N_0 at a particular position in space (x,y,z) is the integral of f over all possible momenta:

$$N_0(x,y,z) = \iiint\limits_{-\infty}^{\infty} f(p_x, p_y, p_z, x, y, z) \, dp_x \, dp_y \, dp_z \equiv \int f \, d\mathbf{p} \qquad (3.33)$$

The current density is given by (3.20), which is completely equivalent to $-N_0 e \langle \mathbf{v} \rangle$. Since $-e$ represents the *charge* trans-

---

[1] The mathematical treatment of conductivity in this and the following section is not essential to an understanding of the later material.

ported by the electron, and E the *energy* transported, the expression for the net *energy flow density* is, accordingly, the same as (3.20), with E substituted for the constant $-e$:

$$\mathbf{J}_W = \int E\mathbf{v}f\,d\mathbf{p} \tag{3.34}$$

In the absence of electric, thermal, or concentration gradients, $f = f_0$. One can readily see that the equilibrium integrals for both $\mathbf{J}$ and $\mathbf{J}_W$ vanish, because the $\mathbf{v}$ factor in the integrand is an odd function of the p_x, p_y, and p_z, while the remaining factors are both even functions independent of the polarity of the momentum. In the presence of fields, however, the density function f will differ from its equilibrium value f_0 by the density perturbation function f_1, which is also a function of the electron coordinates and momenta.

$$f_1 = f_1(p_x,p_y,p_z,x,y,z) \tag{3.35}$$

$f_1 \ll f_0$ is assumed to hold everywhere. At least in metallic conductors, fields and thermal gradients do not measurably alter electron temperature (hence average electron *energy*) or electron density. This further limits f_1:

$$\int f_1\,d\mathbf{p} = 0 \qquad \int E f_1\,d\mathbf{p} = 0 \tag{3.36}$$

These relations will be satisfied if f_1 is an *odd* function of one or more of the momentum components.

If electrons did not suffer collisions, initial velocity distribution and the effect of applied fields could cause a time rate of change of the electron density function f. These effects are usually called "drift" and are expressible in terms of a partial derivative:

$$\frac{\partial f}{\partial t_{\text{drift}}} = \frac{\partial f}{\partial x}\frac{dx}{dt} + \frac{\partial f}{\partial y}\frac{dy}{dt} + \frac{\partial f}{\partial z}\frac{dz}{dt} + \frac{\partial f}{\partial p_x}\frac{dp_x}{dt} + \frac{\partial f}{\partial p_y}\frac{dp_y}{dt}$$
$$+ \frac{\partial f}{\partial p_z}\frac{dp_z}{dt} \tag{3.37}$$

In more compact notation,

$$\frac{\partial f}{\partial t_{\text{drift}}} = \nabla_r f \cdot \mathbf{v} + \nabla_p f \cdot \mathbf{F} \tag{3.38}$$

where the subscripts on the vector operator ∇ indicate the variables of differentiation, and $\mathbf{F}$ is the force $(d\mathbf{p}/dt)$ on the electrons.

Lorentz realized that the density f at a given position and momentum could be changed by *collisions*, in two distinct ways: an electron suffering a collision at a given point in space could have its momentum changed *to a given momentum* **p** from another value (call it **P**), or an electron with the given momentum **p** could suffer a collision altering its momentum *to* **P**. Let us define a function $C(\mathbf{p} \to \mathbf{P}, \mathbf{r})$ representing the probability *per second* that some electron at the point **r**, with momentum **p**, will have its momentum changed *to* the value **P**. Then the probability that an electron will suffer a collision taking it out of the desired momentum range, per second, must be

$$\int_{\text{all } \mathbf{P}} C(\mathbf{p} \to \mathbf{P}, \mathbf{r}) \, d\mathbf{P}$$

The change in *density* at the point and momentum range in question must be this probability, multiplied by the density:

$$\left(\frac{\partial f}{\partial t}\right)_{\substack{\text{collisions} \\ \text{out of } \mathbf{p}}} = -f(\mathbf{p},\mathbf{r}) \int_{\text{all } \mathbf{P}} C(\mathbf{p} \to \mathbf{P}, \mathbf{r}) \, d\mathbf{P} \equiv -a \qquad (3.39)$$

The integral is over *all* possible momenta to which an electron may be transferred by the collision. The entire term, a function of momentum and perhaps of position, will for conciseness be represented by the symbol $-a$.

The change in density due to electrons being transferred *to* the momentum **p** is of different form, for the density appearing in the integral is that at **P**:

$$\left(\frac{\partial f}{\partial t}\right)_{\substack{\text{collisions} \\ \text{into } \mathbf{p}}} = \int_{\text{all } \mathbf{P}} f(\mathbf{P},\mathbf{r}) C(\mathbf{P} \to \mathbf{p}, \mathbf{r}) \, d\mathbf{P} \equiv b \qquad (3.40)$$

The order of the momenta $(\mathbf{P},\mathbf{p})$ in $C(\mathbf{P} \to \mathbf{p}, \mathbf{r})$ indicates that the particle starts with momentum **P** and ends with **p** after the collision. The steady-state requirement that *drift changes of f* (3.38) *exactly compensate the collision-produced changes* (3.39) and (3.40) yields the *Boltzmann transport equation*

$$\nabla_\mathbf{r} f \cdot \mathbf{v} + \nabla_\mathbf{p} f \cdot \mathbf{F} = b - a \qquad (3.41)$$

A simple check of the signs of terms is made by observing (Fig. 3.9) that a group of electrons with constant velocity **v** in the *positive x* direction and *positive* $\partial f/\partial x$ ($\nabla_\mathbf{r} f \cdot \mathbf{v} > 0$) will produce in time a *reduction* of density at a point along the path of motion. The term on the right $(b - a)$ is the *net increase* in $f(\mathbf{p},\mathbf{r})$ due to collisions. When the term on the left is positive, drift causes f to be reduced. When that on the right is

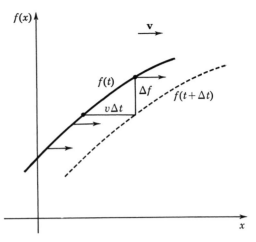

Figure 3.9   A positive density gradient of electrons having positive velocity will produce a reduction of density Δf which must be exactly balanced by an increase in density due to collisions.

positive, collisions cause f to be increased. These two processes are balanced for any position $\mathbf{r}$ and momentum $\mathbf{p}$ if the Boltzmann equation is satisfied.

When the system is in thermal equilibrium $(f = f_0)$, the collisions into and out of a given momentum range are equal; that is, $a = b$. Substituting,

$$f_0(\mathbf{p},\mathbf{r}) \int C(\mathbf{p} \to \mathbf{P}, \mathbf{r})\, d\mathbf{P} = \int f_0(\mathbf{P},\mathbf{r}) C(\mathbf{P} \to \mathbf{p}, \mathbf{r})\, d\mathbf{P} \tag{3.42}$$

In nonequilibrium conditions, therefore,

$$b - a = \int \{ [f_0(\mathbf{P},\mathbf{r}) + f_1(\mathbf{P},\mathbf{r})] C(\mathbf{P} \to \mathbf{p}, \mathbf{r})$$
$$- [f_0(\mathbf{p},\mathbf{r}) + f_1(\mathbf{p},\mathbf{r})] C(\mathbf{p} \to \mathbf{P}, \mathbf{r}) \}\, d\mathbf{P} \tag{3.43}$$

To simplify, we shall assume that collisions between given momenta $(\mathbf{p},\mathbf{P})$ are equally likely in either direction. This will certainly be true if collisions are *elastic* and *isotropic*. This is just what we should expect when electrons collide with fixed defects. The small energy change in electron-phonon collisions also makes the "elastic" assumption reasonable, if not entirely accurate. In an isotropic collision, the deflection angle of the electron's motion is independent of the direction in which the electron is initially traveling (Fig. 3.10). This should also be quite reasonable, at least in cubic crystals.

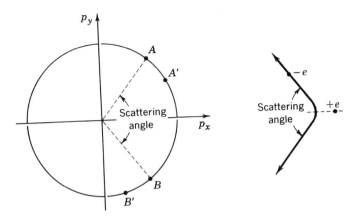

Figure 3.10 An isotropic, lossless collision means that an electron in state A in **p** space will be scattered to point B, lying on the same Fermi surface, with the same probability as for the reverse situation, $B \rightarrow A$, or for $A' \rightarrow B'$. Probability is a function of the scattering angle. The real-space collision corresponding to this momentum-space collision is shown at right.

Our approximation is

$$C(\mathbf{p} \rightarrow \mathbf{P}, \mathbf{r}) = C(\mathbf{P} \rightarrow \mathbf{p}, \mathbf{r}) \qquad (3.44)$$

Using (3.42),

$$b - a = \int [f_1(\mathbf{P},\mathbf{r}) - f_1(\mathbf{p},\mathbf{r})] C(\mathbf{p} \rightarrow \mathbf{P}, \mathbf{r}) \, d\mathbf{P} \qquad (3.45)$$

By conditions (3.36), $f_1(\mathbf{P},\mathbf{r})$ will be an odd function of **P**. Since in the isotropic approximation C is *even* in both **p** and **P**, the first term vanishes in the integration, and

$$b - a = -f_1(\mathbf{p},\mathbf{r}) \int C(\mathbf{p} \rightarrow \mathbf{P}, \mathbf{r}) \, d\mathbf{P} \qquad (3.46)$$

The integral equals the probability per second of an electron of momentum **p** being effectively scattered from **p** to some other momentum value. Its reciprocal is the *mean free time;* therefore, in more concise symbolism,

$$b - a = -f_1/\tau \qquad (3.47)$$

At any point **r**, the mean free time involved in specific collisions $\mathbf{p} \leftrightarrow \mathbf{P}$ is actually a function of *both* **p** and **P**. A function of two vectors is in general a tensor, so τ should truly have tensor form. Since we have not set up the equations to permit this extension, however, we must consider τ a *scalar* function of the momentum; in lossless, isotropic collisions, it is a function only of the electron energy E. The expression (3.47) appears to be generally applicable, even when energy exchange occurs in the collisions, at least at temperatures above the Debye temperature, where the entire phonon spectrum is excited. The Boltzmann equation now takes the completed form

$$\nabla_r(f_0 + f_1) \cdot \mathbf{v} + \nabla_p(f_0 + f_1) \cdot \mathbf{F} = \frac{-f_1}{\tau} \tag{3.48}$$

This is in actuality a nonlinear partial differential equation in f_1, with $\mathbf{F}$ and f_0 the known "driving functions." Past this point, exact analytical solutions are not in general possible. Various techniques can be used for further simplification; in general, they yield little physical insight and have questionable merit, unless leading to recognizable and reasonable-looking solutions. If one is interested only in application of electrical and thermal gradients, terms in f_1 on the left may be neglected, giving immediately an approximate solution

$$f_1 = -\tau(\nabla_r f_0 \cdot \mathbf{v} + \nabla_p f_0 \cdot \mathbf{F}) \tag{3.49}$$

This has the general form of a Taylor-series expansion of the density function f, in which f_0 represents the zeroth-order term and f_1 the first-order term. A higher order of approximation is required to introduce magnetic phenomena (Hall effect, magnetoresistance, etc.). This solution can, however, be used to explain electrical and thermal conduction and electrothermal effects. The electric field enters through $\mathbf{F}$, while a thermal gradient causes the electron momentum distribution f_0 to vary from point to point, yielding a nonzero $\nabla_r f_0$ term.

We can now calculate current and energy flow in response to applied electrical and thermal gradients. Electric fields now appear explicitly, through $\mathbf{F} = -e\mathcal{E}$. Thermal as well as concentration N_0 gradients are implicit in $\nabla_r f_0$. Function f_0 [(3.17)] is *explicitly* related to E, E_f, and T. But E_f depends on N_0 (the electron density) as well as temperature (although in metals the Fermi level is almost constant from absolute zero to temperatures near the melting point). Differentiating (3.17) with respect to one of the cartesian spatial coordinates, x,

$$\frac{\partial f_0}{\partial x} = \frac{2}{h^3} e^{(E-E_f)/kT} \frac{\partial}{\partial x} \left(\frac{E - E_f}{T} \right) (e^{(E-E_f)/kT} + 1)^{-2}$$

$$\frac{\partial f_0}{\partial E} = \frac{1}{kT} \frac{2}{h^3} e^{(E-E_f)/kT} (e^{(E-E_f)/kT} + 1)^{-2} \tag{3.50}$$

The derivative of f_0 with respect to E forms a common factor, since

$$\frac{\partial f_0}{\partial p_x} = \frac{\partial f_0}{\partial E}\frac{\partial E}{\partial p_x}$$

Therefore, including the assumption that E_f is almost independent of T,

$$\mathbf{\nabla}_p f_0 = \frac{\partial f_0}{\partial E}\mathbf{\nabla}_p E$$
$$\mathbf{\nabla}_r f_0 = \frac{\partial f_0}{\partial E}\left[\left(-\frac{E}{T}+\frac{E_f}{T}\right)\mathbf{\nabla}_r T - \frac{\partial E_f}{\partial n_0}\mathbf{\nabla}_r N_0\right]$$

(3.51)

We shall neglect, in our discussion of *metallic* conductors, the concentration gradient $\mathbf{\nabla}_r N_0$. Even a small (percentage) variation of N_0 results in fantastically large space-charge (electric) fields, which will restore charge equilibrium in the order of a few times τ. Using (3.51) in (3.20) and (3.34), we obtain for the current and energy-flow densities

$$\mathbf{J} = e\int\tau\frac{\partial f_0}{\partial E}\mathbf{\nabla}_p E\left[\left(-\frac{E}{T}+\frac{E_f}{T}\right)\mathbf{\nabla}_r T - e\boldsymbol{\varepsilon}\right]\mathbf{v}\,d\mathbf{p}$$
$$\mathbf{J}_W = -\int\tau E\frac{\partial f_0}{\partial E}\mathbf{\nabla}_p E\left[\left(-\frac{E}{T}+\frac{E_f}{T}\right)\mathbf{\nabla}_r T - e\boldsymbol{\varepsilon}\right]\mathbf{v}\,d\mathbf{p}$$

(3.52)

Each now includes terms both in thermal gradient, $\mathbf{\nabla}_r T$, and in $\boldsymbol{\varepsilon}$. These relate in scalar fashion to the current densities, so that in the absence of magnetic fields the relations are of the general form

$$\mathbf{J} = A\,\mathbf{\nabla}_r T + B\boldsymbol{\varepsilon}$$
$$\mathbf{J}_W = C\,\mathbf{\nabla}_r T + D\boldsymbol{\varepsilon}$$

(3.53)

where the integrals A, B, C, and D are properties of the material. In the most general formulation in crystals, A, B, C, and D must be tensors, related to a tensor mean free time τ. This would lead to anisotropic properties. That these relations between currents and driving fields are linear is a direct result of our assumption of small perturbations; happily, Ohm's law of electrical conduction and Joule's law of heat conduction, both linear, apply experimentally over tremendous ranges of field and thermal gradients in metallic conductors.

3.5   One-dimensional Conduction in the Free-electron Model

Limiting discussion to free-electron energy-momentum relations simplifies the current equations (3.52) sufficiently to obtain tractable solutions. We shall assume that only x-directed electrical and thermal gradients are applied. In the free-electron approximations $E = 1/2m^* \times (p_x^2 + p_y^2 + p_z^2)$, $\nabla_p E = \mathbf{v}$; (3.52) then reduce to the scalar forms

$$J_x = -e \int_{\text{all } \mathbf{p}} \tau \frac{\partial f_0}{\partial E} v_x^2 \left[\left(\frac{E}{T} - \frac{Ef}{T} \right) \frac{dT}{dx} + e\mathcal{E}_x \right] d\mathbf{p}$$

$$J_{Wx} = \int_{\text{all } \mathbf{p}} \tau E \frac{\partial f_0}{\partial E} v_x^2 \left[\left(\frac{E}{T} - \frac{E_f}{T} \right) \frac{dT}{dx} + e\mathcal{E}_x \right] d\mathbf{p}$$

(3.54)

Both have the general form

$$\iiint\limits_{-\infty}^{\infty} v_x^2 F(E) \, dp_x \, dp_y \, dp_z = \frac{1}{m^{*2}} \iiint\limits_{-\infty}^{\infty} p_x^2 F(E) \, dp_x \, dp_y \, dp_z$$

where $F(E)$ is a function of energy alone. The integral on the right is not altered if p_x^2 is changed to p_y^2 or p_z^2. Writing this integral in all three alternative forms, adding, and dividing by 3,

$$\frac{1}{m^{*2}} \iiint p_x^2 F(E) \, dp_x \, dp_y \, dp_z$$
$$= \frac{1}{3m^{*2}} \iiint p^2 F(E) \, dp_x \, dp_y \, dp_z$$

The variable of integration may be changed to the absolute momentum p by noting that $dp_x \, dp_y \, dp_z = 4\pi \mathbf{p}^2 \, dp$. A further transformation to the variable E ($= \mathbf{p}^2/2m^*$) gives

$$\iiint v_x^2 F(E) \, d\mathbf{p} = \frac{4\pi 2^{3/2} m^{*1/2}}{3} \int_0^\infty E^{3/2} F(E) \, dE$$

(3.55)

(This step cannot be carried out for *general* E-$\mathbf{k}$ relations, although a similar transformation is possible in the case of ellipsoidal constant-energy surfaces.)

Using (3.55), (3.54) reduce to

$$J_x = \frac{4\pi 2^{3/2} e m^{*1/2}}{3} \int_0^\infty \tau \frac{\partial f_0}{\partial E} E^{3/2} \left[\left(\frac{E}{T} - E_f/T \right) \frac{dT}{dx} + e\mathcal{E}_x \right] dE$$

$$J_{Wx} = \frac{4\pi 2^{3/2} m^{*1/2}}{3} \int_0^\infty \tau \frac{\partial f_0}{\partial E} E^{5/2} \left[\left(\frac{E}{T} - E_f/T \right) \frac{dT}{dx} + e\mathcal{E}_x \right] dE \tag{3.56}$$

Since the particular dependence of τ on E is unknown, it is convenient to express all terms as functions of a set of integrals, I_j:

$$I_j = \frac{4\pi 2^{3/2} m^{*1/2}}{3} \int_0^\infty \tau E^{j+1/2} \frac{\partial f_0}{\partial E} dE \qquad j = 1, 2, 3, \ldots \tag{3.57}$$

Then

$$J_x = -e \left(\frac{I_2}{T} - \frac{E_f I_1}{T} \right) \frac{dT}{dx} - e^2 I_1 \mathcal{E}_x$$

$$J_{Wx} = \left(\frac{I_3}{T} - \frac{E_f I_2}{T} \right) \frac{dT}{dx} + e I_2 \mathcal{E}_x \tag{3.58}$$

I_1, I_2, and I_3 may be treated as constants, determined by collision statistics in the particular conductor.

The (*isothermal*) *electrical conductivity* is defined as

$$\sigma_n = \left(\frac{J_x}{E_x} \right)_{dT/dx=0} \tag{3.59}$$

By (3.58),

$$\sigma_n = -e^2 I_1 \tag{3.60}$$

In the calculation of electrical conductivity, a simple approximation may be made. The function $\partial f_0/\partial E$, which appears in all the integrals I_j, is very small except near $E = E_f$. Over the small significant interval of integration,

$$I_1 \cong \frac{4\pi 2^{3/2} m^{*1/2}}{3} \tau_0 E_f^{3/2} \int_0^\infty \frac{\partial f_0}{\partial E} dE$$

$$\cong \frac{4\pi 2^{3/2} m^{*1/2}}{3} \tau_0 E_f^{3/2} \int_{E \ll E_f}^{E \gg E_f} df_0 \tag{3.61}$$

The constant τ_0 is the mean free time of electrons of energy E_f. Well above $E = E_f$, $f_0 \to 0$; and well below

$E = E_f f_0 \to 2/h^3$; accordingly, the integral reduces simply to $2/h^3$, and

$$I_1 \simeq - \frac{4\pi 2^{3/2} m^{*1/2}}{3} \tau_0 E_f^{3/2} \left(\frac{2}{h^3} \right) \tag{3.62}$$

At absolute zero temperature all states are filled, up to $E = E_{f0}$, and

$$N_0 = \int_{E=0}^{E=E_{f0}} \frac{2}{h^3} d\mathbf{p} \tag{3.63}$$

E_{f0} is the Fermi level at absolute zero. By transformation,

$$N_0 = \frac{2}{h^3} \int_{E=0}^{E=E_{f0}} 4\pi p^2 \, dp = \frac{8\pi \sqrt{2} \, m^{*3/2}}{h^3} \int_0^{E_{f0}} E^{1/2} \, dE$$

$$= \frac{16\pi \sqrt{2} \, m^{*3/2}}{3h^3} E_{f0}^{3/2} \tag{3.64}$$

Using the approximation $E_f \simeq E_{f0}$, which applies well for metals,

$$I_1 \simeq - \frac{n_0}{m^*} \tau_0$$

and

$$\sigma_n \simeq \frac{e^2 N_0 \tau_0}{m^*} \tag{3.65}$$

This is the same as (3.5). The mean free time appearing here is *not* an average for the whole distribution, however, but applies to electrons of energy $E_f \approx E_{f0}$. This emphasizes the point that it is the electrons near the Fermi surface which contribute to metallic conductivity.

Thermal conductivity κ is defined, not for $\mathcal{E}_x = 0$, but at $J_x = 0$, as the energy flow rate divided by the thermal gradient:

$$\kappa = - \left(\frac{J_{Wx}}{\partial T/\partial x} \right)_{J_x=0} \tag{3.66}$$

The negative sign assures κ is positive, since heat flows in the direction of the *negative* temperature gradient. Equations (3.53) indicate that energy may flow even when no temperature gradient is present. Only if heat energy flows *in the presence of a thermal gradient* is there *entropy flow* and true thermal conduction.

From (3.58), setting $J_x = 0$, we find that there must exist an electric field

$$\mathcal{E}_x = -\frac{1}{e}\left(\frac{I_2}{I_1 T} - \frac{E_f}{T}\right)\frac{dT}{dx} \tag{3.67}$$

This is the *electrothermal* (or *Seebeck*) *field*. It is produced because electrons from one end are carried toward the other end of the conductor by a difference in temperature. While the effect is subtly dependent on $\tau(E)$, it is convenient to imagine some of the more numerous high-energy electrons from the hotter end migrating to the colder end. If there is no closed current path, they accumulate to produce a space-charge field of magnitude given by (3.67). This and related phenomena are discussed further in the next section.

Putting (3.67) into (3.58),

$$\kappa = \frac{I_1 I_3 - I_2{}^2}{I_1 T} \tag{3.68}$$

This cannot be evaluated by the earlier approximation of I_1, since the two terms in the numerator would cancel. Using the next degree of approximation to I_j,†

$$\kappa \approx \frac{\pi^2}{3} k^2 T \frac{N_0 \tau_0}{m} \tag{3.69}$$

With (3.65), this gives the famous *Weidemann-Franz ratio*,

$$\frac{\kappa}{T\sigma_n} = \frac{\pi^2}{3}\left(\frac{k}{e}\right)^2 \tag{3.70}$$

This relation is nearly satisfied by simple monovalent metals, but as would be expected, is very approximate in metals of high valency. It should not be surprising that electrical and thermal conductivity are related, since the same electronic "carriers" transport both charge and energy. The thermal conductivity of *metals*, moreover, is almost entirely due to this electronic contribution, only about 10 per cent of the experimental conductivity being due to phonon heat transport. In most insulators, where only phonons may transport heat energy, thermal conductivity is correspondingly smaller.

The electrical conductivity of metals may actually be calculated only if τ_0 is known. Experimental data are there-

† Seitz, *op. cit.*, pp. 140, 177.

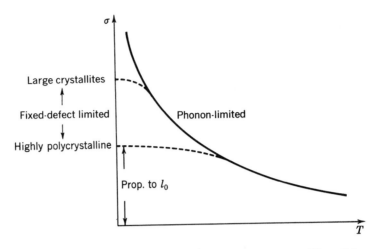

Figure 3.11   Conduction of a metal at low temperatures.   The solid curve represents phonon-limited conductivity, which could be achieved only in an otherwise perfect crystal.

fore more often used to estimate τ_0.   Experiments on metals typically show σ_n versus T as in Fig. 3.11.   This is most easily understood if we express the mean free time as the ratio of a mean free path to velocity:

$$\tau_0 = \frac{l_0}{v_0} \qquad (3.71)$$

where l_0 is the *mean free path* of motion between collisions, and v_0 the electron velocity corresponding to $E = E_f$.   Since E_f changes little with temperature, v_0 can be taken as a constant,

$$v_0 = \sqrt{\frac{2E_{f0}}{m^*}} \qquad (3.72)$$

The mean free path l_0 approaches, at low temperature, an upper asymptote associated with the *fixed defects* in the crystal. It is a strong function of the metallurgical condition of the conductor.   At temperatures above the cryogenic range, however, electron-phonon collisions materially reduce the mean free path.   Since total phonon energy in the crystal, at low temperatures, goes up with the fourth power of T, one might expect very dramatic conduction changes with temperature.   Experimentally, however, resistivity varies almost linearly with temperature, above the *residual resistivity* associated with fixed-defect collisions. This may be explained from detailed electron-phonon collision probabilities. While total phonon density increases rapidly with temperature, the density of phonons which can effectively collide with electrons increases more slowly. Bloch[1] first showed that phonon-limited resistivity should be proportional to T.†

3.6   Electrothermal Phenomena

Solution of the current equations (3.56) for zero electric current, in the presence of a thermal gradient dT/dx, leads to an internal electric field, the Seebeck field [(3.67)]. Across the two ends (x_1, x_2) of a conductor having temperature distribution $T(x)$ will appear a *Seebeck voltage* V_s, the integral of the field:

$$V_s = -\frac{1}{e} \int_{x_1}^{x_2} \left(\frac{I_2}{TI_1} - E_f/T \right) \frac{dT}{dx} \, dx$$

$$= -\frac{1}{e} \int_{T_1}^{T_2} \left(\frac{I_2}{TI_1} - E_f/T \right) dT \qquad (3.73)$$

The voltage depends only on the two particular temperatures at the ends of the conductor; the conductor *length* is unimportant. This is not to say, however, that the Seebeck voltage need be linear in temperature difference, since the Seebeck coefficient (or *thermoelectric power*), which is the integrand of (3.73),

$$\alpha = \frac{1}{e} \left(\frac{I_2}{TI_1} - \frac{E_f}{T} \right) \qquad (3.74)$$

is a function of T.   Room-temperature values of α for simple metals lie scattered over the range $+10$ to -10 $\mu v/°C$.

It is difficult to offer a compilation of values because of the discrepancies between measured values.   The coefficient α in metals is strongly dependent on energy dependence of the mean free path.   The occurrence of both positive and negative values requires interpretation (Fig. 3.12).   While electrothermal effects in metals are subtly dependent on variation of τ with E, these effects are much stronger in semiconductors (Sec. 5.12).

[1] F. Bloch, *Z. Phys.*, **59**:208 (1930).
† Cf. J. M. Ziman, "Electrons and Phonons," pp. 257ff., Clarendon Press, Oxford, 1960.

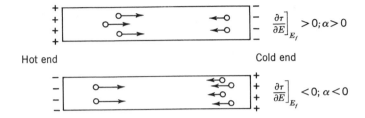

Figure 3.12   In the upper conductor, the mobility of high-velocity electrons is greater than that of low-velocity electrons, and accordingly the negative charge accumulation is at the cold end of the sample.   In the lower situation the low-velocity electrons have greater mobility.

Usual measurement techniques do not measure the absolute Seebeck voltage V_s, because the electrodes connecting the meter with the conductor in question are also under the influence of the same thermal gradient.   Their own electrothermal voltage may oppose that of the conductor.   The usual tabulated voltages (*thermocouple* voltages) are differences between V_s values in two different metals.   Even though in metals these voltage differences are small, the voltage difference is a reliable (and over small temperature ranges, linear) measure of temperature difference.   It is necessary to use a well-prepared sample of the metal to be assured of a reliable calibration, so most thermocouples are made from pairs of specially formulated alloy wires, or a metal vs. an alloy (iron vs. constantan, chromel vs. alumel, platinum vs. platinum-rhodium are accepted combinations, for use over different temperature ranges).   An *inhomogeneous* metal in a thermal gradient will cause errors in temperature measurement, since *the thermoelectric voltage is actually produced in the gradient regions.*

Two other electrothermal effects may be observed in thermal and electric gradients.   In a unit volume of conductor the power due to an electric current is proportional to $\mathcal{E}_x J_x$, while that due to energy flow is $-\partial J_{Wx}/\partial x$.   Thus the *net rate* of heat flow into unit volume is

$$\frac{dW}{dt} = \mathcal{E}_x J_x - \frac{\partial J_{Wx}}{\partial x} \tag{3.75}$$

Substituting from (3.59) and (3.68),

$$\frac{dW}{dt} = \frac{J_x^2}{\sigma_n} + \frac{J_x}{e} T \frac{d}{dx} \left(\frac{I_2}{TI_1} - \frac{E_f}{T} \right) + \frac{d}{dx} \left(\kappa \frac{dT}{dx} \right) \qquad (3.76)$$

The first term is clearly the Joule heat, and the last that heat which would be brought in because of temperature gradient (with no electric current flowing). The central term is the *Thomson heat*, an electrothermal effect. The *Thomson coefficient* σ_T is defined as the negative of the Thomson heat per unit current in a unit thermal gradient. The Thomson heat may be expressed alternatively as

$$- \frac{J_x}{e} T \frac{dT}{dx} \frac{d}{dT} \left(\frac{I_2}{TI_1} - \frac{E_f}{T} \right)$$

whence

$$\sigma_T = - \frac{T}{e} \frac{d}{dT} \left(\frac{I_2}{TI_1} - \frac{E_f}{T} \right) = - \frac{T}{e} \frac{d\alpha}{dT} \qquad (3.77)$$

σ_T is usually masked by other large terms in heat-flow measurements.

Another important thermoelectric phenomenon is *Peltier effect*, the absorption of heat at one junction and emission at the other, when current is passed through two junctions of dissimilar metals. It is the reverse of the Seebeck effect. Phenomenologically, Peltier effect is readily explained: A given electric current passing *isothermally* through a conductor carries with it a certain amount of heat energy. The *same electric current* in a conductor of *different* metal must carry a *different heat current*. At one junction, the current carrying the larger heat flow will "dump" power; electrons entering the opposite junction from the conductor carrying less heat energy must, accordingly, absorb heat from the surroundings. The expression for Peltier heat is again derived from (3.76). Joule heat is liberated at every point in both conductors. Since we have no thermal gradient, however, the final term is zero. The two conductors a and b, however, have different values of α; hence, at the junctions, there will be *discontinuities* in α. Heat exchange between the electrons and the crystal occurs precisely at the junction. The heat generated per unit area of junction is the integral of the volume heat liberation dW/dt across the junction (which we place at $x = 0$; Fig. 3.13). Then the *Peltier coefficient* π_{ab}, the heat

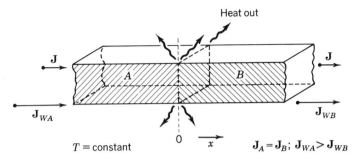

Figure 3.13 The heat and charge-carrying capacity of a composite conductor change abruptly at the junction; hence Peltier heat is liberated (or absorbed) within a few mean free paths of a junction of dissimilar conductors.

liberated or absorbed *per unit current*, is

$$
\pi_{ab} = \frac{T}{e} \int_{0-}^{0+} \frac{d}{dx}\left(\frac{I_2}{TI_1} - \frac{E_f}{T}\right) dx = \frac{T}{e}\left[\left(\frac{I_2}{TI_1} - \frac{E_f}{T}\right)_b \right.
$$
$$
\left. - \left(\frac{I_2}{TI_1} - \frac{E_f}{T}\right)_a\right] = \frac{T}{e}(\alpha_b - \alpha_a) \qquad (3.78)
$$

As much heat is absorbed at one junction as is liberated at the other.   In an actual measurement, it is of course necessary to compensate for Joule heating throughout the conductors, which makes Peltier effect in metals a low-efficiency energy-conversion process.   This situation is much improved in certain semiconductors, as described in Sec. 5.12.   The factor $\alpha = I_2/TI_1 - E_f/T$ appears in each electrothermal effect.   The Peltier and Seebeck effects are thus related directly:

$$
(V_{sa} - V_{sb})_{T_1, T_2} = \int_{T_1}^{T_2} \frac{\pi_{ab}}{T}\, dt \qquad (3.79)
$$

Since π_{ab} is defined for unit current flow, the power output VI from a Seebeck junction pair with a small temperature difference ΔT is related to the Peltier heat transfer by a factor of the form $\Delta T/T$, the same as found in expressions for efficiency of other "heat engines."   Equation (3.79) may be derived, independent of a detailed model, via thermodynamic arguments.[1]

[1] Cf. P. W. Bridgeman, "Thermodynamics of Electrical Phenomena in Metals," p. 56, Dover Publications, Inc., New York, 1961.

The three electrothermal phenomena discussed here represent only a fraction of those which are definable with magnetic, as well as electric and thermal, fields. To describe only a few: A magnetic field applied normal to a thermal gradient will, as in the Hall effect, produce an electric field transverse to both **B** and a thermal gradient $\nabla_r T$, because of the same type of "pile-up" of electrons as in the Hall effect (the *Nernst effect*). When an electric field accompanies a transverse magnetic field, there occurs a transverse thermal gradient (the *Ettingshausen effect*). An applied thermal gradient normal to a magnetic field also causes a transverse thermal gradient, because higher-energy electrons are more strongly deflected by the field (the *Righi-Leduc effect*). None of these seem to be sufficiently strong as to suggest application to energy-conversion devices, however.

3.7 Crystalline Effects in Electronic Conduction

Application of the electronic energy-band theory of solids is needed to explain conductivity in crystalline materials. Setting aside semiconductors and insulators for the present, the chief features of the band theory which affect conductivity are:

1. Nonsphericity of the Fermi surface
2. Nonconstancy of electron (group) velocity over the Fermi surface
3. Variation of the effective mass over the Fermi surface
4. Anisotropy of the phonon momentum distribution, or of defects, leading to different mean free times for electron motion in different directions (Sec. 3.8)
5. Very low or very high effective masses at the Fermi surface
6. Contact of Brillouin-zone boundaries by the Fermi surface
7. Distribution of conduction electrons over parts of two or more energy bands

The detailed analysis is beyond our present scope. We can, however, draw important conclusions from simple study of the Fermi surfaces and energy-band occupation in different materials.

Nonsphericity of the Fermi surface can (in noncubic crystals) lead to anisotropic conductivity. In a two-dimen-

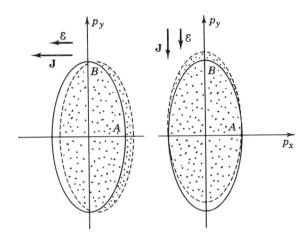

Figure 3.14 Anisotropic conductivity due to elliptical Fermi surfaces. (In cubic crystals there must be a symmetrical set of such elliptical surfaces, which counteract one another's anisotropy.)

sional model, with an elliptical Fermi surface (Fig. 3.14), a possible energy-momentum relation is

$$E = \frac{p_x^2}{2m_x^*} + \frac{p_y^2}{2m_y^*} \qquad (3.80)$$

As drawn, thefi gure implies an m_y^* that is larger than m_x^*. For field-produced motion only in the p_x direction, the effective mass is

$$\frac{1}{m^*} = \frac{\partial^2 E}{\partial p_x^2} = \frac{1}{m_x^*} \qquad (m^*)_x = m_x^* \qquad (3.81)$$

In the p_y direction, $(m^*)_y = m_y^*$. In an applied electric field, say, in the x direction, the Fermi distribution shifts in the x direction by an amount depending on the field strength and the mean free time τ. Assuming τ is constant over the Fermi surface, the amount of shift for given fields in the p_y direction will be the same as in the x direction. At the point $p_x^2/2m_x^* = E_f$, on the Fermi surface (indicated as A in the figure), the electron velocity $v_x = \partial E/\partial p_x = p_x/m_x^* = \sqrt{2E_f/m_x^*}$ is larger than at point B, along the p_y axis. A given field will thence give rise to a larger current density in the x axis than in the y axis. This means anisotropic conductivity. We expect any element having a noncubic lattice to show at least a small degree of anisotropic conductivity. The graphite form of carbon is striking in this respect. Anisotropy between the c axis and the normal plane is 10^4 or more, making accurate measurements difficult. The room-temperature conductivity of single-crystal bismuth is about 1.3 times as large for electric fields applied normal to the hexagonal axis as for fields applied parallel to the axis.

Other anisotropies (effective mass, mean free time) contribute also to anisotropic conduction. All are more or less related, since the *symmetry* of the detailed E-$\mathbf{k}$ variation of electrons is the same as that of phonons. This complicates the problem of separating various sources of anisotropy in the collision processes.

Simple energy-band models (e.g., Fig. 2.10) reveal that effective mass is negative near the maximum-energy limits of bands and positive near the minimum energy. Near the center of a band effective mass may be very high, which is equivalent to saying that the electron velocity does not change rapidly with $\mathbf{k}$. When an electric field shifts a Fermi distribution for which $m^* \gg m_e$ at $E = E_f$, there is very little change of average electron velocity. Accordingly, conductivity is low [substitute $m^* \gg m_e$ in (3.5)]. Measured mobilities ($\mu_e = e\tau/m^*$) of electrons in simple metallic conductors (copper, etc.) are of the order of a few centimeters per volt-second, whereas in semiconductors values of the order of 3,000 to 50,000 are found. Since comparable mean free times would be anticipated, the Fermi surface for many metals must lie in a region of $\mathbf{p}$ space having high effective mass. Since conductivity is the product of charge density and mobility, it is the large valence-electron *density* in metals which permits high conductivities.

In the correct quantum description, the Fermi surface lies in a Brillouin zone. The simple zone, allowing for both spin values, contains only twice as many states as there are unit cells in the lattice. For simple elements containing one atom per unit cell, the first Brillouin zone thus contains twice as many electronic states as there are atoms. Monovalent metals have only *one* valence electron per atom, so that the zone representing the valence-electron band is only one-half full. This reinforces our previous argument of high m^* near band center. A simple monovalent metal might accordingly be expected to have a Fermi surface fitting easily into the (more or less spherical) Brillouin zone. The Fermi surface

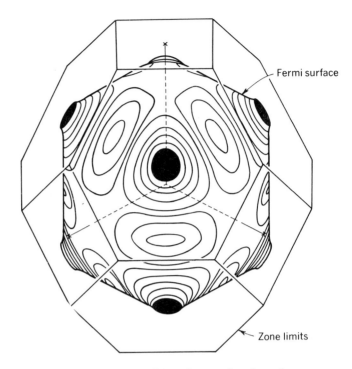

Fermi surface

Zone limits

Figure 3.15   Pippard's model of the Fermi surface of copper.
Note the contact with the zone boundaries.   [*After A. B.
Pippard, Phil. Trans.*, **A250**:325 (1957).]

could be shifted through a considerable change in **p** before any
significant part of the distribution might touch the zone boundary; hence this boundary can have no direct effect on conduction. Even in *copper*, however, the actual constant-
energy surfaces are sufficiently aspherical so that even with
one electron per atom, the Fermi surface contacts the zone
boundary (Fig. 3.15).   When the electron distribution touches
the zone boundary, the *area* of the Fermi surface is lowered.
In an electric field, the parts of the distribution in contact with
a zone boundary cannot shift; hence only the free parts of the
distribution shift.   Fewer electrons take part in the conduction process; hence conductivity should be reduced.   If the
structure is noncubic, anisotropy may be more pronounced.

In an idealized *divalent element*, the two valence electrons
should *completely fill* the valence-band Brillouin zone.   The
Fermi surface is coincident with, or may even lie outside, the
zone boundaries.   When fields are applied, the distribution

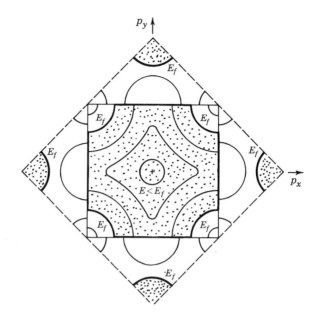

Figure 3.16   Overlap of electrons between two energy bands.   The band of lower overall energy is depicted in the first Brillouin zone of a square lattice, the upper band in the second zone.

cannot shift.   Since *the current density possible in a filled band is zero*, such a material would be expected to have zero electronic conductivity.   This is true of sulfur, selenium, and tellurium, none of which is a good conductor.   It also applies for *tetravalent* elements (C, Ge, Si, Sn, Pb), which are best described as semiconductors (Chaps. 4 and 5).   Divalent *metal* atoms also contain two valence electrons, however.   They would not conduct if the valence-electron energy band were really completely filled.   Since some of these materials are among our better conductors (e.g., beryllium and zinc), there must be energy overlaps between the valence electron band and supposedly "higher-energy" bands, so that *neither* band is completely filled.   Such band overlap is depicted in Fig. 3.16.   Both partly filled bands contribute to electronic conductivity, the result being an *effective* electron density which can be even higher than in a monovalent metal.   For example, suppose that about half of the $2N$ valence electrons spilled over into the adjacent band.   A current would then result from shifting the Fermi surface in *each* band, and the

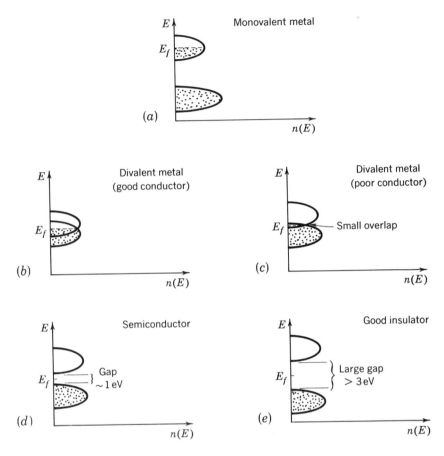

Figure 3.17 Electron populations and band overlapping characterizing various classes of conductors.

effective electron density would be twice that of a monovalent metal.

The most meaningful distinctions between classes of conductors are to be found from their electronic density-of-states functions. Figure 3.17 illustrates different energy-band structures found in (a) monovalent metals, (b) divalent metals which are good conductors, (c) elements which are poor conductors, (d) semiconductors, and (e) insulators. Elements which are poor conductors often exhibit anomalous resistivity-temperature variations (as do graphite and bismuth), which distinguishes them from true metals. The term *semimetals* is sometimes used to describe them.

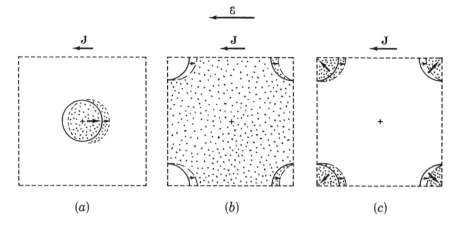

Figure 3.18   (*a*) Shift of electrons in an almost empty band.   (*b*) Shift of electrons in an almost filled band.   (*c*) Equivalent shift of *holes* in the same band as (*b*).   The heavy arrows indicate the velocity, and hence the current associated with each part of the bands. The net current is toward the left in each case.

Although we defer extensive consideration of *hole conduction* to the next chapter, the concept is meaningful even in elements classed as metals.   Let the energy-band overlap in an element of even valence be fairly small.   Only a small fraction of electrons in the valence band (which would normally be filled) may then "spill over" into an overlapping band.   Both bands are represented in the first Brillouin zone (Fig. 3.18).   An electric field causes the electron distribution in the bands to shift.   The higher-energy band approximates the single-band situation described earlier; we can describe conduction in this band via (3.5), in terms of its electron density per cubic centimeter and the effective mass and mean free times of electrons in these states.   In the lower-energy band, each point (in the figure) represents an *occupied* electronic state.   Net current flow associated with the occupied states is the same as that if *positively charged* $(+e)$ particles occupied each *empty* state of the lower band.   That is,

$$- e \int_{\substack{\text{empty}\\\text{states}}} \mathbf{v}\, d\mathbf{p} - e \int_{\substack{\text{occupied}\\\text{states}}} \mathbf{v}\, d\mathbf{p} = 0$$

$$J = -e \int_{\substack{\text{occupied}\\\text{states}}} \mathbf{v}\, d\mathbf{p} \equiv (+e) \int_{\substack{\text{empty}\\\text{states}}} \mathbf{v}\, d\mathbf{p}$$

(3.82)

Current flow in the lower-energy band may be imagined

because of the motion of *positive* "holes," of total density P_0, equal to the density of unoccupied electronic states. Although a hole's positive charge is not attached to a real mass-carrying particle, current flow is properly described by associating with the hole a *positive* effective mass equal in magnitude to the negative effective mass of the particular unfilled electronic state.   The spin of the hole must be opposite that of the particular unfilled electronic state, since the total spin of a band is likewise zero.   While holes are introduced chiefly to describe conduction in the valence band of semiconductors, there is nothing wrong with describing *any* unfilled electronic state as being occupied by a hole.   Where a band is partially filled, we have the option of stating *either* that the lower-energy part of the band is full of electrons *or* that the complementary higher-energy part contains holes.   One naturally expects the energy of positive charges to be higher in potentials where the energy of negative charges is lower; hence *hole distributions* also satisfy Fermi statistics.   The hole concept permits us to neglect the majority of the electronic states in nearly full bands, so as to deal only with those, in the vicinity of the Fermi surface, which affect current flow.

The variation of resistivity with temperature or composition is a function of both of the factors N_0 and μ_n in the conductivity.   In true metals, N_0 is constant, while μ_n decreases inversely with T.   Certain complex metallic alloys (e.g., nickel-chromium), over limited temperature ranges, have almost constant conductivity.   While meaningful analysis of this is well-nigh impossible, the complicated band structures expected in alloys could certainly be expected to lead to unusual conduction effects.   The greatly reduced conductivity of iron as a function of silicon content (Fig. 3.19) demonstrates another effect.   Although no simple theory based on volumetric proportions could explain so big a variation, the silicon atoms acting as fixed defects scatter the conduction electrons and reduce μ substantially even at low concentrations, where the band structure is little affected by the silicon.   Most *disordered* alloys, for this reason, do not normally have as high conductivity as pure metals or *ordered* alloys.

Although the model used to explain conductivity in Sec. 3.4 fails to explain the principle whereby dissipated electron energy is carried off, the fact that at normal temperatures most of it is converted directly into phonon energy leads to some interesting departures from equilibrium phonon behavior.

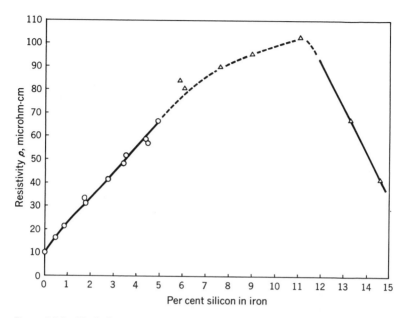

Figure 3.19 Variation of resistivity of iron-silicon alloy with silicon content. (From Bozorth's *Ferromagnetism*, Copyright 1951, D. Van Nostrand Co., Inc., Princeton, N.J.)

In the presence of an electron current flow, the momentum imparted to the electrons by the applied field is transferred by them to the phonons. This results in a larger fraction of phonons with momentum directed opposite to the field than would apply at equilibrium. The phenomenon, known as *phonon drag*, leads to lower-than-expected resistivity and to electrothermal effects of somewhat different values than would occur if the phonon system remained at equilibrium. In a mathematically idealized system, resistance due to phonons would vanish because the electrons would be unable to interact with phonons directed in the same direction of motion. The thermoelectric coefficient would be much larger than would be predicted by the earlier theory. Experimentally, the phenomenon seems to be insignificant in metals, but influences semiconductor thermoelectric properties predictably.

3.8 Geometrical and High-frequency Effects

The conduction theory described thus far applies to a bulk conductor in which all dimensions are large compared with the

Smooth surface (specular reflection)

(*a*)

Rough surface (diffuse reflection)

(*b*)

Figure 3.20   Electrons scattered at the surface of a conductor may be reflected (*a*) specularly or (*b*) diffusely. The surface roughness of most conductors suggests the latter.

electronic mean free path, electrical gradients are small enough so that an electron remains in a uniform field throughout a mean free path, frequencies are low enough that the field does not change appreciably in the mean free time for the electrons, and deviations from thermal equilibrium are small. Thin wires and sheet conductors, particularly at low temperatures, where phonon collisions are infrequent and mean free paths long, can be made smaller than an electron mean free path. Most evaporated films and small drawn wires have large concentrations of defects, however, at spacings as low as 20 to 100 A. Their fixed-defect electron scattering makes it almost impossible to observe true thickness effects. These effects can, however, be studied in specially made thin-sheet single-crystal conductors, at temperatures of a few degrees absolute. Electrons are reflected in some fashion at the sample's boundaries (Fig. 3.20). If boundaries are smooth on a sufficiently small scale, electrons might reflect as from a mirror, but experimental evidence indicates that the electrons mostly reflect *diffusely*. They scatter isotropically from the surface, back into the body of the conductor. A conductor very thin compared with a mean free path may perhaps be described most simply as having a highly anisotropic mean free time, very short for those electrons whose velocities have appreciable components normal to the plane of the conductor. Electrons whose velocities are nearly in the plane can travel distances greater than the bulk mean free path without colliding. This may be represented approximately in a graphical representation in **p** space (Fig. 3.21). If the conductor is, for example, a sheet of thickness t normal to the xy plane,

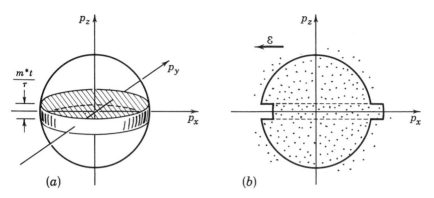

Figure 3.21 In the "ineffectiveness" model only those electrons which should not collide with the surface in a mean free path are considered. They form a thin slablike section of the Fermi sphere, which is shifted as shown in (b), in the presence of an electric field.

lectrons having components of z velocity exceeding

$$|v_z| \cong \frac{t}{2\tau} \tag{3.83}$$

will (starting from the center of the conductor) collide with the wall prior to a mean free time τ. The Fermi swarm of electrons may be separated into two parts, those for which $|v_z| > t/2\tau$ and those for which $v_z < t/2\tau$, as in the figure. Making use of Pippard's empirical "ineffectiveness concept,"[1] we assume that only the electrons in the thin slablike region $|v_z| < t/2\tau$ have normal mean free time; those outside this region are assumed to have such a short mean free time that they contribute negligibly to conductivity. When an electric field is applied to the conductor, only the thin central slab of the distribution shifts. The ratio of thin sheet to bulk conductivity is approximately the ratio of the electrons in the thin slab to those in the entire distribution. In momentum space, using the free-electron approximation $p = m^*v$, the radius of the swarm is $p_0 = (2m^*E_f)^{\frac{1}{2}}$. The thickness of the slab of "effective" electrons is m^*t/τ. The ratio is

$$\frac{\sigma}{\sigma_0} \sim \frac{3m^*t}{4p_0\tau} = \frac{3t}{4v_0\tau} = \frac{3t}{4l_0} \tag{3.84}$$

This is obviously inapplicable when thickness t is more than a tiny fraction of the mean free path.

[1] A. B. Pippard, *Proc. Roy. Soc.*, **A191**:385 (1947).

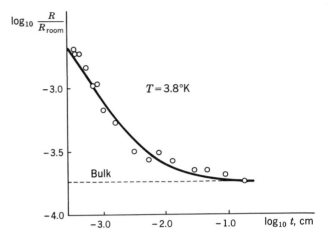

Figure 3.22   Experimental vs. theoretical [(3.85)] resistivity of a thin sheet of tin. [*From E. H. Sondheimer, Advan. Phys.*, **1**:1 (1952).]

A more exact formula for thin-film conductivity[1] fits well the measurable region around $t = l_0$:

$$\frac{\sigma}{\sigma_0} = \frac{3}{4}\frac{t}{l_0}\ln\frac{l_0}{t} \tag{3.85}$$

as shown in Fig. 3.22.

Conduction in thin sheets or wires in the added presence of *magnetic* fields produces effects beyond the usual bulk Hall and magnetoresistance effects, as can be inferred from the graphical model.   In the presence of a magnetic field, the slab of effective electrons is not only shifted but rotated, in a manner and to a degree depending on the direction and strength of the magnetic field.   With field normal to the film plane, thickness effects can in principle substantially enhance the Hall effect.

The addition of these size effects to single-crystal conductors with nonspherical Fermi surfaces leads to even greater complexity.   Considerable information can be obtained about the material in this way by studying the conductivity and magnetic effects for various crystalline orientations.   For example, the ellipsoidal Fermi surface of Fig. 3.14 can be "sliced" in any orientation by a slab of "effective" electrons. By comparing conduction in sheets of various crystalline

[1] E. N. Sondheimer, *Advan. Phys.*, **1**:1–42 (1952).

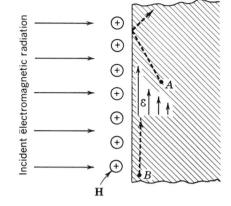

Figure 3.23 At high frequencies, skin effect is "anomalous," i.e., does not satisfy the classical law because electrons such as B, traveling more or less parallel to the surface, are much more affected by the field than electrons such as A, which are near the surface for only a brief interval.

orientations, the volume of the slab, and consequently the cross section of the actual Fermi surface, can be estimated.

In practice, this is easier to apply by measurement of *anomalous skin effect*. Ordinary skin effect is completely classical in origin: When Maxwell's equations are solved for a metal having permeability μ and conductivity σ_n,† current at frequency f is found to penetrate the surface of the conductor according to the relation

$$\frac{J(z)}{J(\text{surface, } z = 0)} = e^{-z/\delta} \tag{3.86}$$

where $\delta = (\pi f \mu \sigma_n)^{-\frac{1}{2}}$

In copper at 10,000 Mc, for example, the room-temperature skin depth δ is less than 10^{-4} cm. In high-quality single-crystal metal at very low temperatures, the mean free path l_0 can be made considerably larger than 10^{-4} cm. Those electrons traveling parallel to the surface in the region very near the surface will move through a uniform field between collisions. Electrons traveling with any appreciable component of their velocity *normal* to the surface will not remain long in the uniform field region (Fig. 3.23). As in very thin film conduction, only the electrons whose velocities are limited to a narrow range of v_z will be highly "effective" in conductivity. Conductivity is anomalously low, and the apparent skin depth appropriately larger. To evaluate this effect it is most convenient to measure the *surface resistance* (ratio of electric to

† Cf. S. Ramo and J. R. Whinnery, "Fields and Waves in Modern Radio," 2d ed., pp. 230ff., John Wiley & Sons, Inc., New York, 1953.

magnetic field at the surface) at low temperatures by micro-wave-loss measurements. Surface resistance will increase if the number of effective electrons is reduced. Using this technique, Pippard[1] developed a description of the Fermi surface in copper (Fig. 3.15).

PROBLEMS

3.1(a) For electrons behaving like free electrons, of energy 10 ev in a conductor having an acoustical wave velocity of 5,000 m/sec, estimate the average change in energy in a collision with a phonon. (HINT: begin by assuming negligible energy change.)

3.1(b) A wafer of sodium metal 0.010 in. thick is cut into the form depicted in Fig. 3.2. The main section is 1.0 cm long and 0.2 cm wide. Room-temperature conductivity is 5×10^{-6} ohm-cm. A magnetic field of 10,000 gauss is available. (1) Define a practical drive current which will not produce excessive heating in air. (2) What Hall voltage should be measured in the given field? (3) Discuss and choose some suitable dimensions for the transverse electrodes and their spacing. (4) What value of balancing potentiometer would be appropriate, and what type of instrument could be used to measure the Hall voltage?

3.2(a) A particular metal may be described using the free-electron approximation. The Fermi level is 10 ev above the zero-electronic-energy state. (1) Find the radius of the Fermi surface in momentum space, mks. (2) Determine the current density at equilibrium associated with that half of the distribution lying in the region $p_x > 0$; that is, find the integral (3.20) over one hemisphere. (NOTE: At equilibrium the contributions from the two hemispheres cancel. Departure from ohmic behavior is to be expected if current densities approach the value calculated here.)

3.2(b) The resistance of a conductor in a transverse magnetic field changes by an amount which at low fields is proportional to B^2. Show that in general the variation should be expressible as $\rho/\rho_0 = 1 + a_2B^2 + a_4B^4 + a_6B^6 + \cdots$, where $a_2 \cdots$ are constants.

3.2(c) Writing the conductivity as a tensor, as in Sec. 1.4, for a field $\mathbf{B} = 1_z B_z$, write the off-diagonal terms as functions of the fields $\mathcal{E}_x$, $\mathcal{E}_y$, $\mathcal{E}_z$ and the Hall constant. Neglect magnetoresistance, which is a second-order effect. Be certain to get signs correct. In what important ways does this differ from the conductivity of an ordinary *uniaxial* crystal without magnetic field?

3.3(a) Sketch two different hypothetical sets of constant-energy contours in a two-dimensional square first Brillouin zone, corresponding to a square lattice. In one, have the lowest-energy point at the

[1] A. B. Pippard, *Phil. Trans.*, **A250**:325 (1957).

center and four highest-energy points in the centers of the four sides. In the second, place four lowest-energy points on the diagonals, equally distant from the origin, with highest-energy points at the corners. Construct also contours directed parallel to the electron velocity (and hence normal to the constant-energy contours).

3.3(b) (1) Show that, in a cubic crystal, any "ellipsoidal" constant-energy surface centered on the origin, $p_x^2/2m_x^* + p_y^2/2m_y^* + p_z^2 2m_z^* = E$, must have $m_x^* = m_y^* = m_z^*$, that is, must be spherical. (2) What limitations are there on such ellipsoidal surfaces in hexagonal lattices? (3) What limitations are there on ellipsoidal surfaces not centered at the origin, in cubic crystals?

3.3(c) Consider an electron traveling along a main diagonal of a Brillouin zone such as that of Fig. 3.7. Let the variation of E with $\mathbf{k}$ along the diagonal be of the form $E = (\Delta/2)[1 - \cos (a/\sqrt{2})k]$, $-\sqrt{2}\,\pi/2 < k < \sqrt{2}\,\pi/a$. Assume that a field $\mathcal{E}$ is applied along this axis and that the electron does not collide. (1) Determine the equation of motion of the center of an electron wave packet by finding $\mathbf{v}$ as a function of time and integrating. (2) For typical $a = 3$ A, what field is required to keep this motion entirely inside a crystal which is a 1-cm-diameter sphere if the width of the band is $(\Delta =) 2$ ev? (3) What length of time is then required for a complete transit of the zone?

3.4(a) It is assumed in the Boltzmann theory that the perturbation f_1 is small compared with f_0 for all values of $\mathbf{p}$. Show that at absolute zero temperature this cannot be correct.

3.4(b) Assuming the presence only of electric and magnetic fields, expand (3.49), using for $\mathbf{F}$ the Lorentz equation (3.30). Substitute this into the expression (3.22) for electric-current density, and show that the term containing the magnetic field vanishes. [This proves the inadequacy of the approximate solution (3.49) for describing magnetic effects.]

3.4(c) Give plausibility arguments for the strong dependence of conduction on those electrons very near the Fermi energy.

3.5(a) The resistivity of a sample of monovalent metal of density 3 g/cm³ and atomic weight 45 is measured versus T. Below 4°K its resistivity approaches a lower limit of 10^{-6} ohm-cm. The free-electron approximation applies: $E = m^*v^2/2$, with $m^* = 5 \times 10^{-31}$ kg. (1) Determine the position of the Fermi energy with respect to the lowest-energy conduction states; (2) estimate crystallite "size," i.e., the mean free path at low temperatures.

3.5(b) From data in, for example, the "Handbook of Chemistry and Physics" (Chemical Rubber Publishing Co.), tabulate for at least four metals the Wiedemann-Franz ratio and compare with the theoretical value (3.70). Use 0°C values where available. Discuss any major deviations from the theory.

3.5(c) Derive (3.69) after the method of Seitz ("Modern Theory of Solids," pp. 176–178), stating all steps.

3.6(*a*) The argument of Fig. 3.12 suggests that thermal conductivities might be substantially different in metals which behave in the two ways described. Explain how thermal conductivity can be (in fact must be) positive, even when net electron transfer is toward the *hot* end of a sample.

3.6(*b*) A power of 0.01 watt is given off from a junction of metals *A* and *B* at 300°K when a 1-amp current is passed through the junction from *A* to *B*. (1) Estimate the thermoelectric voltage of a thermocouple made from these two metals if one junction is immersed in a water-ice mixture and the other maintained at 20°C. (2) Sketch the circuit arrangement and show the polarity of Seebeck voltage developed. Explain the polarity, phenomenologically, simply on the basis of the reversibility of the phenomena.

3.6(*c*) Give a simple phenomenological explanation of the Ettingshausen effect.

3.7(*a*) Indicate qualitatively, in terms of the shift of a *near-spherical* Fermi surface, the effect on conductivity of a shorter mean free path τ for electron motion along one axis than along perpendicular axes. Indicate, as specifically as you can, what details of the phonon distribution might produce such behavior.

3.7(*b*) Assume that a particular *semimetal* has a normally filled and a normally empty band which contact only at their highest and lowest energy points, respectively. There should accordingly be no conduction at absolute zero temperature, because electrons in the filled band cannot shift their momentum. What type of *conductivity vs. temperature* variation would be expected? Explain.

3.7(*c*) Near the top of the lower active band of a hypothetical divalent metal, the *E*-**k** variation can be represented by an isotropic effective mass of $0.5m_e$, and near the bottom of the higher band the effective mass is $0.1m_e$. The overlap is such that, of the total of 2×10^{22} valence electrons/cm³, 10^{21} of these at zero-temperature equilibrium spill over into the upper band. Calculate the conductivity due to both bands if the mean free time is 10^{-13} sec for electrons everywhere in both bands.

3.8(*a*) Develop a simple theory of high-frequency conduction when the mean free time and the inverse of the frequency of the applied signal are comparable, as follows: Consider a single electron in a sinusoidal electric field and solve for its motion as a function of time, as in (3.1). (1) For a constant free time τ, find the velocity in the field direction, and thence conductivity. (2) Indicate *qualitatively* the results of averaging over the actual range of free times. (3) Sketch an expected conductivity vs. frequency variation.

3.8(*b*) Change (3.84) to account for the fact that, as the slab of "effective" electrons becomes thicker, its volume must be corrected to account for the fact that it is a section from a sphere; i.e., the maximum volume is that of the sphere. Compare this theoretical ratio of σ/σ_0 with the experimental data (Fig. 3.22).

GENERAL REFERENCES

Blatt, F. J.: Theory of Mobility of Electrons in Solids, *Solid State Phys.*, **4**:199 (1957). (Semiclassical theory.)

Bridgeman, P. W.: "Thermodynamics of Electrical Phenomena in Metals," Dover Publications, Inc., New York, 1961. (Approached purely from thermodynamic point of view.)

Jan, J. P.: Galvanomagnetic and Thermomagnetic Effects in Metals, *Solid State Phys.*, **5**:1 (1957). (Comparison of theory and experiment.)

Lax, B.: Experimental Investigations of the Electronic Band Structure of Solids, *Rev. Mod. Phys.*, **30**:122 (1958). (Catalogue of band structures studied.)

MacDonald, D. K. C.: "Thermoelectricity: An Introduction to the Principles," John Wiley & Sons, Inc., New York, 1962.

Seitz, F.: "Modern Theory of Solids," McGraw-Hill Book Company, New York, 1940. (A comprehensive treatment of classical theory and briefer treatment of quantum theory.)

Sommerfeld, A., and N. H. Frank: The Statistical Theory of Thermoelectric, Galvano- and Thermomagnetic Phenomena in Metals, *Rev. Mod. Phys.*, **3**:1 (1931). (A readable early treatment.)

Sondheimer, E. H.: The Mean Free Path of Electrons in Metals, *Advan. Phys.*, **1**:1 (1952). (An excellent survey of theory and experiment.)

Ziman, J. M.: "Electrons and Phonons," Clarendon Press, Oxford, 1960. (A comprehensive modern treatment of electronic conduction.)

4
Semiconductors

4.1 Semiconducting Materials

Semiconductors were characterized in the previous chapter as having a filled valence-electron energy band separated by a finite energy band gap from a higher conduction band (Fig. 3.17). This definition could be applied equally well to insulators; these, however, are usually materials with large band gaps and small electronic mobilities. The elements carbon (diamond), silicon, germanium, (gray) tin, tellurium, and selenium are semiconductors. All possess the diamond structure, except the latter two, which have hexagonal structures. Single-crystal germanium and silicon are used extensively in electronic devices. Diamond, however, has not been prepared in electronically valuable form by synthetic crystal-growing techniques, and tin has undesirably low energy band gap and melting point. The complex crystal structures of selenium and tellurium defeat easy growth of good single crystals and discourage single-crystal applications.

A distinguishing characteristic of semiconductor materials is *covalent bonding* (Sec. 1.6), wherein electron pairs are held tightly in the region between adjacent ions. In the characteristic diamond structure, the four nearest neighbors to an atom each contribute one electron to four bonds. The *band gap* E_g (Table 4.1) is the energy required to break an electron out of one of these bonds. The mechanical hardness of the crystal and the band gap are directly related, and both decrease with higher atomic weights (see table).

Table 4.1 Properties of important semiconducting elements and compounds†

Semiconductor	E_g, 0°K, ev	m_n^*/m_e	m_p^*/m_e	μ_n, cm²/volt-sec	μ_p, cm²/volt-sec	Static ϵ/ϵ_0	Minority carrier lifetime τ, μsec	Crystal structure
Ge	0.66	0.55	0.04 0.3	3,800	1,800	16	1,000	D(diamond)
Si	1.08	1.09	0.16 0.5	1,300	500	11.8	2,500	D
GaP	2.4			1,000		8.4		Z(zincblende)
GaAs	1.58	0.072	0.65	8,500	400	13.5	$\sim 10^{-3}$	Z
GaSb	0.80	0.047	0.4	4,000–5,000	850–1,000	15.2		Z
InP	1.34	0.019	0.33	4,600	700	10.6		Z
InAs	0.47	0.013	0.18	30,000	240	11.5		Z
InSb	0.23	0.6–1.0	1.2	70,000	1,000	16.8	3	Z(or hexagonal)
SiC	~3.0	0.27(?)		20–100	10–25	10.2		W(wurtzite) or Z
ZnO	3.3			190		8.5		W or Z
ZnS	3.5–3.7					8.3		Z
ZnSe	2.6							Z
ZnTe	2.15							W
CdS	2.4	0.27(?)	0.07(?)	200		11.6	1,000	W
CdSe	1.74	0.14	0.37	650			10,000	Z
CdTe	1.4–1.6	0.45	0.51	1,250	45	11		Trigonal complex
Bi_2Te_3	0.15	~0.4			515			fcc lattice
PbTe	0.29			~2,500	~1,200			Trigonal
Se	~1.6							Trigonal
Te	0.33			3,000–6,000				Trigonal

† Properties from H. P. R. Frederikse, in D. E. Gray (ed.), "American Institute of Physics Handbook," 2d ed., p. 9-45, McGraw-Hill Book Company, New York, 1963. Lifetime data from A. Coblenz, Semiconductor Compounds, Electronics, Nov. 1, 1957. Value for GaAs inferred from injection-laser (Chap. 10) data.

High-quality germanium and silicon single crystals of large dimensions (up to several inches in diameter and several times as long) can be prepared by one of several techniques, of which the Czochralski method (Fig. 1.22) seems to be the most common. Crystal diameter is limited not only by apparatus size, but by internal stresses set up in very large crystals. These crystals are further purified, for example, by zone refining; desired impurities may be introduced in these processes. Semiconductor crystal growth and refining has developed into a specialized business, and most device manufacturers purchase crystals or slices, for further fabrication.

In addition to elemental semiconductors, an increasing number of *semiconducting compounds* find device application. These compounds are distinguished from metallic alloys in their characteristic crystal structures, where each type of atom occupies particular lattice sites. Although germanium and silicon can easily be alloyed, the *disordered* structure thus formed has very low electron mobility since the structure is not regularly periodic. Silicon and carbon atoms in equal numbers (i.e., the compound silicon carbide SiC) can under proper conditions crystallize into the *zincblende* structure (Fig. 1.15b). SiC crystal growth has alternative forms, which limit its range of usefulness. As would be expected, SiC is not much softer than diamond; it is a common abrasive.

The most important semiconducting compounds are so-called *intermetallic compounds*. These fall into several groups. The III-V ("three-five") compounds form from elements of valence 3 with elements of valence 5 (e.g., gallium and arsenic, indium and antimony, etc.). Most have the zincblende structure; their covalent bonding may be explained on the basis of a total of eight valence electrons possessed by a pair of nearest neighbors. Despite this difference in valence, many of these compounds form structurally unambiguous covalent crystals of substantial energy gap and high melting point. The band gap of a III-V compound is in general higher than that of the tetravalent element lying adjacent (e.g., compare GaAs and InP with Ge, and InSb with Sn). Preparation of high-quality single crystals of these materials is somewhat more difficult than for elemental semiconductors because the zincblende structure, for example, requires alternate (111) planes to contain only one of the two elements. The bonding itself encourages uniform crystal growth; however, if available quantities of one element exceed those of the other, excess atoms of one element may be trapped interstitially in the lattice or may precipitate out to form crystallites (a second phase). Either will damage the perfection of the structure, and accordingly the conduction properties. Gallium arsenide appears to be one of the most useful of these materials, as a competitor for germanium and silicon; even here crystal preparation is much more difficult, for arsenic will evaporate from the molten material unless somehow constrained. Other III-V compounds, while perhaps not so useful for semiconductor junction devices, have characteristics which suit them to particular applications. The successful preparation of large, low-cost, high-quality crystals will usually pave the way to additional applications.

Combinations of the elements in the second and sixth columns of the periodic chart also form semiconducting compounds (II-VI compounds). The sulfides, selenides, and tellurides of zinc, cadmium, and lead may be classed as semiconductors; although these compounds often assume the familiar zincblende structure, their electronic bonding is to a considerable extent ionic. To produce the bonding action, the nonmetallic (valence-6) atoms must lose electrons to the metallic atoms. While the hardness of materials such as ZnS is not comparable with that of covalent bonded semiconductors, the energy band gaps of these materials are still larger than those of the III-V semiconductors of comparable atomic weight. This suits some of these materials very well for applications as luminescent materials (Chap. 10), where large conduction is not of primary importance. These materials, like III-V compounds, suffer from difficulties of growing large crystals. They are not particularly worse from this point of view, however. Since it is simple to produce large single crystals of completely ionic compounds (for example, NaCl), it appears that single crystals whose bonding mechanism is strictly covalent or ionic are easier to produce than those having intermediate types of bonding.

A compilation of known semiconductors includes many compounds of nonzincblende form. Some, like bismuth telluride (Bi_2Te_3), have special properties, fitting them to applications as thermoelectrics (Sec. 5.12). Many metallic oxides show at least some of the generic characteristics of semiconductors. These compounds may have many different atomic ratios (for example, TiO, TiO_2) and associated crystal structures, any or all of which can appear in a polycrystalline sample of the material. The difficulty of maintaining a specified oxygen content during growth of a crystal often makes single-crystal preparation difficult. Similar difficulties are experienced in the preparation of sulfide and telluride crystals.

Since our primary interest in this chapter is with conduction properties, our main concern will be with silicon and germanium. Basic principles discussed apply to other semiconductors, however. Varying degrees of physical perfection of the material may cause some properties (e.g., room-temperature conductivity) to vary over orders of magnitude. In some materials, furthermore, semiconduction may become meaningful only at extremely high or low temperatures, depending on whether the energy band gap is very high or very low. To these natural property limitations one must add the practical requirements of compatibility with available preparation or fabrication techniques and with desirable impurity elements and ease of connection to metallic conductors. The importance and usefulness of a given material are usually controlled ultimately by economic factors in materials preparation and device fabrication.

4.2   Intrinsic Semiconductors

A semiconductor is said to be *intrinsic* if its conduction properties approach those of an ideal pure and perfect single-crystal material having the energy-band characteristics of Fig. 4.1. At zero absolute temperature the valence band should be completely *filled* with electrons and (by the arguments of the previous chapter) cannot conduct; nor can the entirely empty conduction band. The Fermi level, at $T = 0$, lies nearly midway between the two band edges.

As the temperature is raised, some electrons near the top of the valence band are thermally ionized into the lowest levels of the conduction band. The conduction band now contains a few electrons, and the valence band has a few missing electrons, or *holes*. Thermal ionization therefore is said to create hole-electron *pairs*, for there is one hole for each electron. As both electrons and holes transport charge through the semiconductor, they are collectively termed *charge carriers*, or simply *carriers*. The statistics applicable to either are Boltzmann statistics, since the Fermi level lies remote from any occupied electron or hole states. Energy-

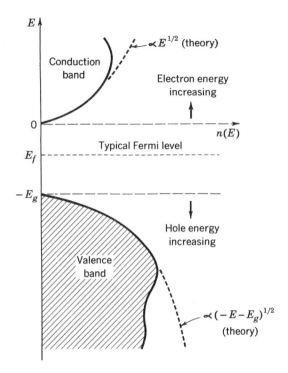

Figure 4.1 Energy bands, with density-of-states functions, for an intrinsic semiconductor.

level diagrams are usually drawn with *electron energy* increasing upward. The converse applies for holes; because of their opposite charge, hole energies increase toward the bottom of the diagram. Diagrams such as Fig. 4.1 have almost complete symmetry with respect to hole and electron distributions, in intrinsic semiconductors.

Since both the electrons in the conduction band and holes in the valence band occupy only very small fractions of the available states, and the mean free time between collisions does not vary rapidly with energy, each electron is equally effective in producing current when the k-space distribution is shifted by application of electric fields. We can accordingly assign a mobility μ_n to all electrons and μ_p to all holes, whose values may best be determined experimentally. With N electrons and P holes per unit volume, by analogy to (3.5) the conductivity is simply

$$\sigma = e(N\mu_n + P\mu_p) \tag{4.1}$$

This relation applies to semiconductors in general. In intrinsic semiconductors, since $N = P = N_i$ (termed the *intrinsic carrier concentration*), conductivity is simply $\sigma = eN_i(\mu_n + \mu_p)$.

Except under the influence of very high electric fields, carriers occupy only narrow energy regions near the conduction and valence band edges. Accordingly, changes in mobility with temperature are associated mainly with changes in the phonon distribution. Variation of mobility in intrinsic samples follows approximately a $T^{-\frac{3}{2}}$ temperature variation. The mobilities of holes are in general smaller than those of electrons, this disparity becoming even more important in compound semiconductors (especially in more nearly ionic compounds).

We now undertake the determination of the intrinsic carrier density N_i, which may be expected to be a strong function of temperature. The first requirement for statistical analysis is the determination of electronic state-density functions $n(E)$ appropriate to conduction and valence. The usual assumption is that the bottom of the conduction band and the top of the valence band may be approximated as having spherical constant-energy surfaces and accordingly effective masses m_n^* and m_p^*. (Throughout the discussion, subscripts and symbols for electrons and holes bear the designations n and p, respectively. It will then be possible to translate expressions for different types of extrinsic semiconductors by interchange of n and p symbols.) That is, if we select the bottom of the conduction band as a reference for energy measure, the E-$\mathbf{k}$ variation will be assumed to be of the form

$$E = \frac{\mathbf{p}^2}{2m_n^*} = \frac{\mathbf{k}^2\mathbf{h}^2}{2m_n^*} \qquad E > 0 \qquad (4.2)$$

While actual constant-energy surfaces of many semiconductors consist of symmetrical sets of ellipsoids whose centers are located away from $\mathbf{k} = 0$, it is satisfactory to use m_n^* as a geometric average of the effective masses over these ellipsoids. Since these semiconductors are cubic crystals, no anisotropy in conductivity results from more detailed theories.

The effective masses of electrons and holes in semiconductors may be determined experimentally by the phenomenon of *cyclotron resonance*. The semiconductor sample is placed in an electromagnetic cavity or waveguide, held at temperatures near zero absolute. An RF electric field is applied in one plane, with a slowly variable magnetic field B_z in the normal direction (Fig. 4.2a). Since the effective mass is assumed constant and isotropic, any *time-dependent* velocity **v** induced by the applied field will be related to the a-c momentum by $\mathbf{p} = m^*\mathbf{v}$. The equation of motion of an electron having an effective mass m^* is thus

$$m^* \frac{d\mathbf{v}}{dt} = -e(\mathbf{\varepsilon} + \mathbf{v} \times \mathbf{B})$$ (4.3)

The electric field is, for example,

$$\mathbf{\varepsilon} = 1_x \varepsilon_x \cos \omega t$$

and B_z is adjusted to the value $\hat{B}_z = \omega m^*/e$. Solving (4.3), assuming for simplicity that the initial velocity of the electrons is zero,

$$\begin{aligned} v_x &= At \cos \omega_c t \\ v_y &= At \sin \omega_c t \end{aligned}$$ (4.4)

where $A \cong -e\varepsilon_x/2m^*$. Application of the electric field thus makes the particles spiral outward (Fig. 4.2b). Velocity in the xy plane is attained through the energy delivered by the electric field. The energy absorbed in this way from the electric field is dissipated in collisions. At this particular setting $(\hat{B}_z = \omega m^*/e)$, power absorption in the electrical circuit will be maximum. At other values of B and fixed RF electric field frequency, the spiraling motion does not occur. From the value $\hat{B}_z$ at which peak absorption occurs,

$$m^* = \frac{\hat{B}_z e}{\omega}$$ (4.5)

This measurement is further refined by using *circularly polarized* electric fields. Electrons and holes must then spiral with opposite senses of rotation in a given magnetic field; with circularly polarized $\mathbf{\varepsilon}$, maximum absorptions for holes and electrons occur with opposite magnetic field polarities (Fig. 4.2c). Cyclotron resonance demonstrates dramatically that holes may be treated as if they were in fact positive-charge, positive-mass particles. The *broad* peaks, indicating a range of effective masses, are due in part to the ellipticity of constant-energy surfaces, and also to the short mean free time between collisions. Experimental curves for both Ge and Si show that the hole states form two degenerate subbands of substantially *different* effective mass. These two groups of states are referred to as *light* holes and *heavy* holes. Cyclotron resonance, however, is one of very few phenomena in

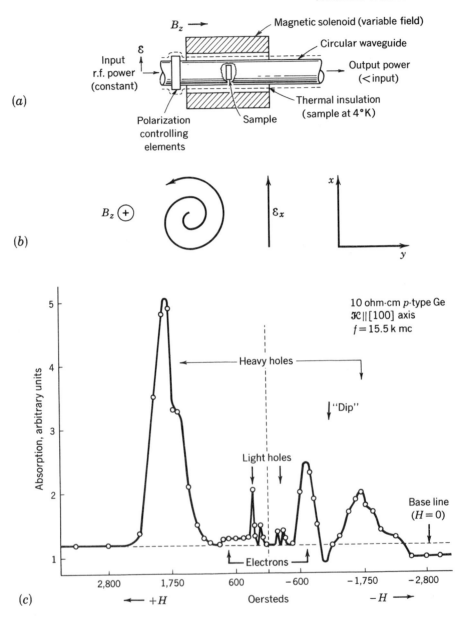

Figure 4.2 Cyclotron-resonance measurement of effective masses. (a) Schematic of measurement apparatus. (b) Path of electron, between collisions, at resonance. (c) Data obtained, power absorption vs. magnetic field. Note that peaks of absorption due to heavy holes appear on both sides, the result of some excitation even with near-circular polarization. "Dip" is attributed to electrons in negative-effective mass states. [*After G. C. Dousmanis et al., Phys. Rev. Letters,* **1**:404 (1958).]

which this detail appears; one ordinarily uses average effective masses for most calculations. Table 4.1 includes effective-mass data for some semiconductors.

In a crystal of unit volume, the volume in momentum space associated with *one electronic state* is, as in Sec. 3.2, $h^3/2$. By the same integration over a spherical p-space volume as used earlier, the total density of conduction-band states at energy E is

$$n(E) = \frac{8\sqrt{2}\,\pi m_n^{*\frac{3}{2}}}{h^3}\, E^{\frac{1}{2}} \qquad \text{(conduction band, } E > 0\text{)} \qquad (4.6)$$

This is as depicted (near the band edge) in Fig. 4.1.

A corresponding density-of-states function is needed for the valence band. The constant-energy surfaces near the *upper* energy limit of the valence band may also be approximated as spherical surfaces (e.g., Fig. 3.7). The density of states, measuring energy *downward* (toward higher hole energy) from the upper valence-band limit, should increase in the same way as that moving *upward* in the conduction band. The shape of $n(E)$ versus E will be a function of the effective mass of electronic states, m_p^*. In terms of the same zero energy reference and the *energy gap* E_g, this inverted distribution may be written

$$n(E) = \frac{8\sqrt{2}\,\pi m_p^{*\frac{3}{2}}}{h^3}\, (-E - E_g)^{\frac{1}{2}}$$

$$\text{(valence band, } E < -E_g\text{)} \qquad (4.7)$$

[The reader should assure himself that this rather awkward-looking relation, together with (4.6), indeed describes the density functions in Fig. 4.1.] Under most conditions, the only states of importance are those within a few kT from the edges of the valence and conduction bands. We shall employ the density functions (4.6) and (4.7) as though they applied in the entire bands, though in fact they are pertinent only near the band edges. Using (C.32), the density of *occupied* states is

$$m(E) = \frac{8\sqrt{2}\,\pi m_n^{*\frac{3}{2}}}{h^3}\, E^{\frac{1}{2}} \left(\frac{1}{e^{(E-E_f)/kT} + 1} \right) \qquad E > 0$$

$$= \frac{8\sqrt{2}\,\pi m_p^{*\frac{3}{2}}}{h^3}\, (E - E_g)^{\frac{1}{2}} \left(\frac{1}{e^{(E-E_f)/kT} + 1} \right)$$

$$\begin{aligned} & E < -E_g \\ = 0 \qquad\qquad & -E_g < E < 0 \end{aligned} \qquad (4.8)$$

We must now calculate the Fermi level E_f, determined by the *total* density of electrons and holes. Matters are simplified by referring, in the valence band, to the density of *unoccupied* electronic states (which is synonymous with occupied hole states):

$$n(E) - m(E) = \frac{8\sqrt{2}\,\pi m_p^{*\frac{3}{2}}}{h^3}(-E - E_g)^{\frac{1}{2}}$$
$$\times \left(\frac{e^{(E-E_f)/kT}}{e^{(E-E_f)/kT} + 1}\right) \qquad E < -E_g \qquad (4.9)$$

In an intrinsic semiconductor, the total density of occupied hole states, P, equals the number of occupied conduction-band electron states, N. We integrate over the entire range of energy, excluding the band gap.

$$P_i = \int_{-\infty}^{-E_g}[n(E) - m(E)]\,dE = \int_0^{\infty}m(E)\,dE = N_i \qquad (4.10)$$

We shall assume at the outset that the Fermi level lies somewhere near the center of the band gap and that the band gap remains far in excess of $6kT$; in intrinsic Ge this condition applies at any temperature below about $1200°K$. The unity term in the Fermi function is then negligible over the conduction-band integration. In the valence band, by the same argument, the unity term predominates; (4.10) is

$$\frac{8\sqrt{2}\,\pi m_p^{*\frac{3}{2}}}{h^3}\int_{-\infty}^{-E_g}(-E - E_g)^{\frac{1}{2}}e^{(E-E_{fi})/kT}\,dE$$
$$= \frac{8\sqrt{2}\,\pi m_n^{*\frac{3}{2}}}{h^3}\int_0^{\infty}E^{\frac{1}{2}}e^{-(E-E_{fi})/kT}\,dE \qquad (4.11)$$

By changing the variable of integration on the left-hand side, both integrals factor out of the equation. After rearrangement,

$$e^{2E_{fi}/kT} = \left(\frac{m_p^*}{m_n^*}\right)^{\frac{3}{2}}e^{-E_g/kT} \qquad (4.12)$$

The Fermi energy in the intrinsic semiconductor, E_{fi}, is therefore

$$E_{fi} = -\frac{E_g}{2} + \frac{3kT}{4}\ln\frac{m_p^*}{m_n^*} \qquad (4.13)$$

The Fermi level is at the center of the band gap, except for a

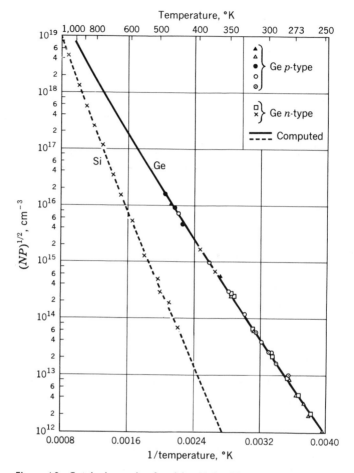

Figure 4.3 Intrinsic carrier densities N_i in silicon and germanium, obtained as best fits to experimental data. Plotted relations correspond to

$$N_i{}^2(\text{Si}) = 1.5 \times 10^{33}T^3 e^{-1.21e/kT}$$

$$N_i{}^2(\text{Ge}) = 3.1 \times 10^{32}T^3 e^{-0.785e/kT}$$

[*After F. J. Morin and J. P. Maita, Phys. Rev.,* **94**:1525 and **96**:28 (1954).]

small displacement of the order of kT, which vanishes if electron and hole effective masses are equal.

Although either side of (4.11) is the total density of electrons (or of holes), it is simpler to evaluate the right-hand side:

$$N_i = P_i = \frac{8\sqrt{2}\,\pi m_n^{*\frac{3}{2}}}{h^3}\, e^{E_{fi}/kT} \int_0^\infty E^{\frac{1}{2}} e^{-E/kT}\, dE \tag{4.14}$$

Substituting E_{fi} from (3.13) and evaluating the definite integral from integral tables,

$$N_i = \frac{4\sqrt{2}}{h^3} (\pi kT)^{\frac{3}{2}}(m_n^* m_p^*)^{\frac{3}{4}} e^{-E_g/2kT} \tag{4.15}$$

The densities of electrons and holes in intrinsic germanium and silicon vs. temperature are described in Fig. 4.3. With a lower energy gap, germanium has substantially more intrinsic electrons and holes at room temperature. Accordingly, the "intrinsic resistivity" of pure germanium at room temperature (300°K) is ~60 ohm-cm, and that of silicon ~230,000 ohm-cm. The degree of perfection and purity of single-crystal semiconductor materials may often be assessed from their actual conductivities. Technical germanium seldom exceeds a value of 20 ohm-cm, and silicon ~1,000 ohm-cm, depending on the extensiveness of impurity removal in a particular sample. Lower resistivity implies more impurities or defects. In those semiconductor materials where high purity and perfection are difficult to achieve, conductivity may not be a reliable measure of purity, for as discussed in Sec. 4.6, there are additional processes which materially reduce the number of active carriers and reduce the apparent conductivity.

4.3 Impurity and Defect States in Semiconductors

Semiconductors are seldom used in intrinsic form, for addition of impurities to produce *extrinsic* material permits control of carrier type and concentration with little reduction of carrier mobilities. Semiconductors are said to be "doped" with these impurities, the basic function of which is to introduce electronic states whose wave functions are highly localized and whose discrete energies lie within "forbidden" energy gaps.

Semiconductors such as germanium and silicon have a uniform covalent-bonded character in which it is relatively easy to introduce localized electronic impurity states of predictable energy. Elements on either side of germanium or silicon in the periodic chart are distinguished in having one fewer or greater valence electrons, but are otherwise very similar to their semiconducting neighbors in dimensions and electronic structure. For example, arsenic atoms added to germanium in minute quantities readily become substitutional impurities. Four of a substitutional arsenic atom's five valence electrons become involved in covalent bonds with the

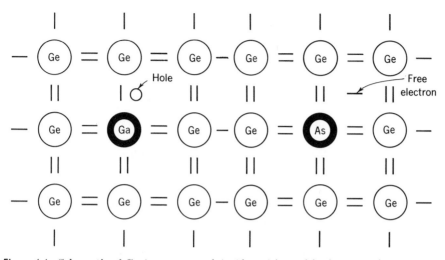

Figure 4.4 Schematic of Ga (acceptor) and As (donor) impurities in germanium.

four nearest germanium atoms (Fig. 4.4).   The fifth arsenic valence electron, not needed for a covalent bond, is more loosely bound to the positive arsenic nucleus.   The strength of this binding can be estimated in a model where the single excess electron is acted on only by a fixed and singly charged nucleus.   The situation is quantum-mechanically comparable with the hydrogen-atom problem if we assume that the periodic potential of the lattice changes only the effective mass of the excess electron.   The increased dielectric constant in the material must also be allowed for.   In the hydrogen atom, the energy level of the ground state is given by [(B.60)]

$$E = - \frac{m^*e^4}{(4\pi\epsilon)^2\hbar^2} \qquad (= -13.6 \text{ ev for hydrogen})$$

Using the microwave dielectric constant, $\epsilon/\epsilon_0 \simeq 16$, for intrinsic germanium, and $m_n^*/m_n \simeq 0.55$, we should thus expect the ground state of the fifth valence electron in the arsenic atom to lie $0.55 \times 13.6/(16)^2 \simeq 0.029$ ev below an ionization state in which the electron is free to move about the germanium crystal.   The lowest-energy free state, in the diagram of Fig. 4.1, corresponds to $E = 0$, the bottom of the conduction band.   The arsenic *impurity state* in germanium lies in the forbidden band with experimental energy

$$E_D \simeq 0.0127 \text{ ev}$$

below the conduction-band edge. As we shall soon show, at room temperature ($kT \simeq 0.025$ ev), most of the excess electrons associated with arsenic atoms in germanium or silicon have sufficient thermal energy to be ionized, or "donated" to the sparsely populated conduction band. Arsenic atoms, and others like them (valence 5), are hence known as (electron) *donors*. The dielectric constant of *silicon* is about 12, m_n^* is larger than in G_e, and donor ionization energies for valence-5 donors are thus ~ 0.05 ev (Fig. 4.5).

A valence-3 substitutional impurity such as gallium has one *less* electron than the four required to complete covalent bonds with four germanium neighbors. While the lattice remains electrically neutral, one of the covalent-bond (valence-band) electrons is missing, and the impurity acts as a possible site for an additional electron. It is easiest to treat the problem of considering the missing valence electron as representing a positively charged *hole*, bound to its site through the same type of electrostatic force and hydrogenlike wave function. This leads, in the same way, to the conclusion that the energy of the localized state lies in the forbidden band, a similar distance ($E_A \approx E_D$) from the valence-band edge at which the bound hole becomes "free." Such a state can, with thermal excitation, *accept* an electron from the nearly filled valence band. (An alternative view is that it donates a hole to the valence band.) Such states are termed *acceptor states*.

By this simple impurity-state theory, we may accordingly expect all valence-5 elements (i.e., nitrogen, phosphorus, arsenic, antimony, and bismuth) to act similarly as donors. Valence-3 atoms, boron, aluminum, gallium, indium, and thallium, act as acceptors. All with the exception of nitrogen are commonly used. The choice of a particular impurity element or elements for a particular device may often be based on fabrication or metallurgical properties or perhaps the ease of introducing the impurity atoms into the solid semiconductor crystal through solid-state diffusion.

Figure 4.5 depicts the energy levels (ionization energies) of a number of impurity atoms in silicon and germanium. Elements of valence 6 have two electrons surplus over those needed to form the covalent bonds of the host lattice. Both of these electrons can be donated to the conduction band. Because the nuclear charge is effectively $+2e$, the first ionization energy is generally higher than for a simple donor (see the levels for sulfur). The second donor electron is even

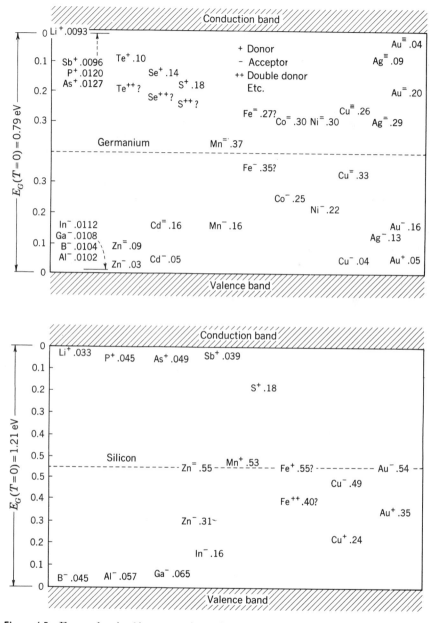

Figure 4.5 Energy levels of important impurity states in germanium and silicon. The polarity signs indicate the state of ionization of the impurity level. (*After N. B. Hannay, "Semiconductors," pp. 341–342, Reinhold Publishing Corporation, New York, 1959.*)

more tightly bound. Such impurities are termed "double donors." Similarly, valence-2 double acceptors have states corresponding to single and double ionization. As discussed in Sec. 4.6, deeper-lying impurity states act more often as electron or hole *traps* than as means to supply carriers to valence or conduction bands.

One may actually use almost any element as an impurity. Elements whose electronic shell structure differs radically from the host might assume either a substitutional or an interstitial site. It is not always possible to predict the energy of an impurity state or even whether it will act as a donor or acceptor. It appears that in silicon and germanium, only substitutional impurities produce significant energy levels in the forbidden band, however.

Impurities in semiconducting compounds follow much the same set of rules as in elemental semiconductors. For example, an atom of *zinc* replacing a *gallium* atom in gallium arsenide has one fewer electron than needed for bond formation and acts as a single acceptor. Likewise, selenium atoms will act as single donors when substituted for arsenic atoms. Since a given impurity may elect one of *two* types of sites, there is the possibility of a variety of states from one impurity. Only by making the impurity "fit" well the desired site, as in the examples given, can one be assured of the results. The same reasoning suggests the use of alkali metals and halogens as single acceptors and donors, respectively, in II-VI compound semiconductors, or as double acceptors and double donors in III-V compounds.

The electronic states associated with *defects* such as vacancies and dislocations may be located in either allowed or forbidden bands; fortunately, however, a given type of point defect always produces states with the same energy levels. The defects introduced by irradiation with high-energy particles can greatly alter the properties of semiconductors and even destroy the usefulness of semiconductor devices exposed to such irradiation. Particular bombarding waves or particles in a given energy range introduce characteristic defect states. Some of these defects are removed by annealing at elevated temperatures (or less rapidly at room temperature).

Whereas in metals electrons are scattered mainly through collisions with phonons, in semiconductors impurities and defects are highly important scatterers of the electron and hole wave packets, reducing electron and hole mobilities. In

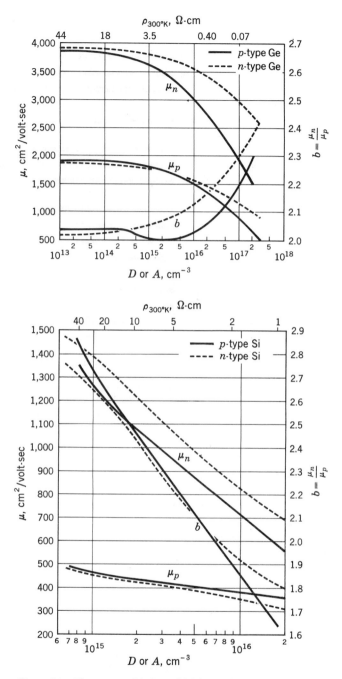

Figure 4.6 Electron and hole mobilities vs. impurity concentration in silicon and germanium. b is the ratio of mobilities. [*After M. B. Prince, Phys. Rev.*, **92**:681 (1953); **93**:1204 (1954).]

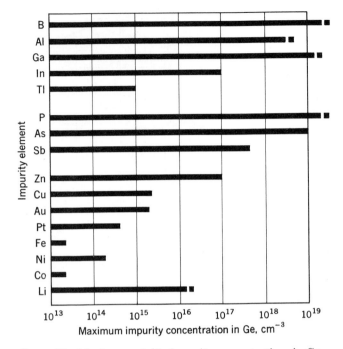

Figure 4.7   Maximum soluble impurity concentrations in Ge. (*Data collected by W. C. Dunlap, "Progress in Semiconductors," vol. 2, p. 167, Heywood and Co., London, 1957.*)

high-quality crystals, the donor and acceptor impurities introduced intentionally may significantly reduce carrier mobilities, particularly at high impurity densities. Figure 4.6 shows typical reduction of electron and hole mobilities in germanium and in silicon as a function of donor or acceptor densities. The mobility limit at low densities is of course due to phonons.

The impurity concentrations introduced into a semiconductor depend mainly on the function of the device. In many devices, satisfactory operation is achieved with doping densities of 10^{17} cm^{-3} or less, but devices such as tunnel diodes (Sec. 5.9) contain impurity densities $\sim 10^{19}$ cm^{-3}. The complex crystal structures of most semiconductors make them unreceptive to alloy formation so that above a *solubility limit* (usually a few per cent) the impurity forms a second phase. Figure 4.7 indicates maximum impurity densities soluble in single-crystal germanium.

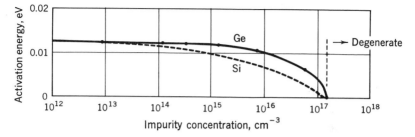

Figure 4.8 Energy required to ionize impurities in Ge and Si, as a function of impurity concentration; this measures the spreading of the impurity levels into bands. Both Si and Ge apparently become degenerate at concentrations slightly greater than 10^{17}. [*After P. P. Debye and E. M. Conwell, Phys. Rev.*, **93**:693 (1954).]

With high impurity concentrations, the impurity atoms are located so near one another that the wave functions of the localized electronic states begin to overlap. Were the impurity atoms arranged in a regular periodic array, the overlap would introduce regular energy bands through coupling of the degenerate impurity states. Though impurities are actually located randomly in the lattice, coupling of impurity states still causes a spread in impurity energy levels which can be described, loosely, as a band. When donor or acceptor density is sufficiently high, the impurity band spreads in energy until finally one side of it reaches the adjacent edge of the valence band (acceptors) or conduction band (donors). A semiconductor with this much, or greater, impurity density is said to be *degenerate*. The effective impurity ionization energy is then zero; the effect is similar to attaching a group of filled states to the conduction band or empty states to the valence band. Figure 4.8 describes the approach of the impurity band edge to the edge of the host-crystal band, as impurity concentration is increased. When degeneracy is reached, the semiconductor has conduction properties not readily distinguishable from those of a poorly conducting metal.

4.4   Conduction in Extrinsic Semiconductors

The conductivity of extrinsic semiconductors is controlled at room temperature largely by the density of impurity atoms and defects. Calculation of N and P is similar to that for intrinsic semiconductors, but they are no longer equal. The conduction formula (4.1) is applicable, with corrections for

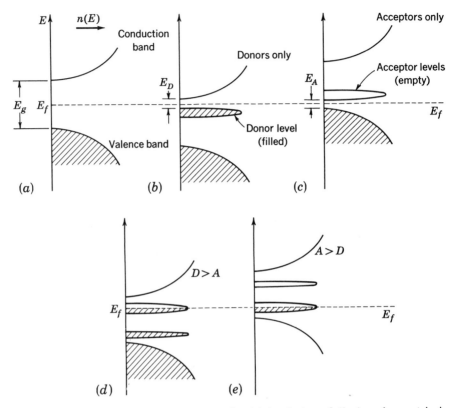

Figure 4.9 Energy and density of states for (a) intrinsic and (b–e) various extrinsic semiconductors. The donor and acceptor bands are exaggerated in width and spacing from band edges for clarity.

reduction of mobility by impurity scattering. The complete density-of-states function may now be represented as in Fig. 4.9. The density of donor states is termed D, that of acceptors A. The energy spread of the impurity bands is assumed small. The important energy constants are the band gap E_g, and E_D and E_A, the impurity *ionization* energies. Simple donors each contribute an extra electron to the crystal, while acceptors contribute an extra hole. The semiconductor as a whole remains electrically neutral, of course.

At zero temperature, all valence-band states will be full and all conduction-band states empty. Acceptor states, in a semiconductor with *only* acceptor impurities, will contain no electrons, and donor electrons in donor-doped material will remain nonionized. As in the intrinsic case, the Fermi energy will in each case lie nearly halfway between adjacent filled and empty bands. If material contains *both* donors and acceptors, with densities D and A, respectively, at zero temperature electrons will fill all the lowest available states. The acceptor states will be partially filled if $D < A$, but totally filled if $D > A$. The donor states will be partially filled and completely empty, respectively, under these conditions. Semiconductors having both impurity types are said to be *compensated*. When fully compensated ($D = A$), the semiconductor is very similar to an intrinsic semiconductor. In general, then, it is the *excess* impurity concentration which controls the semiconductor: when $D - A > 0$, the semiconductor behaves as if it had only $D - A$ *donor* atoms; and the converse is true.

At some high temperature, a function largely of the energy gap E_g, an extrinsic semiconductor will produce intrinsic (thermal) carriers so numerous as to far exceed the net doping density $|D - A|$. The effect of impurities then becomes negligible. The Fermi level approaches the center of the energy gap, as in the purely intrinsic semiconductor. This is usually too extreme an upper temperature limit for meaningful device operation; transistor devices operate well only at temperatures where $N_i < |D - A|$, for example. In the intervening temperature range, the Fermi energy must move uniformly from near the band edge toward the center of the band gap (Fig. 4.10).

The intrinsic-semiconduction calculations of N_i ($= P_i$) of the preceding section were based on the assumption that E_f lay far from the conduction and valence band edges. Since the calculation of N and P in (4.11) is *independent* of any state lying *within* the band gap, the two sides of this expression may be used in the *same* form to express *separately* the *extrinsic* values of N and P. In terms of extrinsic and intrinsic Fermi energies, N and P may be expressed as

$$N = N_i e^{(E_f - E_{fi})/kT}$$
$$P = N_i e^{-(E_f - E_{fi})/kT} \tag{4.16}$$

By direction multiplication,

$$NP = N_i^2 \tag{4.17}$$

These expressions, as before, apply only in thermal equilibrium. Any *increase* of N produced by the presence of donors or of P by acceptors will automatically *reduce* in the

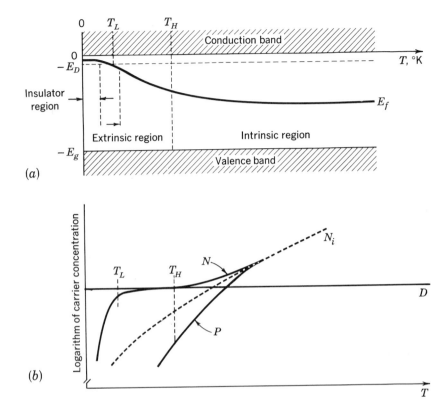

Figure 4.10   (a) Variation of E_f with temperature in an extrinsic semiconductor. (b) Variation of N_i, N, and P with temperature.   In this logarithmic plot, N and P lie equal distances above and below N_i, according to (4.17).

same proportion the concentration of the opposite type of carrier.

Let us investigate electron and hole densities as a function of temperature, in a donor-doped material (Fig. 4.10). At absolute zero neither electrons nor holes are available to conduct.   When temperature reaches the value where the Fermi energy has shifted to the center of the donor band, just one-half of the donors are ionized.   Since the valence band has very few empty states at this low temperature, these $D/2$ donor electrons must lie in the conduction band.   The conduction-electron density N now closely approximates $D/2$. We can define this particular temperature, T_L, quantitatively, using (4.15) and (4.17).   Then, within the limits of accuracy of the approximation used in evaluating the Fermi integral, i.e., for sufficiently low T_L so that E_D is several times kT,

$$\frac{D}{2} = \frac{4(2)^{\frac{1}{2}}}{h^3}(\pi k T_L)^{\frac{3}{2}}(m_n^* m_p^*)^{\frac{3}{4}}e^{-E_D/2kT_L} \qquad (4.18)$$

This demands trial-and-error solution. For $D = 10^{15}$ and a typical value for silicon, $E_D \simeq 0.05$ ev, we find $T_L \cong 60°K$. For Ge, $T_L \cong 15°K$, assuming $E_D \simeq 0.01$ ev. This low-temperature limit T_L is determined mainly by E_D. If *only* low-temperature operation is important, materials of low band gap E_g and correspondingly low E_D (or E_A) are selected. Although degenerate semiconductors conduct even to $T = 0$, they are of limited usefulness because of low mobilities.

When E_f drops to $3kT$ *below* the donor levels, only $e^{-3} \approx 5$ per cent of the donors are not ionized. In the high-temperature range, which applies at room temperature and above for Ge and Si, use may be made of the equation of charge neutrality: $N - P = D - A$. With all impurities ionized, any differences in density of holes and electrons must equal the net impurity density. Substituting (4.17),

$$N - \frac{N_i^2}{N} = D - A \qquad \text{(high temperatures)}$$

Solving for N and P,

$$N = \frac{D-A}{2} + \sqrt{\frac{(D-A)^2}{4} + N_i^2}$$

$$P = N_i^2\left[\frac{D-A}{2} + \sqrt{\frac{(D-A)^2}{4} + N_i^2}\right]^{-1} \qquad (4.19)$$

$$\frac{N}{P} = \left[\frac{D-A}{2N_i} + \sqrt{\frac{(D-A)^2}{4N_i^2} + 1}\right]^2 \qquad (4.20)$$

A practical upper limit of semiconductor-device operation requires that *majority carriers* (which are electrons in donor-doped material) must greatly outnumber *minority carriers*. If we decide upon a limiting ratio $N/P > 10$ (a practical limit will be set by the actual device in question, and its application), (4.20) indicates a limit $(D - A)/N_i > 2.84$. In silicon with a net impurity density $D - A = 10^{15}$, $N_i(\text{max}) = 3.5 \times 10^{14}$. Using Fig. 4.3, this limit is just slightly over 200°, for silicon. For germanium, on the other hand, the limit for $D - A = 10^{15}$ is only about 75°C, demonstrating the high-temperature superiority of silicon. Materials of even higher band gap, such as SiC ($E_g \cong 3$ ev), although not yet suitable for devices (such as transistors) demanding great crystalline perfection, have extremely high practical operating temperatures.

Over the useful operating range of most semiconductor devices, the Fermi energy is remote from both band edges and impurity states. One may readily estimate its position from (4.16) and (4.17). We employ the relations $\ln (N/N_i) = (E_f - E_{fi})/kT$ and $N \cong D - A$; in silicon at 100°C, $N_i = 10^{12}$; then with $D - A = 10^{15}$, $\ln (N/N_i) \cong 7$. The Fermi energy lies about $7kT$ ($\sim$0.25 ev) above the center of the band gap. This is well above center gap, but still remote from both donor states and band edges.

Although in the above calculations we did not solve in detail the equations determining E_f, all essential information for normal semiconductor operating ranges could be obtained by simple approximations. The examples deal with donor-doped material, but apply equally well to acceptor-doped material, replacing N by P, D by A, etc. Since the donor-doped material is characterized by a majority of negative carriers (electrons), it is termed an *n-type semiconductor*. Acceptor-doped semiconductor material is termed *p-type*.

Majority-carrier concentrations in extrinsic semiconductors are relatively insensitive to temperature over broad operating ranges. Conductivities as given by (4.1) should likewise be nearly constant, as is borne out experimentally. While the relations $N \cong D$ or $P \cong A$ would suggest that conductivity should be proportional to impurity density, the reduction of carrier mobility (μ_n or μ_p) by impurity scattering causes conductivity to increase less rapidly than impurity concentration.

4.5 Semiconductor Hall Effect

Hall effect in semiconductors originates from motion of both electrons and holes. With an applied electric field and a transverse component of magnetic field, both electrons and holes are deflected transversely toward the *same* side of the sample (Fig. 4.11). The total current density J_x, from (4.1), is

$$J_x = e(N\mu_n + P\mu_p)\mathcal{E}_x \qquad (4.21)$$

(Small changes in mobility due to magnetoresistance are neglected.) The Hall angle θ_H is again given by (2.8), for

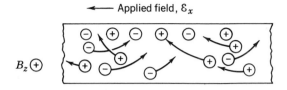

Figure 4.11   Electron and hole motion in combined electric and magnetic fields tends to reduce Hall effect in intrinsic semiconductors.

electrons and holes, respectively:

$$(\theta_H)_{\text{electrons}} = B_z \mu_n \qquad (\theta_H)_{\text{holes}} = B_z \mu_p$$

Because mobility is so much larger than in metals, Hall effect in semiconductors is orders of magnitude greater. With an electron current density $J_{xn} = eN\mu_n\mathcal{E}_x$, the transverse electron current J_y is

$$J_{yn} = \theta_H J_{xn} = B_z \mu_n (eN\mu_n\mathcal{E}_x)$$

The transverse hole current is, similarly,

$$J_{yp} = -B_z u_p (eP\mu_p\mathcal{E}_x)$$

The total transverse current density is the sum of these:

$$J_y = eB_z\mathcal{E}_x(N\mu_n{}^2 - P\mu_p{}^2) \tag{4.22}$$

A Hall field $\mathcal{E}_{yH}$ is required to make the *net y* current zero.   The ratio $\mathcal{E}_{yH}/\mathcal{E}_x$ is thus the same as J_y/J_x:

$$\mathcal{E}_{yH} = B_z\mathcal{E}_x \frac{N\mu_n{}^2 - P\mu_p{}^2}{N\mu_n + P\mu_p} \tag{4.23}$$

The Hall constant R is given by

$$R = \frac{\mathcal{E}_{yH}}{B_z J_x} = \frac{1}{e} \frac{N\mu_n{}^2 - P\mu_p{}^2}{(N\mu_n + P\mu_p)^2} \tag{4.24}$$

This relation is like that for a metal [(3.13)] if the semiconductor is extrinsic ($N \gg P$ or $P \gg N$).   Measurements of σ and R for strongly p-type and n-type extrinsic semiconductors permit determination of *Hall mobilities* (μ_{nH} and μ_{pH}) from (4.24) and (4.1).   Since N, P, μ_n, and μ_p are all temperature-dependent, Hall effect in a semiconductor exhibits wide temperature variations, corresponding to the increase of intrinsic carriers at higher temperatures.

Semiconductor Hall effect has a number of applications. With given drive voltage the potential difference (Hall voltage) developed in a four- or five-contact sample (e.g., like Fig. 3.2) is proportional to magnetic field. Magnetic field measuring probes having dimensions of the order of 1 mm can be constructed. Fields of 1 gauss or less are measurable using sensitive voltage amplification and an a-c drive voltage. Hall devices have also been used as electronic analog multipliers of two electrical signals; one signal is impressed as a current through the element, while the other drives a magnetic solenoid to produce a proportional magnetic field at the semiconductor. The Hall voltage, proportional to the product of the two signals, requires substantial amplification. Other applications include wattmeters, in which a voltage V and a current I are likewise multiplied and averaged by a d-c voltmeter measuring the Hall voltage. Such a device is operable over wide frequency ranges and is insensitive to waveform.

4.6 Carrier Generation, Trapping, and Recombination

Electron and hole concentrations are maintained, at thermal equilibrium, by opposing processes of thermal *ionization* and *recombination*, between band and impurity states. In normal operation of semiconductor devices, however, carrier concentrations are altered from the equilibrium values; it is important to be able to analyze these deviations from equilibrium.

When electrons are moved into conduction-band states, or out of valence-band states, carriers are said to be "generated." The major source of carrier generation in many devices is ionization of impurity states by thermal phonons. A second source, important in photodevices, or whenever radiant energy illuminates a semiconductor, is "pair production"; a photon of sufficient energy acting upon an electron in the valence band can move it at once to the conduction band. This produces *two* carriers, an electron and a hole, both of which must ordinarily possess nonzero momentum to satisfy energy-momentum conservation in the photon-absorption process. Because this conservation is essential, a transition between the extreme edges of the conduction and valence bands is in most semiconductors incompatible with a photon of energy equal to the band-gap energy. This is demonstrated by Fig. 4.12. The crystal momentum **k** of

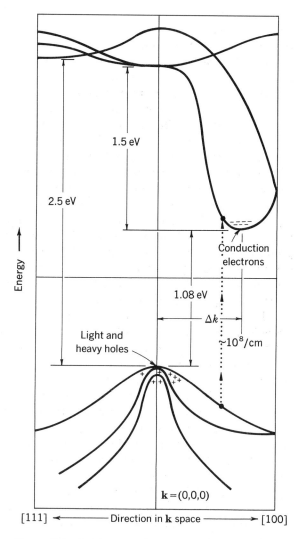

Figure 4.12 Sections through Brillouin zone in **k** space. Lowest-energy conduction-band levels lie at energy 1.08 ev above highest-energy valence-band states. Momentum transfer of the order of $\Delta k = 10^8$ is required for the transition.   Since photons of this energy have momentum of only about 10^4, radiative transitions are not possible.   (*After H. Brooks, Advan. Electronics and Electron Phys., vol. 7, 1955.*)

highest-energy electronic states in the *valence* bands of typical semiconductors such as silicon and germanium is zero; i.e., the hole-state constant-energy surfaces are spheres near the origin of the Brillouin zone. The lowest-energy conduction-band states, however, lie within a set of ellipsoidal constant-energy surfaces at some distance away from the origin in the first Brillouin zone. The figure represents a section of the Brillouin zone for silicon. For simplicity the upper part denotes the conduction band; the lower part, the valence band. States near the band *energy extrema* are connected by large *momentum differences* which are completely incompatible with the small momenta of photons. Only by a transition such as shown (dotted), between states remote from the band edges, can a photon be absorbed or released. Accordingly, it is necessary to use radiant energy with $E = \hbar\omega$ well *above E_g* to produce pairs. The lowest photon energy which will produce absorption is sometimes termed the *optical band gap*. This is invariably larger than the band gap estimated from the carrier density vs. temperature variation.

In simple semiconductors, pair production is the only possible means of absorbing photons of energy just above the optical band gap. Each photon entering the surface of a sufficiently thick bulk sample must therefore eventually produce a hole-electron pair. The material is said to have a *quantum efficiency* of unity. If irradiating photons have energy substantially *above E_g*, however, the energetic efficiency of pair production is reduced, since the excess energy of the carrier pairs produced is yielded to phonons in subsequent collisions. For irradiation by high-energy waves or particles, the efficiency of pair production may typically be of the order of one pair per $3E_g$ to $4E_g$ of irradiating energy.

The thermal-*phonon* carrier-generation processes in a semiconductor act mainly to maintain *majority*-carrier density. In many devices, however, minority carriers are more important. As we shall show, these are introduced in various ways, generally from adjacent regions of opposite semiconductor type. It is essential, in many devices, that these minority carriers be allowed to move through the semiconductor without strong likelihood of being removed from the band in which they are moving. In semiconductor parlance, "loss" of a carrier means simply the return of a conduction-band electron to a localized state or the valence band, or the elimination of a hole by an electron dropping to the valence band. We should distinguish here between *trapping* of carriers and *recombination*. Trapping is the *temporary* removal of a carrier from a band to a localized state. A trap will eventually return the carrier to the band; if the carrier represents signal information, however, it may return too late to represent the desired signal. In this connection one can distinguish between "fast" and "slow" traps; the former return the carrier to the band in a short time (often as little as 10^{-7} sec), while the latter may retain the carrier for seconds, or even hours. It is such slow traps, in fact, which make possible luminescence of some phosphor materials long after excitation has ceased, as for example on radiant clock faces (Chap. 10).

Recombination, on the other hand, implies the permanent loss of the carrier. *Direct recombination* means that an electron in the conduction band drops directly into the valence band. Energy is released generally in the form of a photon. While it is the major source of recombination in some compound semiconductors (GaAs, InAs), direct recombination is of very low probability in Si and Ge, because most of the electrons and unoccupied valence-band states (holes) cannot satisfy the energy-momentum requirements of Fig. 4.12. The predominant recombination processes then make intermediate use of localized states in the forbidden band. A conduction-band electron first drops down to such an intermediate state, releasing energy in the form of one or more low-energy phonons. From the intermediate state, after some random time interval, the electron is "nudged" by phonons and drops into an unoccupied state in the valence band, again releasing one or more phonons. This final step may be described equally well as a hole falling into the intermediate state. The localized state is accordingly sometimes termed a recombination *center*. Figure 4.13 depicts these several trapping and recombination processes.

Localized states in the band gap are clearly the key to many processes. From the arguments of Sec. 2.6, the degree of localization of a state in the band gap depends upon how "deep" it lies from the band edges. The deepest states, near center gap, have generally the most localized electronic wave functions, while "shallow" states such as the usual donor and acceptor states have wave functions extending over many lattice constants. This localization controls the probability of trapping or recombination, for an electron must normally come very close to the imperfection representing a deep state

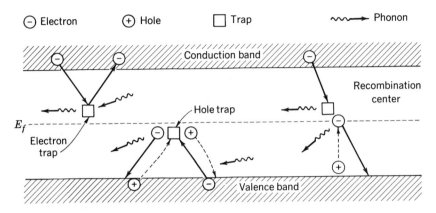

Figure 4.13   Schematic of important trapping and recombination processes in semiconductors.   At left, an electron becomes trapped, releasing a phonon.   It is driven out by the absorption of another phonon.   At center, a hole undergoes a similar process (dashed arrows); an alternative description is in terms of an electron (solid arrows).   At right, an electron drops successively from conduction band to localized state to valence band, releasing phonons in both steps.   In the final stage it annihilates a hole.

to interact with it.   (An exception is a surface state, which we discuss later.)   Once an electron is in such a state, however, the probability (per unit time) of its leaving is again smaller than in a "shallow" state.

Trapping and recombination states occur even in pure semiconductors, as a result of lattice defects.   Highly defected single crystals or polycrystalline semiconductors may have so many such states that it is sometimes difficult to identify their semiconducting nature.   Dislocations are more effective as traps than are point defects; grain boundaries and actual crystal surfaces constitute even larger trapping regions. Modern crystal-growing technology, however, has been developed to the point that very high quality crystals of germanium, silicon, and other semiconductors may be produced, so that traps and recombination centers are not the problem they were in early devices.   In some devices, in fact, deep-lying states must be purposely introduced to remove undesired carriers or to trap space charge into a given region. A common impurity to remove unwanted holes in silicon is gold (Fig. 4.5), although, as will be noted from the figure, other impurities should also have this character.

The dynamic influence of traps and recombination centers can be understood through simple probabilistic arguments. Let us consider for purposes of explanation an intrinsic semi-

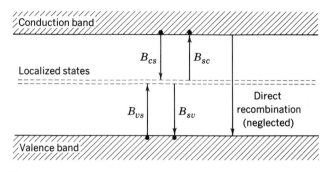

Figure 4.14   Definition of the transition probabilities used in the text.

conductor having a single set of trapping or recombination centers located in the forbidden band at an energy level E_s. We define the various transition probabilities, *per second*, as follows (see Fig. 4.14):

B_{cs}: the probability that a single electron in the conduction band makes a transition to a given unfilled localized state

B_{sc}: the probability that an electron in a given localized state makes a transition into the conduction band

B_{vs}: the probability that any electron in the valence band makes a transition into a given unfilled localized state

B_{sv}: the probability that an electron in a given localized state makes a transition into the valence band

It should be noted that B_{cs} and B_{vs} have a somewhat different interpretation from that of B_{sc} and B_{sv}, since there are essentially infinitely many available states in the conduction band and very many electrons in the valence band but a relatively small number of localized states. The parameters B_{cs} and B_{vs} also imply electrons moving into the proximity of localized states; B_{sc} and B_{sv} do not.

With these definitions, and a localized state density of S (of which S_u are unfilled and S_f filled by electrons), the time rate of transition from the conduction band to localized states is just $NB_{cs}S_u$. There will in turn be a reverse flow of electrons at a rate S_fB_{sc}. Neglecting direct recombination, as is most appropriate in the elemental semiconductors, the net rate of change of electron density N is given by

$$\frac{dN}{dt} = -NB_{cs}S_u + S_fB_{sc} \tag{4.25}$$

There is, similarly, a time rate of change of hole density P, given by

$$\frac{dP}{dt} = -PB_{sv}S_f + B_{vs}S_u \tag{4.26}$$

The rate of change of density of *filled* localized states is just the difference of these:

$$\frac{dS_f}{dt} = NB_{cs}S_u - B_{sc}S_f + B_{vs}S_u - PB_{sv}S_f \tag{4.27}$$

If there were carrier-pair generation by the introduction of photon energy, a generation rate G (carrier pairs per second) would be merely added to both (4.25) and (4.26).

In the condition of thermal equilibrium, the rate of electron and of hole density change must both be zero, and we obtain from (4.25) and (4.26)

$$\frac{NB_{cs}}{B_{sc}} = \frac{S_f}{S_u} = \frac{B_{vs}}{PB_{sv}} \quad \text{(at equilibrium)} \tag{4.28}$$

That is, the relative transition probabilities between pairs of states are related. Since at equilibrium the ratio S_f/S is given by the Fermi factor $\{1 + \exp\left[(E_s - E_f)/kT\right]\}^{-1}$, the transition probabilities are related in a calculable way.

The nature of a particular set of localized states is dependent on the relative transition probabilities between them and the conduction and valence bands. If, for example, B_{vs} and B_{sc} are comparable in magnitude, the states act as recombination centers. Let us imagine a semiconductor having equilibrium carrier densities N_0 and P_0; electron density is raised to $N = N_0 + n'$ at time $t = 0$. This could, for example, be a result of electrons injected into the semiconductor from an adjacent conductor or semiconducting region. It is convenient to assume that $n' \ll S_u$, in which case the unfilled localized states are numerous enough to accommodate all the extra electrons without altering the density of available recombination states appreciably. Equation (4.25) may be written with $N = N_0 + n$; the equation for the perturbation is

$$\frac{dn}{dt} = -nB_{cs}S_u \tag{4.29}$$

Treating the unfilled state density S_u as a constant, the solution of (4.29) is simply

$$n = n'e^{-t/\tau_n} \tag{4.30}$$

The parameter $\tau_n = (B_{cs}S_u)^{-1}$ is termed the *electron bulk lifetime*, for this example. It is inversely dependent on the density of unfilled localized recombination states. In practical semiconductors, which are most often extrinsic, it is mainly the *minority* carriers which are used to carry signal information from input to output of the device. Since majority-carrier density changes are offset by electrons from donor or acceptor states, but minority carriers cannot be replenished in this way, we are most often interested in *minority-carrier lifetimes*. These are dependent on the degree of purity and perfection of a crystal; the data given in Table 4.1 are no more than representative values for high-quality material. The very low lifetime in GaAs is due almost entirely to direct recombination and depends little on perfection.

In contrast to a recombination center, a *trap* is characterized by much higher transition probabilities from the localized state to one band than to the other band. In fact, because of energy-momentum conservation requirements, it is quite possible for B_{cs} and B_{sc} to be zero, or alternatively, for B_{vs} and B_{sv} to be zero. An *electron trap* has relatively high conduction-band–localized-state transition probability with low state–valence-band transition probability; a hole trap is just the opposite. Electrons trapped in electron-trapping states are immobilized and therefore unable to contribute to conductivity. Unlike the case of a recombination center, however, these electrons may eventually return to the conduction band. A trapped electron will remain for an average time of $(B_{sc})^{-1}$ in the trap. This parameter can vary over many orders of magnitude, from as little as perhaps 10^{-8} sec to hours or days. Since phonon activity is the chief motivation for electrons to leave traps, the trapping time of a given trapping state decreases at higher temperatures.

Whether particular trapping states are important depends to some extent on the frequency response required in a given device. In a device which is to operate at a frequency of a few cycles per second, traps which release electrons after a few milliseconds average time will not appreciably deteriorate performance. On the other hand, in a device which must operate at megacycle frequencies, the released carriers would appear at times much too late to contribute to signal currents.

Another characteristic exhibited by carrier traps is *saturation*. In Eq. (4.29), we assumed that the perturbations in electron density were small compared with the density of unfilled localized states. If this is not the case, as will often be true in semiconductor devices, occurrence of a large increase of carrier density will rapidly fill most of the unfilled localized states. Once this happens, there are no further traps to immobilize carriers, and any additional excess carriers contribute fully to conductivity. Although it is never really possible to saturate recombination centers, the density of unfilled recombination centers can be reduced in the presence of large increases of carrier density, so that the effective carrier lifetime is increased. The reader will note that the governing differential equations become nonlinear when both N and S_u (or P and S_f) are variables.

While our major practical concern with traps is their immobilization of charge carriers desired for signal processes, they are also important in another way. The presence of high densities of (for example) electron traps in a particular part of a semiconductor produces a high negative space-charge density in this region, and therefore alters the electrical-potential distribution in a device. This is particularly pertinent at crystal surfaces, which may incorporate trapping as well as recombination states. Some types of semiconductor diode devices are based on the existence of such trapping states (Sec. 5.5).

The energy levels of localized states, within the forbidden band, influence their activity. Consider, for example, an electron-trapping state (B_{cs} large). If the Fermi energy lies below the energy of the state ($E_f < E_s$), most of the states may be unfilled by electrons. Since S_u is large, the trapping probability is high. If, on the other hand, $E_f > E_s$, few states will be empty at equilibrium, and trapping probabilities will be lower. This makes it possible to study localized states in semiconductors by varying the temperature of a lightly doped material. With proper choice of dopant and density, the Fermi energy may be made to rise from very near the valence band (in p-type material) to near center gap; n-type doping permits covering the upper part of the forbidden band. Typically, one studies the conductivity produced by pair production from a constant light source; when E_f passes through E_s for a particular set of states, a significant change in conductivity is observed, as a function of temperature.

Since there are usually several sets of localized states, carrier losses due to all will determine the overall bulk lifetime. By extending (4.29) to a number of sets of states designated by subscript i $(i = 1, 2, \ldots)$, we have

$$\frac{dn}{dt} = -nB_{cs1}S_{u1} - nB_{cs2}S_{u2} - \cdots \qquad (4.31)$$

whence

$$\tau_n = \left(\sum_i \frac{1}{\tau_{ni}}\right)^{-1} \qquad (4.32)$$

where $\tau_{ni} = (B_{csi}S_{ui})^{-1}$.

The *bulk* trapping and recombination effects we have been discussing thus far have been associated with localized states in what has been implicitly assumed to be a very large crystal. Semiconductor devices, however, are generally small and contain relatively large surface areas. Often the effect of surface-located trapping and recombination states is more significant than those in the bulk. There can in fact be many more such surface states than localized impurity states if surfaces of the semiconductor are prepared incorrectly. Imagine a device built from a wafer of silicon 0.01 cm thick and 0.1 cm square. The surface area is $\sim 2 \times 10^{-2}$ cm^2, the volume 10^{-4} cm^3. If *each* atom on a (100) face introduced only *one* surface state, the wafer would contain about 10^{13} such states. In the volume, with a doping of 10^{16}, there would be only 10^{12} majority carriers. With an unfavorable surface, conduction could be materially affected.

When recombination occurs at surfaces, the geometrical situation introduces as a recombination measure not a lifetime, but the so-called *surface recombination velocity*. Assume that recombination is confined to a layer of thickness l at a surface (Fig. 4.15). If the electron density is N, and in this surface region the electron lifetime is τ_{sn} (which may be different from the bulk lifetime τ_n), the equation for *total* charge recombination in the region, per unit area, is

$$\frac{d(eNl)}{dt} = -\frac{eNl}{\tau_{sn}} \qquad (4.33)$$

The quantity $-eNl$ is the charge per unit surface area in the surface layer. The time derivative of this charge is therefore the charge reaching the surface per second, for the charge

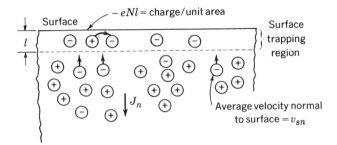

Figure 4.15   Recombination and trapping of charge in a surface layer.

recombined must enter from the body of the semiconductor. Thus

$$J_n \text{ (normal to surface)} = -eN \frac{l}{\tau_{sn}} = \rho_e v_{sn} \qquad (4.34)$$

where $\rho_e = -eN$ is the electron charge density moving at average velocity

$$v_{sn} \equiv \frac{l}{\tau_{sn}} \qquad (4.35)$$

toward the surface. The surface recombination velocity v_{sn} (or v_{sp}, in the case of holes) is more readily measured than l or τ_{sn}, by measurement of current into the surface. The value of v_s is highly dependent on surface treatment. In germanium, values of v_s as high as 10^5 cm/sec result from a surface sandblast treatment, as low as 200 from a sodium hydroxide electrolytic etch. Comparable values are attainable with silicon. Here, the most effective surface treatment appears to be formation of a thin thermally produced oxide (SiO_2). Significance of these parameters can best be appreciated in actual device configurations, where certain surfaces may act as "sinks" for carriers. If, for example, carriers flow through a semiconducting bar at average velocity v when surface recombination is neglected, they will have additional components of velocity v_s toward the surfaces of the bar due to recombination. If the bar is too long, so that the total velocity (the vector combination of the two components) carries carriers to the surfaces, only a small fraction of the minority-carrier current entering one end may be able to reach the other end.

4.7 Photoconductivity

A near-intrinsic semiconductor with $E_g \gg kT$ has very few conduction carriers and therefore high resistivity. If radiant energy at photon energies above E_g illuminates it, carrier pairs are generated. A pair of metallic contacts on two faces of a sample, connected through a battery and meter, will read a current. If the voltage does no more than sweep out the carriers generated, the total number of electrons passing through the external circuit cannot exceed the number of photons absorbed by the semiconductor. In fact, with recombination losses in the bulk and at the surfaces, the charge flow will likely be much smaller.

With carrier trapping action in semiconductor materials, the total current which can be passed through can be much larger. Assuming a material with hole traps which permit recombination only after long times and that all holes generated are rapidly trapped, the trapped-hole density will vary with time by a relation something like

$$\frac{dP_t}{dt} = -\frac{P_t}{\tau_{pt}} + G \qquad (4.36)$$

where G is the rate of generation, and τ_{pt} the lifetime of a trapped hole. With trapped-hole space-charge density, $+eP_t$, an equal concentration of *mobile* electrons exists in the conduction band, to satisfy electrical-charge neutrality. Intimately connected metallic contacts can be made to emit electrons into the semiconductor, by the processes described in Sec. 5.5. So long as trapped-hole density is maintained, therefore, the material is conductive ($\sigma = eN\mu_n = eP_t\mu_n$). The current which can be drawn, by a given voltage across a device, will be proportional to $P_t\mu_n$. For a given geometry, let the current be $I = \zeta P_t\mu_n$, with ζ a constant. Then, since G is proportional to light flux, $dI/dt = -I\tau_{pt} - G/\zeta\mu_n$. The response to high-frequency light variations is found by letting G have a time dependence $e^{j\omega t}$, whence solution of the foregoing differential equation gives a sensitivity

$$\frac{|I|}{|G|} = \frac{\tau_{pt}}{\zeta\mu_n} (1 - \omega^2\tau_{pt}^2)^{-\frac{1}{2}} \qquad (4.37)$$

The response is proportional to τ_{pt} because the density of holes stored at any time depends on their rate of recombination. On the other hand, at high frequencies ($\omega\tau_{pl} > 1$) the response decreases inversely with frequency. Accordingly, a limited sensitivity-bandwidth product is characteristic.

Photoconductivity occurs in all semiconductors. Photoconductive devices for various light-sensing applications have employed a wide range of materials, including II-VI compound semiconductors, such as cadmium sulfide and other sulfides, selenides, and oxides which cannot easily be produced in single crystal-form. The high defect-density characteristic of polycrystalline materials is often a source of trapping states and may actually be desirable. Naturally, mobilities in highly defected materials will be much smaller than those of single crystals, so that these photoconductors do not yield low-resistance devices. Applications most frequently employ thin layers of polycrystalline, or even amorphous material, where the electrical path through the layer is very short but the area may be very large. Some materials trap mainly holes and conduct via electrons, while others have mainly hole conduction.[1]

In many applications, long decay time is no problem. In one technique of xerography, a thin coating of amorphous selenium, having a "dark" resistivity of about 10^{16} ohm-cm, is applied to a metal surface (Fig. 4.16). On the opposite surface, a charge can be built up using a high-voltage corona discharge near the surface. Because of the high resistivity, this charge remains on the surface until the conductivity of the selenium is raised by light falling on its surface. Those parts which are illuminated discharge; the unilluminated parts remain charged. In selenium, electrons are trapped, while holes form the mobile carriers. A powder of fine resin (pigment) particles dusted over the surface clings only to the charged region. The powder is then transferred to paper and fused thereto by heat, leaving an image of the light pattern on the paper. A second scheme employs paper coated with a special zinc oxide powder, which acts directly as a photoconductor.

The photoconductive television camera tube represents an application where time-response and sensitivity requirements must be compromised. Light impinges on a thin photoconductive layer, e.g., of selenium. The layer is photoconductive to an extent, depending on the local light intensity.

[1] For tables of photoconductors, see P. Gorlich, Problems of Photoconductivity, *Advan. Electronics and Electron Phys.*, vol. 14, 1961.

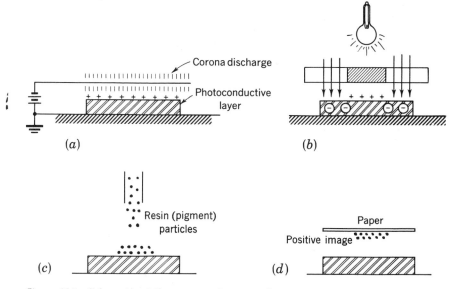

Figure 4.16 Schematic of the process of xerography. (*a*) Surface is charged; (*b*) illumination produces trapped carriers and photoconduction; (*c*) remaining charge attracts pigment resin; (*d*) pigment is transferred to paper.

The insulated rear surface of the photoconductor is scanned by an electron beam, which attempts to charge the surface to zero potential by depositing electrons on the surface (Fig. 4.17). Where the surface is conductive, deposited charge is neutralized by holes originating from a transparent conductor upon which the photoconductor has been deposited. On its next visit to a particular point on the surface, the electron beam deposits a surface charge dependent on the amount of the charge which has leaked away since its last visit to that point. The remaining beam current is electrostatically reflected by the surface charge and collected elsewhere. The current deposited on the surface by the beam is a measure of the light intensity at each point on the surface. Because of trapping, the total current through the photoconductor is much larger than the photon current which excites it. The signal current is a measure of the total photocurrent flow during the time interval between visits of the electron beam to a particular point of the surface. Changes in the television picture can occur only as rapidly as trapping permits; response speed is inferior to that in some other types of television camera tubes. The latter devices must, however,

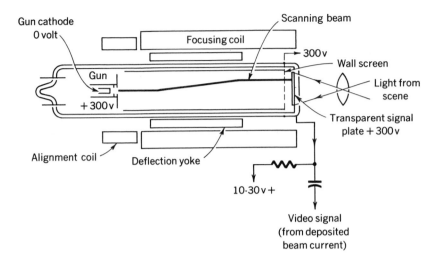

Figure 4.17 Schematic of the Vidicon (television camera tube). The electron beam restores charge to the surface of a photoconductor which has been illuminated. The charge required to recharge the surface is measured as the television video signal. (*After P. K. Weimer et al., Electronics*, May, 1950.)

employ expensive and complex electron multipliers to achieve comparable sensitivity.

Since actual photoconductors are often quite complicated materials, trapping states are many and varied. A multiplicity of trapping time constants, working in concert, may give rise to photoconductive decay of the form

$$P_t = P_1 e^{-t/\tau_1} + P_2 e^{-t/\tau_2} + \cdots$$

Thus, while most of the trapped carriers may be released in a short time, a small fraction may remain trapped for much longer times. This, for example, may give rise to a persistent "afterimage" from a television camera tube. The exponential-decay process is also not the only one observed for trap-saturation effects, and electron transfer from one type of trap to another can give rise to other time dependency, such as functions of the empirical form t^{-n}.

Preparation of photoconductive materials is largely in the realm of physical chemistry, except for simple materials such as selenium. "Tailoring" of materials can be done through introduction of impurities to establish particular trapping characteristics. Major efforts have been made to reduce the "dark current" which flows in the absence of incident light.

This is due to either intrinsic conduction or extrinsic behavior enabled by defects or impurities acting as donors or acceptors.

4.8 Nonuniform Carrier Densities

In metals, electron densities are so high that any substantial percentage changes in density are prohibited by the large space-charge fields which must accompany them. In semiconductors the concentration of carriers, particularly minority carriers in extrinsic material, may be so small that modest electric fields allow order-of-magnitude changes in the carrier densities. Also important are the variations in carrier density where doping in a single semiconductor crystal varies from n type to p type within a small device.

An important mechanism of (minority) carrier flow in semiconductors, not, however, significant in metals, is *diffusion*. Diffusion occurs whenever a *nonuniform* concentration of mobile particles of any sort exists in a thermal environment. Random motion carries the particles throughout the system; unless controlled by other forces (such as fields), diffusion eventually results in a uniform concentration. For example, while diffusion of dye molecules of low molecular weight, in water, results in a uniformly tinted solution, *heavy* dye particles largely stay near the bottom because of the gravitational field. Electric fields in semiconductors act, likewise, on electrons or holes, to prevent them from distributing uniformly through a device.

The governing equations for flow by diffusion may be found using (3.51). The spatial gradient of the density function f_0, in the absence of temperature gradients, is

$$\nabla_r f_0 = -\frac{\partial f_0}{\partial E}\frac{\partial E_f}{\partial n_0}\nabla_r N$$

or in one dimension,

$$\frac{\partial f_0}{\partial x} = -\frac{\partial f_0}{\partial E}\frac{\partial E_f}{\partial N}\frac{\partial N}{\partial x}$$

The expression for the **p**-space density perturbation f_1, with a thermal gradient, is

$$f_1 = -\tau\left(-\frac{\partial f_0}{\partial E}\frac{\partial E_f}{\partial N}\frac{dN}{dx} - e\frac{\partial f_0}{\partial E}\mathcal{E}_x\right)v_x$$

$$= \tau v_x \frac{\partial f_0}{\partial E}\left(\frac{\partial E_f}{\partial N}\frac{dN}{dx} + e\mathcal{E}_x\right) \tag{4.38}$$

The parentheses contain both the concentration gradient and the field. Only the other factors contain the energy E, which is the variable of integration when the current J_x is determined as in (3.54). Accordingly, the current flow produced by a concentration gradient dN/dx is precisely as large as that produced by an electric field $\mathcal{E}_x = \dfrac{1}{e} \dfrac{\partial E_f}{\partial N} \dfrac{dN}{dx}$. Since we have used mobility μ_n to represent empirical factors in the electronic conductivity, in a semiconductor the electron current, including the effect of concentration gradients, may be written

$$J_{xn} = \mu_n N \left(e\mathcal{E}_x + \frac{\partial E_f}{\partial N} \frac{dN}{dx} \right) \tag{4.39}$$

The relation for N in terms of Fermi level (4.16) permits us to evaluate $\partial E_f / \partial N$:

$$dN = \frac{N_i}{kT} \exp \left(E_f - \frac{E_{fi}}{kT} \right) dE_f \qquad \frac{\partial E_f}{\partial N} = \frac{kT}{N}$$

It follows that

$$J_{xn} = e \left(\mu_n N \mathcal{E}_x + D_n \frac{\partial N}{\partial x} \right) \tag{4.40}$$

where

$$D_n = \frac{\mu_n kT}{e} \tag{4.41}$$

is termed the *diffusion constant*, for electrons in the semiconductor. This relation was first established by Einstein. A corresponding relation may be established for holes, except that the current produced by a given concentration gradient is of the opposite sign. The diffusion constant measures specifically the carrier density of flow across a plane when the carrier concentration has a unit gradient ($\partial N/dx = 1$) normal to the plane. The corresponding three-dimensional transport equations for electrons and holes are, by simple extension of (4.39),

$$\begin{aligned} \mathbf{J}_n &= e(\mu_n N\mathcal{E} + D_n \, \boldsymbol{\nabla} N) \\ \mathbf{J}_p &= e(\mu_p P\mathcal{E} - D_p \, \boldsymbol{\nabla} P) \end{aligned} \tag{4.42}$$

The part of the current due to the field is termed the *drift current;* that due to the concentration gradient, the *diffusion current*. The difference in signs of the diffusion terms may be explained by reference to Fig. 4.18. If the concentration

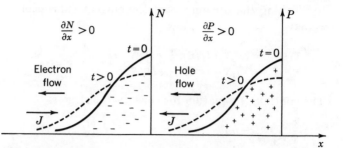

Figure 4.18 Diffusion of electrons (left) and holes (right) with positive density gradients. Dashed curves show densities at a later time due to diffusion. Resulting currents are of opposite sign.

gradient of electrons is in the positive x direction ($\partial N/\partial x > 0$), the resulting redistribution through diffusion carries electrons to the left, current to the right (positive). The same concentration gradient for holes will carry holes and current to the left (negative).

The relation governing diffusion of neutral particles is fundamentally the same as for charged particles, except that electric fields are of course ineffective. The central equation of diffusion (Fick's first law) is

$$\text{Particle current} = \mathbf{J}_M = -D\,\nabla M \tag{4.43}$$

where M is the density, and $\mathbf{J}_M$ the flow rate, of the particles concerned. This relation also applies to solute atoms in a solvent, impurity atoms in a solid, etc. D is always temperature-dependent; in the case of semiconductor carriers this dependence appears in the factors μT, as in (4.41).

Fick's *second* law simply expresses the fact that the partial time derivative of the density of any indestructible particles equals the divergence of the particle current:

$$\frac{\partial M}{\partial t} = -\nabla \cdot \mathbf{J}_M \qquad \text{[applied to (4.43)]}$$

$$= D\,\nabla^2 M \qquad \text{(Fick's second law)} \tag{4.44}$$

In the next chapter we deal exclusively with inhomogeneous semiconductors, wherein the concentration and type of impurity vary from point to point. Equilibrium carrier concentrations, as well as current flow in the presence of applied fields, must be found from self-consistent solution of equations relating current, charge, and electric field.

Taking the divergence of the current expressions (4.42), we have

$$\nabla \cdot \mathbf{J}_n = e\mu_n \nabla \cdot (N\mathcal{E}) + eD_n \nabla^2 N$$
$$\nabla \cdot \mathbf{J}_p = e\mu_p \nabla \cdot (P\mathcal{E}) - eD_p \nabla^2 P \qquad (4.45)$$

The continuity equation for conserved charge is

$$\nabla \cdot \mathbf{J} = \frac{-\partial \rho}{\partial t}$$

where ρ is the charge density. In this sense, however, semiconductor carriers are not conserved, but may be lost by recombination. Letting $N = N_0 + n$ and $P = P_0 + p$, where n, p are excess carrier densities and N_0, P_0 the equilibrium values at a given position in the material, the continuity equations may be corrected for recombination and carrier generation:

$$\frac{\partial N}{\partial t} \equiv \frac{\partial n}{\partial t} = \frac{-n}{\tau_n} + \frac{1}{e}\nabla \cdot \mathbf{J}_n + G_n$$
$$\frac{\partial P}{\partial t} \equiv \frac{\partial p}{\partial t} = \frac{-p}{\tau_p} - \frac{1}{e}\nabla \cdot \mathbf{J}_p + G_p \qquad (4.46)$$

where G_n, G_p are (usually equal) rates of carrier generation, e.g., by photon absorption. The inclusion of trapping phenomena requires the addition of terms expressing the loss of carriers to the various trapping states, as well as additional terms representing the return of trapped carriers from the various traps. It is then necessary to treat additional carrier densities P_t and N_t which are trapped. The "bookkeeping" involved soon gets beyond the needs of simple device solutions, unless further approximations are made.

Combining (4.45) and (4.46) and expanding the divergence terms,

$$\frac{\partial n}{\partial t} = \frac{-n}{\tau_n} + \mu_n(N\nabla \cdot \mathcal{E} + \mathcal{E} \cdot \nabla N) + D_n \nabla^2 N + G_n$$
$$\frac{\partial p}{\partial t} = \frac{-p}{\tau_p} - \mu_p(P\nabla \cdot \mathcal{E} + \mathcal{E} \cdot \nabla P) + D_p \nabla^2 P + G_p \qquad (4.47)$$

The electric field ($\mathcal{E}$) in the semiconductor is determined by the net space-charge density through Poisson's equation $\nabla \cdot \mathcal{E} = \rho/\epsilon$. If we represent trapped electron and hole densities by N_t and P_t, respectively, this becomes

$$\nabla \cdot \mathbf{\mathcal{E}} = \frac{e}{\epsilon} [(P - N) + (P_t - N_t) + (D - A)] \tag{4.48}$$

The combination of Eqs. (4.47) and (4.48) in principle makes possible the solution of semiconductor-device field configurations from the known equilibrium solutions. Equations (4.42) then make it possible to find the carrier currents which flow. Surface recombination effects must be added through introduction of boundary conditions on current flow to surfaces.

The relations are made nonlinear by the product terms including carrier density and field; for large variations, even lifetimes are dependent on carrier concentrations. This makes exact solution quite tedious and obtainable only by numerical analysis. Often, however, complexity may be reduced by assumptions which simplify and linearize the equations. A simple case in point is the diffusion of excess holes introduced at one boundary plane of a semi-infinite n-type semiconductor. We assume the hole density always so low that *charge neutrality* is maintained by a small rearrangement of majority-carrier (electron) distribution. The field can therefore be assumed zero throughout. We are interested here only in the steady-state solution, where $\partial p/\partial t = 0$. Equation (4.47), for holes, is greatly simplified to the homogeneous differential equation

$$\frac{p}{\tau_p} = D_p \nabla^2 p \tag{4.49}$$

If excess holes are introduced uniformly across the plane ($x = 0$) (Fig. 4.19), the problem becomes one-dimensional:

$$\frac{p}{\tau_p} = D_p \frac{d^2 p}{dx^2} \tag{4.50}$$

This simple linear differential equation has the general solution

$$p = A e^{x/L_p} + B e^{-x/L_p} \tag{4.51}$$

where $L_p = (\tau_p D_p)^{\frac{1}{2}}$. L_p is termed the *diffusion length* (an important distance measure for device calculations in the next chapter). The constants A and B are established by the

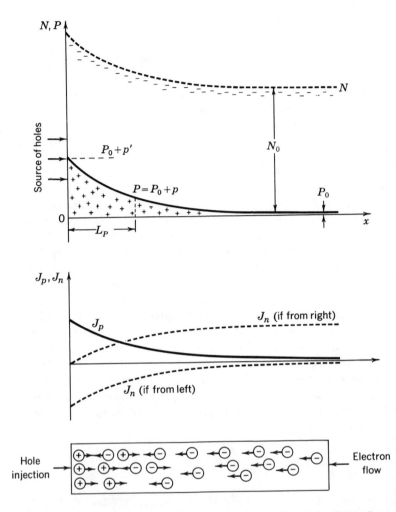

Figure 4.19 Carrier densities and currents produced when holes diffuse from a source at left into n-type material at right. Requirement on current is that total current be constant. It can be zero if electrons also diffuse from the left. If recombination electron current flows from the right, however, net current flows to the right, as shown at bottom.

boundary conditions: $p(x = 0) = p'$, $p(x = \infty) = 0$. Then

$$p(x) = p'e^{-x/L_p} \tag{4.52}$$

The shorter the carrier lifetime τ_p and the smaller the diffusion constant D_p $(= \mu_p kT/e)$, the shorter the distance that the excess hole density extends into the $x > 0$ region.

The solution implies that holes move in the region through diffusion and disappear through recombination processes. There is by (4.42) a *minority-carrier current* of holes moving to the right:

$$J_p = -eD_p\frac{\partial P}{\partial x} = -eD_p\frac{\partial p}{\partial x} = e\left(\frac{D_p}{\tau_p}\right)^{\frac{1}{2}}p'e^{-x/L_p} \tag{4.53}$$

The hole current is largest at $x = 0$ and vanishes at large positive x. The hole-current flow to the right requires at least a minimum accompanying electron flow to transport those electrons which recombine with the holes, as shown in the figure. The *total* electron flow may be in *either* direction. Since we have precluded charge storage by neglecting electric fields, the *total* current in any plane x must be uniform, as shown. A large electronic *majority-carrier current* may be set up by the presence of a very small electric field, because of the relatively large concentration of electrons in the n-type material. This situation forms an important part of the semiconductor-junction theory in the following chapter.

4.9 High-field Phenomena in Semiconductors and Insulators

In metals, the concentration of electrons is so large that during conduction the electron drift velocity is only a small fraction of the thermal velocity. This explains the high degree of ohmic linearity exhibited by metals. Extrinsic semiconductors can also have fairly large carrier concentrations, so again only a small field is necessary to set up very substantial ohmic current densities. As in metals, the onset of *nonlinear* conduction (in homogeneous material) would occur at current and power densities so high that power dissipation under continuous operation is destructive. In semiconductors with low impurity densities, however, so few carriers may be present that very high electric fields may safely be applied. It becomes possible to observe nonohmic conductivity as well as effects due to the space charge of unneutralized carriers. At even higher fields, electrical *breakdown* effects will occur.

We consider first current flow in an insulator or an intrinsic semiconductor, with carriers introduced from adjacent extrinsic material or metal. For simplicity, it will be assumed that only one type of carrier (e.g., electrons) is involved. Presence and density of the opposite carriers depend on gen-

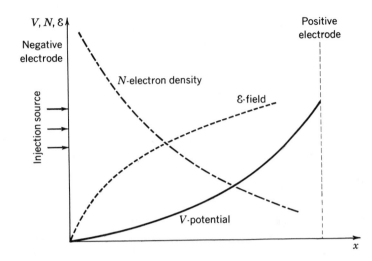

Figure 4.20   Electron density, field, and potential variation in space-charge-limited electron flow in an insulator or intrinsic semiconductor.   Diffusion and trapping are neglected.

eration and trapping processes and the nature of the contacts at the ends of the intrinsic material, as should be made clear in the next chapter. The current-transport equation (4.42) reduces to

$$\mathbf{J} = \mathbf{J}_n = eN\mu_n \mathcal{E} \tag{4.54}$$

The diffusion term may be omitted if concentration gradients are small. It will generally enhance the current flow to some extent. The space-charge equation is simply

$$\nabla \cdot \mathcal{E} = -\frac{eN}{\epsilon} \tag{4.55}$$

since there are assumed to be no donors, acceptors, holes, or trapped carriers present. In one dimension, combining the two expressions,

$$\mathcal{E}\frac{d\mathcal{E}}{dx} = \frac{-J}{\mu_n \epsilon} \tag{4.56}$$

In a one-dimensional steady-state solution, current density must be independent of x. After multiplying through by dx, the equation is integrated directly:

$$\mathcal{E}^2 - \mathcal{E}_0{}^2 = \frac{-J}{\mu_n \epsilon}(x - x_0) \tag{4.57}$$

The most appropriate boundary conditions are $x_0 = 0$, $\mathcal{E}_0 = 0$. If electrons enter at $x = 0$ with zero velocity, this is the correct condition. The field is then given by

$$\mathcal{E} = -\left(\frac{J}{\mu_n \epsilon} x\right)^{\frac{1}{2}} \qquad\qquad (4.58)$$

Defining potential at $x = 0$ as zero, the potential at x is found by integration:

$$V(x) = \frac{2}{3}\left(\frac{J}{\mu_n \epsilon}\right)^{\frac{1}{2}} x^{\frac{3}{2}}$$

The current density through a given thickness t of an intrinsic semiconductor is therefore proportional to the *square* of the applied voltage:

$$J = \frac{9}{4}\frac{\mu_n \epsilon}{t^3} V^2 \qquad\qquad (4.59)$$

The situation is reminiscent of the vacuum-diode solution, in which $J \propto V^{\frac{3}{2}}$. The difference occurs because electron motion is governed here by collisions rather than solely by acceleration (Fig. 4.20).

The square-law voltage-current characteristic can sometimes be observed in "leakage current" in semiconductors and insulators below breakdown voltages; diffusion is not significant. When both electrons and holes are present and trapping must be accounted for, considerably more complex relations are obtained. Solutions relating J and V may even be multivalued, giving rise to the "negative-resistance" effects observed in thin layers of insulating materials such as niobium oxide (Nb_2O_5).

All preceding analysis has assumed the mobility of the electrons to be independent of field. Where fields are of the order of thousands of volts per centimeter, this is no longer accurate. The mobility μ was found in Chap. 3 to be expressible as $e\tau/m^*$, where τ is mean free time between collisions. In metals, the velocity picked up from the electric field between collisions ($\sim e\tau\mathcal{E}/m^*$) is small compared with the thermal velocity, since the important (Fermi-surface) electrons have thermal velocities of the order of 10 ev. In semiconductors, at the band edges, electron and hole velocities are zero. Since electron- and hole-velocity distributions are essentially Boltzmann distributions, the average electron energy is $3kT/2$, and average thermal velocity is given approximately from $(m^*\langle v \rangle^2)/2 = \frac{3}{2}kT$. As in metals, electron mean free time and mobility at low fields are determined by phonon collisions. One may argue for a constant mean free time on the basis that if the electron is moving slowly, a phonon will come along to collide with it about every τ sec. At high applied fields, the *distance* that the carrier travels in this constant interval becomes large; even a carrier brought to rest by a previous collision travels a distance $\sim at^2/2 = (e\mathcal{E}/2m^*)\tau^2$ in time τ. With $m^* = 0.2m_e$ and τ $(\simeq m^*\mu_n/e) = 10^{-11}$ sec, in a field of 10^3 volts/cm this distance is about 50,000 A. With distances this large, the carrier may more often collide with fixed impurities or defects than with phonons. Accordingly, the description at higher fields should be in terms of a constant mean free path l_0, rather than the mean free time. The mean free time then becomes field-dependent; if we set

$$l_0 = \frac{e\mathcal{E}}{2m^*}\tau^2 \quad \text{then} \quad \tau = \sqrt{\frac{2m^*l_0}{e\mathcal{E}}}$$

and

$$\mu = \sqrt{\frac{2el_0}{m^*\mathcal{E}}} \tag{4.60}$$

There exists a range of fields in which the mobility is approximately proportional to the inverse square root of the field, and the carrier drift velocity to the square root of the field. As might be expected from (4.60), mobility reduction is greater with carriers of higher effective mass (Fig. 4.21).

At even higher electric fields, further reduction of mobility is observed, culminating in what appears to be a limiting value of drift velocity, near the onset of breakdown processes. This is usually explained as due to the interaction of electrons with optical-band phonons, which at low electron energies play no significant role. At the high fields for which these processes take place, the usual statistical descriptions of conduction processes become quite inaccurate. Phonons will be "dragged" along by the electron flow. The effective electron temperature will become much greater than that of the lattice. The carriers are said to be "hot." The collision and recombination statistics are also greatly different from those for the usual "cold" carriers, and none of the simple analyses apply. These high-energy particles may suffer collisions which deflect their paths only slightly; hence a mean free path between collisions

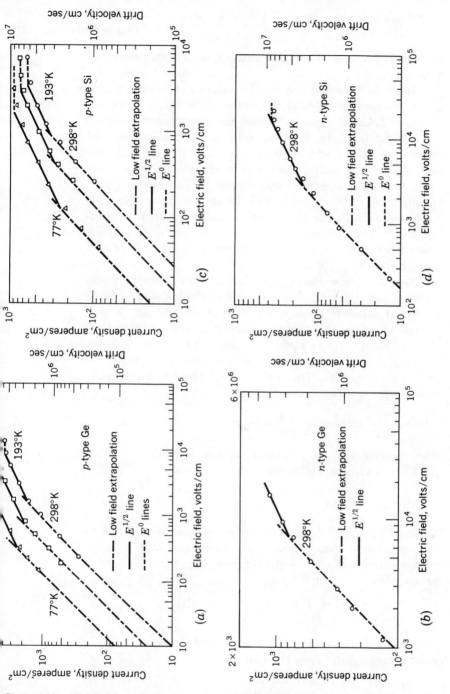

Figure 4.21 High-field conduction in germanium and silicon. (*a*) *p*-type germanium; (*b*) *n*-type germanium; (*c*) *p*-type silicon; (*d*) *n*-type silicon. [*After E. J. Ryder, Phys. Rev.*, **90**:766 (1953).]

may no longer be a meaningful measure of forward progress of a carrier.

Intrinsic semiconductors and insulators experience breakdown processes at fields of the order of 10^5 to 10^7 volts/cm. At these fields, electron and hole energies in nearly perfect crystals can build up, between collisions with impurities and defects, to values which can exceed E_g. It is possible for such a carrier to ionize directly an electron from the valence band into the conduction band, creating a hole-electron pair. Quantitatively, this process may be described by the *pair-creation probability* per unit length of path parallel to an electric field. More often, the inverse is specified: α_n or α_p, pairs created per centimeter of carrier travel, as a function of field strength $\mathcal{E}$.

Let us suppose that a high field is applied across a thin region of near-intrinsic semiconductor of thickness w, carrying an initial intrinsic or injected current density J. A pair created by one of these original carriers at some intermediate plane x_p constitutes an electron which will continue on to the anode, at $x = w$; and the associated hole will move toward the cathode, at $x = 0$. This pair will create additional pairs numbering

$$I = \int_{x_p}^{w} \alpha_n(\mathcal{E}) \, dx + \int_0^{x_p} \alpha_p(\mathcal{E}) \, dx \tag{4.61}$$

As a simplification, we assume $\alpha_p = \alpha_n = \alpha$. Each pair then produces *directly* an additional number of pairs

$$I = \int_0^w \alpha(\mathcal{E}) \, dx$$

Each *pair* moving through the semiconductor represents an external-circuit charge flow $-e$. Beginning with a single carrier introduced at $x = 0$ or $x = w$, the eventual current produced is

$$M = 1 + I(1 + I\{1 + I[1 + I(\cdot \cdot \cdot)]\})$$
$$= 1 + I + I^2 + I^3 + \cdots$$

Expressing this infinite series in closed form, the *carrier multiplication factor* M is therefore

$$M = (1 - I)^{-1} \tag{4.62}$$

Since the generation rate α must be determined empirically, it may be found by measuring M for a variety of field strengths

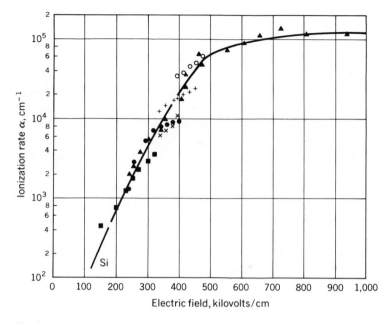

Figure 4.22 Avalanche-ionization data for silicon.   Points were obtained
via three different measurement techniques.   [*After K. G. McKay,
Phys. Rev.,* **94**:877 (1954).]

in the material. I is then found by inverting (4.62).   Data
are given in Fig. 4.22, for silicon.   Separate data on α_p and
α_n have also been obtained.[1]   As a function of applied voltage,
with a given configuration (usually a junction, as described in
Sec. 5.8), the current varies with voltage as shown in Fig. 4.23.
Since, when $I = 1$, the multiplication becomes infinite, a very
steep characteristic is typical.   It is limited only by series
resistance in adjacent semiconductor material.   The process,
because of its similarity to a well-known natural process, is
termed *avalanche breakdown*.   While the term avalanche is
generally reserved for processes in which high-energy carriers
produce hole-electron pairs directly, there can be related
processes in extrinsic semiconductors.   While, for example,
gold impurity states in germanium (Fig. 4.5) are deep enough
in the forbidden band so that little *thermal* ionization takes
place at cryogenic temperatures, high-energy carriers can
ionize these states with much lower energy than that of the
full band gap.   The relatively low fields required for ioniza-

---

[1] Cf. S. L. Miller, *Phys. Rev.,* **105**:1249 (Feb. 15, 1957).

tion permit large device dimensions; the unequal electron- and hole-generation rates, and the ever-present carrier traps introduce space-charge and recombination-time effects not observed in simple avalanche processes.

Breakdown of common insulators, most of which have polycrystalline (ceramics) or amorphous (glasses, plastics) structures, is not well explained by semiconductor avalanching theory. Although very thin sections of some insulators, up to perhaps 10,000 A in thickness, behave roughly according to avalanche theory, on the whole, breakdown processes in solid insulators involve electrically weak regions or defected "channels." These allow applied fields to act upon sections much thinner than the apparent insulator thickness. Many insulators, including most ceramics, are ionic solids of very high band gap. Because in addition they are highly defected, electron energies can often not reach values which permit

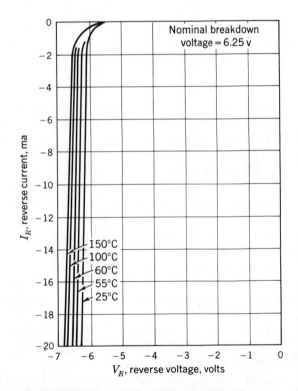

Figure 4.23 Characteristics for a typical voltage-regulator (Zener) diode. [*Data shown are for Texas Instruments, Inc., type* 652C (*August,* 1960).]

avalanching. On the other hand, the charged ions, also under the influence of the field, can have appreciable mobility at fields in the range 10^6 to 10^7 volts/cm. Many ionic solids even have substantial ionic conductivity at low fields. (This disqualifies most of the simpler ionic solids such as alkali halides from application as electrical insulators.) Ion mobility is usually field-dependent because of the activation energy required to lift an ion out of a stable crystalline site. Once freed from its site, however, an ion may collide very effectively with other ions in the material, breaking them loose also. Such an ionic *breakdown* process is far more violent than electronic processes, for electrons can transfer only very small fractions of their energy to the nuclei. The result of ionic breakdown, in an insulating solid such as an oxide, frequently removes oxygen ions to a sufficient extent so that the remaining material in a breakdown channel is conductive. The process is normally destructive. For this reason liquid insulation is preferred at very high voltages, for the products of liquid-dielectric breakdown are usually gases, and the insulator is self-healing. Relatively little is known about ionic-breakdown processes in solids, partly because rapidity and nonrepeatability of these effects make detailed electrical measurement very difficult. Local temperatures can rise so high as to make the material more like a gaseous plasma than a solid conductor. These breakdown processes, characterized by tremendous release of energies, are often termed *collective breakdown*, implying that the process cannot be understood in terms of the independent motion of electron or ions, but only through collective action of large numbers of particles.

PROBLEMS

Use values from Table 4.1 unless otherwise specified.

4.1(*a*) The energy band gap of semiconductors is observed to vary with temperature (for example, $dE_g/dT = 3.6 \times 10^{-4}$ ev/°C for Si and 2.2×10^{-4} for Ge). Show that a positive temperature coefficient (of E_g) may be expected, from the arguments of Prob. 2.7*a* and Fig. 2.14.

4.1(*b*) The *melting points* of ionic crystals (e.g., sodium chloride) are in general lower than those of many covalent semiconductors. The band gap of these materials (as observed by optical absorption) is generally much higher than that of silicon or germanium. Discuss this in terms of the relation between the electron bonding in the crystal and the crystal cohesion.

4.2(a) Show that if constant-energy surfaces in the conduction band are ellipsoidal about $\mathbf{k} = 0$, with effective mass m_x^*, m_y^*, m_z^* along the three major axes, the effective-mass factor in the density-of-states function (4.6) will be of the form $(m_x^* m_y^* m_z^*)^{\frac{1}{2}}$.

4.2(b) Determine intrinsic carrier densities at $T = 300°K$ for (1) GaAs, (2) IsSb, within the accuracy possible using the tabulated data.

4.2(c) (1) If the density-of-states functions were simply uniform densities $n(E) = N_c$ in the conduction band and $n(E) = N_v$ in the valence band, find the expression corresponding to (4.15) for the intrinsic carrier density N_i. (2) If this theory were fitted to the data for Ge in Fig. 4.3, with $E_g = 0.785$ ev, at $T = 300°K$, by what factor would it differ from the more exact theory at $T = 400°K$?

4.2(d) Derive Eqs. (4.4). What is the nature of the electron motion in an electric field of frequency *slightly different from* the cyclotron frequency $B_z e/m^*$?

4.3(a) The hydrogenlike solution for the ionization energy of impurities gives values for single ionization of donors or acceptors. How might the ionization energy for the *second* electron or hole compare with that for the first, according to the simplest one-electron theory? Compare with experimental values for zinc and cadmium in Ge (Fig. 4.5).

4.3(b) List groups of possible simple donor and acceptor impurities for (1) III-V compounds, (2) II-VI compounds, and (3) alkali halides. (4) In each case, what order of donor or acceptor (double donor, triple donor, etc.) is produced by a *vacancy*, of each type of atom in the compound? (5) What will determine the effect of a group IV impurity in a III-IV compound?

4.4(a) Make estimates of the maximum operating temperatures, for the condition $N/P = 3$, for n-type semiconductor with 10^{17} cm^{-3} doping, with the following materials: (1) GaAs, (2) IsSb, and (3) SiC.

4.4(b) (1) Using the parameters for germanium in Table 4.1, plot T_L [defined by Eq. (4.18)] as a function of D over a range of D from 10^{13} to 10^{17}. Assume $E_D = 0.01$ ev and use the heavy-hole effective mass value. (2) What is the maximum impurity density at which (4.18) may be considered fairly accurate?

4.5(a) Sketch an approximate plot for the room-temperature Hall constant of germanium, as a function of *acceptor* density, beginning from intrinsic material. Determine enough points to show the nature of the variation.

4.5(b) A 0.010-in.-thick germanium wafer 3 mm square is used as a "Hall probe" to measure a magnetic field of 100 oe. Contacts are attached along two edges and at the centers of the other two edges. With a 10-volt d-c drive available, specify a practical impurity concentration (explain) and the resultant Hall voltage.

4.6(a) Derive an expression for the time decay of an initial carrier density in an intrinsic semiconductor, by the action of direct recombination (or by fast-acting recombination centers).

4.6(b) Some of the states illustrated in Fig. 4.5 are more correctly termed trapping or recombination centers than donors or acceptors. Indicate which ones could be put into this category for germanium at room temperature. Note that, in general, the cross section of a state for ionization by a photon or phonon is smaller if (1) it has a position near the center of the band gap, and (2) it has a high ionization energy. With this in mind, discuss the possible effects of each of the Au states in both n-type and p-type germanium. At *high* temperatures in germanium, what will be the most likely ionization state of Au impurity atoms?

4.6(c) In a hypothetical p-type semiconductor with acceptor density of 10^{15}, $N_i = 10^{12}$, a density of 10^{14} trapping states lies centered in the band gap. You may assume $m_n^* = m_p^*$. (1) At equilibrium, how many of these electron traps are occupied by electrons? (2) If by photon illumination the electron density suddenly were raised momentarily to 2×10^{10} and B_{cs} were known to be 10^{-11}, how long would it take for the electron density to decay to 10^{10}?

4.6(d) If the surface recombination velocity is 500 cm/sec, in a cylindrical bar of intrinsic silicon 1 mm in diameter and 5 mm long, estimate the electric field which must be applied along the axis to permit 90 per cent of the electrons injected at one end of the bar to reach the other end. Use simple approximation throughout, neglecting bulk recombination.

4.7(a) The mobility of electrons in a particular photoconductor is 50 cm²/volt-sec. A sample of a photoconductor $10 \times 10 \times 1$ mm has a voltage of 10 volts applied across the small dimension. A flux of 10^{10} photons is applied in a very short time, producing a uniform trapped-hole density. (1) Assuming that the trapping time constant is 10^{-3} sec and that all photons are effective, determine the total charge transferred and compare with a similar photoconductor having no traps. (2) Compare the (drift) time constant of the nontrapping device, operated at 10 volts, with that of the trapping photoconductor, using the assumption that electron mobility is the limiting factor in the trap-free device.

4.7(b) A photoconductive layer 10,000 A thick is charged initially to a potential difference of 1,000 volts between its two surfaces. Dielectric constant is 20, and electron mobility is 5 cm²/volt-sec. Incident monochromatic light of 2,536 A wavelength is absorbed in the material with an intensity attenuation exp $-20z$, where z is the thickness of penetration in centimeters. Each photon creates a pair, of which the hole is assumed to be trapped for an average time of 0.005 sec. Neglecting transient effects, what light flux (watts) is required to discharge an area 8.5 by 11 in. in area to a voltage of 50 volts during a 1-sec exposure?

4.8(a) (1) Write the general form of the solution (M versus x) to the diffusion of nonvanishing particles in a one-dimensional cartesian case. Let the plane $x = 0$ be a constant source ($M = M_0$) and the plane $x = a$ be a sink ($M = 0$) and determine the solution. (2) Repeat for concentric cylindrical source and sink. (3) Repeat for concentric spherical source and sink.

4.8(b) Equations (4.47) show that, in general, a semiconductor is nonlinear, i.e., that under some circumstances one would not expect a current flow to be proportional to the voltage producing it. (1) Explain the reason for this in the simplest possible terms.   (2) Show from the equations under what conditions the conduction processes might be expected to be linear; give an example of a linear semiconduction process. (3) Under what conditions should the nonlinearity be most apparent?

4.8(c) In silicon, as described by Table 4.1, what hole density at a plane $x = 0$ is required to produce a hole diffusion current of 1 amp/cm²? If the precise number of electrons to recombine with this hole current come from the right (Fig. 4.19), through a uniform cross section of semiconductor 0.5 cm long, what *donor density* would be required in the n-type region to keep the total voltage drop (calculated from the conductivity) in this region ($0 < x < 0.5$ cm) less than 0.1 volt?   Consider both electron and hole conductivity.

4.9(a) From the data of Fig. 4.21, using (4.60) and effective-mass data from Table 4.1, estimate the mean free path of electron travel between collisions with fixed defects or impurities, in silicon. (Observe that the results apply only to the particular sample tested.)

4.9(b) If the voltage applied to an avalanching semiconductor can be raised rapidly enough, it can be made to exceed the $I = 1$ condition [in Eq. (4.61)] for a brief interval. (1) Explain this. (2) The field is raised abruptly to the value giving $I = 3$, in a silicon semiconductor 10^{-3} cm thick, with uniform field distribution. Estimate the time constant of the increasing current, using limiting drift velocity obtained from Fig. 4.21. Use a simple model, beginning with a single electron.

4.9(c) In many insulators, even in thin-film form, it is not possible to observe avalanche-type breakdown, for destructive breakdown processes occur at lower fields. Discuss factors which may control whether breakdown occurs destructively or reversibly: carrier mobility, crystal perfection, temperature, ionizable impurity content, rate of rise of voltage, duty cycle of pulsed test voltage, insulator thickness, etc.

GENERAL REFERENCES

blished literature in the area of semiconduction is especially
ious. Theoretical work is to be found in *Physical Review*,

more recently in *Journal of Applied Physics*. Descriptions of devices have appeared most copiously in *Proceedings of the IRE*, with much early work in *Bell System Technical Journal*. The interested reader is especially directed toward *Proc. IRE*, vol. 40, November, 1952, and vol. 46, June, 1958, review issues on semiconductors. See also A. F. Gibson (ed.), "Progress in Semiconductors," John Wiley & Sons, Inc., New York, 1956. A number of pertinent articles, also of a review nature, have appeared in various volumes of *Solid State Physics* and in volumes of *Advances in Electronics and Electron Physics*.

Bube, R. H.: "Photoconductivity of Solids," John Wiley & Sons, Inc., New York, 1960.

Dunlap, W. C.: "An Introduction to Semiconductors," John Wiley & Sons, Inc., New York, 1957. (Nontheoretical and thoroughly readable; concentrates on technology.)

Hannay, N. B. (ed.): "Semiconductors," Reinhold Publishing Corporation, New York, 1959. (Comprehensive in properties of elementary and compound semiconductors; much material on preparation.)

Shockley, W.: "Electrons and Holes in Semiconductors," D. Van Nostrand Company, Inc., Princeton, N.J., 1950. (Suffers from unusual organization, but has very interesting use of analogs in developing semiconductor theory.)

Valdes, L. B.: "The Physical Theory of Transistors," McGraw-Hill Book Company, New York, 1961. (An excellent treatment at a readable level.)

Ziman, J. M.: "Electrons and Phonons," Clarendon Press, Oxford, 1960. (A detailed treatise of transport properties.)

5

Semiconductor junctions and devices

5.1 Understanding Inhomogeneous Semiconductors

Almost all semiconductor devices are comprised of a single-crystal semiconductor incorporating two or more semiconducting regions of different impurity density. The electric fields and carrier densities associated with the boundaries between differently doped regions, termed *junctions*, permit a wide variety of essentially nonlinear conductivity effects, in devices incorporating two, three, or more distinct regions.

Most devices can be understood through one-dimensional models in which the various regions are like the components of a large-area "sandwich." All variables are made functions of a single distance parameter z normal to the faces of the sandwich. The only major neglect is usually the surface-recombination effects at the edges (the "crusts" of the sandwich), which cannot be well accounted for in one-dimensional analysis. Since the important semiconductors have cubic structure, their conduction properties are isotropic; hence anisotropy does not limit the usefulness of one-dimensional models.

The conventional way of representing inhomogeneous semiconductors graphically is by an *energy-level diagram*, which can also describe variations of electric field and of Fermi energy. These diagrams (e.g., Figs. 5.2, 5.6, etc.) are used throughout the chapter. While equations such as (4.47) and (4.48) describe the electrical operation of a semiconductor, energy-level diagrams translate the complex equations into a

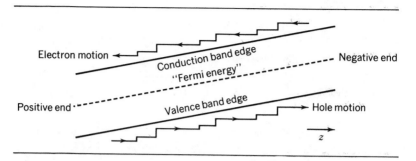

Figure 5.1   Schematic of electrons and holes moving in a semiconductor under the influence of a field. In actuality, the motion is more random, like Fig. 3.1, but this is a convenient model.

more readily visualized form. We have observed earlier that energies involved in electronic processes can seldom be defined absolutely. This is still the case, but we must define the potentials in semiconductor material with respect to z in order to determine the forces making electrons and holes move through the device. Suppose that in an otherwise uniform semiconductor (Fig. 5.1) a small electric field exists. The amount of energy a carrier picks up from the field (and returns to the lattice vibrations in collisions) is $e\mathcal{E}_z$ per unit z distance. In the energy-level diagram, therefore, if we *tilt* the band edges, electrons not colliding move horizontally, as shown. Electrons will pick up kinetic energy, so they must rise from near the bottom of the conduction band to higher levels. This is correctly depicted via such horizontal paths. At the same time, holes moving (in the direction of the field) will also pick up kinetic energy and drop *lower* in the electronic states of the valence band. With collisions, both electrons and holes give up this excess kinetic energy (remaining an average of $3kT/2$ away from the band edges). The figure shows electron and hole "trajectories," much exaggerated, because the actual mean free paths between thermalizing collisions are usually very small. In an energy-level diagram, therefore, electrons tend to "sink" toward the bottom of the conduction band, while holes tend to "float" toward the top of the valence band. On the basis of these arguments, in energy-level diagrams, electric fields, *whatever their source*, are represented by *slope of the band edges*.

When the material is inhomogeneous, the Fermi energy appropriate to different parts of the material must vary. In

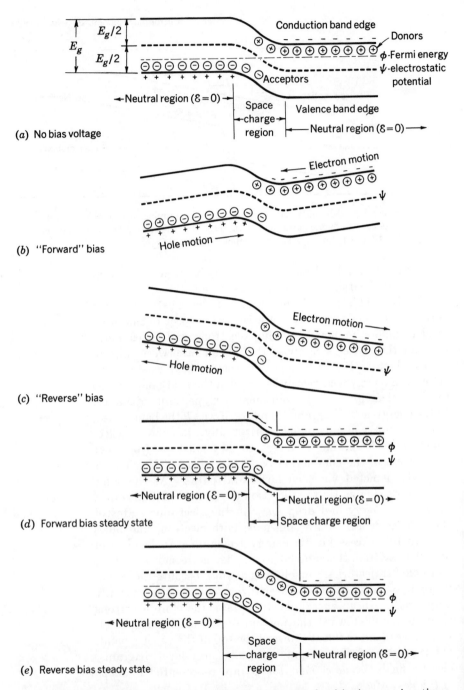

Figure 5.2 Energy levels and carrier and ionized-impurity densities in a p-n junction (a) at equilibrium; (b) immediately after application of a forward voltage; (c) immediately after application of a reverse voltage; (d) steady state with forward voltage; (e) steady state with reverse voltage. In (e), note how carriers have pulled back from the junction region.

n-type material it is nearer the edge of the conduction band, in p-type material nearer the edge of the valence band. At equilibrium, all parts of the semiconductor in contact with one another must have the *same* Fermi energy. Thus, in Fig. 5.2, which represents a semiconductor junction between n-type and p-type material, a line ϕ representing the Fermi energy must be horizontal, at equilibrium. When the semiconductor has applied fields and is therefore not in thermal equilibrium, one may still formally define the Fermi energy, for a particular carrier, as that energy for which the probability of occupation of electronic states is one-half. This energy will then be a function of z, $\phi = \phi(z)$.

In Fig. 5.2, which conveniently has an energy scale in electron volts, we construct a curve which lies parallel to the band edges but midway between them, which we term $\psi(z)$, the *electrostatic potential*. The field and charge density are now expressible in terms of derivatives of ψ. With the sign convention that electron energy increases toward the top of the diagram,

$$\nabla\psi\left(=\frac{d\psi}{dz}\right) = \mathcal{E} \qquad \nabla^2\psi\left(=\frac{d^2\psi}{dz^2}\right) = -\frac{\rho}{\epsilon} \tag{5.1}$$

There should be no confusion with the symbol ψ for a quantum wave function, within the context of this chapter. The *equilibrium* densities of electrons and holes may be expressed [following (4.16)] by

$$N = N_i e^{e(\phi-\psi)/kT}$$
$$P = N_i e^{-e(\phi-\psi)/kT} \tag{5.2}$$

Since $N = P = N_i$ when $\psi = \phi$, there is implicit in (5.2) an assumption of equal effective masses for electrons and holes. A more precise relation would introduce unwarranted "bookkeeping" complexity and add little to the value of results.

We can show that ϕ, not ψ, determines the potential measured by an outside observer, by considering the circuit of Fig. 5.3. Suppose that metal conductors A and B are connected to each end of the semiconductor sample, as shown. The interior parts of the semiconductor need not be at equilibrium. The Fermi level of A must become equal to that at one end of the semiconductor, while B must have the same Fermi level as the other end of the semiconductor. If the two uniform ends (A and B) of the semiconductor are long

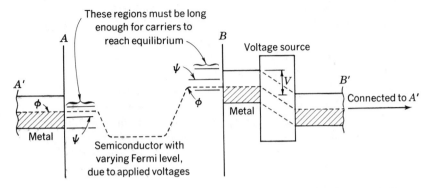

Figure 5.3   Where the semiconductor is in equilibrium, the Fermi energy indicates the potential which is measured by attached contacts.

enough, junctions in the central region will have little influence on electron and hole densities at the ends. The *potential difference* between A and B can be measured by connecting between them a voltage source which raises the potential of all electrons on end A above that of electrons on end B by an amount eV. If this potential is the same as the difference between the Fermi energies at the ends of the semiconductor (and hence in the metal), there will be no fields across the metal conductors. No current will flow; hence $V \equiv \phi_B - \phi_A$ is the *measured* voltage drop in the semiconductor.

A semiconductor energy-level diagram may, for descriptive purposes, be embellished with additional information. Electron and hole densities and the density of ionized impurities may be represented by the use of polarity signs, with the immobile ionized impurities represented by circled symbols, as in Fig. 5.2. While this does not aid analysis, it often improves visualization.

5.2   *p-n* Junctions: Qualitative Behavior

At the heart of most semiconductor devices are one or more junctions of p-type and n-type material. Junctions may be formed in a variety of fashions, as described in Sec. 5.13. In simple junctions, the electric resistance is a function of the direction and magnitude of an applied voltage; current flows more readily in one direction than oppositely. This is the desired property of a diode rectifier. It can be appreciated qualitatively by use of energy-level diagrams.

Figure 5.2a represents a p-n junction with no applied voltage. We assume henceforth that all impurity atoms are ionized, which is reasonable in many practical situations. Far away from the actual junction, majority-carrier density equals the donor or acceptor density. Precisely at the junction, the *net* impurity density is zero. Since there is adjacent material which is extrinsic, however, it is not necessary, even at equilibrium, that $P = N = N_i$, but only that $PN = N_i{}^2$. We cannot have a discontinuous step in ψ at the junction, for this would represent an *infinite* field. For the present, we shall assume only that ψ varies smoothly in the immediate vicinity of the junction, as shown. The density of electrons is naturally greater on the n side, while holes are more numerous on the p side. Some of the electrons on the right will have sufficient thermal energy to surmount the energy barrier and diffuse into the p region, while some of the majority holes on the left will diffuse into the n region. At the same time, the slope in ψ *favors* drift of the few (minority) electrons on the left into the n-type region; the holes on the right drift into the p-type region. At equilibrium, no net current can flow, so that these electron and hole currents due to drift and those in the opposite direction due to diffusion will exactly cancel.

Equilibrium is disturbed by application of a voltage across the ends of the junction. At the instant voltage is applied, the field distributes itself uniformly across the semiconductor, causing the energy-level diagram to "tilt" as shown in Fig. 5.2b, for the application of one polarity of voltage, and Fig. 5.2c, for the opposite polarity. *Majority* carriers react to the field by rushing *toward* the junction in Fig. 5.2b and away in Fig. 5.2c. The potential barrier at the junction prevents free motion of electrons into the p-type material and holes into the n region. There is, however, a redistribution of charge at the junction. For Fig. 5.2b a charge distribution is established which *reduces* the local field across the junction, whereas in Fig. 5.2c the charge distribution *increases* the field at the junction. Carriers flowing from the external circuit restore near-equilibrium hole and electron distributions in the homogeneous material at each end. Almost the entire applied potential drop appears near the junction, resulting in the steady-state situations of Fig. 5.2d and e. In the first case, the total potential differences which majority electrons and holes must surmount to diffuse across the junction is decreased, while in the second it is increased. At equilibrium the current

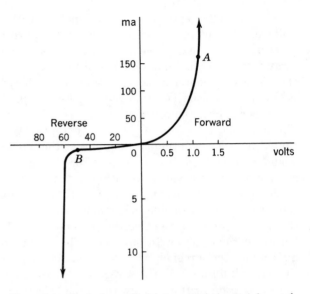

Figure 5.4 Typical *p-n* diode characteristic: *O-A* forward current with low voltage drop in the extrinsic regions; above *A*, resistance causes curve to approach straight line; *O-B* low reverse current; below *B*, avalanche breakdown.

of the majority carriers diffusing across the potential barrier just equaled the drift current in the opposite direction.   The minority-carrier drift current does not depend appreciably on the barrier height, only on the *supply* of minority carriers diffusing from the bulk material to drift across the junction. When the barrier height is reduced, the diffusion current increases, but the opposing minority-carrier drift current does not change appreciably.   A large resultant current flows; this direction of current flow is termed the "forward" direction. When the opposite polarity ("reverse" voltage) is applied, the barrier height *increases*.   The small minority-carrier drift currents continue to flow as before, but the diffusion current is reduced greatly.   The diffusion, or "injection," process is similar to thermionic emission; carriers must surmount a potential barrier to be injected across the junction.   The diffusion current, like thermionic currents, may be expected to depend exponentially on the barrier height, and thus on the applied voltage.   The total current density should be of the form

$$ J = \underset{\substack{\text{injection} \\ \text{current}}}{J_0 e^{eV/kT}} - \underset{\substack{\text{drift} \\ \text{current}}}{J_0} \tag{5.3} $$

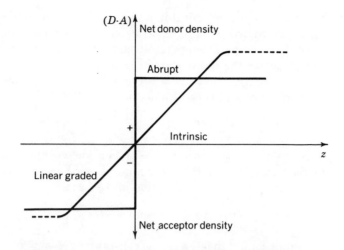

Figure 5.5   Idealized impurity concentrations of abrupt and linear-graded junctions.   In the graded junction, the significant region in which space-charge effects occur is a very small fraction of the total width of the graded region.

This type of V-J variation is obtained in the detailed solution in Sec. 5.4.   The exponential voltage-current characteristic is typical of semiconductor rectifiers.   At high forward voltages, current is somewhat limited by the ohmic resistivity of the material.   In the reverse direction, at high applied voltages, some form of breakdown will occur.   The overall voltage-current characteristic of a junction diode thus appears as in Fig. 5.4.

5.3   Theory of the Equilibrium *p-n* Junction; the Depletion Layer

Junctions are produced in a variety of ways.   In *diffused* junctions (Sec. 5.13) the impurity concentrations vary gradually from one region to the other; hence so does $D - A$. Junctions formed by alloying or by epitaxial deposition, on the other hand, have a nearly discontinuous, or "abrupt," change in impurity density.   Though it is possible to calculate the electrical characteristics of a junction with arbitrary impurity distribution, two idealized models, the *abrupt* junction and the linear-*graded* junction (Fig. 5.5), are most often assumed, for calculations.   Although an abrupt junction is in truth only a mathematical idealization, it is a reasonable approximation to the more abrupt of physical junctions. The impurity density in a linear-graded junction is assumed to be a linear function of the distance parameter; significant effects generally occur entirely *within* the linear slope region.

Space charge and ψ are at every point related by Poisson's equation. For any type of junction,

$$\nabla^2\psi = \frac{d^2\psi}{dx^2} = \frac{e}{\epsilon}[(D - A) + (P - N)] \tag{5.4}$$

where the impurity density $D - A$ is a known junction of z but the carrier charge $P - N$ is not. Equations (5.2) permit us to express $P - N$ as a function of $\psi - \phi$:

$$\frac{d^2\psi}{dx^2} = \frac{e}{\epsilon}\left[(D - A) + 2N_i \sinh\frac{e(\psi - \phi)}{kT}\right] \tag{5.5}$$

At equilibrium, since ϕ is a constant, $\nabla^2\psi \equiv \nabla^2(\psi - \phi)$. Using a normalized potential $u = e(\psi - \phi)/kT$ simplifies the relation to the form

$$\frac{d^2u}{dz^2} = \frac{e^2}{kT\epsilon}[(D - A) + 2N_i \sinh u] \tag{5.6}$$

Since (5.6) is a nonlinear, inhomogeneous second-order differential equation, we may not expect to obtain solutions except through approximation or by numerical analysis.

At or near the center of the actual junction, $\phi - \psi$ must pass through zero, which from (5.2) implies that the net carrier density $P - N$ must be zero. Over a region near this point, $P - N$ is much smaller than $D - A$. Accordingly, (5.6) may there be approximated by

$$\frac{d^2u}{dz^2} = \frac{e^2}{kT\epsilon}(D - A) \tag{5.7}$$

where $D - A$ is given from Fig. 5.5. Considering first an *abrupt junction*, we obtain as solutions to (5.7), near the center of the junction:

$$\text{For } z > 0 \qquad D - A = D \qquad u \cong D\frac{e^2}{kT\epsilon}z^2 - c_1z + c_2$$

$$\text{For } z < 0 \qquad D - A = -A \qquad u \cong -A\frac{e^2}{kT\epsilon}z^2 - c_3z + c_4 \tag{5.8}$$

where $c_1, \ldots, c_4$ are constants of integration, to be evaluated from the boundary conditions. Since (5.7) is just an electrostatic equation for a potential u and no lumped charge exists at the origin $z = 0$, u and its first derivative must both be continuous there. This requires $c_1 = c_3$ and $c_2 = c_4$.

The useful range of z for this approximation [which is that $(P - N) \ll (D - A)$] may be determined by substituting into the original Eq. (5.6); at least where $e(\phi - \psi)$ is only a few kT, since $N_i \ll D$ or A in a useful junction, the approximation is altogether valid. It can in fact be verified, by detailed numerical computation, that a reasonable overall solution is obtained by separating the junction into three regions (Fig. 5.6): (I) a uniform-potential p region $(-\infty <$

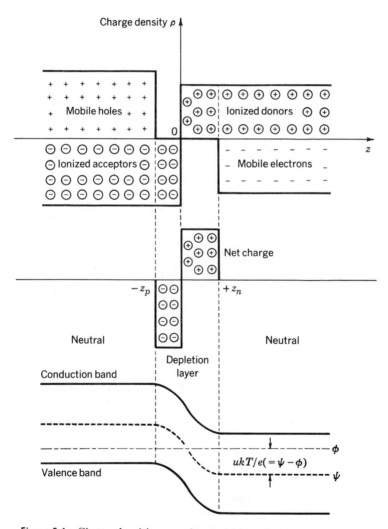

Figure 5.6 Charge densities, net charge, and potential variations in the approximate (depletion-layer) solution to the abrupt junction.

$z < -w_p$); (II) a region in which (5.7) and its solutions (5.8) apply $(-w_p < z < +w_n)$; and (III) a uniform-potential n region $(+w_n < z < +\infty)$.

The solution for u (and ψ) is completed by determining the values of c_1 and c_2 which allow solutions to be matched at the boundaries of the three regions. The solutions in regions I and III are obtained from (5.6) by setting $d^2u/dz^2 = 0$, whence

$$z \leq -w_p: \qquad u(z) = u(-w_p) = \sinh^{-1}\frac{-A}{2N_i} \cong -\ln\frac{A}{N_i}$$

$$z \geq w_n: \qquad u(z) = u(+w_n) = \sinh^{-1}\frac{D}{2N_i} \cong \ln\frac{D}{N_i} \qquad (5.9)$$

$$z \leq -w_p,\ z \geq w_p: \qquad \frac{du}{dz} = 0$$

The logarithmic approximation is valid, since $D/N_i \gg 1$ and $A/N_i \gg 1$. Substituting into (5.8), we obtain

$$w_n = \left[\frac{\ln(AD/N_i^2)}{D(e^2/kT\epsilon)}\right]^{\frac{1}{2}}$$

$$w_p = \left[\frac{\ln(AD/N_i^2)}{A(e^2/kT\epsilon)}\right]^{\frac{1}{2}} \qquad (5.10)$$

The resulting variation of ψ is shown in Fig. 5.6, along with the assumed space-charge densities. Although the exact solution has no such abrupt changes of charge density, there is still a substantial region of z over which the net mobile carrier density $(P - N)$ is nearly zero. This reduction of carrier charge is of course required because the Fermi energy moves toward the center of the band gap; each kT/e displacement of ψ produces a reduction of carrier density by a factor $\sim e = 2.718$. This region, near the junction, is termed the *depletion layer*, or *depletion region*. In any case, the *total* negative impurity-ion charge w_pA in the p part of the depletion layer equals the positive charge in the n part of the depletion layer, w_nD. This is required in order that fields vanish except near the junction.

In a typical junction with $A = D = 10^{15}$, $N_i = 10^{12}$, at $T = 300°K$, the total depletion layer width $(w_n + w_p)$ is of the order of 4×10^{-5} cm, as calculated from (5.10). If the change from p-type to n-type material takes place over a comparable or larger distance, it is more appropriate to apply the linear-graded-junction solution.

The approximate solution for the *graded junction* makes use of the same (depletion) approximation, where now the impurity density near the center of the junction may be expressed as

$$D - A = \frac{N_i z}{L_a}$$ (5.11)

The parameter L_a measures the gradient of impurity density, being the distance from junction center to a point at which the impurity density equals N_i. Using further normalization: $y = z/2L_a$ is taken as a (dimensionless) length parameter; $L_D{}^2 = kT\epsilon/2e^2N_i$ is also a characteristic length, termed in kinetic theory of plasmas the *Debye length*. Then the general relation (5.6) becomes

$$\frac{d^2u}{dy^2} = \frac{4L_a{}^2}{L_D{}^2}(y + \sinh u)$$ (5.12)

If L_a is *very* long, the junction is extremely slow-graded, and the assumption $\sinh u \ll y$ is nowhere valid. If L_a is short, however, so that $4L_a{}^2/L_D{}^2 \ll 1$, we may proceed as before, neglecting the $\sinh u$ term in the depletion region near $y = 0$. Thus, integrating (5.12) with $\sinh u$ omitted,

$$u = \frac{2L_a{}^2}{3L_D{}^2}y^3 - c_1 y + c_2$$ (5.13)

Because of the expected symmetry of the solution around $z = 0$, $c_2 = 0$. The constant c_1 may be used to fit the solution at the ends of the depletion layer: If we represent the depletion-layer limits as $\pm y_d$, equality of u and its first derivative at $y = +y_d$ requires

$$-\sinh^{-1}(y_d) \approx -\ln(2y_d) = \frac{2L_a{}^2}{3L_D{}^2}y_d{}^3 - c_1 y_d$$

$$-\mathrm{sech}\,(y_d) \approx -(1 + y_d{}^2)^{-\frac{1}{2}} = \frac{2L_a{}^2}{L_D{}^2}y_d - c_1$$ (5.14)

(The approximations to $\sinh^{-1}$ and sech apply for large y_d.) These may be solved readily by trail-and-error approximation. For example, in a germanium junction with $L_a = 10^{-5}$ cm, $N_i = 10^{12}$, at room temperature ($L_D = 1.2 \times 10^{-4}$ cm), one finds a depletion layer of width $(2y_d =)$ 13. Physical width is $(4L_a y_d =)$ 2.6×10^{-4} cm. If the material in the uniform regions had $D = A = 10^{15}$, the *total* length of the graded region would be at least $1,000L_a = 10^{-2}$ cm. The actual depletion region, typically, extends over only a small fraction of the graded region. An exact solution of the potential is plotted, together with the approximate solution obtained with our complete-depletion approximation, in Fig. 5.7.

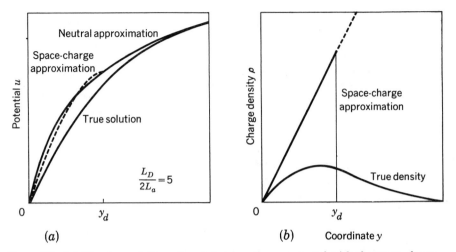

Figure 5.7 (*a*) The true solution of a graded junction, compared with the space-charge approximation (developed in the text) and the solution assuming $y = -\sinh u$. (*b*) The assumed space-charge distribution for the approximation used in the text (triangular) and the space-charge distribution of the true solution. [*Reprinted by permission of the copyright owner, American Telephone and Telegraph Company, and the authors S. P. Morgan and F. M. Smits. This figure originally appeared in the Bell System Tech. J.*, **39**:1573–1603 (1960).]

In both abrupt and graded junctions, the region over which the depletion layer extends is typically very small. This permits simplification of the nonequilibrium theory of junctions in the following sections.

5.4   Current Flow in *p-n* Junctions

When an electric field is applied to a semiconductor, charge carriers are no longer in thermal equilibrium with the lattice; diffusion and drift of majority carriers, into regions where they become minority carriers, upset the thermal-equilibrium relation $NP = N_i^2$. Although, in general, nonequilibrium situations resist precise statistical analysis, carrier-concentration calculation in semiconductors is simplified by the fact that within conduction and valence bands, carriers usually have almost normal *energy distributions*. (This is violated when fields approach 10^5 to 10^6 volts/cm, however.) Figure 5.8 shows typical equilibrium and nonequilibrium carrier distributions. The change in carrier density in nonequilibrium is the same as though the Fermi energy ϕ had moved toward,

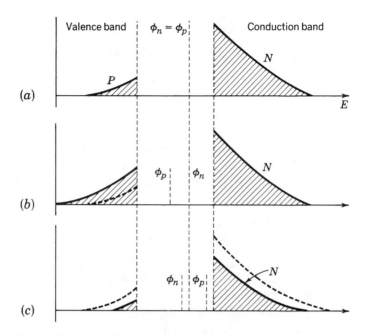

Figure 5.8 (*a*) Equilibrium carrier concentrations vs. energy *in an n-type semiconductor*, near a *p-n* junction. (*b*) Concentration as when holes are injected from *p*-type material (equilibrium concentration dashed). Note shift of ϕ_p away from ϕ_n. (*c*) Concentration as when junction is reverse-biased. Note that both ϕ_p and ϕ_n move away from their respective band edges.

or away from, one or both band edges. This makes it possible to represent the carrier densities by *quasi Fermi levels* (also called *imrefs*) ϕ_n and ϕ_p, *defined separately for electrons and for holes*. Using the symbolism of the previous section, but letting ϕ_p and ϕ_n represent the imrefs, *the carrier densities define the imrefs* by

$$N = N_i e^{e(\phi_n - \psi)/kT}$$
$$P = N_i e^{e(\psi - \phi_p)/kT}$$

(5.15)

In a part of the semiconductor remote from junctions, the carrier densities can be related by the equilibrium condition $NP = N_i^2$; the two imrefs converge to the true Fermi level. Where an excess or deficiency of carriers exists, however,

$$NP = N_i^2 e^{e(\phi_n - \phi_p)/kT}$$

(5.16)

Thus $\phi_n > \phi_p$, in a semiconductor containing *excess carriers* of either or both types. In a semiconducting region containing more or fewer carriers than in equilibrium, a metallic conductor in contact with the semiconductor can have no potential at which electrons do not transfer to, or from, the semiconductor.

The current transport equations of a semiconductor,

$$\mathbf{J}_p = e(\mu_p P \mathbf{\varepsilon} - D_p \nabla P)$$
$$\mathbf{J}_n = e(\mu_n N \mathbf{\varepsilon} + D_n \nabla N)$$

(4.42)

can be written much more compactly in terms of the imrefs. Since $\mathbf{\varepsilon} = \nabla \psi$ and Einstein's relation $\mu = eD/kT$ [Eq. (4.41)] relates mobility and diffusion constant, the current densities can be reduced to the forms

$$\mathbf{J}_p = e\mu_p P \nabla \phi_p$$
$$\mathbf{J}_N = e\mu_n N \nabla \phi_n$$

(5.17)

The absence of current flow, in the equilibrium case, is thus understood from the constancy of $\phi_p \equiv \phi_n \equiv \phi$.

A *forward* junction voltage sweeps extra minority carriers into the regions on both sides of the junction, making ϕ_n exceed ϕ_p in the vicinity. Even with substantial forward current, however, a depletion region still exists. Let its boundaries be $z = -z_p$ and $z = +z_n$, as defined in Fig. 5.9. We shall make the assumption that the regions to left and right of the depletion region are electrically neutral, which requires that ψ be constant. Consider first the n region to the right of the junction. We may safely presume that the density of minority carriers (holes) at point z_n differs from the equilibrium value, because of either injection of extra carriers or loss to the p region. The density of *majority* carriers, on the other hand, should be changed but little by the flow of current across the junction. The majority-carrier density can easily adjust itself to changes of minority-carrier density, to preserve electrical neutrality. If we define the hole density at $z = z_n$ as $p(z_n)$, then, by the diffusion theory of Sec. 4.8, in the region to the right of z_n the excess carrier density will be

$$\left[p(z_n) - \frac{N_i^2}{D} \right] e^{-(z-z_n)/L_p}$$

with a corresponding hole current given by (4.53) as

$$J_p = \frac{eD_p}{L_p} \left[p(z_p) - \frac{N_i^2}{D} \right] e^{-(z-z_n)/L_p} \qquad z > z_n$$

(5.18)

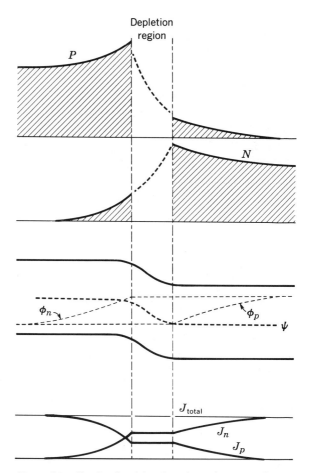

Figure 5.9 Carrier densities, imrefs, and current densities vs. position in a forward-biased p-n junction.

The corresponding solution for ϕ_p in the n-type material is shown in Fig. 5.9. Since the total current through the junction is a constant, the electron current is given by $J_n = J - J_p$, as shown. There is a slight correction in ϕ_n necessary to motivate the electron current flowing in the n region, but this is best accounted for simply by adding later the resistivity of the p-type and n-type material. One can show by substituting into (5.17) that, at moderate current densities, ϕ_n has only a very slight slope in the n region. We may, in the same fashion as above, solve for the ϕ's and excess-electron current in the p region, arriving therefore at complete solutions in regions on each side of the depletion layer (Fig. 5.9).   The electron current in the p region is given in terms of $n(-z_p)$ by

$$J_n = \frac{eD_n}{L_n} \left[n(-z_p) - \frac{N_i^2}{A} \right] e^{(z-z_p)/L_n} \qquad z < -z_p \tag{5.19}$$

Since the depletion region is narrow, there is little recombination of excess carriers there; hence the currents are not altered in passing through.   The *total* current density J is then simply the sum of the electron current at the left-hand boundary of the depletion region and the hole current at the right-hand boundary.

$$J = \frac{eD_n}{L_n} \left[n(-z_p) - \frac{N_i^2}{A} \right] + \frac{eD_p}{L_p} \left[p(z_n) - \frac{N_i^2}{D} \right] \tag{5.20}$$

It remains to determine the properties of the depletion region, so that we may determine the values of $n(-z_p)$ and $p(z_n)$, minority-carrier densities at the edges of this region, as functions of applied voltage.   The NP product is given everywhere by (5.16).   We shall assume first, then prove on the basis of the results obtained, that at least in the forward voltage region the variation of the imrefs across the depletion region is extremely small.   To good approximation $\phi_n - \phi_p$ equals the *applied* forward voltage V across the junction.   Then

$$NP = N_i^2 e^{eV/kT}$$

Since at $z = -z_p$, $P \cong A$, and at $z = z_n$, $N \cong D$, we then obtain

$$p(z_n) = \frac{N_i^2}{D} e^{eV/kT} \qquad n(-z_p) = \frac{N_i^2}{A} e^{eV/kT} \tag{5.21}$$

The total current may then be obtained from (5.20):

$$J = J_0(e^{eV/kT} - 1) \tag{5.22}$$

where $J_0 = eN_i^2(D_n/L_nA + D_p/L_pD)$.   The limiting current density at large reverse voltages, J_0, is usually termed the *reverse saturation current density*.   The fact that this current depends exponentially on temperature and on band gap through N_i^2 makes thermal stability a serious device problem, particularly in germanium diodes and transistors.   Silicon devices have a substantial advantage due to their much lower N_i^2.

Returning to the assumption of constancy of ϕ_p, observe that $\mathbf{J}_p = e\mu P \boldsymbol{\nabla}\phi_p$.   Thus $d\phi_p/dz = J_p/e\mu_p P$ has a maximum value when P is a *minimum*. The smallest value of P in the entire depletion region is at $z = z_n$, where it is given by (5.21). Thus $d\phi_p/dz$ (max), substituting the relation for J_p, is

$$\frac{d\phi_p}{dz} \text{ (max)} = \frac{kT}{eL_p} (1 - e^{-eV/kT}) \tag{5.23}$$

The factor with the exponential can be no more than unity with forward voltages. At room temperature, kT/e is about $\frac{1}{40}$ volt while L_p will typically be much larger than the depletion-layer width. The biggest *slope* that ϕ_p can have is $\frac{1}{40}$ volt per L_p distance; over the entire depletion-region width this must be much less than kT/e. The assumption that ϕ_p (and ϕ_n, by the same argument) is near-constant in the depletion regions is justified. When V is large negative, this argument is clearly not valid. The physical argument for existence of a reverse saturation limit and a J-V characteristic as given by (5.22) has been made in a previous section, however.

If desired, the relation (5.22) may be corrected for junction resistance due to potential drops in the p-type and n-type material. To good approximation,

$$V = V_{\text{applied}} - J\left(\frac{l_p}{e\mu_p A}\right) + \frac{l_n}{e\mu_n D} \tag{5.24}$$

The expression in parentheses is the ohmic resistance of the material of length l_p and l_n on either side of the depletion region. Actually, this is slightly pessimistic, for in the minority-carrier diffusion regions near the depletion region, *both* carriers contribute to the total current flow.

In carrying out this derivation, there was implicitly assumed to be a depletion region. If the impurity "grading" is so gradual that no depletion region exists, then the entire semiconductor will conduct ohmically, with conductivity appropriate to the equilibrium carrier density in each portion of its length. While such a spread-out junction has no particular value, the impurity density in actual devices is sometimes graded gradually from high to low values with the *same* type of impurity. A semiconductor region which is more highly doped than an adjacent n-type or p-type region is often termed an n_+ or p_+ region. Such doping introduces no depletion region and no junction effects as such. It can be effective in reducing ohmic voltage drops; in some devices it may serve to confine the depletion-region fields into a relatively thin region while maintaining a relatively high reverse-bias break-down voltage. These device requirements are discussed in later sections.

5.5 Metal-Semiconductor Contacts

Simple junctions, or *bonds*, between metals and semicon-ductors are required to bring currents into and out of semi-conductor devices. This type of contact should be *ohmic;* i.e., the resistance should be independent of the direction of cur-rent flow. Obviously, such connections should also have a low overall resistance, for efficient device performance.

Intimate bonds between dissimilar materials such as metals and semiconductors generally involve some amount of alloying and/or interdiffusion of the metals into one another. To what extent an alloy is formed depends on the bonding process. Ohmic contacts to semiconductors are generally of two types. One employs a material which is itself a practical impurity agent in the semiconductor. Then, even if the material is alloyed or interdiffused appreciably, if the type of semiconductor formed (*n* type or *p* type) is the same as that in the material connected to, there will be no observed junction effect. The best contacts to semiconductors are made using metals which alloy well with the semiconductor at reasonable temperatures; many are those used for metal-to-metal solder-ing (e.g., tin, indium). Gold, nickel, and aluminum are well suited for high-temperature operation. Contacts are often applied by electroplating (e.g., nickel) or by vacuum evapora-tion (aluminum). Particularly in these two processes, semi-conductor surface cleanliness is very important.

When care is not taken to secure an adequately cleaned surface on the semiconductor, rectification often takes place between a metal and semiconductor. Metal point contacts pressed against a silicon surface exposed to air develop con-duction characteristics similar to those of a semiconductor *p-n* junction. Several phenomena can lead to these rectifying metal-semiconductor junctions. They can roughly be sepa-rated into two groups, in one of which holes take a considerable part, while in the other only electrons are significant. Holes have real significance only in a semiconductor. Therefore, in order for holes to be important in a metal-semiconductor con-tact, an initially *n*-type semiconductor must somehow develop at least a narrow *p*-type region. Figure 5.10 illustrates a way

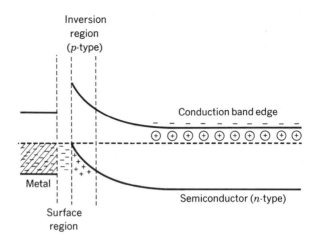

Inversion
region
(*p*-type)

Conduction band edge

Metal

Semiconductor (*n*-type)

Surface
region

Figure 5.10   Charge-trapping model of metal-semiconductor junction.   Attrition of free and valence-band
electrons from *n*-type material adjacent to junction produces an inversion region which conducts by hole motion.

in which this is thought to take place.   A semiconductor
surface, treated properly, will have a high density of surface
states which trap carriers.   In the *n*-type semiconductors
used for many such rectifiers, the trapping states have such an
attraction for electrons that they can hold a substantial surface
charge.   In moderately doped *n*-type semiconductors, the
surface states may deplete electrons from the inner material
to the surface so strongly that not only is donor charge exposed,
but some electrons are even removed from the valence band,
giving this material a *p*-type character.   The figure shows an
appropriate equilibrium charge density and potential diagram.
The region just inside the surface is said to be *inverted* to *p*-type
behavior.   The semiconductor in fact acts like a *p-n* junction,
even without the metal contact.   A metal contact applied by
pressing it against the surface makes contact to the inverted
surface region.   Application of forward and reverse voltages
then produces currents like those of a normal semiconductor
junction.   The particular contact metal does not influence
appreciably the conduction characteristics; it may be chosen
for mechanical hardness or stiffness (e.g., tungsten).

   Another explanation of metal-semiconductor junction
rectification suggests that the relative *work functions* of the
metal and semiconductor may be involved in the action.

Work function is the energy required to move an electron from the material into the vacuum. If the metal has a larger work function than the semiconductor, the metal will presumably have an affinity for the electrons of the semiconductor. This leads to a variation in potentials near the junction. Here, however, it is usually presumed that the field variations take place over extremely short distances, so that there is really no appreciable part of the semiconductor to which p-type character may be assigned (Fig. 5.11). Analysis of operation is based on the equations of thermionic emission: electrons sur-

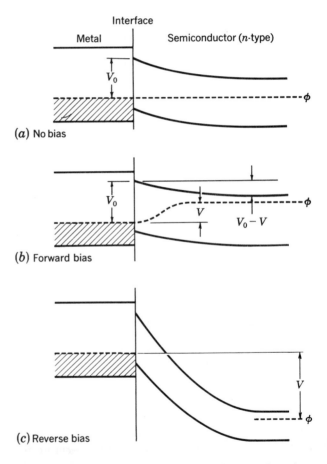

Figure 5.11 Work-function barrier model of metal-semiconductor junction, having no inversion region and operating much like a thermionic diode.

mounting a barrier of height V_0 will produce a *Schottky-emission* current density

$$J_{m \to s} = A T^2 e^{-eV_0/kT} \tag{5.25}$$

where A is the usual thermionic constant (120 amp/cm²-°K²). Electrons in the metal, according to the diagram, will experience such a barrier V_0 related to the work functions of the metal and semiconductor. Electrons in the (n-type) semiconductor, on the other hand, must surmount a barrier of only $V_0 - V$, with V the applied voltage. Electron current "emitted" from semiconductor into metal will therefore be

$$J_{s \to m} = A T^2 e^{-e(V_0 - V)/kT} \tag{5.26}$$

The total current is the difference of the two components,

$$J = A T^2 e^{-eV_0/kT}(e^{eV/kT} - 1) \tag{5.27}$$

which is the same form obtained for the *p-n* junction (5.22).

While details of the electron-injection process at the barrier do not appreciably alter the voltage-current relation, the presence of an insulating layer between the metal and semiconductor in some diodes makes it necessary to explain electron transit via quantum tunneling (Sec. B.2). This of course alters the value of the current from (5.27).

For many years, large-area rectifiers utilizing polycrystalline semiconductors such as copper oxide and selenium have been manufactured. These operate as metal-semiconductor junctions. In some cases actual insulating layers placed between the metal and the semiconductor have been found empirically to improve rectification. Because these rectifiers can carry only low current densities (because of low mobilities), they have been largely superseded by silicon junction rectifiers, which are smaller and much more efficient.

At *microwave frequencies*, a rectifying diode capacitance of the order of 1 $\mu\mu f$ represents a very sizable susceptance. At 30,000 Mc/sec, such a capacitance has a reactance of only about 50 ohms. The capacitance of the depletion layer of a practical-sized junction (say, 10^{-2} cm in diameter) may be considerably more than this, as we show in the section following. The forward resistance of a typical small-area diode, due mostly to the resistance of the connecting metallic conductors, may be a few ohms, while the reverse resistance may be limited by surface currents, etc., to a few hundred ohms (values fairly typical of microwave diodes). If the high reverse resistance, which is the property most useful in detection and mixing, is not to be short-circuited by an excessively high capacitance, the junction area must be made very small. Such a small junction area is made cheaply and easily by use of a tungsten "cat's whisker" which has been sharpened by electrolytic etching. The actual contact dimensions of the wire pressed against the semiconductor may be of the order of 0.0001 in. or less. The n-type silicon used as the semiconductor in microwave diodes is heavily doped (0.001 to 0.1 ohm-cm). The low electron mobility due to the impurity concentration is of little importance in a diode, where only resistivity counts. Thus practical radio-frequency diodes may even be made from polycrystalline materials. Early diodes were adjusted by hand to the proper contact-position pressure for best rectification. Many modern diodes have hermetically sealed mountings, which are assembled automatically.

The point-contact form of diode is relatively cheap, for no critical high-temperature processing is required during assembly. Consequently, certain types of low-power, high-voltage (of the order of 100 volts maximum reverse bias), power-rectifying diodes use this same principle. Higher-voltage diodes of this construction use less strongly doped semiconductor material, so that the junction region is broader.

Point-contact diodes have served as useful detectors for radiation at wavelengths of 1 mm, although at that wavelength it seems necessary to hand-build and adjust the contact for best performance; detector life, stability, and reliability are very poor, because of the microscopic dimensions of the metal contact. Even with their fragility, however, point-contact diodes are the only semiconductor devices which can operate well upward of 10,000 Mc. Some diodes are formed using gold-alloy contacts. These can be electrically fused to the semiconductor by passing a momentary high current. The resulting tiny junctions are much more sturdy than those using pressure contact, and with suitable technology frequency response is nearly as high as in pressure-contact units.

5.6 Device Principles Involving Control of Depletion-region Width

The depletion region in an idealized semiconductor p-n junction is characterized by a "double layer" of charge (i.e., as in

Fig. 5.6). Since the width of the depletion region increases as reverse voltage is applied across the junction, charge is carried through the external circuit as it would in a circuit containing a capacitance. If the amount of charge were directly proportional to the applied voltage, we could characterize the reverse-biased junction by a constant capacitance in shunt with a "leakage" resistance. Such a linear relationship does not exist, as we shall now demonstrate, thus leading to the interesting concept of a voltage-dependent capacitance. Devices built to exploit this behavior are termed varactor (*variable-reactor*) diodes.

The voltage dependence of depletion-layer capacitance can be found by calculating the width of the depletion region as reverse voltage is applied. In the linear-graded-junction theory, the solution for the depletion-layer width in the presence of bias may be carried out approximately, by again assuming that the region is completely depleted of carrier charges, and the *difference* of the *electrostatic potential* across the depletion layer equals V' (Fig. 5.12a). Letting u represent *only* $e\psi/kT$, as from (5.4), solution (5.13) is applicable.

Starting from (5.13), u is again zero at $y = 0$, but equals $[(e/kT)V']/2$ at y_d. Approximately, $du/dy = 0$ at y_d. The relation between V' and y_d is then

$$\frac{e}{kT}\frac{V'}{2} = \frac{4}{3}\left(\frac{L_A}{L_D}\right)^2 y_d^3$$ (5.28)

The capacitance at a given voltage V' is determined by changing the voltage by an amount dV' and measuring the change in the charge dQ on one plate of the "capacitor," i.e., the ion charge exposed on each side of the junction by the displacement of the boundaries of the depletion layer.

$$dQ = e\frac{N_i z}{L_a}dz = 4eN_i y_d L_A\, dy_d$$ (5.29)

The voltage dV' required to move the depletion-layer boundary a distance dy_d is obtained by differentiating (5.28), whereby

$$dV' = \frac{8kT}{e}\left(\frac{L_A}{L_D}\right)^2 y_d^2\, dy_d$$ (5.30)

Dividing the previous relation by this,

$$\frac{dQ}{dV'} = \frac{eN_i^2}{4kT}\left(\frac{L_D}{L_A}\right)^2\frac{L_A}{y_d}$$

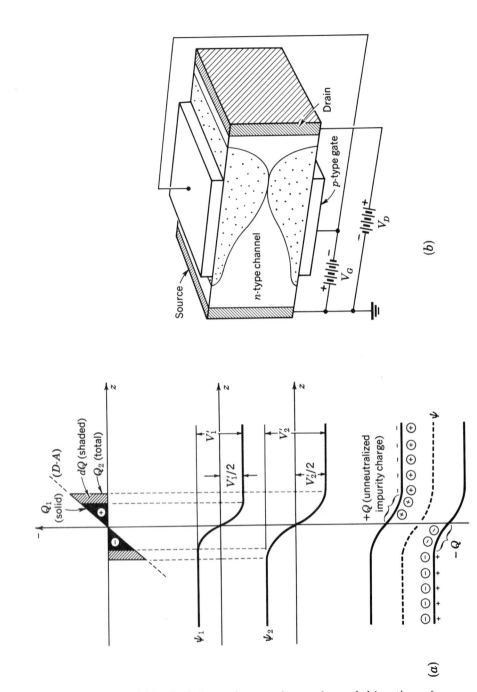

Figure 5.12 (a) Model for depletion-region capacitance of a graded junction. Increase of reverse voltage causes withdrawal of mobile carriers from the junction, removing charge dQ. Q_1, Q_2 and V_1, V_2 represent two different charge and voltage conditions. (b) The unipolar transistor uses the expansion of depletion regions to close off a conducting channel. [*G. C. Dacey and I. M. Ross, Proc. IRE,* **41**:970 (1953).]

Returning to (5.28), we obtain y_d as a function of V'; thence

$$C = \frac{dQ}{dV'} = \left(\frac{e\epsilon^2 N_i}{12 L_A}\right)^{\frac{1}{3}} \left(\frac{1}{V'}\right)^{\frac{1}{3}} \qquad \text{per unit area} \qquad (5.31)$$

If a similar calculation is carried out for an abrupt junction, one finds

$$C = \left[\frac{e\epsilon D A}{4(D + A)}\right]^{\frac{1}{2}} \left(\frac{1}{V'}\right)^{\frac{1}{2}} \qquad \text{per unit area} \qquad (5.32)$$

To be precise, V' is the difference in the *electrostatic potential* across the junction. Reference to Fig. 5.12a shows that the actual applied voltage is less than this by an amount

$$\sim \frac{kT}{e} \ln \frac{DA}{N_i^2}$$

With particularly low applied voltages (or forward voltage), therefore, one should use

$$V' = V_{\text{applied}} + \frac{kT}{e} \ln \frac{DA}{N_i^2} \qquad (5.33)$$

It is instructive to calculate a typical capacitance at the zero-bias point. Assuming an abrupt junction with $E_g = 0.7$ ev, $N_i = 10^{12}$, $D = A = 10^{18}$, and $\epsilon = 15.7\epsilon_0$ (germanium), the capacitance C is 0.35 μf/cm². A junction of area 0.002 $\times$ 0.002 cm would have $C = 1.4$ $\mu\mu$f. Junctions of this size and even smaller can be produced for microwave applications.

Since the most important characteristics of varactor diodes are large relative capacitance change and low resistive current, an abrupt junction provides a superior varactor diode compared with a graded junction; this may be understood intuitively in terms of the easier forcing back of the depletion-layer boundary in the abrupt junction. Low saturation current J_0 is compatible with large capacitance change, for the saturation current (5.22) will be low if the diffusion length is long, the impurity density great, and the mobility small. Low-loss diodes are therefore feasible. A high impurity density also reduces the resistance of the p- and n-type regions which are electrically in series with the junction. This is very important in high-frequency applications, since a variable capacitance in series with a resistance has a parallel equivalent circuit having an effectively smaller reactance change at higher frequencies.

Varactor diodes have several interesting applications. At radio and higher frequencies, they are used in adjusting the frequency of a tuned inductance-capacitance circuit by varying a biasing voltage across the varactor diode. These elements can also be used in *parametric amplifiers* and as highly efficient harmonic generators. Small junctions are formed by alloying a small gold-alloy wire directly to form the junction or by selectively etching a larger junction area. Effective operation at high gigacycle frequencies can be achieved.

The variation of depletion-layer width can also be used in an amplifying device, the *unipolar* transistor. Figure 5.12*b* shows a schematic form of one such device. A region of semiconductor of one majority-carrier type is sandwiched between regions of the opposite type. Metal contacts termed the "source" and "drain" (usually interchangeable) connect to the two ends of the central region, or "channel." Reverse bias applied simultaneously to the two outer ("gate") regions permits no current to be drawn, but increases the width of the two depletion regions. The conducting cross section of the channel is thereby reduced, increasing the resistance appearing between source and drain. These electrodes form the output circuit, permitting the current through a load resistor to be varied. As shown in the figure, the effective reverse bias on the channel can be enhanced by the power supply voltage to produce a sort of positive feedback. Because the width of a depletion region is relatively small, device dimensions are necessarily small. Impedances are relatively high as compared with those of other solid-state amplifiers.

It has been found that similar modulation of channel conductance can be produced even when the gate region is a metal electrode isolated from the channel proper by a thin insulating layer. This type of device is called a *"field-effect" transistor*. No gate current flows, despite the polarity of the gate voltage. The depletion effect here is due to trapping of carriers at the semiconductor-insulator boundary, where the surface charge must correspond to the charge on the capacitor formed by the insulator. This type of device can be made using single-crystal material or with evaporated-film semiconductors such as cadmium sulfide. Although power capacity is low because of the dimensions involved, operation extends to frequencies of hundreds of megacycles in some units. The upper frequency limit is determined by a combination of capacitance effects and the conductance of the channel, so that materials of high mobility give superior high-frequency performance.

5.7 Minority-carrier Transport: The Transistor

Transistors are by far the most useful of semiconductor devices because of their three-terminal (isolated input and output) character. In our previous discussions of junction diodes, it was assumed that the homogeneous regions on each side of the junction proper were sufficiently long to permit minority carriers to recombine. A transistor, however, is characterized by two or more junctions separated by distances *much less* than the diffusion length (L_p or L_n). Carrier lifetimes attained in transistor materials, of the order of 1 msec, lead to diffusion lengths of the order of 0.1 cm. Junction spacings less than 0.001 in. are possible with some techniques, so that it is possible to have very little minority-carrier recombination between a pair of junctions.

For purposes of explanation, we consider a *p-n-p transistor* containing *p*-type semiconducting material on each end, *n*-type material in a narrow center region, and abrupt junctions separating the three regions. The detailed nature of the junctions or depletion layers will not enter into the static arguments if we assume the depletion layers to be narrow. The choice of the *p-n-p* configuration, rather than *n-p-n*, is arbitrary. All procedures and relations of the *p-n-p* solution can also be used for the *n-p-n*, in most cases by interchanging all *p*'s and *n*'s in the equations. Construction is assumed to be planar, as used in most modern high-quality transistors.

The central region is termed the *base*. One of the outer regions is termed the *emitter*, the other the *collector*. The emitter and collector are to a large degree interchangeable, except where nonuniform base impurity density is employed. Collector size and placement often reflect the fact that most power dissipation occurs in this region. In operation, a large reverse-voltage bias is placed on the base-collector junction, thereby defining its function. The impurity level in the base region is made substantially smaller than in the emitter, to reduce the amount of nonuseful carriers (electrons) injected from it. The impurity level of the collector is based on the current and voltage desired; high breakdown voltage requires low impurity content, while high current requires a short length plus high impurity content. Representative values of room-temperature conductivity are a fraction of an ohm-centimeter in the emitter and collector and several ohm-centimeters in the base.

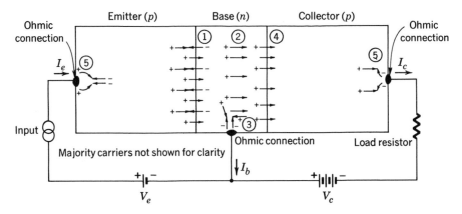

Figure 5.13   Schematic of p-n-p junction transistor operation.   Emitter-base junction is forward-biased, base-collector junction reverse-biased.   (1) Many holes are injected into base region, electrons into emitter region.   (2) Holes *diffuse* across base region, some recombining with electrons from the base contact (3).   Some holes reach collector (4), representing useful output current which can be a substantial fraction of emitter current.   (5) Holes in emitter and collector combine with electrons in metallic contacts to permit current flow to external circuit.   (The circuit shown is termed "common-base"; owing to its low current gain, it is used only where maximum emitter-collector isolation is required, as, for example, at high frequencies.)

Here is a simple explanation of transistor action (Fig. 5.13): The collector junction is reverse-biased with respect to the base.   In the absence of injection (hole) current in the base, therefore, only the reverse saturation current density J_{0c} flows in the collector circuit.   The emitter is normally forward-biased with respect to the base, injecting large numbers of holes into the base and a smaller number of electrons from the base into the emitter.   Many of the holes diffuse across the base, which will be an electrically neutral (constant-potential) region if uniformly doped.   These holes flow readily into the collector to produce current in the collector circuit.   Collector current is essentially independent of the collector voltage.   Current injected from a low-impedance source in the emitter circuit can be collected by a high-impedance load circuit, producing voltage and power gain.   The most popular transistor circuit configuration, the *common-emitter circuit*, applies a signal current input between base and emitter.   A much larger current flows in the base-collector load circuit.   This results in a higher input impedance, and both current and voltage gain.   In this circuit the transistor is analogous to a vacuum triode, the base corresponding to the triode's control-grid electrode.

In the analysis we must carefully discriminate between the *total* minority-carrier density (N,P) and the *excess* density (n,p). The excess density is defined as the difference between the total and that which would appear in the absence of applied potentials, for example, $p_n = N_i^2/D$. The steady-state equation governing the motion of the holes in the base region is, from (4.50),

$$L_p^2 \frac{\partial^2 p}{\partial x^2} = p$$

Following Middlebrook's treatment,[1] the general solution in the base region $(-w_0 < x < w_0)$ can be written in hyperbolic functions:

$$p = A \sinh \frac{w_0 - x}{L_p} + B \sinh \frac{w_0 + x}{L_p} \qquad (5.34)$$

where x is measured from the center of the base region; (5.34) is completely equivalent to $C_1 e^{-x/L_p} + C_2 e^{x/L_p}$, but is simpler in the subsequent determination of the coefficients A and B from the boundary conditions. At the emitter junction, the B term vanishes, while at the collector junction the A term vanishes. The total hole densities at the base side of the emitter and collector junctions depend upon the voltages applied to the junctions; according to Eqs. (5.21),

$$
\begin{aligned}
P(-w_0) &= p_n e^{eV_e/kT} \\
P(w_0) &= p e^{eV_c/kT}
\end{aligned}
\qquad (5.35)
$$

The voltages as before are positive when in the forward direction. The total hole density in the base at the *collector* junction will be negligibly small at large *negative* V_c. Referring to Fig. 5.13 the large reverse bias "sucks" all holes from the vicinity of the junction because of the highly favorable potential distribution. Substituting (5.35) into (5.34) yields the excess hole density in the base region:

$$p = \frac{p_n(e^{eV_e/kT} - 1) \sinh \dfrac{w_0 - x}{L_p} - p_n(1 - e^{eV_c/kT}) \sinh \dfrac{w_0 + x}{L_n}}{\sinh \dfrac{2w_0}{L_p}} \qquad (5.36)$$

[1] R. D. Middlebrook, "An Introduction to Junction Transistor Theory," p. 133, John Wiley & Sons, Inc., New York, 1957.

Substituting this into (4.42) then gives the hole diffusion-current density in the base:

$$J_p = \frac{\dfrac{eD_p}{L_p} p_n(e^{eV_e/kT} - 1) \cosh \dfrac{w_0 - x}{L_p} + p_n(e^{eV_c/kT} - 1) \cosh \dfrac{w_0 + x}{L_p}}{\sinh \dfrac{2w_0}{L_p}}$$

$$-w_0 < x < w_0 \qquad (5.37)$$

The hole current density at each junction can be obtained by substituting for $x = \pm w_0$:

$$J_p(w_0) = \frac{eD_p}{L_p} \left[p_n(e^{eV_e/kT} - 1) \operatorname{csch} \frac{2w_0}{L_p} + p_n(1 - e^{eV_c/kT}) \coth \frac{2w_0}{L_p} \right]$$

$$J_p(-w_0) = \frac{eD_p}{L_p} \left[p_n(e^{eV_e/kT} - 1) \coth \frac{2w_0}{L_p} + p_n(1 - e^{eV_c/kT}) \operatorname{csch} \frac{2w_0}{L_p} \right]$$

$$(5.38)$$

These relations are sufficiently complicated so as to convey little meaning in mathematical form. Figure 5.14 therefore illustrates, for base width $2w_0$ somewhat less than L_p, how the hole density and diffusion current will vary across the base.

In addition to the hole current which flows into the base from the emitter and in part continues through the base into the collector, there are also electron injection currents flowing from the base into the forward-biased emitter and into the collector. It is assumed that the metal contacts joining emitter and collector to *external* circuits are ohmic, so that no additional rectifying action can take place. It is convenient to assume that the overall lengths of emitter and collector regions are much greater than the diffusion length. The electron current density injected into the emitter and the collector can be inferred from (5.22), with proper substitutions for the emitter and collector voltages:

$$J_n(\text{emitter}) = en_{pe} \frac{D_{ne}}{L_{ne}} (e^{eV_e/kT} - 1)$$

$$J_n(\text{collector}) = en_{pc} \frac{D_{nc}}{L_{nc}} (e^{eV_c/kT} - 1) \simeq - \frac{en_{pc}D_{nc}}{L_{nc}}$$

$$(5.39)$$

where

$$n_{pe} = \frac{N_i^2}{P_e} \simeq \frac{N_i^2}{A_{\text{emitter}}}$$

$$n_{pc} = \frac{N_i^2}{P_c} \simeq \frac{N_i^2}{A_{\text{collector}}}$$

The diffusion constants $(D_{ne},\ D_{nc})$ and diffusion lengths $(L_{ne},\ L_{nc})$ are identified separately for emitter and collector, since they will be influenced by differing impurity densities.

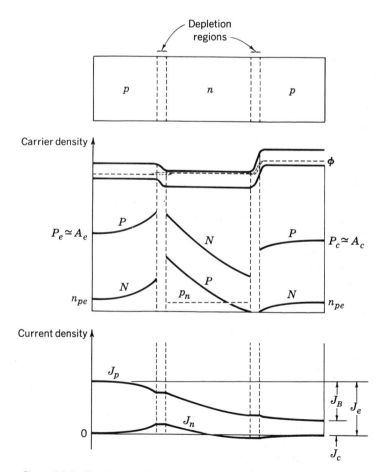

Figure 5.14   Carrier densities and current densities in a p-n-p junction transistor with forward-biased emitter junction.   Recombination of holes in the base is much exaggerated.

The total current flow at the emitter and collector junctions is the sum of electron and hole currents, or

$$J_{\text{emitter}} = \left(\frac{en_{pe}D_{ne}}{L_{ne}} + \frac{ep_nD_p}{L_p} \coth \frac{2w_0}{L_p} \right) (e^{eV_e/kT} - 1)$$

$$+ \frac{ep_nD_p}{L_p} \operatorname{csch} \left(\frac{2w_0}{L_p} \right) (1 - e^{eV_c/kT})$$

$$J_{\text{collector}} = \frac{ep_nD_p}{L_p} \operatorname{csch} \left(\frac{2w_0}{L_p} \right) (e^{eV_e/kT} - 1)$$

$$+ \left(\frac{ep_nD_p}{L_p} \coth \frac{2w_0}{L_p} - \frac{en_{pc}D_{nc}}{L_{nc}} \right) (1 - e^{eV_c/kT})$$

$$(5.40)$$

The emitter-base current is composed partly of useful holes and partly of useless electrons. The ratio $J_p(-w_0)/J_{\text{emitter}}$, from Eqs. (5.38) and (5.40), is termed the *injection efficiency*. This depends on the ratio of doping in the base and emitter, and may be increased through increase of emitter doping. Of the holes injected at the emitter, only part arrive at the collector and are useful. This fraction, termed the *transport factor*, is obtained by dividing $J_p(w_0)/J_p(-w_0)$, from (5.38). In the limit where the forward emitter voltage is much greater than kT, and the *reverse* collector voltage likewise, this ratio becomes sech $(2w_0/L_p)$, or for narrow base width $\approx [1 + (2w_0/L_p)^2]^{-1}$. This clearly indicates the need for a narrow base region.

In the application of transistors to electronic amplification, efficient injection and transport of holes from emitter to collector is all-important. Transistors, like vacuum tubes, are generally characterized by small-signal, or incremental, parameters. The *short-circuit current gain* α_{FB} is the change in collector current per unit change in emitter current with all applied voltages maintained at constant bias levels. Of more interest in common-emitter circuits is the *forward current transfer ratio*, h_{FE}, defined as the collector current change per unit base current change at fixed biases $[h_{\text{FE}} = \alpha_{\text{FB}}/(1 - \alpha_{\text{FB}})]$. While α_{FB} never attains a unity value, h_{FE} can have values in the hundreds.

Equations (5.40) define the nonlinear static characteristics of this idealized transistor model. The base "current density" can be found as the difference of emitter and collector current densities. The area from which total base *current* is calculated must be that of the *junctions*, and not that through which the base current is actually introduced (transversely) from an external circuit.

Actual device characteristics, as suggested by (5.40), are

nonlinear.   Device curves (Fig. 5.15) have significant linear regions, however.   The almost complete independence of collector current on collector voltage is of course due to the fact that fields from the collector do not extend far enough into the base region to affect the diffusion of holes across the base.

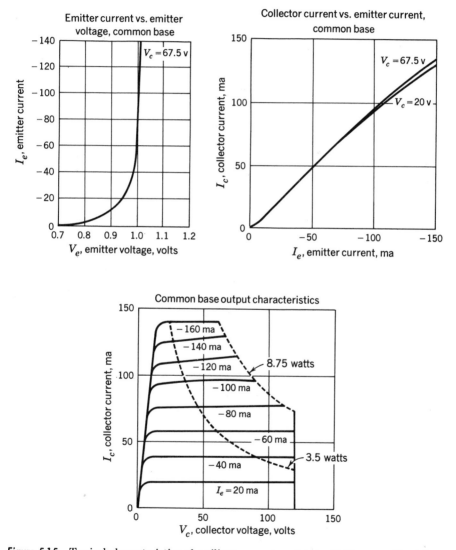

Figure 5.15   Typical characteristics of a silicon *n-p-n* transistor.   Ratings are $V_e \leqq 1$ volt, $V_c \leqq 120$ volts, 8.75-watt dissipation at 25°C.   (*Texas Instruments, Inc., type* 2N122.)

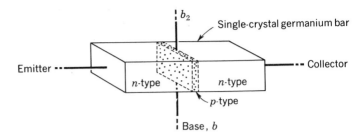

Figure 5.16   A tetrode transistor arrangement permits control of the gain through application of a field across the base region in a direction *transverse* to carrier diffusion.

In actual transistors, processes more subtle than those described by Eqs. (5.40) also influence the transport of minority carriers through the base region. It is now typical to have nonuniform doping in the base regions, in which case electric fields occur in this region and produce drift as well as diffusion of the carriers. This is discussed briefly in Sec. 5.11. Another principle which increases collector current is an enhanced minority-carrier flow from the collector into the base region, produced by the ohmic voltage drop caused by the hole currents injected across the base. Without the primary transport current, there is almost no field in the collector region, and minority-carrier flow into the base is diffusion-limited, but with the field there can be increases of 10 per cent or more in the collector current. This helps to offset the current lost because of low injection efficiency at the emitter, making possible very high values of h_{FE}.†

The transistor is most commonly a simple three-terminal device, as described above. There are other forms, however, such as the *tetrode* transistor pictured in Fig. 5.16. Two base connections are brought out, from the two ends of a long narrow base region. Application of a voltage *across* this region, between contacts B_1 and B_2, has the effect of changing emitter-junction bias on parts of the emitter. In the *p-n-p* device shown, if the control voltage is increased, the upper part of the emitter junction is reverse-biased and cannot inject carriers. The control action is thus a *gain* control, something like that in a tetrode vacuum tube. The low conductivity required in the base region, plus the need for current supplied

---

† These and other properties of transistors are discussed in L. P. Hunter (ed.), "Handbook of Semiconductor Electronics," sec. 4, McGraw-Hill Book Company, New York, 1962.

in the control circuit, limits the application of this type of device. Such factors, in addition to the greater complexity of this and other hybrid devices, have made the simple p-n-p and n-p-n junction transistors by far the most important semiconductor-amplifier devices.

Because of the extensive application of transistors in linear and nonlinear circuits, extensive parameterizations have been made. This permits detailed characterization, as demanded, for example, in applications in high-reliability circuits. This parameterization is described in several of the listed references. For certain applications, primarily in computer switching circuits, the transistor is best viewed in its circuit function as a *charge-control* device: charge supplied to the base region controls collector-circuit charge which charges the internal and circuit capacitances.[1]

5.8   Avalanching Junctions; *p-n-p-n* Devices

With sufficiently large reverse bias, any junction will suffer a "breakdown" in which current increases well beyond the J_0 value defined in the simple junction theory. This can be the result of either of two processes. In very highly doped junctions, particularly more abruptly graded ones, a quantum tunneling effect (similar to that discussed in the following section) can occur. Where the electric fields are smaller, in a graded or lightly doped junction, avalanche processes prevail. The tunneling process was first postulated by Zener. The term *Zener diode* is, however, applied to all voltage-limited diodes, most of which actually operate via avalanche processes.

In a junction with reverse applied voltage, the depletion layer becomes wider than at equilibrium. Using the abrupt-junction depletion-region theory of Sec. 5.3, with the difference in the electrostatic potential across the region given by V', the width of the region (for $D = A$) is approximately

$$w = \left(\frac{2V'\epsilon}{eD}\right)^{\frac{1}{2}} \qquad (5.41)$$

The field in the region is nearly uniform; if it were precisely so, it would be given by V'/w; that is,

$$\mathcal{E} \cong \left(\frac{eDV'}{2\epsilon}\right)^{\frac{1}{2}} \qquad (5.42)$$

---

[1] For a charge-control analysis of the transistor, cf. D. leCroisette, "Transistors," Prentice-Hall, Inc., Englewood Cliffs, N.J., 1963.

The field accordingly varies with the $\frac{1}{2}$ power of the voltage and the impurity density in the material. For $D = 10^{16}$ in germanium, the field reaches 2×10^5 volts/cm with an applied voltage of about 20 volts. The depletion-layer width at this point is therefore about 10^{-4} cm. The actual voltage at which current should become infinite may be estimated, since in uniform field the condition becomes $\alpha w = 1$ (where α is the average pair-generation probability of Sec. 4.9):

$$\alpha = \frac{1}{w} = \left(\frac{eD}{2V'\epsilon}\right)^{\frac{1}{2}} \cong \frac{eD}{2\epsilon\mathcal{E}} \tag{5.43}$$

By plotting this relation between α and $\mathcal{E}$ against a curve of ionization probability α (e.g., Fig. 4.22a) vs. field, the intersection of the two curves gives breakdown field and voltage as functions of impurity density D. A similar procedure may be carried out for graded junctions.

A major application of avalanche junctions is as voltage-regulator diodes. Operated well up on the current-multiplication curve, the voltage across a Zener diode is constant except for a slight slope in the voltage-current characteristic produced by the ohmic resistance of the p and n regions (cf. Fig. 5.4). Such diodes are generally built with substantial heat-dissipating capacity, for this mode of operation requires power dissipation far greater than in normal rectifier application.

All junctions suffer breakdown at high reverse voltages. Unless a unit is constructed specifically with this in mind, however, the precise voltage at which breakdown occurs will not be uniform from one unit to the next. Voltage-regulator diodes are generally produced by diffusion (Sec. 5.13), which permits accurate control of impurity concentration and allows breakdown voltage to be reduced in one or more processing steps, to a desired value.

Avalanche processes also occur in transistor junctions when high reverse-bias voltages are applied. The maximum collector voltage which may be applied to a transistor is often limited by this effect. Even below the voltage at which substantial avalanche multiplication takes place, however, a small current multiplication due to avalanching can increase the effective transport efficiency of a transistor, permitting the unit to exhibit a considerably higher h_{FE} than at lower collector voltage. This is clearly not a highly stable point of operation, however, since small collector-voltage changes can strongly affect the multiplication factor. Another voltage-limiting factor in transistors is known as "punch-through." This occurs, particularly in lightly doped or graded-junction units, when the base-collector depletion layer is so broadened by reverse collector bias that it extends to the emitter-base depletion layer. Holes can then travel directly between emitter and collector without control action of the base voltage. This phenomenon, like the avalanche-breakdown process, is nondestructive so long as power dissipation does not become so high as to melt semiconductor or contacts or cause undesirable diffusion of impurities within the operating device.

Devices incorporating three junctions in a p-n-p-n configuration exhibit behavior resembling breakdown phenomena. The three junctions are located close enough to one another so that minority-carrier diffusion can take place over the entire region (Fig. 5.17a). A voltage is applied across the outer

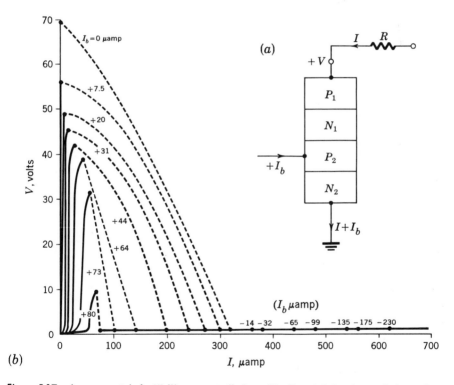

Figure 5.17   A p-n-p-n triode ("silicon controlled rectifier").   (a) Device and electrode arrangement; (b) characteristics, for various values of bias current I_b.   [$After\ I.\ M.$ $Mackintosh,\ Proc.\ IRE,$ **46**:1229 (1958).]

terminals, so that the central junction is reverse-biased and the outer junctions forward-biased. When the voltage is raised to a value causing breakdown of the central junction, the outer junctions inject carriers toward the central regions. While the central junction remains slightly reverse-biased, the diffusion of these carriers permits a large current to flow with only a low voltage on the device. The *V-I* characteristic (Fig. 5.17*b*) is similar to that of a gas-discharge diode. Control is achieved through external connection to one of the central regions (either *p* or *n*), so that one of the end junctions may be forward-biased. The diffusion of carriers from this junction reduces the voltage at which "breakdown" occurs, resulting in the family of curves shown in the figure. Since only very low control voltages are required to cause the device to break down by this mechanism, the device may be thought of as a controlled switch. It has many applications in power control. Silicon devices carrying 300 amp or more are available. In 60-cycle power control applicatons, the unit recovers from the breakdown condition when the voltage reverses, reverse-biasing the twŏ outer junctions.

5.9   Quantum Tunneling in Semiconductor Junctions

Semiconductor junctions can exhibit high-field phenomena never observed in metallic conductors, because the very narrow width of the depletion region sustains the entire reverse applied voltage. Under most conditions, high-current characteristics above critical voltages are associated with avalanche-breakdown processes. In certain devices, however, electrons may quantum-mechanically *tunnel* directly across the depletion region.

The basic phenomenon of tunneling is described in Sec. B.2, where the example shows that tunneling through regions of more than a few tens of angstroms, with energy in the tunneling region of the order of 1 ev above the electron energy, is so improbable as to lead to almost negligible electron transit. One requirement, therefore, is an extremely narrow depletion region. With a depletion-region width w less than 100 A, furthermore, avalanche multiplication is small, because even with substantial pair-generation probabilities, α, the product $\alpha w \ll 1$.

A second, and almost obvious, requirement for tunneling is that electrons in states on one side of the depletion region lie directly opposite *empty* electronic states on the opposite side. This will clearly be true in a very strongly reverse-biased junction. It is also true, *in parts of the forward-voltage region*, for junctions so heavily doped as to be *degenerate*. Where in a normal semiconductor the Fermi energy at room temperature lies between the impurity band and the center of the band gap, in a degenerate semiconductor it will normally lie *within* the allowed bands. A rough approximation to the position of the Fermi energy may be made by estimating the density of electronic states in a conduction band. With spherical constant-energy surfaces as an approximation, and with an effective mass m^*, the total number of states in the conduction band up to an energy E_0 above band bottom is given by [cf. Eq. (C.34)]

$$\frac{8\pi(2m^*)^{\frac{3}{2}}E_0^{\frac{3}{2}}}{3h^3}$$

Taking as an example $m^* = 0.1m_e$ and $E_0 = 0.06$ ev, we find only 2×10^{18} states up to this level. At absolute zero, the Fermi energy of a degenerate n-type semiconductor lies *above* the bottom of the conduction band, between it and the top of the impurity band. At higher temperatures, it will even rise, if the density of states in the conduction band is low.

Figure 5.18 gives a crude picture of the operation of a *tunnel diode* (often termed an Esaki diode, after its inventor). The energies of filled and of empty states are shown for purposes of the explanation. It may be helpful to think in terms of $T = 0°\text{K}$ operation, which is not different in principle from operation at ordinary temperatures. The band edges shown are not the edges of the normal valence and conduction bands, for degeneracy extends the bands toward the center of the band gap. With large negative voltages (Fig. 5.18a), electrons in the p region are brought to energy levels above the uppermost filled states in the n region, and we find large tunneling currents. At zero voltage (Fig. 5.18b) the electrons of both bands lie opposite one another, and no tunneling takes place. As voltage is increased positive, electrons in the n region come opposite unfilled states (mainly those associated with the acceptor band) in the p region, and electron current flows to the left via tunneling. This current reaches a maximum at approximately the voltage, V_{peak}, described by Fig. 5.18c, where a maximum of electrons lie opposite unfilled states. As the voltage is increased even further, the number of electrons

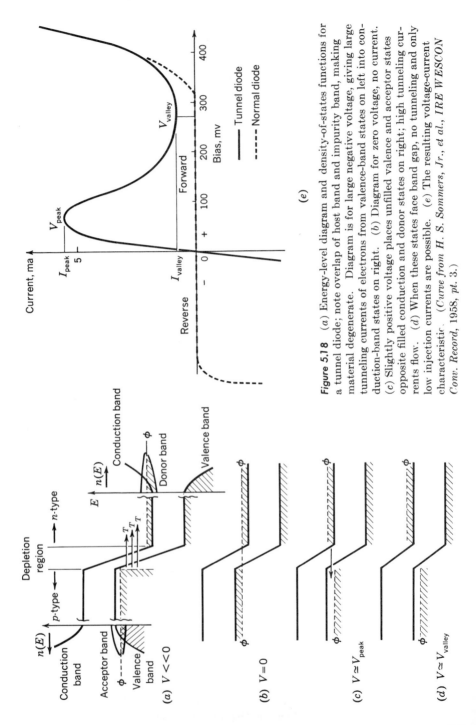

Figure 5.18 (a) Energy-level diagram and density-of-states functions for a tunnel diode; note overlap of host band and impurity band, making material degenerate. Diagram is for large negative voltage, giving large tunneling currents of electrons from valence-band states on left into conduction-band states on right. (b) Diagram for zero voltage, no current. (c) Slightly positive voltage places unfilled valence and acceptor states opposite filled conduction and donor states on right; high tunneling current flow. (d) When these states face band gap, no tunneling and only low injection currents are possible. (e) The resulting voltage-current characteristic. (*Curve from H. S. Sommers, Jr., et al., IRE WESCON Conv. Record, 1958, pt. 3.*)

lying opposite unfilled states is decreased because of the forbidden band. Finally, at the voltage V_{valley} (Fig. 5.18d), no further tunneling is possible. At higher voltages, however, the diode begins to carry its normal forward diffusion current due to thermal carriers surmounting the potential barrier. This will occur only at substantially greater junction voltages than in a normal junction, since the expression for current in a junction (5.22) contains the impurity density in the denominator. Accordingly, the resultant voltage-current characteristic is something like that shown in Fig. 5.18e. The exact shape of the curve must be a function of the precise distance the electrons must tunnel, the shape of the potential barrier, and the densities of electrons and states available to them. While in many tunnel diodes it is possible to achieve close approximations to theoretically predicted curves, there is often a much larger "tail" on the tunneling characteristic than can be readily predicted. Since electrons can tunnel only at constant energy, this cannot be attributed to oblique motion of electrons across the barrier. It is rather the result of tunneling of electrons in impurity or defect states within the forbidden band. Peak-current–valley-current ratio is an important practical measure of tunnel diodes. Ratios of 10:1 or even higher can be produced. Typical valley voltage for germanium or silicon tunnel diodes is $\sim$0.25 volt.

It is interesting to check roughly the tunneling probabilities, using a simple theory. The depletion layer of an abrupt junction, according to (5.10), has a width for $D = A$, at zero applied voltage given by

$$2L_D \left(\frac{2N_i}{D}\right)^{\frac{1}{2}} \left(\ln \frac{D^2}{N_i{}^2}\right)^{\frac{1}{2}}$$

Using $L_D = 10^{-4}$ cm as appropriate for germanium near room temperature, with $N_i = 10^{12}$, $D = 10^{19}$, the width is about 50 A. Using the expression derived in Sec. B.2, for tunneling across a triangular potential barrier, with effective field given by the band gap ($\sim$0.6 ev) divided by the depletion region width, $\mathcal{E}_z \cong 10^6$ volts/cm. The tunneling probability, according to (B.25), is of the order of

$$\exp\left[-\frac{4}{3}\frac{(2m)^{\frac{1}{2}}}{e\mathcal{E}_z \hbar} V_0{}^{\frac{3}{2}}\right] \simeq e^{-10}$$

We may estimate the current approaching the barrier by assuming that one-half of the carriers are moving at thermal velocity $(kT/2 = m^*v_T{}^2)/2$ *toward* the barrier, giving $v_T \approx 1.5 \times 10^7$ cm/sec. $J_{\text{incident}} \cong eDv_T/2 \approx 1.2 \times 10^7$ amp/cm². With e^{-10} probability of passage, we predict current densities of 500 amp/cm², in reasonable agreement with observed values. Even higher doping gives current densities as great as 100,000 amp/cm².

As contrasted to avalanching, tunneling is an extremely *rapid* phenomenon, suited therefore to microwave-frequency devices. Small oscillators delivering milliwatt powers have been constructed well above 1,000 Mc/sec, using a single tunnel diode. The devices are also of interest as computer elements because of the bistable character when connected to a voltage supply through a high resistance. Here again rapid switching is important. The very low voltage at which the device operates and the large current densities obtained in small devices can make it less attractive, since power capabilities are extremely small, while impedances are low.

Tunneling can also be observed in comparably thin insulating films. While these materials, in thicker layers, do not exhibit the classical characteristics of semiconductors, the tunneling process does not require a single-crystal sample.

5.10   Junction Photodevices

Electron-hole pair generation in semiconductors is utilized in a variety of devices, both for photosensing and for energy conversion. While many explicit forms of devices have been constructed, they generally fall into three categories. The first and simplest are merely *p-n* diodes, operated with reverse voltage bias. Photons impinge, producing pairs, near the semiconductor junction. The majority carrier of the generated pair is ineffective, but once the minority carrier diffuses to the actual junction, it will be swept over and into the other side (Fig. 5.19a). Passage of a carrier produces a current in the external circuit. If the minority carrier recombines before diffusing to the junction, it is not recorded. Accordingly, only those pairs generated within less than a diffusion length from the junction are effective. *Surface* recombination can be a serious problem, because the carriers are generated near the illuminated surface.

A second class of photodevices takes advantage of a transistorlike geometry, where the *base* region is illuminated, but not connected to an external circuit. In the absence of

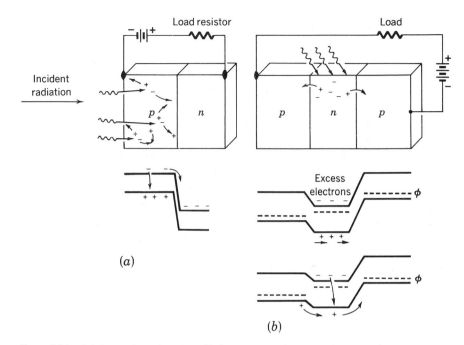

Figure 5.19   (*a*) Operation of a photodiode; (*b*) operation of a phototransistor.

illumination, the collector junction is reverse-biased (Fig. 5.19*b*) and little current flows.   Minority carriers released by photon pair production in the base region can diffuse to the emitter and collector regions, leaving a surplus of majority carriers (see figure) whose space charge *forward-biases* the emitter junction.   This permits injection of additional minority carriers across the junction.   Those diffusing minority carriers which recombine in the base region eventually neutralize the remaining excess majority charge.   There will result an increase of collected current by a factor the same as h_{FE}, that factor by which the collector current exceeds the base current in a conventionally operated transistor.   As in photoconductivity (Sec. 4.7), the response time of the device is nearly inversely proportional to the amplification factor, since slow recombination of the charge "trapped" in the base region is required for high gain.

The third, and certainly the most important, type of photodevice is the *photovoltaic* (energy-conversion) cell. This, too, is a simple junction diode, generally constructed

with very large surface area to collect a large photon flux.
Minority carriers generated within a diffusion length of the
junction diffuse to the junction, as in the simple photodiode.
The minority carrier is carried across by the electrostatic field
$\nabla\psi$ in the depletion layer.   This field will still be present,
however, even when a *forward* voltage difference approaching
the band gap appears across the junction (Fig. 5.20b).   For
the two carriers to recombine, an electron must move through
the external circuit.   If there is no external-current path,
majority-carrier excess charge will build up on both sides of
the junction, tending to reduce the step in the electrostatic
potential.   Figure 5.20a shows a short-circuited photovoltaic
junction, Fig. 5.20b the junction in the open-circuit condition, where the electrostatic potential variation is almost
canceled by the space charge.   Figure 5.20c is an intermediate
condition in which there are both an external voltage generated
and current flow in an external circuit.

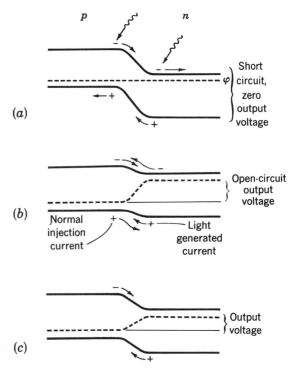

Figure 5.20 Photovoltaic diode.

The open-circuit voltage V_0 of the diode is determined by observing that the light-generated current J_L flows in the opposite direction to the normal forward-bias diode current and is almost totally insensitive to junction voltage. The junction will pass a forward current given by (5.22). When the cell is open-circuited, the two opposing currents must be equal; hence

$$J_0(e^{eV_0/kT} - 1) = J_L$$

and

$$V_0 = \frac{kT}{e} \ln\left(\frac{J_L}{J_0} + 1\right)$$

(5.44)

From (5.22), note that lightly doped high-carrier-lifetime semiconductors will produce a larger open-circuit voltage. Although Eqs. (5.44) do not apply if the calculated V_0 nears or exceeds the band-gap voltage, with solar illumination of actual devices the voltage does not approach this level. An open-circuit voltage of 0.5 volt or less is typical of silicon diodes. These are the most commonly used units, because of their relatively large band gap and the ease of producing a large-area oxidized surface with low surface recombination velocity. Only a small fraction of the photon energy of the usual source, sunlight, is utilized in pair production. Accordingly, theoretical limiting conversion efficiencies of these devices as "solar cells" are only about 20 per cent.

5.11 Transient and Time-dependent Effects

The discussion of junction phenomena and devices has thus far been limited to the steady state. A number of characteristic effects may control the dynamic performance of devices. Among these are junction capacitance, diffusion velocity, drift velocity, initial transients required to establish excess carrier density in forward-biased junctions, and transients required to remove carriers when reverse bias is applied.

Junction capacitance is of particular concern in high-frequency or switching transistors and diodes. The emitter-base capacitance shunts the input circuit directly; with the conductance of the emitter-base junction, this sets a limit on the product of gain and bandwidth of an amplifier using a transistor. The position of the base-collector capacitance in the transistor circuit may place it as a feedback element

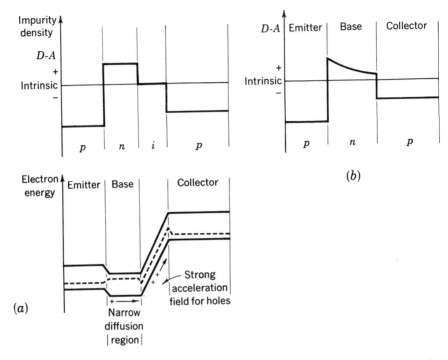

Figure 5.21 (*a*) Impurity concentration and energy-level diagram of a *p-n-i-p* transistor; (*b*) impurity concentration of a graded-base transistor.

between input and output. In transistor *switching circuits*, the input current to the base electrode must charge this capacitance, increasing the time delay of the circuit. The junction capacitances depend on the abruptness of the junctions and the impurity density on each side of the junction; a lower density or a broader junction will reduce the capacity, but a broader base region leads to lower gain and longer diffusion time. This consideration led to the *p-n-i-p* (or alternatively, *n-p-i-n*) transistor (Fig. 5.21*a*), incorporating an intrinsic region between actual base and collector. This may be viewed as an extended base-collector junction. Capacitance is substantially reduced, and the usual depletion-layer electrostatic field is spread out over the intrinsic region. Carrier drift time across the intrinsic region is small compared with the time required for carriers to diffuse an equal distance. The base region can be made somewhat narrower than in a simple *p-n-p* transistor, but an excessively narrow base width increases the resistance of the current path from the base contact. A further modification is the incorporation of a graded impurity density in the base (Fig. 5.21*b*). Here, fields of the collector-junction depletion region extend far into the base region. All modern high-frequency and switching transistors employ base grading to some degree. Conduction by *drift* takes place at an average velocity

$$v_{\text{drift}} = \mu \mathcal{E}$$

A current injected into a region of width w in which a field ($\mathcal{E}$) exists will thus cross the region in a time

$$\tau \cong \frac{w}{\mu \mathcal{E}} \tag{5.45}$$

For example, holes having mobility of 1,000 cm²/volt-sec will cross a region 10^{-4} cm wide in a field of 10^4 volts/cm in 10^{-11} sec. This time, typical of depletion-layer transit, is small compared with the transit time through uniformly doped base regions, which minority carriers must cross by diffusion. The equation of motion of excess holes in a field-free (diffusion) region is given by [Eq. (4.47)]

$$\frac{\partial p}{\partial t} = -\frac{p}{\tau_p} + D_p \frac{\partial^2 p}{\partial x^2} \tag{5.46}$$

It is instructive to imagine propagation of "waves" of excess holes, of the form

$$p = p_0 e^{j\omega t} e^{-kz} \tag{5.47}$$

Substituting into (5.46) yields for k, the "propagation constant,"

$$k^2 = j \left(\frac{\omega}{D_p} - \frac{j}{D_p \tau_p} \right) \tag{5.48}$$

At the high frequencies of interest, the first term is the only one which need be considered. The propagation of small-amplitude signal "waves" across the diffusion region is, accordingly, of the form

$$\exp j \left[\omega t - \left(\frac{\omega}{D_p} \right)^{\frac{1}{2}} z \right] \exp \left[-\left(\frac{\omega}{D_p} \right)^{\frac{1}{2}} z \right] \tag{5.49}$$

The group velocity, hence the velocity at which signals propagate through the region, is found by differentiation and inversion of the propagation constant $(\omega/D_p)^{\frac{1}{2}}$.

$$v_{\text{group}} = 2(\omega D_p)^{\frac{1}{2}} \tag{5.50}$$

For example, at 100 Mc/sec, in an n-p-n silicon device, signals propagate at a velocity of 3.4×10^5 cm/sec. In a base region of width 10^{-3} cm, however, such signals would suffer a total phase shift of about 1.9 rad and from (5.49) would have an associated attenuation of the order of $e^{-1.9}$. This serves to demonstrate the very serious problems encountered in the design of high-frequency transistors and the need to go to extremely thin and graded-impurity base regions to achieve high-frequency response. If a collector-base voltage of 10 volts can be distributed uniformly across the same 10^{-3}-cm base region, Fig. 4.21 suggests that the carrier drift velocity can be increased to about 6×10^6 cm/sec, reducing the signal loss and phase shift to manageable values. It is possible, using graded-base techniques, to attain useful transistor operation at many hundreds of megacycles.

In extrinsic regions like the emitter and collector material of a transistor, it is not necessary for carriers to *diffuse* to produce a current in the output conductor because conduction is largely via majority carriers, just as in a metal. An important parameter in this connection, however, is the "relaxation time" of *majority* carriers in the device. The arrival from the base of a burst of minority carriers into the collector region momentarily unbalances the space-charge neutrality of the region. A field is established by this space charge, upon which majority carriers rearrange themselves to neutralize the field. Other carriers move in from the collector contact to represent current flows in the external metallic circuit. The characteristic time required for majority carriers to neutralize this space-charge field is called the *relaxation time* τ_r. The *total* current density in the charge-rearrangement process is zero:

$$\nabla \times \mathfrak{IC} = J_{\text{total}} = 0 = J_{\text{convection}} + \epsilon \frac{\partial \mathcal{E}}{\partial t}$$

where $J_{\text{convection}} = e\mathcal{E}(\mu_p P + \mu_n N) = \sigma\mathcal{E}$. The solutions of $\sigma\mathcal{E} + \epsilon(\partial\mathcal{E}/\partial t) = 0$ are of the form $e^{\pm(t/\tau_r)}$, where

$$\tau_r = \frac{\epsilon}{\sigma} \tag{5.51}$$

In 1-ohm-cm germanium, relaxation time is $\sim$14 nanosec (14×10^{-9} sec). In transistors and other devices operating at frequencies of 100 Mc/sec or more, therefore, the assumption of electrically charge-neutralized emitter, base, and col-

lector regions may not be justified.   Use of short emitter and
collector regions, high-conductivity material, and short connection wires minimizes high-frequency effects.

The effects known collectively as "minority-carrier storage effects" refer to the high excess minority-carrier densities
which occur in a junction which is strongly forward-biased,

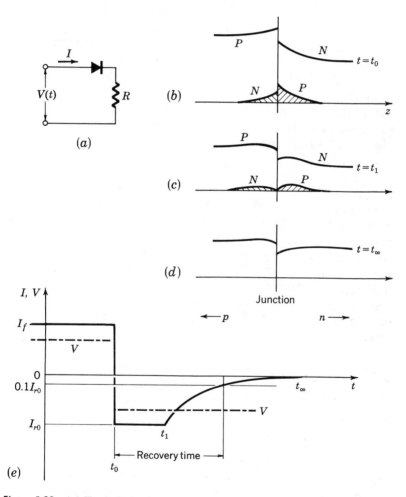

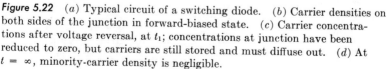

Figure 5.22   (a) Typical circuit of a switching diode.   (b) Carrier densities on
both sides of the junction in forward-biased state.   (c) Carrier concentrations after voltage reversal, at t_1; concentrations at junction have been
reduced to zero, but carriers are still stored and must diffuse out.   (d) At
$t = \infty$, minority-carrier density is negligible.

as compared with the equilibrium or the reverse-bias state. The phenomenon causes difficulties primarily in switching diodes and transistors, when a junction is abruptly switched from a condition of substantial forward current flow toward high reverse voltage. The relatively large minority-carrier density on both sides of the junction is a source of large transient currents, as these carriers return across the depletion layer (Fig. 5.22). Reverse voltage is generally applied through a resistor in the external circuit; during part of the transient "recovery" period the junction acts almost as a short circuit, the current being determined by the reverse drive voltage and this series resistance. The integrated transient current can almost equal the minority carriers "stored" in the junction. If the peak transient current is large, a large fraction of the stored minority carriers can return. If, however, the transient extends for a time comparable with the carrier lifetime or longer, a large fraction of the carriers will recombine without returning.

All conventional transistors depend on minority-carrier injection into the base; hence minority-carrier storage effects must retard high-speed switching somewhat. In switching diodes and transistors it is common to introduce gold, an impurity which acts as a recombination center, to decrease carrier lifetime. In narrow-base transistors, gain is slightly reduced, but switching time is greatly decreased. Metal-semiconductor diodes of the surface-barrier type, employing only one type of carrier, do not exhibit minority-carrier storage, explaining why high-microwave-frequency operation is possible.

5.12   Semiconductor Thermoelectrics

Thermoelectricity in semiconductors is a much more significant effect than it is in metals. Figure 5.23 should help explain this. An n-type semiconductor is shown connected via an ohmic junction to a metallic conductor. Passage of electron current from the semiconductor to the metal causes lowering of the energy of the transported electrons. Heat is given off in the process. When the current is reversed, only the higher-energy electrons from the metal pass into the semiconductor. Heat must be supplied to reestablish the proper thermal distribution of the electrons of the metal. The amount of heat absorbed or given off, per electron transferred, may be of the

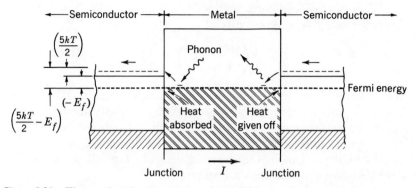

Figure 5.23   Thermoelectric effect at junctions of metal and n-type semiconductor.

order of $E_g/2$. This contrasts strongly with the far more subtle effects in metals.

The transport theory of Chap. 3 may again be applied, since it was based on a generalized electron-energy distribution $f_0(E)$. The Seebeck coefficient α is then given by (3.74), where the I_j represent the integrals (3.57). The derivative of f_0,

$$\frac{\partial f_0}{\partial E} = \frac{2}{h^3}\frac{1}{kT}\,(e^{(E-E_f)/kT} + 1)^{-2}e^{(E-E_f)/kT}$$

can be approximated closely, throughout the conduction band of an n-type semiconductor, by

$$\frac{\partial f_0}{\partial E} = -\frac{2}{h^3}\frac{1}{kT}\,e^{-(E-E_f)/kT} \tag{5.52}$$

The integrals I_j may now be evaluated.

$$I_j = \frac{4\pi 2^{\frac{3}{2}}m^{*\frac{3}{2}}}{3}\int_0^\infty \tau E^{j+\frac{3}{2}}\frac{\partial f_0}{\partial E}\,dE$$

$$\cong \text{const} \times \tau \int_0^\infty E^{j+\frac{3}{2}}e^{-E/kT}\,dE \tag{5.53}$$

The constant will not be needed further. The mean free time τ is removed from the integral because its variation over the occupied electronic states of the conduction band is very small. Using integral tables,

$$\int_0^\infty E^{j+\frac{3}{2}}e^{-E/kT}\,dE = \Gamma\left(\frac{j+3}{2}\right)(kT)^{j+\frac{5}{2}} \tag{5.54}$$

where $\Gamma(x)$, the *gamma function*, satisfies $\Gamma(x+1) = x\Gamma(x)$.

With the Seebeck coefficient α defined as in Chap. 3, we obtain for extrinsic n-type material

$$\alpha = \left(\frac{I_2}{TI_1} - \frac{E_f}{T} \right) = \frac{1}{T} \left(\frac{5kT}{2} - E_f \right) \tag{5.55}$$

In a wide-band-gap semiconductor which is lightly doped, the energy in parentheses may be close to $E_g/2$. Strictly speaking, since the theory was based on elastic and isotropic scattering, it applies only when impurity scattering dominates electronic mobility. Changes in the coefficient of kT result when other scattering mechanisms are assumed.

The relation between the electronic parts of electrical and thermal conductivities may also be obtained:

$$\frac{\kappa}{T\sigma_n} = \frac{1}{e^2 T^2} \left(\frac{I_2{}^2}{I_1{}^2} - \frac{I_3}{I_1} \right) = \tfrac{7}{2} \left(\frac{k}{e} \right)^2 \tag{5.56}$$

This may be compared with the corresponding relation for metals [(3.70)]. Of course, in a lightly doped semiconductor, which would give a maximum Seebeck coefficient, a major part of the thermal conductivity could be due to phonon transport.

In a p-$type$ semiconductor, the same line of reasoning indicates the Seebeck coefficient to be *opposite in sign*, for when electrons leave a metal conductor to enter p-type material, they shortly recombine with holes to release energy. It is easily shown, by electron-hole symmetry, that the Seebeck coefficient for p-type material is proportional to the difference between the Fermi energy and an energy $5kT/2e$ *below* the top of the valence band. The Seebeck coefficient of a semiconductor is reduced at high temperatures, for although E_f moves toward center band, minority carriers work in opposition to the majority carriers.

A simple semiconductor thermoelectric cell may consist of two simple bars of semiconductor material, one of p-type and the other of n-type material, joined across both ends by ohmic contacts to metal bars acting as heat source and sink, respectively (Fig. 5.24). The external electrical circuit is closed via one of the metal endpieces. The thermal gradient between hot and cold junctions will be distributed, more or less uniformly, across the bars. Such a thermoelectric device may be used to refrigerate, by transport of heat from one junction to the other through the Peltier effect, or to transform heat

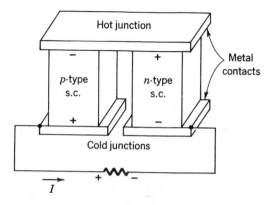

Figure 5.24 A simple semiconductor thermoelectric device, which may be used as either a generator (as shown here) or a refrigerator.

into electrical power, using the Seebeck effect. The open-circuit voltage of a thermoelectric generating cell is simply the thermoelectric voltage difference between the n-type and p-type legs. Since the individual thermoelectric voltages across these legs are of opposite polarity, the voltage output is much larger than that observed between two metals in the familiar bimetallic thermocouple. Seebeck coefficients in semiconductors can exceed 1 mv/°C, but values of 100 to 300 μv/°C are more typical for the low-band-gap materials usually employed.   Let the Seebeck coefficients of the two legs of the circuit of Fig. 5.24 be α_1 and $-\alpha_2$, respectively. The total open-circuit voltage, for a small temperature difference ΔT, over which α may be assumed constant, will be

$$V = (\alpha_1 + \alpha_2)\, \Delta T$$

where α is presumed given in volts per degree Kelvin. The resistance of the element, assuming semiconductor legs of length l, area S, and conductivities σ_1 and σ_2, will be

$$R = \frac{l}{S}\left(\frac{1}{\sigma_1} + \frac{1}{\sigma_2}\right)$$

We neglect the resistance of end straps and external circuit. From d-c circuit theory, the maximum power deliverable by a generator of voltage V and internal resistance R is

$$P_{o,\text{max}} = \frac{V^2}{4R}$$

achieved when internal and load resistances are equal. The maximum power output of the thermoelectric generator will be

$$P_{o,\max} = \frac{(\Delta T)^2 (\alpha_1 + \alpha_2)^2}{(4l/S)(1/\sigma_1 + 1/\sigma_2)} \tag{5.57}$$

At the same time, thermal conduction through the two legs is

$$P_{\text{th}} = \frac{\Delta T S}{l} (\kappa_1 + \kappa_2) \tag{5.58}$$

with κ_1 and κ_2 the thermal conductivities of the two legs, respectively. The ratio of power output to thermal losses is a useful measure of thermal efficiency:

$$\frac{P_{o,\max}}{P_{\text{th}}} = \frac{\Delta T}{4} \frac{(\alpha_1 + \alpha_2)^2}{(\kappa_1 + \kappa_2)(1/\sigma_1 + 1/\sigma_2)}$$

Although this is not per se the device efficiency, it is a measure thereof. Setting $\kappa_1 = \kappa_2$, $\sigma_1 = \sigma_2$, and $\alpha_1 = -\alpha_2$, it reduces to the form

$$\frac{P_{o,\max}}{P_{\text{th}}} = \frac{\Delta T}{4} \left(\frac{\alpha^2 \sigma}{\kappa} \right) \tag{5.59}$$

The temperature difference is merely a parameter of device operation, while the factor in parentheses is an important characteristic of the thermoelectric material. The same factor appears in efficiency expressions for thermoelectric refrigerators. This factor, $Z = \alpha^2 \sigma / \kappa$, is commonly employed as a *figure of merit* for thermoelectric materials.

From (5.55), the Seebeck coefficient α is large for materials of high band gap and decreases to very small values for metals (which have no band gap). Figure 5.25 plots α and the other pertinent parameters involved in the figure of merit Z versus carrier concentration. There is a clear one-to-one relationship between α and carrier concentration, where the density of states in the conduction band, for example, is comparable in all materials considered. As E_f approaches the band edge, α will decrease proportionately, as shown. The electrical conductivity σ, neglecting variations of mobility, varies linearly with carrier density. That part of the thermal conductivity κ due to the electrons is, by (5.56), proportional to σ and carrier density. The thermal conductivity due to phonons may be approximated as constant, as in the figure, although it varies considerably among semiconductors. The product $\alpha^2 \sigma / \kappa = Z$

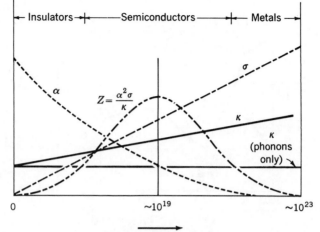

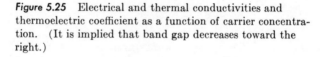

Increasing carrier density

Figure 5.25 Electrical and thermal conductivities and thermoelectric coefficient as a function of carrier concentration. (It is implied that band gap decreases toward the right.)

will accordingly reach a maximum value at a carrier density of the order of 10^{19} cm^{-3}. The actual criterion of a maximum Z is best met, not by classical semiconductors such as Ge or Si, but by II-VI compounds such as zinc telluride, bismuth telluride, etc. These rather "exotic" materials are considerably superior to Si and Ge in figure of merit largely because of much smaller thermal (phonon) conductivities. Since phonon conductivities are not readily calculable, an empirical search was required to optimize the material properties.

It is not even necessary to use single-crystal material to enjoy the advantages of these materials, thus permitting parts of thermoelectric devices to be cast into desired shapes. While relinquishing the single-crystal requirement clearly reduces cost, the intrinsic cost of the best materials still makes large-scale devices fairly expensive and appears to have discouraged application to home refrigeration and other ordinary uses.

Because they are so highly doped and connected via ohmic contacts, thermoelectric semiconductors demand no detailed junction theory as do the classical devices. In actual operation, in fact, they resemble semimetals. There is, correspond-

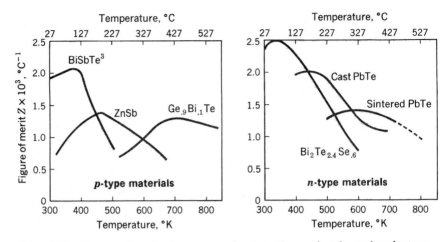

Figure 5.26   Figures of merit of some n- and p-type thermoelectric semiconductors. (*After R. R. Heikes and R. W. Ure, Jr., "Thermoelectricity: Science and Engineering," pp. 537–538, Interscience Publishers, Inc., New York, 1961.*

ingly, less difficulty in making ohmic contacts from the metal to the semiconductor. Because of the massiveness and brittleness of typical elements, however, care must be taken to avoid thermal or mechanical stresses.

Different temperature ranges of operation are best satisfied by materials of different energy gap and/or doping density. Melting points could also be a consideration. Figure 5.26 shows typical figures of merit for several p-type and n-type materials. Devices covering large temperature ranges can be made from stacked segments of different materials, to optimize the performance of each part.

5.13   Semiconductor Junction Device Fabrication

All semiconductor junction devices require closely defined regions of p-type material and of n-type material. Device fabrication is mainly involved with techniques for obtaining a desired impurity density in every part of a device.

Bulk semiconductor material is generally pulled from a doped melt in ingots 1 in. or more in diameter. Zone-melting operations may be carried out on the pulled ingot to establish impurity density and/or make it more uniform. Ingots of silicon and germanium are commonly pulled in a [111] direction established by the "seed" used to initiate crystal growth.

There is nothing to be gained electronically by this orientation, but [111] surfaces provide a better base for alloying operations in silicon and germanium. The ingot is usually sliced transversely into wafers a few mils in thickness. A single wafer may serve for a large number of transistors or diodes, and can be further divided by sawing, sandblasting, or scoring and cracking (as in "cutting" glass).

Subsequent processing is highly varied. The significantly different doping techniques are (1) alloying, (2) diffusion, and (3) epitaxial growth. In producing an *alloyed junction*, a small piece (e.g., a few mils on a side) of a desired impurity metal may be placed on a semiconductor wafer having the opposite type of impurity. The combination is then heated in a nonoxidizing atmosphere, above the melting point of the eutectic alloy formed between the semiconductor and the impurity, for example, about 580°C for aluminum on silicon (Fig. C.1). In some instances, the impurity may be entirely melted. The semiconductor and impurity interdissolve to form an alloy. The impurity may also diffuse slightly into the solid semiconductor, but this is not the major effect. After a predetermined time interval, the wafer is allowed to cool. The molten semiconductor-metal alloy closest to the semiconductor recrystallizes, in the same crystalline form as the semiconductor. The remaining impurity metal is found to have made an ohmic contact to the semiconductor. That part of the impurity which has alloyed with the semiconductor produces a *p-n* junction of the type shown in Fig. 5.27. The junction can be nearly abrupt.

It is necessary to control carefully the time and temperature of the process if the *p-n* junction is to lie a desired distance inside the semiconductor. A second alloyed junction may be placed simultaneously on the opposite side of a very thin wafer, to form an *alloyed-junction transistor*. The first and still the more numerous transistors of alloyed construction are germanium *p-n-p* units. This reflects strongly the desirable metallurgical properties of indium and tin as impurities in germanium. These elements melt at low temperature, but have low diffusion into germanium at their melting points, permitting abrupt junctions. A low vapor pressure at the alloying temperature precludes excessive evaporation during alloying.

Diffusion of impurity materials in the base semiconductor is the controlling factor in many fabrication tech-

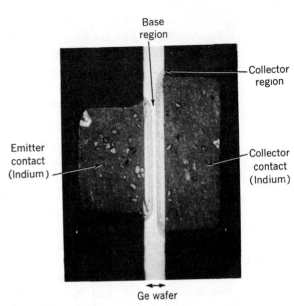

Base
region

Collector
region

Emitter
contact
(Indium)

Collector
contact
(Indium)

Ge wafer

Figure 5.27   Micrograph of a section of an alloyed
germanium transistor, clearly showing the recrystallized
p regions forming emitter and collector.   [*Courtesy of
J. A. Decker, Western Electric Company, Allentown, Pa.*]

niques.   It is probably the most common procedure in use.
This diffusion is described, in uniform semiconductors and at
low impurity densities, by the same diffusion equation (4.43)
which governs carrier motion through the material.   Impurities, however, diffuse much more slowly than electrons.   At
room temperature the significant impurities diffuse so slowly
that the useful lifetime of completed semiconductor devices is
not limited by migration of impurities; excessive overheating
does create trouble, however.   Diffusion coefficients for various impurities in silicon and germanium, as functions of temperature, are given in Fig. 5.28.   A peculiar but valuable
property is that donors diffuse more rapidly in germanium,
while acceptors diffuse more rapidly in silicon.   This has a
profound influence on the types of devices which can be fabricated most simply from germanium or silicon in p-n-p or
n-p-n configurations.   Some devices, in a given semiconductor
element, can be made only in one of the two configurations.

The dynamics of diffusion are described on one dimension
by Fick's equation,

$$\frac{\partial M}{\partial t} = D \frac{\partial^2 M}{\partial x^2} \tag{4.44}$$

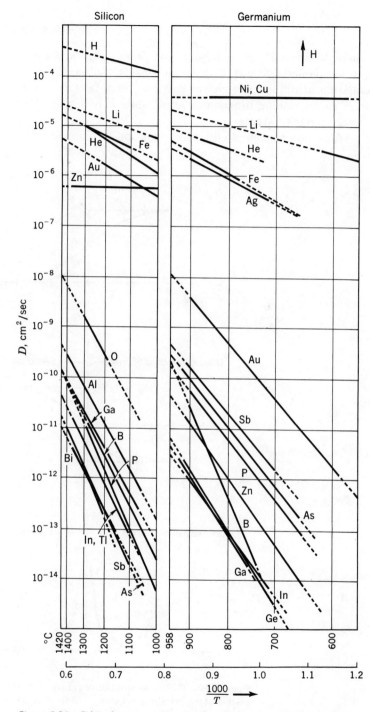

Figure 5.28 Diffusion constants of a number of impurities in silicon and germanium, as functions of temperature. [*After A. van Wieringen and W. Warmoltz, Physica, **22**:849 (1956).*]

where M is the impurity density, and D its diffusion constant (at low concentration). Although this is the same as the equation of diffusion of charge carriers, there is of course no term corresponding to recombination, since it is impossible to "lose" impurity atoms.

Although the simple diffusion equation for constant D is

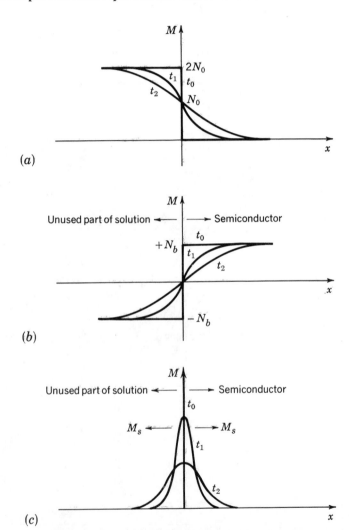

(a)

(b)

(c)

Figure 5.29 Diffusion-equation solutions. (a) Initial concentration step; (b) displaced step, representing out-diffusion if solution for $x > 0$ is used; (c) planar concentration, representing initial surface concentration M_s if solution for $x > 0$ is used.

linear and only of second order, it is not solved as readily as the steady-state form we used in describing carriers in junctions. Boundary conditions must be stated for both time and positions. An *initial concentration step* (Fig. 5.29a) yields a solution of the form

$$M = 2(\pi)^{-\frac{1}{2}} M_0 \int_{\frac{x}{2(Dt)^{\frac{1}{2}}}}^{\infty} e^{-\xi^2} d\xi = M_0 \operatorname{erfc} \frac{x}{2(Dt)^{\frac{1}{2}}} \tag{5.60}$$

Tables of the *complementary error function* erfc z are to be found in any comprehensive book of mathematical tables. This particular distribution occurs in certain processes where an initial-step impurity distribution is established, e.g., in growing the crystal, and subsequent heating is used to distribute impurities.

The process of *out-diffusion* consists in heating an impurity semiconductor, which we assume to be uniformly doped, so that the impurities vaporize from the surface. Assuming that any impurity atom that reaches the surface will vaporize, the density at the surface will always be zero. The solution here can be found by adding a constant [also an admissible solution of Eq. (4.44)] to the solution of (5.60) to yield the result shown in Fig. 5.29b. The mathematical expression is

$$M = M_0 \operatorname{erf} \frac{x}{2(Dt)^{\frac{1}{2}}} \tag{5.61}$$

The error function erf z is simply $1 - \operatorname{erfc} z$. A third useful solution is that of a "planar source." If a planar concentration of impurities M_s (measured by the total number of atoms per *square* centimeter) lies at the plane $x = 0$ at time $t = 0$, then at times $t > 0$ the impurity becomes distributed according to

$$M = \frac{M_s}{(\pi Dt)^{\frac{1}{2}}} \exp \frac{-x^2}{4Dt} \qquad x > 0 \tag{5.62}$$

Here M_s is the initial surface concentration of impurities. This solution is plotted in Fig. 5.29c. An impurity material can be applied to a surface by plating, etc., in known quantity (M_s per unit area). If the surface is then covered by an impermeable coating, or if the vapor pressure of the impurity is sufficiently low, *in-diffusion* proceeds without appreciable loss of the impurity material.

Diffusion of *all* impurities in a crystal occurs when the material is heated. An impurity having lower D will diffuse

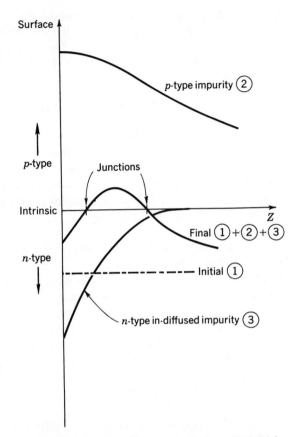

Figure 5.30 Double-diffused transistor. (1) Initial uniform donor density. (2) In-diffused, rapidly diffusing acceptor density. (3) In-diffused, rapidly diffusing donor density. Final curve contains two junctions.

more slowly, and changes in its distribution can sometimes be neglected.   Figure 5.30 illustrates successive steps of diffusion of impurity atoms into a thin n-type silicon wafer to form two p-n junctions.   The accuracy of diffusion depth is even greater than the obtainable parallelism of two faces of a wafer.   Diffusion from only one face of a wafer is thus a better-controlled process for producing transistors.

It is clear from the figures that concentration gradients achieved by diffusion yield junctions anything but abrupt. The *rate-growing process* can produce abrupt junctions, however, without the low-temperature limitation inherent in alloyed devices. The technique makes use of the dependence of *segregation coefficient* on rate of growth (Sec. 1.9). When the crystal is pulled very slowly from the molten material, the segregation process is essentially in equilibrium, and the density of impurities in the solid is the product of the density in the melt and the segregation coefficient. When the crystal is grown rapidly, as by lowering the temperature of the melt, however, impurity material is taken into the crystal in *larger* quantities than it would in slow growth. An impurity which can diffuse rapidly in the melt will not build up its concentration to as great a degree during rapid growth. A melt of semiconductor material is doped with *both* donors and acceptors, in quantities such that at slow crystal-growing rates (growth can be stopped completely by further heating the molten material) there is a predominance of acceptors in the solid crystal. At faster growth rates, more of the slow-diffusing donors get imprisoned in the solid. Alternatively fast and slow growth yields an ingot with alternating *p*-type regions. This process can be continued as frequently as desired; thickness of the resulting regions can be made less than a mil. Fabrication of devices is completed by cutting the material into bars and attaching ohmic contacts. The location of the junctions is generally determined by electrical measurement before the ingot is cut. Mainly because of the difficulties of cutting and of locating electrodes, this technique is now little used.

If single-crystal semiconductor material at suitable temperatures is exposed to vapor of the same material, *epitaxy* occurs (Sec. 1.8). Elemental or even compound semiconductors can be deposited, including impurities. It becomes possible to lay down a thin layer of material of specified resistivity on top of another of much different resistivity. The thickness of epitaxially deposited layers can be much smaller than in other techniques, which suggests high-frequency devices. Both epitaxial deposition and multiple in-diffusions have been employed to form planar multicomponent devices in so-called *microcircuits*. Figure 5.31 illustrates the formation of resistors, capacitors, and transistors in *silicon planar technology*. Device areas are defined by etching away unwanted material or by preventing diffusion in some areas by means of a silicon oxide coating, produced by thermal oxidation of areas not covered by a protective coating (later removed). This technique, with many variations, permits large numbers of transistors or more

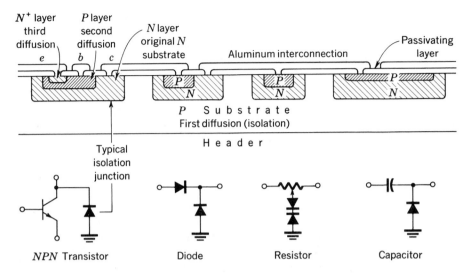

Figure 5.31   Triple-diffusion technology for producing microelectronic planar devices. Electrical isolation is obtained by reverse biasing of elements. "Passivating layer" is thermally grown SiO_2, which covers those silicon surfaces not contacted by the aluminum film interconnection. (*After Signetics Corp. Bulletin* 8001, *January*, 1963.)

complex "integrated" circuits to be fabricated on a single silicon wafer.

The materials used in doping semiconductors need not be pure impurity elements. It is quite common to use alloys containing several different impurities. Each impurity acts almost independently. Use of a particular alloy may be dictated largely by metallurgical considerations, such as melting point and the ease with which the semiconductor is "wet" by the material. Some devices have even used a compound alloying material, one element of which produces an alloy contact, another diffusing into the semiconductor to produce a second junction.

The preparation of semiconductor surfaces before and after device fabrication is an extensive technology. Cleanliness is essential in fabrication stages. The completed device must be protected against surface contamination and the resulting high surface-recombination velocity. Silicon surfaces may easily be protected by "passivating" with a thin oxide (SiO_2) coating, thermally formed. Most devices are in addition sealed into containers which prevent damage or surface contamination and provide rigid support for connecting electrodes.

PROBLEMS

Since the properties of semiconductor materials are subject to wide variations and the configurations of modern semiconductor devices likewise, these problems are intended to serve mainly as an exercise. They should also contribute to the reader's understanding of how material parameters and device dimensions are interrelated. Unless instructed otherwise, the student should use the representative materials data presented in Table 4.1.

5.1(a) Explain in your own words the meanings of and difference between the electrostatic potential ψ and Fermi energy ϕ. Why are both needed to describe an inhomogeneous semiconductor?

5.1(b) Make the necessary changes in (5.2) for a semiconductor in which the Fermi energy in intrinsic material lies above the center of the band gap by a distance δ ev.

5.3(a) Figure 5.7 identifies a "neutral solution" for the graded junction, one for which $(D - A) + (P - N) = 0$. Find the corresponding solution for the abrupt junction and plot along with the approximation (5.8), for the case $D = A = 10^{17}$, $N_i = 10^{12}$, $\epsilon/\epsilon_0 = 12$.

5.3(b) Consider the related problem of an abrupt junction between intrinsic and extrinsic (e.g., n-type) semiconductor material. (1) Show why a "depletion" solution exactly like that in the text is no longer admissible. (2) Show that u must have an inflection point at the junction. (3) In one imaginable solution, the entire change in u is distributed at essentially constant field in the intrinsic material; show that this results in an incorrect charge balance. (4) Show that it is, however, reasonable that a relatively small part of the change in u occurs in the extrinsic material.

5.4(a) An abrupt junction in a silicon bar has 10^{15} doping density on both sides. The material on *each* side of the junction is 0.2 cm long, and the bar is 0.05 cm square in cross section. Plot I versus V for positive and negative voltages, accounting for the potential drops in the ends of the device, at 300°K.

5.4(b) If a hole current of 10 amp/cm² is flowing in a junction, with $p(-z_p) = 10^{15}$ and $p(z_n) = 10^{14}$: (1) Estimate the fraction of injected holes which are lost by recombination in the depletion layer itself. The depletion layer is 2×10^{-4} cm wide. (HINT: What is total hole recombination rate in the depletion region?) (2) Are any or all holes which recombine in the depletion layer useless? Assume $\tau_p = 10^{-3}$ sec.

5.4(c) In the high-reverse-voltage region of a junction's operation, (5.21) suggests that the minority-carrier densities at the boundaries of the depletion region become zero, that is, $p(z_n) = n(-z_p) = 0$ in the limit $V = -\infty$. Explain the meaning of the remaining terms in (5.20), in terms of minority-carrier diffusion in the p and n regions. Illustrate by sketching densities of majority and minority carriers in this situation.

5.4(d) A germanium abrupt-junction diode is operated over a wide range of temperature. Describe performance qualitatively (1) near absolute zero, (2) near the temperature at which the Fermi energy crosses the donor and acceptor energies, and (3) in the intrinsic region. (HINT: The depletion-layer assumption may not always be valid.) (4) How might one design a germanium diode for maximum temperature range, allowing all parameters to be adjusted with this goal in mind?

5.5(a) What barrier voltage is required in order that a metal-semiconductor diode carry the same current density as a silicon junction diode with $D = A = 10^{16}$? (The constant $A = 120$ amp/cm²-°K².) Assume $T = 300$°K.

5.5(b) A hypothetical silicon surface has electron traps averaging one trap in an area 100 A square. The bulk material is doped n type with a density of 10^{15} cm⁻³. The effect of the traps will be assumed to produce a uniform hole density of 10^{16} in a region of thickness t. (1) Calculate the inversion-layer thickness t. (2) Using a simple space-charge solution, determine the potential barrier (i.e., change in ψ) associated with such a space-charge configuration. (3) By what equation(s) could a more exact solution for potential configuration be obtained at equilibrium?

5.5(c) A point-contact diode is often subject to very high pulse currents, in microwave radar applications. This can cause "burnout." Presuming that burnout occurs when the tungsten contact point reaches 1200°C and that the pulses are so short that no heat redistribution occurs during the pulse, what current can a device with a point 10^{-4} cm in diameter withstand for a 1-μsec interval? ($c_p = 0.034$ cal/g, $\rho = 25 \times 10^{-6}$ ohm-cm, approximate average values over the range 0 to 1200°C for tungsten. Specific density is 19.3 g/cm³.)

5.6(a) Prove, using the approximations of Sec. 5.3, that the depletion-layer width of a reverse-biased *abrupt* junction is

$$w = w_p + w_n = \left(\frac{\epsilon V'}{e}\right)^{\frac{1}{2}} \left[\left(A + \frac{A^2}{D}\right)^{-\frac{1}{2}} + \left(D + \frac{D^2}{A}\right)^{-\frac{1}{2}}\right]$$

where V' is the electrostatic potential drop across the junction. [HINT: The function u can be used to represent merely $e\psi/kT$, whereupon (5.8) is an applicable solution.]

5.6(b) Derive Eq. (5.33) using the relation of the previous problem for depletion-region widths.

5.6(c) Determine parameters for a silicon unipolar transistor with abrupt junctions and equal doping densities which will close off the channel with 20 volts bias on the gates. Specify a doping density and the thickness of the gate region. Define dimensions which will yield zero-bias channel resistance of 10,000 ohms. (HINT: Use results of Prob. 5.5a.)

5.7(a) An abrupt-junction germanium p-n-p transistor is to have (at room temperature) 0.1-ohm-cm emitter, 2-ohm-cm base, and 1-ohm-cm collector regions. (1) Find the required doping densities by successive approximation. (2) At large forward emitter bias and reverse collector bias, what base length is tolerable for a *transport factor* of 0.98?

5.7(b) A silicon n-p-n transistor whose cross section is 1 mm² has collector doping of 2×10^{16} and base doping of 10^{16}. Upper limit of operating temperature is to be set by reverse saturation collector current of 100 μa. Estimate the temperature for this condition, neglecting change of mobility with T.

5.7(c) (1) In the limit $2w_0 \ll L_p$, show that the effective velocity of holes across the base of a p-n-p transistor is given by D_p/w_0. Take the velocity to be the ratio of the current density to the average (excess) hole charge density. (2) If surface-recombination velocity is 10^3 cm/sec, estimate the fraction of hole current lost by surface recombination in a transistor having a base region 0.002 cm wide by 0.04 by 0.04 cm square cross section. Assume $D_p = 40$ cm²/sec.

5.7(d) (1) Find a simple expression for the short-circuit current gain α under the condition $2w_0 \ll L_p$. (2) Discuss means of increasing this parameter and the resulting influence on other performance characteristics.

5.7(e) If an excessively large collector voltage is applied to a transistor of thin base region, when the collector-base depletion region contacts that of the emitter-base junction, a high current is drawn in the phenomenon known as "punch-through." (It is generally not destructive.) (1) Draw an energy-level diagram illustrating the phenomenon. (2) For an n-p-n silicon transistor with abrupt junctions, with $D_c = 10^{16}$, $D_e = 10^{16}$, $A_b = 10^{15}$, and base width of 10^{-3} cm, estimate (for zero emitter-base voltage) the collector voltage at which the two depletion layers make contact. Use 300°K constants; see Prob. 5.5a for a pertinent relation.

5.8(a) (1) Using the uniform-field approximation, show that each point on Fig. 4.22 corresponds to a diode of breakdown voltage $V = \mathcal{E}/\alpha$. (2) Using the approximation (5.43), plot silicon-diode breakdown voltage as a function of impurity density.

5.8(b) Draw energy-level diagrams, plus carrier-density curves, for a p-n-p-n diode (no control current) at the same voltage in (1) the low-current state and (2) the high-current state.

5.9(a) What parameters must be altered, in a tunnel diode, to produce a "valley region" extending to higher voltage?

5.9(b) Transistors are sometimes described as "minority-carrier" devices. A tunnel diode, on the same terms, is a "majority-carrier" device. (1) Explain the significant phenomenological differences. What type of device is (2) a unipolar transistor, (3) a silicon diode, (4) a *p-n-p-n diode?*

5.9(c) What are the main requirements for tunnel-diode construction, in regard to (1) the semiconductor material, (2) the impurity? (3) Discuss the possible usefulness of various impurities in germanium tunnel diodes.

5.10(a) (1) Calculate and plot the voltage-current density characteristic of a photovoltaic junction at room temperature, neglecting resistive voltage drop in the semiconductor. Let $J_L = 10^4 J_0$. (2) Estimate the operating condition for maximum output power, under the same assumption.

5.10(b) The intrinsic current flow in a junction photodevice sets sensitivity limits. (1) In a silicon reverse-biased junction device of 10^{15}-doped material at room temperature, what photon flux and radiant power density at $\hbar\omega = E_g$ produce a signal just equal to the "dark current"? (2) How could this sensitivity be improved?

5.11(a) A silicon *n-p-n* transistor has base width of 0.02 cm. (1) Using intrinsic mobility and lifetime values, estimate the base-region phase delay at 20 Mc/sec, by (5.49). Neglect depletion-region width. (2) If the final 0.015 cm of base, next to the collector, is replaced by an intrinsic semiconductor (to a *p-n-i-p* configuration), what is the total phase delay from emitter to collector, with 10-volt negative collector-base voltage? (3) Estimate the avalanche-breakdown voltage of the collector in this latter case.

5.11(b) An *n-p-n* silicon abrupt-junction transistor has a cross section of 0.1 by 0.1 cm, an emitter length of 0.05 cm, and base-region length of 0.01 cm. Doping is 10^{16}-10^{15}-10^{16}. (1) Calculate the zero-emitter voltage capacitance of the emitter junction. (2) Calculate the emitter series resistance and that of the base (approximately) if connected by a contact along one 0.1-cm-long side. Neglect depletion-region thickness. (3) A voltage is applied between a full-area emitter contact and the base contact; the effective junction voltage is that which appears across the capacitance of the junction. At what frequency will this voltage be only 0.707 of that applied?

5.11(c) A silicon abrupt-junction diode of 10^{-4} cm^2 area is formed from 10^{16}-doped material. (1) With a forward current of 10^9 times the reverse saturation current, what is the total stored (excess) minority-carrier charge (electrons plus holes)? (2) If the diode is used in series with a 1,000-ohm resistor and a reverse voltage of 20 volts applied suddenly: (i) About how long will the reverse current remain at a constant value? (ii) Approximately how much of the stored charge will be recovered? (Assume lifetimes are 500 μsec.)

5.12(a) If both electron and hole conduction are considered, the Seebeck coefficient of a semiconductor may be expressed as $\alpha = (\alpha_n \sigma_n + \alpha_p \sigma_p)/(\sigma_n + \sigma_p)$. Calculate the variation of Seebeck coefficient in p-type silicon, as a function of impurity concentration, at $T = 300°K$ from intrinsic to 10^{18} cm^{-3}.

5.12(b) Design a thermoelectric generator with one p-type and one n-type leg, operating with a 200°C temperature difference. An electrical output power of 1 watt is desired, operating at a maximum power-output condition. Heat source and sink are 1 in. apart. Neglect thickness of end electrodes, insulators, etc. Give area of legs, voltage and current output, and efficiency. In the calculation, use values of $\alpha = \pm 200$ $\mu v/°C$, $\rho = 10^{-3}$ ohm-cm, and $\kappa = 0.016$ watt/cm-°C (typical of bismuth telluride).

5.13(a) A silicon crystal doped with arsenic is grown in a crystal-pulling furnace in which the rate of pulling has a sinusoidal time variation. Accordingly, the doping density is uneven, having a variation $D = D_0 + D_1 \sin (2\pi x/10^{-2})$ along its length (x in centimeters). The crystal is subsequently heated in an oven at 1300°C. (1) Show that the initial impurity density variation will be reduced exponentially with time. (2) How long will it take for the variation to be reduced to one-tenth of its initial value?

5.13(b) A wafer of germanium is uniformly doped with indium to a density of 10^{15} cm^{-3}. A surface coating of 10^{12} cm^{-2} arsenic atoms is added and prevented from evaporating from the surface. Assuming that the indium does not diffuse appreciably at the temperature of heating, determine the deepest possible penetration of a p-n junction into the wafer.

5.13(c) A thick block of silicon is doped uniformly with 10^{15} cm^{-3} arsenic atoms and 10^{16} cm^{-3} aluminum atoms. Assuming that the aluminum atoms leave the surface immediately as they arrive (so that the surface is a sink for them) and neglecting diffusion of the arsenic, at 1300°C, how long does it take for a p-n junction to form to a distance 10^{-3} cm inside the surface?

5.13(d) A silicon bar containing uniform concentrations of impurities, 10^{16} cm^{-3} of antimony and 10^{15} cm^{-3} of boron, is melted along half its length and then allowed to resolidify. Neglecting diffusion, sketch the resulting impurity distributions and the net density D-A versus length, giving approximate densities and critical dimensions. Discuss use of this bar as a transistor. Use data from Table 1.3.

GENERAL REFERENCES

The progress of semiconductor technology has been so rapid that much has not yet been recorded in book form. The periodical literature has also failed to keep record of the advances, in part because of the proprietary nature of processing techniques. Most device literature is to be found in *Proceedings of the IRE* and in the *Transactions of the Professional Group on Electron Devices* (IRE). Additional sources are *Bell System Technical Journal, Solid State Journal,* and *RCA Review.* Most presently produced devices were conceived in the period 1949–1955; some are continually reinvented.

Biondi, F. J. (ed.): "Transistor Technology," vols. I–III, D. Van Nostrand Company, Inc., Princeton, N.J., 1958. (The most comprehensive treatment of processing and technology of materials and devices.)

Heikes, R. K., and R. W. Ure, Jr.: "Thermoelectricity: Science and Engineering," Interscience Publishers, Inc., New York, 1961. (In our opinion, the best of a group of books written at the peak of popularity of thermoelectricity.)

Hunter, L. P. (ed.): "Handbook of Semiconductor Electronics," McGraw-Hill Book Company, New York, 1962. (Strongest in applications, but includes highly useful device-design considerations.)

Linvill, J. G.: "Models of Transistors and Diodes," McGraw-Hill Book Company, New York, 1963. (Stresses development of equivalent-circuit models from the underlying theory.)

Valdes, L. B.: "The Physical Theory of Transistors," McGraw-Hill Book Company, New York, 1961. (Excellent treatment of device theory.)

6
Superconductivity

6.1 Superconductivity and Related Phenomena

Superconductivity was discovered in mercury in 1911, by H. Kamerlingh Onnes, who only three years earlier had succeeded in liquefying helium (boiling point, 4.2°K). Mercury and many other metals as well were found to become perfect electrical conductors, at least at ordinary low frequencies, below *critical temperatures* a few degrees above absolute zero. A large number of metallic elements and innumerable alloys have later been shown to exhibit this remarkable property. While for many years there were doubts as to the absolute vanishing of electric resistance, experiments in which continuously circulating currents in superconductors were found to maintain their initial value for at least $2\frac{1}{2}$ years have verified this property.

Shortly after his discovery of the phenomenon, Onnes also discovered that magnetic fields applied to a superconductor also affect the onset of perfect conductivity. In fact, even at absolute zero, there is a critical magnetic field which may be applied to render the material a normal conductor. For many superconductors, the relation between the critical field and temperature takes the approximate form

$$\left[\frac{T_c(\mathcal{3C})}{T_c(0)} \right]^2 = 1 - \left[\frac{\mathcal{3C}_c(T)}{\mathcal{3C}_c(0)} \right]^2 \tag{6.1}$$

This relationship is shown in Fig. 6.1; the appropriate values of $T_c(0)$ are given in Table 6.1 for all known superconducting

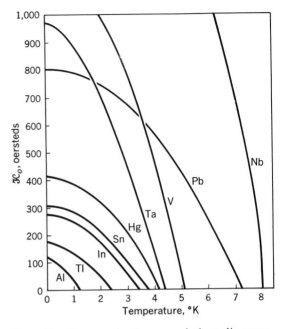

Figure 6.1 Superconducting-normal phase diagrams
for a number of superconducting elements. Measurements are made with field along the axis of a
rod-shaped specimen. [*After D. A. Buck, Proc.
IRE,* **44**:482 (1956).]

metals and a number of alloys.   Values of $\mathfrak{K}_c(0)$ are also given,
where available.   The figure may be viewed as a *phase* diagram, the region inside the curve representing the superconducting phase, and that outside, the normally conducting
phase.   The transition from normal to superconducting state,
or the converse, may be treated thermodynamically as a phase
transition.

In 1933, Meissner and Ochsenfeld discovered another
property of all superconductors, one which has further significance in understanding their electrical properties.   If a bulk
sample of (typically) centimeter dimensions is cooled while in
a magnetic field to below the value of critical temperature corresponding to that field, magnetic flux is repelled from the body
of the superconductor, so that it becomes *perfectly diamagnetic*
($B = 0$ or $\mu = 0$; see Sec. 8.1).   This is in marked contrast to
the behavior of a material which is merely an ideal conductor,
for such a conductor would retain the flux that was in it prior

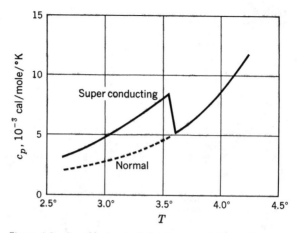

Figure 6.2   Specific heat of tin–4 per cent bismuth alloy, illustrating the typical behavior of c_p. The normal curve was taken with the use of a magnetic field exceeding $\mathfrak{IC}_c$. [*After K. Mendelssohn and J. R. Moore, Proc. Roy. Soc. (London),* **A152**:34 (1935).]

to its conversion to perfect conductivity. This *Meissner effect* in superconductors must therefore be treated, in classical theories, as a separate property. The Meissner effect is *reversible* in simple superconductors; i.e., if a field is applied before cooling, the end result after cooling is the same as that obtained if the sample is first cooled, then brought into a field.

Experimentally (see Fig. 6.2) the specific heat of superconductors portrays a *second-order* phase transition, when the temperature is changed in the absence of a magnetic field (i.e., something like Fig. C.3 for ferromagnetic materials, which also have a second-order transition). In the presence of a magnetic field, however, there is a heat of transition, indicating a first-order transition. This can be understood by simple thermodynamics.

The Gibbs free energy of a magnetic material may be expressed, in differential form (Sec. C.1), as

$$dG = -S\,dT + V\,dp - \mu_0 \mathbf{M} \cdot d\mathfrak{IC} \tag{6.2}$$

Neglecting the $V\,dp$ term, at constant temperature G can be found by integrating from zero field:

$$G(T,\mathfrak{IC}) = G(T,0) - \mu_0 \int_0^{\mathfrak{IC}} \mathbf{M} \cdot d\mathfrak{IC} \tag{6.3}$$

Table 6.1   Critical fields and temperatures of elemental and some compound superconductors

Element	T_c, °K	$\mathcal{K}_c(0)$, oe	Element	T_c, °K	$\mathcal{K}_c(0)$, oe	Compound	T_c, °K	$\mathcal{K}_c(0)$, oe
Al	1.196	99	Pb	7.175	802.6	AlNb$_3$	18	
Cd	0.56	30	Re	1.699	201	BaBi$_3$	5.69	740
Ga	1.091	51	Ru	0.49	66	Bi$_2$Pt	0.16	10
Hf	0.165		Sn	3.74	305	CoSi$_2$	1.40	105
Hg(α)	4.153	412	Ta	4.483	780	GeIr	4.70	
Hg(β)	3.949	339.3	Tc	11.2		InLa$_3$	10.4	
In	3.407	293	Th	1.37	162	Nb$_3$Sn	18.07	
Ir	0.14	19	Ti	0.39	100	SiV$_3$	16.8–17.1	
La(α)	5.0		Tl	2.36	171			
La(β)	5.95	1,600	U(α)	0.6–0.7	~2,000			
Mo	0.92	98	V	5.3	1,310			
Nb	9.25	1,944	Zn	0.91	53			
Os	0.655	65–82	Zr	0.55	47			

Data collected by B. W. Roberts, in D. E. Gray (ed.), "American Institute of Physics Handbook," chap. 9, p. 110, McGraw-Hill Book Company, New York, 1963. Compound superconductors listed represent only a tiny fraction of the hundreds of compounds and alloys studied, to illustrate the range of materials which exhibit superconductivity.

But by the Meissner effect and using the relation $\mathbf{B} = \mu_0(\mathbf{M} + \mathcal{K})$ defined in Sec. 8.1, in a superconductor,

$$\mathbf{M} = -\mathcal{K} \tag{6.4}$$

Substituting into (6.3) and integrating,

$$G_s(T,\mathcal{K}) = G_s(T,0) + \mu_0 \frac{\mathcal{K}^2}{2} \tag{6.5}$$

Along the phase boundary (Fig. 6.1) between normal and superconducting phases, it must be possible to move electrons from superconducting to normal condition without changing the Gibbs free energy G. Accordingly, along that phase boundary, the normal phase has free energy

$$G_n(T,\mathcal{K}_c) = G_s(T,0) + \mu_0 \frac{\mathcal{K}_c^2(T)}{2} \tag{6.6}$$

But it should be noted that in the *normal* phase the free energy cannot be dependent on $\mathcal{K}$ to any appreciable extent, since the conductor is nonmagnetic in nature. So (6.6) applies for *any* field, not only $\mathcal{K}_c$.

The entropy of a system is given [via (6.2)] as

$$S = -\frac{\partial G}{\partial T} \text{ (const } p, \mathcal{K}) \tag{6.7}$$

Accordingly, the *difference* in entropy between a superconducting and a normal phase may be found by differentiating both (6.5) and (6.6). The dependence of $\mathfrak{X}_c$ on T (as noted from the figure) must be recognized.

$$S_n - S_s = -\mu_0 \mathfrak{X}_c \frac{d\mathfrak{X}_c}{dT} \tag{6.8}$$

The difference in the entropy, multiplied by the temperature, is the superconducting-normal transition heat:

$$Q_{s \to n} = -\frac{\mu_0 T}{2} \mathfrak{X}_c \frac{d\mathfrak{X}_c}{dT} \tag{6.9}$$

From the figure, $d\mathfrak{X}_c/dT$ is zero at $T = T_c(0)$, indicating a second-order transition, but becomes negative at other temperatures, indicating a positive heat of transition. This result may be viewed most simply by noting that in a transition caused by raising temperature in the presence of a magnetic field, the heat supply must provide the energy required to fill the superconductor with magnetic field.

Before adequate microscopic theories of superconductivity were proposed, much of the analytical activity in the area was of a thermodynamic nature. Beginning with empirical relations such as (6.1), one can derive expressions for specific heat and other thermodynamic properties. Unfortunately, the empirical relations chosen were too simple to represent the electronic processes actually taking place, so that there is a considerable amount of published material prior to circa 1957 which has no current validity. The reader should be aware of this situation when using the literature.

While the properties of liquid helium have apparently little in common with those of superconducting metals, this liquid is so important a commodity for superconductor studies that it deserves some consideration here.

Helium boils at 4.2°K; hence a container of liquid helium at atmospheric pressure will maintain an immersed specimen at 4.2°K until the He has entirely evaporated. If the pressure of gaseous helium over the liquid is reduced, the boiling point is lowered (just as water's boiling point is lowered at high altitudes). Temperature of an immersed specimen can therefore be conveniently controlled, down to 1 to 2°K, by reduction of the helium pressure using a vacuum pump (the boiling point is 3.2° at 200 mm Hg absolute pressure, 1.4° at 3 mm Hg). A simple pressure regulator can be relied upon to hold temperature within about $10^{-3}\,^{\circ}$K.   The supply of liquid helium in this country has been sufficient, so that little scavenging of the helium gas has been carried out, but it is common practice in Europe to conserve the gas for reliquefication.   At 2.2°K, normal liquid helium undergoes a transition which, from a molecular point of view, is strongly analogous to superconductivity.   Below the critical temperature the liquid, or at least a part of it, becomes a "superfluid" capable of escaping through the tiniest cracks in a vessel.   Superfluid helium has also a very high *thermal* conductivity.   To explain these effects, one may assume that the transition produces a fluid of zero viscosity.   Analogously, the *electrons* in a superconductor may also be characterized as having zero viscosity.   Thermodynamically, the superfluid state of helium may be looked upon as a "condensation" of the Bose-Einstein particles into a lowest-energy state, as mentioned in Sec. C.7.   In apparent support of this concept is the fact that the helium *isotope* having only a single neutron does not have a superfluid state; these particles have a net nuclear spin and should accordingly satisfy not Bose-Einstein, but Fermi-Dirac statistics.   Although a superfluid makes a very poor experimental environment for most purposes, the high cost of the lighter isotope prohibits its use except in very specialized experiments.

6.2   The London Two-fluid Theory

The properties of *normal* conductors may be explained reasonably well using the simple conduction relation

$$J_n = \sigma \mathcal{E} \tag{6.10}$$

This provides adequate results, except in the case of conduction in very thin films, and of course in high-frequency applications where the anomalous skin effect more correctly describes actual electronic processes.   Knowledge of the validity of a relation such as (6.10), however, still does not give us a means of studying microscopic processes.

In superconductors, a similar conduction relation can be derived, as well as a relation describing the Meissner effect, without any knowledge of the microscopic processes.   The brothers London derived a macroscopic theory, in 1934.[1]   The hypotheses they invoked were (1) that the superconductor con-

[1] F. London and H. London, *Proc. Roy. Soc. (London)*, 1935, p. 149.

tains a density n_s of electrons which move without loss, and (2) that the Meissner effect is to be described.

The superconducting electrons are assumed to respond to electric fields just as free electrons:

$$m \frac{d\mathbf{v}}{dt} = -e\boldsymbol{\varepsilon} \tag{6.11}$$

Statistical distributions of electron velocity were neglected. The supercurrent density $\mathbf{J}_s$ is the superelectron charge density times velocity:

$$\mathbf{J}_s = -en_s\mathbf{v} \tag{6.12}$$

By differentiating (6.12) and substituting (6.11), we obtain

$$\dot{\mathbf{J}}_s = \frac{n_s e^2}{m} \boldsymbol{\varepsilon} \tag{6.13}$$

This is the basic relation describing the absence of resistance. Since no electric field occurs unless the current is changing, steady currents may be set up without any electric field. Only if electric fields exist does the presence of nonsuperconducting electrons make itself felt, for only in the presence of an electric field can these be accelerated and produce ohmic losses. Equation (6.13) therefore suggests that the lossless character of superconductivity exists only for steady currents. We shall return later to high-frequency properties.

The equally important Meissner effect may be represented by the use of the Maxwell equation

$$\nabla \times \boldsymbol{\varepsilon} = -\frac{\partial \mathbf{B}}{\partial t} = -\mu_0 \frac{\partial \mathfrak{IC}}{\partial t} \tag{6.14}$$

The final form assumes that the material has a linear magnetic character, a reasonable assumption except for some special compounds which are simultaneously superconductive and ferromagnetic. The substitution of the curl of (6.13) into (6.14) gives

$$\nabla \times \dot{\mathbf{J}}_s = -\frac{\mu_0 n_s e^2}{m} \frac{\partial \mathfrak{IC}}{\partial t} \tag{6.15}$$

Time integration gives

$$\nabla \times \mathbf{J}_s = -\frac{\mu_0 n_s e^2}{m} (\mathfrak{IC} - \mathfrak{IC}_0) \tag{6.16}$$

The field $\mathfrak{K}_0$ is a constant of integration. Since Meissner effect prohibits fields in the superconductor, the constant must be zero. The second London equation is, accordingly,

$$\nabla \times \mathbf{J}_s = -\frac{\mu_0 n_s e^2}{m} \mathfrak{K} \tag{6.17}$$

The nature of the equations, at least for the d-c case, becomes clearer if a simple solution is investigated. Take the curl of (6.17) and substitute from Maxwell's equation:

$$\nabla \times \mathfrak{K} = \mathbf{J}_n + \mathbf{J}_s + \frac{\partial \mathbf{D}}{\partial t} \tag{6.18}$$

For the d-c case both $\mathbf{J}_n$ and $\partial \mathbf{D}/\partial t$ are neglected.

$$\nabla \times \nabla \times \mathbf{J}_s = -\frac{\mu_0 e^2 n_s}{m} \mathbf{J}_s$$

We make use of the general vector relation

$$\nabla \times \nabla \times \mathbf{J}_s = \nabla(\nabla \cdot \mathbf{J}_s) - \nabla^2 \mathbf{J}_s$$

Since no steady accumulation of charge could be anticipated, we must have $\nabla \cdot \mathbf{J}_s = 0$, whereupon

$$\nabla^2 \mathbf{J}_s = \frac{\mathbf{J}_s}{\lambda^2} \tag{6.19}$$

where $\lambda^2 = m/\mu_0 n_s e^2$. The parameter λ has dimensions of *distance*, and is termed the *penetration depth*. The meaning of this depth can be understood from the solution of the one-dimensional equation

$$\frac{d^2 J_s}{dx^2} = \frac{J_s}{\lambda^2}$$

Solutions are

$$J_s = A e^{x/\lambda} + B e^{-x/\lambda} \tag{6.20}$$

The values of the constants A and B depend on boundary conditions. Consider an infinitely thick superconductor ($x > 0$) with planar surface $x = 0$. The solution with positive exponential would involve infinite currents; hence the other must be correct. B is the current density J_0 at the surface, which clearly cannot have an x component (out of the surface). The

total current per unit width normal to the direction of current
flow is

$$I = \int_0^\infty J_0 e^{-x/\lambda} \, dx = J_0 \lambda \tag{6.21}$$

The penetration depth is, accordingly, the effective thickness
of the current-carrying layer if the current were uniform with
the current density at the surface.   The analogy to the normal
"skin depth" of electromagnetic theory is apparent.   The current integral of (6.21) may even be used to define "penetration
depth" if the attenuation of current with distance does not
follow the exponential law, as in more accurate theories.

The value of λ may be estimated using for n_s a value of
the order of the number of atoms per cubic centimeter ($\sim 10^{23}$)
and for m the free-electron mass (though, as we know from
band theory, the effective mass may be quite different).   This
yields $\lambda = 200$ A, which is something like a practical *lower*
limit to λ.   The penetration of magnetic field into a superconductor is found by substitution of (6.20) into (6.17); the x
dependence of $\mathcal{3C}$ is the same as that of J_s.   Thus we see that
the Meissner effect (magnetic flux expelled from a superconductor) is only an approximation.   In fact, if a dimension of the
superconductor is of the order of λ, very little field reduction
can take place in the interior.   The field reduction is brought
about by supercurrents flowing to shield the interior of the
conductor from fields.

Since λ contains n_s, the unknown density of superconducting electrons, one should not be surprised that it varies with
temperature.   Above T_c, n_s must be zero.   At zero temperature, n_s attains some maximum value, when all electrons which
can become superconducting have done so.   The depth λ is
therefore a minimum at $T = 0$ and approaches infinity at
$T = T_c$.   Many experimental data fit

$$\lambda \cong \frac{\lambda_0}{[1 - (T/T_c)^4]^{\frac{1}{2}}} \tag{6.22}$$

where $\lambda_0 = \lambda \, (T = 0)$.   The variation of λ with applied magnetic field has been studied using very thin superconductors;
it was concluded by Pippard that there is only a few per cent
change of λ with $\mathcal{3C}$, even up to $\mathcal{3C}_c$.   This is of the form

$$\lambda(\mathcal{3C}) = \lambda_{(\mathcal{3C}=0)} \left(1 + \gamma \, \frac{\mathcal{3C}^2}{\mathcal{3C}_c{}^2} \right) \tag{6.23}$$

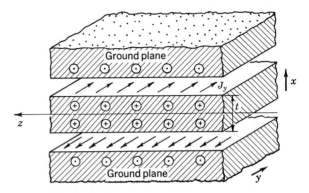

Figure 6.3 Geometry of a strip superconductor between superconducting "ground planes." Current must flow in the ground planes, in a direction opposite that in the conductor.

where $\gamma \approx 0.02$. This result is encouraging, since one would not expect the presence of a magnetic field to alter materially the distribution of electrons over normal and superconducting electronic states.

It is now elementary to obtain the d-c solution for current density in a superconducting conductor in the form of a thin strip (Fig. 6.3). Practical thin-film superconductors may be approximated over most of their width by this type of geometry. Let the current flow be in the y direction and the strip have a thickness t in the x direction and (so far as we are concerned) be infinitely wide in the z direction. The solution for current density is again given by (6.20). We assume that the conductor's external environment is symmetrical about $x = 0$, as, for example, a strip conductor between two ground planes (see the figure). The supercurrent J_y is thus symmetrical with respect to $x = 0$, through the center of the strip. In a strip of infinite width there is no reason to expect the current density to be z-dependent. Since $J_y(x) = J_y(-x)$ by symmetry, $A = B$, and $J_y = 2A \cosh (x/\lambda)$. If I is the total current per unit width in the z direction, then

$$I = 2A \int_{-t/2}^{t/2} \cosh \frac{x}{\lambda} \, dx \qquad (6.24)$$

The final expression for current density,

$$J_y = \frac{I \cosh (x/\lambda)}{2\lambda \sinh (t/2\lambda)} \qquad (6.25)$$

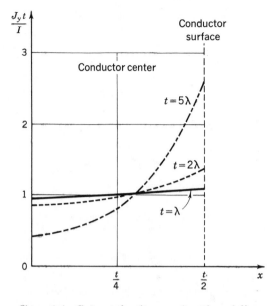

Figure 6.4 Current density as a function of distance across the conductor of Fig. 6.3, for thickness of λ, 2λ, and 5λ (London theory).

follows from evaluation of the integral and substitution.   This function is plotted in Fig. 6.4.   When the thickness of the superconducting strip is *much less than* the penetration depth λ, the current is almost uniformly distributed through the metal and the field is scarcely "excluded."

Using (6.17), the magnetic field accompanying this current distribution can readily be calculated:

$$\mathfrak{IC} = \mathbf{1}_z \mathfrak{IC}_z = \mathbf{1}_z \frac{I}{2} \frac{\sinh (x/\lambda)}{\sinh (t/2\lambda)} \tag{6.26}$$

The field at the surfaces of the conductor $(x = \pm t/2)$ is $\mathfrak{IC}_z = \pm I/2$.   This is of course independent of the current *distribution*.

The current (and field) distributions of other geometries of conductors may in principle be calculated using (6.19).   In round cylindrical conductors, the current density and field are expressed in terms of Bessel functions, etc.   In many situations where the geometry is excessively complicated to permit analysis, analogs may be used.   Where a superconductor is large compared with the penetration depth, and two-dimensional in form, the magnetic field at the surface of the conductor (which

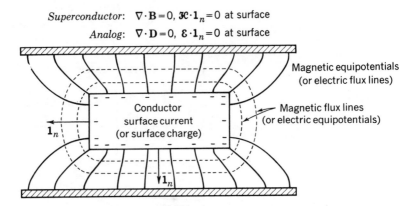

Superconductor: $\nabla \cdot \mathbf{B} = 0$, $\mathfrak{K} \cdot \mathbf{1}_n = 0$ at surface

Analog: $\nabla \cdot \mathbf{D} = 0$, $\mathcal{E} \cdot \mathbf{1}_n = 0$ at surface

Figure 6.5   A bulk superconductor (or its electrostatic analog).

is in turn equal to the current flowing in the conductor at that point) may be found using an *electrostatic* model. The requirements on the magnetic field around a large bulk superconductor are (1) that it have no component normal to the surface, and (2) that it satisfy Laplace's equation. The equipotential lines around an electrically charged conductor of the same shape satisfy these same requirements. Thus (Fig. 6.5) the field lines must be the same.

When the conductor is small (only a few λ in some dimension), so that the currents are no longer a good approximation to surface currents, this analog is not accurate. A more refined analog requires that a current which is an exponential function of time be passed through a *normal* conductor. In this case Maxwell's equation

$$\nabla \times \mathcal{E} = -\frac{\partial \mathbf{B}}{\partial t}$$

may be written

$$\nabla \times \mathbf{J} = -\sigma \frac{\partial \mathbf{B}}{\partial t}$$

All quantities are assumed to vary as $e^{\alpha t}$, so that

$$\nabla \times \mathbf{J} = -\alpha\sigma \mathbf{B} \tag{6.27}$$

This is a direct analog to London's Eq. (6.17), identifying $\alpha\sigma \rightarrow 1/\mu_0\lambda^2$. Construction of conductors with dimensions of a few inches and drive signals of millisecond time constant make it possible to simulate superconducting thin-film-device

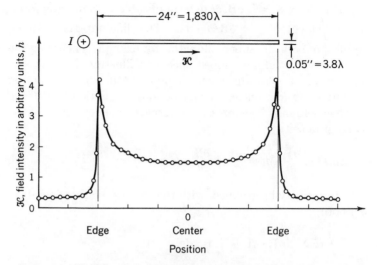

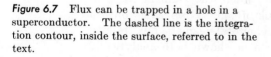

Position

Figure 6.6 Fields at the surface of a thin superconductor, determined by the exponential-time-function analog.   The return wire in the analog was 39 in. above the center of the strip conductor.   [*After N. H. Meyers, Proc. IRE,* **48**:1603 (1960).]

geometries.   Special exponential-rise generators and measuring instrumentation are required; the actual exponential time functions used can be only a few time constants long, limiting the accuracy of the procedure.   Figure 6.6 shows a field distribution of a thin-strip superconductor obtained by this procedure.   Effects due to the finite width of the strip are apparent.   If a superconductor in the form of a thin strip over a ground plane is many times wider than the intervening insulation's thickness, edge effects may safely be neglected.

A most interesting application of London's theory is the superconducting loop, or more generally, a hole in a superconducting specimen (Fig. 6.7).   We shall assume Maxwell's

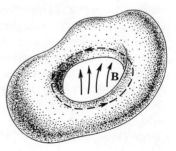

Figure 6.7 Flux can be trapped in a hole in a superconductor.   The dashed line is the integration contour, inside the surface, referred to in the text.

equation $\nabla \times \mathcal{E} = -\partial B/\partial t$ to be applicable. In integral form, it is $\oint \mathcal{E} \cdot dl = -\int_s \partial B/\partial t \cdot ds$. The line integral will be applied only in the superconductor, for example, encircling the hole in the doughnut-shaped specimen illustrated. The surface integral *must*, however, include both superconducting material and free space. From London's equation (6.13), the electric field may be expressed in terms of the derivative of the current density:

$$\mu_0 \lambda^2 \oint \frac{\partial J_s}{\partial t} \cdot dl = -\int_s \frac{\partial B}{\partial t} \cdot ds \qquad (6.28)$$

The terms may be grouped, with the time derivative operating on both:

$$\frac{\partial}{\partial t} \left(\mu_0 \lambda^2 \oint J_s \cdot dl + \int_s B \cdot ds \right) = 0 \qquad (6.29)$$

The expression in parentheses must accordingly be a constant, so long as the material remains superconducting.

$$\Phi_c = \mu_0 \lambda^2 \oint J_s \cdot dl + \int_s B \cdot ds = \text{const} \qquad (6.30)$$

Φ_c is a quantity characteristic of the path of integration c. London terms it the "fluxoid" of the path, since it has dimensions of magnetic flux. Applying this relation to a bulk superconductor, for paths of integration which are always a few λ inside the superconductor, J_s is effectively zero. Thus, for such paths, *the total magnetic flux through the path must remain constant*. There will be little flux through the superconductor deep in the material, as we have seen, so this flux may be associated with the hole.

The constancy of Φ_c does not apply if the material passes through a superconducting-normal transition. We may consequently introduce flux into a hole in a superconductor by cooling it below T_c in an applied magnetic field or by increasing an applied field to greater than $\mathcal{3C}_c$, so that the material becomes normally conducting and the field permeates the specimen. When the field is again reduced below the critical field, part of the flux lines passing through the sample will escape to the outside, but some to the inside, where they remain trapped. Once flux is trapped in the hole, (6.30) is applicable until a field exceeding $\mathcal{3C}_c$ is applied. The total magnetic flux trapped (more correctly, the fluxoid) can be shown both analytically

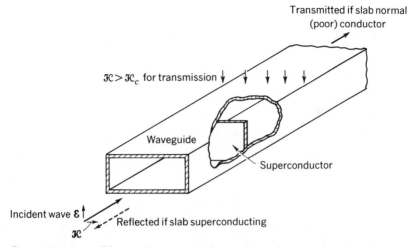

Figure 6.8   A possible use of a superconductor as a microwave switch.   The superconducting slab placed across the waveguide reflects almost all the incident power until it is made normally conducting.

and experimentally to be *quantized*, in quanta of $hc/e = 4 \times 10^{-7}$ gauss-cm^2.   These quanta are known as *fluxons*.

The behavior of superconductors at direct current is described using only Eq. (6.17), since superconducting electrons *prevent* any steady electric field from being established. Under high-frequency conditions, even the superconducting electrons must be accelerated (losslessly) by the electric field. They therefore introduce a *reactive* impedance, the presence of which "unmasks" the normally conducting electrons in the superconductor, since there are now electric fields in the material.   High frequencies in superconductors are of possible interest in certain applications; for example, a thin film of superconducting material might be placed transversely across a waveguide (Fig. 6.8).   When a magnetic field is applied, the material goes normal.   In this case a larger fraction of incident microwave power can be transmitted past the film than when the film is superconducting.   The important property here is the propagation of microwaves through the material.   Beginning with one of Maxwell's equations and London's equation (6.13),

$$\nabla \times \mathfrak{IC} = \mathbf{J}_{\text{total}} = \mathbf{J}_s + \mathbf{J}_n + \epsilon \frac{\partial \mathcal{E}}{\partial t}$$

$$\frac{\partial \mathbf{J}_s}{\partial t} = \frac{\mathcal{E}}{\mu_0 \lambda^2}$$

we assume all fields and currents sinusoidal. Then $\partial/\partial t \equiv j\omega$. Using $\mathbf{J}_n = \sigma_n \mathbf{\mathcal{E}}$, the right-hand side of the first equation above can be written exclusively in terms of $\mathbf{\mathcal{E}}$:

$$\nabla \times \mathbf{\mathcal{H}} = \left(\sigma_n + j\omega\epsilon - \frac{j}{\omega\mu_0\lambda^2} \right) \mathbf{\mathcal{E}} \tag{6.31}$$

Take the curl of (6.31), and substitute another Maxwell equation, $\nabla \times \mathbf{\mathcal{E}} = -\mu_0 \dfrac{\partial \mathbf{\mathcal{H}}}{\partial t} = -j\omega\mu_0\mathbf{\mathcal{H}}$:

$$\nabla \times \nabla \times \mathbf{\mathcal{H}} = \nabla(\nabla \cdot \mathbf{\mathcal{H}}) - \nabla^2\mathbf{\mathcal{H}} = j\omega\mu_0 \left(\sigma_n + j\omega\epsilon - \frac{j}{\omega\mu_0\lambda^2} \right) \mathbf{\mathcal{H}}$$

Since $\nabla \cdot \mathbf{B} = 0$ and $\mathbf{B} = \mu_0\mathbf{\mathcal{H}}$, $\nabla \cdot \mathbf{\mathcal{H}} = 0$. Then

$$\nabla^2\mathbf{\mathcal{H}} = \left(\frac{1}{\lambda^2} - \omega^2\mu_0\epsilon + j\omega\mu_0\sigma_n \right) \mathbf{\mathcal{H}} \tag{6.32}$$

This includes both low-frequency and high-frequency behavior. If $\omega = 0$, $\mathbf{\mathcal{H}}$ varies according to London's penetration law for superconductors. If $\lambda \to \infty$ and $\mathbf{J}_n = 0$, it is the usual electromagnetic wave equation [whose solutions include $e^{\pm j\omega(\mu_0\epsilon)^{\frac{1}{2}}z}$, for one-dimensional (plane) waves in a dielectric (μ_0, ϵ)]. The inclusion of $\mathbf{J}_n$ introduces loss, as in a conductor or a lossy dielectric. The term $\omega^2\mu_0\epsilon \equiv (2\pi/\lambda_0)^2$, where λ_0 is the electromagnetic wavelength. At least through microwave frequencies, it is typically much less than the penetration-depth term $1/\lambda^2$, and may be neglected. The form of the high-frequency supercurrents and fields is, accordingly,

$$e^{j\omega t} \exp\left[\pm \frac{z}{\lambda} (1 + j\omega\mu_0\sigma_n\lambda^2)^{\frac{1}{2}} \right] \tag{6.33}$$

The superconductor attenuates waves impinging on it. Like the attenuation of a "cutoff" waveguide, however, the attenuation is reactive and represents reflection of the incident waves. The normal conductivity σ_n introduces power dissipation.

Another high-frequency property of interest is the *surface impedance* of a superconductor, the ratio of the tangential electric field to the current flowing per unit width in a surface, as inside an electromagnetic cavity. The penetration of magnetic field can be described by (6.33):

$$\mathbf{\mathcal{H}}_x(z) = \mathbf{\mathcal{H}}_0 e^{-(1/\lambda^2 + j\omega\mu_0\sigma_n)^{\frac{1}{2}}z}$$

where $\mathfrak{3C}_0$ is the field at the surface. From (6.31), the electric field is given in terms of the magnetic field by

$$\mathcal{E} = \frac{1}{\sigma_n - j/\omega\mu_0\lambda^2} \, \nabla \times \mathfrak{3C}$$

The curl has only a y component, and substituting $\mathfrak{3C}_x$ from above,

$$\mathcal{E}_y = \frac{-j\omega\mu_0}{(1/\lambda^2 + j\omega\mu_0\sigma_n)^{\frac{1}{2}}} \, \mathfrak{3C}_x$$

By drawing a closed integration path through the surface, one can show that the total current J_y per unit width of surface of the superconductor equals the field $\mathfrak{3C}_x$ at the surface, as in (6.26). The ratio $\mathcal{E}_y/\mathfrak{3C}_x = Z_s$ is the surface impedance, in this case

$$Z_s = \frac{j\omega\mu_0}{(1/\lambda^2 + j\omega\mu_0\sigma_n)^{\frac{1}{2}}} \tag{6.34}$$

When λ is infinite, the formula is that for a normal metal $[Z_n = (j\omega\mu_0/\sigma)^{\frac{1}{2}}]$, as a result of classical skin effect. While the surface impedance of normal conductors at high frequencies always yields a 45° phase angle (equal resistance and reactance, from the factor $j^{\frac{1}{2}}$), the surface impedance of superconductors even at high microwave frequencies is more nearly reactive. For λ much less than the normal skin depth, (6.34) may be approximated by

$$Z_s = R_s + jX_s = \frac{\omega^2\mu_0{}^2\lambda^4\sigma_n}{2} + j\omega\mu_0\lambda^2 \tag{6.35}$$

which shows the resistive part increasing with the square of frequency.

In normal metals, anomalous skin effect (Sec. 3.8) plays a major role when the skin depth becomes smaller than electron mean free paths. In superconductors, similar effects, discussed briefly in the next section, lead to anomalies in the behavior. At or above microwave frequencies, results of the London theory become inadequate to explain experimental behavior. Prior to the development of an adequate microscopic theory, experimentalists had determined empirical relations which seemed to fit observed data. These relations are usually expressed in terms of the ratio of the surface *resistance* (determined by the "lossy" part of Z_s) in the super-

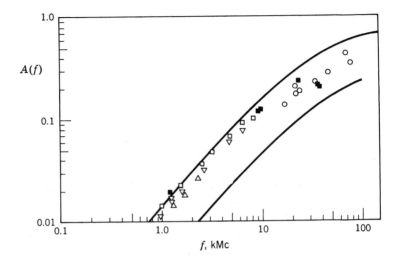

Figure 6.9   Frequency-dependent function in the surface-resistance formula (6.36).   The experimental data, for a variety of materials, may define a universal curve.   [*After P. B. Miller, Phys. Rev.*, **118**:928 (1960).]

conducting state to that in the normal state.   The empirical form given by Pippard is

$$\frac{R_s}{R_n} = A(f) \frac{t^4(1 - t^2)}{1 - t^4} \tag{6.36}$$

where $t = T/T_c$.   The function $A(f)$ is slightly different for each metal, but goes approximately as the $4/3$ power of frequency.   Values of $A(f)$ versus f are given in Fig. 6.9.

The low electrical losses of superconductors suggest the possibility of using them for d-c power-transmission lines or in resonant cavities at microwave frequencies.   The transmission-line application is of somewhat academic interest, because of the problem of carrying the necessary refrigeration for great distances.   Cavities for accurate frequency control are more interesting.   Practically speaking, it is extremely difficult to achieve suitably smooth superconductor surfaces by machining, but a value of quality factor (inverse of fractional bandwidth), $Q = 8 \times 10^6$, has been reported at 9,200 Mc/sec in a machined lead cavity.[1]

[1] C. J. Grebenkemper and J. P. Hagen, *Phys. Rev.*, **86**:673 (1952).

6.3   Modern Microscopic Theories

Phenomenological theories such as the London theory of superconductivity seldom give any clues to the underlying electronic processes, no more than does Ohm's law. From the outset, theorists had an awareness that complex and basically different electronic processes were at work. Fritz London looked at the persistent current in a superconducting ring as analogous to a single atom in which electrons can move forever without loss. While this view is too simple and somewhat misleading, the problem is indeed one of explaining how superconducting electrons can move through the lattice without giving up energy as they would in a normal metal. Although this particular point is not explained satisfactorily even today, strides have been taken in understanding the basic phenomenon. The important theories evolved are complex beyond the level of this text, and can be described here only in much simplified terms. The reader who has understood the manipulations of London's theory should not give up hope, however, for the London theory is adequate for major conclusions of superconductivity phenomena and a good source of device equations. Its chief failing (in device analysis) is inaccurate description of the detailed nature of field penetration, which, like anomalous skin effect, is not truly exponential.

A few important experimental facts led to the presently accepted fundamental views. One which may seem odd is that the transition temperature of a superconductor is a function of the atomic weight M; that is, if two *isotopes* of the same metal are compared, the transition temperature varies as

$$T_c \propto M^{-\frac{1}{2}} \tag{6.37}$$

What is so strange is that nowhere in the theory of metals do the fine details of the lattice vibrations (phonons) play an essential role. This "isotope effect," predicted in 1950 in a theory of Fröhlich,[1] actually led the way to the present theories.

An effect first discovered experimentally was the absorption of infrared photons by superconductors, even near absolute zero temperature, where the majority of active electrons are superconductive. Even if one made the assumption that the number of normally conducting electrons did not approach zero, there would be no ready explanation for the observed sharp absorption edge for radiation below wavelengths cor-

[1] H. Fröhlich, *Proc. Phys. Soc.*, **A63**:778 (1950).

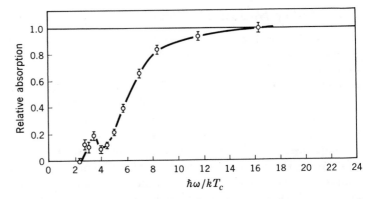

Figure 6.10 Conductivity of superconductors vs. frequency (expressed in terms of the ratio of photon energy to kT_c), measured in thin lead films. [*After R. E. Glover and M. Tinkham, Phys. Rev.*, **108**:243 (1957).]

responding to $\hbar\omega \gtrsim 3.5kT_c$ (Fig. 6.10). This absorption is similar to the photon absorption which produces electron-hole generation in a semiconductor. The latter corresponds to ionization of valence electrons across the energy gap. The observed infrared absorption edge gave support to the existence of a similar but very narrow (for example, 3 mv for $T_c = 10°\mathrm{K}$) energy gap in superconductors. The unusual exponentially varying specific-heat contribution found in superconductors, difficult to explain in terms of earlier models, is of the kind expected from a transition corresponding to the excitation of electrons across an energy gap. The energy-gap concept has now become a fundamental aspect, along with superconductivity and Meissner effect. Superconducting-electron states lie below the energy gap, and normal states above it. This energy gap, however, unlike the near-constant energy gap in semiconductors, depends strongly upon temperature. At T_c its value goes to zero; above T_c, superconducting states cannot even exist in a bulk semiconductor.

The now-famous *BCS theory*[1] was the first truly successful microscopic quantum theory; it explains the energy gap and Meissner and isotope effects. This theory also yields a theoretical value for the energy gap which compares closely with experiment. In the theory it is recognized that phonons do

[1] J. Bardeen, L. N. Cooper, and J. R. Schrieffer, *Phys. Rev.*, **108**:1175 (1957).

play a major role in superconductivity.   They are found to
enter via the *coupling* they provide between *pairs* of electrons.
The reader may recall that the wave motion of a particle is
perturbed by any type of field; for example, the energy of a
spinning electron in a magnetic field is perturbed either positively or negatively, depending on its orientation (Sec. B.8).
A phonon which disturbs the lattice periodicity interacts
strongly with a *single* electron when the frequency and wavelength of the phonon are correct to couple two one-electron
states (as discussed in Sec. 2.8).   In the BCS theory, it was
suggested that a phonon may interact simultaneously with
two electrons, perturbing the motion of both without ever
being fully transferred from one to the other.   This *virtual
phonon* binds the electrons together to a certain extent.   This
interaction is strongest when both the moment and the spins
of the electrons in the pair are opposite ($\mathbf{k}_1 = -\mathbf{k}_2; \mathbf{s}_1 = -\mathbf{s}_2$).
Below T_c such a pair, with individual momenta corresponding
to values of $\mathbf{k}$ at the Fermi surface, has energy less than twice
the energy of a single electron at the Fermi surface.   Since
the important conduction electrons are those very near E_f, a
small energy gap separates the normally conducting one-electron states from the new two-electron states.   Bardeen and
colleagues, studying only "optimized" pairs with opposite $\mathbf{k}$-
and $\mathbf{s}$-value electrons, found an energy gap at $T = 0$ of $E_g =
3.52kT_c$, remarkably close to the experimental values.

An experimental result which gives direct evidence of the
energy gap is a *quantum tunneling* observation of Giaever.[1]   A
thin-film superconductor is deposited on a smooth glass surface
by evaporation.   The surface of the material is covered by an
insulating layer 100 A or less in thickness; this can be done in
the case of aluminum by oxidizing the metal first deposited.   A
second metal coating, either normal or superconducting, is then
added atop the insulator.   Electrodes connected to the two
metal strata register a voltage-current curve indicative of the
band structure, as in a tunnel diode.   In Fig. 6.11a is depicted
a metal-insulator-metal "sandwich," wherein each of the
metals is a superconductor, one of higher band gap than the
other.   A voltage is applied between the superconductors such
as to raise the electron energy of superconductor II, as shown.
The current which flows at modest voltages in this polarity is
due to electrons tunneling from the normal-electron band at
top right through the insulator and into the normal band on

[1] I. Giaever and K. Megerle, *Phys. Rev.*, **122**:1101 (1961).

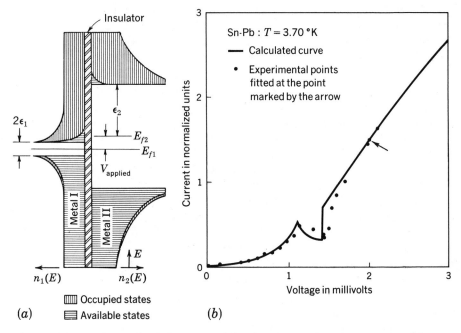

Figure 6.11 (*a*) Energy-level diagram and density-of-states functions postulated for superconductor-insulator-superconductor "sandwich." The critical temperature of superconductor II is greater than that of superconductor I. (*b*) Experimental and calculated tunneling current through the insulator, for a tin-lead combination. [*After S. Shapiro et al., IBM J.*, **6**:34 (1962).]

the left. This explains the initial rise of the current, in Fig. 6.11*b*. The more rapid rise is presumably due to the tunneling of superconductive-band electrons (at lower right) into the superconductive band on the left. At $V_{ap} \simeq \epsilon_2 - \epsilon_1$, the upper edges of the superconducting bands are aligned. Above this voltage and up to a voltage $\epsilon_1 + \epsilon_2$, the most plentiful electrons (at the top of the superconducting band) face no available states; hence the tunneling current is reduced. Above $\epsilon_1 + \epsilon_2$, however, the superconducting electrons on the right can tunnel directly into normal band states in the left. The voltage-current relations actually observed support the values of superconducting-normal band-gap energy observed through infrared absorption and predicted theoretically.

The most important concept in the BCS theory is the *correlation* of motions of the two electrons forming a superconductive pair. Electrons so paired can maintain coupled motion when separated by a distance termed the "correlation length," $\xi \sim 10^{-4}$ cm. This very substantial distance (large in relation to usual electron mean free paths in room-temperature conductors) may also be viewed as a two-electron wave-packet dimension. Whenever the penetration depth λ calculated from London's theory is *large* compared with this distance, the London calculation is fairly accurate. If, however, the London theory predicts a change of current over distances much shorter than this correlation length, it must be wrong. This is the same type of limitation relating normal skin effect and anomalous skin effect (Sec. 3.8). Superconductors for which $\lambda < \xi$ are now termed type I superconductors, and those for which $\lambda > \xi$ are termed type II superconductors. In addition to affecting the field-penetration law, this distinction has major effect on the nature of superconducting-normal transitions, as discussed in the following section. Several phenomenological theories, principally due to Pippard and to Ginzburg and Landau,[1] give more accurate relations for field penetration. Although these are not microscopic quantum theories, they contain appropriate parameters which can be adjusted to fit the results of the BCS theory. The solution due to Pippard[2] begins by observing that Eq. (6.17) may, upon substitution of the vector potential $\mathbf{A}$ ($\mathbf{B} = \nabla \times \mathbf{A}$), be written

$$\mathbf{J}_s = -\frac{\mathbf{A}}{\mu_0 \lambda^2} \tag{6.38}$$

The Londons assumed that the superconducting current density at a point depends only upon the magnetic vector potential *at that point*. In the Pippard theory, the superconducting current density is defined, not only by the vector potential at that point, but by a weighted average of the vector potential at all points surrounding the point in question. Pippard replaces (6.38) by

$$\mathbf{J}(\mathbf{r}) = \frac{3}{4\pi \mu_0 \lambda^2 \xi_0} \int \frac{\mathbf{R}[\mathbf{R} \cdot \mathbf{A}(\mathbf{r}')]e^{-R/\xi_0}}{R^4} \, d\mathbf{r}' \tag{6.39}$$

where the integral is over the space of $\mathbf{r}'$, and $\mathbf{R}$ is the vector joining points $\mathbf{r}$ and $\mathbf{r}'$ ($\mathbf{R} = \mathbf{r} - \mathbf{r}'$). The relation includes the effect of $\mathbf{A}$ at a point a distance $\mathbf{R}$ away, with the weighting factor $R^{-2}e^{-R/\xi_0}$. The parameter ξ_0 corresponds to the cor-

[1] V. L. Ginzburg and L. D. Landau, *JETP, U.S.S.R.*, **20**:1064 (1950).
[2] A. B. Pippard, *Proc. Roy. Soc. (London)*, **A216**:547 (1953).

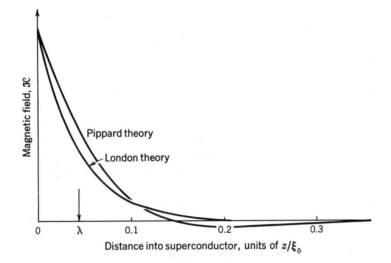

relation length; the exponential approximates the form of the superconducting electron wave packet $|\psi^2|$.   If $A(r)$ does not vary rapidly, over a range of several ξ_0, it may be removed from under the integral; the resultant integration yields (6.38). The solutions of (6.39) lead to currents which *do not decay exponentially* vs. distance into a superconducting surface. Figure 6.12 is a comparison of London's exponential decay with a calculation of Pippard for his type of penetration law, for the case $\lambda = 0.04\xi_0$.   The results suggest that we should expect the major effects predicted by London theory to be within reason.

Pair correlation of electrons can also explain the absence of resistivity in superconductors.   The particular nature of the paired-electron state makes it impossible for the pair, as such, to lose kinetic energy in phonon collisions.   As discussed in Sec. 2.8, even normally conducting electrons are in certain circumstances unable to interact with phonons which may be present.   Only when a superconducting electron pair achieves a sufficiently large kinetic energy are energy-exchange collisions possible.   This results in "splitting" of the pair into two normally conducting electrons and represents the sort of superconducting-normal transition which occurs when an applied field is increased above the critical value. The applied field increases kinetic energies, for the paired electrons must move faster to produce current required to exclude higher fields.

6.4   Superconducting-Normal Transitions

In Sec. 6.1, a phase diagram (Fig. 6.1) related the critical temperature and critical field for a long rod-shaped specimen aligned parallel to the field. By the application of either heat or a magnetic field, superconductivity in a metal may be reversibly "switched" on and off. The field may be entirely external, or it may be partly or wholly produced by current in the superconductor itself. Many electronic applications of superconductors depend upon these transition properties. Here we consider some aspects of the transition process, first in regard to slow changes and then to more rapid transitions, in simple type I superconductors such as pure tin and lead. The somewhat different behavior of type II superconductors is discussed briefly.

An enlightening example of a superconductor transition is that of a sphere in a uniform magnetic field $\mathcal{3C}_0$ (Fig. 6.13). The magnetic field in the vicinity of a perfectly diamagnetic sphere (a good approximation for a completely superconducting sphere) is described in many electromagnetism texts;[1] the solution for a dielectric sphere is formally identical with that of a magnetic sphere. In the region outside the sphere ($r > a$), $\mathcal{3C}$ may be derived as the gradient of a scalar potential U:

$$U = \mathcal{3C}_0 r \cos \theta - \frac{\mathcal{3C}_0}{2} \frac{a^3}{r^2} \cos \theta \qquad (6.40)$$

While the *field* at the poles is zero, that at the equator is $\frac{3}{2}\mathcal{3C}_0$. If a magnetic field $\frac{2}{3}\mathcal{3C}_c$ is applied, the field at the equator of the superconductor will equal $\mathcal{3C}_c$. For fields above $\frac{2}{3}\mathcal{3C}_c$, the field at the equator exceeds $\mathcal{3C}_c$ and at least *part* of the volume of the sphere must become normally conducting. We should intuitively expect a small band at the equator to become normal, leading to the field configuration suggested in the figure. If this were so, however, the field *everywhere* in the normal region must be greater than $\mathcal{3C}_c$; otherwise the material could not *remain* normally conducting. A sketch of the mag-

---

[1] See, for example, W. R. Smythe, "Static and Dynamic Electricity," pp. 140–141, McGraw-Hill Book Company, New York, 1950.

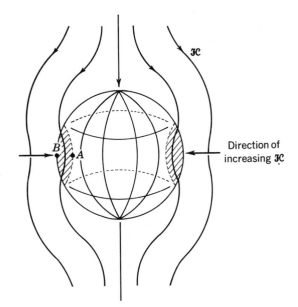

Direction of
increasing $\mathfrak{K}$

Figure 6.13 Superconducting (e.g., lead) sphere in a
magnetic field. The field configuration shown is for
the hypothetical situation where a continuous band
around the sphere might turn superconductive.
Since magnetostatic theory shows that the field is
greater at A than at B, this is not a stable
configuration.

netic field lines in such a condition indicates that flux lines
would be concave toward the center of the sphere. Where
such a field configuration exists, the field must, as a solution of
Laplace's equation ($\nabla \cdot \mathbf{B} = 0$), always *increase toward the
origin*. The field must therefore be greater than $\mathfrak{K}_c$ at the
normal-superconducting boundary, since this would be the
greatest field in the material. Such a field distribution is
therefore not consistent with our original assumptions.

The actual behavior of the superconducting sphere as the
field exceeds $\frac{2}{3}\mathfrak{K}_c$ is to form randomly located *domains* of normal material, starting from the edge of the sphere. These,
sketched in Fig. 6.14, carry just enough magnetic flux to make
the field at the superconducting-normal boundaries equal $\mathfrak{K}_c$.
As the external field is increased further, the regions of normal
material grow at the expense of superconducting regions, still
maintaining a random domain structure. When the *applied*
field equals or exceeds $\mathfrak{K}_c$, the entire sphere becomes normally
conducting. The process should be completely *reversible;* that

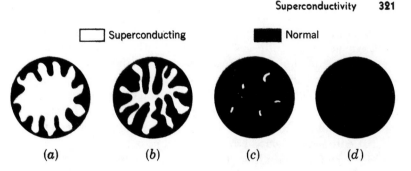

☐ Superconducting   ■ Normal

(a)   (b)   (c)   (d)

Figure 6.14   Section normal to the magnetic field through sphere of Fig. 6.13, showing likely domain configurations.   Sketches a to d are for successively increasing fields.   [*See also* W. DeSorbo and V. L. Newhouse, J. Appl. Phys., **33**:1004 (1962).]

is, as the field is slowly decreased from $\mathcal{3C}_c$, domains of super-conducting material appear, expand, and force the flux from the sphere.   The transition phenomenon was observed some years before this domain behavior was understood.   A super-conductor which contains some domains of normally conduct-ing material is said to be in "the intermediate state"; this early terminology, while not particularly descriptive, remains with us.

The spatial *scale* of the domain structure may be of importance in device application.   The controlling factors in the establishment of domain structure are (1) the magnetic stored energy in the normal regions, and (2) the energy required to maintain domains of given dimensions.   The interface between normal and superconducting domains carries a cir-culating current, which represents the motion of superelectrons in a region of thickness $\sim\lambda$.   This current involves electrons, which carry kinetic energy.   Each unit area of domain *bound-ary* represents a given kinetic energy.   In the intermediate state, the distribution of magnetic flux in normally conducting domains through the specimen involves an energy which depends on the magnetic-flux *distribution*.   This magnetic energy is minimum when the domains are infinitesimal in "thickness" and varies with the domain dimensions in some monotonic fashion.

The free energy G, which seeks a minimum at equilibrium, thus contains two domain-dependent terms:

magnetic stored energy, decreases with l
$$\downarrow$$
$$G = G_0 + G_1 + G_2 \leftarrow \text{domain surface energy, increases with } l \qquad (6.41)$$
$$\uparrow$$
domain-independent

Domain dimensions may be characterized by a length parameter l, which measures in a crude way the average transverse dimension of domains; equilibrium demands some finite average l, as shown in Fig. 6.15, if both G_1 and G_2 are *positive* functions. While the computation of G_1 and G_2 is not usually feasible, experimental measurements of domains in soft, ductile pure semiconductors such as tin, lead, and mercury show characteristic dimensions in the range of 1 mm to 1 cm.

This behavior is altogether altered if energy associated with the domain boundaries is not positive, but *negative*, i.e., if the presence of the boundaries actually lowers the energy of the electrons in the vicinity. This predicts infinitesimal domain dimensions; in light of the quantization of flux, the domains cannot be smaller than the size sufficient to carry a quantum of flux through the superconductor. This type of behavior is exhibited by type II superconductors.

The hypothesis that the magnetic field required to destroy superconductivity is the same whether derived from external or self-produced fields can be tested simply by the application of a magnetic field $\mathcal{3C}_0$ parallel to a long current-carrying conductor of circular cross section. The self-produced field is then $\mathcal{3C} = I/2\pi r$. With this shape, the field at the supercon-

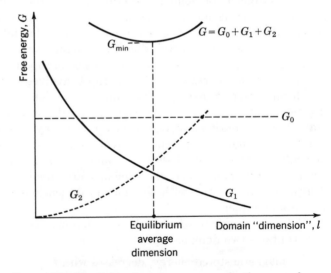

Figure 6.15 The fixing of average superconducting-normal domain dimensions in a type I material, that is, one having positive surface energy in the boundary.

ductor boundary due to applied field equals the applied field. At the superconductor surface the two fields are perpendicular; hence the critical current and field should be related by

$$\mathcal{3C}_c{}^2 = \left(\frac{I}{2\pi a}\right)^2 + \mathcal{3C}_0{}^2 \tag{6.42}$$

This is indeed found true when the superconductor is of type I and has dimensions $a \gg \lambda$. In small-diameter conductors or thin films of type I, although an expression of the form (6.42) still applies approximately, the apparent value of $\mathcal{3C}_c$ can be many times the value applicable to bulk material. Superconducting electrons can make a transition into normally conducting states when their *kinetic energy* is increased to a sufficiently large value. The effect of a magnetic field applied to a superconductor is to induce supercurrents on the surface. The field producing the supercurrent is the usual one due to time rate of magnetic-flux change. When the magnetic field becomes larger, the kinetic velocity must increase (for the numbers of superelectrons can be increased only by lowering the temperature). Above the critical field, the onset of normal conductivity moves the normal-superconducting boundary, in the direction of weaker fields.

In the presence of a magnetic field, in the plane of a thin-film superconductor [same geometry as for Eq. (6.25)], a current exists in the superconductor, of the form

$$J_z = A \sinh \frac{x}{\lambda} \tag{6.43}$$

where the zero of x is at the center of the film (Fig. 6.4). The internal magnetic field, by the London theory, is

$$\mathcal{3C}_y = \lambda^2 \frac{\partial J}{\partial x} = A\lambda \cosh \frac{x}{\lambda}$$

The relation between the current density and field at the surface is obtained by eliminating A and substituting $x = t/2$:

$$\mathcal{3C}_y = \lambda J_z \frac{\cosh (t/2\lambda)}{\sinh (t/2\lambda)} \tag{6.44}$$

If we presume that when the kinetic velocity of the surface superelectrons reaches a value giving an energy of the order of the band-gap energy, the electrons become normal, $J \propto$ velocity $\propto (E_{\text{gap}})^{\frac{1}{2}}$. There should, by this elementary thinking, be a critical current density J_{crit} which is the maximum tolerable before transition occurs. Since in the case of a thin-film superconductor the maximum current density occurs at the surfaces ($x = t/2$), then

$$\mathcal{3C}_{crit} = \lambda J_{crit} \coth \frac{t}{2\lambda} \tag{6.45}$$

The limit of $\coth (t/2\lambda)$ as $t/2\lambda \to \infty$ (i.e., the *bulk* limit) is unity; hence

$$\frac{\mathcal{3C}_c \text{ (film)}}{\mathcal{3C}_c \text{ (bulk)}} \approx \coth \frac{t}{2\lambda} \tag{6.46}$$

This general form of variation is observed experimentally.

The *critical current* of a thin film may also be calculated by the same method as for (6.46). Here London's equations yield, as shown earlier,

$$J_y = \frac{I}{2\lambda} \frac{\cosh (x/\lambda)}{\sinh (t/2\lambda)} \tag{6.25}$$

At the surface, $x = t/2$, the current and current density are related by

$$I = 2J_{y,\text{at surface}} \lambda A \tanh \frac{t}{2\lambda} \tag{6.47}$$

The critical current is found by substituting J_{crit}, and as before,

$$\frac{I_c \text{ [thickness } (t)]}{I_c \text{ (large thickness)}} = \tanh \frac{t}{2\lambda} \tag{6.48}$$

The current is, of course, based on the superconductor surface area, and not on the volume. While critical field increases, critical current *decreases*, in thinner films. To assure that critical field and critical current in a device assume values near their *bulk* values, it is necessary to make conductor thickness *several times* λ.

While zero-temperature critical fields of pure superconductors such as lead and tin are of the order of a few hundred oersteds, those of higher-melting metals and alloys (niobium, etc.) may be tens of thousands of oersteds. Early researchers classified the materials into two groups, "soft" (type I) and "hard" (type II), the soft materials being of low melting point and high ductility and the hard being high-melting and difficult to produce in strain-free form. This distinction is now known to be inaccurate, for supposedly "soft" superconductors, when severely strained, can be made to exhibit much higher $\mathcal{H}_c$ values and lower associated critical currents. Type II characteristics can also be produced by the addition of impurity elements to normally "soft" materials. The most dramatic distinction between the two types of behavior is seen in the way in which magnetic flux is repelled from the interior of long-rod samples of the two types of material (Fig. 6.16a). Type I supercon-

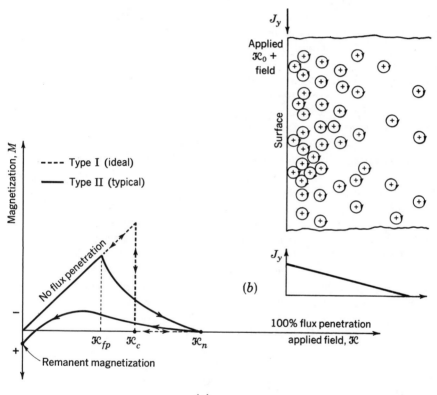

(a)

Figure 6.16   (*a*) Flux penetration as a function of applied field in type I and type II superconductors (the existence of a magnetization equal to the negative of the applied field, i.e., a 45° line, indicates that no flux penetrates the specimen). Whereas flux penetration occurs abruptly in type I superconductors, flux penetrates at lower fields ($\mathcal{H} \gtrsim \mathcal{H}_{fp} \cong 2^{-\frac{1}{2}}\mathcal{H}_c$) but does not completely fill a type II superconductor until very high fields ($\mathcal{H} > \mathcal{H}_n$) are attained. When field is removed, flux does not leave the superconductor reversibly, leading to the hysteresis effect shown. (*b*) A schematic of fluxon penetration in type II superconductors. Each flux quantum is represented by a flux line (+) with associated circulating currents. The current J_y corresponds to a gradient in fluxon density. Additional fluxons may be forced into the surface when the gradient becomes sufficiently large.

ductors, i.e., relatively undefected simple metals or ordered alloys, will change abruptly from superconducting to normal at a critical field $\mathfrak{K}_c$. Behavior of type II superconductors shows that the field does not completely penetrate the material up to very high fields and that the amount of superconducting material remaining decreases slowly as the field is increased. This corresponds to the forcing into the superconductor of individual quantized fluxons, rather than the large domains characteristic of pure undefected material. As fields are *reduced*, furthermore, the flux does not reversibly leave the superconductor. There is hysteresis in the process, and accordingly there are *losses* associated with even very slow transitions produced by application of field or change of current in the type II superconductor.

A description of field penetration into a type II superconductor is somewhat different from that of the pure elemental superconductors described earlier. Fluxons are prevented from entering the material by what may be described as "surface tension," up to a field which is of the order of 0.707 times the critical field corresponding to type I behavior (Fig. 6.16a). At higher fields, fluxons are forced into the surface by the applied field. Since (Fig. 6.16b) there will be a gradient of fluxon density ($\nabla \times \mathfrak{K} \neq 0$), there must accordingly be a current flowing in the surface; a uniform fluxon density would require no currents in the superconductor. The existence of a *critical current* for a type II superconducting wire implies that there is a critical fluxon gradient which will cause the fluxons to move deeper into the wire, reducing the area of superconducting material and causing the current to flow in a smaller portion of the wire, leading finally to normal conductivity. This critical current may correspond to a current density much larger than that found by applying $\mathfrak{K}_c \approx I/2\pi r$ at the wire surface, however, because the current flows in a region much thicker than the typical penetration depth of a type I superconductor.

The theory of type II superconductors has been developed more recently than that of pure elemental semiconductors. It has been well established that the addition of other metals to an elemental superconductor introduces type II behavior, in principle due to the reduction of mean free paths of electrons in alloys. The only clear exceptions would appear to be *ordered* alloys having a regular crystal structure. Applications in devices where magnetic fields must alter a superconductor to the normal state are essentially limited to type I superconduc-

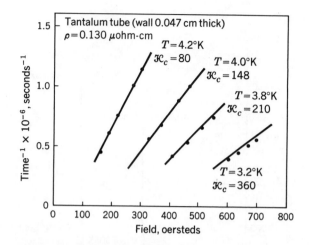

Figure 6.17   Time for the superconducting-normal phase boundary to penetrate the 0.0047-cm thickness of a tantalum tube, at various values of temperature and drive field. [*From W. B. Ittner, Phys. Rev.*, **111**:1483 (1958).]

tors.   Such applications are described in Sec. 6.5.   Type II superconductors, in the main mechanically "hard" metals and alloys in highly strained condition, are used in high-field magnets and similar applications (Sec. 6.6).

When a magnetic field exceeding $\mathcal{H}_c$ is applied *suddenly* to a type I superconductor, the resultant transition does not occur instantaneously.   As can be predicted from the London formulation, there is a limited velocity of motion of the domain boundaries, due to the eddy currents produced by the changing magnetic fields in the *normal* region.   While electric fields must be zero in the superconducting phase, the electrons in the normal region experience a magnetic field which increases from $\mathcal{H}_c$ to $\mathcal{H}_a$ (the driving field) as the domain boundary passes them.   Since it is the excess field ($\mathcal{H}_a - \mathcal{H}_c$) which causes the boundary to move, eddy currents oppose change of $\mathcal{H}$.   The normal electrons oppose the motion of the boundary and reduce its velocity to relatively low values.   Figure 6.17 shows data on the penetration time of a tantalum sample by fields of various intensities.   Since the equation of field penetration has the form of a *diffusion equation*, the time required for the field to penetrate a distance d is of the form

$$\tau = f\left(\frac{\mathcal{H}_a}{\mathcal{H}_c}\right)\frac{d^2}{\rho} \tag{6.49}$$

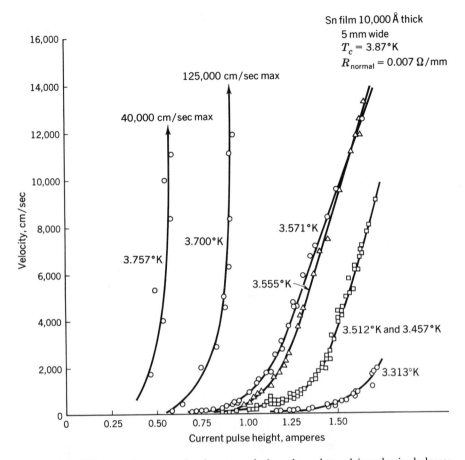

Sn film 10,000 Å thick
5 mm wide
$T_c = 3.87°K$
$R_{normal} = 0.007 \ \Omega/mm$

125,000 cm/sec max

40,000 cm/sec max

Figure 6.18 Velocity of superconducting-normal phase boundary, driven by joule losses in the normal region when pulsed by high-current pulses. (*From W. H. Cherry and J. I. Gittleman, Proc. Symp. on Superconductive Techniques for Computing Systems, OTS Document 161763, Office of Naval Research, p. 75, 1960.*)

where ρ is the resistivity in the normal phase, and the function $f(\mathfrak{3C}_a/\mathfrak{3C}_c)$ is transcendental, decreasing monotonically with increasing $\mathfrak{3C}_a$. The reduction of thickness to a few times λ makes this delay, in thin films, only of nanosecond duration.

Transitions can also be produced by *heating* a superconductor, from adjacent normally conducting material; it is in fact essential in transition-rate measurements to take these heating effects into account. If the superconductor is mounted in such a way as to be heated by adjacent material having previously made the transition to normal, the domain

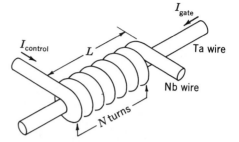

Figure 6.19 A wound-wire cryotron.

boundary will propagate. This effect is most pronounced when the superconductor has low thermal mass and carries a large current. The normal region may be initiated thermally or by using the field of another conductor. Although the thermal propagation is mainly dependent on the support and environment, the experimental results shown in Fig. 6.18 are probably typical.

6.5 Superconductive Amplifying and Switching Devices

The first superconductor device for electronic switching applications was the so-called *wound-wire cryotron*. This device consists of a superconducting wire of low critical field around which are wound several turns of a superconducting wire of higher-critical-field material (Fig. 6.19). The latter acts as a solenoidal electromagnet. When a current of sufficient magnitude is applied to the coil, the enclosed wire becomes normally conducting. Its resistance therefore changes from zero to some finite value. Output power is obtained by connecting this variable resistance into an output circuit.

The theory of this device is very simple. The current through the solenoidal wire (the "control") produces a magnetic field NI_c/L, where N is the number of turns, I_c is the *control current*, and L the length of the winding. The current I_g in the controlled wire (the "gate") produces a circumferential field at the surface $\mathcal{3C} = I_g/2\pi a$, where a is the radius of the gate. The gate wire becomes normally conducting when the total field exceeds $\mathcal{3C}_c$; the condition is

$$\mathcal{3C}_c{}^2 = \left(\frac{I_g}{2\pi a}\right)^2 + \left(\frac{NI_c}{L}\right)^2 \tag{6.50}$$

This relation is conveniently described by a curve relating the critical I_c and I_g, as in Fig. 6.20. Such a curve is also a phase

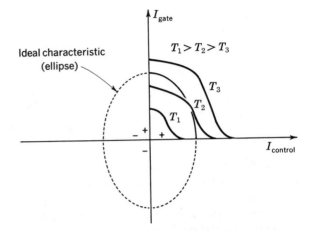

Figure 6.20   Ideal and typical characteristics of simple cryotrons involving gate and control conductors at 90°. Operating currents are controlled by helium-bath temperature.

diagram, for the gate is superconducting for all values of I inside the curve.   The control wire is always superconducting, since its material is such that its critical field far exceeds that of the gate.   The curve is completely symmetrical for negative currents as shown by dashed lines.

The ratio of I_g at zero control current to I_c at zero gate current is termed the *gain* of the device, though not a current gain in a traditional sense.   For the twisted-wire cryotron, values of this gain of 10 or more can be obtained.   It is possible to develop even higher effective gains by biasing the control current so that in the absence of an input signal, the control current is only slightly below the value needed to switch the gate to normal.

This early cryotron, like most of the devices which have followed it, was basically a switching device; the gate resistance was either *on* or *off*.   A *linearly* controlled device can be made in several ways, as by the use of a tapered-pitch control winding.   When the control current is applied, the part of the gate under the most closely spaced control winding becomes resistive at lower control currents than does the part experiencing a weaker control field.   The linearly controlled gate resistance may be used to control current in another circuit.   A practical limitation stems from the low resistances attainable; this is of

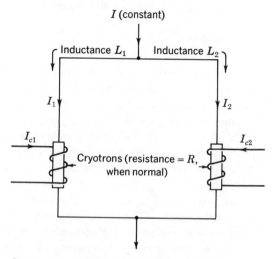

Figure 6.21   Simple cryotron flip-flop circuit.
There is electrical isolation between input and
controlled elements.

less concern where many cryogenic amplifier stages are cascaded, however.

Cryotron *switching* devices show considerable promise in large-scale computer applications, for in digital computers such large numbers of elements are required that the cost and trouble of maintaining a low-temperature environment may be offset by the simplicity and small size of the basic elements.

A binary computer switching element should be a device having two stable conditions of operation, means for altering its condition, and the ability to drive several other similar elements from one operating condition to another. Figure 6.21 is a schematic of the most common computer circuit configuration using cryotrons, analogous to the "flip-flop" of electron tube or transistor circuits. Two cryotron gate elements are used, and a constant current I is applied across the circuit. Assuming that both of the cryotrons are superconducting at the time current is applied, the current I will divide into the two arms in the inverse ratio of the inductances of the two arms: During the current build-up there is a voltage $L \, dI/dt$ across each arm.

$$ L_1 \frac{dI_1}{dt} = L_2 \frac{dI_2}{dt} $$

Since $I_1 + I_2 = I$, solving simultaneously yields

$$I_1 = I \frac{L_2}{L_1 + L_2} \qquad I_2 = I \frac{L_1}{L_1 + L_2} \qquad (6.51)$$

In computer circuits of this type the two arms are usually made to have equal inductances, to divide current equally. If the gate in arm 1 is made resistive by a control current, since the other arm is still superconducting, I shifts to flow completely in arm 2. If the control current across arm 1 is then removed, the current may not shift back but remains in arm 2. When the active arm, arm 2, is later made resistive momentarily, the current does shift back to arm 1. This shifting of current from arm 1 to arm 2 is the basis of operation of this circuit component. The two stable states, in which all current flows in one of the arms, are equivalent to those of a flip-flop.

The switching time, for causing all current to shift from one arm to another, is a major limiting characteristic of this element. Assuming that the input current I is constant, one must solve

$$I_1 + I_2 = I$$
$$I_1 R + L_1 \frac{dI_1}{dt} = L_2 \frac{dI_2}{dt}$$

for the shift of current from arm 1 to arm 2, subject to the boundary condition at $t = 0$: $I_1 = I$, $I_2 = 0$. The solution is a simple exponential:

$$I_1 = I e^{-Rt/(L_1 + L_2)}$$
$$I_2 = I(1 - e^{-Rt/(L_1 + L_2)}) \qquad (6.52)$$

R is the resistance of the gate when normally conducting. This result demonstrates the importance of reducing the circuit inductance, particularly since the controllable resistance is at best small.

The most practical configuration for cryotron elements is a thin superconducting film, deposited on a smooth surface such as glass, generally by evaporating the source material at high temperature in vacuum. The materials commonly used have been lead (Pb) for the connecting and control elements and tin (Sn, which has lower T_c and $\mathfrak{IC}_c$) for the gate elements (which should of course exhibit the abrupt transition of type I behavior). Operating temperature is maintained $\sim 0.1°$ below the critical temperature of the gate electrode ($\sim 3.8°$K), by maintaining constant pressure over a boiling liquid-helium bath. Under these conditions the control currents required are in the tens of milliamperes for typical elements having widths of the order of 0.005 to 0.025 in. and thickness of several thousand angstroms.

The cryotron elements themselves are of two basic types, the crossed-film cryotron and the in-line cryotron, both shown in Fig. 6.22. The crossed-film cryotron has a nominal gain (as defined earlier), without bias, equal to the ratio of widths of gate and control conductors, w_g/w_c. The magnetic field of a thin-strip conductor is large only between the conductor and a returning conductor such as the superconducting ground plane used in cryotron thin-film circuits. The magnetic field, from simple electromagnetic considerations, equals the current per unit *width* of conductor. The cryotron gate element is subject to fields in perpendicular directions, from its own current and that of the control element. When either field or the vector combination reaches $\mathcal{3C}_c$, the gate will conduct normally. The gain, as defined earlier, is the ratio of current in gate and

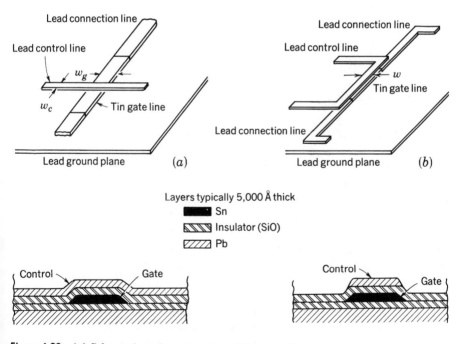

Figure 6.22   (a) Schematic and section view of "crossed-film" cryotron element; (b) "in-line" cryotron.

control (separately) which causes transition, which is just the width ratio. Since the gate can be made very wide, substantial current gains are possible. As the gate is increased in width, the resistance introduced into the circuit is reduced proportionately. If the gate resistivity in the normally conducting condition is ρ, and gate thickness is t_g, the normal gate resistance is

$$R = \rho \frac{l}{A} = \rho \frac{w_c}{t_g w_g} \tag{6.53}$$

The inductance of thin-film conductors may be calculated approximately, assuming that λ is small compared with the insulation thickness separating the conductor from the ground plane. For a conductor of width w, separated from a superconducting ground plane by an insulator t_d thick,

$$\mathcal{K} = \frac{I}{w}$$

Since $LI^2 = \int \mu_0 \mathcal{K}^2 \, d(\text{volume})$ and

$$\frac{\text{Volume}}{\text{Unit length}} = w t_d$$

hence

$$L = \frac{\mu_0 \mathcal{K}^2}{I^2} \times \text{volume} = \frac{\mu_0 w t_d}{w^2} = \frac{\mu_0 t_d}{w} \qquad \text{per unit length} \tag{6.54}$$

The inductance of the circuit is reduced by widening the conductor and making insulation thinner. A practical insulation is of the order of 5,000 A thick, the same order of thickness used for lead conductors and tin gates. We can estimate L/R for practical cryotron flip-flops, assuming the width of the control and connection conductors to be 0.005 in., a dimension convenient to achieve by simple masking procedures. The resistivity of the gate in the normal region depends upon its condition of strain, crystallite size, etc., and may be estimated at about 10^{-6} ohm-cm. Accordingly, if $w_g/w_c = 5$ and the entire switching element is assumed to be $l = 2$ cm in total length,

$$\frac{L}{R} = \frac{l \mu_0 t_d t_g w_g}{\rho w_c^2} \approx 2.5 \times 10^{-8} \text{ sec} \tag{6.55}$$

The control width is used for inductance calculation here, since the wider gate element occupies usually only a short fraction of the length of the complete device. Inductance due to cur-

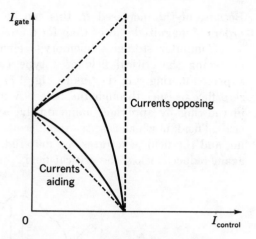

Figure 6.23   Control characteristic of an in-line
cryotron.   The angled characteristics are ideal,
the rounded curves characteristic of actual
devices.

rent penetration into the superconductors can often increase L
by the order of 20 per cent.

The in-line cryotron cannot have current gain greater
than unity, without bias, for the control conductor must cover
the gate completely to control it.   Making the control much
wider than the gate is unnecessary.   The I_c-I_g phase diagrams for real and idealized in-line cryotrons are given in
Fig. 6.23.   Gate current may be made twice as large with I_c
present as in its absence; i.e., in the second quadrant the field
of the control opposes that of the gate.   If the gate is biased
near the maximum current, an effective gain greater than unity
may be realized.   Generally speaking, however, in-line cryotrons are used only for higher output voltages.   The resistance of in-line cryotrons can be much larger than that of
crossed-film units; hence the time constant is much smaller.
Quantitatively, if l_g is the effective gate length of that part
which turns resistive,

$$R = \rho \frac{l_g}{w_g t_g}$$

$$L \cong \frac{\mu_0 t_d l}{w_g}$$

$$\tau = \frac{L}{R} \cong \frac{\mu_0}{\rho} \frac{t_d t_g l}{l_g}$$

(6.56)

Because of the increased R, this can be as much as several orders of magnitude lower than for a crossed-film cryotron.

Computer storage ("memory") elements are based on exceeding the critical field of a type I superconductor. A superconducting ring (i.e., as in Fig. 6.7) will ordinarily have zero flux passing through the hole. A flux may be induced in the ring by applying, momentarily, a field exceeding the critical field, in which case the ring becomes normally conducting and the field penetrates the material. When the field is again reduced below the critical field, the flux in the ring is

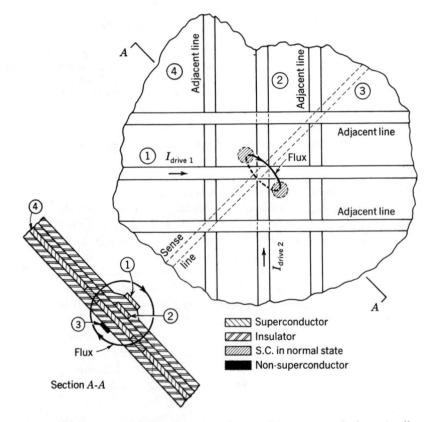

Figure 6.24 Plan and section views of continuous-sheet memory device. Application of high currents to two 90° conductors produces fields large enough to break through the adjacent continuous sheet of tin and render two regions normally conducting. Flux is trapped in the loop shown until current is reversed. (1) Drive conductor; (2) second drive conductor, at 90° to first; (3) 45° sense conductor, a normally conducting material, senses the linked flux; (4) continuous tin sheet. Other sense lines, not shown, pass under each junction.

expelled toward both the center and the outside, leaving a flux through the hole. Although we have postulated a physical hole in a superconducting ring, this process works as well when an inhomogeneous field (Fig. 6.24) is applied to a continuous superconducting sheet. The field "punches" a normally conducting "hole" in the material, leaving a ring of current flowing around the hole and flux passing through it. The magnetic field strength in the normal region must be equal to or slightly larger than $\mathcal{K}_c$ and of course equal to $\mathcal{K}_c$ at the superconducting boundary. If the field were greater than $\mathcal{K}_c$ at the boundary, the normally conducting region would enlarge; if smaller, it would contract, since it is a general property of a superconducting domain (at equilibrium) that the field at the normal-superconducting boundary must equal $\mathcal{K}_c$.

In one embodiment of the superconducting memory, many superconducting-memory elements are on a continuous thin film. Two sets of magnetic field–producing conductors above this sheet, as in Fig. 6.24, cross one another. The fields of the conductors (themselves superconducting) have maximum values at the corners of the crossing as shown. When the currents in these conductors (which are provided with drive signals by a selection circuit) are both positive, a large field is produced in the locations shown. This produces two small superconducting regions; when the drive current is removed, a magnetic flux will continue to pass through the two regions and close on itself. For computer-memory purposes, there may be many thousands of such crossings, each representing storage of a binary digit. The flux through the normal regions always flows in one direction or the opposite direction, one representing a binary *zero*, the other a *one*. The memory is interrogated by applying a pair of positive current pulses to conductors forming a particular crossing. If a one is present at the crossing, nothing will happen. If a zero is present, the flux must reverse, and the changing flux may be sensed by another set of conductors. The element can be set or reset to a one or zero condition by application of positive drive pulses to its common drive lines. This system has potentially very-high-density storage capabilities.

The application of superconducting devices to electronic systems has only recently become a practical possibility. A very serious problem in superconducting-device application, of course, is the extremely low temperature environment required ($4°K$ or less). If adequate supplies of liquid helium are available, satisfactory operation is achieved through vacuum pumping to reduce the helium temperature. Limited natural supplies of helium gas make it desirable for broad-scale applications to incorporate closed-cycle refrigeration. Small helium liquefiers have been developed which operate on complex multistage refrigeration processes, and can provide a few watts of heat capacity at 4°K. While this is a very small power capacity, a very large computer ($\sim 10^7$ cryotrons) using all-cryotron construction would generate only about one watt of electrical heat dissipation.

Superconductivity offers, in addition, a variety of device possibilities based upon onset of normal conductivity, variable-inductance devices, means of displacing flux, etc.[1]

6.6 Applications of High-critical-field Superconductors

Several type II superconducting elements and a wide variety of compounds are characterized by low ductility, high melting point, high critical temperatures (up to about 20°K), and especially high critical fields (many thousands of oersteds, in some cases). These materials are particularly useful in certain applications involving high magnetic fields. Figure 6.25 shows critical fields and currents for such materials. Since, as mentioned earlier, these transition properties are in part associated with strains in the material, it is difficult to state *intrinsic* properties for the more interesting materials. The measured data are strongly dependent on particular processing techniques, which are sometimes quite complex. Some of the materials, for example, must be heat-treated after formation into the final device (e.g., wire-wound solenoidal magnets).

Superconducting magnets formed from these superconductors are often long uniform-diameter solenoids (Fig. 6.26). The straightforward magnetostatic solution for the field of an infinitely long solenoid indicates that the magnetic field inside the inner diameter should be constant ($\mathfrak{IC} = NI/l$). The magnet wire in the innermost layer is in the field of maximum intensity. The field experienced by outer layers decreases with radius, and is essentially zero at the outermost layer. To develop a field of, say, 60,000 oe, it is necessary to have a material which can withstand high magnetic fields without

[1] The interested reader is directed to V. L. Newhouse, "Applied Superconductivity," John Wiley & Sons, Inc., New York, 1964, for description and analysis of these devices.

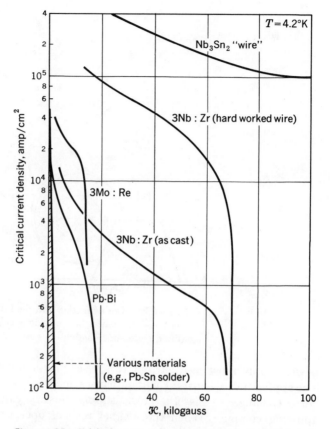

Figure 6.25   Critical current density vs. magnetic field for a variety of high-field (type II) superconductors.   [*After J. E. Kunzler, J. Appl. Phys.*, **33**:1042 (1962).]

losing its superconductivity.   In a simple solenoid wound with the same wire throughout, a high current-carrying capacity permits less wire to be used, which is important because these materials are expensive.   Because of the typical sharp knee of the field-current curves of Fig. 6.25, the most favorable design point lies just above the knee of the curve.   Since outer layers do not experience so large a field, they may be formed from a material of higher current density and lower critical field (e.g., an inner Nb_3Sn solenoid and an outer Mo-Re solenoid).

Operation of superconducting magnets affords some unusual problems.   Even a magnet of a few pounds weight will store a large amount of energy in its field.   The operating

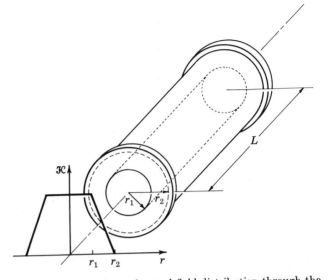

Figure 6.26   Configuration and field distribution through the windings and center hole of a long solenoid, like those wound from superconducting wire.

power supply must feed current to a resistance-less inductor. The application of constant voltage causes linear $(V = L \, dI/dt)$ current change, so that the power supply must be capable of applying voltage.   When the magnet reaches operating current, the voltage must be zero; a constant-current power supply is desirable for long-term stability.   While it is possible in principle to eliminate constant-current feed via a superconducting switch across the magnet terminals, in most applications field control is desirable.   Care must be taken not to "break" the current rapidly, since the large inductive voltage can, as in other magnets, damage the windings of a superconducting magnet.   Some superconducting magnets have actually used gold as the sole insulating material between turns; since its finite but small resistance is still infinitely larger than that of the superconductor, steady current flows *only* in the superconductor.   Power is dissipated in initially exciting the magnet, however.   In all superconducting magnets, care must be taken not to permit any part of the magnet to become resistive during normal operation, for the rapid dissipation of stored energy could cause permanent damage.

Because of the very high cost of raw materials and processing, not to mention the difficulties of supplying a suitable low-temperature environment, superconducting magnets are most useful in those applications where their high fields can be obtained in no easier way or where very light weight at moderate field strengths is important. Possible applications include beam focusing of millimeter-wave microwave tubes and constraint of high-temperature plasmas, as well as scientific research applications.

Devices for handling of large power, such as transformers and transmission lines, can in principle be constructed using superconductors in place of the usual copper conductors. At the usual power-transmission frequencies, superconductor losses due to normal-electron motion would be negligible. Unless type I superconductors were used, there would be losses due to hysteresis of fluxon movement in the superconductor. As in many other potential applications, however, the problem of refrigeration of a large device to cryogenic temperatures is a controlling factor. Despite progress in closed-cycle refrigeration, the continuous refrigeration of high-volume devices is still prohibitively expensive. Even after initial cooling, the biggest heat loss is via conductors passing into room-temperature regions. The refrigeration alone requires $>1,000$ times as much primary energy as the amount of heat removed from the cryogenic system.

PROBLEMS

6.1(a) Assuming that the critical field and temperature are related as in Eq. (6.1), determine the corresponding differences in entropies between normal and superconducting conditions.

6.1(b) One may test the validity of zero resistivity in a superconductor by producing a circulating current and observing the reduction of current with time. Suppose that a circulating current were set up in a lead tube 1 cm in diameter and 10 cm in length, with 0.05 cm wall thickness. If after one year a current set up in this tube had decayed no more than the $\frac{1}{2}$ per cent accuracy of the measuring instrument, what is the largest possible value of the bulk resistivity of the material? Neglect end effects, assume that the current flow is entirely circumferential, use the long-solenoid relation for the magnetic field inside the tube, and neglect fields outside of the tube. (HINT: Stored energy per unit volume = $\mu_0 \mathfrak{3C}^2/2$. Total is $LI^2/2$.)

6.1(c) Describe what happens physically when a small permanent magnet is brought near (1) an ideal conductor ($\rho = 0$); (2) a perfect diamagnet ($\mu = 0$). Indicate forces and/or currents involved.

6.2(*a*) In normal conductors and polarizable materials, the equation of state is a single equation (for example, $\mathbf{J} = \sigma\mathbf{\mathcal{E}}$, $\mathbf{D} = \epsilon\mathbf{\mathcal{E}}$). In London's theory, however, two equations of state are required to describe superconductivity. Discuss the significance of this point.

6.2(*b*) A round superconducting wire 1 cm in diameter carries a 60-cps current. (1) Using the static solution (6.20), on the assumption that the wire diameter is many times larger than the penetration depth, combine with (6.18) to find the electric field vs. depth from the surface of the wire. (2) With this result, calculate the power loss in a 100-mile transmission line using two such wires to carry a 60-cps current of peak value 1,000 amp. Let $n_n = n_s = 10^{23}$ cm^{-3}; assume the electronic mass to be that of free electrons; and let mean free time of normal electrons between collisions be 10^{-10} sec.

6.2 A long horizontal strip of superconducting material 10 cm wide and 1 mm thick has its long axis in an east-west direction. A straight horizontal conducting wire carrying a d-c current in a north-south direction is lowered to a distance of 1 cm from the surface of the strip. Discuss the distribution of induced supercurrent in the strip by the aid of sketches. Can the current flow on both sides of the strip? Where are the return currents? Does a strip of finite length behave differently from an infinite one?

6.2(*d*) A long superconducting lead tube of circular cross section and 1 in. internal diameter is cooled in a strong magnetic field parallel to its axis. The field is then reduced below $\mathcal{3C}_c$ ($= 500$ oe). (1) How much flux is trapped in the inside? (2) Draw a sketch showing direction of fluxes, and supercurrent flow on all pertinent surfaces.

6.3 (1) State the pieces of experimental evidence for the existence of a finite "band gap" between superconducting and normal states of electrons. (2) Would a simple energy-band model, based on the explanation of semiconduction, be able to explain the disappearance of superconductivity when the band gap was reduced to zero? Explain. (3) Is it likely that the disappearance of superconductivity is associated with the average thermal expansion of the lattice, *directly?* Explain.

6.4(*a*) A variable magnetic field can be applied either (1) parallel or (2) normal to the axis of a long round superconducting lead wire. Discuss, for each case, whether normal resistance should appear abruptly or gradually as a function of magnetic field. Explain in terms of expected domain configurations.

6.4(*b*) If the density of superconducting electrons in a bulk-metal sample is 10^{22} cm^{-3}, their effective mass equals the free-electron mass, and $\mathcal{3C}_c = 200$ oe, estimate the kinetic energy in the superconducting-normal interface per square centimeter of area. The kinetic energy of the superelectrons required to establish the interface may be found from $v = J/n_s e$, by integrating $(mv^2/2)\, dn$ over all superconducting electrons. Compare with the magnetic energy $\mu_0 \mathcal{3C}^2/2$ integrated over this same region.

6.4(c) Consider a crude model for relating T_c and $\mathfrak{IC}_c(0)$, as follows: Assume that when the kinetic energy of the electrons at the superconductor surface reaches $3.5kT_c$, transition takes place. Relate the velocity to the current density at the surface by $v = J/n_s e$ and the kinetic energy to velocity via the free-electron relation. Then find the values of n_s necessary to explain the tabulated values of Table 6.1.

6.4(d) Estimate qualitatively the effect on the velocity of thermal expansion of a normal region in a superconducting film, caused by the following: (1) high-substrate (support) conductivity; (2) low-substrate specific heat; (3) poor thermal contact of film to support; (4) application of a magnetic field (when at a given current level); (5) entire element in a vacuum.

6.5(a) A hypothetical cryotronlike device comprises a coaxial structure with central control wire and concentric surrounding gate. If, at operating temperature, $\mathfrak{IC}_c$ (gate) = 100 oe and $\mathfrak{IC}_c$ (control) = 500 oe, also r_{control} = 0.5 mm, r_{gate} (inner) = 1 mm, and r_{gate} (outer) = 1.2 mm, calculate and plot the idealized control characteristic. The tubular gate element is a short section with small wire connections at each end.

6.5(b) A particular cryotron flip-flop operates at 30 ma supply current. The total length of each arm is 0.25 in., which includes two gate elements each 0.025 in. in length. The gate elements are 0.025 in. wide, while the remainder of the conductor is 0.005 in. wide. Dielectric thickness is 5,000 A, and the normal resistivity of the gates is 10^{-6} ohm-cm. (1) Calculate the switching time constant of the device. (2) Calculate the energy required to perform a single switching operation. (3) If a system containing 10^7 such devices had a cooling capacity at operating temperature of 1 watt (available for dissipation of switching power), at what average rate (operations per second) could each device operate?

6.5(c) Using the data in Table 6.1, select materials which might be used as gate conductors in crossed-film cryotron circuits operating in the range 3 to 4.5°K. In each case, assume that (6.1) applies, and calculate the operating temperature at which a current of 100 ma in a 0.01-cm-wide control conductor would be able to switch a gate carrying no current.

6.6(a) A magnet producing high fields has large forces on its conductors, which may be calculated from the formula $\mathbf{f} = I \, d\mathbf{l} \times \mathbf{B}$, where $d\mathbf{l}$ is a differential length of conductor directed along the direction of current flow. A long superconducting solenoid produces 50,000 gauss in a 2-cm-diameter inner hole and is 8 cm in outside diameter. If it is uniformly wound with 2,000 turns/cm length, calculate the current and the total radial pressure (psi) produced by all the conductors and acting on the outer shell of the device; neglect restraining action of the wire.

6.6(b) A supply of Nb_3Zr wire (as described in Fig. 6.25) is available, having a diameter of 0.025 cm (total diameter with insulation, 0.03 cm). A magnet is to be constructed with inner diameter of the winding of 2 cm and a length of 20 cm. Assume that the winding is composed of uniform layers (layer thickness = wire diameter). Working at the limit given in the curve, plot the field attainable vs. the number of pounds of alloy used. Assume a density of 8 g/cm³, and use the long-solenoid formula to derive the field.

GENERAL REFERENCES

From a theoretical point of view, the field of superconductivity is the least mature of those considered in this text. The earlier treatments were either thermodynamic or phenomenological; only since about 1957 has the theory taken a turn for the better. The device area became active about 1956, peaked in 1958, and continues at a slow rate because of the technological problem of cryogenic refrigeration. Most papers will be found in *Physical Review*, with a few in *Journal of Applied Physics* and a few device papers in *Proceedings of the IEEE*. An extensive survey appeared in *Reviews of Modern Physics*, vol. 36, January, 1964.

IBM J. Res. Develop., vol. 6, January, 1962. (Special issue on superconductivity; papers by J. Bardeen and many others.)

London, F.: "Superfluids: Macroscopic Theory of Superconductivity," Dover Publications, Inc., New York, 1961. (Theory forms the foundations of device analyses and a simple basis for comparison with more modern theories.)

Lynton, E. A.: "Superconductivity," Methuen & Co., Ltd., London, 1962. (An excellent modern survey, with references.)

Newhouse, Vernon L.: "Applied Superconductivity," John Wiley & Sons, Inc., New York, 1964. (A device-engineering treatment which includes discussions of modern theories.)

Office of Naval Research: Symposium on Superconductive Techniques for Computing Systems, OTS Document 161763, Washington, D.C., 1960. (A compendium of device technology and concepts.)

Schafroth, M. R.: *Solid State Phys.*, **10**:293 (1960). (A coherent but advanced discussion of theories of superconductivity.)

7
Dielectrics

7.1 Polarization of Solids

In the conduction processes described in Chaps. 3 to 6, electrons were required to move bodily through the solid. Dielectric and magnetic phenomena are more subtle, requiring only slight shifts in position of electrons; in ionic solids, furthermore, ion motions may make a substantial contribution in observed dielectric phenomena. As we show later, if electrons are permitted to move freely through the solid, their contribution to the dielectric properties is *opposite in sign* to the major contributions made by electrons and ions which are only slightly displaced in the presence of an electric field.

In order to appreciate the microscopic aspects of dielectric behavior, it is necessary to comprehend the classical theory. In a classical dielectric, the *electric flux density* **D** differs from that in free space, in the presence of a given electric field, because of *polarization* of the material. This is the induction of electric dipole moments, or the orientation of existing dipoles, by the field. In the continuum (classical) theory the solid is imagined to contain infinitely many small *electric dipoles* of infinitesimal dimensions. An electric dipole (Fig. 7.1a) may be visualized as a set of two opposite charges, $\pm q$, displaced a vector distance **d** from one another. The *electric dipole moment* is defined as $\mathbf{p}_e = q\mathbf{d}$, directed as shown. The electrostatic potential V, associated with an electric dipole, at distances **r** large in comparison with **d**, is given by

$$V = \frac{\mathbf{p}_e \cdot \mathbf{r}}{4\pi\epsilon r^3} = \frac{|\mathbf{p}_e|\cos\theta}{4\pi\epsilon r^2} \tag{7.1}$$

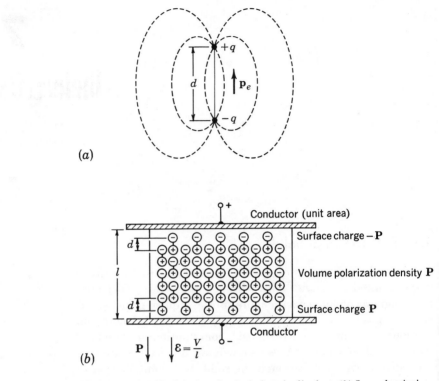

(a)

(b)

Figure 7.1   (a) Model of a classical electric dipole.   (b) In a classical dielectric with applied field, the dipoles may be arranged to cancel one another's long-range fields, so that only the surfaces of the dielectric normal to the applied field have uncompensated charges.

When an electric field $\mathbf{\mathcal{E}}$ is applied to a dielectric slab by a pair of large-area parallel plates, one imagines that infinitely many such infinitesimal dipoles are induced into being (Fig. 7.1b). Because the field is uniform in this geometry (in a non-crystalline or otherwise isotropic dielectric) these field-induced dipoles are all oriented in the field direction. Within the slab of dielectric, the dipoles' electric fields cancel, for we are at liberty to imagine the positive charges of one layer of dipoles to coincide with the negative charges of the next layer. At the electrode surfaces this is not possible; hence the uppermost and lowest layers of charge do not cancel. The electric flux density $\mathbf{D}$ in the dielectric consists of two components, one which would be present *in the absence of the dielectric*, $\mathbf{D} = \epsilon_0 \mathbf{\mathcal{E}}$, the other due to the immobile induced surface charge. The uncompensated charge in each surface constitutes a layer of ipoles of length d, which have per unit area of surface a charge ensity $\mathbf{P}d/d = \mathbf{P}$. This so-called *depolarization charge* there-)re produces an electric flux density $\mathbf{D}$, through the dielectric etween the positive and the negative charge, equal in ration- lized units to $\mathbf{P}$. The total electric flux density in the con- inuous dielectric is, accordingly,

$$\mathbf{D} = \epsilon_0 \mathbf{\mathcal{E}} + \mathbf{P} \tag{7.2}$$

trictly speaking, this result applies only for infinitesimal ipoles, for which it is a *point relation* applicable at any point ו a dielectric. The field $\mathbf{\mathcal{E}}$ is a *macroscopic* field, and does not וclude the high *local* fields present in an actual solid containing iscrete electronic and nuclear charges.

In actual crystalline dielectrics, the dipole moment den- ity, or polarization per unit volume, is a *linear* function of lectric field strength, for fields of practical value. It need not e a scalar relation, however. A constant tensor χ_e, termed the *ielectric susceptibility*, may be used to define this relationship:

$$\mathbf{P} = \epsilon_0 \chi_e \mathbf{\mathcal{E}}$$

ח its cartesian components,

$$\begin{aligned}
P_x &= \epsilon_0(\chi_{11}\mathcal{E}_x + \chi_{12}\mathcal{E}_y + \chi_{13}\mathcal{E}_z) \\
P_y &= \epsilon_0(\chi_{21}\mathcal{E}_x + \chi_{22}\mathcal{E}_y + \chi_{23}\mathcal{E}_z) \\
P_z &= \epsilon_0(\chi_{31}\mathcal{E}_x + \chi_{32}\mathcal{E}_y + \chi_{33}\mathcal{E}_z)
\end{aligned} \tag{7.3}$$

'he components χ_{ij} have the symmetry imposed on all such econd-rank tensor properties in crystals (Table 1.2). In iso- ropic or polycrystalline materials, χ_e is simply a scalar. While usceptibility is a true material property, materials are more ·ften described through the permittivity $\epsilon = \epsilon_0(1 + \chi_e)$ or the 'dielectric constant" $k = 1 + \chi_e$.

Actual electrostatic solutions of fields in dielectrics can be nade using (7.2), which is completely general, along with a elation between $\mathbf{\mathcal{E}}$ and $\mathbf{P}$ [in lineard ielectrics, the relations 7.3)]. For example, consider the dielectric slab located ·etween two remote electrodes, which in the absence of the lab produce a uniform field $\mathcal{E}_a$ (Fig. 7.2a). If the dielectric is sotropic, the field in the dielectric should be in the same direc- ion as the applied field. Electric flux enters normal to the lab face. Applying the usual boundary condition that the lectric flux density $\mathbf{D}$ has a continuous normal component hrough the surface of a nonconductor, the flux density must ·e the same in the dielectric and outside. In a *linear* dielectric,

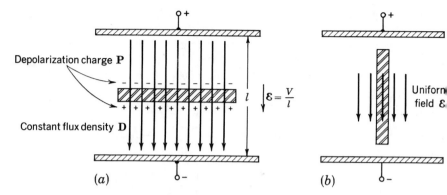

Figure 7.2 (*a*) A thin slab of dielectric in a uniform field. (*b*) A dielectric in the form of a long rod, or a slab parallel to the field; the tangential electric field, being continuous across the boundary, must be the same in the dielectric as in the free-space region█

we have $D = \epsilon \mathcal{E}$; accordingly, the field in the dielectric $\mathcal{E}$ is related to the applied field through $\epsilon_0 \mathcal{E}_a = \epsilon \mathcal{E}$; hence $\mathcal{E} = (\epsilon_0/\epsilon)\mathcal{E}_a$. The field in the dielectric ($\epsilon/\epsilon_0 > 1$) is therefore less than the applied field.

While this method of solution is always successful, there is an alternative way of calculating the field in a dielectric. The depolarization charge P, which by the arguments applying to Fig. 7.1*b* appears at the surface of the dielectric slab, is of such polarity as to *reduce* the field in the dielectric. Taking into account simply the applied field and that due to this surface charge, the field in the dielectric is

$$\mathcal{E} = \mathcal{E}_a - \frac{P}{\epsilon_0} \tag{7.4}$$

If the linear relation $P = (\epsilon/\epsilon_0 - 1)\mathcal{E}$ is substituted, the expected result is obtained. The two methods are equivalent.

The field in a dielectric of any shape can be found by considering the influence of the applied field and that of the induced surface charges. When the field internally is non-uniform, it will usually be necessary to introduce a charge density within the dielectric (these charges are referred to as "free poles"). There are a great variety of shapes which a dielectric sample may take for specific device applications. It is frequently desired that the internal electric field in a sample be uniform. It may be shown[1] that internal fields are uniform

[1] See J. A. Stratton, "Electromagnetic Theory," p. 211, McGraw-Hill Book Company, New York, 1941.

only in *isolated ellipsoidal samples*. An ellipsoid is a body whose surface can be described, from an origin at its center, by a relation

$$\frac{x^2}{a^2} + \frac{v^2}{b^2} + \frac{z^2}{c^2} = \text{const} \tag{7.5}$$

A sphere is a limiting form $(a = b = c)$. The thin disk, or long rod of circular or elliptical cross section, is a good approximation to a limiting form of ellipsoid, the rod being represented by $a \to \infty$, the disk by $b = c \to \infty$.

In an isotropic dielectric ellipsoid, fields applied along each of the major axes produce *different* polarization-charge fields. The relations corresponding to (7.4) are

$$\mathcal{E}_x = \mathcal{E}_{ax} - \frac{\mathcal{D}_x P_x}{\epsilon_0} \qquad \mathcal{E}_y = \mathcal{E}_{ay} - \frac{\mathcal{D}_y P_y}{\epsilon_0} \qquad \mathcal{E}_z = \mathcal{E}_{az} - \frac{\mathcal{D}_z P_z}{\epsilon_0} \tag{7.6}$$

where $\mathcal{D}_x$ is termed the *depolarization factor* for the x direction, etc. $\mathcal{D}_x$, $\mathcal{D}_y$, and $\mathcal{D}_z$ depend on the shape of the ellipsoid, i.e., on a, b, and c; it can be shown that *their sum is unity*. (In unrationalized units, $\mathcal{D}_x + \mathcal{D}_y + \mathcal{D}_z = 4\pi$.) The $\mathcal{D}$ applicable in Fig. 7.2a is unity, as in (7.4); if the same slab is oriented as in Fig. 7.2b, inspection shows $\mathcal{E} = \mathcal{E}_a$; hence $\mathcal{D} = 0$. For a *sphere*, $\mathcal{D}_x = \mathcal{D}_y = \mathcal{D}_z = \frac{1}{3}$, by symmetry. For a long thin z-directed rod of circular cross section, $\mathcal{D}_z = 0$, $\mathcal{D}_x = \mathcal{D}_y = \frac{1}{2}$, etc. Dielectric configurations of many actual devices are nonellipsoidal; here the relatively simple concept of depolarization factor must be replaced by an actual calculation of the *nonuniform* field distribution. It is, however, often important, as, for example, when studying high-frequency behavior of materials, to be certain that the field is uniform and in a known direction in the sample. In *anisotropic* dielectrics, relations (7.6) apply if ϵ_{ij} is diagonalized and the crystal axes coincide with the ellipsoid axes. The favored crystal shapes in this kind of study are thin flat plates, thin rods of round cross section, and (particularly with anisotropic materials) spheres.

7.2   Microscopic Polarization Processes

The classical relations of the previous section define a polarization density **P** which appears in response to a macroscopic field $\mathcal{E}$, but do not describe how the polarization is brought about. There are three basically different sources of polarization in solids:

1. The *rotation* of molecules, or parts of molecules, such that negative ions are pulled in a direction opposite to that of the local field and positive ions in the direction of the local fields (rotational polarization)

2. The *displacement* of ions, in ionic solids, such that positive and negative ions are displaced, against the natural restoring force of the crystalline cohesive forces (ionic polarization)

3. The *perturbation* of electron orbits in the direction opposite to an applied field (electronic polarization)

Figure 7.3 illustrates each of these effects. The distinction between rotation and displacement of an ion is not a sharp one; the former description is generally reserved for ions which have little or no restoring force against the motion in question. Water (H_2O), even slightly below its freezing point, shows substantial polarization due to the rotation of the two hydrogen ions about the heavier oxygen ion.

The ionic polarization (of an ionic solid) in a given electric field depends upon the strength of the restoring forces which tend to hold the ions in equilibrium positions. The "stiffer" these forces, the smaller the ionic displacements can be, and the less the polarization in a given field. As implied in Fig. 7.3b, when all ions have their equilibrium locations, the solid is defined to be unpolarized.

Figure 7.3c describes a crude model whereby the polarization of an atom (not an ion) due to the displacement of its orbital electrons can be estimated. While a more detailed quantum-mechanical description of electronic polarization is given in the section following, an estimate using this model is enlightening. A uniform-density electron cloud, of total charge $-Ze$, is imagined to form a sphere of fixed radius a, surrounding a positive nuclear charge $+Ze$ (Fig. 7.3c). When the center of the electronic charge and the point-charge nucleus coincide, there is no force between the nucleus and the (supposedly undeformable) electronic charge cloud, and of course there are no external fields. When the centers of the opposite charges are displaced by a distance $\mathbf{r}$, however, the nucleus finds itself in a field

$$\mathbf{\varepsilon}' = \frac{-Ze\mathbf{r}}{4\pi\epsilon_0 a^3}$$

as can be shown simply by determining the field in the uniform electronic space charge. In a field $\mathbf{\varepsilon}_l$, the electronic charge is

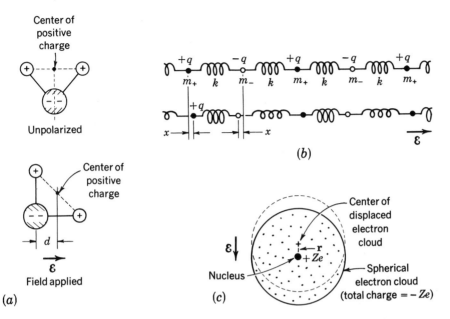

Figure 7.3 Schematic representation of the three types of electric polarization. (a) Ions in a molecule, if free to rotate to some extent, will do so in an electrical field, thus producing a polarization. (b) A linear-chain representation of an ionic solid. The charge of each ion, multiplied by the amount of shift of its position in the presence of a field, represents its contribution to electric dipole moment. (c) Electrons surrounding a nucleus will shift their center of motion in the presence of a field.

displaced from the supposedly fixed nucleus by such a distance that the two fields cancel ($\mathcal{E}_l + \mathcal{E}' = 0$). We define the *polarizability* α of this "atom" as the electrical dipole moment it produces for a unit local field, divided by ϵ_0:

$$\alpha = \frac{p_e}{\epsilon_0 \mathcal{E}_l} \tag{7.7}$$

Here the polarization is simply Zer; hence

$$\alpha = 4\pi a^3 \tag{7.8}$$

The result, interestingly, does not depend on the total charge.

A polarizability may be defined similarly for *each type of ion* in an ionically polarizable solid if a suitable model for the springlike ionic restoring forces is available. This is discussed further in Sec. 7.4. In the case of rotational polarizability, the approach must be somewhat different for without restoring forces it would appear that the slightest field would produce a large polarization, and α should be infinite. Here it is not springlike forces which restore the ions to equilibrium positions, but rather the thermal activation of the rotational modes. An electric field must work against the natural tendency for phonons to put the molecule into a nonpolarized orientation. A quantum perturbation theory is necessary to obtain meaningful results.

In defining polarizability, the field $\mathcal{E}_l$ in which the atom or ion is polarized is a *local* field, which is generally quite different from the macroscopic field $\mathcal{E}$, not only because of surface polarization charge (as discussed in the last section), but because of the fields of the discrete atomic or molecular dipoles surrounding the atom or ion in question. Although the precise solution for the polarization properties of an actual dielectric would involve extremely weighty quantum calculations, approximate classical models have been employed with fair success to define qualitative behavior of dielectrics.

To determine the local field, we shall associate with *each atom* of the solid an electric dipole moment $\mathbf{p}_e$ (Fig. 7.4a). All atoms will be assumed to have the same moment; it will of course be necessary for the entire dielectric sample to have a simple shape, such as a thin slab, so that the electric field is uniform. Each atom will be assumed to have a polarizability α. The analytical argument will be carried out for an elemental solid. (In the case of an ionic solid, it will be necessary to define a polarizability for each type of ion and calculate fields at each.) We shall assume that the polarizability is isotropic, i.e., that the atom is not more readily polarized along one axis than along others. We must now find the *total* local field, that due to (1) applied field, (2) surface charges, and (3) surrounding atomic dipoles. This last contribution is best found by dividing the atoms into two groups, one a small sphere surrounding the particular atom in question, the other the remainder of the atoms in the sample. (This treatment is attributed to Clausius and Mosotti.)

The field reduction due to the depolarization charge on the outer surfaces of the sample will, as in (7.6), be $-\mathfrak{D}\mathbf{P}/\epsilon_0$, where $\mathfrak{D}$ is the appropriate depolarization factor for the external geometry. If we remove the small sphere surrounding the point in question, there must be a surface charge on the *inside* surface of the spherical *cavity* (Fig. 7.4b) which produces a field of sign opposite to that of the surface depolarizing field. Since the missing sphere has a uniform depolarization factor of $\frac{1}{3}$,

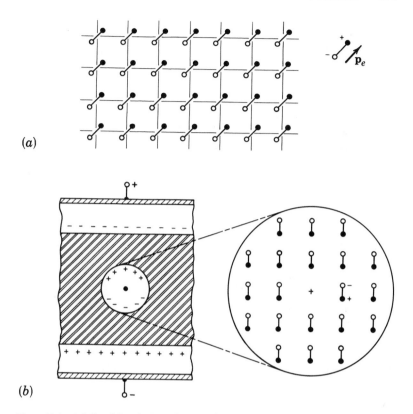

Figure 7.4   (*a*) Semiclassical model of a dielectric, in which a dipole $\mathbf{p}_e$ is associated with each atomic site.   (*b*) Construction for derivation of the Clausius-Mosotti relation.   Only the detailed atomic fields of the small sphere surrounding the point in question need be considered, while the remaining material is treated as a continuum.

the total field due to all atoms *except* those in the missing sphere will be $\mathcal{E}_a - \mathfrak{D}\mathbf{P}/\epsilon_0 + \mathbf{P}/3\epsilon_0$.   (If the sample were itself spherical, the field inside the hollow sphere is precisely the applied field.)   The final contribution to $\mathcal{E}_l$ is that of the atomic dipoles inside the small sphere.   Since these are in the immediate vicinity of the atom in question, their detailed field variations (7.1) must be considered.   If the radius vector joining the atom at the center of the sphere with the ith atomic dipole is $\mathbf{r}_i$, the field due to atoms in the small sphere will be of the form

$$\mathbf{p}_e \cdot \sum_i \frac{\mathbf{r}_i}{|\mathbf{r}_i|^3} \times \text{const}$$

The sum is taken over all atomic dipoles. If the crystal structure has a center of symmetry, there will be a neighbor at $-\mathbf{r}_i$, for each neighbor $\mathbf{r}_i$; hence the potential and field due to these neighbors must cancel. It can further be shown that all *cubic* structures have zero near-neighbor dipole field contributions. In this case

$$\mathbf{\mathcal{E}}_l = \mathbf{\mathcal{E}}_a - \frac{\mathfrak{D}\mathbf{P}}{\epsilon_0} + \frac{\mathbf{P}}{3\epsilon_0} \qquad \mathbf{P} = N\alpha\mathbf{\mathcal{E}}_l\epsilon_0 \tag{7.9}$$

The field, polarization, and flux density are related through (7.2), which, however, relates to the *macroscopic field*, not the applied field. But the macroscopic field $\mathbf{\mathcal{E}}$ is just $\mathbf{\mathcal{E}}_a - \mathfrak{D}\mathbf{P}/\epsilon_0$. With this in (7.9),

$$\mathbf{D} = \epsilon_0\mathbf{\mathcal{E}}\frac{1 + 2N\alpha/3}{1 - N\alpha/3} = k\epsilon_0\mathbf{\mathcal{E}} \qquad k = \frac{1 + 2N\alpha/3}{1 - N\alpha/3} \tag{7.10}$$

In terms of the dielectric constant k,

$$\alpha = \frac{3}{N}\frac{k - 1}{k + 2} \tag{7.11}$$

This suggests that we can *determine* the atomic polarizability α, knowing the density and the dielectric constant. It is of interest to use the simple electronic-polarizability theory (7.8), in which case the polarizability may be related to density. Imagining the atoms to be close-packed spheres, the efficiency of packing is only 74 per cent (of total volume filled). The density of atoms of radius a is, in such a close packing, $N = 0.74 \times 3/4\pi a^3$. The polarizability, by (7.8), will be $\alpha = 0.74$ $(3/N)$. This predicts a dielectric constant $k = 9.6$. Unfortunately, there is no close-packed cubic insulator to compare. We can also estimate the polarizability for spherical atoms in the diamond structure (also that of germanium and silicon), which has a packing efficiency of 34 per cent. The dielectric constant predicted is $k = 2.5$, well below the values for C, Ge, and Si, but at least of a reasonable order of magnitude.

Equation (7.10) indicates that the dielectric constant will become infinite when $\alpha = 3/N$. This situation is avoided by the spherical-atom model, as indicated above. The interpretation of this phenomenon is simply that the *local fields* produced by a given polarization are themselves great enough to maintain that polarization, so that an applied field of negligible magnitude can produce a large polarization. This is reminiscent of the "bootstrap" effect observed, for example, in applying positive feedback to an amplifier. The polarization is assumed to be linear in the local field, but practically speaking, it will be limited by the onset of nonlinearities. Thus a more adequate theory would indicate that the polarization becomes limited at a certain "saturation" value. The material should exhibit a *remanent* polarization whenever $\alpha > 3/N$. Certain complex *ionic* solids, known as *ferroelectrics*, do have such behavior (Sec. 7.7).

7.3   Quantum-theoretical Description of Electronic Polarization[1]

The electronic energy-band theory (Chap. 2) is required to explain conductivity in metals and semiconductors. Description of electrons by Bloch wave functions implies that the electrons move constantly through the lattice. The electronic properties of dielectrics and of many magnetic materials are best explained by assuming the electrons associated with particular nuclei. While this appears to be a basic weakness of the band theory, it should be observed that the Bloch functions are not a unique set of wave functions for a periodic structure. Even in a conductor it is more appropriate to represent deeper-lying electronic states as "bound," rather than "band," states. Accordingly, in treating the dielectric properties of solids, the electron wave functions can be treated in much the same fashion as if the atoms were independent of one another.

The influence of electric fields on electrons in a nonconducting solid depends on the frequency of the fields. At such high frequencies that individual photons of electromagnetic energy can produce electronic quantum *transitions*, dielectrics are extremely "lossy"; i.e., they absorb a large part of the radiation. At lower frequencies, no such transitions are possible. The high-frequency case is treated by *time-dependent* quantum perturbation theory, as in Chap. 10. At lower frequencies, electronic response to electric fields is almost the same as for steady (d-c) fields. In this *quasi-static* situation, electronic polarization may be explained satisfactorily in terms of the static perturbations in electron wave functions and

---

[1] The quantum-theoretical treatment in this section is included to demonstrate the dependence of electronic polarization on the detailed electron state of an atom; it is not essential to an understanding of the other material in the chapter.

energy levels, in an electric field. With the magnitudes of the electric fields typically applied to practical dielectrics, these energy changes are truly small perturbations, and the simplest quantum perturbation theory may be used. Following an approach somewhat similar to that of Sec. B.9, we presume that an electron in the unperturbed atom is described by single-electron wave functions ψ_{0j} and an unperturbed hamiltonian energy function H_0. The index j represents all possible combinations of single-electron quantum numbers (n, l, m, s). The energy of an electron having the state ψ_{0j} is E_{0j}. The time-independent form of the Schrödinger wave equation may be expressed, in operator notation, as

$$H_0\psi_0 = E_0\psi_0 \tag{7.12}$$

In this *time-independent perturbation theory*, we shall choose to pay no attention to electron-energy degeneracies, which are not known to be important in dielectric phenomena.

If an electric field $\mathcal{E}_l = \mathbf{1}_x \mathcal{E}_l$ is applied, the energy of an electron when at radius vector $\mathbf{r}$ from the nucleus as origin is perturbed by an amount $H_1 = -e\mathcal{E}_l \cdot \mathbf{r} = -e\mathcal{E}_l x$. The *perturbed* wave equation may be expressed as

$$(H_0 + H_1)\psi_j' = E_j'\psi_j' \tag{7.13}$$

The new energy levels E_j' are to be determined. Since the field magnitude $\mathcal{E}_l$ is a variable, the perturbation will be a function of $\mathcal{E}_l$, and we may expand the perturbed wave functions and energy levels in power series:

$$
\begin{aligned}
E_j' &= E_{0j} + \mathcal{E}_l E_{1j} + \mathcal{E}_l^2 E_{2j} + \mathcal{E}_l^3 E_{3j} + \cdots \\
\psi_j' &= \psi_{0j} + \mathcal{E}_l \psi_{1j} + \mathcal{E}_l^2 \psi_{2j} + \mathcal{E}_l^3 \psi_{3j} + \cdots
\end{aligned}
\tag{7.14}
$$

Whereas the energy parameters E_{1j}, E_{2j}, etc., are sets of undetermined *constants*, the ψ_{ij} are undetermined *wave functions* of the coordinates of the electron motion. Substitution of (7.14) into the wave equation (7.13) gives

$$
\begin{aligned}
(H_0 - e\mathcal{E}_l x)&(\psi_{0j} + \mathcal{E}_l \psi_{1j} + \cdots) \\
&= (E_{0j} + \mathcal{E}_l E_{1j} + \cdots)(\psi_{0j} + \mathcal{E}_l \psi_{1j} + \cdots)
\end{aligned}
\tag{7.15}
$$

With $\mathcal{E}$ an independent variable, the coefficients of each power of $\mathcal{E}_l$ must vanish *separately*. This yields a series of equations:

$$
\begin{aligned}
&\text{Constant:} && H_0\psi_{0j} = E_{0j}\psi_{0j} && j = 1, 2, \ldots \\
&\text{Coefficient } \mathcal{E}_l: && H_0\psi_{1j} - ex\psi_{0j} = \psi_{1j}E_{0j} + \psi_{0j}E_{1j} \\
&\text{Coefficient } \mathcal{E}_l^2: && H_0\psi_{2j} - ex\psi_{1j} = \psi_{2j}E_{0j} + \psi_{1j}E_{1j} + \psi_{0j}E_{2j} \\
&\text{Etc.}
\end{aligned}
\tag{7.16}
$$

The first is simply a restatement of the original unperturbed equation. In describing the unknown functions ψ_{1j}, ψ_{2j}, etc., we may make use of the fact that (barring degeneracies) the ψ_{0j} form a *complete orthogonal function set* (Sec. B.4). For convenience, they will also be assumed to have been *normalized* so that the integral of $|\psi_{0j}{}^2|$ is unity, for all j. The new functions ψ_{ij} can therefore be expanded as Fourier series in these presumed known functions ψ_{0j}. Let

$$\psi_{1j} = \sum_{i=0}^{\infty} f_{1ij}\psi_{0i} \qquad \psi_{2j} = \sum_{i=0}^{\infty} f_{2ij}\psi_{0i} \qquad \text{etc.} \qquad (7.17)$$

Our problem is now reduced to finding only the constants f_{1ij}, etc. Finally, we define another set of coefficients X_{ij} such that

$$H_1\psi_{0j} = -e\mathcal{E}_l x\psi_{0j} = -e\mathcal{E}_l \sum_{i=0}^{\infty} X_{ij}\psi_{0i} \qquad (7.18)$$

The second equation of (7.16) can be expanded, in terms of these definitions:

$$\sum_i f_{1ij}H_0\psi_{0i} - e\sum_i X_{ij}\psi_{0i} = \sum_i f_{1ij}E_{0j}\psi_{0i} + E_{1j}\psi_{0j} \qquad (7.19)$$

Making use of (7.12) and rearranging,

$$-e\sum_i X_{ij}\psi_{0i} + \sum_i [f_{1ij}(E_{0i} - E_{0j})\psi_{0i}] - E_{1j}\psi_{0j} = 0 \qquad (7.20)$$

We next multiply the above by ψ_{0j}^* and integrate over the appropriate space variables, using the orthonormality conditions; the result is

$$f_{1ij} = \frac{-eX_{ij}}{E_{0i} - E_{0j}}$$
$$E_{1j} = -eX_{jj} \qquad (7.21)$$

We may expand in a similar fashion the third equation of (7.16). The same procedure is followed in multiplying through and integrating, resulting in

$$E_{2j} = \sum_i \frac{e^2 X_{ij}X_{ji}}{E_{0i} - E_{0j}} - \frac{e^2 X_{jj}{}^2}{E_{0j} - E_{0j}} \equiv \sum_{i \neq j} e^2 \frac{X_{ij}X_{ji}}{E_{0i} - E_{0j}} \qquad (7.22)$$

The process can be carried further; however, *second-order* perturbation theory (including terms to $\mathcal{E}_l{}^2$) is sufficient to explain *linear* dielectric properties. The energy of the electron in the perturbed state ψ'_j is therefore

$$E'_j = E_{0j} - e\mathcal{E}_l X_{jj} + e^2\mathcal{E}_l{}^2 \sum_{i \neq j} \frac{X_{ij}X_{ji}}{E_{0j} - E_{0j}} + \cdots \qquad (7.23)$$

The constants X_{ij} are clearly important parameters. Using the definition (7.18), multiplying through by ψ^*_{0i}, and integrating, we find

$$X_{ij} = \int_{\text{all space}} \psi^*_{0i}x\psi_{0j}\,dv \qquad (7.24)$$

For $i = j$, the integral (X_{jj}) is just the *expectation* of the electron's x coordinate (with respect to the nucleus) in the *unperturbed* wave function. Since an electron in a real atom normally spends as much time on one side of the nucleus as the other, X_{jj} will therefore be zero. We should expect the energy of a *permanent* electric dipole in an electric field $\mathcal{E}_l$ to be $-\mathbf{p}_e \cdot \mathcal{E}_l$, in this instance precisely $-e\mathcal{E}_l X_{jj}$. The central term in (7.22) therefore represents the field-interaction energy of permanent electric dipole moments. The field also *induces* an electric dipole moment, as described roughly by the space-charge model of the previous section. If we continued and found the perturbed wave function ψ'_j, it could be shown to have an expected shift in electronic position: $\langle x \rangle \propto \mathcal{E}_l$. This manipulation does not add significantly to our analysis, and will be left as an exercise for the reader. This represents a dipole moment $p_e = \langle x \rangle e = \epsilon_0 \alpha \mathcal{E}_1$. The energy associated with the induced moment is

$$\int_0^{\mathcal{E}_1} \mathbf{p}_e \cdot d\mathcal{E} = \epsilon_0 \alpha \int_0^{\mathcal{E}_l} \mathcal{E}\,d\mathcal{E} = \epsilon_0 \frac{\alpha}{2}\mathcal{E}_l{}^2 \qquad (7.25)$$

(The energy here is positive, because it requires energy to displace the electron from its unperturbed position.) Comparing with (7.23), the polarizability α of the electron must be

$$\alpha = 2\frac{e^2}{\epsilon_0}\sum_{i \neq j}\frac{X_{ij}X_{ji}}{E_{0i} - E_{0j}} \qquad \text{(electron initially in state ψ_{0j})} \qquad (7.26)$$

The quantities X_{ij} are termed *matrix elements*, in more sophisticated quantum theory. Like other such "coupling integrals," they are small if the two coupled wave functions ψ_{0i} and ψ_{0j} do not overlap appreciably. With a given wave-function overlap, however, the greatest part of the polarizability is associated with pairs of unperturbed electronic states (ψ_{0i}, ψ_{0j})

which are close together in energy, i.e., those for which the denominator $E_{0i} - E_{0j}$ is smallest. Accordingly, the outermost electrons of the atom should be most important, for the differences between electronic energy levels in this region are smallest. This agrees with the intuitive concept that less strongly bound electrons should be easiest to displace. These, unfortunately, are also the most difficult to analyze accurately; hence actual calculation of electronic dielectric constants of most solids is difficult.

If those electrons nearest to being free are the greatest contributors to polarization, it could be imagined that truly *free* electrons would contribute substantially, particularly if they did not collide frequently (as compared with the frequency at which the dielectric is to be used). The equation of motion of free electrons in a sinusoidal field $\mathbf{\varepsilon} = \mathbf{1}_x \varepsilon_x e^{j\omega t}$ is simply

$$m\ddot{x} = -e\varepsilon_x e^{j\omega t} \tag{7.27}$$

Neglecting entirely the collisions, the trajectory of the electrons will be oscillatory; hence integration of (7.27) is equivalent to division by $j\omega$, and

$$\dot{x} = \frac{je\varepsilon_x}{m\omega} e^{j\omega t}$$

The electronic *convection current* is simply charge density Ne times velocity. Adding the displacement current density $j\omega\epsilon\varepsilon_x$,

$$J_x(\text{total}) = \left(j\omega\epsilon - \frac{je^2N}{\omega m}\right)\varepsilon_x = j\omega\epsilon\left(1 - \frac{\omega_0^2}{\omega^2}\right)\varepsilon_x \tag{7.28}$$

where ω_0, the electron *plasma frequency*, equals $(e^2N/m\epsilon)^{\frac{1}{2}}$. Free electrons therefore introduce a *negative electric susceptibility*.

7.4 Frequency Dependence of Dielectric Properties

One of the most striking characteristics of dielectrics is the relationship between dielectric constant and dielectric losses and frequency. Each of the types of polarization described in the previous section has a characteristic frequency response, and each gives rise to dielectric power absorption (loss) in characteristic frequency ranges.

It is conventional, in the phenomenological treatment of frequency dependence, to use imaginary exponential notation

($e^{j\omega t}$) for sinusoidal time functions. Thus, if a field $\mathcal{E}$ is applied to a dielectric, a displacement current density $\epsilon\, d\mathcal{E}/dt = j\omega\epsilon\mathcal{E}$ (representing the charging of the electrode surfaces) flows in the connecting circuit and in the dielectric itself. If the dielectric has loss mechanisms, the current flow is not entirely in time quadrature (90° in time-phase difference) with the field. This may be represented phenomenologically by permitting ϵ to be a complex number. Then

$$J_{\text{displacement}} = j\omega\epsilon\mathcal{E} \equiv j\omega(\epsilon' - j\epsilon'')\mathcal{E} \tag{7.29}$$

While the loss parameter ϵ'' produces the same results as electronic conductivity, no conduction electrons need be present. Both ϵ' and ϵ'' are strongly frequency-dependent; they are closely related to one another, as we shall show.

The loss properties of a dielectric may be represented by plotting ϵ'' versus frequency. More commonly, the ratio

$$\tan \delta = \frac{\epsilon''}{\epsilon'} \tag{7.30}$$

termed the *loss tangent*, is stated. This is the tangent of the angle by which the current in the dielectric differs from time quadrature with the electric field. Another common description is in terms of the *quality factor* Q, defined for any electrical reactance device or network as

$$Q = \frac{\text{maximum energy stored during sinusoidal cycle}}{\text{energy dissipated per cycle}} \cdot 2\pi \tag{7.31}$$

Where the network contains only a capacitance made using the given dielectric (ϵ',ϵ''), the Q is simply the inverse of the loss tangent of the dielectric.

The frequency dependence of molecular rotational polarization may be described simply, by observing that an applied field cannot instantly polarize the molecule. Rather, when the field is applied, polarization increases nearly linearly with time, as the rotational motion swings the ions around into a polarized orientation. Thus, in the absence of collisions, we have a molecular polarization given approximately by

$$\frac{d\mathbf{p}_e}{dt} = \left(\frac{\alpha_0\epsilon_0}{\tau}\right)\mathcal{E} \tag{7.32}$$

The constant in parentheses will be identified shortly, but is for the moment simply a constant. At high frequencies, where the field changes through several cycles between collisions of the molecule and phonons, the polarizability is given directly from (7.32), substituting sinusoidal dependence $(d/dt = j\omega)$.

$$\alpha \equiv \frac{p_e}{\epsilon_0 \mathcal{E}} = \frac{\alpha_0}{j\omega\tau} \qquad \text{(high-frequency limit)}$$

That is, the heavy ions cannot follow the instantaneous field variations. At lower frequencies, however, and in static fields, collisions restore a nonpolarized orientation at intervals averaging a mean collision free time or relaxation time τ (which is a function of the dielectric and of temperature). Accordingly, in static fields, integrating (7.32) from $t = 0$ to $t = \tau$ and averaging over all values of free time between collisions, we obtain p_e (average) $= \alpha_0\epsilon_0\mathcal{E}$; this represents a static polarizability of α_0. When the static and high-frequency behavior is combined, the polarizability can be represented by the function

$$\alpha = \frac{\alpha_0}{1 + j\omega\tau} \qquad \text{(molecular rotation)} \qquad (7.33)$$

This part of the total polarizability generally becomes insignificant above audio frequencies, because of the inertia of the ions involved. It can, however, produce extremely large contributions to dielectric constant. For example, water at room temperature has a static dielectric constant of about 80. Figure 7.5 shows the polarizability contributions from this source, at low frequencies.

Ionic displacements are characterized by the same high-inertia movements of heavy ions, but the springlike restoring forces of the lattice alter the frequency response. Consider the linear-chain model of Fig. 7.3b, presuming that the two types of ion are equally but oppositely charged and of the same mass. When a field is applied, the displacement of each ion by a distance x produces a restoring force, from each of the "springs" of constant k. Each spring is deformed a distance $2x$, so that the restoring force on the ion is $4xk$. This must be offset by the force on the ionic charge $q\mathcal{E}$; hence the displacement is related to the field by

$$x = \frac{q\mathcal{E}}{4k}$$

The polarization produced by *each* ion is qx; hence the ionic polarizability at low frequencies is

$$\alpha_0 = \frac{q^2}{4k\epsilon_0} \qquad (7.34)$$

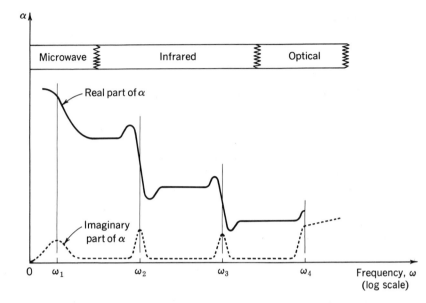

Figure 7.5 Schematic for the variation of polarizability with frequency. The variation near ω_1 is due to ionic dipoles, those near ω_2 and ω_3 to electronic transitions between discrete states and/or narrow energy bands, and that near ω_4 to transitions from or to a broad energy band. The imaginary part of α represents response in quadrature time phase to the exciting field, which corresponds to dielectric losses.

The response of this system to fields of high frequency may be found by writing a complete force equation

$$m\,\frac{d^2x}{dt^2} + 4kx + q\mathcal{E} = 0$$

With sinusoidal fields, using exponential symbolism,

$$x = \frac{q\mathcal{E}}{4k - \omega^2 m}$$

Polarizability can be expressed in terms of α_0:

$$\alpha = \frac{\alpha_0}{1 - \omega^2 m/4k} = \frac{\alpha_0}{1 - \omega^2/\omega_0{}^2}$$

The critical frequency $\omega_0{}^2 = 4k/m$ corresponds to the upper frequency limit of the optical phonon band. As discussed in Sec. 2.8, in this frequency range electromagnetic energy and acoustical energy can exchange quanta. Accordingly, there are dielectric losses associated with the phonon absorption of electric energy near the critical frequency ω_0. A more correct expression for the polarizability due to ionic motion is therefore given by

$$\alpha = \frac{\alpha_0}{1 - (\omega^2/\omega_0^2) + j\omega\tau} \quad \text{(ionic displacements)} \quad (7.35)$$

This contribution produces polarization up to the appropriate optical absorption region. Note, however, that the higher the value of ω_0 (due to "stiffer" lattice forces), the lower will be the low-frequency polarizability α_0, from (7.34). This term accounts for the rather large dielectric constants of some ionic solids, extending usefully above the microwave region in some cases. Of course, an actual solid may have several modes of acoustical resonance, each of which will contribute to low-frequency polarization and each of which fails, above its resonance frequency. The relaxation time τ depends on the solid, its degree of crystalline perfection, and the temperature. Elemental dielectrics will lack this contribution entirely, and in polycrystalline or amorphous solids the resonance will be broadened because of nonuniform ω_0.

The remaining contribution is electronic. Because electronic orbital perturbations are essentially elastic, the frequency dependence will resemble that of the ionic displacements. Since electronic masses are far less, however, the "resonances" occur at higher frequencies. A detailed treatment is possible, using time-dependent quantum-perturbation theory. When applied to individual electrons which can make a transition from one discrete energy level to another, the theory gives results equivalent to (7.35). The "loss" is actually energy absorption, when electrons make such a transition. Because their relaxation from an excited state to their ground state is generally phonon-produced, the absorbed energy is dissipated as heat. Figure 7.5 illustrates an electronic-transition contribution to polarizability at ω_2 and ω_3. Solids may have many such transitions, at frequencies ranging from a few tenths of a volt photon energy up to many electron volts. As in the ionic case, the transitions of higher frequency can contribute less to low-frequency polarization. This is observable in (7.23).

Where electrons can make transitions between discrete-energy states and energy bands, or between two bands, absorption occurs over a wide range of frequencies, as shown in Fig.

7.5, at ω_4. While absorption bands do not permit use as loss-less dielectrics, both broad and narrow bands can be used to permit filtering of unwanted frequencies from broad-band radiation when it passes through the material.

The form of the polarizability relations (7.33) and (7.35) resembles relations for the complex electrical impedance of electrical networks.   In fact, it is possible to form an electrical-network analog of a dielectric.   Figure 7.6 represents the molecular rotational polarization by a series resistance-capacitance circuit, ionic and electronic resonance terms by RLC circuits, and the electronic absorption band by a high-pass filter circuit which absorbs power above its cutoff frequency. At very low frequencies, the effective capacitance is $C_1 + C_2 + C_3 + C_4$; this is reduced, at higher frequencies, where R_1, then L_2, etc., dominate their parts of the circuit.   While such a model has pedagogical value, the reader should remember that the dielectric constant is related to the polarizability through a relation which depends on the local fields [e.g., as in (7.10)]; the actual variation of ϵ' and ϵ'', therefore, could not be expected to follow exactly the frequency dependence of capacitance in the analog.

With these principles in mind, one can often surmise con-siderable about the dielectric properties of a material from a knowledge of its structure.   While, for example, the low-fre-quency dielectric properties of the semiconductors silicon and germanium are retained up to frequencies corresponding to photons of band-gap energy (in pure materials), the high static dielectric constants found in many liquid dielectrics can cer-tainly not be applied at substantial frequencies.   At optical wavelengths, in fact, the refractive indices of transparent mate-

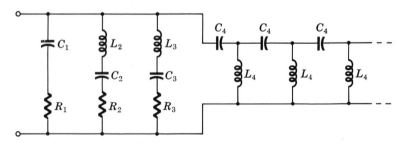

Figure 7.6   Electric circuit analog representing the frequency variation of Fig. 7.5; one may think of this circuit as representing a capacitance con-structed using the material described.

rials range over a relatively narrow range of values. This is not surprising if we note that electronic polarizability is little dependent on atomic number [as suggested by the simple theory of Eq. (7.8)].

7.5 Anisotropy and Nonlinearity in Optical Dielectrics

Any crystalline dielectric which is of noncubic structure may, by the arguments of Sec. 1.3, be expected to have anisotropic properties. While this is in general the case, dielectric properties are so largely associated with small perturbations of inner-shell electrons that anisotropies are generally quite weak. While ordinarily insignificant in low-frequency applications, nevertheless, at optical frequencies, anisotropy gives rise to the so-called *birefringence* of certain materials. In some materials, *electrically produced* birefringence (electrooptic effect) is the consequence of slight dielectric *nonlinearity*.

Optical description of dielectrics is generally in terms of the *refractive index* $n = (\epsilon/\epsilon_0)^{\frac{1}{2}}$ rather than permittivity ϵ. In isotropic materials, Maxwell's equation yields waves of velocity $(\mu\epsilon)^{-\frac{1}{2}}$, which for nonmagnetic materials may be expressed as $(\mu_0\epsilon_0)^{-\frac{1}{2}} \cdot (\epsilon/\epsilon_0)^{-\frac{1}{2}} = c/n$. The refractive index is therefore the ratio of the velocity of light in free space to that in the dielectric. The permittivity in noncubic crystals is a tensor, which means that the refractive properties are dependent on the direction of the electric field of the electromagnetic waves.

In a general crystalline dielectric, assuming linearity, the polarization is related to the electric field by (7.3). The total energy stored in a dielectric by the application of electric fields may be obtained by integrating $\mathbf{D} \cdot d\mathbf{\mathcal{E}}$, from zero field. In a linear dielectric, this yields $\frac{1}{2}\mathbf{D} \cdot \mathbf{\mathcal{E}}$. Substituting from (7.2) and (7.3), letting $\epsilon_{ij} = 1 + \chi_{ij}$, this total energy is

$$W = \frac{1}{2}(\epsilon_{11}\mathcal{E}_x^2 + \epsilon_{22}\mathcal{E}_y^2 + \epsilon_{33}\mathcal{E}_z^2 + 2\epsilon_{12}\mathcal{E}_x\mathcal{E}_y + 2\epsilon_{13}\mathcal{E}_x\mathcal{E}_z + 2\epsilon_{23}\mathcal{E}_y\mathcal{E}_z) \tag{7.36}$$

The constant-energy surfaces ($W = $ const) in "$\mathcal{E}$ space" are ellipsoidal, since (7.36) is the expression of an ellipsoid with center at $\mathcal{E} = 0$. Such an ellipsoid must have three major-axis directions. If we rotate the field coordinates to new axes (x',y',z') corresponding to these major directions, in the new coordinates W will have the form

$$W = \frac{1}{2}(\epsilon'_{11}\mathcal{E}_{x'}^2 + \epsilon'_{22}\mathcal{E}_{y'}^2 + \epsilon'_{33}\mathcal{E}_{z'}^2) \tag{7.37}$$

The energy W is of course invariant to such coordinate rotations. This means that, in the new coordinates, the polarization expressions have the form

$$P_{x'} = \epsilon'_{11}\mathcal{E}_{x'} \qquad P_{y'} = \epsilon'_{22}\mathcal{E}_{y'} \qquad P_{z'} = \epsilon'_{33}\mathcal{E}_{z'} \qquad (7.38)$$

Along these axes, accordingly, the electric flux density will lie parallel to the electric field. Operation of anisotropic optical dielectrics is best understood through expressing the entire electric (or electromagnetic) field in terms of its components in the x', y', z' axes. Each of these components will then propagate with the velocity appropriate to the particular field direction [$c/n = c(\epsilon_0/\epsilon'_{11})^{\frac{1}{2}}$, for fields in the x' direction, etc.].

In treating optical propagation in dielectrics, the concept of the *indicial ellipsoid* has been found useful. One imagines the ellipsoidal surface

$$\epsilon_{11}x^2 + \epsilon_{22}y^2 + \epsilon_{33}z^2 + 2\epsilon_{12}xy + 2\epsilon_{13}xz + 2\epsilon_{23}yz = \epsilon_0 \qquad (7.39)$$

The major-axis directions of the ellipsoid, corresponding to crystalline axes in all instances except monoclinic and triclinic lattices, have half-axis lengths of $(\epsilon_0/\epsilon'_{11})^{\frac{1}{2}}$, $(\epsilon_0/\epsilon'_{22})^{\frac{1}{2}}$, and $(\epsilon_0/\epsilon'_{33})^{\frac{1}{2}}$ in the x', y', and z' directions, respectively; hence the length of the ellipsoid axis is a measure of the velocity of light propagation for fields along that axis. Figure 7.7 illustrates such an ellipsoid, somewhat exaggerated from the usual axial ratios differing by a few per cent in, for example, hexagonal crystals.

The phenomenon of birefringence is observed when light is passed through the crystal in such a way that part of the light-wave electric field is parallel to the optic axis (the c axis of hexagonal, trigonal, etc., crystals) and part is at right angles to the optic axis. The two components will propagate with different wave velocities; if the refractive index for a given wave is n, the total phase shift in passing through a length of crystal l is $\theta = 2\pi n l/\lambda$. (The parameter λ is the free-space wavelength.) Accordingly, the difference in phase shifts of two orthogonally polarized components is

$$\Delta\theta = \frac{2\pi(n_\| - n_\perp)l}{\lambda} \qquad (7.40)$$

The refractive indices along field directions parallel and perpendicular to the optic axes are represented by $n_\|$ and $n_\perp$, respectively. As shown in Fig. 7.7, if an incident light wave is *linearly* polarized at 45° to the optic axis, its two components will form a circularly polarized resultant wave when $\Delta\theta = 90°$

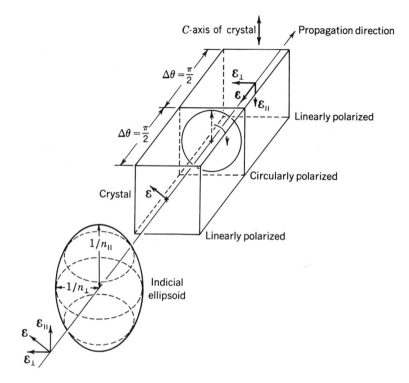

Figure 7.7 Schematic showing the indicial ellipsoid for a uniaxial (e.g., hexagonal) crystal. Light polarized at 45° to the c axis is altered after travel through a given length into circularly polarized radiation, and after twice that distance into linear polarized radiation at 90° to the original configuration, because of the different velocities of the two orthogonal components.

and a wave of polarization at 90° to the original when $\Delta\theta = 180°$. For light of a given wavelength, one can prepare a section of crystal to perform these functions; one for 90° phase-shift difference is termed a *quarter-wave plate*, for 180° a half-wave plate.

Crystalline dielectrics are at best only weakly *nonlinear* in normal optical field strengths. That is, the components ϵ_{ij} are to a very slight extent functions of the field $\mathbf{\mathcal{E}}$. While non-linearities can be observed even at microwave frequencies, they become usefully large only at such high fields that dielectric losses or dielectric breakdown preclude significant device applications such as efficient harmonic generation. Only with the relatively recent availability of intense pulsed light sources (lasers) have nonlinear effects been observable at optical wavelengths. Since, however, very tiny changes in the refractive index produce meaningful optical phase shifts, high-voltage *low-frequency* signals can produce large enough changes in dielectric constant to *modulate* optical signals. Small field-produced birefringence (represented by slight *distortion* of the indicial ellipsoid) can be used in a manner similar to Fig. 7.7. A modulator may consist of a polarizer, followed by a field-sensitive dielectric and a second polarizer at right angles to the first. If we assume no birefringence, with zero modulating voltage, no light will pass. When sufficient voltage is applied to produce $\Delta\theta = 180°$, the output all passes the output polarizer giving 100 per cent modulation.

A cubic crystal will ordinarily be isotropic, and hence have a spherical indicial ellipsoid. With large applied fields, however, in some cubic crystals of the class $\overline{4}3m$ (which includes diamond and zincblende), the indicial ellipsoid is distorted as shown in Fig. 7.8a. The nature of the distortion is determined completely by the point-group symmetry of the crystal and the direction of the applied field, while the magnitude is a function of the particular material. The refractive index for the optical component polarized *parallel* to the application of a strong

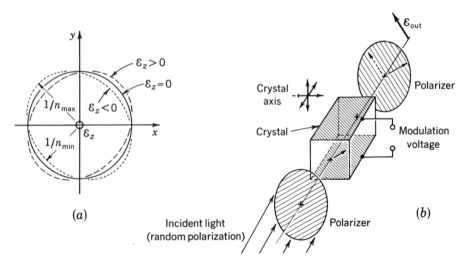

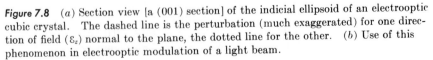

Figure 7.8 (a) Section view [a (001) section] of the indicial ellipsoid of an electrooptic cubic crystal. The dashed line is the perturbation (much exaggerated) for one direction of field ($\mathcal{E}_z$) normal to the plane, the dotted line for the other. (b) Use of this phenomenon in electrooptic modulation of a light beam.

electric field in a [001] direction is to first order unchanged, while that of components normal to the direction of the applied field is slightly altered. Since the distortion of the ellipsoid for a field of *opposite polarity* is of the form shown dotted, the change of refractive index in a direction normal to the field is a *linear* function of applied field. This phenomenon is termed the *linear electrooptic effect*, or *Pockels' effect*. Figure 7.8b illustrates a device mode whereby this material is used to modulate a light beam. A strong electric field is applied along one of the crystalline axes; incident light is polarized in a [011] direction. The refractive index of the component of light parallel to the field is not altered, whereas that normal to the field is changed.

The electrooptic properties of materials are often described by the voltage which must be placed across the crystal to produce a relative optical phase difference of 180°. This "$\lambda/2$ voltage" is typically of the order of 10^4 volts in useful materials, giving some idea of the very small degree of dielectric nonlinearity. Since the polarization altered by the applied fields must be electronic in origin to vary at optical wavelengths, light may readily be *modulated* at microwave frequencies.

Strong linear electrooptic effects are also found in dihydrogen phosphate crystals (KH_2PO_4 and $NH_3H_2PO_4$), which have a tetragonal structure of point-group class $\overline{4}2m$). These crystals have of course a naturally uniaxial character and natural birefringence. The electrooptic properties of these crystals have been studied extensively.[1] Though soft and water-soluble, very large crystals of high transparency can be grown more readily than crystals of the cubic materials.

Another common electrooptic effect is the *Kerr effect*, or *quadratic electrooptic effect*. The indicial sphere of an isotropic material is distorted by high fields into an ellipsoid, with major axis coincident with the field. The change, however, is *independent* of the electric field *polarity*, so that in simple series approximation the refractive index in the direction of the applied field is $n = n_0 + n_1 \mathcal{E}^2 + \cdots$. In solids this effect is ordinarily so weak as to be unsuitable for electrooptic-device applications. Certain liquids (CS_2, nitrobenzene) have, however, been used in Kerr electrooptic modulators up to microwave modulation frequencies.

Dielectric anisotropies and nonlinearities are so dependent on material and structure as generally to defy theoretical prediction of quantitative material properties. Many of the

[1] Cf. B. H. Billings, *J. Optical Soc. Am.*, **42**:12 (1952).

important electrooptic materials, piezoelectrics, and low-loss insulators, furthermore, are organic compounds. From an applicational point of view, this complicates application of many of these materials, for in general solid organics should be kept below softening or dissociation temperatures. Water-soluble crystals must be prevented from dissolving in humid environments, and crystals which are hydrated prevented from losing their water of hydration in hot or dry environments.

7.6 Piezoelectricity

While most dielectrics are only weakly anisotropic, weakly nonlinear, and weakly sensitive to mechanical strain, electromechanical effects are still large enough to be of practical value in electrically driven acoustical resonators and in a variety of electromechanical transducer applications. The entire field of electromechanical phenomena in dielectrics is termed *piezoelectricity*.

Piezoelectricity is evidenced by an induced polarization and an electric charge appearing on the surface of a mechanically *strained* dielectric. In Fig. 7.9, we use a two-dimensional model of an ionic solid to demonstrate that piezoelectricity *cannot occur* in crystals having a center of symmetry. (This can be shown generally through symmetry operations; see Prob. 7.6a.) The dipole moment is determined using an ion plus a fraction of each of its nearest neighbors (here we take one-third of each of the charges of the three nearest neighbors). The square lattice in Fig. 7.9a, when strained, still retains complete cancellation of dipole moment, whereas the structure of Fig. 7.9b develops net dipole moments due to each atom and its neighbors. Only 20 of the 32 crystal classes can be piezoelectric; all centrosymmetric classes (Fig. 1.9), as well as class 432, are excluded for reasons of symmetry. Practical piezoelectric materials, however, are limited to a small number of natural and synthetic compounds. While many dielectrics are piezoelectric, most applications are satisfied either by quartz (SiO_2), Rochelle salt (sodium potassium tartrate tetrahydrate, $NaKC_4O_6 \cdot 4H_2O$), or ammonium (or potassium) dihydrogen phosphate $(KH_2PO_4, NH_3H_2O_4)$. Other materials, often termed "piezoelectric," such as barium titanate $(BaTiO_3)$, are really ferroelectrics operating by another mechanism (discussed in the next section).

Piezoelectricity in materials such as quartz is a *linear*

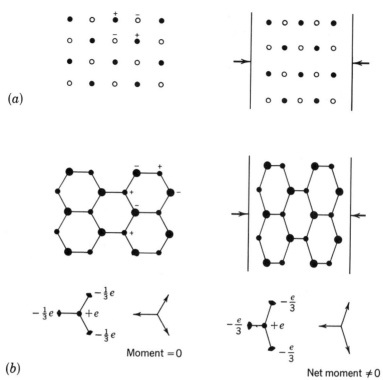

Figure 7.9 (*a*) Compression of, for example, a simple cubic crystal such as NaCl, which has a center of symmetry, produces no polarization. (*b*) A crystal without a center of symmetry can be distorted in such a way as to produce a strain-dependent polarization.

effect; an opposite strain will result in the induced dipole moment being oppositely directed. There are *quadratic* effects which are not so demanding of crystal structure; that is, even a centrosymmetric crystal will in general *expand* in an applied field. Reversal of the field does not, however, result in reversal of the strain. Expansion takes place here merely because the free energy (the sum of the mechanical strain energy and the electrostatic energy) is made *smaller* when the volume expands slightly, reducing ϵ. This typically weak effect is termed *electrostriction*. It permits, however, no converse strain-induced polarization, as does true piezoelectricity.

The governing equations of linear piezoelectricity may best be derived by expansion of a suitable energy function (Sec. C.1). With the variables polarization, field, stress, and strain, there are a number of such functions. If, for example, we choose the energy function having field and strain as its independent variables, for small fields and strains the function must be expandable as follows:

$$E(\mathcal{E},\mathbf{S}) = \frac{1}{2} \sum_{i=1}^{6} \sum_{j=1}^{6} c_{ij}S_iS_j + \frac{\epsilon_0}{2} \sum_{i=1}^{3} \sum_{j=1}^{3} \chi''_{ij}\mathcal{E}_i\mathcal{E}_j$$

$$+ \sum_{i=1}^{3} \sum_{j=1}^{6} e_{ij}\mathcal{E}_iS_j \qquad (7.41)$$

This expansion is completely general. Higher-order terms would be required to describe nonlinear properties. The c_{ij} are the same *compliance* components defined in Sec. A.5, but measured in this case in the absence of electric fields (whether applied or induced). Similarly, the susceptibility components χ''_{ij} are to be measured at zero strain. Although achieving these conditions may be difficult in practice, electromechanical coupling in many materials is so small that compliance and susceptibility measurements may be made in the usual way with little error.

A second energy function used in piezoelectricity is that which is a function of *stress* and field quantities. It may be expressed as

$$E(\mathcal{E},\mathbf{T}) = \frac{1}{2} \sum_{i=1}^{6} \sum_{j=1}^{6} s_{ij}T_iT_j + \frac{\epsilon_0}{2} \sum_{i=1}^{3} \sum_{j=1}^{3} \chi'_{ij}\mathcal{E}_i\mathcal{E}_j$$

$$+ \sum_{i=1}^{3} \sum_{j=1}^{6} d_{ij}\mathcal{E}_iT_j \qquad (7.42)$$

Again, it should be recognized that the elastance s_{ij} and susceptibility χ'_{ij} used here are to be evaluated at zero field and stress, respectively.

The partial derivative of $E(\mathcal{E},\mathbf{S})$ with respect to a given strain component, while holding other strains and the field constant, is simply the corresponding stress: $\partial E(\mathcal{E},\mathbf{S})/\partial S_i = T_i$. Likewise, the partial with respect to the field is merely the corresponding component of polarization **P**, whence we obtain the basic linear equations

$$T_i = \sum_{i=1}^{6} c_{ij}S_j + \sum_{j=1}^{3} e_{ji}\mathcal{E}_j$$

$$P_i = \sum_{j=1}^{6} e_{ij}S_i + \epsilon_0 \sum_{j=1}^{3} \chi''_{ij}\mathcal{E}_j$$

$$(7.43)$$

In the absence of the electromechanical coupling terms e_{ij}, these are simply the equations of linear elastic and dielectric media.

In the same fashion, the derivatives of $E(\mathbf{\mathcal{E}},\mathbf{T})$ yield expressions for the strain and polarization, in terms of the stress and the field:

$$S_i = \sum_{j=1}^{6} s_{ij}T_j + \sum_{j=1}^{3} d_{ji}\mathcal{E}_j$$

$$P_i = \sum_{j=1}^{6} d_{ij}T_i + \epsilon_0 \sum_{j=1}^{3} \chi'_{ij}\mathcal{E}_j$$

(7.44)

Nothing more is involved in the derivation of these equations than the assumption of linearity and the existence of electromechanical coupling. The two (tensor) forms e_{ij} and d_{ij} are a bit unusual, for they couple a vector and a second-rank tensor. As with other such properties, each crystalline point group has its characteristic form of the d_{ij} and e_{ij} components, related to a standardized orientation of x, y, and z axes with the crystalline axes. For quartz (group symbol 32; see Fig. 1.9), the pertinent components are

$$
\begin{array}{c|cccccc}
 & 1 & 2 & 3 & 4 & 5 & 6 \\
\hline
x & e_{11} & -e_{11} & 0 & e_{14} & 0 & 0 \\
y & 0 & 0 & 0 & 0 & -e_{14} & -e_{11} \\
z & 0 & 0 & 0 & 0 & 0 & 0 \\
\end{array}
$$

$$
\left|\begin{array}{cccccc}
d_{11} & -d_{11} & 0 & d_{14} & 0 & 0 \\
0 & 0 & 0 & 0 & -d_{14} & -2d_{11} \\
0 & 0 & 0 & 0 & 0 & 0 \\
\end{array}\right|
$$

(7.45)

Fields or polarizations in the z axis (which is defined as the major axis of this trigonal crystal) are *not* coupled to stresses or strains ($d_{3j}, d_{j3} = 0$). Fields in the x or y directions, however, are coupled simultaneously to *several* stress or strain components. Suppose, to a quartz crystal which is unclamped, we apply a static field $\mathbf{\mathcal{E}} = 1_x\mathcal{E}_x$. By (7.44) and (7.45) there will be strains consisting of expansion in the x direction, S_1, an equal contraction in the y direction, S_2, and a yz-plane shear, S_4. Any or all of these three strains may be used to couple to mechanical vibrations. The only way to separate them, for static or low-frequency motion of the crystal, is by shaping the crystal to accentuate the motion in a desired direction. That is (Fig. 7.10), a plate may be cut very thin in the x direction

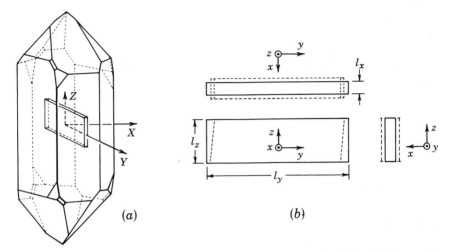

Figure 7.10   (*a*) An *X*-cut crystal in the parent quartz crystal.   (*b*) Distortion, much exaggerated, of an *X*-cut crystal with a positive-*x*-directed field. For the example in the text, noncontacting metal plates adjacent to the large (*yz*) faces permit coupling to an external circuit.

(l_x), long ($l_y \gg l_x$) in the y direction, but narrow in the z direction ($l_z < l_y$). The total change in the y length due to an applied field, $\mathcal{E}_x$, is $-d_{11}\mathcal{E}_x l_y$. The change in l_x will be only $|d_{11}\mathcal{E}_x l_x| \ll |d_{11}\mathcal{E}_x l_y|$. The effect of the shear will be minimized by the narrow z width.

The room-temperature values of the piezoelectric coefficients of quartz, as given by Cady,[1] are

$$d_{11} = 2.3 \times 10^{-10} \text{ cm/volt} \quad d_{14} = -6.7 \times 10^{-11} \text{ cm/volt}$$
$$e_{11} = 1.7 \times 10^{-1} \text{ coul/cm}^2 \quad e_{14} = 4.0 \times 10^{-2} \text{ coul/cm}^2$$

For example, a field of 100 volts/cm applied in the x axis of quartz will cause a strain of $2.3 \times 10^{-10} \times 10^2$, or only 2 parts in 10^8. This is a very small effect, but even the strongest linear piezoelectric materials have constants only about ten times as large.

Use of a plate such as that of Fig. 7.10 as a piezoelectric resonator is best understood by describing, first, its acoustical resonances, then polarizations produced by the resonance, and finally, the electrical coupling circuit. In Appendix A, we investigate waves in *isotropic* elastic solids and show that only in shear-wave modes can the motion be expressed in terms of a

[1] W. G. Cady, "Piezoelectricity," p. 219, McGraw-Hill Book Company, New York, 1946.

single stress and strain [discussion preceding Eq. (A.52)]. Quartz, however, has elastic constants of the more complicated form

$$
\begin{vmatrix}
s_{11} & s_{12} & s_{13} & s_{14} & 0 & 0 \\
s_{12} & s_{11} & s_{13} & -s_{14} & 0 & 0 \\
s_{13} & s_{13} & s_{33} & 0 & 0 & 0 \\
s_{14} & -s_{14} & 0 & s_{44} & 0 & 0 \\
0 & 0 & 0 & 0 & s_{44} & 2s_{14} \\
0 & 0 & 0 & 0 & 2s_{14} & 2(s_{11} - s_{12})
\end{vmatrix}
$$

$$
\begin{vmatrix}
c_{11} & c_{12} & c_{13} & c_{14} & 0 & 0 \\
c_{12} & c_{11} & c_{13} & -c_{14} & 0 & 0 \\
c_{13} & c_{13} & c_{33} & 0 & 0 & 0 \\
c_{14} & -c_{14} & 0 & c_{44} & 0 & 0 \\
0 & 0 & 0 & 0 & c_{44} & c_{14} \\
0 & 0 & 0 & 0 & c_{14} & \tfrac{1}{2}(c_{11} - c_{12})
\end{vmatrix} \tag{7.46}
$$

where at room temperature

$$s_{11} = 1.27, s_{33} = 0.97, s_{44} = 2.01, s_{12} = -0.17, s_{13} = -0.15,$$
$$s_{14} = -0.43, s_{66} = 2.9 \; (\times \; 10^{-12} \, \text{cm}^2/\text{dyne})$$
$$c_{11} = 87.5, \; c_{33} = 107.7, \; c_{44} = 57.3, \; c_{12} = 7.6, \; c_{13} = 15.1,$$
$$c_{14} = 17.2, \; c_{66} = 39.9 \; (\times \; 10^{10} \, \text{dynes/cm}^2)$$

It is not possible to separate y-axis compression S_2, the main term of interest in the plate of Fig. 7.10, from other components. In fact, a shear stress T_4 as well as stresses T_1, T_2, T_3 will be produced by such a strain. If the dimensions of the plate are small in all but the y direction, however, the kinetic energy involved in the resulting S_1, S_3, and S_4 vibrational strains will be small, so that the velocity given in (A.24) will be reasonably accurate. With

$$v \cong (s_{11}\rho_d)^{-\frac{1}{2}}$$

the density $\rho_d = 2.651$ g/cm^3, and $s_{11} = 1.27 \times 10^{-12}$ cm^2/ dyne, the longitudinal-wave velocity is approximately 5.4×10^5 cm/sec. A plate $l_y = 1$ cm in length will oscillate at half-wavelength resonance at a frequency of approximately

$$f = \frac{v}{\lambda} = \frac{v}{2l_y} = 2.7 \times 10^5 \text{ cps} = 270 \text{ kc}$$

With the crystal undergoing a strong compressional oscillation $S_2(y,t)$ in the y axis as shown in Fig. 7.10, (7.43) indicates that there will be a polarization $P_x = e_{12}S_2 = -e_{11}S_2$ due to this component of motion, as well as a contribution $P_x = e_{11}S_1$

from the x-directed accompanying strain. Since S_1 and S_2 will be opposite in polarity, these polarizations will aid, and produce a substantial polarization charge on the yz faces of the plate. This charge will induce a voltage on the conducting plates and couple thereby to the external circuit.

The design of quartz oscillator crystals has through long experience been reduced to the use of standard formulas. Analysis of particular modes is very similar to determination of field configurations and resonant frequencies of electromagnetic cavity resonators. Because of the many orientations in which a crystal can be cut (that described is called an X-cut plate), many variations are possible. A single crystal may oscillate at two or even three alternative frequencies, which are almost independently determined. Any crystal, like an electromagnetic cavity, has many possible oscillation modes. Good crystal design requires that unwanted modes be remote in frequency from the desired mode, or be strongly damped by the friction of the mechanical supports.

A major improvement in quartz oscillator crystals occurred with the development of special "cuts" which compensate for temperature change of the elastic and piezoelectric constants. Although some of the elastic constants of quartz change as much as 10^{-3} per degree centigrade, some changes are positive while others are negative. Using a mode of vibration which is a function of two such elasticity components, it is possible to reduce substantially the temperature rate of change of resonant frequency. In the now common AT cut, the temperature coefficient of frequency change is below about 2×10^{-6} per degree centigrade from 0 to 50°C. When such a crystal is held at near-constant temperature in an environmental oven, frequency stability can be extremely good.

A major reason for the value of quartz as an acoustical oscillator is its low acoustical loss. The much more complex hydrated salts have substantially greater crystalline disorder, hence more opportunity for phonon scattering and other loss processes. Excessive loss not only reduces the effective quality factor [Q, Eq. (7.31)] of an acoustical resonator, but can lead to undesirable internal heating in high-energy transducers.

7.7 Ferroelectrics

If, in the simple theory of Sec. 7.2, the polarizability equals or exceeds ($\alpha =$) $3/N$, a self-polarization of the dielectric will occur.   Actually, at large polarization, the relation between atomic or ionic polarization p_e and local electric field $\mathcal{E}_l$ becomes nonlinear, with a "saturation" character (Fig. 7.11).   If, however, the initial polarizability (slope of p_e, or $Np_e = \mathbf{P}$, near zero $\mathcal{E}_l$) is large enough, with zero applied field, the straight line $\mathcal{E}_l = P/3\epsilon_0$ intersects with the polarizability relation.   The intersection marks the *remanent polarization*, characteristic of *ferroelectric* materials.

The term ferroelectric is an odd analogy to ferromagnetic materials, which have magnetic polarization remanence; otherwise there is nothing "ferro" about ferroelectric materials. Actual materials are considerably more complicated than can be explained by the simple theory of (7.10), since they are ionic solids.   Apparently only the high polarizability of ionic motions is sufficient to permit ferroelectric behavior, since it is not known to occur when only electronic polarization is involved.   Accordingly, the frequency response of ferroelectric materials does not permit their use (as ferroelectrics) at microwave and higher frequencies without substantial losses.

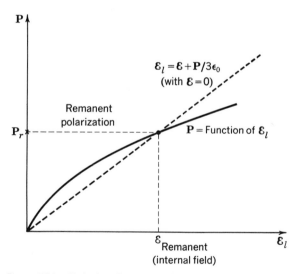

Figure 7.11   Relation demonstrating the finite remanent polarization in a ferroelectric crystal.   The straight line is the *local field* produced in a spherical sample because of polarization charge, with zero macroscopic field.   The curve is the polarization *produced by a given local field*.   The intersection of the two defines the remanent polarization.

All known ferroelectrics have properties which are highly anisotropic and structure-dependent. Furthermore, ferroelectric behavior is observed only over certain temperature ranges. Above a transition temperature T_c, the material becomes simply a normal dielectric. The behavior *above* the transition temperature may be understood through observing that the polarizability is temperature-dependent. In the case of ions having low restoring forces, a statistical analysis indicates that polarizability should be inversely dependent on temperature: $\alpha = C/T$. If this is substituted into (7.10), the dielectric susceptibility ($\chi_e = k - 1$) takes the form

$$\chi_e = \frac{NC}{T - NC/3}$$

which is generally written as the *Curie-Weiss law*

$$\chi_e = \frac{C'}{T - T_c} \tag{7.47}$$

The high dielectric constant at temperatures just above T_c is evidence of the assistance given an applied field by self-polarizing fields. There is also very substantial dielectric loss, associated with large ionic motions. Above critical temperatures, actual ferroelectrics behave very nearly as described by (7.47) (cf. Fig. 7.14).

While the simple isotropic dielectric theory is useful in explaining the causes of ferroelectricity, these materials can really be understood only by careful study of their crystal structures. For example, one finds that remanent polarization is always directed along some major crystalline axis. This is a consequence of the rather large ionic displacements which take place in the ferroelectric regime. While electronic polarizability is almost isotropic, ionic polarizability is highly anisotropic; a given ion fits its crystalline site so snugly that it can be displaced much more easily in some directions than in others. These structure-dependent properties can best be appreciated by studying an example. By far the most commonly used ferroelectric material is *barium titanate* ($BaTiO_3$). In this particular structure, depicted in Fig. 7.12, motion of the body-centered titanium ion is a crucial part of the ferroelectric process. At temperatures *above* the Curie point, the lattice of $BaTiO_3$ is simple cubic. Since it has a center of symmetry, it is not even piezoelectric. As temperature drops below about 120°C, the crystal structure deforms slightly (to the tetragonal

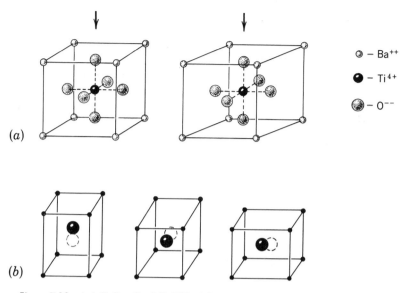

$$\bigcirc - Ba^{++}$$
$$\bullet - Ti^{4+}$$
$$\circledast - O^{--}$$

(a)

(b)

Figure 7.12   (a) Unit cell of $BaTiO_3$ (the *perovskite* structure), stereo pair. (b) The cubic unit cell, below 120°C, can be elongated to tetragonal form in any of three axes, producing any of six polarization directions.

class $4mm$). No abrupt *volume* change occurs, however. At the same time, electric polarization appears spontaneously, along *any one* of the three equivalent [100] axes of the original cubic structure. Detailed structural studies have revealed the existence of a *shift* of the titanium ion *in the direction of polarization.* Along with this shift, there is readjustment of the positions of the oxygen atoms and a corresponding elongation of the entire structure. By application of a sufficiently large electric field ($\sim 10^3$ volts/cm), in some other equivalent direction ([010], [001], or oppositely along the original axis, polarization shifts to the new direction. Elongation is now found along the new axis.

As the temperature is further reduced, at about 0°C another transition occurs, in which the crystal distorts further to orthorhombic. Although polarization now appears in [011] and equivalent directions, microscopically it probably remains in a combination of [010] and [001] directions. Below $-90°C$, a further transition occurs, remanent polarization now appearing along the original [111] axes. The crystal now deforms to the trigonal class, as would be expected from a cubic crystal strained along a *body diagonal.* Figure 7.13 shows the rema-

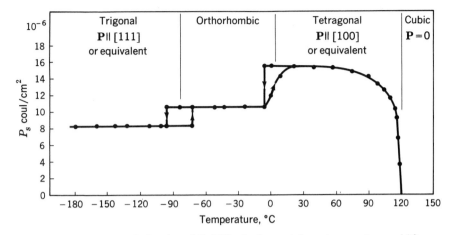

Figure 7.13   Remanent polarization of BaTiO₃ single crystal vs. temperature.   [*After W. J. Merz, Phys. Rev.*, **76**:1221 (1949).]

nent polarization of $BaTiO_3$ as a function of temperature. Above 120°C, the material can be said to be *paraelectric* (as indeed are all simple dielectrics). The hysteresis in the transitions at 0 and $-90°$ are to be expected, just as water does not freeze spontaneously at 0°C. The observed polarization of barium titanate at room temperature would correspond to the displacement of each Ti ion by about 0.15 A, a substantial fraction of the 4-A lattice constant. Actually, the displacement is known to be considerably less than this because of *electronic* polarization and displacements of the oxygen ions surrounding the titanium ion.

The dielectric properties of ferroelectrics depend strongly on the state of remanent polarization. Figure 7.14 shows small-signal dielectric constants in $BaTiO_3$ as a function of temperature. The lower curve is taken perpendicular to the polarization axis $\epsilon_\perp$, and the upper curve along the polarization axis $\epsilon_\parallel$. Above the highest transition temperature, properties are isotropic, as expected from the cubic structure. The very large anisotropy, in the ferroelectric regime, indicates the relative ease with which the titanium ion may be displaced along the polarization axis, in contrast to its "stiffness" in normal directions. The increase in ϵ *above* each transition fits closely a Curie-Weiss law.

If *high* fields are applied to a large or polycrystalline sample of $BaTiO_3$, *hysteresis* appears (Fig. 7.15a) in the $\mathcal{E}$-P

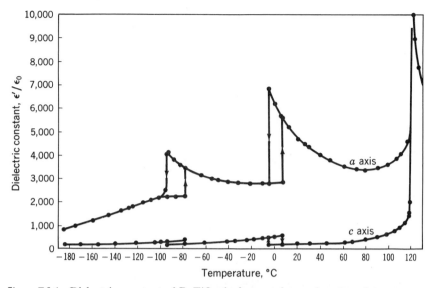

Figure 7.14   Dielectric constant of $BaTiO_3$ single crystal, as a function of temperature.   The c axis is the elongated axis of the tetragonally modified lattice.   [*After
W. J. Merz, Phys. Rev.*, **76**:1221 (1949).]

relation.   This is explained in terms of macroscopic *domains*,
regions of uniform polarization separated by narrow boundaries
from regions of another direction of polarization.   At room
temperature there are six different directions of spontaneous
polarization which a crystal of barium titanate can assume.
If, however, a large crystalline sample assumes a uniform **P**,
large external electric fields and electrostatic stored energy
$[\int(\varepsilon\mathcal{E}^2/2)\ dv]$ result.   Transition regions (domain boundaries)
between domains of different **P** directions have a high *surface
energy*, as in magnetic materials or superconductors (Secs. 9.3
and 6.4).   The free energy of a macroscopic crystal is, however,
lowered by division into domains, which lowers the electrostatic energy.   Rhombohedral domains, such as depicted in Fig.
7.15*b*, are typical of single-crystal $BaTiO_3$.   As a field is
applied, the polarization will attempt to align with the field,
for the interaction energy of the applied field and P would then
be smallest ($-\mathbf{P}\cdot\mathbf{E}$ will be a minimum).   Domains of one
polarization grow at the expense of the others, just as in fer-
romagnets (Sec. 9.3).   This process leads to the hysteresis in
the $\mathcal{E}$-P relation.   For time-varying fields above a few megacycles, the hysteresis curve degenerates to a narrow ellipse, and

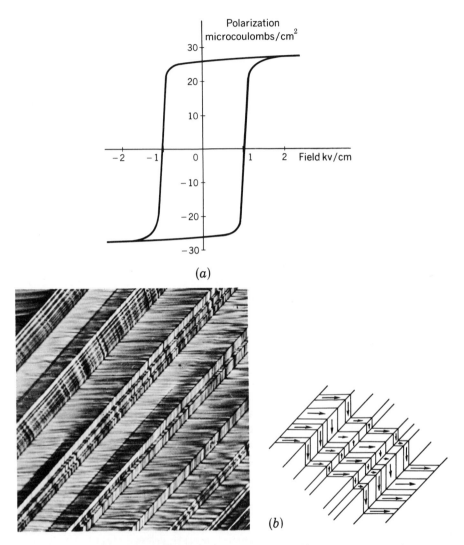

Figure 7.15 (a) D-ε characteristic of polycrystalline $BaTiO_3$ at room temperature, illustrating hysteresis. [*After J. M. Herbert, J. Electronics and Control*, **5**:170 (1958).] (b) Domain patterns observed in single-crystal $BaTiO_3$. [*After W. J. Merz, Phys. Rev.*, **95**:690 (1954).]

finally to nearly a straight line corresponding to linear permittivity. The domain-boundary motion is simply unable to keep pace with high-frequency field variations. The comparable properties of magnetic domain-boundary motions are much better understood (taken up in some detail in Sec. 9.3).

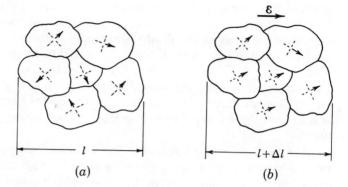

Figure 7.16 Schematic of polycrystalline $BaTiO_3$ in unpolarized and polarized states.   Crystalline axes shown as if in plane of sketch, for convenience.   (a) Unpolarized state, random arrangement of polarizations of crystallites.   (b) Polarized state, each crystallite having **P** nearest direction of polarized field, crystallites on the average elongated in field axis, relative to state (a).

Both ferroelectrics and ferromagnetics, however, suffer from comparable frequency limitations on the boundary-motion processes, which effectively limit device applications, using the hysteresis property to frequencies of the order of a megacycle.

An important use of barium titanate is as a "piezoelectric" transducer.   When a piece of barium titanate (usually poly-crystalline, for low cost) is "polarized" by application of an electric field of the order of 10^3 volts/cm, it will produce polari-zation changes upon being strained; conversely, application of fields will cause changes in the length of a sample.   The opera-tion may be understood in terms of the tetragonal distortion of the crystallites.   An unpolarized sample has its crystallites polarized in more or less arbitrary directions (Fig. 7.16a). When a field is applied, some of the crystallites are realigned in directions nearer that of the field, producing at the same time some remanence (Fig. 7.16b).   At some critical field value, all the crystallites are polarized in [001] directions near-est the field, and further elongation is only slight.   When the field is relaxed, because of internal strains the sample will relax toward an unpolarized state, but will retain some remanence. If to this sample an alternating field is applied, its length in the direction of the field will expand and contract, like a true piezoelectric.   Like a true piezoelectric, it will also produce a surface polarization charge in response to tensile stresses, as a result of the crystallite tetragonal axes being forced into the direction of the strain. It is necessary first to polarize the sample, however, since if half of the crystallites are polarized one way and the other half opposite, there will be no *observed* polarization. This is an important key to the operation of the material, and in most applications it is necessary to have a bias field applied to prevent depolarization with repeated strains or overcome the consequences of accidental overheating past 120°C.

For small fields and strains the "piezoelectric" properties are nearly linear. One can define d_{33} and d_{31} ($= d_{32}$), respectively, as the per unit strains, per unit field, parallel and perpendicular to the field. Typical values at room temperature are of the order of $d_{31} = -10^{-8}$, $d_{33} = 2 \times 10^{-8}$ cm/volt (about 100 times those for quartz). Thus a 10-cm-long sample with 100 volts/cm field along its length would deform about 2×10^{-5} cm (in length). Length would *increase* with field in the original polarization direction, decrease for opposite fields. Excessive fields will of course produce irreversible changes, as the operation follows a hysteresis curve similar to Fig. 7.15a. Since titanates are hard ceramic materials, unaffected by environment so long as temperature stays in the proper range, they make very useful transducers. Particularly important is the fact that they can be made to deform in any axis along which one can apply a field and in the normal directions as well.

Other major ferroelectric materials include Rochelle salt, which exhibits ferroelectricity only over the amazingly narrow range of 255 to 297°K. The remanent polarization appears along the major axis of this uniaxial crystal, therefore has only two possible orientations. Potassium and ammonium dihydrogen phosphates are ferroelectric only up to about 150°K, but at room temperature still display strong ionic polarizability, from the "tail" of a Curie-Weiss relation. Linear piezoelectric constants are also very high in this region, showing the connection between strong piezoelectricity and ferroelectric behavior (in noncentrosymmetric crystals). Although Rochelle salt has long been used in phonograph devices as a low-frequency piezoelectric transducer, its largely ionic polarization does not permit it to compete with quartz at higher frequencies.

While there are relatively few ferroelectrics of practical value, a number of complex solids exhibit behavior which suggests that they have internal ferroelectric behavior. If, however, internal or surface conductivity is large, the surface charge indicative of remanent polarization may be neutralized. When some of these materials are heated through their transition temperature, however, surface charges appear momentarily as the *internal* polarization is released. These materials have been termed *pyroelectric;* the tourmaline crystal is the classic example. Other materials, primarily tantalates and niobates, have internal polarization which cancels (as in antiferromagnetism) over several unit cells, and is detectable through the typical specific-heat variation characteristic of second-order phase transitions. These materials are said to be *antiferroelectric.*

The analogy of ferroelectric to ferromagnetic behavior is so striking that it is only natural that ferroelectric devices should have been proposed on similar principles to ferromagnetic devices. Although the hysteresis and domain phenomena are closely analogous, many important magnetic phenomena cannot appear analogously in dielectrics. The magnetic dipole, for example, exhibits a natural resonance, in a magnetic field, not present with electric dipoles. The strength of magnetic effects, in terms of the interaction energy of the polarized material in a field $(-\mu_0 \mathbf{p}_m \cdot \mathcal{K})$, is much greater, *per unit volume* of material, than the corresponding dielectric quantity $(-\mathbf{p}_e \cdot \boldsymbol{\mathcal{E}})$, *at reasonably attainable fields.* There is no electrical analogy to the transformer, for there is no such thing as a "magnetic current," of "magnetic charge," which would set up an *electric* field, as an *electric* current sets up a *magnetic* field in a transformer. Magnetic materials can perform at very high frequencies, because of the low inertia of the spinning electrons. Large *electric* polarizations, on the other hand, are associated mainly with ionic displacements; the high inertia of the ions prevents phenomena such as large nonlinear susceptibility from being observed at high frequencies. For these reasons and others, in energy-conversion applications dielectric materials play mainly the important but peripheral role of electrical insulators. Capacitor *energy banks* also use dielectrics to store energy for correction of power factor of power systems and for activation of the high-intensity gas discharge lamps used in pulsed-laser operation and high-speed photography. Because capacitors can store energy constantly with almost zero dissipation, they have a decided advantage over magnetic devices, which store energy only owing to the circulation of an electric current in a conductor.

7.8   Thermal Dependence of Dielectric Properties

The dielectric constants of simple elemental dielectrics show relatively small temperature dependence, since there is relatively little change in electronic structure. The nature of the change is generally toward an increase of dielectric constant at higher temperatures, brought about by the expansion of the lattice. Of course, if the dielectric is a semiconductor, temperature increase may raise the free carrier density to introduce conduction losses. In ionic dielectrics, however, very substantial increases in dielectric constant are brought about at high temperatures because of the loosening of the bonds which hold ions in place. This is illustrated by Fig. 7.17a, for a steatite (magnesium silicate)-based dielectric. That the increased dielectric constant is largely due to ionic motions is demonstrated by the negligible increase observed at high frequencies. Figure 7.17b shows that this increase is not obtained without substantial increase in the losses (tan δ).

Some dielectrics, particularly those based on titanates, exhibit a negative temperature coefficient of dielectric constant, as is apparent at low temperatures in Fig. 7.17c; at higher temperatures, the same ionic-polarization increase is observed as in steatites. Although the negative-temperature-coefficient behavior is applicable up to very high frequencies, it is no doubt related to the Curie-Weiss variation (7.46) typical of ferroelectrics above their transition temperatures.

Capacitors for electronic circuit applications are formulated from mixed ceramics, so that the composite material may have a positive, negative, or zero temperature coefficient. This is useful in compensating for undesirable thermal variations of resonant circuits in radio and other applications.

At extremely high temperatures, most dielectrics will conduct substantially, through either electronic or ionic conduction mechanisms. Since most solid dielectrics are used in polycrystalline or amorphous (glassy) form, electronic mobilities are generally so low that electronic conductivity is normally of little consequence. When very substantial voltages are involved, however, nonuniformities in an insulator can produce extremely high electric fields in localized regions. Any current flow can produce heating, which results in increased carrier densities and can ultimately result in "breakdown" of the insulator. If temperatures and fields become sufficiently large so that appreciable ion flow is possible, irreversible breakdown

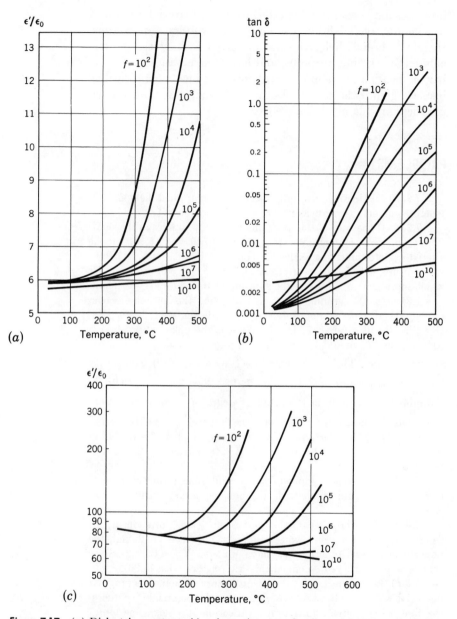

Figure 7.17 (a) Dielectric constant ϵ'/ϵ_0 of steatite ceramic (*Centralab Corp. type* 302) versus T; (b) loss tangent of this material versus T; (c) dielectric constant of titania ceramic (*American Lava Corp. type* N750T96) versus T. (*After A. R. von Hippel,* "*Dielectric Materials and Applications,*" *pp. 383, 384, 389, John Wiley & Sons, Inc., New York,* 1954.)

processes may occur in which the insulating material is reduced to a conductive medium. In many high-voltage applications, therefore, liquid dielectrics are preferred. They can be circulated for cooling purposes, and have the advantage of flowing to "heal" a momentary breakdown. Since most dielectric insulating liquids are hydrocarbon-based oils, breakdown products are mainly harmless gases.

PROBLEMS

7.2(a) Distinguish carefully between (1) applied field $\mathcal{E}_a$, (2) macroscopic field (in a dielectric) $\mathcal{E}$, and (3) local field $\mathcal{E}_l$.

7.2(b) If the sum of the fields due to nearby dipoles in the small sphere about a point is not zero, formulas (7.9) and (7.10) will be altered. Determine the dielectric constant if this sum is $\beta \mathbf{P}/\epsilon_0$, where β might be positive or negative. Are there conditions under which more general forms of the sum might be required? Explain.

7.2(c) In the ground state of hydrogen, the actual electron probability density is not uniform, but varies as $|\psi|^2 \propto e^{-2r/r_0}$ [Eq. (B.82)]. By modifying (7.11): (1) What is the polarizability? (2) At what field $\mathcal{E}_l$ should 1 per cent nonlinearity in the p_e-$\mathcal{E}_l$ relation appear? [HINT: The field is found by setting $4\pi r^2 \epsilon_0 \mathcal{E} = \int_0^r \rho(r) 4\pi r^2 \, dr$. Let $\rho(r)$ be proportional to $e^{-2r/r_0} \cong 1 - 2r/r_0 + \cdots$. Obtain the proper constant from the definite integral $\int_0^\infty x^2 e^{-cx} \, dx = 2/c^3$. Carry out the indefinite integral with the first two terms of the series, obtaining $\mathcal{E}_l \cong (ar + br^2)/\epsilon_0$. Then $\mathcal{E}_l \cong a p_e/e\epsilon_0 + b p_e{}^2/e^2\epsilon_0$. Find $\alpha \cong (a/e)^{-1}$, and the $\mathcal{E}_l$ for which $|br^2| = 0.01|ar|$. Recall that $r_0 = 0.529$ A.]

7.2(d) At a steady applied electric field, does a dielectric come into thermal equilibrium with its nonconducting surroundings? Explain.

7.3(a) (1) Show that the perturbed wave function $\psi_j' \cong \psi_{0j} + \mathcal{E}_l \psi_{1j}$ has a nonzero expectation $<x> \propto \epsilon_l$, even though the unperturbed wave functions ψ_{0j} have $<x> \equiv X_{jj} = 0$. (2) Show that $\alpha \equiv -e<x>/\epsilon_0 \mathcal{E}_l$, defined this way, agrees with (7.26).

7.3(b) For an electron in the lowest-energy state in a rectangular potential well of width $a = 1$ A, determine the polarizability due to the first three nonvanishing terms. (Section 10.1 has some useful integrals.) Compare with the result obtained in the spherical-charge-cloud model.

7.4(a) The resonance phenomena described by (7.35) may occur with resonance frequencies ω_0 spaced close together. To determine the influence of this, plot the real and imaginary parts of the sum of two such terms of equal values of α_0. One has $\omega_0 = 10^{12}$, and the other, $\omega_0 = 1.1 \times 10^{12}$. Each has $\tau = 10^{-13}$.

7.4(b) For a dielectric which can be described using (7.9), but where α and k are recognized to be complex numbers ($k = k' - jk''$), derive expressions for the real and imaginary parts of α, in terms of k' and k''. Give also approximations applicable when $(\tan \delta)^2 \ll 9$.

7.4(c) At low frequencies, α can be written as $\alpha \cong \alpha_0 + \alpha_1(1 + j\omega/\omega_0)^{-1}$, where α_0 is a real constant. Using the 300°C data of Fig. 7.17a with (7.10), fit at several frequencies to find values for $N\alpha_0$, $N\alpha_1$, and ω_0. Using these values, substitute into (7.10) to find $\tan \delta$, and compare with Fig. 7.17b.

7.5(a) Describe the nature of the probable change of dielectric constants when an originally unstrained homogeneous *amorphous* dielectric has a mechanical stress T_1 (positive) applied (give the tensor permittivity form) and indicate which terms will likely increase and which decrease from their value in the unstrained dielectric.

7.5(b) In a particular crystal specimen, the z axis is coincident with a major axis of the crystal. Along that axis, an applied field $\mathcal{E}$ will produce an x-directed electric flux density $D_z = 4\epsilon_0 \mathcal{E}_z$. In the xy plane, however, D and $\mathcal{E}$ are related via

$$\frac{D_x}{\epsilon_0} = 3\mathcal{E}_x - 0.5\mathcal{E}_y$$

$$\frac{D_y}{\epsilon_0} = -0.5\mathcal{E}_x + 2\mathcal{E}_y$$

(1) Determine the directions of the major axes x' and y' (along which $D \parallel \mathcal{E}$), in relation to the given axes. (2) Write the components of the susceptibility tensor for the xyz and $x'y'z'$ coordinates.

7.5(c) The electrooptic crystal (point-group) classes mentioned ($\overline{4}3m$ and $\overline{4}2m$, described in Fig. 1.9) have diad (twofold) rotational axes. (1) Show that a field applied to a crystal *along* a fourfold or sixfold rotational axis *could not* produce Pockels' effect. (HINT: Use the equivalency of the four orientations, together with the elliptical form of a section of the indicial ellipsoid.) (2) Accordingly, state several classes which, accordingly, could not have linear electrooptic properties with field along a major axis.

7.6(a) Show, by the methods of Sec. 1.4, that crystals having a center of symmetry must have all d_{ij} or e_{ij} coefficients identically zero. (HINT: Use the transformations $x' = -x$, $y' = -y$, $z' = -z$ on stress, strain, field, and polarization components.)

7.6(b) A 1-cm cube of quartz has faces normal to the conventional X, Y, and Z axes of the crystal. (1) A pair of noncontacting electrodes is used to measure the capacitance across each of the three parallel pairs of faces; what are these values, neglecting fringing of the fields? (2) By use of (7.38) and (7.39), estimate the capacitance values which would be obtained from the same quartz cube in a clamped (unstrained) condition. (NOTE: Susceptibilities in *unstressed* conditions are $\chi'_{11} = 3.5$, $\chi'_{33} = 3.6$.)

7.6(c) A quartz cube like that in the previous problem is used as an electromechanical transducer, with noncontacting electrodes across the X dimension covering the yz faces. Mechanical contacts on the Y dimension drive a *viscous* load which relates stress and deformation through $T_2 = -R \, dS_2/dt$. (1) Show that, from the viewpoint of the electrical contacts, the crystal and mechanical elements have an equivalent electrical circuit constituting a capacitance across the contacts, with a series resistance-capacitance combination also across the contacts. [HINT: Set up (7.39) for this case. It consists of two equations involving only S_2, T_2, $\mathcal{E}_1$, and P_1. Using the $T_2 = S_2$ relation given, find a differential equation relating only $\mathcal{E}_1$ and P_1. The current in the electrical circuit may be identified as dP_1/dt.] (2) From the equivalent circuit, explain why it is difficult to use such an element effectively for energy conversion.

7.6(d) A long bar of quartz is clamped at one end, and the other end is attached to a mechanical linkage which *bends* the crystal in a direction normal to its length. Describe how the crystal could be cut and where electrodes should be fastened for producing an output proportional to the bending. (Note that bending produces both positive and negative tensile stresses in the bar, while the shear is of the same sign throughout.)

7.7(a) A polycrystalline sample of KH_2PO_4 has crystallites oriented randomly. At some $T < T_c$, after removal of a polarizing field, all crystallites have polarization along their c axes *closest* to the direction of the field. What fraction of single-crystal remanent P appears? (HINT: Average over a random distribution of polarizations directed in all directions over a 2π solid angle.)

7.7(b) (1) Determine the *depolarizing field* on a thin (100) slab of single-crystal $BaTiO_3$ polarized normal to a slab face, at room temperature (25°C). (2) A total field of 500 volts/cm applied to a macroscopic specimen of this material can reverse polarization. Can spontaneous polarization be maintained normal to the slab, in the absence of an applied field? Explain.

7.7(c) A polycrystalline sample of $BaTiO_3$ is initially in a non-remanent state. A field is applied along a given axis, sinusoidal with peak value just exceeding the field for polarization reversal. (1) Sketch roughly the change of length ($l \parallel \mathcal{E}$) versus time, for the *initial* cycle of voltage, and in the steady state. (2) Sketch also the nature of the change in a dimension normal to the field, on the same time axis.

7.8 If the diffusion constant of zinc in the insulator ZnO is $D = 1.3e^{-3.2e/kT}$ cm²/sec, estimate the ionic conductivity at 1000°C. Assume that a 5 per cent excess of Zn^{++} ions is present and contributes to conduction. Density of pure ZnO is 5.68 g/cm³. [HINT: Use (4.42).]

GENERAL REFERENCES

The field of dielectrics has had a slower and steadier evolution than many others. Except for the fields of ferroelectrics and electro-optics, most work has been reported in physical and chemical journals. Some device work has appeared in *Proceedings of the IRE*. The progress in materials technology is reported in review in *Progress in Dielectrics*, vols. 1–5 (through 1963). Most material relating to optical properties appears in the *Journal of the Optical Society of America*.

Clark, F. M.: "Insulating Materials for Design and Engineering Practice," John Wiley & Sons, Inc., New York, 1962. (A comprehensive encyclopedia of all types of practical dielectrics.)

Fröhlich, H.: "Theory of Dielectrics," Clarendon Press, Oxford, 1958.

Jaynes, E. T.: "Ferroelectricity," Princeton University Press, Princeton, N.J., 1953. (An early study indicating the various approaches to the theory, still largely pertinent.)

Känzig, W.: Ferroelectrics and Antiferroelectrics, *Solid State Phys.*, vol. 4, 1957. (An excellent, thorough, and very readable review of all aspects of the subject.)

Katz, H. W. (ed.): "Solid State Magnetic and Dielectric Devices," John Wiley & Sons, Inc., New York, 1959. (Indicates the possible uses of dielectric phenomena in devices.)

Mason, W. P.: "Piezoelectric Crystals and Their Application to Ultrasonics," D. Van Nostrand Company, Inc., Princeton, N.J., 1950. (Design of quartz crystal transducers.)

Von Hippel, A. R.: "Dielectric Materials and Applications," John Wiley & Sons, Inc., New York, 1954. (A good basic introduction plus much information on materials and applications.)

Wood, E. A.: "Crystals and Light," D. Van Nostrand Company, Inc., Princeton, N.J., 1964. (An excellent introductory treatment of point-group symmetry and anisotropic optical properties.)

8

Magnetism

8.1 Magnetic Polarization

Since magnetism is a polarization phenomenon involving magnetic dipoles, it is described formally in much the same way as dielectric phenomena. The concept of field strength, flux density, and polarization density all have their counterparts:

	Electric	Magnetic
Field intensity:	$\mathcal{E}$	$\mathcal{3C}$
Flux density:	D	B
Polarization (per unit volume):	P	M

The electrostatic equations in the absence of free *charge* and the magnetostatic equations in the absence of convection current are almost identical:

	Rationalized units	*Unrationalized units, e.g., cgs gaussian*	
Electric:	$\nabla \cdot \mathbf{D} = 0; \quad \mathbf{D} = \epsilon_0\mathcal{E} + \mathbf{P}$	$\mathbf{D} = \mathcal{E} + 4\pi\mathbf{P}$	(8.1)
Magnetic:	$\nabla \cdot \mathbf{B} = 0; \quad \mathbf{B} = \mu_0(\mathcal{3C} + \mathbf{M})$	$\mathbf{B} = \mathcal{3C} + 4\pi\mathbf{M}$	

In our formulation, the forms of the electric and magnetic equations are slightly different, because the electric polarization is defined in terms of electric charge while magnetic polarization is defined in terms of electric current (dimensions of M are current $\times$ area/volume).

Because of the equivalence of the controlling equations (8.1), all the polarization-charge and depolarization-factor concepts of Sec. 7.1 can be applied directly. Magnetic problems are often more complex, however, because of the complex relationship between **M** and $\math3C$ in many materials.

Although dielectric publications show no accord on unit systems, the bulk of magnetics literature employs "gaussian" (cgs unrationalized) units. We continue here as elsewhere in the text with rationalized mks units, but reproduce the significant equations in both systems of units, when the two forms differ.

The major units used in the two systems are:

	Gaussian	*Rationalized mks*
Field strength $\math3C$:	1.0 *oe* $\equiv$	$\dfrac{10^3}{4\pi}\ amp/m$
Flux density **B**:	1.0 *gauss* ($\equiv$ 1.0 *maxwell/cm²*) $\equiv$	$10^{-4}\ weber/m^2$
Permeability of free space:	$\mu_0 = 1$	$\mu_0 = 4\pi \times 10^{-7}$

While some unrationalized relations contain the velocity of light, c, and rationalized ones contain 4π or μ_0, dynamic relations such as those in Secs. 8.8 and 8.9 take the same form in either system.

For those magnetic materials whose polarization is linearly dependent on magnetic field strength, a *magnetic susceptibility* χ_m and permeability μ may be defined:

$$\mathbf{M} = \chi_m\math3C \qquad \mu = \mu_0(1 + \chi_m) \qquad (\text{cgs: } \mu = 1 + 4\pi\chi_m) \tag{8.2}$$

Whereas *linear dielectric* materials may have dielectric constants ϵ/ϵ_0 much larger than unity, an important limitation of truly linear magnetic materials is that the susceptibility for most of these materials may be found in the range $-10^{-5} < \chi_m < 10^{-5}$. Materials with negative susceptibility are termed *diamagnetic*, and those with positive susceptibility are termed *paramagnetic*. *All* solids not having strongly nonlinear magnetic behavior are either diamagnetic or paramagentic. In dealing with magnetic or electromagnetic behavior of such materials, however, the very small magnetic susceptibility is generally neglected.

The magnetic materials of broadest practical importance resemble ferroelectrics in that they have remanent polarization, even in the absence of a field. The magnetostatics of these materials cannot be described by a linear susceptibility, although the general polarization relations (8.1) always apply. We show in this chapter and the next that the *magnetization* (magnetic polarization) **M** is influenced by magnetic fields not linearly, but in such ways that the magnitude of **M** in the so-called ferromagnetic and ferrimagnetic materials remains substantially constant, while only its *direction* is varied. This behavior introduces many types of magnetic effects not possible in linearly polarizable materials.

8.2 Origins of Diamagnetism and Paramagnetism[1]

Conduction electrons can be shown to exhibit paramagnetic ($\chi_m > 0$) behavior. Whereas, in the absence of a magnetic field, free electrons have energies independent of their spin orientations, a magnetic field $\mathcal{3C}_z$ alters the electron energy, according to (B.72). Instead of representing the entire conduction band, e.g., of a metal as a single electron distribution, the two *half-bands* representing electrons with the two values of spin (parallel and antiparallel to the field) have energies different by the small amount $\Delta E = \mu_0 e\hbar\mathcal{3C}_z/m$. The situation

[1] Appendix B, particularly Sec. B.8, is introductory to this material.

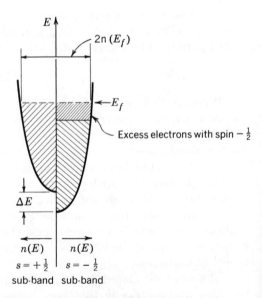

Figure 8.1   Density-of-states functions and electron population of the two half-bands ($s = \pm\frac{1}{2}$) of conduction electrons in a metal.

is described, much exaggerated, in Fig. 8.1. The two half-band electronic-state-density functions are identical but for a *shift* (ΔE) in energy level. There are, therefore, slightly more electrons in the band of spins *parallel* to the field, since electrons must fill both half-bands up to the same (Fermi) energy level. In metals the state density $n(E)$ is a slowly varying function of energy near the Fermi energy; hence it may be assumed uniform at least over a range of a few kT. The *excess* density of electrons in the lower-energy state ($n_- - n_+$) is simply $n(E_f)$ times the energy difference ΔE. According to the arguments of Sec. B.8, each excess electron contributes a component of magnetic moment in the field direction: $\mathbf{p}_m \cdot \mathbf{1}_z = e\hbar/2m_e = \beta:(9.273 \times 10^{-24}\,\text{joule/weber/m}^2)$ (cgs: $\beta = e\hbar/2mc = 9.27 \times 10^{-21}\,\text{erg/gauss}$). This important magnetic quantum is called a *Bohr magneton*. The total magnetic polarization of a solid of conduction-electron density N is therefore $|\mathbf{M}| = 2\beta^2 n(E_f)\mu_0 \mathcal{3C}_z$; accordingly, the paramagnetic susceptibility is

$$\chi_m = \frac{M}{\mathcal{3C}} = 2\beta^2 n(E_f)\mu_0 \qquad \text{(free electrons)} \tag{8.3}$$

This is much smaller ($\chi_m \approx 10^{-5}$) than would be predicted by application of Boltzmann statistics. As can be predicted directly from Fig. 8.1, the free-electron paramagnetic susceptibility of metals is almost independent of temperature.

While conduction electrons make a paramagnetic contribution to magnetic susceptibility, electrons in *closed* electronic shells are the source of diamagnetic susceptibility. A complete electronic shell has all orbital and spin-angular momenta "paired off," so that the *total* angular momentum of the atom due to each such shell ($1s$, $2s$, $2p$, etc.) is precisely zero. The orbital motion of these electrons is, however, slightly perturbed by a magnetic field. This perturbation can readily be understood on purely classical grounds. Consider an electron moving classically about a nucleus, at constant angular velocity ω and linear velocity v, in a circular orbit of radius r ($= v/\omega$). The orbit will here be assumed to have its angular momentum parallel to a z-directed magnetic field. The field is initially zero and is then increased [$\mathcal{3C}_z = \mathcal{3C}_z(t)$]. In the circular orbit of the electron, there will be an induced *electric* field, just as if the electron were moving in a conductor; the electric field experienced by the electron is the orbit area πr^2 times the rate of change of flux density, $\mu_0\, d\mathfrak{IC}_z/dt$, divided by the orbit length $2\pi r$:

$$\varepsilon = -\frac{r}{2}\,\mu_0\,\frac{d\mathfrak{IC}_z}{dt} \tag{8.4}$$

The negative sign is inherent in Maxwell's equations. The field produces a force on the orbiting electron, and consequently a torque

$$T = \text{force} \times \text{radius} = \frac{\mu_0 e r^2}{2}\,\frac{d\mathfrak{IC}}{dt} \tag{8.5}$$

which causes the electronic motion to *precess* (like a gyroscope) in what is termed the *Larmor precession*. Since torque is time rate of change of angular momentum L and magnetic moment is related to L through $p_m = -eL/2m$,

$$\frac{dp_m}{dt} = -\frac{\mu_0 e r^2}{4m}\,\frac{d\mathfrak{IC}}{dt} \tag{8.6}$$

We may integrate, observing that for the sample as a whole, p_m is zero when $\mathfrak{IC}$ is zero. Hence

$$p_m = -\frac{\mu_0 e r^2}{4m}\,\mathfrak{IC} \tag{8.7}$$

The initial orbital moment is not observed, because it is canceled by another electron in the shell, of opposite moment. *Both* are similarly perturbed by the field so that the perturbation (8.7) describes either one. The diamagnetic contribution to susceptibility is, for N atoms per unit volume,

$$\chi_m = -\frac{N\mu_0 e}{4m}\sum_i r_i^2 \tag{8.8}$$

The sum is over all closed-shell electrons, r_i being the effective orbital radius of the ith electron. In quantum form, the parameter r^2 becomes $\langle x^2 + y^2 \rangle$, a calculable quantity if the wave functions are known. Clearly, the *outermost* electrons in an atom are most significant. The negative sign means that the perturbation of the electron motion sets up a field *opposing* the change in applied magnetic field. This is equivalent to *Lenz's law* in circuit theory, which states that current induced in a conductor is directed to *oppose* a change of magnetic flux.

A rough estimate of the magnitude of diamagnetic susceptibility can be made by assuming that r is about 1 A, whence, from (8.8), $\chi_m \approx 10^{-5}$ for $N \approx 10^{29}\ m^{-3}$.

Measured values of χ_m for *nontransition* (closed-shell) metals range from the order of -1×10^{-6} for beryllium to the order of 3.6×10^{-6} for lithium, indicating that diamagnetic and paramagnetic (conduction electron) contributions are usually comparable and nearly cancel.

8.3 Paramagnetism in Transition and Rare-earth Elements[1]

Whereas the magnetic susceptibilities of conduction and closed-shell electrons in solids are small, elements which have incomplete electronic shells can exhibit stronger magnetic behavior. Of the transition and rare-earth elements, the most strongly magnetic are those with incomplete $3d$ or $4f$ subshells, the so-called *iron-group* and *lanthanide-group* elements, respectively.

There are at least five distinguishable environments in which these elements display their magnetic properties: (1) as elemental solids and alloys, (2) as impurity ions in crystalline insulating solids of low inherent susceptibility, (3) as major constituents of ionic solids, (4) in large metalloorganic molecules, and (5) as gaseous atoms or ions. The *state of ionization* of the atom is always extremely important, for *removal* of electrons from an unfilled shell alters greatly the magnetic properties. It is therefore conventional to refer always to the ionic state, that is, Fe^{++}, Fe^{3+}, etc., except in metals and alloys. This indicates that the magnetic properties of the iron ions thus described are due to six and five $3d$ electrons, respectively (Table B.1). In metals and alloys, it is almost impossible to define precisely the number of electrons associated with a given nucleus; hence we cannot define an ionized state.

The detailed magnetic properties of transition-metal or rare-earth ions depend largely on the degree to which incomplete-shell electrons are electrostatically "screened" from electric and magnetic fields due to neighboring ions. Since the $3d$ wave functions (Fig. B.9) are less well screened (in iron-group atoms) than are $4d$ or $5d$ electrons (in the other transition-metal series), iron-group $3d$ electrons are more

---

[1] Application of the phenomena described here is made in *maser* devices (cf. Sec. 10.7).

sensitive to their crystalline environment and to the nature of neighbor atoms. This makes the magnetic significance of iron-group elements surpass that of all others. Next in importance are the lanthanides, with their missing $4f$ electrons. While they are even magnetically stronger than any iron-group elements, these materials are strongly magnetic only at low temperatures.

Let us consider briefly a *free* metal ion, as might exist in a metal-vapor "gaseous discharge." The ground state of the ion consists of the electronic configuration described by Table B.1, less the appropriate number of ionized electrons. A free chromium (Cr^{3+}) ion has only three remaining electrons, in $3d$ orbits. Which, then, of the *ten* possible one-electron states in the $3d$ subshell do these electrons occupy? Even without an external magnetic field there exist spin-orbit coupling effects, as discussed in Sec. B.8. The coupling of three electrons is complicated and not amenable to exact analysis. It has been found empirically that in elements toward the left-hand side of the periodic chart (and including the transition elements and lanthanides) the internal spin-orbital coupling is much weaker than the coupling between spins or between orbital motions. This situation has been termed Russell-Saunders, or LS *coupling*. The electronic spin angular momenta are the most strongly coupled and therefore quantize themselves *internally* against a common axis. So, in turn, do the orbital momenta. In the Cr^{3+} ion, the three electron spins line up along a common axis, and the orbital moments also line up along a second internal axis (Fig. 8.2). Spectrographic data prove that the arrangement of the electrons over the states of different (m,s) is such as to maximize the overall spin angular momentum along its axis ($S = \frac{3}{2}$ measures the spin of the ion). Since all spins are already paralleled, only *one* orbital moment can have the angular momentum $m = 2$ along the common orbital axis, while the others have, respectively, $m = 1$ and $m = 0$. The resulting overall orbital angular momentum is defined by the quantum index $L = 2 + 1 + 0 = 3$. Vectors are used to represent S and L, with the appropriate lengths $|\mathbf{L}| = \hbar[L(L + 1)]^{\frac{1}{2}}$ and $|\mathbf{S}| = \hbar[S(S + 1)]^{\frac{1}{2}}$. The remaining electrons, in their closed subshells, do not contribute to paramagnetic properties of the ion. The orbital and spin angular momenta then couple further to produce an overall angular momentum index J, which is found empirically to be $J = |L - S|$ for ions with less than half filled subshells and $J = L + S$ for ions with greater than half filled subshells. These empirically determined relations are known as *Hund's rules*. In the case of Cr^{3+}, therefore, $J = 3 - \frac{3}{2} = \frac{3}{2}$. In Ni^{++}, having *eight* $3d$ electrons, $S = \frac{5}{2} - \frac{3}{2} = 1, L = 2 + 1 = 3, J = 4$. In any such ion, the *total* angular momentum vector $\mathbf{J}$, in a weak magnetic field, has possible angular momentum of $J_z = J\hbar, (J - 1)\hbar, \ldots, -J\hbar$ *along the field axis*.

The contribution of spin angular momentum to magnetic moment is relatively *twice* as large as that of orbital angular momentum (Sec. B.8). While the spin moment lies parallel to the spin angular momentum vector $\mathbf{S}$ and the orbital magnetic moment is itself parallel to $\mathbf{L}$, the total magnetic moment cannot be parallel to $\mathbf{J}$ (Fig. 8.2). While $\mathbf{J}$ has field-direction components $J_z = J\hbar, (J - 1)\hbar, \ldots, -J\hbar$, the corresponding magnetic moment has corresponding values $(p_m)_z = (g/2)\beta[J, (J - 1), \ldots, -J]$; the constant g is termed the *Landé g-factor*, or *spectroscopic splitting factor*. It has the value 2.0 for free electrons, 1.0 for purely *orbital* angular momentum, and the general value

$$g = 1 + \frac{S(S + 1) + J(J + 1) - L(L + 1)}{2J(J + 1)} \tag{8.9}$$

While the concept of the g-factor is well founded in spectroscopy, it is often used elsewhere in magnetism to explain deviation of an observed magnetic moment from theoretical values.

When an iron-group ion is located in an insulating crystal, electrostatic fields of its neighbors play a major role in defining "orbital" motion of $3d$ electrons. As a result, the orbital angular momentum of $3d$ electrons is almost completely eliminated, or "quenched." We can show this using simple wave concepts. Imagine an electronic wave function which, like the hydrogen-atom wave functions of Sec. B.7, has an *azimuthal* variation $e^{jm\phi}$. With the time factor $e^{-jEt/\hbar}$, this represents a *rotating* electron wave about the polar axis of the atom. This wave function, however, is derived in a *central-force field*. If we place an atom in the strong electrostatic fields of neighboring atoms, the $3d$ electrons have a perturbation potential V, with the symmetry of the site. The electronic wave functions of $3d$ electrons in this situation are *strongly* perturbed. A perturbed wave function can, at least formally, be expressed as a sum over unperturbed wave functions, as in (B.84). Hence

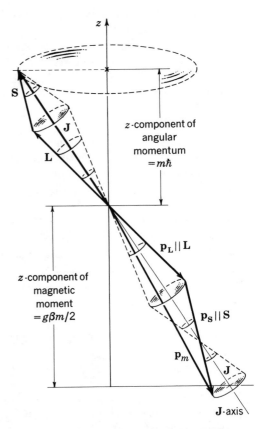

Figure 8.2   Free-ion magnetism.   In LS coupling, the total orbital-angular-momentum vector **L** (the vector sum of electronic orbital momenta) and the corresponding total spin vector **S** can be thought to combine vectorially in an isolated ion to form a constant total angular momentum vector **J**; **L** and **S** precess randomly about **J**. The orbital-magnetic-moment vector $\mathbf{p_L}$ always remains opposite in direction to **L**, and $\mathbf{p_S}$ to **S**. But $\mathbf{p_S}$ is relatively *twice* as long as $\mathbf{p_L}$, for given momentum.   Accordingly, the combination of $\mathbf{p_L}$ and $\mathbf{p_S}$ precesses about a vector opposite to **J**.   In a magnetic field, **J** precesses randomly about the field axis; its component along that axis is fixed.   The component of $\mathbf{p}_m$ is projected on $-\mathbf{J}$, and this projected on the field axis, to define the measurable magnetic moment.

a perturbed wave function is at least symbolically of the form

$$\psi = \sum_{m=-l}^{+l} A_m e^{jm\phi} \tag{8.10}$$

where A_m are a set of coefficients like those defined in a perturbation theory.

The resulting wave function should contain either equal or opposite coefficients $A_m = \pm A_{-m}$, when the perturbation has cubic or hexagonal symmetry, for example. Accordingly, ψ can be written

$$\psi \propto \sum_{m=0}^{l} A_m \begin{Bmatrix} \sin \\ \cos \end{Bmatrix} m\phi \tag{8.11}$$

The wave functions sin $m\phi$ or cos $m\phi$ are now *standing waves*, implying *no* observable orbital angular motion. This means that when neighboring-atom fields are large, *orbital angular momentum of outer electrons about their nucleus is no longer a constant*. This should not be surprising, for angular momentum is only a constant for isolated particles and central-force fields. Iron-group ions in crystalline ionic solids therefore behave as though their $3d$ electrons have little or no orbital angular momentum (hence $g \cong 2$).

In a free hydrogen atom, with unpaired electron spin, the two possible spin states ($s = \pm\frac{1}{2}$) are *degenerate* in the absence of a magnetic field. This is not, however, the case for paramagnetic ions such as Cr^{3+}, for example, in ruby (Al_2O_3). The quenching of the orbital angular momentum permits the description of the ground state of the ion solely in terms of the spin-angular-momentum state. Along any field axis, $S_z = \frac{3}{2}, \frac{1}{2}, -\frac{1}{2},$ or $-\frac{3}{2}$. There would be *four* degenerate states in the absence of magnetic field, were it not for the *crystalline fields* of the neighboring ions in the solid. The Cr^{3+} ion in ruby lies in a site which has an axis of symmetry. In the absence of an external field, the spin will quantize itself against this internal axis, with the quantized component of angular momentum S_z along the axis. The states $S_z = \pm\frac{1}{2}$ are identical, from the crystal's point of view, since there is no internal *direction* defined in the site. So are the two states $S_z = \pm\frac{3}{2}$. The two pairs of states, however, are perturbed differently by the fields of the neighboring ions, so that the four degenerate spin states are *split* into two groups of two (Fig. 8.3). The crystalline field splitting ($\mathcal{H}_z = 0$) is small, amount-

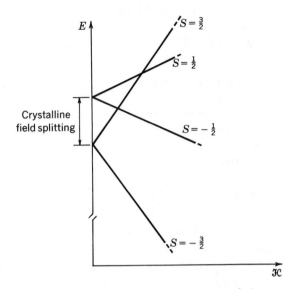

Figure 8.3   Energy levels of Cr^{3+} in Al_2O_3 (ruby) vs. magnetic field $\mathfrak{IC}$.

ing to an energy difference (specified in terms of the photon frequency $f = \Delta E/h$) of 11.6 kilomegacycles, or about 4×10^{-5} ev.

When a magnetic field is applied *along the same crystalline axis*, there will be an *additional* perturbation of the simple form

$$E_{S_z} = g\mu_0\beta\mathfrak{IC}_z S_z \tag{8.12}$$

linear in the field. When the magnetic field is applied in a direction oblique to the crystalline axis, the two perturbations no longer work together, and the resultant energy levels vary in somewhat different fashion. The result is amenable to calculation.[1]

The magnetic susceptibility of these strongly paramagnetic solids varies approximately inversely with temperature, unlike the paramagnetic contributions of conduction electrons. For illustration, consider a hypothetical ion having only a single unpaired spinning electron. Where the ion is separated from other ions of its kind by other nonparamagnetic ions and is unaffected by crystalline fields, the two energy levels in a magnetic field are given by (8.12) with $S_z = \pm\frac{1}{2}$. With the

[1] Cf. A. A. Vuylsteke, "Elements of Maser Theory," chap. 6, D. Van Nostrand Company, Inc., Princeton, N.J., 1960.

presumed independence of separated ions, Boltzmann statistics apply. The densities of ions in the lower and upper spin states, of energies E_- and E_+ $(= -E_-) = \mu_0 g \beta \mathfrak{IC}_z / 2$, respectively, will be

$$n_- = N \frac{e^{-E_-/kT}}{e^{-E_+/kT} + e^{-E_-/kT}} \qquad n_+ = N \frac{e^{-E_+/kT}}{e^{-E_+/kT} + e^{-E_-/kT}}$$

where N is the total ion density. The resultant excess of ions with spin parallel to the field $(n_- - n_+)$ produces a magnetic polarization

$$M = (n_- - n_+) p_m = \frac{N \beta g}{2} \tanh \frac{\mu_0 g \beta \mathfrak{IC}_z}{2kT} \tag{8.13}$$

For T large enough, the argument is small and

$$M \cong \frac{N \mu_0 \beta^2 g^2 \mathfrak{IC}_z}{4kT}$$

The susceptibility is, accordingly,

$$\chi_m = \frac{M}{\mathfrak{IC}} \cong \frac{N \mu_0 \beta^2 g^2}{4kT} \tag{8.14}$$

With an ionic density, for example, $N = 10^{27}$ m^{-3}, at room temperature, χ_m is of the order of 10^{-5}, comparable with experimental values. At cryogenic temperatures it can be much larger, because of the $1/T$ variation. While the statistics of an n-level system (for example, Cr^{3+} ions have four levels) involve more detailed calculation, the susceptibility increases by a factor almost the square of the number of magnetically active electrons.

8.4 Paramagnetic Cooling

Many experimental techniques require a very low temperature environment. Maintaining temperature of a specimen or device involves placing it in some sort of heat bath. At atmospheric pressure dry ice (CO_2, which sublimes at $\sim 200°K$), liquid nitrogen (which boils at $77°K$), and liquid helium (which boils at $4.2°K$) form safe and convenient constant-temperature baths. Temperature slightly below $4.2°$ can be obtained with liquid helium by reducing the pressure over it with a vacuum pump. This technique has its limits, because of the increasing difficulty with which enough evaporation can be produced, at the lower vapor pressures.

A *cyclic* magnetization (isothermal) and demagnetization (adiabatic) of a large paramagnetic sample (as refrigerant) can be used in a refrigeration cycle at these very low temperatures. The full cycle consists of four steps:

1. The sample is brought into contact with a heat sink such as liquid helium.
2. A strong magnetic field is applied (heat given off to the heat sink).
3. Removal of contact with the heat sink.
4. Removal of the magnetic field (temperature drops).

To understand how this process works, one must examine the several contributions to specific heat of a paramagnetic solid at the low temperatures in question. Such materials as iron ammonium alum [$FeNH_4(SO_4)_2 \cdot 12H_2O$] are insulators; hence conduction-electron contributions are absent. The lattice vibrations contribute a term of order T^3, very small at temperatures of 1°K or lower. This means that lattice vibrations are virtually "frozen out." In the absence of an applied magnetic field (and neglecting crystalline fields), all spin states are degenerate. In the presence of a magnetic field, paramagnetic ions have energy levels such as given by (8.12). At temperatures or fields where the energy differences are *large* compared with $kT/2$, almost all the spins will be aligned parallel to the field. At fields where the energy difference is much smaller than $kT/2$, there will be approximately equal numbers of ions in each state. The situation is depicted in Fig. 8.4 for a two-level ion. The spins are coupled, through phonon collisions, to the crystal-lattice vibrations. The device to be refrigerated, generally of much lower mass than the paramagnetic crystal, is placed in good thermal contact with the paramagnet.

In the first step the paramagnet is brought into contact with the heat bath; this brings both spins and lattice to equilibrium at the heat-bath temperature. The application of a magnetic field ($\mathcal{3C} \gg kT/2\mu_0\beta g$) causes the originally degenerate energy levels of the spins to be split. Most of the spins in the upper level then drop to the lower level by giving off their energy to lattice vibrations. These in turn transfer it to the heat sink. If the field is applied abruptly, the heat given off is

$$\Delta Q \cong n_+(E_+ - E_-) \cong \frac{N}{2} \mu_0\beta\mathcal{3C}g \tag{8.15}$$

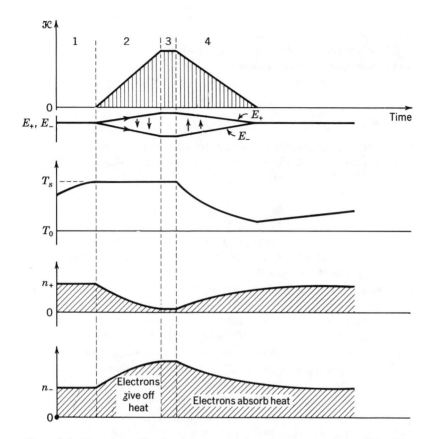

Figure 8.4 Steps in cooling by demagnetization of a paramagnetic solid. The numbered intervals correspond to the steps described in the text. The final, cooling, step is *adiabatic*, since the system cannot exchange heat with its surroundings.

The third step is accomplished by moving the paramagnetic sample or a thermal contact element so it is no longer in contact with the bath.   As the field is removed, the energy levels of the spins again return to their degenerate condition.   During the field reduction, electrons in the lower level can be excited by lattice vibrations to the higher energy level.   The spin-system *entropy* increases, that of the lattice decreases, and consequently the lattice is cooled.   For most effective cooling the sample should be strongly paramagnetic and the field large. High-iron salts are employed, and magnetic fields of 10,000 oe or more are desirable.   Several pounds of paramagnetic material may be required to keep the cooling cycle usefully long.

The temperature to which a sample may be cooled by this technique is limited ultimately by the crystal-field splitting of the electron-spin levels (as in Fig. 8.3). Where the energy-level differences due to crystalline fields, with no applied field, become of the order of kT, electrons will remain in the lower-energy states at all times and not make the necessary transitions; hence the material becomes useless for lower temperatures. The coldest temperature obtained is $\sim 0.001°K$, in a single-stage paramagnetic cooler; multiple-stage devices have been contrived; even these do not overcome the ultimate crystalline-field splitting limit.

8.5   Ferromagnetism

There is found to be *remanent* magnetic polarization in pure iron, nickel, and cobalt, as well as in many transition-metal alloys, in useful temperature regions well above room temperature. Metals and alloys having this property are said to be *ferromagnetic*. At cryogenic temperatures additional elements from the lanthanide (rare-earth) group become ferromagnetic. Just as in ferroelectricity and superconductivity, the ferromagnetic property disappears completely above a critical temperature, termed the *Curie temperature*. Above this, these materials are only paramagnetic. Table 8.1 lists the ferromagnetic elements, their Curie temperatures, and saturation magnetizations (in cgs units, $4\pi M_s$ = gauss). It is particularly interesting that some iron-group metals not ordinarily ferromagnetic, in combination with other elements, form

Table 8.1   Ferromagnetic elements†

Element	Saturation magnetization $4\pi M_s$, gauss at 0°K	Curie temperature T_c, °K	Bohr magnetons per atom n_B, 0°K
Fe	21,900	1043	2.219
Co	16,100	1404	1.715
Ni	5,690	631	0.604
Gd	25,100	289	7.12
Tb	17,200	230	4.95 (or 9.10)
Dy	23,250	85	6.84
Ho	28,700	20	8.54
Er	...	20	7.2

† Data from R. M. Bozorth, T. R. McGuire, and R. P. Hudson, "American Institute of Physics Handbook," 2d ed., chap. 5, p. 164, McGraw-Hill Book Company, New York, 1963.

ferromagnetic alloys such as bismuth-manganese and platinum-chromium alloys. Here, however, the local order of the crystals is very important, stressing the fact that ferromagnetism is highly dependent on the nature and location of neighbor atoms.

Following the approach used in dielectric theory, first attempts to understand ferromagnetics were based on local fields produced by the atoms' dipole moments. Whereas free Fe^{++} ions have six $3d$ electrons and the net spin angular momentum of four electrons, the observed magnetization of 2.3β per atom suggests that this is a more appropriate value to assume in estimating the possible dipole interaction. The magnetic field of a magnetic dipole $\mathbf{p}_m$, at a distance $\mathbf{r}$, is by magnetostatic theory[1]

$$\mathcal{3C}(\mathbf{r}) = \frac{3(\mathbf{r}/r)[(\mathbf{r}/r) \cdot \mathbf{p}_m] - \mathbf{p}_m}{4\pi r^3} \tag{8.16}$$

The *maximum* interaction energy between two such dipoles spaced r is, for similarly and oppositely directed dipoles, respectively,

$$E_{\pm} = \pm \frac{\mu_0 p_m{}^2}{2\pi r^3} \tag{8.17}$$

Setting $p_m = 2.3\beta$ and giving r a typical value of 2 A, the interaction energy is $\Delta E = E_+ - E_- \cong 2 \times 10^{-24}$ joule $\cong 10^{-5}$ ev. This is so far below kT at room temperature ($\frac{1}{40}$ ev) that it would be impossible for dipoles coupled this way to remain coupled above $\sim 10^{-3}\,°K$. Thus, unlike ferroelectricity, ferromagnetism could not be explained by dipole interaction.

Lacking quantum theory, physicists then turned to phenomenological theories. P. Weiss, in 1907, proposed that the *local* magnetic field $\mathcal{3C}_l$ include a strong "molecular field" directed parallel to the direction of magnetization. He then expressed the local field as

$$\mathcal{3C}_l = \mathcal{3C}_a + \lambda \mathbf{M} \tag{8.18}$$

where $\mathcal{3C}_a$ is the macroscopic field, $\mathbf{M}$ the magnetization, and λ a dimensionless constant, to be determined empirically. As with dielectrics (Sec. 7.1), this theory demands that a magnetic polarizability α be defined for the atom. Using the

[1] Cf. J. D. Jackson, "Classical Electrodynamics," p. 147, John Wiley & Sons, Inc., New York, 1962.

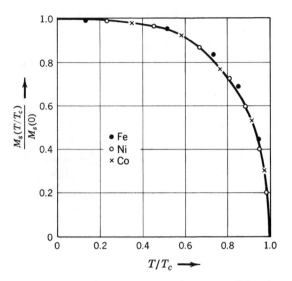

Figure 8.5 Relative magnetization versus T for the three ferromagnetic elements of the iron group. (*After R. F. Soohoo, "Theory and Application of Ferrites," p. 43, Prentice-Hall, Inc., Englewood Cliffs, N.J., 1960.*)

paramagnetic susceptibility relation (8.14) as a guide, we might let $\alpha = \alpha_0 T_0/T$, so that $\mathbf{M} = N\alpha\mathcal{JC}_l$. Substituting into (8.1) and (8.18),

$$\left|\frac{M}{\mathcal{JC}_a}\right| = \chi_m = \frac{N\alpha_0 T_0}{T - N\alpha_0 T_0\lambda} \equiv \frac{C}{T - T_c} \tag{8.19}$$

The behavior of ferromagnetic materials above the Curie temperature T_c follows this Curie-Weiss law fairly well. This, unfortunately, does not suggest the actual microscopic mechanism responsible for the effective "molecular field" $\lambda\mathbf{M}$, however.

Below the Curie point, the remanent magnetization $|\mathbf{M}|$ drops to zero at T_c in the typical manner illustrated in Fig. 8.5. Since the change is not discontinuous, the loss of magnetism is describable as a *second-order* phase transition, as borne out also in experimental specific-heat data (Fig. C.3). Weiss's theory can even be made to predict this behavior. The paramagnetic theory of (8.13) indicates that the magnetization *saturates* at sufficiently high fields ($\tanh \infty = 1$). Remanence $\mathbf{M}$, in the Weiss formula, is the value of $\mathbf{M}$ in the absence of $\mathfrak{K}_a$: $\mathbf{M} = \mathfrak{K}_l/\lambda$.   If we therefore identify $\mathfrak{K}$ in (8.13) as the $\mathfrak{K}_l$ of the Weiss theory and solve the two relations simultaneously,

$$M = \frac{N\beta g}{2} \tanh \frac{\mu_0 \beta \lambda M g}{2kT} \tag{8.20}$$

The transcendental solution, most readily performed graphically, shows a variation $M(T)$ very similar to that of Fig. 8.5. The value of local field (or Weiss molecular field, as it is often called) λM necessary to fit observed Curie temperature values and other data in iron is in the vicinity of 10^6 oe.   Even though local electric fields in crystals can be large, there can be no *magnetic fields* of such large magnitude.   This anomaly led eventually to the correct quantum interpretation that ferromagnetism is really controlled by *electrostatic* forces, as explained in the next section.

8.6   Quantum Theory of Ferromagnetism[1]

The development of quantum theory paved the way for the discovery of the true source of ferromagnetism.   Not even to this day, however, has theory been developed to a point permitting precise calculation.   This reflects the very complicated situation in which the $3d$ electrons of iron, nickel, and cobalt participate not only in magnetic phenomena, but probably also in conduction.   Neither the bound-electron model nor a one-electron energy-band description is correct.   The band model is desirable because of the fact that the electrons per atom contributing to ferromagnetism in metal and alloys are nonintegral in number.   It is simplest to attempt to explain this by band-overlap concepts (like Fig. 3.18) and/or field-shifted subbands (like Fig. 8.1).   The most important feature of ferromagnetism, however, is a short-range *electron-electron interaction*.   Similar interactions are involved in the theory of superconductivity.   Whereas superconducting electron pairs are mobile, however, ferromagnetism is more easily explained in terms of more nearly localized electron pairs, situated on adjacent atoms.

We present here the formal aspects of a development of the type first suggested by Dirac.[2]   Two electrons, presumed

---

[1] The derivation in this section is not essential to the understanding of following material.   It is in essence a plausibility argument for the classical theory of Secs. 8.8 to 8.10.

[2] P. A. M. Dirac, *Proc. Roy. Soc. (London)*, **112A**:661 (1926).

located on adjacent atoms, have an overlap in their orbital wave functions. A quantum wave function describing *uncoupled* electrons will then be a product of one-electron wave functions, each factor representing an electron orbiting one of the two nuclei. This can be expressed formally as

$$\psi_{n_A,l_A,m_A}(x_1,y_1,z_1) \cdot \psi_{n_B,l_B,m_B}(x_2,y_2,z_2) \cdot S(\mathbf{s}_1) \cdot S(\mathbf{s}_2)$$

The ψ factors represent orbital wave functions with indices n_A, etc., centered on the nuclei A and B. The coordinates x_1, y_1, z_1 are those of an electron we shall call "electron 1," and x_2, y_2, z_2 those of "electron 2." The spin factors $S(\mathbf{s}_1)$ and $S(\mathbf{s}_2)$ are functions of the "spin coordinates" $\mathbf{s}_1$ and $\mathbf{s}_2$ of the two electrons.

This system of two electrons on two atoms is degenerate, for it would have the same energy if electron 1 orbited nucleus B and electron 2, nucleus A, with the wave function

$$\psi_{n_A,l_A,m_A}(x_2,y_2,z_2) \cdot \psi_{n_B,l_B,m_B}(x_1,y_1,z_1) \cdot S(\mathbf{s}_1) \cdot S(\mathbf{s}_2)$$

When we actually take into account the interaction between the two electrons, we can use degenerate perturbation theory (Sec. B.9) and find that the interaction splits the degeneracy. The two resulting wave functions may be written

$$\psi_{\text{I}} = [\psi_A(x_1,y_1,z_1) \cdot \psi_B(x_2,y_2,z_2)$$
$$+ \psi_A(x_2,y_2,z_2) \cdot \psi_B(x_1,y_1,z_1)]S_{\uparrow\downarrow}(\mathbf{s}_1,\mathbf{s}_2)$$
$$\psi_{\text{II}} = [\psi_A(x_1,y_1,z_1) \cdot \psi_B(x_2,y_2,z_2)$$
$$- \psi_A(x_2,y_2,z_2) \cdot \psi_B(x_1,y_1,z_1)]S_{\uparrow\uparrow}(\mathbf{s}_1,\mathbf{s}_2)$$

(8.21)

The combined spin functions $S_{\uparrow\downarrow}(\mathbf{s}_1,\mathbf{s}_2)$ and $S_{\uparrow\uparrow}(\mathbf{s}_1,\mathbf{s}_2)$ are, respectively, antisymmetrical and symmetrical to exchange of the pair of electrons $\mathbf{s}_1 \Leftrightarrow \mathbf{s}_2$, so that the *complete* wave functions are properly antisymmetrical, as required by the exclusion principle for the entire system wave function (Sec. B.10). While the relations resemble (B.88), the two factors ψ_A and ψ_B in this case represent functions associated with two different nuclei.

Even if the spin coupling due to magnetic fields produced is very small, as is the case, there can be a large difference in the *orbital energies* in solutions I and II. According to the perturbation theory, the energies for the two nondegenerate states are given by (B.82). The coupling energy which figures in this is mainly the electrostatic energy of repulsion of the electrons.   Accordingly, by (B.82), the system energy is $E_0 + J_{11} + J_{12}$ for state ψ_I, and $E_0 + J_{11} - J_{12}$ for state ψ_{II}. The energy difference $2J_{12}$ is termed the *exchange energy*.   It is the energy which would be required merely *to reverse the spin of one of the electrons*.   Because of the exclusion principle, this *cannot* be done without also making a transition from one function (ψ_I, ψ_{II}) to the other.   Thus it is *not* the dipole coupling which controls ferromagnetism, but a much larger electrostatic energy.   We now proceed formally, without giving a full justification of the quantum theory used.[1]

Representing the interaction energy of the two electrons {mainly the electrostatic energy contribution $e^2/[4\pi\epsilon_0(\mathbf{r}_1 - \mathbf{r}_2)^2]$} by the perturbation function H_1, the wave equations for the perturbed wave functions ψ_I and ψ_{II}, expressed in operator form, are

$$(H_0 + H_1)\psi_I = (E_0 + J_{11} + J_{12})\psi_I$$
$$(H_0 + H_1)\psi_{II} = (E_0 + J_{11} - J_{12})\psi_{II}$$

(8.22)

Operators relating *only* to the spin also satisfy characteristic operator equations.   Just as the relation $H\psi = E\psi$ [cf. Eq. (B.74)] means that the operator H operating on ψ produces E times ψ, the operator which corresponds to the square of the sum of spins of the two electrons, $(\mathbf{s}_1 + \mathbf{s}_2)^2$, has characteristic values

$$(\mathbf{s}_1 + \mathbf{s}_2)^2\psi_I = 0$$
$$(\mathbf{s}_1 + \mathbf{s}_2)^2\psi_{II} = \hbar^2(1)(1 + 1)\psi_{II}$$

(8.23)

The first expression is interpreted as indicating that the total spin is zero in ψ_I.   It has a magnitude squared of $\hbar^2 S(S + 1)$, with $S = 1$ in ψ_{II}, where the two spins are parallel.   Since the *square* of the spin angular momentum is $\hbar^2(\frac{1}{2})(\frac{1}{2} + 1)$ for either electron, in *either* ψ_I or ψ_{II}, we have also $\mathbf{s}_1{}^2\psi_I = \hbar^2(\frac{3}{4})\psi_I$, $\mathbf{s}_2{}^2\psi_I = \hbar^2(\frac{3}{4})\psi_I$, $\mathbf{s}_1{}^2\psi_{II} = \hbar^2(\frac{3}{4})\psi_{II}$, and $\mathbf{s}_2{}^2\psi_{II} = \hbar^3(\frac{3}{4})\psi_{II}$. By straightforward algebra, *subtracting* these from (8.23),

$$[(\mathbf{s}_1 + \mathbf{s}_2)^2 - \mathbf{s}_1{}^2 - \mathbf{s}_2{}^2]\psi_I = \hbar^2(2 - \tfrac{3}{4} - \tfrac{3}{4})\psi_I$$
$$[(\mathbf{s}_1 + \mathbf{s}_2)^2 - \mathbf{s}_1{}^2 - \mathbf{s}_2{}^2]\psi_{II} = \hbar^2(0 - \tfrac{3}{4} - \tfrac{3}{4})\psi_{II}$$

Since the operators are linear, the brackets on the left may be

[1] The interested reader is referred to a text such as L. I. Schiff, "Quantum Mechanics," McGraw-Hill Book Company, New York, 1955, for a more detailed treatment of electron spin.

expressed as $2s_1 \cdot s_2$, whence

$$(s_1 \cdot s_2)\psi_I = \frac{\hbar^2}{4} \psi_I$$

$$(s_1 \cdot s_2)\psi_{II} = -\frac{3\hbar^2}{4} \psi_{II}$$

(8.24)

We now multiply (8.24) by $2J_{12}/\hbar^2$, transpose all terms to the left side, transpose (8.22), and finally add the two sets of expressions,

$$\left(H_1 - J_{11} + J_{12} + \frac{2J_{12}}{\hbar^2} s_1 \cdot s_2 - \frac{J_{12}}{2} \right) \psi_I = 0$$

$$\left(H_1 - J_{11} - J_{12} + \frac{2J_{12}}{\hbar^2} s_1 \cdot s_2 + \frac{3J_{12}}{2} \right) \psi_{II} = 0$$

(8.25)

Since the identical operator functions (in parentheses) on the left, operating on ψ_I and ψ_{II}, produce zero results in each case, it is concluded that the corresponding classical variables are also zero, and the hamiltonian is written in the form

$$H_1 = J_{11} - \frac{J_{12}}{2} - 2 \frac{J_{12}}{\hbar^2} s_1 \cdot s_2$$

(8.26)

The interaction energy H_1 thus contains, in addition to non-spin-dependent parts J_{11} and $-J_{12}/2$, a term $-2J_{12}s_1 \cdot s_2/\hbar^2$, representing the influence of the coupled spins.

In (8.26), if J_{12} is positive, the state of lowest energy, ψ_{II}, has the spin vectors parallel. When J_{12} is negative, the anti-parallel situation, ψ_I, is of lowest energy. The case $J_{12} > 0$ leads to *ferromagnetism*, $J_{12} < 0$ to *antiferromagnetism* (Sec. 8.7).

Dirac implied from the result (8.26) that if *each* pair of available electron spins of adjacent atoms in the solid were coupled in this way, ferromagnetism could be explained by the strong tendency for *all pairs* of adjacent-atom electron spins to remain parallel. The dot product $s_1 \cdot s_2$ suggests that the pair of spins may have *any* relative angular orientation, not merely parallel. With only two electrons, however, quantization of the *system* requires that the relative configurations be either parallel or antiparallel. Where many electrons are all coupled together through this mechanism, however, electrons in a large sample are quantized *as a group*. A pair of adjacent electrons can then have *any* angle between their spin vectors. One interprets the $s_1 \cdot s_2$ expression to apply for arbitrary

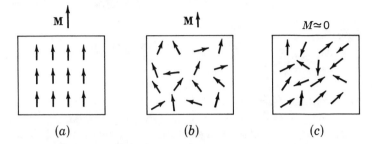

Figure 8.6 Schematic of the orientation of spins in a ferromagnet. (a) Near zero temperature, all spins nearly aligned; (b) just below the Curie temperature T_c, spins oscillating wildly but still partly aligned; (c) above T_c, spins randomly oriented.

directions of s_1 and s_2. In so doing, one must imagine the spin-angular-momentum vectors s_1 and s_2 to behave like classical vectors. While this raises some question as to what magnitude to assign to these vectors, the reader should not be overly concerned. The only use we shall make of (8.26) is in development of a qualitative theory, where the constants are handled by fitting empirical data. There is, however, much experimental evidence that adjacent spins are coupled by just such an expression; a torque is produced whenever s_1 and s_2 are caused to depart from parallelism. Properties of a large sample are explained in terms of such interactions between the spins of each pair of adjacent atoms.

A chief aim of a theory of ferromagnetism should be the prediction of Curie temperature T_c. It should somehow be possible to relate the parameter controlling the strength of the ferromagnetic exchange coupling J_{12} to T_c. Unfortunately, one would need to deal with coupling between the spin of an atom and those of all its neighbors, then develop a model predicting under what conditions of thermal agitation the coupling would finally give way and leave the spins rotating independently of one another. Figure 8.6 shows what probably happens: near zero temperature, the spins are all nearly parallel through a macroscopic portion of a sample; the magnetization has its maximum value. Near T_c, adjacent spins are swinging through angles near 180° with respect to one another. Above T_c, the spins are rotating in a random fashion. We might estimate the "breakaway" energy by imagining a single atomic spin to be required to invert completely its orientation in the presence of z near-neighbor atoms. This would require an energy $2zJ_{12}$. If the available thermal energy were of the order of kT, then setting the two energies equal at T_c yields

$$T_c = \frac{2zJ_{12}}{k}$$

(8.27)

For a simple ferromagnetic metal with T_c of 400°C, this suggests that J_{12} is of the order of 10^{-3} ev per atom pair. Such a term could easily arise from electron-orbital overlap and should be (as it is indeed) a strong function of the particular atoms involved and their interatomic spacing.

8.7 Antiferromagnetism and Ferrimagnetism; Ferrites

While iron, nickel, and cobalt, according to the quantum theory of ferromagnetism, have positive exchange energy $(J_{12} > 0)$, chromium and manganese could be said to have *negative* exchange energy. This gives rise to the phenomenon called *antiferromagnetism*, where electronic spins of *adjacent* atoms are held in *opposite* orientations by the exchange forces. There is, naturally, no observed magnetic polarization, for it is locally canceled. In chromium (body-centered cubic), the body-centered atomic spins are directed opposite to those (of equal numbers) on the cube corners. Antiferromagnetics are characterized by a transition temperature called the *Néel temperature* T_N, at which the exchange forces can no longer resist thermal attempts to make the spins independent. Chromium, for example, has $T_N = 475°K$, the value of which is ascertained from specific-heat data.

Most antiferromagnetic materials are ionic compounds in which nonmagnetic ions play an essential role in a process termed *superexchange*. An oxygen ion often lies more or less directly between two transition metal ions (Fig. 8.7a). The theory of superexchange holds that the oxygen atom takes only a single electron from its neighbors. It is itself paramagnetic, not having a closed $2p$ subshell. This ion is then able to couple the two metallic neighbor ions so as to align their spins in opposite directions. While oxygen is the element most often responsible for superexchange, sulfur, selenium, tellurium, and even halogens also form antiferromagnetic compounds, but most have Néel temperatures well below room temperature.

While antiferromagnetic materials appear to be mainly curiosities, there is an important group of closely related oxides,

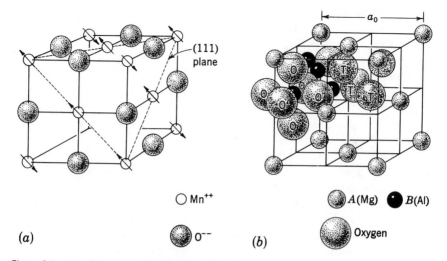

(a)   (b)

○ Mn⁺⁺   ⬤ O⁻⁻   🔘 A(Mg)   ⚫ B(Al)

🔘 Oxygen

Figure 8.7   (a) The magnetic Mn^{++} ions in MnO are arranged in two sets of equal number whose spins cancel and which are separated by an O^{--} ion. The (111) orientation of the spin sets can be determined by magnetic-resonance measurements. (b) A unit cell of the *spinel structure*. The basis is fcc, shown here with A (Mg) ions at the lattice points. The O^{--} ions are shifted slightly from an fcc arrangement by the presence of the ions. Only four of the sixteen B (Al) ions in this unit cell are shown. Four others are located in the lower right-hand octant nearest the viewer, four others in the far upper right, etc. The four A ions not on the cell exterior are near the centers of the remaining four octants. The six oxygen ions marked O form an octahedral site, while the four marked T form a tetrahedral site. [*After* D. Polder, *Proc. IEEE (London)*, **97**(pt. II):246 (1950).]

termed *ferrimagnetic* materials (the name stems from the word *ferrites*, the most important group of ferrimagnetic materials). These also operate via superexchange, with groups of transition-metal ions whose spins are oppositely directed. Unlike antiferromagnetics, however, ferrimagnetics are composed of two or more sets of *different* transition-metal ions; there are generally different *numbers* of ions in each set. While the electron spins of the opposing groups do partially cancel, they still present a net magnetization which can be quite large. Ferrimagnetic oxides are generally quite poor electrical and thermal conductors. This has benefits, for they may accordingly be used in high-frequency devices, where magnetic fields must penetrate them. Because the magnetic electrons in ferrites are truly *localized*, an Fe^{++} ion with six $3d$ electrons will have four unpaired electron spins, and an Mn^{++}, five unpaired spins, as do these ions in paramagnetic materials. This tends to make the net magnetization of ferrites larger, per transition-metal ion, than in ferromagnetic metals and alloys. The magnetizations are yet considerably smaller than those of iron, cobalt, or nickel, because most of the volume is filled with non-contributing oxygen ions.

Ferrites are also often termed "ferrospinels," for their crystal structure is like that of the natural mineral spinel ($MgAl_2O_4$) (Fig. 8.7b). It is convenient to think of the spinel structure as a close-packed oxygen structure into the interstices or voids of which metal ions are packed. Figure 1.19 shows that an fcc structure has two types of voids, tetrahedral and octahedral. There are two tetrahedral voids and one octahedral void per oxygen atom. Since per "molecule" ($MgAl_2O_4$) there are only three metal ions, only one-quarter of all voids are filled. In spinel itself, *divalent* magnesium ions occupy the smaller tetrahedral voids, of which only one-eighth are filled, while *trivalent* aluminum ions fill one-half of the larger octahedral voids. The unit cell consists of eight "molecules." It is common to refer to the tetrahedral sites as "*A* sites" and the octahedral ones as "*B* sites." While we have based the description on the concept of an ideal fcc oxygen basis, the presence of metal ions in some voids causes shrinkage of unoccupied voids; overall, cubic symmetry is maintained. The lattice constant of *ferrites* is to some extent dependent on the metal-ion content, varying with different metal ions from a cube side of about 8.3 to about 8.5 A.

As a group, ferrites may be thought of as derivatives of *magnetite* (Fe_3O_4), which contains two ferric (Fe^{3+}) ions and one ferrous (Fe^{++}) ion, for each *four* O^{--} ions. Trivalent (Fe^{3+}) ions occupy *all* tetrahedral *A* sites and half of the *B* sites, while divalent ions occupy the other half of the *B* sites. This peculiar structural situation is called an *inverse spinel*. The distribution of the divalent and trivalent ions over the *B* sites is apparently random; this disorder has a profound effect on both resistivity and magnetic properties, particularly magnetic losses. Furthermore, it means that ferrites could not be expected to show high crystalline symmetry. Fe_3O_4 has much lower resistivity than many other ferrite materials (about 7×10^{-3} ohm-cm at room temperature), explained by the distribution of Fe^{++} and Fe^{3+} on equivalent octahedral voids. Conduction results when an electron "hops" from a divalent to a trivalent ion (both on *B* sites). The energy for this particular process is so low that it is thermally activated at room temperature.   A more useful ferrite material is nickel ferrite ($NiFe_2O_4$), in which divalent nickel ions occupy half of the B sites.   Resistivity here is of the order of 10^6 ohm-cm, because the Fe^{3+} and Ni^{++} ions cannot readily trade electrons.   There are infinitely many possible ferrites, since there are almost unlimited ion combinations on A and B sites.   A wide range of ions may be used: Fe, Ni, Co, Mg, Mn, Cu, because of their nearly equal sizes, may be added to occupy all eight B sites per unit cell.   A combination of two or more of these may also be used.   Certain ions, such as Na, Li, Ca, do not "fit" as well.   These may be included only in a smaller fraction of sites, the rest being filled by more appropriate ions from the iron group.

Néel first pointed out[1] that the magnetic moment of a ferrimagnetic material should be the *difference* of the moments of A and B ion systems.   If we attribute 5 Bohr magnetons to Fe^{3+} and 4 to Fe^{++}, then for Fe_3O_4, which contains Fe^{3+} in the A sites (5 magnetons per "molecule") and Fe^{++} and Fe^{3+} in the B sites $(5 + 4 = 9$ magnetons per "molecule"), the net moment should be $(9 - 5 = 4)$ magnetons per molecule.   The experimental value of 4.1 indicates excellent agreement with this principle.   Nickel ferrite ($NiFe_2O_4$), which by the same token should have 2 magnetons per molecule, actually has 2.3.   The difference is usually attributed to g-factors which differ from the value 2 for free electrons.

In ferrites containing strongly paramagnetic ions such as Mn, Co, Ni, replacement of some of these ions with, for example, zinc ($Mn_{1-x}Zn_xFe_2O_4$) can actually *increase* magnetization [$\sim 5(1 + x)$ magnetons per molecule].   This is understandable from the relatively small zinc ions' ability to displace Fe^{3+} ions from the tetrahedral sites.   Since the spin of ions in the tetrahedral locations is subtracted from that of the octahedral ions, the addition of zinc reduces the tetrahedral-site magnetization and increases the overall M.   The arrangement is $Mn_{1-x}^{++}Fe_{1+x}^{3+}$; $Zn_x^{++}Fe_{1-x}^{3+}$; $p_m \cong [5(1 - x) + 5(1 + x) - 0 - 5(1 - x)]\beta$ per molecule.   This proceeds up to about 50 per cent filling of the tetrahedral sites ($x = 0.5$), at which point the magnetization and Néel temperature are reduced appreciably because of the inability of the nonmagnetic zinc ions to contribute to the necessary exchange interaction.

The antiferromagnetic interaction between metal ions separated by an oxygen ion lying *directly* between them is

[1] L. Néel, *Ann. Phys.*, **3**:137 (1948).

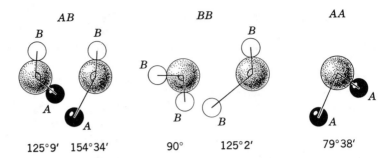

AB	BB	AA
125°9′ 154°34′	90° 125°2′	79°38′

Figure 8.8   The most important contributions to superexchange coupling in ferrospinels are due to the ion arrangements shown. In general, the coupling is strongest when the metal ions are nearly 180° apart and not far from the oxygen ion. The A-A coupling is therefore the weakest, and the A-B coupling strongest. The angles are indicated in the figure, and the spacings are approximately to scale. (*After J. Smit and H. P. J. Wijn, "Ferrites," p. 149, John Wiley & Sons, Inc., New York, 1959.*)

probably the strongest contributor to ferrimagnetism. A number of different exchange interactions take place in ferrimagnetics (Fig. 8.8). Normally, the strongest interaction is between the spins of an A ion and an antiparallel B ion. Slightly weaker interactions couple pairs of B ions (B-B interaction); the weakest are usually the A-A interactions, unless the B sites have many nonmagnetic ions, in which case A-A interaction may be stronger than B-B interactions. Since all interactions are presumably negative-exchange-energy interactions, the very existence of magnetization indicates that the A-B interaction is strong enough to override the others, for otherwise the materials would be antiferromagnetic.

The presence of two *partly* independent coupled spin systems, the A system and the B system, leads to certain interesting effects not observed in ferromagnetic metals and alloys. If one supposes first that the antiferromagnetic B-B interaction is stronger than the A-A interaction, the Weiss "molecular field" acting on the B ions can be thought to be proportional to the *difference* between the opposing A-B and B-B forces, and therefore *smaller* than the net molecular field which A ions experience. The net magnetization due to B ions therefore decreases more rapidly than that of the A system, as temperature increases. The B system will usually have larger magnetization than the A system, since it has *twice* as many ions. The net magnetization, as a function of temperature, can

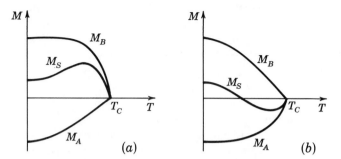

Figure 8.9 The weakening of one spin subsystem relative to the other, at elevated temperatures (but below T_c), reduces its magnetization and may permit the net magnetization M_s (a) to have a maximum or (b) to be zero, at some intermediate temperature.

behave as shown in Fig. 8.9. Magnetic remanence finally disappears at the same Néel temperature for both A and B systems since it is governed by the A-B interaction. At some temperature below transition, however, the contributions of the two partial spin systems A and B can be equal (but opposite) and $M = 0$. If in some particular material the A-A interaction is stronger, the magnetization may behave as in Fig. 8.9a, producing a *larger* M at elevated temperatures. The detailed properties of ferrites, as we have seen, depend entirely upon what metal ions fill the tetrahedral A sites and octahedral B sites. A particular type of ion will generally have greater affinity for one type of site than for the other. Zn^{++} and Cd^{++} prefer A sites, while Ni^{++} and Cr^{3+} prefer B sites. The ferrite most valuable in a given application will depend on the particular application, from permanent-magnet applications to microwave devices and computer-memory elements.[1]

The preparation of ferrite materials begins with mixing of finely ground particles of various metallic oxides having the overall concentrations of metal ions desired in the final ferrite. This material is then fired at temperatures of the order of 1000°C, which serves mainly to homogenize the oxides. It is then again powdered, and pressed into the desired shape. The second firing (1200 to 1400°C, or slightly below the melting point) forms the material into a dense polycrystalline body.

[1] Extensive tables of various ferrite materials and their characteristics appear in D. E. Gray (ed.), "American Institute of Physics Handbook," 2d ed., chap. 5g, p. 5-164, McGraw-Hill Book Company, New York, 1963.

Grinding of the surfaces of the finished piece is required where close tolerances must be held. All steps of the preparation can be critical in determining material properties; for example, other crystalline oxide structures can result, if the proper oxygen content is not maintained.

In addition to the ferrospinels, there are a variety of other complex ferrimagnetic oxide compounds. Compared with some of these (for example, $Ba_3Ni_2Fe_{24}O_{41}$), the spinel structure is relatively simple. As might be expected, such complex materials may contain crystalline phases of completely different properties. (These variants are best identified by x-ray-diffraction measurements.) Materials which are hexagonal in lattice symmetry can exhibit large anisotropy of magnetic properties, which are beneficial in some application (Sec. 9.5).

The rare-earth–iron *garnet* group, typified by yttrium–iron garnet (sometimes called "Yig"), is of interest because of its unambiguous structure. The oxygen lattice on which the structure is built is again of cubic close-packed form, with a unit cell containing eight molecules ($Y_3Fe_5O_{12}$). The large yttrium ion "pushes back" oxygen ions to form a site neighbored by eight oxygen atoms. *All* sizable existing voids are then occupied by yttrium or iron ions, and there is, accordingly, no randomness in the ion distribution. Although both ferrites and ferrimagnetic garnets can be produced in single-crystal form by growth from a molten-salt solvent, the magnetic *losses* of the completely ordered structures are substantially lower than those of ferrites. This can be particularly important in applications where a very distinct magnetic-resonance phenomenon is required, as in certain microwave power devices.

8.8 Spin Dynamics

Since most magnetic devices operate via *change* in the direction of magnetization, we require dynamic equations describing ferro- and ferrimagnetic materials. The lack of complete success in quantum-theoretical description of the phenomenon might imply that accurate macroscopic equations cannot be obtained. This is fortunately not so. A very useful dynamic theory can be formulated, based on the following principles:

1. Magnetic dipole moments of electrons can change their orientations, but not their magnitudes.
2. Magnetic spin moments of adjacent atoms are tightly

bound in common orientation, with an energy of the form $-2J_{12}\mathbf{s}_1 \cdot \mathbf{s}_2/\hbar^2$.

3. Each magnetic dipole also has angular momentum.

In a fairly small but macroscopic region, many spin angular momenta are oriented parallel, or nearly so. They are strongly coupled, each to the next, by exchange forces; hence the quantum "system" which we deal with is a large group of electrons of *total* angular momentum $\gg \hbar$. For any angular coordinate measure the uncertainty in the angle, $\Delta\theta$, is no more than 2π. From the uncertainty principle, the corresponding uncertainty in any component of angular momentum need be no more than $\Delta L_x = h/\Delta\theta = \hbar$. This implies that we may treat a system with angular momentum $\gg \hbar$ as *classical* if we are willing to accept *an uncertainty of the order of* $\hbar$ in any cartesian component of angular momentum. While this is catastrophic in single-atom systems, with large numbers of coupled electrons it becomes a very good approximation. We therefore define $\mathbf{M}$, the magnetization (density) of a ferromagnet, as a vector whose *local direction* may change but whose *magnitude is fixed* and equal to the saturation magnetic polarization of the magnet. Unless we are dealing with temperature changes or with inhomogeneous materials, $M = |\mathbf{M}|$ is assumed to be strictly constant.

The angular momentum and magnetic moment of electrons are oppositely directed; according to (B.69), there will be an angular momentum density $\mathbf{L}$, where

$$\mathbf{M} = -\left(\frac{eg}{2m}\right)\mathbf{L} \qquad \left[\text{cgs: } \mathbf{M} = \left(\frac{-ge}{2mc}\right)\mathbf{L}\right] \tag{8.28}$$

The factor $g/2$ is unity for electrons whose entire momentum is due to spin. Since orbital angular momentum may not be completely quenched, g is retained as an empirical factor which can be adjusted to fit a particular material. Classical mechanics then gives an equation relating a torque $\mathbf{T}$ on the spins to the change of $\mathbf{L}$:

$$\frac{d\mathbf{L}}{dt} = \mathbf{T} \tag{8.29}$$

Combining (8.28) and (8.29),

$$\frac{d\mathbf{M}}{dt} = -\frac{eg}{2m}\mathbf{T} \tag{8.30}$$

The torque due to a magnetic field $\mathcal{3C}$ can be found from the classical energy of interaction of a magnetic dipole moment $\mathbf{p}_m$ with the field:

$$E = -\mu_0 \mathbf{p}_m \cdot \mathcal{3C} \equiv -\mu_0 p_m \mathcal{3C} \cos \theta_{p_m,\mathcal{3C}} \qquad (\text{cgs}: E = -\mathbf{p}_m \cdot \mathcal{3C}) \qquad (8.31)$$

The torque exerted on the dipole is zero when the spin is parallel to the field, and a maximum when perpendicular. The torque is readily shown to have a magnitude $dE/d\theta = \mu_0 p_m \mathcal{3C} \sin \theta$. In correct vector form, for a unit volume of material $(p_m = M)$,

$$\mathbf{T} = \mu_0 \mathbf{M} \times \mathcal{3C} \qquad (\text{cgs}: \mathbf{T} = \mathbf{M} \times \mathcal{3C}) \qquad (8.32)$$

It is instructive to find solutions for this simplest form of dynamic relation involving only an applied d-c magnetic field with an initial deviation of $\mathbf{M}$ from its lowest-energy orientation parallel to the field. Let the field be $\mathcal{3C} = 1_z \mathcal{3C}_0$ and let $\mathbf{M}$ be represented by its cartesian components M_x, M_y, M_z. Then, letting $\gamma_e = -\mu_0 g e/2m$ (cgs: $\gamma_e = -ge/2mc$), the dynamic equation

$$\frac{d\mathbf{M}}{dt} = \gamma_e \mathbf{M} \times \mathcal{3C} \qquad (\text{cgs: same, with } \gamma_e \text{ as defined}) \qquad (8.33)$$

found by combining (8.30) with (8.32), has only two non-vanishing components,

$$\dot{M}_x = \gamma_e M_y \mathcal{3C}_0$$
$$\dot{M}_y = -\gamma_e M_x \mathcal{3C}_0$$

Solving simultaneously,

$$\ddot{M}_x = -\gamma_e^2 \mathcal{3C}_0^2 M_x$$

General solutions are

$$M_x = A \sin \gamma_e \mathcal{3C}_0 t + B \cos \gamma_e \mathcal{3C}_0 t$$
$$M_y = A \cos \gamma_e \mathcal{3C}_0 t - B \sin \gamma_e \mathcal{3C}_0 t \qquad (8.34)$$
$$M_z = \text{const}$$

Both general solutions correspond to the M vector being in gyroscopic precession about the field, at *constant* precession angle, at *fixed* angular velocity $\gamma_e \mathcal{3C}_0$, and in a *fixed* rotation direction. The only way to alter the sense of rotation is by changing the sign of the field. This precession is an important property of magnetic spin systems, further distinguishing magnetic polarization behavior from that of dielectrics. The

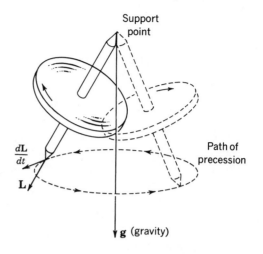

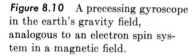

Figure 8.10 A precessing gyroscope in the earth's gravity field, analogous to an electron spin system in a magnetic field.

gyromagnetic resonance frequency $\omega_0 \equiv \gamma_e \mathfrak{IC}_0$, for electrons whose orbital motion is completely quenched ($g = 2$), is ($\mu_0 e/m =$) 2.8 Mc/oe. The motion is identical with that of a gyroscope supported at one end in a gravitational field (Fig. 8.10). Both the spins and the gyroscope have angular momentum; the gyroscope's mass interacts with a gravitational field in just the manner given for the magnetic spin system by (8.31).

The magnetic spin system, like a gyroscope, is found experimentally to be slightly lossy, so that the precession angle about an abruptly applied field will eventually be reduced. The magnetization will finally align with the field. As in most solid-state loss mechanisms in crystals, the culprits are phonons and imperfections. (The electron spins are, however, the least sensitive to this kind of disturbance, of all aspects of electronic motion.) The method of introducing the damping torque into Eq. (8.33) must guarantee that changes introduced into **M** by damping do not change its *magnitude*. Damping forces must therefore act normal to the vector **M** at all times, suggesting that they include a cross product with **M**. The earliest form of damping term was introduced by Landau and Lifschitz; in a field $\mathfrak{IC}$,

$$\frac{d\mathbf{M}}{dt} = \gamma_e \mathbf{M} \times \mathfrak{IC} + \frac{\alpha\gamma_e}{M} \mathbf{M} \times (\mathbf{M} \times \mathfrak{IC}) \tag{8.35}$$

In another useful form, introduced by T. Gilbert, the field does not appear in the damping term. This is preferred for solving problems in which the precession frequency is produced not by

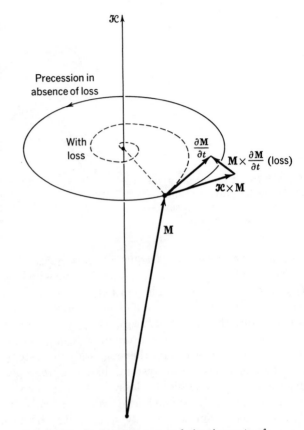

Figure 8.11 Various torques and the time rate of change of **M**, which appear in the equations for a precessing spin system.

a field, but by anisotropy, as discussed in Sec. 9.4:

$$\frac{d\mathbf{M}}{dt} = \gamma_e \mathbf{M} \times \mathfrak{IC} + \frac{\alpha}{M} \mathbf{M} \times \frac{d\mathbf{M}}{dt} \tag{8.36}$$

The two relations are equivalent for small variations of **M**. Figure 8.11 defines the several terms and their directions. The loss parameter α is dimensionless and must be empirically determined. Still other formulations have also been used to solve particular problems. Since the value of α is defined by experiment, it is not in general possible to identify "correct" damping relations for all experimental situations.

The dynamic equations as presented have the implicit assumption that all electron spins in the entire specimen move

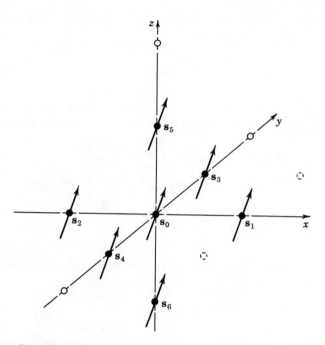

Figure 8.12   Model used for the exchange-torque calculation.

in unison. While this is often reasonable, it is equivalent to assuming that exchange coupling of adjacent atomic electron spins is infinitely strong. Any change in orientation, from one spin to that of an adjacent atom, produces a *torque*, according to the classical interpretation of (8.26). If, however, the orientation of **M** changes at a uniform rate through the solid, the exchange torque on each spin is zero. The complete expression for torque must therefore involve some *second-derivative* measure of **M**. Consider, for example, a spin vector s_0, surrounded by six similar spin vectors not necessarily oriented in the same direction, with (for simplicity) the sixfold symmetry of nearest neighbors in a simple cubic lattice (Fig. 8.12). The exchange energy of s_0 with s_1 is $2Js_0 \cdot s_1/\hbar^2$, where J is the exchange energy. The torque on s_0 due to s_1 is zero when the two are parallel, has a maximum value when they are perpendicular, and is directed normal to both s_0 and s_1. By comparison with (8.32), the torque must have the form

$$T = \frac{2Js_0 \times s_1}{\hbar^2} \tag{8.37}$$

The *total* exchange torque on s_0, from all six surrounding spin vectors, is therefore

$$T(s_0) = \frac{2J}{\hbar^2} s_0 \times \sum_{i=1}^{6} s_i \tag{8.38}$$

Letting the nearest-neighbor distance be a, the laplacian of s (treated now as a variable vector) is defined by the limit

$$(\nabla^2 s)_{s=s_0} = \lim_{a \to 0} \frac{(s_1 - s_0) - (s_0 - s_2)}{a^2}$$
$$+ \frac{(s_3 - s_0) - (s_0 - s_4)}{a^2} + \frac{(s_5 - s_0) - (s_0 - s_6)}{a^2}$$

$$\therefore (\nabla^2 s)_{s_0} \cong \frac{1}{a^2} \sum_{i=1}^{6} s_i - \frac{6 s_0}{a^2}$$

Since the cross product of s_0 with itself is zero, the torque (8.38) can be written

$$T(s) = \frac{2Ja^2}{\hbar^2} s \times \nabla^2 s \tag{8.39}$$

We omit the subscript on s_0 and interpret s as the spin at the point in question.   This is now a *point relation* for the torque on *one* spin.

We may relate the exchange torque to the Weiss field λM by imagining the situation in which we *fix* the spin orientations of six surrounding atoms in the same direction s and allow s_0 alone to change.   The torque exerted on s_0 will then be

$$T(s_0) = \frac{2J}{\hbar^2} s_0 \times (6s) \tag{8.40}$$

But this is *equivalent to* the effect of the Weiss field λM on s_0; by (8.32), recognizing that $p_m = -(eg/2m)s_0 = \gamma_e s_0/\mu_0$,

$$T(s_0) = \gamma_e(\lambda M \times s_0) \tag{8.41}$$

We obtain by comparison of the two expressions for exchange torque, (8.40) and (8.41),

$$\lambda M = \frac{-6(2J)s}{\gamma_e \hbar^2} \tag{8.42}$$

The torque T per unit volume is $1/a^3$ times the torque per spin:

$$T = \frac{1}{a} \frac{2J}{\hbar^2} \cdot s \times \nabla^2 s \tag{8.43}$$

But the spin per atom **s** and the magnetization per unit volume **M** are also related by

$$\mathbf{p}_m = \frac{\gamma_e \mathbf{s}}{\mu_0} = a^3 \mathbf{M} \tag{8.44}$$

Substituting this and (8.42) into (8.43), we obtain

$$\mathbf{T} = \frac{a^2 \lambda \mu_0}{z} \mathbf{M} \times \nabla^2 \mathbf{M} \tag{8.45}$$

where z is the number of nearest neighbors, in this case six.

In the presence of a general macroscopic field $\mathfrak{K}$ (which may be nonuniform) and the exchange forces, the overall dynamic expression, combining (8.32) and (8.45), is the partial differential equation

$$\frac{\partial M}{\partial t} = \gamma_e \mathbf{M} \times \mathfrak{K} + \frac{\lambda a^2}{z} \mathbf{M} \times \nabla^2 \mathbf{M} + \text{(damping term)} \tag{8.46}$$

We make use of this relation in discussing spin waves (Sec. 8.10).

8.9 Ferrimagnets in High-frequency Fields

Because of their high conductivity, ferromagnetic metals and alloys are not useful at frequencies above a few megacycles, except in the form of very thin films. Ferrites, however, are usually poor conductors, having resistivities of the order of 10^4 ohm-cm or higher. In the microwave region, furthermore, *dielectric* losses of many ferrimagnetic materials are low. Domain-wall motion (Sec. 9.3) need not be considered above a few megacycles, since fields which can be applied at high frequencies are seldom large enough to produce substantial wall motion. Analysis of high-frequency behavior may accordingly be carried out using the dynamic equation (8.35) or (8.36). The magnetic fields in a low-power microwave device are usually small compared with d-c fields which are applied to adjust frequency-sensitive behavior. For example, in free space, the electromagnetic power flow per unit area equals $\left(\frac{\mu}{\epsilon}\right)^{\frac{1}{2}} \frac{\mathfrak{K}_m{}^2}{2}$ in a plane electromagnetic wave having *peak* magnetic field $\mathfrak{K}_m$. For a power density of 1 watt/cm², $\mathfrak{K}_m = 7.29$ amp/m, or only 9.15×10^{-2} oe.

In applications of ferrites in RF magnetic fields, the

steady-state orientation of the magnetic spins is aligned by a bias field (or by an equivalent anisotropy). This produces a precession resonance which is generally set near the operating frequency. The small RF fields must be applied in a direction nearly normal to the bias field, for components parallel to **M** produce no torque (**M** × $\mathfrak{K}$). If the RF magnetic field is linearly polarized (for example, $\mathfrak{K} = 1_z\mathfrak{K}_0 + 1_x\mathfrak{K}_1 \sin \omega t$), it produces a small circular precessional motion of the magnetization in its natural direction. This precession has maximum amplitude when $\omega = \gamma_e\mathfrak{K}_0$. If the magnetization naturally precesses in a particular sense and the field is *circularly* polarized with the *same* sense, the magnetization will be strongly acted upon by the field and will precess twice as strongly as in a linearly polarized field of the same amplitude. If, on the other hand, the magnetization's natural sense of precession is *opposite* to that of the RF field, the field has little influence on the magnetization, since it cannot couple to it effectively. There is also strongly different magnetic behavior, above and below resonance, from that near the resonance.

To show all these effects analytically, we must derive the relationship between the time variations of **M** and a small applied RF field. The static orientation of **M** will be assumed in the positive z direction. The applied RF field will consist of an x component ($h_x e^{j\omega t}$) and a y component ($h_y e^{j\omega t}$), where we make use of the complex notation. If h_x and h_y are allowed to be complex numbers, any type of polarization can be constructed; i.e., if h_x and h_y are related by a *real* constant factor ($h_x = c_1 h_y$), the wave is linearly polarized, but where $h_x = \pm j h_y$, the field is circularly polarized. We shall assume the resonance to be derived solely from an applied field $\mathfrak{K}_0$ along the z axis. In the result, $\gamma_e\mathfrak{K}_0$ may be replaced by a general resonance frequency ω_0, with complete generality. The resonance frequency will be altered by magnetic anisotropies of any kind (Sec. 9.4). The appropriate equation for spin motion, using Eq. (8.36) and assuming the magnetization of the specimen moves coherently ($\Delta^2 \mathbf{M} = 0$), is

$$\frac{d\mathbf{M}}{dt} = \gamma_e(\mathbf{M} \times \mathfrak{K}_0) + \gamma_e(\mathbf{M} \times \mathbf{h}) + \frac{\alpha}{M}\left(\mathbf{M} \times \frac{d\mathbf{M}}{dt}\right) \tag{8.47}$$

It is now necessary to *linearize;* i.e., we assume that $\mathbf{M} \cong 1_x m_x + 1_y m_y + 1_z M$, where the x and y components of **M** are small compared with the z component and the variation of M_z can be neglected. In these terms, (8.47) reduces to the scalar equations

$$\dot{m}_x = \gamma_e(m_y\mathfrak{K}_0 - Mh_y) - \alpha\dot{m}_y$$
$$\dot{m}_y = \gamma_e(-m_x\mathfrak{K}_0 + Mh_x) + \alpha\dot{m}_x$$

(8.48)

Presuming that the magnetization components m_x and m_y also have sinusoidal time dependence, a time derivative is equivalent to the factor $j\omega$; rearranging terms,

$$\gamma_e M h_y = -j\omega m_x + (\gamma_e\mathfrak{K}_0 - j\omega\alpha)m_y$$
$$\gamma_e M h_x = (\gamma\mathfrak{K}_0 - j\omega\alpha)m_x + j\omega m_y$$

(8.49)

Solving simultaneously,

$$m_x = \gamma_e M \frac{j\omega h_y - (\gamma_e\mathfrak{K}_0 - j\omega\alpha)h_x}{\omega^2 - (\gamma_e\mathfrak{K}_0 - j\omega\alpha)^2}$$
$$m_y = \gamma_e M \frac{-j\omega h_x - (\gamma_e\mathfrak{K}_0 - j\omega\alpha)h_y}{\omega^2 - (\gamma_e\mathfrak{K}_0 - j\omega\alpha)^2}$$

(8.50)

For the small fields typical of many microwave applications of ferrites, a *linear tensor permeability* $\boldsymbol{\mu}$ may be defined by the small-signal RF relation

$$\mathbf{b} = \mu_0(\mathbf{h} + \mathbf{m}) \equiv \boldsymbol{\mu}\mathbf{h}$$

We have from (8.50)

$$\frac{b_x}{\mu_0} = \left[\frac{-\gamma_e M(\gamma_e\mathfrak{K}_0 - j\omega\alpha)}{\omega^2 - (\gamma_e\mathfrak{K}_0 - j\omega\alpha)^2} + 1\right]h_x$$
$$+ \left[\frac{j\omega\gamma_e M}{\omega^2 - (\gamma_e\mathfrak{K}_0 - j\omega\alpha)^2}\right]h_y$$
$$\frac{b_y}{\mu_0} = \left[\frac{-j\omega\gamma_e M}{\omega^2 - (\gamma_e\mathfrak{K}_0 - j\omega\alpha)^2}\right]h_x$$
$$+ \left[-\frac{\gamma_e M(\gamma_e\mathfrak{K}_0 - j\omega\alpha)}{\omega^2 - (\gamma_e\mathfrak{K}_0 - j\omega\alpha)^2} + 1\right]h_y$$
$$\frac{b_z}{\mu_0} \cong 0$$

(8.51)

Letting

$$\mu = \mu_0\left[1 - \frac{\gamma_e M(\gamma_e\mathfrak{K}_0 - j\omega\alpha)}{\omega^2 - (\gamma_e\mathfrak{K}_0 - j\omega\alpha)^2}\right]$$
$$\kappa = \frac{\mu_0\omega\gamma_e M}{\omega^2 - (\gamma_e\mathfrak{K}_0 - j\omega\alpha)^2}$$

the RF permeability tensor may be written

$$\boldsymbol{\mu} = \begin{bmatrix} \mu & j\kappa & 0 \\ -j\kappa & \mu & 0 \\ 0 & 0 & 0 \end{bmatrix}$$

(8.52)

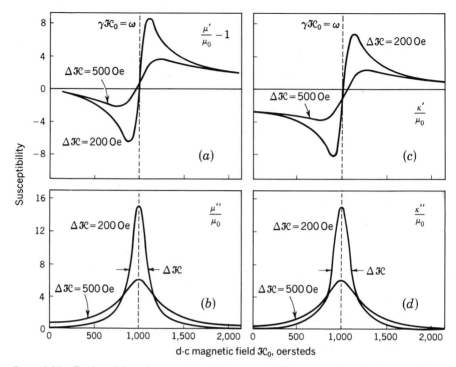

Figure 8.13   Real and imaginary parts of the permeability tensor for a ferrimagnetic material, *as a function of magnetic field,* for two different values of magnetic loss (line width).   The resonance frequency is assumed to be 2,800 Mc/sec, and the saturation magnetization ($4\pi M_s$, cgs) is 3,000 gauss.   (*From B. Lax and K. J. Button, "Microwave Ferrites and Ferrimagnetics," p. 155, McGraw-Hill Book Company, New York, 1962.*)

From the terms of (8.52), a number of important properties of ferrites may be derived.   Recall that the tensor conductivity and permittivity are always symmetrical ($\epsilon_{ij} = \epsilon_{ji}$, $\sigma_{ij} = \sigma_{ji}$, from Sec. 7.4).   The RF permeability tensor here, however, is *antisymmetrical,* since the xy and yx terms are not equal, but opposite.   Inequality of such coefficients is a necessary condition for nonreciprocal devices; of the nonconductive processes, *only* magnetic phenomena are suitable for such devices.

In Fig. 8.13 the real and imaginary parts ($\mu = \mu' - j\mu''$, $\kappa = \kappa' - j\kappa''$) of the elements of the permeability tensor are plotted against field ($\mathfrak{K}_0$) for several values of α.   This is slightly reminiscent of Fig. 7.5 for a dielectric near a "resonance."   Observe that μ' is positive (inductive effect) only when the resonance $\gamma_e \mathfrak{K}_0$ is *above* the operating frequency. The actual measurement of ferrite materials can be made in a fixed-frequency microwave-measuring setup, where $\mathfrak{K}_0$ is varied from values above ω/γ_e to values below ω/γ_e, yielding from the reactance variation that of μ' and μ''. The difference in fields, $\Delta\mathfrak{K}_0$, between which the power absorbed is more than one-half its maximum value, is commonly termed the *line width* of the material. This can be shown to be related directly to α; the imaginary part of μ is

$$\mu'' = \mu_0 \frac{\omega\alpha\gamma_e M(\omega^2 + \gamma_e^2\mathfrak{K}_0^2 + \omega^2\alpha^2)}{[(\omega - \gamma_e\mathfrak{K}_0)^2 + \omega^2\alpha^2][(\omega + \gamma_e\mathfrak{K}_0)^2 + \omega^2\alpha^2]} \tag{8.53}$$

With the assumption that α is much less than unity (it may in practice be near 0.01 in single-crystal ferrites, and perhaps 0.1 in polycrystalline materials) the maximum value of μ'' occurs at $\omega = \gamma_e\mathfrak{K}_0$:

$$\mu''_{\max} = \frac{\mu_0 M}{2\alpha\mathfrak{K}_0} \tag{8.54}$$

With the same degree of approximation, the rapidly varying part of μ'' is due only to the bracketed expression on the left of the denominator, which *doubles* at a field for which

$$(\omega - \gamma_e\mathfrak{K}_0)^2 + \omega^2\alpha^2 = 2\omega^2\alpha^2$$

or

$$\omega - \gamma_e\mathfrak{K}_0 = \pm\omega\alpha \qquad \mathfrak{K}_0 = \frac{\omega}{\gamma_e}(1 \pm \alpha)$$

The line width when measured at frequency ω is therefore

$$\Delta H = 2\alpha\mathfrak{K}_0 \tag{8.55}$$

By solving (8.48) as time-dependent equations, one can show that initial perturbations of M decrease with a relaxation *time constant*

$$\tau_r = \frac{1}{\gamma_e\mathfrak{K}_0\alpha} \tag{8.56}$$

The most interesting situations arise with *circularly* polarized fields. Here we are interested in circular-polarization components of the magnetization. The calculation may be dealt with readily using complex notation. Let $h_x = h_+$ and $h_y = -jh_+$ for one sense of polarization, and $h_x = h_-$, $h_y = jh_-$ for the opposite direction of polarization. Then $h_x = h_+$ +

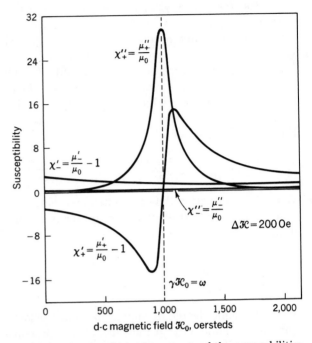

Figure 8.14 Real and imaginary parts of the permeabilities for circularly polarized waves in the ferrite described by Fig. 8.13. (*From B. Lax and K. J. Button, "Microwave Ferrites and Ferrimagnetics," p.* 156, *McGraw-Hill Book Company,* 1962.)

h_-, $h_y = -j(h_+ - h_-)$. In like fashion, define $b_x = b_+ + b_-$, $b_y = -j(b_+ - b_-)$. By substitution in Eqs. (8.51), we obtain

$$b_+ + b_- = (\mu + \kappa)h_+ + (\mu - \kappa)h_-$$
$$b_+ - b_- = (\mu + \kappa)h_+ - (\mu - \kappa)h_-$$

and finally

$$b_+ = (\mu + \kappa)h_+ \qquad b_- = (\mu - \kappa)h_- \tag{8.57}$$

The new quantity $\mu_+ = \mu + \kappa$ may accordingly be defined as the *permeability* for (b_+, h_+) waves, while waves of opposite polarization sense have an effective permeability $\mu_- = \mu - \kappa$. These two functions are remarkably different, as is shown in Fig. 8.14. The h_- solution has little reactive or loss effects due to spin resonance, while the h_+ solution (for field and natural precession in the same sense) is strongly resonant. This characteristic is most useful in ferrite microwave devices, where in

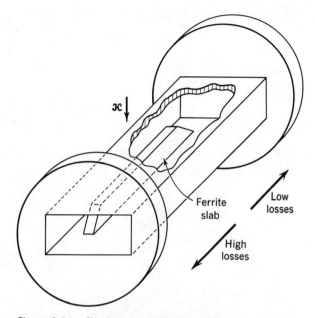

Figure 8.15 Configuration of a microwave waveguide isolator, using a ferrite slab set off center. Static field is usually supplied by a permanent-magnet assembly external to the waveguide. Waves traveling through the guide in one direction are strongly attenuated, while waves pass through almost losslessly in the opposite direction.

a given waveguide waves traveling in opposite directions can be given opposite directions of polarization. It is then possible for one wave to excite strong resonance losses, while an opposite-traveling wave is scarcely affected.

Figure 8.15 illustrates the construction of a simple form of microwave *isolator*, or nonreciprocal transmission line. The ferrite element is placed in the waveguide, and a magnetic bias field applied externally. Pure circularly polarized fields of a given rotation are found only in one plane through the waveguide, for given frequency; the ferrite slab is located in this plane and must therefore be relatively thin. Waves traveling in one direction in the ferrite slab have one sense of circular polarization, while those in the opposite direction have the other. This device can also be made into a sort of modulator, or switch, by switching the amplitude or direction of the biasing magnetic field, respectively. In simple isolator service, attenuation ratios of 40 db in one direction to 0.5 or 1 db in the

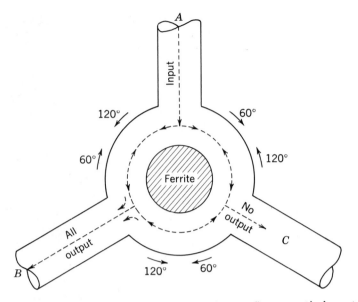

Figure 8.16 Schematic of a ferrite circulator. Some practical devices employ a single cylinder of ferrite as shown; RF field configurations around the ferrite are complex.

opposite direction can be obtained, generally over fractional bandwidths of 10 or 20 per cent. Microwave isolators have also been constructed by making use of the large ratio of μ' for the two polarizations, well *away from* resonance. A waveguide, usually circular in cross section, is nearly filled with ferrite material. For the polarization having lower permeability the waveguide has a higher cutoff frequency than in the opposite polarization. In the region between the two cutoff frequencies the waveguide is unidirectional. The energy which is not propagated here is largely *reflected* back to its source, not absorbed. This overcomes in part the limitation imposed on the conventional isolator by heating. Since Curie temperatures of typical ferrites are below those many metallic magnetic materials, temperature rise produced by power dissipation is a serious problem in high-power ferrite devices.

Ferrites in waveguide configurations can also be used as field-dependent, and therefore magnetically controllable, phase shifters or as phase shifters which shift phase of electromagnetic waves of different polarization by different amounts. An important related application is the so-called *circulator*. The device schematized in Fig. 8.16 passes out through waveguide port B most of the signal into port A. Signals into B come out of C; those into C come out of A. This is possible if the phase shift between ports is 60° in one direction, but 120° in the opposite direction. The symmetry of the device divides the input at any port into two paths. Recombining at each of the two other ports, the two halves of the signal are 180° out of phase at one, but exactly in phase at the other. Other special combinations of phase shift can be made to work equally well, though if the total phase shift is more than 2π, the device becomes more frequency-dependent.

Ferrites can also be used in devices for power-limiting and harmonic generation, employing *nonlinearities* neglected in our derivation of tensor permeability. One of many such nonlinear effects occurs because the RF component of magnetization precession is only linearly proportional to drive when the precession is small, and becomes nonlinear at high drive levels.

8.10 Spin Waves

Equation (8.46) describes dynamics of a magnetic medium in which spins are coupled to one another by nearest-neighbor forces. This is analogous to the coupling between nuclei which leads to acoustical waves (phonons). A field perturbation applied at one edge of a macroscopic sample could not be expected to produce changes immediately at the other edge because the intermediate spin momenta cannot respond instantaneously. The *inertia* of the spin angular momenta and the springlike exchange forces combine to set up wave motion (Fig. 8.17).

Let us consider here small-amplitude wave solutions, which are termed *spin waves*. This wave system can support uniform plane waves; hence let

$$\mathbf{M} = \mathbf{M}_0 + \mathbf{m}e^{j(\omega t - \mathbf{k}\cdot\mathbf{r})} \qquad \mathfrak{K} = \mathfrak{K}_0 + \mathbf{h}e^{j(\omega t - \mathbf{k}\cdot\mathbf{r})} \qquad (8.58)$$

where $\mathbf{k}$ and $\mathbf{M}$ are constant vectors, and $|\mathbf{m}| \ll |\mathbf{M}_0|$. Since $\nabla^2(e^{j\mathbf{k}\cdot\mathbf{r}}) = -k^2 e^{j\mathbf{k}\cdot\mathbf{r}}$, we obtain, upon substitution into (8.46), neglecting losses,

$$j\omega\mathbf{m} = \gamma_e \left[\mathbf{m} \times \mathfrak{K} + k^2 \left(\frac{a^2\lambda}{z} \right) \mathbf{m} \times \mathbf{M}_0 \right] \qquad (8.59)$$

An important part of the solution is the time-varying magnetic field $\mathbf{h}(x,y,z,t)$ produced by the spin motion. Since a-c magnetization $\mathbf{m}$ is a function of position, *internal* demagnetizing

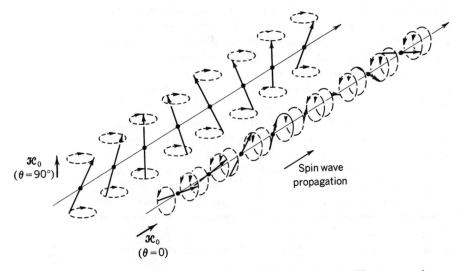

$\mathcal{3C}_0$
$(\theta = 90°)$

Spin wave
propagation

$\mathcal{3C}_0$
$(\theta = 0)$

Figure 8.17   Spin-wave motion of spin vectors.   The upper drawing illustrates a situation where the static field is normal to the wave propagation; in the lower drawing, they are parallel.

fields are required by Maxwell's equations, even in an infinite medium.   We shall presume that the spin waves have velocities much less than the velocity of light; this means that any accompanying electric field may be neglected.   With zero conductivity, Maxwell's equation $\nabla \times \mathcal{3C} = \mathbf{j} + \partial \mathbf{D}/\partial t$ becomes

$$\nabla \times \mathbf{h} = 0 \tag{8.60}$$

There is the additional requirement

$$\nabla \cdot \mathbf{B} = \mu_0(\nabla \cdot \mathcal{3C} + \nabla \cdot \mathbf{m}) = 0 \tag{8.61}$$

We have assumed a form for the magnetization variation and must now find the field which it produces.   (This is analogous to the problem of finding the electric field due to a charge distribution.)   We shall avoid the details of determining the field and simply state the result:[1]

$$\mathbf{h} = -\frac{\mathbf{k}(\mathbf{k} \cdot \mathbf{m})}{k^2} e^{j(\omega t - \mathbf{k} \cdot \mathbf{r})} \tag{8.62}$$

The reader may quickly prove its accuracy by substitution, using $\nabla e^{-j\mathbf{k} \cdot \mathbf{r}} = -j\mathbf{k} e^{-j\mathbf{k} \cdot \mathbf{r}}$.   The field (8.62) is applicable only when external sample boundaries are far removed.   It is there-

[1] Cf. R. Soohoo, "Theory and Application of Ferrites," p. 232, Prentice-Hall, Inc., Englewood Cliffs, N.J., 1960.

fore a good approximation when the wavelength of the spin waves is much smaller than the sample dimensions.

Applying (8.62) to the torque equation (8.59) and neglecting second-order products of the form $\mathbf{m} \times \mathbf{h}$, the governing equation is

$$j\omega\mathbf{m} = \gamma_e \left[\mathbf{M}_0 \times \mathbf{h} + \mathbf{m} \times \left(\mathfrak{K}_0 + \frac{k^2 a^2 \lambda}{z} \mathbf{M}_0 \right) \right] \tag{8.63}$$

With little loss of generality, we assume $\mathbf{M}_0 \cong 1_z M$, $\mathfrak{K}_0 = 1_z \mathfrak{K}_0$, obtaining two equations from (8.63),

$$
\begin{aligned}
j\omega m_x &= \gamma_e \left[-M h_y + m_y \left(\mathfrak{K}_0 + \frac{k^2 a^2}{z} \lambda M \right) \right] \\
j\omega m_y &= \gamma_e \left[M h_x - m_x \left(\mathfrak{K}_0 + \frac{k^2 a^2}{z} \lambda M \right) \right]
\end{aligned}
\tag{8.64}
$$

Substituting h_x and h_y from (8.62),

$$
\begin{aligned}
j\omega m_x &= \gamma_e \left[\frac{M k_y}{k^2} (k_x m_x + k_y m_y) + m_y \left(\mathfrak{K}_0 + \frac{k^2 a^2}{z} \lambda M \right) \right] \\
j\omega m_y &= \gamma_e \left[-\frac{M k_x}{k^2} (k_x m_x + k_y m_y) - m_x \left(\mathfrak{K}_0 + \frac{k^2 a^2}{z} \lambda M \right) \right]
\end{aligned}
\tag{8.65}
$$

This pair of homogeneous simultaneous algebraic equations has a solution only if their determinant vanishes. This condition is

$$\omega = \gamma_e \left[\left(\mathfrak{K}_0 + \frac{k^2 a^2}{z} \lambda M \right) \left(\mathfrak{K}_0 + \frac{k^2 a^2}{z} \lambda M + M \frac{k^2 - k_z^2}{R^2} \right) \right]^{\frac{1}{2}}$$

(We have used $k_x^2 + k_y^2 + k_z^2 = k^2$.) Expressing the *angle* that $\mathbf{k}$ makes with the z axis as θ, $k_z = k \cos \theta$; the last term in the brackets simplifies to $M \sin^2 \theta$.

$$\omega = \gamma_e \left[\left(\mathfrak{K}_0 + \frac{k^2 a^2}{z} \lambda M \right) \left(\mathfrak{K}_0 + \frac{k^2 a^2}{z} \lambda M + M \sin^2 \theta \right) \right]^{\frac{1}{2}} \tag{8.66}$$

This *dispersion relation* determines the propagation constant as function of frequency and direction of propagation. The spin-wave spectrum may best be understood through a plot of ω versus k (Fig. 8.18). Plots for $\theta = 0$ ($\mathbf{k} \parallel \mathfrak{K}_0$) and $\theta = 90°$ ($\mathbf{k} \perp \mathfrak{K}_0$) are given. With the waves propagating in the direction of the d-c field ($\theta = 0$), waves of infinite wavelength ($\mathbf{k} = 0$) have frequency $\gamma_e \mathfrak{K}_0$, just the natural resonance frequency. The "cutoff" frequency is $\gamma_e \mathfrak{K}_0$, because the spins

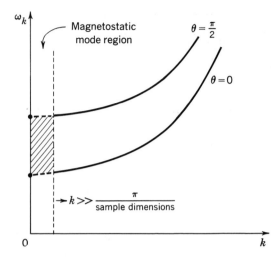

Figure 8.18 Spin-wave ω-k relations. In the region near $k = 0$, the wavelength is comparable with the sample dimensions, and a magnetostatic-mode (standing-wave) description is more appropriate.

can precess no slower than this. For $\theta > 0$, the magnetic fields produced by the spin-wave motion provide an additional restoring torque which increases the minimum spin precession frequency.

In a finite sample, waves of low **k** (long wavelength) must be combined into standing waves, geometry-dependent *resonances*, of frequency above the natural gyromagnetic resonance. These are termed *magnetostatic modes*. They bear the same relation to spin waves that resonant-cavity modes bear to propagating electromagnetic waves. Accurate calculation must take into account not only precise geometry, but also the properties of surface spins. Although in actuality all spin-wave motions of a finite sample are resonant modes, when the dimensions exceed a few tens or hundreds of spin wavelengths, the resonances will spread so as to become indistinguishable, because of the magnetic losses neglected in (8.66).

It is informative to estimate spin-wave parameters. For example, consider a sample with 1-cm dimensions, at a wavelength of $\frac{1}{100}$ cm: $k = 200\pi$; let the atomic spacing a be of the order of 3 A and $\lambda M/z = 10^6$ oe (typical of many magnetic materials). The term $k^2 a^2 \lambda M/z$ is about 3.5×10^{-4} oe.

For $\theta = 0$, the spin waves of $\frac{1}{100}$-cm wavelength lie only about $2.8 \times 10^6 \times 3.5 \times 10^{-4} = 10^3$ cycles *above* the gyromagnetic resonance frequency $\gamma_e\mathcal{3C}_0$. It is much easier to measure spin-wave resonances in smaller samples, which have accordingly greater frequency separation between resonant modes.

Spin waves are the natural vibrations of an electron spin system, analogous to lattice vibrations (phonons) in crystals. Spin waves are therefore quantized ($E = \hbar\omega$); the quanta are sometimes called *magnons*. The spectrum shown in Fig. 8.18 is only the lower end of the magnon spectrum; there will be, in exact analogy to lattice vibrations, an upper cutoff frequency corresponding to alternate atoms having spin motion in opposite phase. This condition occurring in a simple cubic lattice at $k = \pi/a$ corresponds to $\omega \simeq \gamma_e(\mathcal{3C}_0 + k^2a^2\lambda M/z) \approx \gamma_e\pi^2\lambda M/z \approx 10^7\gamma_e$; since $\gamma_e = 2.8$ Mc/oe, $\omega_{\text{cutoff}} \approx 2.8 \times 10^{13}$ cps, above the optical spectrum. At normal temperatures, only the lower part of the spin-wave spectrum is excited.

The thermal behavior of magnetic material, as well as magnetic losses, can in principle be explained by spin waves. Thermodynamically, we should expect these waves to be excited more strongly at higher temperatures. The existence of spin waves implies that average magnetization will be slightly reduced, for with any precession of the spins, the component of magnetization in the direction of a bias field cannot be equal to its full magnitude M. At higher temperatures, the higher-frequency spin waves are excited more strongly and the observed magnetization decreases. On this basis F. Bloch showed that the observed saturation magnetization must vary at low temperatures as $M = M_0[1 - (T/T_c)^{\frac{3}{2}}]$. Since spin waves are linear only at small amplitudes, Bloch's theory fails well below the Curie temperature.

Losses in magnetic materials can be described as the excitation of spin waves from a *time-varying* magnetization. Any time-varying-magnetization motion can be expressed as a sum of spin-wave and magnetostatic modes. The nonlinearities of high-amplitude spin waves permit energy conversion to other frequencies. Hysteresis losses in low-frequency operation of magnetic materials are the result of establishment of spin waves by nonuniformities in the magnetization of an inhomogeneous specimen. These spin waves carry away energy, which is incapable of being reconverted and extracted from the solid. The spin waves couple first to one another, and then eventually to the lattice, by magnon-phonon coupling, whence they finally appear as heating of the lattice. Structural imperfections scatter spin waves and enable them to convert to phonon energy more rapidly.

PROBLEMS

8.1 The definition of the magnetic moment of a current loop is the product of its current and area. From this, show that $\mathbf{B} = \mu_0(\mathfrak{IC} + \mathbf{M})$, and *not* $\mathbf{B} = \mu_0\mathfrak{IC} + \mathbf{M}$, is the correct form.

8.2(a) Assuming an effective mass equal to the free-electron mass in the conduction band of a metal having 10^{23} electrons/cm^3, find at $T = 0$ the value of $n(E_f)$, and calculate the paramagnetic susceptibility using (8.3).

8.2(b) (1) Estimate the room-temperature paramagnetic susceptibility of a semiconductor, due to an electron density of 10^{17} cm^{-3}. Assume the electrons act magnetically just like free electrons, so that Boltzmann statistics control the populations of $s = \frac{1}{2}$ and $s = -\frac{1}{2}$ states. (2) How would the additional presence of 10^{17} holes/cm^3 alter the paramagnetic susceptibility? (3) With what class of magnetic materials might an intrinsic semiconductor be associated?

8.2(c) A solid is composed of 10-electron atoms in a close-packed crystal structure. Each atom is represented as a uniform-density spherical electron cloud surrounding the nucleus. Find the solid's diamagnetic susceptibility, calculating the value per atom by determining the average square of the electron radius in the charge cloud, $\langle r^2 \rangle = \langle x^2 + y^2 \rangle$. Atomic radius is 1.5 A.

8.3(a) Using the vector model of Fig. 8.2, prove (8.9). (HINT: First find the projection of the $\mathbf{p}_m$ vector on the $\mathbf{J}$ axis.)

8.3(b) Use Hund's rule to calculate the theoretical values of L, S, and J for the rare-earth elements listed and use (8.9) to calculate g. Compare the theoretical maximum magnetic moment per atom gJ (magnetons) with the experimental values listed: Ce, 2.4; Pr, 3.5; Nd, 3.5; Sm, 1.5; Eu, 3.4; Gd, 8.0; Tb, 9.5; Dy, 10.6; Ho, 10.4; Er, 9.5; Tm, 7.3; Yb, 4.5.

8.3(c) A paramagnetic sample placed in a nonuniform magnetic field experiences forces which tend to make it move toward regions of higher field. (1) Explain this in terms of energy of the sample versus position. (2) If the field in a given region varies approximately proportional to z ($\mathfrak{IC} = az$), determine the z-directed force on a small sample of volume V, as a function of z and its (scalar) χ_m.

8.4(a) At slow field reduction, demagnetization of a paramagnetic salt is adiabatic, the *sum* of the lattice and paramagnetic-electron entropies remaining constant. By the Debye theory the low-temperature lattice entropy is proportional to T^4. (1) Using $dS = dQ/T$ and finding $dQ/dt = (d/dt)[\Delta E(n_+ - n_-)]$ by (8.13) (where $\Delta E = 2\mu_0\beta\mathfrak{3C}$, the difference in the two energy levels), integrate dS/dt to find an integral relation for S versus T. Show that this S is a function of $\Delta E/kT$, is monotonic, and saturates at large enough temperatures. (2) Sketch the lattice entropy and the sum of lattice and paramagnetic entropies at both very high and very low fields. Show on the sketch the magnetization-demagnetization cycle followed in paramagnetic cooling.

8.4(b) Paramagnetic cooling is possible in part because of the relatively large specific heat of paramagnetic electrons at very low temperatures. The energy of a paramagnetic system of two spin levels per atom ($S_z = \pm\frac{1}{2}$) is just the energy difference times the number of atoms in the excited state ($E_p = 2\mu_0\beta\mathfrak{3C}n_+$). The specific heat is the derivative of this with respect to temperature. (1) Calculate and plot the variation of $c = dE_p/dt$ versus the normalized energy difference $2\mu_0\beta\mathfrak{3C}/kT$, noting the temperature at which c is maximum. (2) If the lattice energy is given by the Debye theory, $E = 3\pi^4NkT(T/T_D)^3/5$, at what low temperature are the specific heats of lattice and paramagnetic electrons equal at $\mathfrak{3C} = 1,000$ oe and a Debye temperature $T_D = 400°K$?

8.5(a) Find the relation between $\lambda.lI = \lambda N\beta$ and T_c, using (8.20). (This applies directly only to the one-electron-per-atom model.)

8.5(b) (1) Show that in an actual crystal (two dimensions are sufficient), the dipole-dipole coupling of spins is not in all cases such as to promote *parallel* alignment of spins. (2) Show that in a centrosymmetric structure (i.e., a crystal having a center of symmetry) there can be no *net* dipole-dipole interaction.

8.6(a) The interaction leading to ferromagnetism is usually described in terms of nearest-neighbor atoms only. Explain why the localized-electron concept is important in this regard.

8.6(b) By (8.21), it would appear that when the quantum numbers of the two electrons (l,m,n) are equal, the function ψ_{II} would vanish. Explain clearly why this is not so, whereas what appeared to be a similar argument is used in Appendix B to illustrate the exclusion principle.

8.7(a) (1) Plot the theoretical magnetic moment (per molecule) of $Ni_xFe_{3-x}O_4$ versus the parameter x, if the Ni^{++} ions prefer B sites of the ferrite. (2) Repeat for $Cr_xFe_{3-x}O_4$. Let x run from 0 to 1.

8.7(b) Most oxides of the form XO (X being a transition-metal ion) are antiferromagnetic, whereas oxides of the form ZX_2O_4, $Z_3X_5O_{12}$, etc., are ferrimagnetic. Give an explanation in support of this.

8.7(c) Explain *phenomenologically* what happens in a ferrite when the magnetization goes through zero *below* the transition temperature, as described in Fig. 8.9. (Show by a sketch the possible orientations of spins at some particular instant.)

8.8(a) Derive (8.36) from (8.35). (HINT: Cross $d\mathbf{M}/dt$ with $\mathbf{M}$.)

8.8(b) Repeat a derivation similar to (8.34) but including the loss term of (8.36) to show that small initial precession decays with a time constant $\tau = (\gamma_e \alpha \mathcal{3C}_0)^{-1}$. Assume $\alpha^2 \ll 1$. (HINT: Approximate M_z by the constant M, with a field applied in the z direction.)

8.8(c) From the classical descriptions of atomic electric and magnetic dipoles, contrast the behavior of the two kinds of dipoles when a torque is applied to each, at right angles to an applied static field.

8.8(d) Consider a one-dimensional *line* of coupled spins in the absence of a magnetic field. The spin direction may be taken at right angles to the line. (1) Show that if the spin at one end of the line is twisted through an angle θ, the steady-state solution has the twist distributed evenly along the line. (2) What happens if the twisted end is released?

8.9(a) A *symmetrical* tensor (describing crystal permittivity, for example) can be diagonalized by rotation of coordinates. Show that the tensor permeability (8.52) is not diagonalizable by, but is in fact *invariant* to, rotations about the z (field) axis.

8.9(b) A ferrite sample with $M = 300$ (cgs), $g = 2$, $\epsilon/\epsilon_0 = 10$, $\alpha = 0.1$ is placed in a d-c field which produces 10,000 Mc/sec resonance. (1) If linearly polarized electromagnetic waves ($\mathcal{3C}_{RF} \perp \mathcal{3C}_0$) pass through the material at the resonance frequency (propagating as $e^{j(\omega t - \omega\sqrt{\mu\epsilon}\,z)}$), determine the attenuation per centimeter length of travel. (2) If the RF field amplitude is 0.1 oe at a given point, determine the absorption power density. [HINT: With sinusoidal fields, calculate the energy input per unit volume: $\int B \, d\mathcal{3C} = \int B \, (d\mathcal{3C}/dt) \, dt$ over a 1-sec period.]

8.9(c) The material described in Fig. 8.13, with $\Delta\mathcal{3C} = 500$ oe, is placed into a TEM-mode transmission line (e.g., coaxial circular cylindrical conductors) so that it completely fills the cross section. The d-c magnetic field is applied along the direction of propagation, so that the RF magnetic field is linearly polarized and normal to the d-c field. If the dielectric constant at the operating frequency of 2,800 Mc/sec is 15 and dielectric losses are neglected, plot the approximate variation of the phase shift per meter and the loss per meter in decibels over the significant range of d-c fields. Data may be taken from the curves.

8.10(a) (1) Determine, in a material for which $\lambda M a^2/z = 10^{-9}$ (cgs), at what frequencies magnon and phonon energies and momenta are comparable. (Take the simplest case, of $\mathcal{3C}_0 = 0$ and $\theta = 0$.) (2) Repeat for the magnon-photon case. (3) With an applied magnetic field of the order of 1,000 oe, what wavelengths of photons and of phonons will interact most strongly with the spin waves? Assume $v_{photon} = c/5$, $v_{phonon} = 4 \times 10^5$ cm/sec.

8.10(b) A magnetic thin film 1,000 A in thickness has an applied field, in the film plane, of 500 oe. Assume that $4\pi M = 10,000$ gauss and that $\lambda M a^2/z$ has an effective value of 5×10^{-10} (cgs). If the behavior of the spins at the film edge is such that the spin-wave amplitude is zero there, calculate the frequencies of the three lowest-frequency magnetostatic modes. (HINT: Let k be such that the film contains one, two, or three half-wavelengths.)

GENERAL REFERENCES

Periodical publications in magnetism appear in both physical and metallurgical journals. Proceedings of the Annual Conference on Magnetism and Magnetic Materials are published in the *Journal of Applied Physics*, as a supplement to an early-spring issue. Results of another symposium appeared in *Reviews of Modern Physics*, vol. 25, 1953.

American Society for Metals: "Magnetic Properties of Metals and Alloys," 1959. (Contains excellent reviews of many phases of magnetics, by a number of experts.)

Bates, L. F.: "Modern Magnetism," 4th ed., Cambridge University Press, New York, 1961. (Simple descriptions of magnetism; stresses measurements.)

Bozorth, R. M.: "Ferromagnetism," D. Van Nostrand Company, Inc., Princeton, N.J., 1951. (An encyclopedia of materials properties, with readable descriptions of physical basis.)

Lax, B., and K. J. Button: "Microwave Ferrites and Ferrimagnetics," McGraw-Hill Book Company, New York, 1962. (A comprehensive treatment of phenomena and device applications.)

Rado, G. T., and H. Suhl (eds.): "Magnetism," Academic Press Inc., New York, 1963. (An encyclopedic work in three volumes, with articles by many contemporary experts.)

Van Vleck, J. H.: "The Theory of Electric and Magnetic Susceptibilities," Clarendon Press, Oxford, 1932. (Deals with the essentials; although written shortly after the advent of quantum theory, accurate even today.)

9

Domain magnetics

9.1 Magnetic Anisotropies

While the exchange coupling between electron spins is the salient feature of ferro- and ferrimagnetic materials, *magnetic anisotropies* control most of the macroscopic properties of these materials. Anisotropy of magnetic properties means that the spin energy is a function of the *direction* of **M**. Directions of lowest energy are termed "easy" directions, while directions of highest energy are termed "hard" directions. The energies involved in anisotropy are *much smaller* than the exchange energy. Because many spins are so strongly exchange-coupled into a single spin system, the system can manifest anisotropy representing much less than kT per atom.

An *isotropic* ferro- or ferrimagnet in the form of a small sphere of $\lesssim 10^{-5}$ cm diameter would direct its magnetization in an arbitrary direction. It would be at the whim of the tiniest magnetic field applied. Since anisotropy is always present, zero-field magnetization of a small sphere will lie in one of the easy directions. That of a larger sample, as we shall show, breaks up to form a number of *magnetic domains* whose sizes and arrangement are controlled by the nature and amount of anisotropies present. The influence of an applied field depends on the extent to which it produces torques on the spin system to overcome the anisotropy forces.

Magnetic anisotropies occur on all spatial scales. Major sources of anisotropy in magnetic materials are, in decreasing spatial scale:

1. Nonspherical shape of a complete magnetic sample (shape anisotropy)

2. Anisotropic stress of parts or all of the sample (stress anisotropy)

3. Anisotropy due to a local ordering of some of the atoms in a normally disordered alloy or ferrimagnetic compound (directional-ordering anisotropy)

4. Anisotropy due to crystalline fields (crystalline anisotropy)

Shape anisotropy occurs whenever a ferro- or ferrimagnetic specimen (or a complete device) is of nonspherical form. One often considers shapes which are limiting cases of ellipsoidal geometry (plates, rods). In devices, toroidal (doughnut-shaped) magnetic elements are quite common. Shape anisotropy is also evident when many elongated or foreshortened crystallites are to some extent magnetically isolated from one another (as discussed in Sec. 9.5). This and other anisotropies are conveniently discussed in terms of the variation of *free energy* (which we shall simply term E) with the configuration of magnetization. At equilibrium, the configuration will assume that form for which the free energy is a minimum. There may be several possible minimum-energy configurations, in which case past history may determine which is attained. We assume for the present that the magnetization in the entire sample is directed in the same direction; this is truly meaningful only for ellipsoidal samples, but these will serve to demonstrate the principles. Analysis of cube-shaped, toroidal, etc., samples is at best only approximate, but the general principles may be applied to empirical solutions for these more complex shapes. Following (7.6), the applied magnetic field may be separated into cartesian components parallel to the major axes of the ellipsoid. The internal field components ($\mathfrak{IC}_x$, etc.) are then related to applied field components ($\mathfrak{IC}_{ax}$, etc.) by

$$\mathfrak{IC}_x = \mathfrak{IC}_{ax} - \mathfrak{D}_x M_x \qquad \mathfrak{IC}_y = \mathfrak{IC}_{ay} - \mathfrak{D}_y M_y$$
$$\mathfrak{IC}_z = \mathfrak{IC}_{az} - \mathfrak{D}_z M_z \qquad (9.1)$$

where $\mathfrak{D}_x$, etc., are the three depolarization factors (whose sum is unity). The differential of the free energy of any solid characterized by a magnetization **M** and a magnetic field $\mathfrak{IC}$, at constant temperature and pressure, is given from Sec. C.1 by

$$dE = -\mu_0 \mathbf{M} \cdot d\mathfrak{IC}$$

From (9.1), $d\mathcal{3C}_x = d\mathcal{3C}_{ax} - \mathfrak{D}_x \, dM_x$, etc. Substituting in the above differential and integrating, the integral over $\mathcal{3C}_{ax}$ can be carried out with M in fixed orientation; since the reference point of the free energy is arbitrary, the lower limit of integration over M_x, M_y, and M_z is also arbitrary, and

$$E = -\mu_0 \mathcal{3C}_a \cdot \mathbf{M} + \frac{\mu_0}{2} \left(\mathfrak{D}_x M_x{}^2 + \mathfrak{D}_y M_y{}^2 + \mathfrak{D}_z M_z{}^2 \right) + \text{const} \tag{9.2}$$

The first term is the direct interaction with the applied field, while the second represents shape anisotropy. Suppose, for example, we have a long circular-cylindrical sample ($\mathfrak{D}_z = 0$, $\mathfrak{D}_x = \mathfrak{D}_y = \frac{1}{2}$). The z direction is parallel to the long axis of the sample. When $M_z = M$, $M_x = M_y = 0$, (9.2) indicates that the energy will be a minimum (in zero field). In fact, in this case the anisotropy energy may be expressed in the form

$$E_{\text{shape}}(\text{long rod}) = \frac{\mu_0}{4} \left(M_x{}^2 + M_y{}^2 \right)$$

$$\equiv \frac{\mu_0}{4} M^2 \sin^2 \theta \qquad (\text{cgs: } \pi M^2 \sin^2 \theta) \tag{9.3}$$

where θ is the angle of $\mathbf{M}$ with the z axis. This is the simplest mathematical function for a *uniaxial* anisotropy. The magnetization prefers to lie along an axis, but not in a preferred direction along that axis. By way of contrast, the influence of the applied field alone may be said to produce a *unidirectional* anisotropy, for with this alone (e.g., a spherical sample), the only preferred magnetization direction is parallel to the field. In a thin circular *disk* ($\mathfrak{D}_z \cong 1$), the preferred orientations are in the plane of the disk. The anisotropy energy is

$$E_{\text{shape}}(\text{thin disk}) = \frac{\mu_0}{2} M^2 \cos^2 \theta \tag{9.4}$$

A phenomenological explanation of the shape anisotropy is instructive. When the magnetic flux emerges from a small-area face (the end) of a rod, there is less total stored magnetic field energy ($\mu_0 \int \mathcal{3C}^2 \, dv/2$) in the region around the sample than when flux emerges from the much larger cross sections in the x or y directions (Fig. 9.1). A similar argument demonstrates lowest energy when flux emerges from the edge of the disk. In thin needlelike crystallites or thin films, shape anisotropy is often the controlling factor in magnetic behavior.

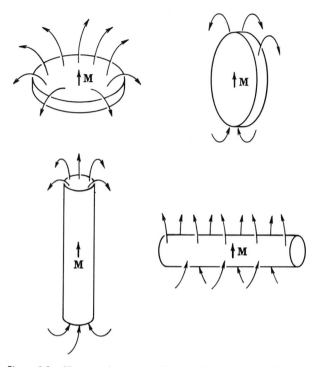

Figure 9.1   Shape anisotropy of long rod-shaped and thin disk-shaped samples. The magnetic stored energy which their magnetization produces is less when it emerges through a smaller-area face.

The free-energy contributions arising from ellipsoidal shape anisotropy and similar energies in more complex magnetization configurations are termed *magnetostatic energy*, i.e., energy which resides in magnetostatic fields.

The shape anisotropy of *toroidal* samples of ferro- or ferrimagnetic material is not expressible in closed form, although it is easy to see that the magnetization configuration of Fig. 9.14a is one involving no external magnetic fields. While the two magnetization states of azimuthal magnetization are minimum-energy configurations, any non-minimum-energy configuration is unlikely to have a mathematically simple form. In such instances, and also ones involving configurations such as that of Fig. 9.21, it is common to make simplifying assumptions; for example, in high-permeability materials, the magnetic flux is often assumed to remain in the magnetic material except at an actual "air gap." This *magnetic-*

circuit approach to magnetostatic calculations, while very approximate, has great engineering value.

Stress anisotropy is related to *magnetostriction*, which is taken up in Sec. 9.6. When a tensile stress **T** is applied in a given direction to a polycrystalline sample, the resulting strain of the material causes the magnetization to prefer either the axis along which the stress is applied *or* any direction in the plane normal to that axis. For a simple tensile stress, the anisotropy energy is of the approximate form (derived in Sec. 9.6)

$$E_{\text{stress}} = \tfrac{3}{2}\lambda_s T \sin^2 \theta \tag{9.5}$$

where θ is the angle between the magnetization **M** and the axis of stress. This also has the uniaxial form. The *saturation magnetostriction constant* λ_s is defined in Sec. 9.6. If λ_s is positive (as for iron), the application of tensile forces on a sample causes the magnetization to prefer the stress axis ($\theta = 0$, $E_{\text{stress}} = 0$). If λ_s is negative, as in nickel, the magnetization prefers the plane normal to the stress ($\theta = \pi/2$). While the theory can be generalized to include a full complement of stresses ($T_i, i = 1, \ldots, 6$) the added complexity is not justifiable here. The constant λ_s is relatively large ($\sim -50 \times 10^{-6}$) in nickel and smaller in iron ($\sim 10^{-5}$). For some alloy compositions, for example, 81.5 per cent Ni–18.5 per cent Fe (by weight), it is almost zero; this composition is highly useful when the magnetic material may be strained and no change of magnetic properties is tolerable.

Directional-ordering anisotropy is, for example, observed in nickel-iron alloys, where a magnetic field applied during heat-treatment causes pairs of iron atoms to align more or less parallel to the applied field (Fig. 9.2). The induced anisotropy is uniaxial, corresponding to the axis of the magnetic-anneal field. The energy per unit volume can be expressed, to first order, by

$$E_{\text{directional ordering}} = K_u \sin^2 \theta \tag{9.6}$$

Values of K_u vary tremendously with material and processing and range up to about 10^4 ergs/cm³ in Ni-Fe alloys.

Directional-ordering anisotropy is also obtained during magnetic heat-treatment in *ferrites* containing cobalt ions. The octahedral *B* sites (Sec. 8.7) have slightly uniaxial distortion along the [111] axes, due to small shifts of the oxygen ions from the positions they would occupy if they formed an

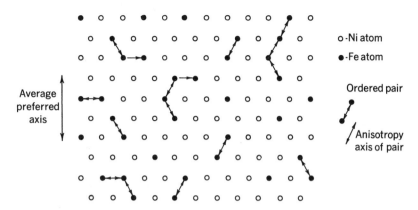

Figure 9.2   Induced anisotropy, in nickel-iron and related alloys, due to "pairing" of some of the iron atoms.   There are slightly more pairs oriented parallel to the field than in the other orientations.   Each pair has a strongly axial spin-direction anisotropy, which influences its neighbors through exchange coupling.

ideal face-centered cubic oxygen sublattice.   There are, however, equal numbers of occupied octahedral sites distorted along *each* of the four [111] axes.   When a cobalt-containing ferrite is heated in a magnetic field, cobalt ions diffuse to sites which allow them to have lowest energy.   Cobalt ions have intrinsically higher anisotropy than the iron ions, hence will strongly favor those sites with uniaxial distortion nearest to the applied field direction.   This process can lead to an extremely high uniaxial anisotropy constant (for example, $K_u = 2 \times 10^6$ ergs/cm^3, in the ferrite $Co_{0.7}Fe_{2.3}O_4$).

Crystalline anisotropy appears in all ferromagnetic and ferrimagnetic materials.   This phenomenon is due basically to spin-orbit coupling effects, like those discussed in Sec. B.8.   There is also a contribution due to dipole-dipole coupling of the type described by (8.17).   In the free atom, the effective magnetic field at the spinning electron, due to the motion in the electric field of the nucleus, gives rise to a magnetic spin-orbit coupling (cf. Fig. B.11).   In a solid, even though the spinning electron has an "orbit" with little or no net angular momentum about its associated nucleus, it nevertheless experiences magnetic fields in its motion in the presence of the surrounding nuclear charges.   Certain spin orientations therefore cause the spin-orbit perturbation of electron energy to be greater than in other orientations.   The energy of the

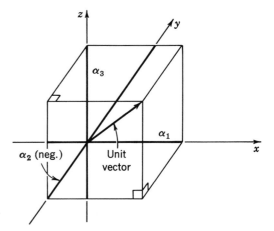

Figure 9.3 Definition of the *direction cosines* α_1, α_2, and α_3 in terms of a unit vector. In the case shown, α_2 is negative.

electron will accordingly be a *function* of the spin's orientation *with respect to the crystal axes*. The crystalline anisotropy energy, as a function of spin orientation, must possess the full *rotational* symmetry characteristic of the crystal.

Whereas the anisotropy of the permittivity and conductivity of crystals may be described by a maximum of six coefficients (Sec. 1.4), the dependence of crystalline anisotropy energy on spin orientation is described by a function limited only to proper symmetry. The anisotropy energy may, however, be expanded in a series of terms, to as high an order as required. The pertinent coordinates for the cubic structure typical of many magnetic materials are *direction cosines* of the spin orientation. We can define the *orientation* of **M** by the projections of the unit vector **M**/M on the three major cartesian axes of the cubic crystal (Fig. 9.3). These projections are the three direction cosines $M_x/M = \alpha_1$, $M_y/M = \alpha_2$, $M_z/M = \alpha_3$. The two lowest-order terms in a series expansion of *cubic* anisotropy energy are then

$$E_{\text{crystal}} = K_1(\alpha_1{}^2\alpha_2{}^2 + \alpha_2{}^2\alpha_3{}^2 + \alpha_3{}^2\alpha_1{}^2) + K_2(\alpha_1{}^2\alpha_2{}^2\alpha_3{}^2)$$
$$+ \cdots \qquad (9.7)$$

The direction cosines are not all independent, since the squares of the cartesian projections of a unit vector must equal unity: $\alpha_1{}^2 + \alpha_2{}^2 + \alpha_3{}^2 = 1$. Along a [100] axis, for example, $\alpha_1 = 1$, $\alpha_2 = \alpha_3 = 0$, and $E = 0$. Along a body diagonal,

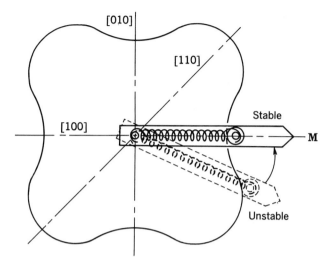

Figure 9.4 Analog of anisotropy energy variation with orientation. The figure represents E versus θ as in a (001) plane, for iron. The moving arm of the analog, pivoted at the center, has a spring which causes it to seek an orientation at which the spring is least extended (and has therefore the least energy). There are four equally preferred orientations.

all $\alpha^2 = \frac{1}{3}$; each term is a maximum. Since K_1 and K_2 can be either positive or negative, we can represent crystals with preferred spin orientations along either [001], [111], or [011] axes by different combinations of K_1 and K_2. The measured values, at room temperature, for nickel and iron are

$$\text{Iron: } K_1 = 420 \times 10^3 \qquad K_2 = 150 \times 10^3 \text{ ergs/cm}^3$$
$$\text{Nickel: } K_1 = -34 \times 10^3 \qquad K_2 = 53 \times 10^3 \text{ ergs/cm}^3$$

Thus, in iron, **M** prefers [001] axes, while in nickel, [111] axes are preferred. The composition 75 per cent Ni–25 per cent iron has $K_1 \approx 0$, and addition of a few per cent of molybdenum appears to reduce anisotropy to an even higher order.

The apparent maze of possible sources of anisotropy in magnetic materials makes understanding particular materials something of a puzzle where several anisotropies are present simultaneously. From a heuristic point of view, it is easiest to imagine an energy surface such as shown in Fig. 9.4. A mechanical analogy is depicted in the figure. The equilibrium orientation(s) of **M** will be the ones in which the energy is lowest. In the following sections we consider several combinations of anisotropies leading to important material properties, especially the domain concept.

9.2 Magnetic Domains

Magnetic samples much over 1,000 A in dimensions find it possible to lower their free energy by separating into several *magnetic domains*, in each of which the magnetization is uniformly directed. With this sort of arrangement, external fields can be eliminated. Adjacent domains will usually have magnetization directions displaced by 90 or 180° (Fig. 9.7). Within each domain, magnetization is directed so as to minimize anisotropy energy, i.e., along preferred axes. In the iron crystal described by the figure, these axes are mutually perpendicular ([001], etc.). Materials with uniaxial anisotropies (e.g., cobalt, or materials with induced anisotropy) have only a single axis, so that adjacent domains must be oppositely magnetized.

The domain properties are closely connected with the boundary regions, or *domain walls*, separating adjacent domains. Whereas in the figures these walls are drawn as lines, they are actually hundreds of lattice constants in thickness, with characteristic internal spin arrangements.

Bloch[1] was apparently the first to recognize some of the forms that domain walls could take. In a *Bloch wall* (Fig. 9.5), as a function of distance normal to the wall, each successive *plane* of spins is oriented at a slightly different angle to those adjacent to it so that the total change of direction of magnetization is comprised of a large number of small angles between adjacent spins. Because of exchange coupling $(-2J\mathbf{s}_1 \cdot \mathbf{s}_2/\hbar^2)$, energy must be supplied to spins to produce this alignment. Because of exchange energy, therefore, the domain wall *prefers to be as wide as possible* so that the "twist" is distributed over many atomic layers. The orientations of the domains separated by the wall are determined by crystalline or other anisotropies. Spins in the wall are in *nonpreferred* orientations with respect to this anisotropy. The anisotropy contribution to wall energy is therefore a minimum *when the wall is of zero width* and is more or less proportional to wall width. Since the two energy contributions work in

[1] F. Bloch, *Z. Phys.*, **74**:295–335 (1932).

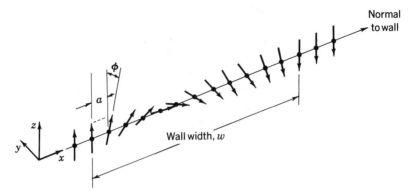

Figure 9.5 A simple Bloch domain wall, wherein the magnetization, as one passes through the wall, rotates about a normal to the wall plane. The actual angular "twist" between spins of adjacent atoms (ϕ) in a real wall may be of the order of one degree.

opposition, the actual wall width will be that at which the *sum* of the anisotropy contributions is a minimum.

A detailed analysis of the variation of the spin orientations in a wall can be carried out by the use of (8.46), with an appropriate torque representing anisotropy. This leads to a nonlinear differential equation which requires numerical solution; we shall make use of a more approximate theory, which yields comparable results. The model employed is a simple cubic structure of lattice constant a, with one-electron spin on each atom. A Bloch wall (Fig. 9.5) will be assumed to lie normal to the z axis, so that an entire (100) *plane* of atoms has each spin orientation. The wall will be assumed to distribute a 180° "twist" of the spins *uniformly* over width w, so that *each* angle between in adjacent spin planes is $\phi = 180°/(w/a)$. Each spin in a given plane couples to four others in its own plane, but with no extra energy involved here, because the atoms all have like-directed spins. Each atom, however, couples to one nearest-neighbor atom in each of the two adjacent planes. The exchange energy involved here is $J(1 - \cos \phi)$, since the energy required to make $\phi = 180°$ is defined as $2J$, where J is the exchange energy. The total exchange energy in unit area of the wall represents one such pair-interaction-energy term from *each* of the $(1/a^2) \times (w/a)$ atoms. The energy in the wall due to exchange is, per unit area,

$$E_{\text{ex}} = \frac{Jw}{a^3} (1 - \cos \phi) \cong \frac{Jw}{2a^3} \phi^2 \qquad (9.8)$$

for the small ϕ appropriate to the expected solution, for which $\cos \phi \approx 1 - \phi^2/2$.

The anisotropy will be assumed to be of some origin having the form (9.6), with $\theta = 0$, $180°$ in the two adjacent domains. The preferred axis is thus the z axis of Fig. 9.5. The anisotropy energy appropriate to the first plane of reoriented spins will be $a^3 K_u \sin^2 \phi$ per atom, that of the second plane $a^3 K_u \sin^2 (2\phi)$, etc. The total anisotropy energy in the wall per unit area is therefore

$$E_{an} = K_u a \sum_{n=0}^{w/a} \sin^2 n\phi$$

which can be put into the integral form

$$E_{an} = K_u \int_0^w \sin^2 \frac{\pi x}{w} \, dx = \frac{K_u w}{2} \tag{9.9}$$

In the exchange energy, substituting $\phi = \pi a/w$ leads to an expression for total energy which is a function of w only:

$$E_{\text{wall}} = \frac{K_u w}{2} + \frac{\pi^2 J}{2wa} \tag{9.10}$$

The equilibrium wall width w is that giving the smallest wall energy, found by differentiating E_{wall} with respect to w:

$$\frac{dE_{\text{wall}}}{dw} = \frac{K_u}{2} - \frac{\pi^2 J}{2w^2 a} = 0$$

At equilibrium, therefore,

$$w = \pi \left(\frac{J}{K_u a}\right)^{\frac{1}{2}} \qquad E_{\text{wall}} = \pi \left(\frac{K_u J}{a}\right)^{\frac{1}{2}} \tag{9.11}$$

One-half of the wall energy is due to each energy term.

As a crude estimate of the values involved, let us assume $a = 2.5 \times 10^{-8}$ cm and $K_u = 5 \times 10^5$ ergs/cm^3. Using the approximate relation (8.27), let $J \cong kT_c/2z$ correspond to $T_c = 600°$K in this simple cubic ($z = 6$) model; $J = 6.9 \times 10^{-21}$ joule $= 6.9 \times 10^{-14}$ erg. Then

$$E_{\text{wall}} \cong 3.7 \text{ ergs/cm}^2 \qquad w \cong 1{,}000 \text{ A}$$

These values are comparable with experimental values, which may only be inferred from indirect measurements.

Many forms of domain walls are known to exist, as a result of special materials and configuration limitations.

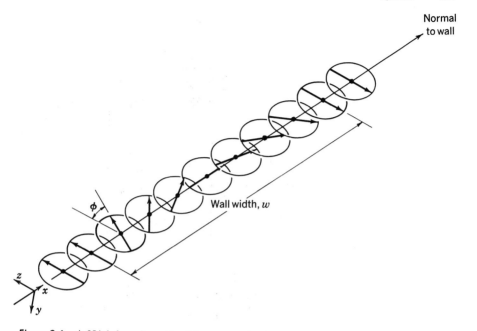

Normal
to wall

Wall width, w

ϕ

Figure 9.6   A Néel domain wall.   The magnetization remains in a plane.

Whereas the simple Bloch wall of Fig. 9.5 has magnetization directions which depart from a plane through the wall, in very thin ($\lesssim 800$ A) magnetic films the planar-shape anisotropy is so strong that a Néel wall (Fig. 9.6) has lower energy than a Bloch wall.   In single-crystal samples (e.g., Fig. 9.7), other variations are encountered, having different relations between the plane of rotation and a normal to the wall.

A macroscopic ferromagnetic specimen of centimeter dimensions may contain many thousands of domains.   The arguments of Sec. 9.5 show that above a critical particle size a multidomain configuration should have lower free energy than a single domain.   In large samples, subdivision into many small domains yields lower free energy due to stress anisotropy and magnetostriction.   In a large single crystal of iron, each domain is oriented very nearly along a [001] or equivalent axis, to minimize the crystalline anisotropy energy.   If, as in Fig. 9.7, *closure domains* exist at the ends of the sample, no magnetostatic energy term is present.   Yet, in a sample of centimeter dimensions, many small domains (of submillimeter dimensions) are observed.   Why are there not merely four domains, as in the small specimen of Fig. 9.19?   The culprit

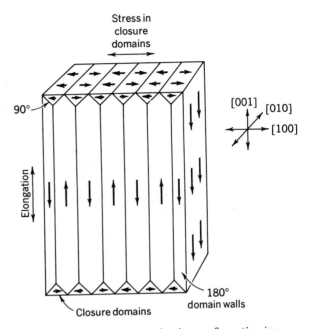

Figure 9.7   A possible magnetization configuration in a single iron crystal of millimeter dimensions. Each domain is magnetized parallel to a preferred direction of the crystalline anisotropy.

is another energy term which has thus far been neglected. As discussed in Sec. 9.6, the alignment of spins in a given direction produces magnetostrictive *strain* which attempts to *elongate* iron in a [001] direction of magnetization. Here, those domains running the length of the sample can elongate without constraint, but attempted expansion of the closure domains sets up *internal* stresses as shown. If the closure domains are large, the associated stress anisotropy [e.g., Eq. (9.5)] is large; further subdivision of domains, even with the addition of more domain-wall area, can yet reduce the *total* energy. Equilibrium-domain dimensions in an actual ferromagnet therefore depend on the magnetostriction elastic constants, the exchange energy, and crystalline anisotropy, as well as the exact shape of the sample. Meaningful domain calculations for practical materials are almost hopelessly complicated. In some typical bulk materials, domains are experimentally found to be of the order of 0.1 to 1.0 mm in average dimension. The *shapes* of magnetic domains vary

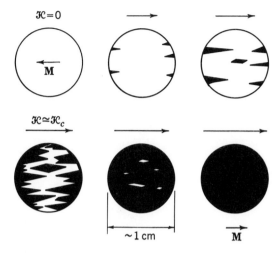

Figure 9.8 Magnetization reversal by domain-wall motion in a typical thin magnetic film, as field is increased in the direction opposite to the initial magnetization. Arrows show the strength of the applied field.

greatly with material, geometry, and environment. Commonly, domain boundaries are comprised of a number of planar wall sections, each section lying parallel or normal to crystalline or other anisotropy axes.

9.3 Domain-wall Motion

At frequencies up to a few hundred kilocycles, many magnetic materials alter their magnetization directions by the process of *domain-wall motion*.   As illustrated by Fig. 9.8, application of a magnetic field in a direction opposite to the remanent magnetization causes small reversed-magnetization domains to make themselves apparent.   As the field is increased, these grow, reaching a condition of zero *average* remanent magnetization at a field usually termed the coercive force $\mathcal{3C}_c$, and eventually expanding to encompass almost the entire sample. The figure represents the fairly simple situation in a thin magnetic film, where crystalline and stress anisotropies are almost zero, and uniaxial anisotropy [(9.6)] in the plane governs domain configuration.

Let us examine the characteristics of a domain wall moving under the influence of a magnetic field.   We take as an

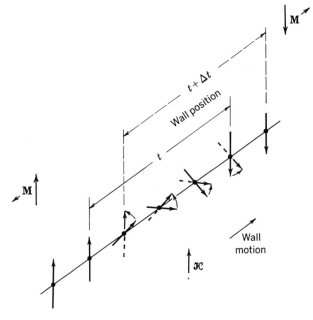

Figure 9.9   Motion of a domain wall in response to an
applied field.   The spin rotation advances the wall position
as shown (dashed) at $t + \Delta t$.

example a (180°) magnetic domain wall in a material having
only uniaxial anisotropy.   Since the magnetization prefers to
lie along a single axis, domains are oriented as shown in Fig.
9.9.   In the absence of any applied field, the energy of individual spins on the left of the wall is exactly the same as of
those on the right, since both are oriented along the preferred axis.   So long as the material is microscopically uniform, furthermore, the energy per unit area associated with
the wall [(9.11)] is independent of the wall location.   An exception must be made if the motion of the wall causes a change
in magnetostatic energy; if the sample is large, however, a
small wall motion should cause no appreciable change in the
magnetostatic energy.   If now a field $\mathcal{3C}$ is applied in the direction shown, spins on the right of the wall have higher energy
than those on the left.   The field interaction energy
$(-\mu_0 \mathcal{3C} \cdot \mathbf{M})$ makes it profitable for the wall to move to the
right.   This displacement requires 180° reversal of the orien-
tation of *each* spin as the wall passes by it.   The rate of

reversal of the spins is, however, limited by the viscous damping described in Sec. 8.8.   The faster a given spin reverses, the more energy is expended in the process.   The energy source "driving" the wall is the $2\mu_0\mathfrak{IC}M$ energy difference (per unit volume) between spins on opposite sides of the wall. The velocity of the wall depends directly on the energy available per unit displacement, and therefore on the applied field. To obtain a semiquantitative result, let us make use of the dynamic equation for spin motion in the form (8.36).

In Fig. 9.9, while the wall is passing a particular spin, the spin executes a change of angular orientation with time, approximated in the Bloch wall model of Fig. 9.5 by

$$\theta = \frac{\pi t}{\tau} \qquad 0 < t < \tau \tag{9.12}$$

where θ is the instantaneous angular orientation.   The wall thus begins passing over the spin at $t = 0$ and completes its passage at $t = \tau$.   In (8.36) the vector $d\mathbf{M}/dt$ is always at right angles to $\mathbf{M}$, simplifying the calculations.   In the present case the *magnitude* of the vector $d\mathbf{M}/dt$ is just $M\,d\theta/dt$, and therefore the magnitude of the loss torque T (per unit volume) is

$$T_{\text{loss}} = \frac{\pi\alpha M\mu_0}{\gamma_e\tau} \tag{9.13}$$

The energy dissipated owing to this damping torque is simply the integral of the torque over the angle:

$$W_{\text{loss}} = \int_0^\pi T_{\text{loss}}\,d\theta$$

Since $d\theta = \pi/\tau\,dt$,

$$W_{\text{loss}} = \frac{\mu_0}{\gamma_e}\int_0^\tau \frac{\pi^2\alpha M\,dt}{\tau^2} = \frac{\pi^2\alpha M\mu_0}{\gamma_e\tau} \tag{9.14}$$

This is presumed to be the loss *per unit volume* caused by uniform motion of a wall through the volume.   Because in reality the spins may precess for several cycles in performing the inversion of direction, this result may be somewhat in error; experimentally, wall-motion losses are several times higher.   In an applied field $\mathfrak{IC}$, this energy must equal the available (input) energy per unit volume, $2\mu_0\mathfrak{IC}M$; hence

$$\frac{\pi^2 M\alpha\mu_0}{\gamma_e\tau} = 2\mu_0\mathfrak{IC}M$$

If the wall width is w, the *velocity* v_w at which the wall moves is just w/τ; so, finally,

$$v_w = \frac{2w\gamma_e\mathfrak{K}}{\pi^2\alpha} \tag{9.15}$$

For the motion of 180° walls in nickel-iron films, for which

$$\alpha \cong 0.1 \qquad w \cong 1,000 \text{ A}$$

the wall velocity is $\sim$200 cm/sec *per oersted*, by Eq. (9.15). This means that with a 1-oe available field to drive the wall and domains of 1-mm dimensions, reversal by wall motion might require $\sim$10^{-3} sec, quite a slow process by comparison with the rotation process described in Sec. 9.4. We have here neglected the additional losses due to *eddy currents*. In a magnetic material which is also an electrical conductor, the time rate of change of magnetization which accompanies wall motion will, according to Maxwell's equations, induce electric fields proportional to the rate of magnetization change. These produce currents which flow in the material, with an additional loss which is also describable as a "viscous" loss, and change the constant in (9.15). To overcome this, magnetic materials are often used in the form of thin sheets (laminations) or ribbons (tape). In other cases, small powder particles may be compacted in such a way that the magnetic properties are little affected but the conductivity is materially reduced. Because of their small dimensions, thin magnetic films ($\sim$1,000 A thick) have negligible eddy currents and associated losses. This effect is of course almost totally absent in ferrites, which generally have very high resistivity.

In a homogeneous magnetic material, even the slightest magnetic field should produce motion of domain walls; hence one would expect that the field required to initiate wall motion would be almost zero. If, however, magnetic anisotropy *varies* along the path of a moving domain wall, the energy of the wall (which is a function of the anisotropy) is larger when the wall is in a region of high anisotropy energy and smaller in a region of low anisotropy energy. It will naturally prefer a low-energy location. In a very low field, a wall already in existence will be prevented from moving farther when it reaches a high-anisotropy region, as shown in Fig. 9.10. If the wall is to be driven across this barrier, the field must be raised high enough to impart to the spins in the high-anisotropy region sufficient energy ($2\mu_0 M\mathfrak{K}$) to increase the wall

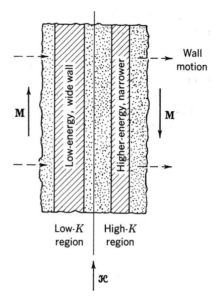

Figure 9.10   An inhomogeneous magnetic material requires a *coercive force*, for wall motion.   When a wall must advance into a high-anisotropy region, additional magnetic field is required, to provide the increased wall energy.

energy enough to let it pass the barrier.   If the anisotropy constant is K on one side and $K + \Delta K$ on the other, for example, the wall energy, by (9.11), must increase from $(\pi^2 JK/a)^{\frac{1}{2}}$ to $[\pi^2 J(K + \Delta K)/a]^{\frac{1}{2}}$ in a distance of travel of only $w \cong (\pi^2 J/aK)^{\frac{1}{2}}$.   The energy *per unit volume* which must be added, to move the wall, is therefore approximately

$$\left(\frac{\pi^2 J}{a}\right)^{\frac{1}{2}} \frac{(K + \Delta K)^{\frac{1}{2}} - K^{\frac{1}{2}}}{(\pi^2 J/aK)^{\frac{1}{2}}} \cong \frac{\Delta K}{2} \quad \text{for small } \Delta K/K$$

Letting $2\mu_0 M \mathfrak{K}_c = \Delta K/2$, the field required to "coerce" the wall into moving is

$$\mathfrak{K}_c \cong \frac{\Delta K}{4\mu_0 M} \tag{9.16}$$

This, then, should be the coercive field, or *coercive force*, of the material.   Equation (9.16) indicates that $\mathfrak{K}_c$ is lower in more uniform material.   Some nickel-iron-molybdenum alloys in the form of well-annealed thin tapes exhibit $\mathfrak{K}_c$ as low as ~ 0.01 oe.

If a field *exceeding* $\mathfrak{K}_c$ is applied, the excess of field will be available to drive the wall across the region.   When the wall later emerges from the high-anisotropy region into a lower-anisotropy region, wall motion can become very rapid.   The progress of the wall in the presence of a constant drive field is therefore very erratic. The magnetization along the applied-field axis as a function of time contains random jumps due to this erratic motion. This effect, which can be observed in the output of high-frequency transformers, is called *Barkhausen noise*. It has a broad spectrum in the kilocycle region.

The rate of magnetization reversal by domain-wall motion will be *zero* at fields less than the coercive force. Any *additional* field will produce an average wall velocity. The resulting wall motion takes place at an average velocity given by

$$v_w = \text{const} \times (\mathfrak{IC} - \mathfrak{IC}_c) \tag{9.17}$$

The distance a *single* domain wall must travel during *complete* magnetization reversal is determined by the constitution of the material and by the device configuration. In a given device, the average distance of wall motion required for reversal will usually be a small fraction of the dimensions of the device, of the order of a millimeter or less. With an average wall velocity v_w, the "switching time" required for complete magnetization reversal by wall motion will be of the approximate form

$$t_{\text{switching}} \propto \frac{S}{\mathfrak{IC} - \mathfrak{IC}_c} \tag{9.18}$$

where S is an empirical constant.

Domain-wall motion is ordinarily an irreversible process because of the losses incurred in moving walls past high-anisotropy regions. At very low applied fields, however, *reversible* wall motion can sometimes occur. If the variation of anisotropy energy with position is not abrupt but continuous, as in Fig. 9.11, a wall can be made to move in an applied field, to return reversibly (elastically) when the field is removed. Only a small change of magnetization can occur by this reversible motion, however, for there are bound to be *small-scale* "peaks and valleys" in the anisotropy which cannot be passed over without losses.

Another reversible effect occurring in many materials at low applied fields is *small-angle rotation* of the magnetization in a crystallite at fields lower than those necessary to initiate domain-wall motion. Since the preferred axes of the crystallites are usually randomly oriented with respect to the applied field, the field produces a torque on the spins in each domain, causing all the spins in each domain to rotate in unison, as

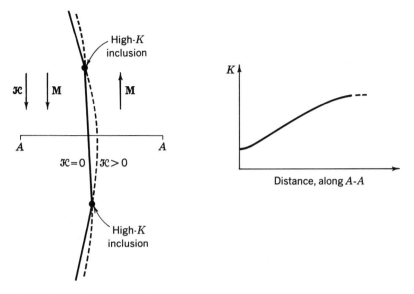

Figure 9.11 In a region where the anisotropy constant K is changing slowly, a wall may move reversibly within certain limits. The wall shown is "pinned" by two imperfections, so that it bulges reversibly with the application of field and returns when the field is removed.

described in Sec. 8.8. Since slower spin motions are required to produce a given magnetization change by rotation than by wall motion, the rotation process is less lossy. At higher drive fields, wall-motion effects can generally take place, so rotational change of **M** is generally limited to small angles.

In practical high-permeability ferromagnetic materials, magnetization reversal is a complex combination of these effects. Crystallite size is very important, for in polycrystalline material of high crystalline anisotropy and small crystallite size, each *crystallite* is a separate domain (Sec. 9.5). In simple materials such as iron or high-iron alloys, however, domain walls can extend over a number of crystallites in intimate contact. If the crystallites are larger than $\sim 1{,}000$ A, each may be composed of *several* domains. The preferred orientation of spins in each crystallite will be along one or more of the preferred axes of the crystallite (in iron [001] axes). An *unmagnetized* specimen might appear as in Fig. 9.12a, with zero net magnetization. The application of field initially produces slight rotation of the crystallite magnetizations (region OA of the hysteresis curve of Fig. 9.13), followed

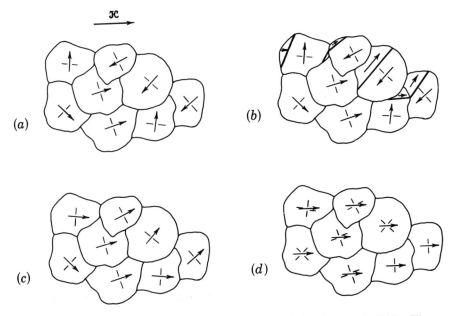

Figure 9.12   The magnetization of a polycrystalline sample by a magnetic field.   The crystalline axes, for convenience, are shown as if oriented in the plane.

at $\mathcal{3C} \gtrsim \mathcal{3C}_c$ by motion of the domain walls across the crystallites (Fig. 9.12b).   This is region AB of the B-$\mathcal{3C}$ characteristic.   At B, the crystallites have magnetizations oriented along the preferred crystalline axis *nearest* in direction to the field direction (Fig. 9.12c).   At even higher fields, the magnetization in each domain is further rotated until at C it is fully aligned with the field (Fig. 9.12d).   When the field is removed, however, the situation again returns to that of point B (Fig. 9.12c).   Application of a reversed field produces mostly slight rotations $(B'-D)$ until the coercive force is reached in the opposite direction.   Then the walls move to a condition E, equivalent to B, but with opposite orientations. Once the material has been magnetically cycled several times, it will repeat a *major hysteresis loop*, as shown.

Various magnetic materials display to different degrees the processes of domain rotation and wall motion, with different degrees of homogeneity and crystalline anisotropy.   These are apparent to some degree in the B-$\mathcal{3C}$ characteristics. These may be taken at various peak flux densities, yielding a *saturation hysteresis loop* plus more or less ellipsoidal *minor*

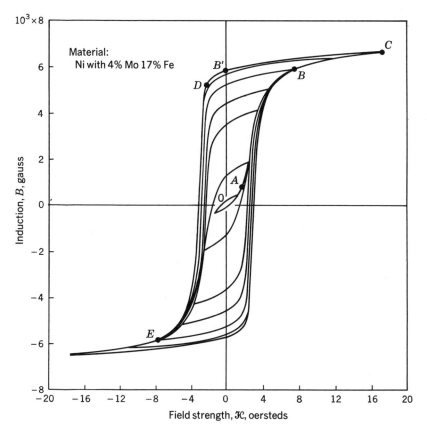

Figure 9.13 Hysteresis curves of 4-79 Permalloy material, a high-permeability alloy with a considerably more "square" loop than high-iron materials. (*From Bozorth's "Ferromagnetism," Copyright 1951, D. Van Nostrand Co., Inc., Princeton, N.J.*)

loops (Fig. 9.13). The area enclosed by a loop is equivalent to an energy loss (hysteresis loss) per unit volume per magnetic cycle. This loss decreases with decreasing field amplitude, until finally, at low fields, the loop area reduces to nearly zero. This is an indication of reversible domain-wall motion and/or small-angle rotation. In applications such as low-level transformers used in communications, a large $(B/\mathcal{3C})_{\mathcal{3C}\to 0} = \mu_i$ (initial permeability) is desirable. In some special-purpose magnetic materials comprising largely iron, nickel, and molybdenum (e.g., supermalloy), initial permeability may be as high as 10^6. This requires not only high homogeneity, but also a near-zero crystalline anisotropy and magnetostriction, the latter to prevent stress anisotropies in normal handling of the material.

An important group of magnetic materials is based on iron containing of the order of 5 per cent silicon. In power transformers and rotating machinery, the magnetic material must offer (1) high saturation magnetization, (2) low losses, and (3) low cost. On the basis of cost and flux capacity, iron is the best available material. The hysteresis losses, while higher than in some expensive specialized alloys, may be kept to about 1 to 2 watts/lb at 60-cycle operation. Addition of a few per cent of silicon substantially reduces eddy-current losses by increasing resistivity of iron (Fig. 3.19), without serious reduction of magnetization. Further additions of tiny amounts of other elements (e.g., phosphorus) permit easier rolling of the material into the usual thin laminations.[1]

Although at low frequencies the usual transformer core materials are iron or nickel-iron alloys, in many applications specially processed manganese-magnesium-zinc *ferrite* materials offer smaller size and lower cost, as well as substantially higher switching speeds. These materials are pressed into desired (often, toroidal) shape and high-temperature-fired to produce the finished component. Most such cores are employed in flux-switching modes of operation. Because of the "square" B-$\mathcal{3C}$ characteristics, little flux change is observed until the current through the core reaches a value $(-\mathcal{3C}_c \times$ flux-path length). Flux then switches abruptly to the opposite direction around the core, producing thereby a rapidly rising voltage, $d\phi/dt$, in each conductor which passes through the hole in the core.

Figure 9.14a illustrates the important application of small ferrite cores as digital-computer memory elements. The direction of flux signifies the memory state (zero or one, clockwise or counterclockwise). Two separate conductors carry drive currents I_x and I_y, each passing through many such cores, but two *particular* conductors only passing through a single core. When each conductor carries current of the same value and direction, the critical field $\mathcal{3C}_c$ is exceeded and the magnetization can reverse, if it was initially in a state

[1] The detailed technology of all metal and alloy magnetic materials is discussed in great detail, along with complete magnetic properties, in R. M. Bozorth's monumental book, "Ferromagnetism," D. Van Nostrand Company, Inc., Princton, N.J., 1951.

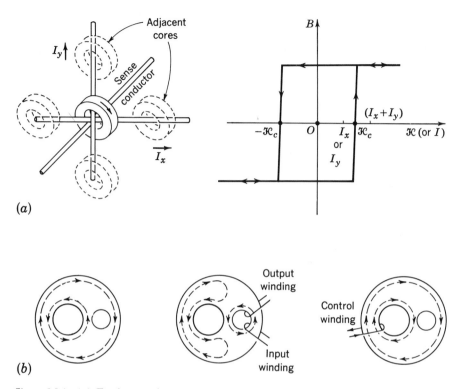

(a)

(b)

Figure 9.14 (a) Ferrite core in orthogonal drive-conductor geometry used for digital-computer memory applications; drive currents I_x and I_y are chosen such that core may not reverse its direction of magnetization until currents flow in both conductors. (b) Flux configurations in the transfluxor (described in the text).

opposing the drive-current field.   When only a single current flows, or the two currents are in opposing directions, no switching can occur.   The "state" of a core is sensed by passing currents through the two conductors in a given direction and ascertaining if switching occurs.   If so, a third conductor also has induced voltage, which is amplified in a "sense" amplifier.   It is then desirable to reset to the original state by passing reversed currents through both conductors.   Memories using this or similar schemes may contain millions of separate cores, each representing one binary digit of information.   Similar cores are also used, with primary and secondary windings, to transform voltage or current.   Since flux changes are not linear functions of applied magnetic field, these transformers are best suited for handling *pulses*.

More complex functions can be performed using ferrite cores of more complex shapes. The core sketched in Fig. 9.14*b* is termed a *transfluxor*.[1] In the situation shown on the left, no *net* flux passes through the left-hand "leg" of the core. The material surrounding the right-hand aperture is magnetized in a clockwise sense. A drive current in the right aperture can reverse the flux around the aperture to produce the situation shown in the center, simply by producing field exceeding $\mathfrak{IC}_c$ around the aperture. When the right-hand drive current is reversed, the situation returns roughly to that shown in the left-hand sketch. If, now, a current is passed through the left-hand aperture sufficient to produce the flux situation shown on the right, current in the right-hand aperture may no longer switch the flux around the aperture, unless the field is big enough to switch an *outer* flux path, a much longer path. In the state shown in the central sketch, the right-hand aperture is used as a pulse transformer, with an input and an output winding. In the right-hand situation, the pulse transformer is "blocked." Intermediate positions may be obtained by careful control of the current in the left-hand aperture, so that the device can be viewed as a transformer of controllable coupling.

The magnetization reversal in these ferrite cores, at fields of the order $\mathfrak{IC}_c \rightarrow 2\mathfrak{IC}_c$, can be described as wall-motion processes. At higher fields, however, other processes begin to play a part, and curves similar to the thin-film switching curve of Fig. 9.15 are observed. The inverse of the slope of the linear portion of the curve is defined, in the manner described by (9.18), as the *switching coefficient S*. Properly formulated ferrite switching cores have values of S as low as 0.5 oe-μsec.

9.4 Magnetization Rotation

In the wall-motion process, the viscous-damping forces limit the speed of magnetization changes. When the magnetization of the sample rotates simultaneously, damping is no longer a serious limitation. Switching speeds of the order of 10^{-9} sec may be realized in some materials, even at fields of only a few oersteds.

Figure 9.15 is a typical experimental magnetic switching-speed characteristic (as a function of drive field) observed in a thin magnetic film. The curve consists of three more or less

---

[1] Cf. J. A. Rajchman and A. W. Lo, *Proc. IRE*, **44**:321 (1956).

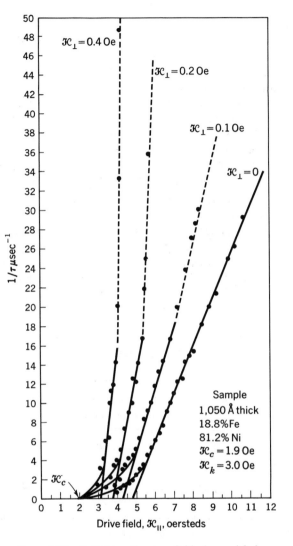

Figure 9.15 Switching time vs. fields for a nickel-iron thin film, showing three characteristic regions. Application of a field component $\mathfrak{K}_\perp$ makes M lie slightly oblique to the drive field $\mathfrak{K}_\parallel$, increasing the torque on the spins. [*From F. B. Humphrey and E. M. Gyorgy, J. Appl. Phys.*, **30**:935 (1959).]

well defined regions and is similar to those obtained for ferrite bulk materials. Just above the coercive force $\mathfrak{IC}_c$, it represents wall motion, where by (9.18) the reciprocal of the switching time should be proportional to $\mathfrak{IC} - \mathfrak{IC}_c$. At much larger fields, the curve is a straight line representing viscous-damped rotation of the sample as more or less a single domain. Here the slope is much steeper. In the intermediate region, the reversal is partly rotational and partly due to wall motion.

The best example of domain-rotational magnetization reversal occurs in magnetic thin films, ferromagnetic alloys (usually $\sim$81 per cent nickel, 19 per cent iron) typically $\sim$1,000 A in thickness. These layers can have only a single domain through their thickness, though there may be several domains covering the surface of a film of millimeter dimensions. The magnetization, because of the film's thinness, is strongly confined to the film plane by a shape anisotropy of the form (9.4). Such films normally are given an induced uniaxial anisotropy (9.6) by a magnetic field applied during deposition. The free energy of a film, with **M** in the film plane, is just the sum of interaction terms due to the uniaxial anisotropy and an applied field:

$$E = -\mu_0 \mathfrak{IC} \cdot \mathbf{M} + K_u \sin^2 \phi \tag{9.19}$$

Here ϕ measures the angle by which the magnetization deviates from a preferred axis ($\phi = 0, 180°$). The applied magnetic field is most usefully separated into a component parallel to the preferred axis ($\mathfrak{IC}_\parallel$) and a perpendicular component ($\mathfrak{IC}_\perp$), both in the film plane. Then per unit volume of the material,

$$E = -\mu_0 \mathfrak{IC}_\parallel M \cos \phi - \mu_0 \mathfrak{IC}_\perp M \sin \phi + K_u \sin^2 \phi \tag{9.20}$$

The usual B-$\mathfrak{IC}$ or M-$\mathfrak{IC}$ curve relates a field component $\mathfrak{IC}$ with the component of magnetization in the same direction. In a film, such a characteristic may be taken with the field at any angle to the preferred uniaxial axis. Two cases of most interest are $\mathfrak{IC}_\perp = 0$ and $\mathfrak{IC}_\parallel = 0$. The former ($B_\parallel$ versus $\mathfrak{IC}_\parallel$) is termed an "easy-axis" characteristic. We establish the equilibrium magnetization in the direction of $\mathfrak{IC}_\parallel$ ($M_\parallel = M \cos \phi$) by setting equal to zero the derivative of E with respect to ϕ:

$$\mu_0 \mathfrak{IC}_\parallel M \sin \phi + 2K_u \sin \phi \cos \phi = 0 \tag{9.21}$$

Two solutions exist ($\sin \phi = 0$ and $\cos \phi = -\mu_0 \mathfrak{K}_\| M/2K_u$). The former corresponds to an energy minimum, the latter to a maximum. What goes on may better be appreciated by plotting the free energy as a function of ϕ for various fields (Fig. 9.16a). With ϕ at an initial value of 180° and positive $\mathfrak{K}_\|$, $\phi = 180°$ continues to be a *local* minimum for the free energy until $\mathfrak{K}_\| > 2K_u/\mu_0 M$, at which point the magnetization reverses rapidly to $\phi = 0$. After that, only when $\mathfrak{K}_\| < -2K_u/\mu_0 M$ can reversal again occur. Only two equilibrium positions of ϕ exist in this case, 0 and 180°. The M-$\mathfrak{K}$ characteristic is the rectangular loop (1) shown in Fig. 9.16b.

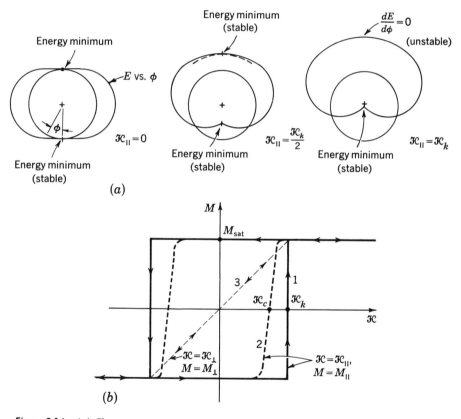

(a)

(b)

Figure 9.16 (a) Energy versus ϕ contours for three different values of field applied parallel to the easy axis. (A constant has been added to E to permit it to remain positive for all fields shown.) (b) Resulting M-$\mathfrak{K}$ or B-$\mathfrak{K}$ "loops": (1) ideal easy-axis loop; (2) observed easy-axis loop, due to wall-motion switching at $\mathfrak{K}_c < \mathfrak{K}_k$; (3) ideal hard-axis loop; observed loops have rounded shape at $\mathfrak{K} = \mathfrak{K}_k$.

When the magnetic field is applied in the "hard" direction, $\mathcal{3C} = \mathcal{3C}_\perp$, the field produces torque tending to align the magnetization parallel to itself. With $\mathcal{3C}_\parallel = 0$, the condition comparable with (9.21) is

$$\frac{\partial E}{\partial \phi} = -\mu_0 \mathcal{3C}_\perp M \cos \phi + 2K_u \sin \phi \cos \phi x = 0 \qquad (9.22)$$

This has a solution $\cos \phi = 0$, which corresponds to an energy maximum, with the energy minima given by $\mu_0 \mathcal{3C}_\perp M = 2K_u \sin \phi$. The corresponding magnetization, $M \sin \phi$, is

$$M_\perp = M \sin \phi = \frac{\mu_0 \mathcal{3C}_\perp M^2}{2K_u} \qquad (9.23)$$

The $M_\perp$-$\mathcal{3C}_\perp$ characteristic is therefore a straight line up to saturation at $M \sin \phi = M$. The curve saturates at the field

$$\mathcal{3C}_\perp = \frac{2K_u}{\mu_0 M} = \mathcal{3C}_k \qquad \left(\text{cgs}: \mathcal{3C}_k = \frac{2K_u}{M} \right). \qquad (9.24)$$

the same point at which the easy-axis curve switches. In practice, the ideal easy-axis curve may not be observable, for if the coercive force $\mathcal{3C}_c$ for wall-motion switching is lower than $\mathcal{3C}_k$, only the wall-motion process occurs.

Figure 9.17 illustrates how the magnetization is switched in computer memory applications of such films. Two conductors produce field components $\mathcal{3C}_\parallel$ and $\mathcal{3C}_\perp$ in the film plane. Application of $\mathcal{3C}_\perp > \mathcal{3C}_k$ first causes ϕ to become 90°; then subsequent application of a small $\mathcal{3C}_\parallel$ moves ϕ to one side or the other from 90°. When $\mathcal{3C}_\perp$ is removed, the only equilibrium orientation available to the magnetization is the one *nearer* to the direction of the applied $\mathcal{3C}_\parallel$. This orientation may be $\phi = 0$ or $\phi = 180°$, representing two different memory states.

While in thin films a viscous-damping mechanism controls the speed of response, this damping can be so small that *oscillations* of the magnetization about its equilibrium position establish a switching-time limit. These oscillations are observed to be damped with a time constant of the order of 10^{-8} sec.

Small-angle rotation is the principle of operation of ferrimagnets at megacycle frequencies, as described in Sec. 8.9. Since these ferrites may exhibit substantial RF permeability at reasonable losses in the radio frequency through UHF

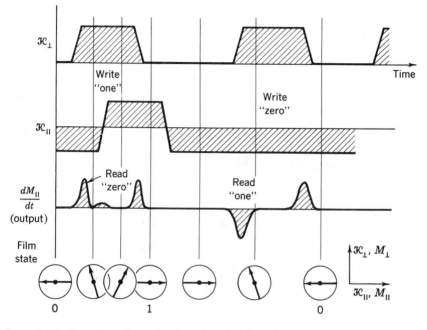

Figure 9.17   Operation of rotational-mode switching thin films in computer memory applications.   Fields in easy and hard directions are applied in sequence to place magnetization along a desired easy-axis direction.   The field sequence is arranged to promote rotation of magnetization and inhibit wall motion.   The small circles show the direction of **M** at each instant, in the film plane.

ranges, they improve efficiency of small-signal high-frequency transformers and inductors.   Figure 9.18 illustrates the RF properties of a series of nickel-zinc ferrites of different compositions.   If one is willing to settle for a permeability of 100 or less, values of $Q(\mu''/\mu')$ of more than 100 may be realized at 1 Mc/sec.

In RF and microwave ferrite applications, one would usually prefer the ferrimagnetic resonance frequency ω_0 to be controlled solely by an applied static magnetic field.   In the presence of magnetic anisotropies, however, resonance is obtained even without a field.   Consider, for example, a material having uniaxial anisotropy (9.6).   With the equilibrium magnetization direction in the z axis ($\theta = 0$), any displacement of magnetization through an angle θ from the preferred axis yields a restoring torque

$$T = \frac{dE}{d\theta} = K_u \sin 2\theta \tag{9.25}$$

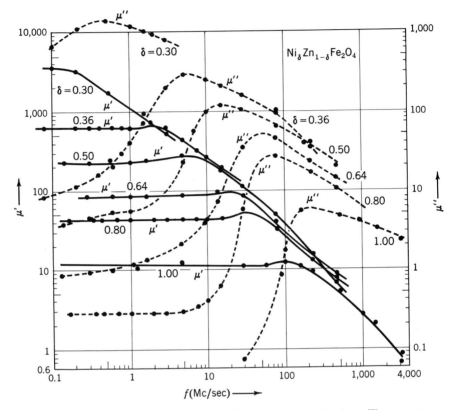

Figure 9.18   High-frequency linear permeability of nickel-zinc ferrite.   The resonance is due to internal anisotropy.   Addition of nickel raises the resonance frequency, lowers low-frequency permeability and losses.   (*From J. Smit and H. P. J. Wijn, "Ferrites," p. 269, John Wiley & Sons, Inc., New York, 1959.*)

To employ the vector spin-dynamics equations, it is necessary to represent such a torque in vector form.   We may do so by observing that for *small* deviations from the preferred axis, $T = 2K_u \sin \theta$.   This has the form of a vector (cross) product; since the torque on the spins is directed so as to return $\mathbf{M}$ to the preferred axis, it may be expressed as

$$\mathbf{T}_{\text{anisotropy}} \cong \frac{2K_u}{M} \mathbf{M} \times 1_z \qquad (9.26)$$

The total torque, in the presence of the anisotropy plus a field $\mathfrak{IC} = 1_z \mathfrak{IC}$, is the sum of (9.26) and (8.32):

$$\mathbf{T} = \mu_0 \left(\mathfrak{IC} + \frac{2K_u}{\mu_0 M} \right) (\mathbf{M} \times 1_z) \qquad (9.27)$$

When spin-dynamics equations are set up, in this case the gyromagnetic resonance frequency will no longer be simply $\gamma_e \mathfrak{K}$, but

$$\omega_0 = \gamma_e \left(\mathfrak{K} + \frac{2K_u}{\mu_0 M} \right) \tag{9.28}$$

Reversal of the magnetic field will reduce the anisotropy-produced resonant frequency, provided of course that the magnetization *remains* directed at $\theta = 0$. With K_u as large as 2×10^6 ergs/cm³ and $M = 500$ (cgs) for cobalt ferrites, the "built-in" resonance due to anisotropy may be above 10,000 Mc/sec. The anisotropy in nickel-zinc ferrite compositions shows up clearly in Fig. 9.18 as the existence of a built-in resonance which is a function of composition. High internal anisotropies are usually avoided in polycrystalline microwave ferrite applications, for the *random orientations* of the crystallites and/or domains will cause a substantial spread in the apparent resonance. At the lower frequencies, there is also added loss due to partial wall-motion processes. It is, in fact, difficult to build an efficient microwave isolator or circulator in the range below $\sim$1,000 Mc because of the natural breadth of ferrimagnetic resonance of polycrystalline materials (evident in Fig. 9.18). With a condition of operation requiring but little *applied* field, the material may become partially demagnetized, leading to increase of loss and breadth of the resonance.

An important advantage of single-crystal ferrimagnetic materials is that the anisotropy of the crystal is more uniform and therefore contributes a constant term to the resonance frequency. Accordingly, sharply resonant devices are possible, for example, using yttrium–iron garnet crystals.

9.5 Small-particle Magnets

The properties of small ferro- or ferrimagnetic particles are very different from those of large crystals. This can best be understood by examining two possible domain configurations in a small cubical piece of iron, a model which is commonly employed.[1] Figure 9.19 shows the particle in a single-domain configuration and in a four-domain configuration. Only the single-domain configuration has magnetostatic energy (field outside the cube itself). A rough estimate of this energy is

[1] Cf. Bozorth, *op. cit.*, p. 830.

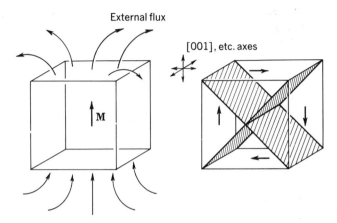

External flux

[001], etc. axes

Figure 9.19   Two possible configurations of magnetization of a small iron cube. The magnetic free energy of the configuration on the left (one domain) is due to the external magnetic fields produced externally; that of the four-domain configuration, to the domain walls.

found by using the magnetostatic energy appropriate to an ellipsoid, from (9.2). The free energy E_1 of the single-domain particle is therefore of the order of $E_1 = \mu_0(M^2\mathfrak{D}/2) \times$ volume. The most reasonable approximation for depolarization factor is that for a sphere ($\mathfrak{D} = \frac{1}{3}$):

$$E_1 \cong \frac{\mu_0 M^2 t^3}{6} \tag{9.29}$$

where t is the cube side.

The four-domain particle, on the other hand, has no demagnetizing field acting on the spins, since no flux emanates from the particle. It does, however, have the surface energy associated with the internal domain walls. The particular four-domain configuration has no energy contributions from magnetostrictive stresses (Sec. 9.6). The only energy contribution, therefore, is the wall energy

$$E_4 = 2^{\frac{3}{2}}t^2 E_w \tag{9.30}$$

Since the energy E_4 varies as t^2, while E_1 varies as t^3, *larger particles* must prefer the four-domain configuration. The critical particle size at which the two configurations have equal energy is

$$t_c \cong \frac{12\sqrt{2}\,E_w}{\mu_0 M^2} \tag{9.31}$$

Critical single-domain particle sizes, according to this theory, are in the vicinity of a few hundred angstroms for most magnetic materials. Though, clearly, the ideal wall structure suggested in Fig. 9.19 could not occur in a particle too small to contain a wall of the typical width calculated in (9.11), experiments show that particles less than $\sim$1,000 A do behave as *single domains*.

If a particle is incapable of containing domain walls, the wall-motion magnetization-reversal process described in Sec. 9.3 cannot apply. Magnetization can change only by rotation of **M** *in the entire particle*. This means that the pertinent magnetic field for reversal is [as described by (9.24)] of the order of $\mathcal{3C}_k = 2K/\mu_0 M$, with K the anisotropy constant. In finely powdered iron, which in bulk form has a domain-wall coercive force of the order of 1 oe, magnetization reversal required experimental fields of the order of 500 oe (while $2K_1/\mu_0 M \cong 2 \times 4 \times 10^5/2 \times 10^3 = 400$ oe). The anisotropy of cobalt is about ten times larger. The widely used alnico (aluminum-nickel-cobalt plus copper) permanent-magnet materials actually are not homogeneous, but consist of very small magnetic crystals separated by nonmagnetic regions. Accordingly, the magnetic regions act like fine particles and have appropriately high coercive forces of 500 to 1,000 oe.

While properly separated small particles in *any* orientation will show a high coercive force, random orientation means that without applied fields the full saturation magnetization is not available: the B-$\mathcal{3C}$ characteristic will have a "rounded" shape, like Fig. 9.13, as contrasted with Fig. 9.16. When applied magnetic fields approach no more than perhaps one-half the coercive force (in a direction opposite to the average direction of magnetization) some particles will reverse their magnetization. This may lead, after further cycling of the demagnetizing field, to serious deterioration of the remanent magnetization, which must be allowed for in any application where there is a chance of field variation. This limitation is, to a large extent, overcome in *oriented* magnets like Alnico V, where additional *uniaxial* anisotropy is induced by a heat-treatment in a magnetic field (in the vicinity of 600°C). The hysteresis characteristic of oriented alnico is very nearly rectangular in the direction of the anisotropy (Fig. 9.20.)

Since in "permanent magnets" the chief goals are to attain high coercive force and/or high remanent magnetiza-

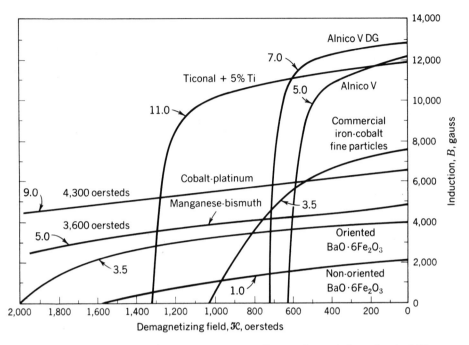

Figure 9.20   Demagnetization curves, corresponding to the second quadrant of Fig. 9.13, for a variety of high-coercive materials.   The number at the knee of each curve indicates the energy products, in millions of gauss-oersteds.   [*After J. J. Becker, Metall. Rev.,* **7**:371 (1962).]

tion, the ultimate would be achieved if one could at the same time align the crystallites with their crystalline preferred axes parallel to the desired field direction, while adding shape anisotropy by giving them the form of needlelike particles. This ideal has not been reached, but in certain ferrimagnetic oxides crystallites can be aligned to develop extremely high coercive forces, as oriented small-particle magnets.   The material $BaFe_{12}O_{19}$, having a *hexagonal* crystal structure, has an extremely strong crystalline anisotropy in the c axis of the crystallites.   Finely ground material takes the form of platelets whose large direction (typical of many hexagonal crystals) is *normal* to the c axis.   This prevents the additional benefit of shape anisotropy, but the crystalline anisotropy is very large.   This powder is pressed into a firm mass at room temperature in the presence of a field of the order of 10,000 oe. The platelets actually move so as to align themselves in this field.   After a carefully controlled sintering process to bind

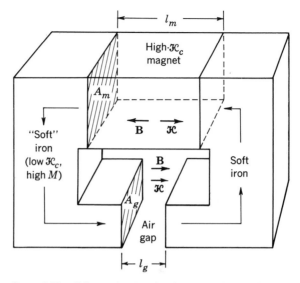

Figure 9.21   Schematic of a simple magnetic circuit to produce magnetic flux density in the air gap. The magnetic flux density and field are opposite in direction only in the high-coercive magnet, which serves the driving force of the circuit.

the mass together, the resultant magnet has so strong an anisotropy that its coercive force may be of the order of 1,500 oe.   Even higher coercive forces may be obtained in bismuth-manganese and platinum-cobalt alloys, characterized by high crystalline anisotropy which may be oriented by suitable heat-treatment.   Such highly processed materials, particularly the platinum-cobalt alloys, can be extremely expensive, however.

In typical applications, these so-called "permanent magnets" provide static magnetic flux in air or a *magnetic circuit*. A representative circuit is shown in Fig. 9.21.   A low-coercive material of sufficiently high magnetization to carry the flux density of the permanent magnet (e.g., soft iron) connects the permanent magnet magnetically to an air gap.   By Maxwell's equations, since the line integral of field around a closed path equals the current passing through it, the summation of $\mathfrak{K} \cdot d\mathbf{l}$ terms around the circuit will be zero.   If we can neglect the contribution of the connecting elements, this gives $\mathfrak{K}_g l_g = -\mathfrak{K}_m l_m$, where the subscripts refer to gap and magnet.   Since the magnetic flux Φ ($= B \times$ area) is common to both elements,

$B_g A_g = B_m A_m$; the magnetic description of the air gap is simply $B_g = \mu_0 \mathcal{H}_g$. By combination of the field and flux relations,

$$\mathcal{H}_m = -\frac{1}{\mu_0} \frac{l_g A_m}{l_m A_g} B_m \tag{9.32}$$

The negative $\mathcal{H}_m$ indicates that the magnet operates *in the second quadrant of its B-$\mathcal{H}$ characteristic* (Fig. 9.20). The magnetic stored energy $\mu_0 \mathcal{H}_g{}^2 A_g lg/2$ in the gap can, by the same relations, be shown equal to

$$W = \frac{\mu_0 B_m \mathcal{H}_m A_m l_m}{2} \tag{9.33}$$

Accordingly, to produce the most useful flux density in the largest volume, the magnet must be operated at a large *energy product* $B_m \mathcal{H}_m$. The largest value of this product occurs just at the "knee" of the curve, but because of the danger of irreversible demagnetization, values of $-\mathcal{H}_m$ are kept somewhat smaller. While the largest values of energy product ($\sim 5 \times 10^6$ gauss-oe) are obtained in alnico materials, the largest useful coercive forces are obtained in ferrites, Bi-Mn, and Pt-Co. Higher saturation magnetization can be obtained in some materials of lower coercive force.

The choice of a particular magnetic material for flux-producing applications depends to a large extent on the geometry and environment. Alnico materials cannot operate efficiently without external soft-iron circuits; such a magnet, faced with an air gap equal to its own length, and of equal area, produces by (9.32) a demagnetizing field large enough to carry it well away from saturation. This problem is overcome in the barium ferrimagnetic materials, because of their lower B and higher $\mathcal{H}_c$. Since the largest possible demagnetizing field is that experienced by a flat magnetic plate magnetized normal to its surface, $\mathcal{H}_{\text{demagnetizing}} = -M$, materials with values of M (or $4\pi M$, in cgs units) well below the coercive force $\mathcal{H}_c$ can remain almost fully magnetized even in the form of thin plates or films.

9.6 Magnetostriction

When a bar of polycrystalline iron is subjected to a magnetic field, its length parallel to the field first increases, then decreases at higher fields by a few parts per million. A bar of *nickel*

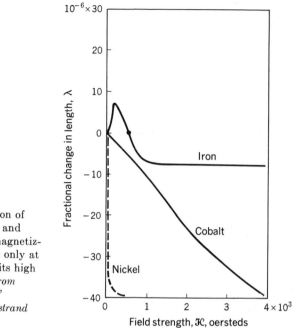

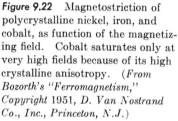

Figure 9.22 Magnetostriction of polycrystalline nickel, iron, and cobalt, as function of the magnetizing field. Cobalt saturates only at very high fields because of its high crystalline anisotropy. (*From Bozorth's "Ferromagnetism," Copyright* 1951, *D. Van Nostrand Co., Inc., Princeton, N.J.*)

under the same condition *shrinks* in length until magnetic saturation is reached. This variation, as a function of applied field, is illustrated by Fig. 9.22. Great experimental variations can occur, depending on the magnetic state of the material and the detailed crystalline state.

This *magnetostriction* is directly related to *stress anisotropy*, discussed in Sec. 9.1. Theoretical discussion is simplified if one thinks of a very small crystallite, where there can be no state of zero magnetization and the only variable is the *direction* of magnetization. In iron-group atoms, the electrons of the partially filled 3d subshell are just beneath the valence 4s subshell; in fact, their orbits actually extend through the 4s orbits. Atomic "dimensions" are thus determined to a considerable extent by the orbits of 3d electrons. There are, therefore, contributions to the crystal's binding energy from these electrons. The binding forces are also, not unexpectedly, dependent on the orientation of the spins. Thus a single-crystal single-domain iron particle cut accurately into spherical form at a temperature above the Curie point, when cooled, will become elongated along a [001] axis along which the spins are oriented. It will simultaneously contract in both of the perpendicular [001] directions; there will be a slight volume increase also, but this is a lower-order effect akin to the electrostriction which occurs in ordinary dielectrics.

If the magnetization of our small spherical iron crystal is reoriented along a [111] axis (*not* a preferred axis), the dimension parallel to the magnetization now *decreases*. This is a particular material property of iron. Nickel, unlike iron, *always* contracts in the direction of the magnetization, most substantially when the magnetization is oriented in the [001] directions, and least in the [111] directions.

In a polycrystalline ferromagnetic sample without special crystallite orientation, the magnetostrictive effect is more complex. Nickel contracts in the direction of the field for *any* orientation of crystallites, explaining its simple λ-$\mathcal{H}$ relation. Iron *expands* at *low fields*, which produce [001]-directed domains aligned in the general direction of the field (Fig. 9.12c). At higher fields, the magnetization in each crystallite throughout the sample rotates into parallelism with the field. In iron, the *majority* of all crystallite orientations *contract* in the field; hence at saturation the sample as a whole contracts. At very large fields, volume expansion becomes apparent, explaining the final expansion evident in the curve.

The simple stress-anisotropy energy [(9.5)] introduced earlier is based on an approximate model with *isotropic* magnetostriction. Elongation (or contraction) along the magnetization axis is assumed to be independent of crystallographic orientation; this model is much better suited to nickel and cobalt than iron. Consider again the small crystalline sphere ground to shape above T_c. At a temperature below T_c, a material with $\lambda_s > 0$ will be slightly *elongated* along the axis of **M**. It will likewise become foreshortened along the axis of **M** if $\lambda_s < 0$. The shape of the resulting *spheroidal* crystal may be expressed in terms of the distance l from its center to the surface:

$$l = A + B \cos^2 \theta \qquad |B| \ll A \tag{9.34}$$

Figure 9.23 depicts such a particle with $B < 0$ (e.g., nickel), placed between pressure pads which exert uniform pressure T. In the absence of magnetic fields which could rotate the axis of magnetization, the pressure will keep the magnetization aligned parallel to the pressure axis. If the magnetization is rotated by an *external magnetic* field, the elongation is no longer parallel to $\theta = 0$, and the *shape* of the particle

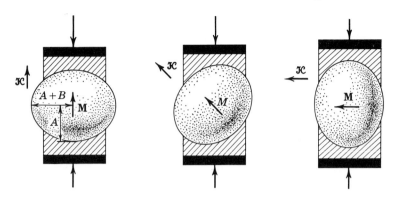

Figure 9.23   Model used in deriving the expression (9.36) for magneto-elastic energy.

changes as shown. The particle moves the pressure pads from a spacing $2(A + B)$ to a spacing $2(A + B \cos^2 \theta)$, all the time exerting constant pressure T. The work done E is $-2T(A + B) + 2T(A + B \cos^2 \theta)$ per unit area. Therefore the change in the free energy of the sample is $E = +2TB(1 - \cos^2 \theta) = 2TB \sin^2 \theta$.

The parameter B/A is related to the observable quantity λ_s. To evaluate B for a particular material, consider the way in which *polycrystalline* λ_s might be measured. The length of a large polycrystalline sample is measured at zero magnetization, and again at full saturation. In the first case, the domains are *randomly* oriented. The average $A + B\langle \cos^2 \theta \rangle$ over all θ is $(A + B/3)$. At saturation, on the other hand, all domains are magnetized in a common direction, and the length will increase in the ratio

$$\frac{\text{Length at saturation}}{\text{Length at zero magnetization}} = \frac{A + B}{A + B/3} = 1 + \lambda_s \qquad (9.35)$$

Therefore $\lambda_s = 2B/3A$.

The energy in the problem above is $E = 3\lambda_s TA \sin^2 \theta$. For a sample of *unit length*, $2A = 1$, one obtains approximately

$$E_{\text{stress}} = \tfrac{3}{2}\lambda_s T \sin^2 \theta \qquad \textit{per unit volume} \qquad (9.36)$$

This deviation is admittedly crude, and aimed clearly at the $\sin^2 \theta$ form of anisotropy energy. Theoretical expressions for λ and E_{stress} for *anisotropic* magnetostriction must contain direction cosines not only for the magnetization, but also for the directions of the crystal axes.

The relatively strong magnetostriction of nickel has applications in ultrasonic transducers. To obtain a maximum change in length, it is necessary to permit almost complete demagnetization, thus introducing large hysteresis losses, as well as eddy currents. The total change in dimensions is considerably less than in some ferroelectric materials, and the need to apply field parallel to the direction of desired motion limits device configurations. The mechanical sturdiness and simplicity of nickel transducers make up for these short-comings, in many applications. Furthermore, at the normal frequencies of operation, above the audible frequency range, it is generally easier to provide drive fields and power via current in a magnetizing coil than to obtain the high voltages required for ferroelectrics. Typical applications are in ultrasonic cleaning baths, where a liquid is vibrated by an attached magnetostrictive element. Ultrasonic abrasion-grinding tools are also based on powerful nickel transducers.

It is worth noting that cobalt ferrites may have magnetostriction constants of -6×10^{-4}, ten times larger than nickel. This suggests possible applications in acoustical or ultrasonic transducers.

PROBLEMS

9.1(a) What is the form of the cubic anisotropy term next above the K_2 term? Express as a function of the direction cosines, and define maximum- and minimum-energy orientations.

9.1(b) A single crystal of iron is cut into the form of a thin disk having (001) faces of circular cross section. It is placed in a *very strong* magnetic field directed in the plane and at an angle θ to the x axis. (1) Show that crystalline anisotropy in the form (9.7) causes a *torque* to be exerted on the disk, directed in the [001] direction, and in the amount $T = (K_1 \sin 4\theta)/2$ per unit volume. (2) Since the magnetically produced torque is given by (8.32) by $\mu_0 \mathfrak{IC} \times \mathbf{M}$, in the case of iron how much field must be applied to ensure that the magnetization direction is within 1° of the field direction?

9.1(c) An alloy having no crystalline anisotropy and a magnetization of $(4\pi M_s =)$ 14,000 gauss has a magnetostriction constant λ_s of $+15 \times 10^{-6}$. If this is formed into a small needle-shaped sample, what type and how large a force must be exerted on the sample in order that the magnetization should not prefer any particular orientation? Is this practical? (Explain.)

9.2(a) Show that in a material having [100], etc., preferred crystalline axes, i.e., like iron, 180° domain walls may lie in any plane parallel to a [100] direction and 90° walls in any plane parallel to a [110] direction, without having unequal normal components of **M** on the two sides of the wall. In a large crystal, why is it energetically unfavorable for large walls to be oriented so that the normal component of **M** is not continuous across the wall?

9.2(*b*) Domain walls observed in thin films (uniaxial anisotropy) have typically a "sawtooth" shape (Fig. 9.8). Show that such a shape reduces magnetostatic energy resulting from flux emanating from the surface of the film at the domain wall.

9.2(*c*) (1) Show that to first approximation the energies of Bloch and Néel walls in a uniaxial material should be the same. (2) Sketch a cross section of a thin film, normal to both the film plane and the wall plane, showing the dipole configuration associated with Bloch and Néel walls in section view. (Let the uniaxial axis be horizontal in your drawing.) Show the nature of the magnetic fields extending out of the film plane, due to the spins near the center of the wall, for each type of wall. (3) By free-energy concepts, explain why very thin films show preference for Néel-type walls. (4) If the wall width (in the film plane) is of the order of 500 A, what film thicknesses would you expect to exhibit each type of wall?

9.3(*a*) The wall-velocity theory of this section is based on simple viscous-damped motion of the spins. (1) With the awareness that real spin motion is oscillatory, describe qualitatively the spin-orientation variations which might be expected in very fast wall motion. (2) If the resonance of the spins is at 300 Mc/sec, estimate the order of magnitude of drive field (with the parameters given in the text example) at which these oscillatory effects might become apparent. (3) In the presence of this oscillatory motion, should wall velocity be greater or less, at given field, than as calculated in the text example? Explain.

9.3(*b*) Energy is required not only to move walls but to establish them. (1) Calculate and compare the energies required to form a wall and to move it 10^{-1} cm, at the velocity given in the text example. (2) On this basis, justify the fact that most magnetic materials form many walls and move them only a short distance in magnetic reversal, rather than moving a single wall.

9.3(*c*) (1) Give qualitative arguments to explain why less energy is required to generate a magnetic domain wall at a crystal surface than in the center of a uniform crystal. (2) Why is the nucleation energy at a grain boundary somewhat higher than at the surface?

9.4(*a*) Derive and plot the M-$\mathcal{3C}$ relation for rotational switching with field applied at 45° to the preferred axis of a uniaxial material (that is, $\mathcal{3C}_{\parallel} = 0.707\mathcal{3C}$, $\mathcal{3C}_{\perp} = 0.707\mathcal{3C}$).

9.4(*b*) What crystalline and material factors should lead to (1) high initial permeability in a magnetic material, (2) high maximum permeability $(dB/d\mathcal{3C}|_{max})$?

9.4(c) The natural resonance of a small spherical iron crystal may be calculated as for a uniaxial crystal in (9.28). (1) Show that the anisotropy torque here, however, is a function of the direction in which **M** is perturbed from a lowest-energy [001] direction. (2) Determine the frequencies associated with the maximum and minimum torques, using (9.7). (3) Would you expect such a crystal to show a very narrow resonance line width if cooled to near $0°K$?

9.5(a) A group of small single-crystal cobalt particles are dispersed in a nonmagnetic matrix. (1) If 70 per cent of the volume is filled by the cobalt particles, estimate the remanent magnetization, assuming the particles are not preferentially oriented. (See Prob. 7.6a for a clue.) (2) Sketch a likely B-$\mathfrak{IC}$ characteristic, estimating the value of $\mathfrak{IC}_c$ from the domain-rotation theory. Assume $K_u = 10^7$ ergs/cm³.

9.5(b) (1) Do the domain arguments, applied here to small ferromagnetic particles in a nonmagnetic matrix, apply also to the converse situation of nonmagnetic particles in a magnetic matrix? Explain. (2) How would one best select elements for such a material?

9.5(c) Round bar magnets of each of the materials described in Fig. 9.20 are magnetized along their length in an air path. Approximately what magnetic flux density is found emanating from the round faces after removing each bar from the magnetizing coil?

9.6(a) (1) How much force is exerted on an immobile object attached to a 1-in.-diameter nickel bar when the bar is taken from the unmagnetized state to saturation along its axis? (2) If such a bar is 10 in. long and attached to an elastic object, what is the maximum energy which can be transferred to the object by the magnetostrictive shrinkage of the bar? (3) If 25 per cent of the energy per cent transferred in this way is converted into useful work, estimate the transducer efficiency, neglecting eddy-current losses. (Use $\lambda_s = -40 \times 10^{-6}$, $s_{11} = 0.5 \times 10^{-6}$ kg/cm², and a hysteresis loss of 2,000 ergs/cm³ for full-cycle hysteresis. Note that a full field cycle produces two force pulsations.)

9.6(b) A "bimetal" strip is made by fastening together, face to face, two $\frac{1}{16}$- by 1-in. cross-section strips. Each is 12 in. long, one of iron, the other of nickel. They are initially unmagnetized. Estimate the deflection of the free end if one end is clamped and a field of more than 1,000 oe is applied along the axis.

GENERAL REFERENCES

The same general sources as cited in Chap. 8 are pertinent here. Those listed below deal specifically with domain properties.

Brown, W. F., Jr.: "Magnetostatic Principles in Ferromagnetism,"
North Holland Publishing Company, Amsterdam, 1962.

Kittel, C.: Physical Theory of Ferromagnetic Domains, *Rev. Mod.
Phys.*, **21**:541 (1949).   (An excellent basic treatment of domain
properties.)

Quartly, C. J.: "Square-loop Ferrite Circuitry," Iliffe Books, Ltd.,
London, and Prentice-Hall, Inc., Englewood Cliffs, N.J., 1962.
(An empirical description of ferrite switching circuits.)

10

Quantum electronics

10.1 Electron Energy-level Transitions

Whereas electronic motion in conductors involves *bands*, of states spaced almost infinitesimally in energy, and polarization phenomena involve mainly the slight perturbation of constant-energy states, in quantum-electronic phenomena the electrons make more or less discrete *transitions* from one energy level to another. While these transitions play roles in semi-conduction (Sec. 4.6), in quantum-electronic applications of semiconducting and insulating solids we are more interested in the energy absorbed, and especially that released in such transitions. Energy may be released in the form of phonons (heat) or photons. Photon energy obtained in this way has value in illumination and display devices; in certain devices a number of electrons may be made to release photon energy in synchronism with an electromagnetic field, making possible oscillators and amplifiers, from microwave through optical frequencies.

Let us consider first a simple example to illustrate the nature of electronic motion during a transition from one constant-energy state to another. An electron is located in a one-dimensional potential well with infinite sides (Fig. B.3). The *normalized* constant-energy solutions, according to the discussion in Sec. B.2, are

$$\psi_m = \left(\frac{2}{a}\right)^{\frac{1}{2}} \sin\left(\frac{\pi z}{a}\right) e^{-jE_m t/\hbar} \qquad m = 1, 2, 3, \ldots \tag{10.1}$$

where the well extends from $z = 0$ to $z = a$. The associated energy is

$$E_m = \frac{\hbar^2}{2m}\left(\frac{\pi m}{a}\right)^2 \tag{10.2}$$

In *any state*, the electronic wave function in the potential well is expandable as a series in the complete orthogonalized and normalized set of functions ψ_m. The coefficients a_m will in general be functions of time:

$$\psi(z,t) = \sum_m \psi_m a_m(t) \tag{10.3}$$

We postulate that, because of some perturbation in the particle energy, as produced for example by time-varying electric fields, the particle makes a transition from its initial state ψ_m to another state ψ_n. Although in exact treatments of such perturbations there are more subtle consequences, we shall presume that the given perturbation produces a time-dependent wave function of the form

$$\psi(z,t) = \psi_m \cos\frac{\pi t}{2\gamma} + \psi_n \sin\frac{\pi t}{2\tau} \tag{10.4}$$

At $t = 0$ the system is in state ψ_m, and at $t = \tau$, it is in the state ψ_n. Note that ψ is normalized, for the wave functions ψ_m and ψ_n are normalized and $\sum_m a_m(t)a_m^*(t) = 1$.

The *expectation* of the system energy may be evaluated, at time t, by using the operator $j\hbar(\partial/\partial t)$ in the usual expectation integral (cf. Sec. B.4):[1]

$$\langle H \rangle = j\hbar \int_0^a \psi^* \frac{\partial \psi}{\partial t}\, dz \tag{10.5}$$

Substituting from (10.4),

$$\langle H \rangle = j\hbar\left(-j\frac{E_m}{\hbar}\cos^2\frac{\pi t}{2\tau} - j\frac{E_n}{\hbar}\sin^2\frac{\pi t}{2\tau}\right) \tag{10.6}$$

We have neglected here the time derivative of the $\pi t/2\tau$ terms, in comparison with the rapidly varying $e^{-jEt/\hbar}$ terms.

$$\langle H \rangle = E_n + (E_m - E_n)\cos^2\frac{\pi t}{2\tau} \tag{10.7}$$

[1] There is some question as to the validity of expectation calculations during a transition, for it is unlikely that measurements could actually be made. Formally, however, there seems to be no objection.

The expected energy changes uniformly from E_m to E_n in the interval $0 \leq t \leq \tau$ (Fig. 10.1). We shall be interested only in this time interval.

We may also calculate the expectation of electron position $\langle z \rangle$. In the initial or in the final state

$$\langle z \rangle = \int_0^a z \psi_m^* \psi_m \, dz = \frac{a}{2} \tag{10.8}$$

i.e., the particle's average position is at the center of the well. During a transition, however,

$$\langle z \rangle = \int_0^a z \left[\psi_m^* \cos\left(\frac{\pi t}{2\tau}\right) \psi_n^* \sin\frac{\pi t}{2\tau} \right]$$
$$\times \left[\psi_m \cos\left(\frac{\pi t}{2\tau}\right) + \psi_n \sin\frac{\pi t}{2\tau} \right] dz$$
$$= \cos^2\left(\frac{\pi t}{2\tau}\right) \int_0^a z \psi_m^* \psi_m \, dx + \sin^2\left(\frac{\pi t}{2\tau}\right) \int_0^a z \psi_n^* \psi_n \, dz$$
$$+ \cos\left(\frac{\pi t}{2\tau}\right) \sin\left(\frac{\pi t}{2\tau}\right) \int_0^a z (\psi_m^* \psi_n + \psi_n^* \psi_m) \, dz \tag{10.9}$$

The first and second terms sum to $a/2$, the expectation in either constant-energy state. The final term can be expressed by (10.4) as

$$\frac{4}{a} \sin\frac{\pi t}{\tau} \cos\left[\frac{(E_m - E_n)t}{\hbar} \right] \int_0^a z \left(\sin\frac{\pi m x}{a} \sin\frac{\pi n z}{a} \right) dz \tag{10.10}$$

The integral is nonzero *only* if the indices m and n differ by odd integers.

$$\langle z \rangle = \frac{a}{2} + \frac{4a}{\pi^2} \sin\frac{\pi t}{\tau} \cos\left[\frac{(E_m - E_n)t}{\hbar} \right] \left[\frac{1}{(m-n)^2} \right.$$
$$\left. - \frac{1}{(m+n)^2} \right] \quad |m - n| = 1, 3, 5 \ldots, 0 \leq t \leq \tau \tag{10.11}$$

Superimposed on its static value $a/2$, the expectation $\langle z \rangle$ has an *oscillation* at the transition frequency $(E_m - E_n)/\hbar$, the amplitude of the oscillation depending on the particular beginning and end states. If the electron were in a suitable time-varying electric field, this oscillation would permit it to give up the energy as a photon (or phonon) (Fig.10.1). A postulated transition between states of indices differing by an even integer does *not* produce an oscillation in the electron's expected position. Such transitions are termed "forbidden" transitions. The rule $|m - n| = 1, 3, 5 \ldots$, defining allowed and for-

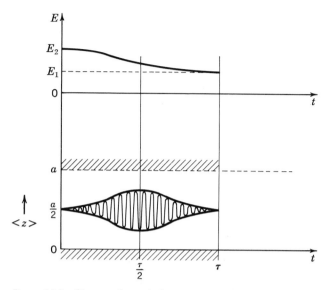

Figure 10.1   Expectations of electron energy and position during transition from a state of energy E_2 to E_1, in a simple potential well.

bidden transitions, is termed a *selection rule*. More complex systems such as real atoms have more complicated selection rules for various kinds of transitions. Allowed transitions are characterized by the nonvanishing of a *matrix element*, in the present case $Z_{mn} = \int z\psi_m^*(\mathbf{r})\psi_n(\mathbf{r})\ dv$. The transition described here is termed an *electric dipole transition*, since the equivalent electron motion produces a dipole moment $-ez$. In a more complicated case, the transition may not produce such a dipole moment and cannot radiate or absorb energy in a uniform time-varying electric field; hence the dipole matrix element Z_{mn} will be zero.

10.2   Classical Radiation and Absorption by Electrons

Classically, an electron may radiate if (1) it moves uniformly through a medium faster than the velocity of light therein (Cherenkov radiation) *or* (2) its motion is rapidly accelerated or decelerated. In electronically active solids, only the latter case appears to be important, since the ordinary motion of electrons does not attain relativistic velocities. A third radiation source, not really classical in origin, is the radiation

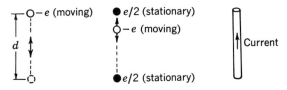

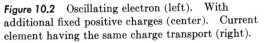

Figure 10.2   Oscillating electron (left).   With additional fixed positive charges (center).   Current element having the same charge transport (right).

produced as a result of time-varying *orientation* of an electron's magnetic (spin) dipole.

The acceleration of electron motion may take several forms; for example, an electron of high energy colliding with a heavy nucleus will have its motion altered so rapidly that it may give off much of its energy in photons over very broad ranges of photon energy.   This again is of little importance to us.

Of more interest is the radiation occurring when an electron is undergoing almost periodic acceleration, as, for example, when it is *classically* orbiting a nucleus.   As the results of the previous section would suggest, from a quantum-theoretical viewpoint an electronic acceleration is predicted, and hence radiation, *only* when the electron is *in transition* between constant-energy states.   The nature of the resulting radiation is described very well by representing classically the expected motion.   Imagine the electron oscillating in a straight line along the z axis about a fixed origin, with sinusoidal motion $z = (d/2) \sin \omega t$ (Fig. 10.2).   This represents, for example, the expected motion of the electron in the example of the previous section.

In a linear homogeneous medium characterized by a phase velocity $c = (\mu\epsilon)^{-\frac{1}{2}}$ for electromagnetic waves, a space charge density $\rho(x,y,z,t)$ and a space current density $\mathbf{J}(x,y,z,t)$ produce electromagnetic fields at some point (x',y',z'), which can be expressed in terms of the *retarded potentials* ϕ and $\mathbf{A}$:[†]

$$\phi(x',y',z',t) = \frac{1}{\epsilon} \int_{\substack{\text{all} \\ \text{space}}} \frac{\rho(t - R/c)}{4\pi R} \, dx \, dy \, dz \tag{10.12}$$

$$\mathbf{A}(x',y',z',t) = \mu \int_{\substack{\text{all} \\ \text{space}}} \frac{\mathbf{J}(t - R/c)}{4\pi R} \, dx \, dy \, dz \tag{10.13}$$

[†] Cf. S. Ramo and J. R. Whinnery, "Fields and Waves in Modern Radio," 2d ed., pp. 198 and 199, John Wiley & Sons, Inc., New York, 1953.

where the parameter R is the distance between the source point (x,y,z) and (x',y',z'): $R^2 = (x - x')^2 + (y - y')^2 + (z - z')^2$.

Electric and magnetic field intensities may be derived from $\mathbf{A}$ and ϕ using Maxwell's equations:[1]

$$\mathbf{B} = \nabla \times \mathbf{A}$$
$$\mathbf{\mathcal{E}} = -\nabla \phi - \frac{\partial \mathbf{A}}{\partial t} \tag{10.14}$$

We need be interested only in the solution at great distances from a small source, for energy radiated must continue traveling outward, whereas local nonradiative fields decay rapidly near the source. The radiative electric and magnetic fields emanating from the charge distribution vary inversely with distance from the radiative source; the square of field quantities, integrated over a large sphere, will hence converge to a constant radiated power. The "far-field" electric and magnetic fields must furthermore be uniquely related in a propagating wave. We can therefore find the fields by determining at first only $\mathbf{A}$, then $\mathbf{B}$, and finally $\mathbf{\mathcal{E}}$ via Maxwell's equations. A *current-carrying conductor* is, from a radiation point of view, equivalent to our moving electron if it carries the same charge over the same distance at the same rate. That is, the charge $-e$ is carried from a point $z = +d/2$ to $z = -d/2$ sinusoidally at the rate ω. Consider a conductor of length d carrying continuous and uniform current along its length:

$$I = \frac{e\omega}{2} \cos \omega t \tag{10.15}$$

At one end of the conductor, a charge $q = \int I \, dt = (e/2) \sin \omega t$ appears. We can make the original oscillating electron situation more nearly equivalent by imagining a stationary positive charge $+e/2$ located at each end of the electron oscillation path (Fig. 10.2). The charge transport produced by the current (10.15) is then the same as that of the oscillating-plus-fixed charges.

The problem is now reduced to finding the radiation fields of a small current-carrying element of length d. (The dimensions of typical electronic orbits are usually small fractions

[1] Cf. S. Ramo and J. R. Whinnery, "Fields and Waves in Modern Radio," 2d ed., pp. 198 and 199, John Wiley & Sons, Inc., New York, 1953.

of a wavelength of the emitted radiation, at least down to optical wavelengths.)

Assuming there are no other sources of radiation, the integral for **A** is merely

$$\mathbf{A} = 1_z \frac{\mu \omega e d}{8\pi R} e^{j\omega}(t - R/c) \tag{10.16}$$

If we assume that the radiating charge is at the origin (Fig. 10.3), R is just a radius vector. In *cylindrical coordinates*, $R = (r^2 + z^2)^{\frac{1}{2}}$,

$$\mathbf{B} = \nabla \times \mathbf{A} = -1_\phi \frac{\partial A_z}{\partial r} = 1_\phi \frac{\mu \omega e d}{8\pi} \left(-j \frac{kr}{R^2} + \frac{r}{R^3} \right) e^{j(\omega t - kR)}$$

where $k = \omega/c$.

In terms of the polar angle θ of *spherical coordinates*, $r/R = \sin \theta$; since $\mathbf{B} \simeq \mu_0 \mathfrak{IC}$, in the materials of interest,

$$\mathfrak{IC}_\phi = \frac{\omega e d}{8\pi} \left(-j \frac{k \sin \theta}{R} + \frac{\sin \theta}{R^2} \right) e^{j\omega(t - R/c)} \tag{10.17}$$

The second term in the parentheses decreases as the *inverse square* of the distance from the source, and is an *induction field*, which does not contribute to radiated power. The radiative field, from the first parenthetical term, may be substituted into Maxwell's equation $\nabla \times \mathfrak{IC} = \partial \mathbf{D}/\partial t$, to determine in polar coordinates the *radiative electric field:*

$$\boldsymbol{\varepsilon} = 1_\theta \frac{j\omega^2 e d \mu}{8\pi R} \sin \theta \; e^{j\omega(t - R/c)} \tag{10.18}$$

The time-averaged power radiated is found by integrating the *Poynting vector* ($\boldsymbol{\varepsilon} \times \mathfrak{IC}$) over the surface of a large sphere. A factor of one-half gives the average of the time factor.

$$P_{\text{rad}} = \oint (\boldsymbol{\varepsilon} \times \mathfrak{IC}) \, da = \frac{1}{2} \sqrt{\frac{\epsilon}{\mu}} \left(\frac{\omega^2 e d \mu}{8\pi R} \right)^2 \int \sin^2 \theta \, da$$

where the differential area da is given by $da = R^2 \sin \theta \, d\theta \, d\phi$.

$$P_{\text{rad}} = \frac{1}{2} \sqrt{\frac{\epsilon}{\mu}} \left(\frac{\omega^2 e d \mu}{8\pi} \right)^2 \times 2\pi \int_0^\pi \sin^3 \theta \, d\theta$$

Finally,

$$P_{\text{rad}} = \frac{\omega^4 (ed)^2 \epsilon^{\frac{1}{2}} \mu^{\frac{3}{2}}}{48\pi} \tag{10.19}$$

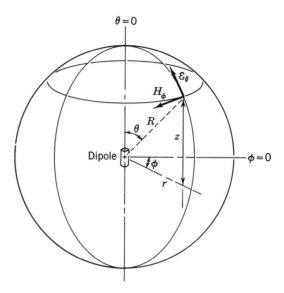

Figure 10.3   Coordinates and field configuration of oscillating dipole or current element.

Figure 10.3 illustrates the nature of the solution. The electric field of the radiated wave, whose direction defines the *polarization* of the wave, is always parallel to 1_θ, while the magnetic field is parallel to 1_ϕ.   Zero power *density* is radiated off the ends of the current element ($\theta = 0, \pi$) and a maximum at $\theta = \pi/2$.   The fields have axial symmetry.   The *rate* of energy radiation by the oscillating electron is proportional to the fourth power of the oscillation frequency and the square of the travel d.

The solution is more useful than might appear.   While it describes only an electron moving linearly, an electron moving in a *circular orbit* is equivalent to *two* such electrons moving in 90° time phase, in linear motion along two perpendicular axes (Fig. 10.4).   The radiation field is just the linear superposition of two solutions such as we have found. The wave radiated *parallel* to the plane of electron motion will be linearly polarized, whereas that radiated *normal* to the plane will be *circularly* polarized.   This polarization property is a measurable characteristic of real atomic radiation.

The electron motion is retarded, during radiation, by the radiated field itself and by externally produced fields (which in atomic radiation are usually much larger).   This retarda-

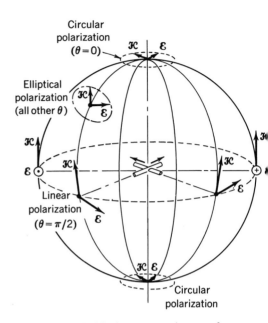

Figure 10.4 Fields due to two time-quadrature current elements at right angles, equivalent to electron in circular trajectory. Circular polarization at $\theta = 0$, π, linear polarization at $\theta = \pi/2$; elliptical polarization at intermediate angles.

tion explains the conversion of electron energy to radiation. In the admittedly nonphysical case of straight-line electron motion, the retardation is entirely along the direction of motion and involves no change in *directed* electron momentum. With a physically more meaningful circular or elliptical orbit, however, retardation reduces the *angular momentum* of the electron. The presence of angular momentum in the radiated electromagnetic wave itself can be exposed by a more detailed analysis. This reveals also that the total angular momentum of a wave having one photon of energy may be, at most, of the order of $\hbar$. In quantum-mechanical treatments of emission (or absorption) of a photon by an orbiting electron, the selection rules *require* that an angular-momentum change occur. If the emitted photon is polarized in the plane *normal to* a special axis (e.g., a static field axis) as in Fig. 10.4, the component of angular momentum $m\hbar$ along that axis must change. Here classical and quantum-mechanical solutions are in agreement.

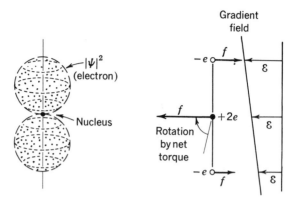

Figure 10.5   Example of a quadripole charge distribution. (Left) The electron distribution of a 2s electronic state. (Right) One form of quadripolar distribution of point charges. In a nonuniform electric field, as shown at right, the total *forces* on the charges cancel, but there is a net *torque* on the charge distribution (clockwise in the figure).

The radiation described by (10.12) to (10.19) is electric dipole radiation. *Orbital* transitions of electrons may involve a time-varying electric dipole moment. The peak a-c dipole moment produced in such a transition will ordinarily be of the order of the orbital dimension times the electronic charge. The interaction energy of an electric dipole of moment $\mathbf{p}_e$ with an electric field $\boldsymbol{\varepsilon}$ is

$$E_{\text{electric pole}} = -\mathbf{p}_e \cdot \boldsymbol{\varepsilon} \qquad (10.20)$$

Any rotation or other change of the dipole in the field causes energy $(-d\mathbf{p}_e \cdot \boldsymbol{\varepsilon})$ to be transferred to or from the dipole. In some atomic transitions, however, the oscillating charge distribution during a transition represents not dipole, but higher-order charge distribution. A *quadripole* is illustrated in Fig. 10.5, for example. This charge distribution does not have an energy of interaction with a *uniform* electric field, but will interact with a *nonuniform* field, for example, $\varepsilon_z \propto z$. A system which produces an (expected) time-varying charge distribution like that shown in Fig. 10.5 is said to have a *quadripole transition*. This type of transition is "forbidden" by selection rules like those in (10.11). The interaction energy of an electron in a nonuniform field $\varepsilon_z = \varepsilon_0 + \varepsilon_1 z + \cdots$ is

$$dE = -\boldsymbol{\varepsilon} \cdot \mathbf{p}_e \cong ez(\varepsilon_0 + \varepsilon_1 z)\, dz$$

If the electron is to interchange energy with this field in a transition, $\langle dE \rangle$ must be nonzero:

$$\langle dE \rangle = (e\mathcal{E}_0 \langle z \rangle + e\mathcal{E}_1 \langle z^2 \rangle)\, dz \qquad (10.21)$$

Thus in the transition described in Sec. 10.1, while for $|m - n| = 2, 4, 6, \ldots$ the transitions are "forbidden," $\langle z^2 \rangle$ has a nonzero oscillation for these transitions. Accordingly, they may occur in a nonuniform field. In solids the presence of neighboring atoms allows nonuniform electromagnetic fields to exist and "forbidden" transitions actually occur. Even in solids, however, radiation and absorption processes involving quadripole moments are far "weaker" than dipole transitions.

Whereas electric dipole transitions account for the higher-energy transitions in solids, *magnetic dipole* transitions are responsible for most transitions in the microwave spectrum. The simplest magnetic dipole transition is the *inversion* of a spin from a state where the magnetic moment of the electron is opposed to a field $\mathcal{3C}$ to a condition where it is parallel to the field. The spin precession is analogous to that of a lossy gyroscope inverting by precession in the gravitational field (Fig. 10.6). The electron, like a gyroscope, *must* process about the field axis. Only if the precession is accompanied by energy loss, as when the electron is radiating energy to an a-c magnetic field, can the spin axis eventually precess to the lower-energy orientation. The magnetic interaction is with an RF magnetic field *normal* to the initial spin axis set by crystalline fields and/or a static field (Sec. 8.9). In a given *electromagnetic* field, electric dipole interaction (10.19) with a typical orbiting electron is much stronger than the magnetic interaction with its spin magnetic moment:

$$E_{\text{magnetic dipole}} \simeq -\mu_0 \mathbf{p}_m \cdot \mathcal{3C} \qquad (10.22)$$

Electric and magnetic fields in a planar electromagnetic wave in free space are related by

$$\frac{\mathcal{E}}{\mathcal{3C}} = \mu_0 c \; (= 377 \text{ ohms, in free space})$$

We may estimate the typical electric dipole moment p_e by a charge $-e$ with a dipole arm of 1 A ($p_e \cong 1.6 \times 10^{-29}$, mks). The magnetic dipole moment of a free-electron spin is shown in Chap. 8 to be $\beta \approx 9 \times 10^{-24}$, mks. Accordingly,

$$\frac{E_{\text{electric dipole}}}{E_{\text{magnetic dipole}}} \simeq \frac{p_e \mathcal{E}}{\mu_0 p_m \mathcal{3C}} \approx \frac{1.6 \times 10^{-29} \times 3 \times 10^8}{9 \times 10^{-24}} \approx 500$$

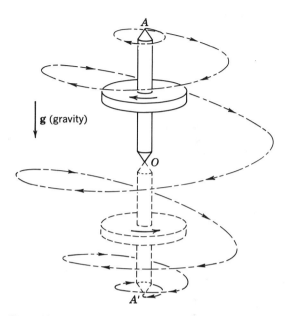

Figure 10.6 Inversion of a gyroscope in a field. If point O is fixed, precession of A will carry it to A'. Where the gyroscope is a magnetic spin, the energy loss which permits the change in precession angle can be due to radiation of a photon.

Roughly speaking, fields 500 times as large, or a *power density* about 10^5 times as large, are required, at a given frequency, to permit radiation or absorption of energy at the same rate by *equal numbers* of electrons by magnetic-spin transitions as by orbital transitions. This is one reason why typical microwave (maser) devices produce only milliwatt or smaller power outputs, whereas optical (laser) oscillators using comparable amounts of solid-state active material can produce instantaneous output powers of more than 10^8 watts. An additional gain of 10^4 is obtained in the photon energy at optical frequencies, as compared with microwaves.

10.3 Stimulation of Transitions by Electromagnetic Fields[1]

The quantum-mechanical treatment of electromagnetic radiation and its effect on atomic systems is, in complete detail,

[1] The details of the theory are not essential to the later material in this chapter; however, the nature of the results [(10.42) and (10.44)] defining transition probabilities is highly significant.

very complex. As in many other problems, it is possible, by approximation, to obtain a useful description of the processes. The quantum "system" describing radiation interacting with an electron is really *two coupled systems*: the electromagnetic (photon) energy system and the electronic system. The coupling may be weak or strong, depending on the strength of the electromagnetic fields experienced by the electron(s) and on how much of the electromagnetic system is occupied by interacting electrons. For example, if an electromagnetic system has available only one photon of energy at an electronic transition frequency, the absorption of this energy by an electron has a profound effect on both the electromagnetic system and the atom. The simple theory here, however, is based on weak coupling between systems containing many electrons and many photons.

For quantum-electronic problems, it is most convenient to describe the electromagnetic fields as confined to an electromagnetic cavity, where they may have only discrete frequencies, according to (C.50). Each resonant mode of the oscillator may be treated quantum-mechanically as a *harmonic oscillator*, because the electric field energy and the magnetic field energy have the same relative positions in the hamiltonian (energy) function as the kinetic and potential energies of the simple pendulum oscillator (Sec. B.2). Each resonant mode, of frequency ω, may have energy levels

$$E(\text{mode of frequency } \omega) = \hbar\omega(n + \tfrac{1}{2}) \tag{10.23}$$

There is a characteristic zero-point energy ($\hbar\omega/2$). In the quantum solution for the cavity fields, there are also zero-point fields; i.e., there is never a state of the cavity resonance in which the fields are precisely zero. By application of Bose-Einstein statistics to such a cavity, it is shown in Sec. C.7 that the thermal energy in such a cavity has density, for frequencies ω well above the lowest resonance,

$$W(\omega) = \frac{\hbar\omega^3}{\pi^2 c^3 (e^{\hbar\omega/kT} - 1)} \tag{10.24}$$

per unit frequency interval. The total field in the cavity may consist of the thermal contribution (10.24), which has random phase, as well as an applied field (for example, $\varepsilon \sin \omega_c t$) supplied from some outside source. At microwave frequencies, it is more appropriate to describe the thermal radiation at *each* cavity resonance separately; (10.24) is accurate only when resonances are closely spaced in frequency.

The system electron(s) may now be described. An electron *not* in the presence of external fields or other disturbances may be characterized by any of a set of wave functions ψ_n with corresponding (fixed) energy levels E_n. Expressing the hamiltonian operator simply as H_0, the time-dependent form of the wave equation may be written

$$H_0\psi = j\hbar \frac{\partial \psi}{\partial t} \qquad (\psi = \psi_n) \tag{10.25}$$

The coupling between fields and electron will be described in a unilateral fashion by considering the field to produce a small perturbation in electron energy, just as in time-independent perturbation theory (Sec. 7.3). Here, however, the perturbation H_1 represents a time-varying field.

$$(H_0 + H_1)\psi = j\hbar \frac{\partial \psi}{\partial t} \tag{10.26}$$

The perturbed wave function ψ may be expanded as a series in the unperturbed ψ_n, with the coefficients a_n, functions of time only.

$$\psi = \sum_n a_n(t)\psi_n \tag{10.27}$$

Substituting into the wave equation (10.26),

$$\sum_n a_n E_n \psi_n + \sum_n a_n H_1 \psi_n = j\hbar \sum_n \left(a_n \frac{\partial \psi_n}{\partial t} + \psi_n \frac{\partial a_n}{\partial t} \right) \tag{10.28}$$

The time dependence of the ψ_n is simply $e^{-jE_n t/\hbar}$, so that $\partial \psi_n / \partial t = -j(E_n/\hbar)\psi_n$. If now we multiply through all terms by ψ_m^* and integrate over the space of the ψ's, the preassumed *normalization* of the ψ_n removes many terms, leaving

$$a_m E_m + \sum_n a_n \int \psi_m^* H_1 \psi_n \, dv = j\hbar \left(-j \frac{E_m}{\hbar} a_m + \frac{da_m}{dt} \right)$$

Finally,

$$\frac{da_m}{dt} = -\frac{j}{\hbar} \sum_n a_n \int \psi_m^* H_1 \psi_n \, dv \tag{10.29}$$

This relation is completely general and is, in fact, a "matrix mechanics" equivalent to the time-dependent Schrödinger equation. We consider here only the influence of the *electric field* on the electron. If the electric field acting on the electron is

$$\mathbf{\mathcal{E}} = -\mathbf{1}_z \, \mathcal{E} \cos \omega t \qquad (10.30)$$

the perturbation H_1 of the energy of an electron whose coordinates are measured from some convenient origin (i.e., the nucleus of its atom) is

$$H_1 = -e \int_0^{\mathbf{r}} \mathbf{\mathcal{E}} \cdot d\mathbf{r} = e\mathcal{E}z \cos \omega t \qquad (10.31)$$

Substituting into (10.29),

$$\frac{da_m}{dt} = -\frac{j}{\hbar} \, e\mathcal{E} \cos \omega t \sum_n a_n \int \psi_m^* z \psi_n \, dv \qquad (10.32)$$

The same integrals appear here as in earlier theory. The integral $\int \psi_m^* z \psi_n \, dv$ may be written $Z_{mn} e^{-j(E_n - E_m)t/\hbar}$, where

$$Z_{mn} = \int \psi_m^*(x,y,z, \ldots) z \psi_n(x,y,z, \ldots) \, dv \qquad (10.33)$$

Unless the atom exhibits a *permanent* electric dipole moment, $Z_{mm} = 0$, as discussed in Sec. 7.3. It will now be assumed that the system has two well-defined unperturbed states ψ_1 and ψ_2, of energies E_1 and $E_2 > E_1$. Other states will be assumed far removed in energy. The perturbed wave function is then approximately

$$\psi = a_1\psi_1 + a_2\psi_2 \qquad (10.34)$$

and the equations determining a_1 and a_2 are

$$\frac{da_1}{dt} = -\frac{j}{\hbar} \, e\mathcal{E} \cos (\omega t) a_2 Z_{12} e^{-j(E_2 - E_1)t/\hbar}$$
$$\frac{da_2}{dt} = -\frac{j}{\hbar} \, e\mathcal{E} \cos (\omega t) a_1 Z_{21} e^{-j(E_1 - E_2)t/\hbar} \qquad (10.35)$$

Z_{11} and Z_{22} are assumed to be zero. All coefficients except a_1 and a_2 will be negligible if the frequency of the perturbation ω is near $(E_2 - E_1)/\hbar$ and we *begin* in state ψ_1 or ψ_2. Considering the *radiative* $E_2 \to E_1$ transition, the system begins in state ψ_2, so that at $t = 0$, $a_2 = 1$ and $a_1 = 0$. Letting $(E_2 - E_1)/\hbar = \omega_0$ and expanding $\cos \omega t$,

$$\frac{da_1}{dt} = -j \frac{e\mathcal{E}a_2}{2\hbar} Z_{12}(e^{j\omega t} + e^{-j\omega t})e^{-j\omega_0 t} \qquad (10.36)$$

We shall assume that the field is applied abruptly at $t = 0$. While exact solution is tedious, we can obtain a solution correct near $t = 0$ by assuming that, in a short time interval, a_2 remains nearly constant $(a_2 \simeq 1)$. Equation (10.36) may then be integrated directly.

$$a_1 \simeq \frac{e\mathcal{E}Z_{12}}{2\hbar} \left[-\frac{e^{j(\omega-\omega_0)t}}{\omega - \omega_0} + \frac{e^{-j(\omega+\omega_0)t}}{\omega + \omega_0} \right]_0^t \tag{10.37}$$

Since we are interested in frequencies near $\omega = \omega_0$, the first term in the brackets is much larger than the second, which may be omitted with little error.

$$a_1 \simeq \frac{-e\mathcal{E}Z_{12}}{2\hbar} \left[\frac{e^{j(\omega-\omega_0)t} - 1}{\omega - \omega_0} \right] \tag{10.38}$$

$$a_1^* a_1 = |a_1|^2 = \left(\frac{e\mathcal{E}}{2\hbar}\right)^2 |Z_{12}|^2 \left[\frac{2 - 2\cos(\omega - \omega_0)t}{(\omega - \omega_0)^2} \right] \text{ (small } t) \tag{10.39}$$

The quantity $|a_1|^2$ is the *probability* that at time t following the onset of a perturbing electric field at $t = 0$, a *single* electron whose transition frequency is $\omega_0 = (E_2 - E_1)/\hbar$ will be found in the lower-energy state. The probability that each of N independent electrons with the same transition frequency will be found in the new state at t is just $N|a_1|^2$. Actual electrons in a solid, however, have transition frequencies ω_0 which are spread over a *range* of frequencies because of lattice imperfections and interactions between nearby electrons. In measuring the spectrum of a solid, we accordingly find that the energy-transition frequencies cover a finite *line width*, described by a factor $g(\omega_0)$ (Fig. 10.7). The fraction of all electrons having transition frequency between ω_0 and $\omega_0 + d\omega_0$ is defined as $g(\omega_0) \, d\omega_0$. Normalization accordingly requires $\int_0^\infty g(\omega_0) \, d\omega_0 = 1$. Likewise, the electric field ($\mathcal{E}$) is not usually at a single discrete frequency and may more properly be expressed as a Fourier spectrum $\mathcal{E}(\omega)$. The quantity $\mathcal{E}^*(\omega)\mathcal{E}(\omega)$ which appears in the modified form of (10.39) must be integrated over all frequencies, $\int_0^\infty d\omega$. Accordingly, with these modifications, the average transition probability at time t *for an ensemble of many atoms* takes the form

$$|a_1|^2 = \frac{e^2|Z_{12}|^2}{2\hbar^2} \iint\limits_0^\infty \left[\frac{1 - \cos(\omega - \omega_0)t}{(\omega - \omega_0)^2} \right] \mathcal{E}^2(\omega)g(\omega_0) \, d\omega \, d\omega_0 \tag{10.40}$$

Unless the natural spectrum of the transition, $g(\omega_0)$, *overlaps* to some extent the spectrum $\mathcal{E}^2(\omega)$ of the exciting radiation,

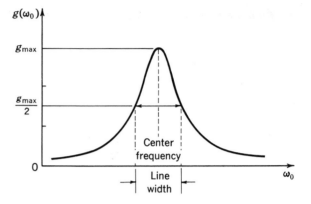

Figure 10.7 Line shape factor $g(\omega_0)$, the distribution function for the transition frequencies of a large number of electrons. Line width may be stated in terms of frequency, wave number, or energy spread of the photons.

there will be no probability of electron transitions. In two special but important cases the complicated integrals in (10.40) can be greatly simplified. In the case of *thermal* radiation acting on the electrons, $\mathcal{E}^2(\omega)$ is nearly uniform over a broad frequency. The line width [the range of ω_0 over which $g(\omega_0)$ is large] covers a much narrower range. In (10.40), $\mathcal{E}^2(\omega)$ may be replaced by $\mathcal{E}^2(\omega_0)$ and removed from the integral; the integration over ω_0 yields the bracketed part intact. The remaining integration, over ω, may be transformed to the form

$$|a_1|^2 = \frac{e^2 \mathcal{E}^2(\omega_0)}{2\hbar^2} \left(\frac{t}{2}\right) \int_{-\omega_0 t/2}^{\infty} \frac{\sin^2 u}{u^2} \, du \qquad (10.41)$$

where $u = (\omega - \omega_0)t/2$. The definite integral $\int_{-\infty}^{+\infty}$ is merely π, and since our limits encompass most of the infinite integral,

$$|a_1|^2 \cong \frac{e^2 \mathcal{E}^2(\omega_0)|Z_{12}|^2 \pi t}{4\hbar^2}$$

The probability that electrons initially in state 2 at $t = 0$ will be in state 1 at t is *proportional to* t. Even though this relation is good only at small t, we may infer that S_{21}, probability *per unit time* of an electron making a transition $2 \to 1$

in the presence of a *broad-band* radiation source of field spectral density $\mathcal{E}^2(\omega_0)$, is the coefficient of t:

$$S_{21} \cong \frac{\pi e^2 \mathcal{E}^2(\omega_0)|Z_{12}|^2}{4\hbar^2} \qquad \text{(broad-band radiation)} \qquad (10.42)$$

If, on the other hand, the radiation inducing transitions is much *narrower* in bandwidth than the line width of $g(\omega_0)$ (e.g., let $\mathcal{E} = \hat{\mathcal{E}} \sin \omega_r t$), its "spectrum" is a Dirac function[1] $\mathcal{E}^2(\omega) = \hat{\mathcal{E}}^2 \delta(\omega - \omega_r)$; the integral of this spectrum is then just the square of the sinusoidal field ($\hat{\mathcal{E}}^2$). The integral (10.40) is now

$$|a_1|^2 = \frac{e^2|Z_{12}|^2}{4\hbar^2} \hat{\mathcal{E}}^2 \int_0^\infty \frac{1 - \cos (\omega_r - \omega_0)t}{(\omega_r - \omega_0)^2} g(\omega_0) \, d\omega_0 \qquad (10.43)$$

The simplest assumption here is that the factor $g(\omega_0) \cong g(\omega_r)$ over the sensible range of integration. It is then removed from the integral, giving for an ensemble of atoms

$$S_{21} \cong \frac{\pi e^2 \hat{\mathcal{E}}^2 g(\omega_r)|Z_{12}|^2}{4\hbar^2} \qquad \text{(narrow-band radiation)} \qquad (10.44)$$

While (10.42) is accurate for thermal radiation, line shape factors $g(\omega_0)$ typical of solid-state spectra are not broad enough to make our final approximation an especially good one. A more exact solution reveals that in narrow-line transitions driven by nearly monochromatic fields, transition probabilities do *not* in fact increase linearly with time. Transient effects occur which do, however, settle down after a period of time to give a transition probability S_{21} which is proportional to $\hat{\mathcal{E}}^2$. If a large number of electrons, N_2, are in state 2, the number which *begin* transition, *per second*, will then be given by $S_{21}N_2$. A similar derivation can be made for the transition from state 1 to state 2. The *stimulated absorption probability* $S_{12} \equiv S_{21}$, as can readily be shown by assuming $a_1 = 1$, $a_2 = 0$, at $t = 0$. The matrix element $|Z_{12}|$, for typical *allowed* transitions, will be of the order of 10^{-8} cm $\times$ $e \cong 10^{-29}$, mks.

Having the probabilities $S_{21} = S_{12}$, we may determine the rate of energy absorption by a set of N electrons, of which N_2 and N_1 are in states 2 and 1, respectively. Since $S_{21}N_2$ per

[1] Defined, for example, by

$$\int_{-\infty}^{\infty} f(x)\delta(x - x_0) \, dx = f(x_0)$$

second will begin a transition $E_2 \rightarrow E_1$, while $S_{12}N_1$ per second will begin a transition $E_1 \rightarrow E_2$, the energy per second absorbed by the entire system is

$$P_{\text{absorbed}} = S_{12}(N_1 - N_2)(\hbar\omega_0) \tag{10.45}$$

To give up or to receive energy from a field, electrons must have motion *in time phase* with the field. This is an important characteristic of field-induced transitions. In maser or laser devices, where the power *absorbed* is made *negative* by setting up the situation $(N_2 - N_1) > 0$ and establishing fields well above noise levels, the emitted radiations from the many atoms are in time phase. The result is a nearly constant output frequency. This radiation is said to be *coherent*.

While the foregoing has dealt with electric dipole transitions, the theory [from Eq. (10.29)] can be adapted to magnetic (spin) dipole transitions, where the perturbing field is magnetic and the interaction energy $E = -\mu_0 \mathbf{p}_m \cdot \mathbf{\mathfrak{K}}$. This is pertinent for microwave paramagnetic (spin) transitions.

10.4 Einstein's Emission-Absorption Theory

Long before the development of quantum wave mechanics, photon emission and absorption was treated thermodynamically by Einstein.[1] His arguments reveal an even more accurate description of the stimulation processes than that described in the preceding section. He considered a system of independent atoms, each having two energy levels E_1 and E_2 $(> E_1)$. N_1 and N_2 are the respective numbers (or densities) of atoms in states 1 and 2 $(N_1 + N_2 = N)$. The stimulated-transition probabilities S_{12} and S_{21} were *assumed* proportional to the *thermal-equilibrium* radiation density $W(\omega_0)$, as given by (10.24); Einstein let $S_{12} = B_{12}W(\omega_0)$, $S_{21} = B_{21}W(\omega_0)$. The number of stimulated transitions per second from state 1 to state 2 is $B_{12}W(\omega_0)N_1$; from state 2 to state 1, $B_{21}W(\omega_0)N_2$. Einstein added a second *emission* term $A_{21}N_2$, independent of the thermal fields, which he termed *spontaneous emission*. We shall shortly see why this is needed. Einstein did *not*, however, include in his analysis any nonradiative (phonon) transitions, which we shall add later. In the steady state, emission and absorption rates must be equal:

$$B_{12}W(\omega_0)N_1 = B_{21}W(\omega_0)N_2 + A_{21}N_2 \tag{10.46}$$

[1] Albert Einstein, *Phys. Z.*, **18**:121–123 (March, 1917).

At *equilibrium* the densities N_2 and N_1 must be thermodynamically related. A Boltzmann distribution (C.37) applies to the independent atoms, requiring

$$\frac{N_1}{N_2} = e^{(E_2 - E_1)/kT} \tag{10.46a}$$

Inserting this into (10.46),

$$W(\omega_0) = \frac{A}{B_{12}e^{(E_2 - E_1)/kT} - B_{21}} \tag{10.47}$$

Since we must assume that at equilibrium the only radiation present is *thermal*, the radiant energy density must satisfy the Planck law (10.24). Since (10.24) and (10.47) must be equivalent,

$$B_{21} \equiv B_{12} = B$$
$$\frac{A}{B} = \frac{\hbar\omega^3}{\pi^2 c^3} \tag{10.48}$$

The *stimulated* emission and absorption probabilities B_{21} and B_{12} are equal, as expected. The *spontaneous emission* coefficient A_{21} is directly related to the stimulated emission coefficient. From (10.47),

$$\frac{\text{Stimulated emission}}{\text{Spontaneous emission}} = \frac{BW(\omega_0)}{A} = \frac{1}{e^{\hbar\omega_0/kT} - 1}$$
$$= \text{thermal photons in cavity mode} \tag{10.49}$$

Since the spontaneous emission equals the stimulated emission divided by the number of thermal phonons which produce it, *the spontaneous emission is just that which would be produced by a single photon in the cavity mode.*

Since from (10.48) the spontaneous-emission probability is proportional to the cube of the emission frequency, spontaneous emission becomes very important at optical wavelengths. Optical spectroscopists refer to the "natural lifetime" of an excited state of an atom as the time which it may be expected to remain in the upper state. In optical-wavelength transitions (e.g., in quantum-electronic devices), spontaneous emission is often the process by which excited-state electrons "relax" to a lower state. Since A_{21} is the probability of spontaneous emission, per second, its reciprocal is the upper-state lifetime. The parameter $B_{21} = S_{21}/W(\omega_0)$ may be found from (10.42) if it is realized that in propagating

waves one-half of the energy is carried by the electric fields
and the rest by magnetic fields; that is,

$$W(\omega_0) = \frac{\epsilon_0 \hat{\mathcal{E}}^2(\omega_0)}{2} + \frac{\mu_0 \hat{\mathcal{H}}^2(\omega_0)}{2} = \epsilon_0 \hat{\mathcal{E}}^2(\omega_0) \tag{10.50}$$

From (10.42) and (10.48),

$$B_{21} = \frac{\pi e^2 |Z_{12}|^2}{4 h^2 \epsilon_0} \qquad A_{21} = \frac{e^2 |Z_{12}|^2 \omega^3}{4 \pi h \epsilon_0 c^3} \tag{10.51}$$

Using $|Z_{12}| = 10^{-8}$ cm, $E_2 - E_1 = 2$ ev, for example,

$$\frac{1}{A} \cong 10^{-8} \text{ sec}$$

This is a typical value for ordinary "allowed" optical transi-
tions. "Forbidden" transitions will have much smaller $|Z_{12}|$
and a correspondingly longer lifetime. At microwave frequencies, where the wavelength is perhaps 10^5 larger, spontaneous emission may generally be neglected; *phonon-induced*
transitions then limit excited-state lifetimes.

One cannot predict spontaneous emission from our perturbation theory of Sec. 10.3 because the field is not quantized
together with the atomic system. A complete quantum-
theoretical solution involves the existence of *zero-point fields*,
which may for purposes of explanation be viewed as the stimulation for spontaneous emission. If we adhered strictly to
the ideas of Sec. 10.3, we should expect both spontaneous emission *and* spontaneous absorption due to these fields. This
leads immediately to a contradiction, however, for at zero
temperature the zero-point energy $\hbar\omega/2$ could certainly *not*
give to the atom a *full* photon $\hbar\omega$, or in fact any energy at all.
By solving quantum relations for the cavity and atom *simultaneously*, one can arrive at the correct result: The spontaneous
emission is that which would be produced by the fields due to
one photon in the resonant mode of the cavity; spontaneous
absorption does not occur. The more detailed theory is
beyond our present treatment.[1]

10.5 Narrow-band Spectra of Solids

While in the previous section we dealt with a transition
between a pair of discrete states of an electron, in an actual
atom many such pairs of states may produce transitions. This

---

[1] Cf. W. Heitler, "Quantum Theory of Radiation," 2d ed., pp. 82ff.,
Oxford University Press, London, 1944.

fairly complex situation is eased somewhat by the fact that most transitions involve only a single electron. Furthermore, many transitions of importance in electron devices occur only between states near the uppermost filled states and ones of more elevated energy. Only when extremely large energies are involved do electrons in electronic shells near the nucleus become involved, as, for example, in x-ray emission by electron-bombarded solids.

The many characteristic transition frequencies are observed in some instances by irradiating the material with narrow-band photon radiation, observing those photon wavelengths which are strongly absorbed by the material. The resulting variation of absorption with wavelength is termed the *absorption spectrum*. Since the lower termini of absorption transitions are mainly the states occupied by electrons at equilibrium, absorption spectra can be relatively simple. More information about electronic transitions may be obtained through an *emission spectrum*, the variation of the emitted photon intensity vs. wavelength. Emission spectra may be excited in various ways; if by high-energy particles or photons, the upper termini of the transitions may extend to very high energies, and the electrons may suffer not one but several radiative transitions during their relaxation to the ground state. Accordingly, emission spectra are in general more complex (i.e., contain more transition frequencies) than absorption spectra and are completely dependent on the means of excitation. While gaseous materials may be studied by excitation in a flame or electrical-plasma discharge, excitation of solids may be carried out nondestructively by photon or electron irradiation (or in some cases by passing conduction electron currents through the material).

The *x-ray* emission spectra of solids are associated with transition of electrons from excited or ionized states to specific levels near the nucleus. These transitions are so sharply definable that the intensity of x-ray emission from an irradiated or electron-bombarded material may be used to measure the concentrations of particular elements in the material. This nondestructive, fairly accurate (1 per cent or better) method of analyzing composition of a solid is known as "x-ray fluorescence." Excitation may be carried out using a very small high-energy electron beam; such an electron microprobe permits study of composition variation over areas of micron (10^{-4} cm) dimensions.

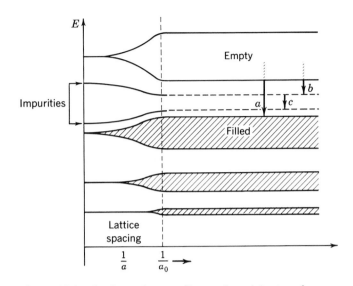

Figure 10.8 Configuration-coordinate plot of host and impurity energy levels in a solid. In general, the broadest line widths may be expected in transitions (*a*) between bands, somewhat narrower line widths from transitions between a band and a localized state (*b*) and the narrowest between localized states (*c*). Transitions between deep-lying electronic states associated with electrons close to the nucleus are normally unlikely because these states are filled.

In a pure and undefected crystal, the atomic electron energy levels are spread, from the atomic levels, into continuous energy bands (Fig. 2.18). Metallic solids, having essentially continuous electronic energy bands in the vicinity of the Fermi energy, are in general not suitable for quantum-electronic applications; they merely act as conductors. Semiconducting and insulating crystals, however, can have substantial energy band gaps between allowed energy bands, and accordingly, transitions can occur only over limited ranges of photon energy (Fig. 10.8). Even here, however, the range of photon absorption (and hence, under the proper conditions, emission) is too broad to be of practical interest. As discussed in Sec. 4.6, there are additional factors in many solids which make improbable the *direct* emission of radiation in many band-to-band transitions. Materials used for quantum-electronic applications, therefore, are almost always impurity-doped insulating or semiconducting materials. The narrowness of the impurity bands in a *lightly* doped material permits one, or even both, termini of the transition to have nearly discrete energy. If it can be arranged that a transition occurs between two such nearly localized states, the observed emission or absorption covers a relatively narrow range of photon energies.

The concepts of greatest importance in regard to actual electronic transitions in quantum-electronic devices, in addition to the photon energy, are the *line width* of a given transition and the *lifetime* of an excited state. In these respects, there are important differences between optical-wavelength and microwave transitions, as a result of the electronic processes important for the two cases.

In an optical transition which (according to usual spectroscopic rules) is "allowed," we have estimated that the spontaneous-emission probability would be of the order of 10^8 sec^{-1}. Under these conditions, the transitions from an excited state (state 2) of low-equilibrium population into the ground state (state 1) could be described by the differential relation

$$\frac{dN_2}{dt} \cong - A_{21}N_2 \tag{10.52}$$

This has the simple solution, if $(E_2 - E_1) \gg kT$,

$$N_2 \propto e^{-A_{21}t} \tag{10.53}$$

This suggests a decay time of the order of $A_{21}^{-1} = 10^{-8}$ sec; the emitted radiation from a group of such electrons might have a time dependence of the nature of $e^{-A_{21}t} \sin \omega_0 t$. Such an exponentially damped signal has a *natural line width* (bandwidth) of $\Delta\omega \cong 2A$. At optical wavelengths, it is more common to refer to the *wave number* (the reciprocal of the photon wavelength) rather than the frequency. The wave number of 1-ev photons is 8,080 (a convenient mnemonic). The line width of $\Delta\omega \cong 10^8$ at this radian frequency of $\omega_0 \cong 2 \times 10^{14}$ corresponds to about 1 part in 10^6. The corresponding wave-number line width is thus about 10^{-2} wave number. Careful optical measurements of line widths during transitions between discrete energy levels in solids, however, seldom reveal line widths less than several wave numbers. The increase in the line width is due to the fact that in the highly perturbed environment of a defected solid, the energy levels are perturbed to a variety of values.

Since the transitions involved in *optical* spectra involve substantial changes of electron energy, these are "orbital" transitions in which the electric dipole moment of the moving electron is active. The transitions involved in *microwave* spectra in solids are derived from electron-spin states of paramagnetic impurity ions and are much less sensitive to perturbing fields of neighboring impurity atoms and defects. There is a relatively small line broadening due to so-called "spin-spin" coupling, the interaction between spins of nearby impurity atoms. One might expect, therefore, that microwave paramagnetic spectra would have extremely narrow line widths. This is not true, at least at room temperature, for although spontaneous emission is a negligible limit to the lifetime of excited states, disturbance of the spins by *phonons* limits the time that a paramagnetic ion will remain in an excited state, at room temperature, to 10^{-8} sec or less. This *spin-lattice* coupling can lead to 100 Mc/sec line width, even in lightly doped materials, unless cryogenic temperatures are employed.

Line broadening in paramagnets is termed *homogeneous* when power absorption is almost uniform over the material. If, however, high (and therefore statistically nonuniform) impurity-ion density or nonuniform applied magnetic fields cause a transition frequency to vary from point to point within a sample, the resultant broadening is termed *inhomogeneous.*

In many quantum-electronic applications, a large natural line width and a short excited-state lifetime are almost equally undesirable. In general, study of a particular transition in a particular material requires measurement of both line width and lifetime.

Both spontaneous-emission and phonon-stimulated transitions reduce the population of excited states, without producing useful output radiation. In phonon-induced transitions, in fact, it is not uncommon to produce no photon emission at all, merely one or several phonons. Unlike spontaneous emission, however, phonon processes can produce absorption as well as emission of energy.

Let P_{12} denote the probability per unit time of an atom in state 1, making a phonon-induced transition to state 2, and P_{21} the converse probability of a $2 \rightarrow 1$ transition. Then, for the thermal-equilibrium two-energy-level system, we have

$$N_2 B_{12} W(\omega) + A N_2 + P_{21} N_2 = N_1 B_{12} W(\omega) + P_{12} N_1 \qquad (10.54)$$

This can apply at equilibrium only if $P_{12} N_1 = P_{21} N_2$, or by (10.46a),

$$\frac{P_{12}}{P_{21}} = e^{-(E_2 - E_1)/kT} \qquad (10.55)$$

At very low temperatures, where the phonons responsible for this "relaxation" are fewer, P will be lower. At microwave frequencies, where $e^{-(E_2-E_1)/kT} \approx 1$, P_{12} and P_{21} are almost equal. At optical wavelengths, however, $P_{12} \ll P_{21}$.

Consider a more general system of N identical and independent impurity atoms, each having many states (E_i, $i = 1, 2, \ldots$). The number of atoms in the ith state changes in time because of:

1. Electrons arriving at state i via stimulated transitions *from* other states (S_{ji})

2. Electrons leaving state i via stimulated transitions *to* other states (S_{ij})

3. Electrons arriving via spontaneous emission from *higher*-energy states (A_{ji}, $j > i$)

4. Electrons leaving via spontaneous emission to *lower*-energy states (A_{ij}, $i > j$)

5. Electrons arriving by relaxation processes, from other states (P_{ji})

6. Electrons leaving by relaxation processes to other states (P_{ij})

A *dynamic equation* can now be written for the ith state:

$$\frac{dN_i}{dt} = \sum_j S_{ij}(N_j - N_i) + \sum_{j>i} A_{ji}N_j - \sum_{j<i} A_{ij}N_i$$
$$+ \sum_i (P_{ji}N_j - P_{ij}N_i) \tag{10.56}$$

The coefficients must of course satisfy $S_{ji} = S_{ij}$, and $P_{ji} = P_{ij}e^{(E_i-E_j)/kT}$. The time derivative dN_i/dt is the *net* change of numbers of atoms in state i, which at equilibrium or in any steady-state condition will be zero. A set of equations such as this for each state of the system, plus the condition on the total numbers of atoms,

$$N = \sum_i N_i \tag{10.57}$$

completes the description of the system. If the stimulation S_{ij} is known at each frequency, the equations may be solved for $N_i(t)$. From the various terms, the *rate* of emission, absorption, etc., may then be determined. For abrupt changes in radiation intensity, the changes in the state populations N_i will to a first order follow simple exponential time variations, since the equations are first-order and linear. Non-linear effects can arise, however, for example as described in Sec. 4.6.

10.6   Principles of Stimulated-emission Devices

By extension of (10.54) to a nonequilibrium situation,

$$\frac{N_2}{N_1} = \frac{S_{12} + P_{12}}{A_{21} + S_{12} + P_{21}} \tag{10.58}$$

As the incident radiation S_{12} is increased, the ratio N_2/N_1 increases from its thermal-equilibrium value (10.46a), to approach unity. Even with infinitely high incident radiation, however, it is not possible to make N_2 exceed N_1. The net stimulated absorption (the absorption less the emission) is given by (10.44). If, and only if, it is possible for N_2 to exceed N_1 is the net power emissive. With $N_2 > N_1$, the nonequilibrium situation termed *population inversion*, an incident electromagnetic energy can be amplified by adding to itself the emission power. We have already argued that if the incident radiation is strong enough, most of the emission will be in phase with it and the output largely coherent (in phase with the input). *Internal* losses of radiation in a device, due to conduction losses, etc., must of course be kept low. This is the principle of *maser* (microwave amplification through stimulated emission of radiation) and *laser* (light amplification, etc.) devices. Earliest masers achieved a population inversion between two molecular states of gaseous ammonia molecules through an electrostatic focusing arrangement which physically separated molecules of two energy states by a nonuniform electric field. This principle was painfully complicated and operated at a fixed frequency.

Masers or lasers, in any form and at any frequency, require certain essential elements: (1) a pair of energy levels ($E_2 > E_1$) spaced by the desired photon energy, with a strongly *radiative* transition (not highly susceptible to release of energy via phonons); (2) means for elevating electrons into the upper state in large numbers via a path *other* than direct stimulated absorption; (3) an electromagnetic system capable of retaining, with low losses, photons of energy ($E_2 - E_1$); and (4) means for bringing the useful electrons into the radiation field (generally by filling a large part of the electromagnetic system with the active material). In addition, the

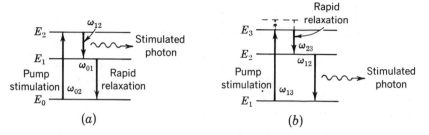

Figure 10.9 Two modes of operation used in three-level stimulated-emission devices.

system may require (5) means for "draining" atoms out of the lower-terminus state, a process termed *depopulation*.

Almost all stimulated-emission devices make use of *additional* energy levels or bands in connection with requirements 2 and 5.   If the energy-elevation process is to not connect E_2 and E_1 directly, a third state *must* be involved.   This gives us the *three-level* maser (or laser), an ingenious scheme devised by N. Bloembergen.   This may take either of two forms, as illustrated in Fig. 10.9.   In Fig. 10.9a, the atoms are first elevated from state 0 to state 2, where they are stimulated to emit and thus drop into state 1.   Relaxation or spontaneous-emission processes carry them quickly to state 0.   This is presumably the ground state, so that the electrons can drop no farther.   They are then "pumped" back into state 2, in a continuous process.   In Fig. 10.9b, state 1 is the ground state and relaxation or spontaneous emission joins states 3 and 2. (Throughout the discussion we shall use 2 and 1 to represent the upper and lower termini of the desired transition.)   The means by which energy elevation is produced is termed the *pump*, a name borrowed from parametric-amplifier jargon, which got it in turn from the process by which a child operates a swing (ah, semantics!).

We show in (10.58) that high-intensity radiation can never invert populations, but it can make the populations at terminal states nearly equal.   When two (or more) such populations are nearly equalized by high-intensity radiation, the transition is said to be *saturated*.   Three-level devices are pumped by saturating the *outer two* energy levels.   If atoms relax rapidly in the unused transition (for example, $E_1 \rightarrow E_0$ in Fig. 10.9a), few atoms will remain in state 1, and there will be *more* in state 2.   In Fig. 10.9a "pumped" atoms, in the absence of stimulation and relaxation losses in state 2, divide about equally in states 0 and 2; in Fig. 10.9b most must be in state 2, with few in states 1 and 3.   The presence of radiation fields at the desired frequency $\omega_{21} = (E_2 - E_1)/\hbar$ will stimulate emission and reduce $N_2 - N_1$.   If these fields are applied abruptly, a large pulse of stimulated emission can occur before $N_2 - N_1$ becomes attenuated.   The system eventually reaches a steady-state situation if fields are applied steadily at ω_{21}.

The presence of relaxation or spontaneous emission between all three pairs of states complicates matters by producing attrition of $N_2 - N_1$ even without stimulated-emission fields.   The random photon emission produced is termed *fluorescence*, while energy from any nonradiative relaxation goes into phonons (heat).   In fact, if the relaxation probabilities P_{21} and P_{20} in Fig. 10.9a are large enough, it may never be possible to attain $N_2 - N_1 > 0$, or if so, only at excessive expense of pump power.

The processes involved in three-level stimulated-emission devices can be represented via a hydraulic analog in which reservoirs represent the energy levels (Fig. 10.10).   Relaxation and spontaneous emission are represented by "leaks" from a reservoir to the others above and below it, and stimulated emission by a circuit allowing fluid to pass from reservoir 2 to reservoir 1.   For simplicity, we neglect phonon-induced *upward* transitions; this is valid at least in optical devices.   The fluid, in this transition, pumps another fluid into another reservoir—the radiant energy into the electromagnetic cavity.   The valve opening is a function of the radiant energy in the electromagnetic system times the difference in levels in reservoirs 2 and 1: $S_{21}(N_2 - N_1)$.   Electromagnetic energy "fluid" flows into the electromagnetic reservoir, while cavity losses leak out, along with output power.   This model (apologies to Rube Goldberg) demonstrates that stimulated emission will not appear if "leaks" are excessive either in the atomic-state "reservoirs" or in the electromagnetic "reservoir."

It is easiest to analyze device behavior in *oscillators*.   Any true energy amplifier must also be capable of oscillating, since if the output power exceeds the input, part of it can be "fed back" as input.   Accordingly, device tests to establish materials parameters usually are based on obtaining oscillations.   A nonoscillating device puts out broad-band output "noise," whereas in oscillation the output becomes virtually

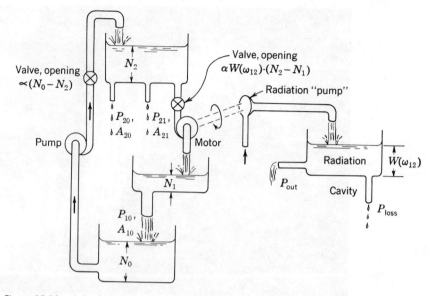

Figure 10.10 A hydraulic analog of three-level-device operation. There must be imagined to be a continuous supply of radiation to the radiation "pump." The analog neglects phonon-induced transitions from lower to higher energy levels (P_{02}, P_{12}).

monochromatic. An oscillator requires as its electromagnetic system only, for example, a low-loss cavity resonant at $\omega_{21} = (E_2 - E_1)/\hbar$. The radiation needed to initiate the oscillations is always present in the form of thermal energy. Only if $N_2 - N_1$ is large enough to offset cavity energy losses can oscillations be sustained. When the cavity is properly tuned, oscillations build up quickly, but may quickly decay in amplitude as $N_2 - N_1$ becomes depleted below the start-oscillation condition. Under some conditions, $N_2 - N_1$ may be built up by the pump faster than fields can be built up in the cavity. We may then expect oscillator output to consist of a series of nearly exponential (decaying) pulses, as is typical of the output variation in many optical-laser oscillators (Fig. 10.11).

A full description of device operation requires dynamic relations for level populations (10.56) and (10.57), as well as separate relations for the electromagnetic system, and the values of coupling parameters. The total stimulated-emission power $S_{21}(N_2 - N_1)\hbar\omega_{21}$ provides both the power loss

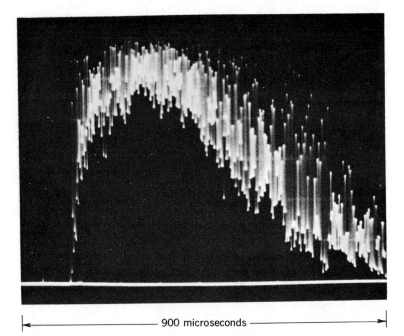

|←——————————— 900 microseconds ———————————→|

Figure 10.11   Variations in the output of a stimulated-emission oscillator.   Output does not commence until the pump has built $N_2 - N_1$ to a high enough level.   Independent operation of different parts of the device as separate relaxation oscillators gives rise to output pulses, typically of microsecond duration in lasers.   (*Photo, courtesy of E. Snitzer, American Optical Co., Southbridge, Mass.*)

and the output power.   Using (10.45), with (10.51) (which also applies in a resonant cavity),

$$S_{21} = B_{21}g(\omega_c)\epsilon\hat{\mathcal{E}}^2 = B_{21}g(\omega_c)\frac{E_{\omega_c}}{V'} \tag{10.59}$$

Since $\epsilon\hat{\mathcal{E}}^2$ is the cavity field energy density, it equals the total cavity-mode energy (E_{ω_c}) divided by a quantity of the order of the cavity volume V' (geometry-dependent).   Equation of stimulated power with the sum of loss and output power gives

$$(N_2 - N_1)B_{21}g(\omega_c)\frac{E_{\omega_c}}{V'} = \frac{P_{\text{loss}} + P_{\text{out}}}{E_2 - E_1} \tag{10.60}$$

The Q of a cavity is defined as the energy stored in the cavity mode divided by the energy lost per radian of the oscillation:

$$Q = \frac{E_{\omega_c}\omega_c}{P_{\text{loss}}} \tag{10.61}$$

Substituting into (10.60),

$$E_{\omega_c} = \frac{V' P_{\text{out}}/\hbar\omega_c}{g(\omega_c)B_{21}(N_2 - N_1) - V'/Q\hbar} \tag{10.62}$$

The population difference $(N_2 - N_1)$ is related to the power output and the loss of the cavity. The "start-oscillation" condition is $P_{\text{out}} = 0$. In order for E_{ω_c} to be able to grow from zero, it is necessary that $N_2 - N_1$ be large enough so that the denominator of (10.62) is zero:

$$\frac{N_2 - N_1}{V'} \geq \frac{1}{Q\hbar B_{21}g(\omega_c)} \tag{10.63}$$

The condition for start of oscillations favors a small cavity of high Q (i.e., low electrical losses), a strong interaction parameter B, and a narrow-line-width transition [$g(\omega_c)$ large]. For $P_{\text{out}} > 0$, $N_2 - N_1$ must be increased, e.g., doubled when the power output just equals the cavity losses. If (10.63) is combined with (10.56) and (10.57), the conditions on state populations, one can obtain oscillation criteria (pump power required, etc.). Amplifier-gain criteria are similar in form.

The physical configurations of both microwave and optical stimulated-emission devices are discussed in the following sections. Although the use of different electronic transitions (paramagnetic in the microwave case, orbital in the optical case) makes requirements somewhat different, these devices are limited at any frequency by considerations of line width, cavity losses, and obtainable population inversion. In every case, the ultimate frequency stability of a stimulated-emission oscillator is determined, not by the transition itself, but by the stability of the resonant frequency of the electromagnetic system. There is no known solid-state transition having "zero line width." In this respect, the operation of stimulated-emission devices is comparable with conventional electronic oscillators and amplifiers, for a "monochromatic" output can be obtained from an electronic oscillator even though the amplification mechanism can operate over a range of frequencies.

10.7   Microwave (Maser) Devices

Substantially different motivations have dictated device development at microwaves as against optical wavelengths. Good vacuum-tube oscillators exist, up to around 100,000 Mc.

With their low photon energy, solid-state stimulated-emission power devices cannot compete with these highly efficient sources. There are needs, however, for low-level low-noise amplifiers which can be well satisfied by maser devices operating at microwatt power levels. While microwave devices can be pumped at *optical* wavelengths, this is highly inefficient, because only one microwave photon can ordinarily be obtained per input optical photon.

Transition energies for microwave frequencies are much lower than for optical transitions; for example, 20,000 Mc/sec photons have energies of only about 10^{-4} ev. *Electron paramagnetic spectra* (Sec. 8.3) have the required energy-level differences and may furthermore be "tuned" by control of external static magnetic fields for alteration of operating frequencies. Spectra utilized in practical masers are often those of chromium or gadolinium ions as dilute impurities in ionic crystals. The most common maser material is pink ruby, Al_2O_3, doped with ($\sim$0.05 per cent) chromium.

Figure 8.3 shows the effect of *crystalline field splitting* and external magnetic field on the spin energy levels. The desired set of three energy levels for a three-level maser operation is available from three of the four levels of the Cr^3 ions. At least one of the three transitions in the three-level maser must involve a change of spin angular momentum by $\Delta S = 2\hbar$, a transition forbidden outside the crystalline environment.

The requirements on the transition frequencies and relaxation probabilities in a three-level microwave maser to develop an inverted population $N_2 - N_1 > 0$ may be derived by setting up kinetic equations for three states. Spontaneous emission is negligible; hence

$$
\begin{aligned}
\frac{dN_1}{dt} &= (-N_1 P_{12} + N_2 P_{21}) + (-N_1 P_{13} + N_3 P_{31}) \\
&\quad + S_{12}(N_2 - N_1) + S_{13}(N_3 - N_1) \\
\frac{dN_2}{dt} &= (-N_2 P_{21} + N_1 P_{12}) + (-N_2 P_{23} + N_3 P_{32}) \\
&\quad + S_{12}(N_1 - N_2) + S_{33}(N_3 - N_2) \\
\frac{dN_3}{dt} &= (-N_3 P_{31} + N_1 P_{13}) + (-N_3 P_{32} + N_2 P_{23}) \\
&\quad + S_{13}(N_1 - N_3) + S_{23}(N_2 - N_3)
\end{aligned}
\tag{10.64}
$$

If the radiation densities at the three frequencies are presumed known, as well as all the relaxation probabilities, the equations may be used to obtain *steady-state* solutions by setting each of the $dN_i/dt = 0$.   Only two of the three homogeneous equations are independent; the third required equation is

$$N_1 + N_2 + N_3 = N \tag{10.65}$$

N_i and N may be defined either as total numbers of ions or as densities.

In terms of new independent variables N_1, $N_2 - N_1$, and N_3, (10.64) and (10.65) may be expressed as

$$N_1(-P_{12} - P_{13} + P_{21} - S_{13}) + (N_2 - N_1)(S_{12} + P_{21})$$
$$+ N_3(S_{13} + P_{31}) = 0$$
$$N_1(P_{13} + P_{23} + S_{13} + S_{23}) + (N_2 - N_1)(P_{23} + S_{23}) \tag{10.66}$$
$$+ N_3(-P_{31} - P_{32} - S_{13} - S_{23}) = 0$$
$$2N_1 + (N_2 - N_1) + N_3 = N$$

With given S_{ij} and P_{ij}, the determination of the N_i is straightforward but lengthy algebra.   Let us, accordingly, consider only those conditions on the pump intensity S_{13} and on P_{ij} required for a minimal degree of inversion ($N_2 - N_1 \geq 0$). We can set both S_{23} and S_{12} at zero, in this limiting condition. The resulting condition will be "start oscillation" only for a lossless cavity, however.

In the solution of (10.66), the same denominator determinant applies for N_1, $N_2 - N_1$, and N_3.   Since only $N_2 - N_1$ may possibly be negative, the *numerator* (of $N_2 - N_1$) contains the only changes of sign.   The numerator of the solution for $N_2 - N_1$ is

$$S_{13}(P_{23} - P_{12} + P_{21} - P_{32})$$
$$+ \text{(products of } P \text{ terms, in pairs)} \tag{10.67}$$

The denominator is negative.   The expression as a whole may be written in the form

$$N_2 - N_1 = \frac{S_{13}(P_{23} - P_{12} + P_{21} - P_{32}) + f_1}{-f_2}$$
$$f_1, f_2 > 0 \tag{10.68}$$

Since the denominator *does not* change sign versus S_{13}, if $N_2 - N_1$ is *ever* to be positive, a necessary (but not sufficient) condition for $N_2 - N_1 > 0$ is

$$P_{21} - P_{12} < P_{32} - P_{23} \tag{10.69}$$

For energy differences small with respect to kT, the exponential (10.55) may be represented by the first two terms of its series; that is, $e^{-\hbar\omega/kT} \cong 1 - \hbar\omega/kT$.   Then

$$P_{12} \cong P_{21}\left(1 - \frac{\hbar\omega_{12}}{kT}\right) \qquad P_{23} \cong P_{32}\left(1 - \frac{\hbar\omega_{23}}{kT}\right)$$

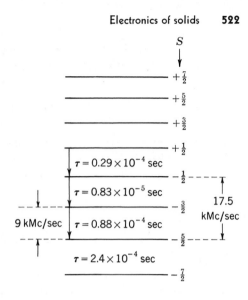

Figure 10.12   Increase of relaxation rate of $(S = -\frac{1}{2}) \rightarrow (S = -\frac{3}{2})$ transition by absorption, using a second impurity. These relaxation times (τ, measured at $4.2°K$) permit operation with a signal frequency more than one-half of the pump frequency. [*After H. E. D. Scovil, G. Feher, and H. Seidel, Phys. Rev.*, **105**:762 (1957).]

The appropriate condition on the relaxation probabilities is now

$$P_{21} \frac{\hbar\omega_{12}}{kT} < P_{32} \frac{\hbar\omega_{23}}{kT}$$

or

$$\frac{P_{21}}{P_{32}} < \frac{\omega_{23}}{\omega_{12}} = \frac{\omega_{\text{pump}} - \omega_{\text{signal}}}{\omega_{\text{signal}}} \tag{10.70}$$

where $\omega_{12} = \omega_{\text{signal}}$, and $\omega_{13} = \omega_{\text{pump}}$. The same relation (10.68) gives a lower limit of $f_1/(P_{32} + P_{12} - P_{23} - P_{21})$ for the pump power S_{13}.

If the relaxation probabilities P_{32} and P_{21} are equal, (10.70) becomes

$$\omega_{\text{pump}} > 2\omega_{\text{signal}} \tag{10.71}$$

Although $P_{32} \approx P_{21}$ is a reasonable approximation (e.g., in ruby), it is possible to enhance one relaxation probability by adding impurity ions which are excited by energy from the active ions and later dumping this energy into phonons. This has actually been done using a gadolinium (Gd^{3+}) ion as the active impurity ion and cerium as a second impurity in lanthanum ethyl sulfate;[1] 9,000 Mc/sec output was obtained, with 17,500 Mc/sec pumping, clearly avoiding (10.71) (Fig. 10.12).

[1] H. E. D. Scovil et al., *Phys. Rev.*, **105**:762–763 (Jan. 15, 1957).

Reduction of the relaxation probabilities P_{ij} improves operation by decreasing the start-oscillation value of pump intensity S_{13}. In microwave-maser-device materials, the excited-state lifetimes for paramagnetic excited states are of the order of 10^{-8} at room temperature, leading to excessive pump-power requirements. By cooling either to liquid-nitrogen temperature (77°K), or preferably to liquid-helium temperature (4.2°K), phonon densities are substantially reduced, increasing relaxation times by orders of magnitude. Bloembergen[1] quotes typical room-temperature and liquid-helium relaxation times for iron-group impurity ions:

Ion	300°K, sec	4°K, sec
Fe^{3+}	10^{-8}	10^{-3}
Mn^{++}	10^{-8}	10^{-2}
Cu^{++}	10^{-8}	10^{-2}
Cr^{3+}	10^{-8}	10^{-1}
Ni^{++}	10^{-9}	10^{-4}
Fe^{++}	10^{-10}	10^{-7}

The natural superiority of the Cr^{3+} ion relative to other iron-group ions is apparent. Operation with these other ions costs additional pump power, roughly in proportion to the inverse of the relaxation times quoted. Even so, the efficiency (output divided by input pump power) of ruby masers is typically less than 0.1 per cent. In low-noise-amplifier applications, however, the maser acts as an amplifier of signal levels near that of thermal noise. Since thermal-noise power at 300°K, in a signal of 10 Mc/sec bandwidth, is about 5×10^{-14} watt, microwatt output levels are adequate. While ruby has been the most common maser material, special applications suggest other materials having a larger group of spin states. One desirable feature is *low-frequency pumping*, enabling masers to operate at frequencies where sufficient pumping power cannot be obtained from vacuum-tube pump sources. The Fe^{3+} ion in rutile (TiO_2) has six spin states ($S_z = \frac{5}{2}, \frac{3}{2}, \ldots , -\frac{5}{2}$). An energy-level diagram vs. applied magnetic field is shown in Fig. 10.13. The field is adjusted so that the energy differences $E_3 - E_1$ and $E_5 - E_3$, as well as $E_4 - E_2$, are exactly the same. (The crystal axes and field must have a particular

[1] N. Bloembergen, D. B. Langmuir, and W. D. Hershberger (eds.), "Foundations of Future Electronics," p. 94, McGraw-Hill Book Company, New York, 1962.

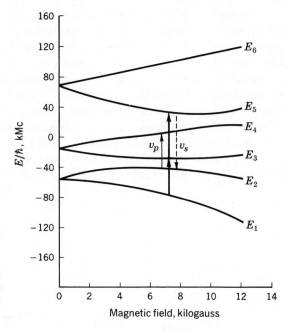

Figure 10.13 Selection of energy levels to provide equally spaced intervals permits pumping in two successive steps and therefore operation at signal frequency less than the pump frequency. [*After* W. E. Hughes, *Proc. IRE*, **50**:169 (1962).]

orientation to achieve this condition.) A single pump at 65,000 Mc/sec not only pumps electrons from E_1 to E_3, but from E_2 to E_4 and E_3 to E_5. At sufficient intensity it will *saturate* the three levels ($N_1 \approx N_3 \approx N_5$). The transition $E_5 \rightarrow E_2$ has a photon frequency of 96,000 Mc/sec. With a suitable cavity the maser will amplify or oscillate at 6,000 Mc/sec, well above the 65,000 Mc/sec pump frequency. The efficiency is invariably lower than that of three-level operation, because of the added numbers of ions making $E_3 \rightarrow E_1$ relaxations.

The simplest form of maser is a simple electromagnetic cavity resonant at the signal frequency, with provision for applying pump frequency to active material in the cavity. This will amplify over a bandwidth corresponding to the line width of the maser material, $\sim g(\omega_0)^{-1}$, or the bandwidth of the cavity, $\sim \omega_c / Q$, whichever is smaller. The cavity acts like a *negative resistance*, from the viewpoint of the signal

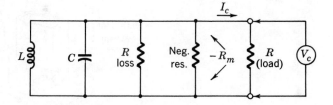

Figure 10.14 Equivalent circuit of a cavity maser. The negative resistance due to the population inversion must overcome the positive loss resistance. If the *net* negative resistance ($-R_m$) overcomes the load resistance R, oscillation occurs.

terminals [(10.60)]. Assuming that the population is sufficiently inverted, there exists a proportionality

$$E_{\omega_c} \propto P_{\text{out}} \tag{10.72}$$

In terms of a fictitious "cavity voltage" V_c, the energy density W at the resonant frequency is proportional to V_c^2 (as is true of any resonant electrical circuit). The output power may be expressed as $V_c I$; (10.72) may be written in the alternative forms

$$V_c^2 \propto P_{\text{out}} = V_c I \qquad I \propto V_c, \text{ or } I = -R_m V_c$$

Under these conditions, power comes *out* of the cavity; hence the cavity may be replaced at its terminals by a *negative electrical resistance* $-R_m$, in parallel with a resonant circuit representing its resonance (Fig. 10.14). In the circuit shown, voltage and power gains can be obtained, with a load resistance R placed effectively in series with the cavity terminals and a signal source. The voltage gain is

$$G = \frac{V_R}{V_{IN}} = \frac{R}{R - R_m} = \frac{P_R}{P_{IN}} \tag{10.73}$$

The condition $R_m \geq R$ permits oscillation.

Maser amplifiers can amplify frequencies over a bandwidth determined ultimately by their material, but often limited by circuit configurations. Bandwidths of a few tens of megacycles near 10,000 Mc/sec center frequency are typical of simple ruby masers. While the line widths of the transitions are increased by increasing the ion density to permit "spin-spin" (dipole) coupling of nearby ions, this has

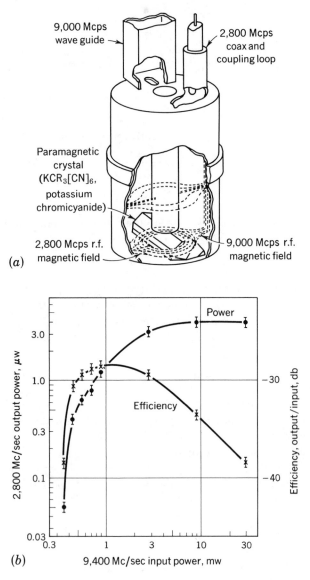

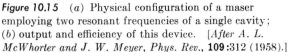

Figure 10.15 (*a*) Physical configuration of a maser employing two resonant frequencies of a single cavity; (*b*) output and efficiency of this device. [*After A. L. McWhorter and J. W. Meyer, Phys. Rev.,* **109**:312 (1958).]

a disadvantage. A small region of high *local* ion density will have transition frequencies so remote from those of more dilute ions that this region will respond only to certain frequencies; local relaxation effects will also be different from those elsewhere.

As in other microwave devices, if attainment of ultimate bandwidth is not possible using a single-cavity device, one employs *traveling-wave* devices in which the cavity resonance is effectively and losslessly broadened by coupling many cavities together. Another way to visualize a traveling-wave device is to imagine the maser's negative resistance distributed along a transmission line to produce a *negatively attenuating* traveling wave.

Some characteristics of a narrow-band maser are given in the schematic of Fig. 10.15. Masers are used in high-sensitivity radar receivers, in radiotelescopes, communication-satellite ground equipment, and similar applications. The need for a liquid-helium environment limits applications; hence in many microwave receivers low-noise varactor-diode (Sec. 5.6) amplifiers are used in place of masers.

10.8   Optical (Laser) Devices

Before the development of the laser, no optical energy source of near-monochromatic output existed. With this type of energy source, new vistas in communications and in spectroscopic research were opened. The new-found ability to focus narrow-band radiation into regions of wavelength dimensions, together with the high-pulsed outputs available from ruby lasers, made possible tremendous energy concentrations.

Although basic principles of three-level masers and lasers are the same, the phenomena involved are different. Here electronic orbital transitions, rather than spin transitions, are used to attain the desired transition energies. There is little chance to alter operating frequencies, except by changing materials. In lasers, spontaneous emission is the most serious relaxation effect. If excited-state lifetimes of 10^{-8} sec (that is, $A \simeq 10^8$) were used, it would be difficult if not impossible to maintain pumping strong enough to overcome these losses. Fortunately, however, transitions which would be termed "forbidden" in a gaseous spectrum have spontaneous-emission probabilities *very much smaller* than 10^8, even at room temperature.

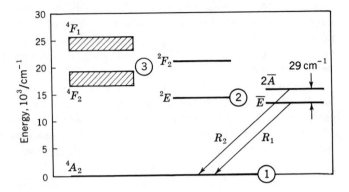

Figure 10.16 Pertinent energy levels of ruby, for laser operation. (1) Ground state; (2) intermediate states; (3) energy bands (upper terminus of pump transition). [*After T. H. Maiman, Phys. Rev.*, **123**:1151 (1961).]

Suitable laser materials cannot in general be predicted entirely on theoretical grounds, and it becomes necessary to study emission spectra of possible candidates to determine laser potentialities. The spectrum will normally contain a great many transitions, of which only a few will be pertinent to a particular device. It is important that others not interfere. A prime requirement is a narrow but strong fluorescent (emission) line with a long decay time after excitation is removed. The narrowness of the line assures that the transition occur between states whose energies are relatively discrete. Otherwise, at a given frequency, relatively few of the active atoms could aid the build-up of stimulated emission. The long decay time assures that P_{21} and A_{21} are small. An additional requirement is a *high quantum efficiency* for the desired transition; i.e., most of the atoms elevated (by pumping) to a higher energy level should return to the ground state through the desired transition. Otherwise much pump power will be wasted on useless transitions.

Materials having suitable emission lines of long relaxation time have been found among ionic solids doped with iron-group or rare-earth impurity ions. There are excited states of these ions, often several electron volts above the ground state, in which the electron wave functions still remain fairly well localized.

The energy levels of pink ruby (Al_2O_3 with ~ 0.05 per cent Cr^{3+}) are depicted in Fig. 10.16. The ground state is really two pairs of states with crystalline field splitting (Fig. 8.3). Above this are a pair of narrow-spaced states, and even higher, broad energy bands. The transition to the ground state from the lower of the two intermediate states ($\lambda = 6{,}934$ A, bright red in color) is a "forbidden" transition having very low spontaneous-emission probability at room temperature, $A_{21} \simeq 200$ sec^{-1}. Furthermore, the relaxation from the *band* to the intermediate state is relatively rapid, with $P_{32} \simeq 2 \times 10^7$. Spontaneous emission from the band to the ground state gives $A_{31} \simeq 3 \times 10^5$. Measurements also indicate that relaxation effects P_{31} and P_{21} are negligible, as compared with spontaneous emission.

The presence of a *band*, rather than a line, at the uppermost level is a tremendous advantage, indeed a necessity, to allow efficient pumping from broad-band sources (e.g., xenon flash lamps or mercury-arc lamps) which are the most efficient known means of supplying optical pumping power. If the upper level were instead a narrow line, only the tiny part of the pump output in its line width could be utilized for pumping. We have, therefore, a further requirement for a laser material: an absorption band of substantial width above the desired transition levels. Ruby has two such bands, both of which dump atoms into the upper stimulated-emission state.

The basic requirements on relaxation times in ruby lasers may be obtained from (10.56) and (10.57). With suitable approximations to take into account the high quantum efficiency of the desired transition, it can be shown[1] that

$$\frac{N_2 - N_1}{N} \simeq \frac{S_{13} - A_{21}}{S_{13} + A_{21} + 2S_{12}}$$

(10.74)

It follows that $S_{13} > A_{21}$ is a minimal requirement on pump power; i.e., the pumping must more than overcome spontaneous-emission losses from state 2 to state 1. Heavens shows that for ruby this is satisfied using an incandescent-pump source of 3300°K or above in thermal contact with the laser material. The *optical* radiation from gas-discharge lamps can be as high as from a thermal-radiation source of 10,000°K, without the attendant infrared (heat) output.

A ruby laser, cooled to liquid-nitrogen temperature, has, for example, been operated continuously at 4 mw output with a gas-discharge lamp requiring 930 watts power input. It is more common, however, to pulse ruby lasers from gas-

[1] O. S. Heavens, Optical Masers, *Appl. Optics*, suppl. 1, 1962.

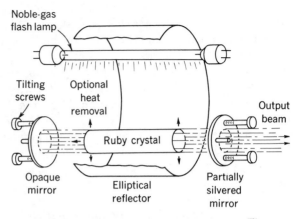

Figure 10.17   One form of pulsed ruby laser. The elliptical reflector has the pump source at one focus and the ruby at the other.

discharge lamps fed by capacitor banks charged to upward of $(CV^2/2 =)$ 100 joules of energy.

One form of a simple pulsed ruby laser is shown in Fig. 10.17.   The ruby crystal is located at the focus of an elliptical mirror system which converges the flash-lamp radiation.   The crystal may be cooled (as required for sequenced pulsing) via end connections, making use of the high thermal conductivity of the material.   The "cavity" is formed by two planar or spherical mirrors, which reflect the light back and forth through the crystal.   While early laser mirrors were formed by depositing metal coatings on the highly polished ends of the ruby crystal, separate mirrors permit adjustment to parallelism and improve efficiency.   Since the mirrors are separated by many thousands of wavelengths at the output frequency, the cavity can support many different modes of oscillation simultaneously, with extremely close frequency spacings. The several modes within the few-hundred-megacycle line width of the transition are the important ones.   Output may be obtained by having one mirror transmit a few per cent of the light incident on it.   When the flash tube (pump) is pulsed, no laser output is observed for $\sim$0.5 msec since $N_2 - N_1$ must have time to build up.   There follows a series of output pulses (as shown in Fig. 10.11).   Instantaneous output power may reach the megawatt level.   Intensity of the radiation is so great that many supposedly stable materials, such as glass lenses used for focusing the output, are visibly damaged after only a few "firings."

A major characteristic of stimulated-emission devices is *coherence*. If the output signal from a 1-cm-diameter ruby laser were all *in phase* across the output mirror, it would act like a "dish" antenna $1/0.00006934$ ($\simeq 14,000$) wavelengths in diameter. Since the beam width (solid angle Ω) of an antenna of cross section a is given[1] by $\Omega = \lambda^2/a$, the half-angle θ of the (conical) spread of the beam of radiation should be $\theta = \dfrac{4}{\sqrt{\pi}}\dfrac{\lambda}{\text{diam}}$, or about 0.15 mrad. Actual beams of radiation from lasers are found to be broader, as might correspond to radiation from an "antenna" $\sim 100\ \mu$ in diameter. Detailed studies of the output show that in this case the laser does not oscillate as a whole, but regions in the ruby $\sim 100\ \mu$ in diameter may oscillate independently of others. We have, therefore, a series of *paralleled* oscillators, not all producing simultaneous output pulses. The resulting radiation has a beam spread corresponding to any one such independent oscillator. This independent operation of different parts of the laser may be reduced by using spherical mirrors, even further by focusing the radiation, inside the laser, through a small aperture. The elimination of subsidiary modes of oscillation, as, for example, by the case of special mirror systems, is of major importance in practical communication applications.

If there is *no* cavity resonance at the transition frequency, $N_2 - N_1$ will build to a very high value $[N_2 - N_1 \to N$, by Eq. (10.73)], limited by spontaneous emission (A_{21}). When the resonance is restored, oscillation can build rapidly to a much higher value than usual. Figure 10.18 shows an experimental arrangement for detuning the cavity, with a resulting "giant pulse" of output radiation.

A somewhat similar procedure is used in laser *amplifiers*, where the optical resonant cavity may be dispensed with. While the high excess population ($N_2 - N_1$) cannot produce oscillations in very weak thermal radiation, it can be stimulated to emit by the incidence of light from a separate laser oscillator. The output radiation travels in the same direction as the input because of phase coherence of emission and incident radiation. Correct adjustment and timing of pump pulses to both amplifier and oscillator are essential. The power

[1] J. D. Kraus, "Antennas," pp. 53ff., McGraw-Hill Book Company, New York, 1950.

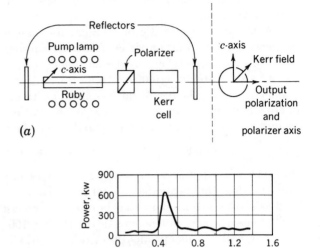

Figure 10.18   (a) An arrangement for "Q-spoiling" a ruby laser to allow $N_2 - N_1$ to build up. When the Kerr electrooptic cell is pulsed, light is allowed to pass through the polarizer and a "giant pulse" is obtained. (b) Output vs. time; note the absence of the small individual pulses seen in Fig. 10.11. [*After F. J. McClung and R. W. Hellwarth, J. Appl. Phys.*, **33**:828 (1962).]

theoretically attainable in such a large pulse is fantastic. In a ruby crystal of, say, 50 cm³, there are $\sim 10^{21}$ chromium atoms, each with available energy of ~ 1 ev. A total of $\sim 10^{-19} \times 10^{21}$ joules can be made available. With a pulse length of, say, 10^{-8} sec, peak power output could be $\sim 10^{10}$ watts. An actual peak output power approaching 10^9 watts has been obtained in an oscillator-amplifier system using the giant-pulse technique.

Lasers have also been constructed using many other materials, of which uranium-doped (U^{3+}) calcium fluoride (CaF_2, Fig. 1.15) is a good example. The lanthanide and actinide (rare-earth) metals, in general, have complex spectra. As one might expect, there are more energy levels between the ground state and energy bands than in ruby. While this provides a variety of possible transitions, transition energies are generally *lower* than in ruby (for example, $CaF_2:U^{3+}$ has output in the infrared, at $\lambda = 26,130$ A). The narrowness of

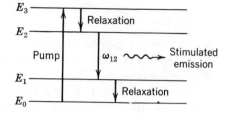

Figure 10.19   Schematic of the four-level laser. The lowest state E_0 serves merely to drain the lower-terminus state E_1.

absorption bands at the wavelengths where available flash tubes have large outputs may require increased pumping power, without improving laser output. Despite this, it is possible to obtain laser action from $CaF_2:U^{3+}$ at 77°K with only 2 joules of flash-lamp input energy, because of the degree to which the pertinent electrons in the uranium ion are shielded from neighbors. The relatively high degree of shielding of the absorbing electrons in rare-earth ions makes it possible in some instances to get laser action from these ions, even when not sited in a single crystal. Ions (e.g., neodymium) incorporated into glasses can be made to "lase" (i.e., produce coherent output), albeit with some increase of threshold pumping power. The incorporation of rare-earth ions (e.g., terbium or europium) into large stable metalorganic molecules called *chelates* also permits laser action, because of the constant near-neighbor relations provided by the other atoms of the molecule. These molecules may be dispersed in a liquid or plastic.

Many laser materials suffer from having excessive relaxation from upper states to the ground state. If the ground state is the lower terminus of the desired transition $(E_2 \rightarrow E_1)$, N_1 may accordingly remain large, even with high pump power, since it is the lower terminus of many relaxations. This is avoided in the *four-level laser*, which has, in addition to the upper band E_3, a ground state E_0 *below* E_1. Operation is described in Fig. 10.19. The pump causes the transition $E_0 \rightarrow E_3$, whereupon rapid relaxation causes the drop to E_2. Stimulated emission then takes electrons to E_1. They must then drop rapidly to E_0 by relaxation, P_{10}; at room temperature, however, P_{10} and P_{01} $(=e^{-(E_1-E_0)/kT}P_{10})$ may be nearly equal, and at equilibrium $N_1 \simeq N_0$. The problem is solved by cooling the laser so that $E_1 - E_0 \gg kT$. This will *depopulate* N_1 and permit laser action with a lower N_2. Most of the rare-earth-doped lasers operate by this scheme.

Semiconductor Lasers

Another very important laser-device principle, quite different from those described thus far, is the *recombination-radiation* or *injection laser*, which is based on a semiconductor junction diode. While electron-hole recombination in elemental semiconductors (Ge, Si) occurs largely by "indirect" (*phonon*) processes, this is true to a much lesser extent in some of the compound semiconductors. A major part of the recombination in GaAs, InAs, InP, and other "direct"-recombining compounds is due to photon emission. The main feature permitting this is the location of low-energy conduction-band states and high-energy valence-band states in near proximity in the first Brillouin zone. [Silicon and germanium have high-energy valence-band states, i.e., hole states, near $\mathbf{k} = 0$, but lowest-energy electron states are far removed from $\mathbf{k} = 0$ (Fig. 4.12).] Conduction electrons of low momentum can drop into impurity states, or perhaps directly into low-momentum valence-band states, liberating simultaneously (low-momentum) photons. The band gap and phonon spectrum also figure in the radiative-recombination probability. If there are no intermediate states below the conduction band by an energy less than the *upper limit* of phonon frequency, radiative transition will be more likely. At least one of the two terminal states involved in the radiative-recombination process in GaAs is thought to be localized, most probably *acceptor* states. The upper-terminus states must also belong to a narrow band of energies, to explain the relatively narrow line width of the recombination fluorescence (Fig. 10.20*b*).

In the recombination-radiation laser, pump action is obtained merely by forward-biasing the *p-n* junction diode. This injects large numbers of minority carriers across the junction (Sec. 5.4) which then recombine, in GaAs giving off characteristic near-infrared radiation centered at 8,383 A. The forward-biased junction voltage may be relatively small; in fact, must be less than E_g. This introduces an apparent anomaly, since the applied voltage carries one minority carrier across the junction for each electronic charge fed into the device. A small junction voltage thus yields energy output per carrier almost equal to the band-gap energy. Energy required for a carrier to pass across the junction potential barrier is supplied by its being on the thermal high-energy "tail" of the Boltzmann energy distribution. The photon

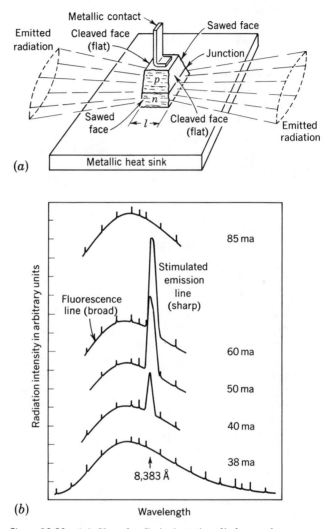

(a)

(b)   Wavelength

Figure 10.20   (a) Use of a GaAs junction diode as a laser.
The particular diodes used have impurity concentrations
above 10^{17} (Zn: Te or Se).   The dimension l may be less than
1 mm.   Reflective coatings need not be used because of the
high refractivity of the material.   (b) Operation of a GaAs
laser at 2°K with d-c input.   Oscillation is detected by the
narrowing of both the spectral output and the radiated-beam
angle.   Small peaks are calibration marks of the spectrometer.
Junction area was 5.4 × 10^{-4} cm².   [*After W. E. Howard
et al., IBM J.*, **7**:74 (1963).]

energy which leaves the diode as recombination radiation therefore carries heat away from the junction. In practice, this heat-to-radiation energy conversion is not appreciated, because of the ohmic losses in the diode.

The gallium arsenide diode has two of three major requirements for laser action: two states producing a sharp transition, and a pumping means. An electromagnetic "cavity" is formed in the diode wafer itself (Fig. 10.20a). Since the output wavelength is greater than that corresponding to band-gap energy, the crystal is essentially transparent to the output radiation. With the crystal polished, or natively cleaved, to produce two flat parallel surfaces, oscillations build up at the junction plane. The emitted radiation has the narrow beam angle which characterizes true laser action. The device, when cooled, may be operated continuously. Figure 10.20b shows how the radiation output assumes a narrow spectral line width when the condition for self-sustaining oscillations, i.e., the critical junction current, is surpassed. Were there a *broader* natural line width, the start-oscillation condition would occur only at higher power levels. A major advantage of this laser over those of the radiation-pumped variety is that only a d-c supply is required. Since *each* electron flowing in the power circuit produces a recombination-radiation photon, efficiency is high (up to 20 to 30 per cent in low-temperature-pulsed operation). Undoubtedly, many modifications of this principle will be exploited, for different wavelengths and power levels.

Optical-laser devices are also constructed using purely gaseous spectra. They operate well at room temperature (though in the actual discharge, electron temperature is around $10^4\,°K$). They can produce milliwatts of *continuous* output. Pumping occurs because of electron excitations in the discharge itself. These devices will not be discussed further here, since they make no active use of solid-state materials.

10.9 Broad-band Luminescence in Solids

Under appropriate excitation, many nonmetallic solids exhibit *luminescence*, i.e., the emission of radiation with a spectrum different from that of an incandescent body. In practice, one is usually most interested in visible radiation. Luminescence of various kinds is often categorized in terms of the source of *exciting* energy:

Photoluminescence occurs when the energy is introduced in the form of photons, usually of higher energy than those emitted.

Cathodoluminescence occurs because of bombardment by high-energy electrons, as in a television picture tube.

Electroluminescence occurs when electric fields (usually a-c) cause excitation of electrons (Sec. 10.10).

Thermoluminescence occurs as a result of heating, when electrons in metastable states make radiative transitions.

Chemiluminescence occurs in certain exothermal chemical reactions, where energy is released in photon form rather than heat.

The first three of these categories are the most important in electronic applications.

Materials are said to *fluoresce* if the emitted radiation ceases within $\sim 10^{-8}$ sec after excitation is removed; if radiation persists after a time long compared with spontaneous-emission relaxation times, the material is more properly said to *phosphoresce*, and is termed a *phosphor*. Most luminescent materials are phosphors in which intermediate electronic energy transfers delay decay of radiation output, in some cases many hours, but more typically milliseconds.

Luminescent solids include impurity-doped or defected ionic or covalent compounds, such as alkali halides, and many semiconducting compounds. Silicates and other mixed oxides can be useful luminescent materials. Practically any non-metallic material will luminesce under some conditions, but the more useful materials have special properties which enable high luminosity to be obtained in a desired region of the spectrum, with a desired method of excitation. Empirical methods for obtaining these properties have been developed over a period of many years. Although the field of luminescent solids has much in common with semiconductors, different groups have done research work in the two areas. Whereas semiconductors have become a field for engineers, phosphors remain primarily the work of chemists.

Luminescence in Wide-band-gap Semiconductors

Luminescence may occur in solids through any number of sequential electronic energy transfers. Two broad classes of materials appear to exist, however, usually discussed via different models. In one, primary exciting energy creates *free electrons.* Semiconductor theory may be used to describe the resulting phenomena. In the second, electronic transitions take place in the *localized* environment of an impurity or defect.

The class of luminescent materials in which free electrons play a major role is typified by ZnS. Wide-band-gap materials (ZnS has $E_g \cong 3.7$ ev) are desired, so that transitions somewhat less than the full band-gap energy fall into the *optical* range of $\sim$1.8 to $\sim$3.0 ev. The terminology of luminescence differs from that of semiconduction, though many concepts are common. As in semiconductors, one introduces two different types of impurities, here termed *activators* and *coactivators.* Activators, having energy levels near the valence band, are located in a fashion analogous to acceptor states in a conventional semiconductor, but serve primarily as *hole traps* or *recombination centers.* Coactivators are located near the conduction band and serve primarily as electron traps. Since pair generation (by incident radiation or high-energy particles) is the primary source of carriers, donors and acceptors in the usual sense are not required. In ZnS phosphors, copper is commonly employed as an activator, with chlorine a possible coactivator. The processes yielding emission in ZnS and related II-VI compounds are just the trapping and recombination processes (Sec. 4.6) in semiconductors. Whereas the elemental semiconductors Ge and Si usually release recombination energy via radiationless (phonon) transitions, some of the III-V compounds (e.g., GaAs, used in junction lasers, in single-crystal form) and many II-VI compounds recombine electrons and holes primarily by direct photon-emissive transitions. In the wider-band-gap compounds, the explanation lies partly in the fact that E_g, the band gap, is much greater than the highest phonon energies. In general, the emitted energy is far from monochromatic, because of the perturbing effects of phonons, imperfections, and impurities. Incident radiation or high-energy bombarding electrons elevate electrons from the valence to the conduction band. Here they may, for example, fall into activator levels, releasing photons immediately. The subsequent short drop into the valence band is nonradiative. Recombination may be delayed if electrons fall into traps (coactivator states). Undesired impurities may have states located in the band gap, enabling phonon transitions to occur. These are termed "quenching," or "poisoning," centers and are

quivalent to the recombination centers in Ge or Si. These
vill inhibit radiative recombination and reduce light output.

Luminescent materials are used mainly in the form of
very small crystallites, a few microns in dimensions. Prepara-
ion involves purification of the materials, grinding to desired
ineness, mixing, and heating to permit different components
o interdiffuse. Sometimes heating in a gas atmosphere is
used, to introduce impurities such as chlorine. By largely
mpirical means, materials can be produced having wide
variations in emission properties and response to different
timulations.

In luminescent solids, the external properties of most
nterest are:

1. The emission spectrum
2. The absorption spectrum
3. The energy-conversion efficiency
4. The decay time

The *emission spectrum* is of primary importance, in many
applications such as color television, where the spectral con-
ent of the resulting emission must be accurately controlled.
Figure 10.21 illustrates the emission spectra of the three
(cathodoluminescent) phosphors used in color television. The
eye distinguishes these broad spectra only as a "red," a "blue,"
and a "green"; their combination appears white, when excited
in the proper ratio. A common method of shifting wavelengths in an emission spectrum is to mix two compounds of
different band gap, such as ZnS and ZnSe, in varying propor-
ions. The control of type and amount of activators and
coactivators also determines spectral content, as well as conversion efficiency. Emission at the shorter wavelengths
(toward blue and UV) in general yields higher conversion
efficiency in such phosphors. The photon-emissive transition
then covers almost the entire band gap of the material; there
is less phonon competition; and the "shallowness" of the
mpurity states means larger cross sections for the interception
of conduction-band electrons. At longer wavelengths, i.e.,
in the red portion of the spectrum, the need for deeper-lying
impurities promotes phonon processes and reduces light
output.

Absorption spectra, the measure of the relative absorption
of a range of incident wavelengths, are also of great importance. For example, in "fluorescent" lamps the primary

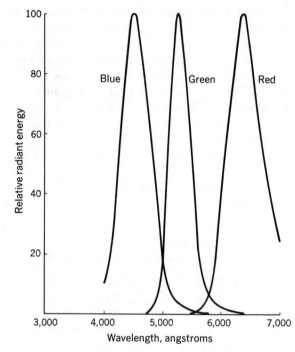

Figure 10.21   Spectral output of the group of three phosphors (termed P22) used in producing color television images.   (*Courtesy of RCA*.)

excitation﹒is mainly blue and ultraviolet radiation from a mercury-glow discharge.   This is converted by phosphors into visible radiation approximating a white (or other) "color." Unless a phosphor can absorb much of the available excitation, efficiency must be low.   Absorption is controlled largely by the band gap of the crystal, for the absorptive transitions are mainly from the valence band into the conduction band. Figure 10.22 illustrates absorption spectra of several typical (II-VI) phosphors, along with the resulting emission.   Radiation-induced luminescence is equivalent to three-level laser operation (Fig. 10.9), though line widths are much broader in typical phosphors.

Energy-conversion efficiency is a very complex function of the nature of the material and of the method of excitation. A phosphor intended for cathodoluminescence (as in a television picture tube) is compounded very differently from one which is to be radiation-excited.   In the former, there may

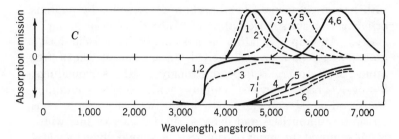

Figure 10.22 Emission and absorption spectra of ZnS phosphors (1–3) and ZnSe phosphors (4–7) with different activators and coactivators. (*After H. W. Leverenz, "Luminescence of Solids," p. 162, John Wiley & Sons, Inc., New York, 1950.*)

be processes such as x-ray generation competing for the available electron energy. Once the incident energy excites an electron to a conduction-band state, efficiency is determined by the likelihood of nonradiative transitions. Typical energy-conversion efficiency in a cathodoluminescent phosphor is only a few per cent (light energy out/electrical energy in), although there is almost unity quantum efficiency (one photon per hole-electron pair).

Decay time of light emission is normally in the micro-second or millisecond range unless electrons (or holes) are trapped in deep-lying electronic states. Trapped electrons radiate only after release from the trap, which can be seconds to hours after removal of excitation. The process is again typified in Fig. 4.13. Luminescence decay generally follows either an exponential law ($\sim e^{-t/\tau}$) or a power law ($\sim t^n$, where $n \approx -1$). Blue and ultraviolet phosphors have in general shorter decay times than red-emitting phosphors, because in the usual host crystals they require shallower activator and coactivator states. Major efforts in materials research have resulted in improved materials for this part of the spectrum, in general using more complex ionic solids as hosts.

Luminescence in Strongly Ionic Solids

While semiconductor energy-band theory is adequate for the treatment of photon emission and absorption effects in the II-VI compounds, a modified description is needed for ionic solids such as the alkali halides and many oxides such as silicates, phosphates, etc. Any measurable electrical conduction in these materials is attributable to the motion of ions rather than electrons.   Irradiation of these solids by photons or particles results in excitation of *localized* defect or impurity states.   An impurity atom in a strongly ionic solid has a ground state and several excited states, almost like a free atom.   State energies depend strongly on the surroundings, however.   Laser devices employ ionic solids containing transition-metal and rare-earth impurities.   Interest here is on simpler impurities and defects, since a narrow line width is not required, in many phosphors.   A simple divalent metal atom substituting for a sodium atom in NaCl, for example, will have a single electron in excess of a filled shell.   A *chlorine vacancy* also has an associated excess electron.   Such vacancies, which can, for example, be produced by irradiation which establishes Frenkel defects, are called *F centers*.   Alkali halides, while not completely typical of ionic luminescent solids, can, however, be produced readily in single-crystal form.   Under these conditions point defects of different kinds can be identified via their absorption and emission characteristics.

The excess electron of the F center has energy levels reminiscent of a hydrogen atom.   The "system" here consists not only of the electron, but also of the nearby (sodium) ions.   The equilibrium positions of the neighbor ions depend appreciably on the electronic state of the excess electron.   With the electron in a high-energy orbit in which its wave function spreads over many lattice constants, nearby ions probably recede toward their outer neighbors (Fig. 10.23a).   With the electron in a small (low-energy) orbit (Fig. 10.23b), however, the ions are attracted toward it into new equilibrium positions.   This situation is best depicted by plotting energy levels as functions of the distances of the neighbor ions from the vacancy center, as in Fig. 10.23c.   The energy represented is that of the entire moving system, the electron plus the neighbor ions.   We make use of the same hypothetical construction as, for example, in Fig. 2.14, a *configuration-coordinate plot*.   The absolute minimum energy occurs with the electron in the ground state and at a certain ion position r_1.   With the electron in its next-higher state, the minimum energy occurs at a larger ion spacing r_2.

An electron can make radiative transitions much more rapidly ($\sim 10^{-8}$ sec) than ions can readjust their positions.   If the system begins in the ground state with ion spacing r_1, absorption of an incident photon of energy $\sim \hbar\omega_1$ permits the

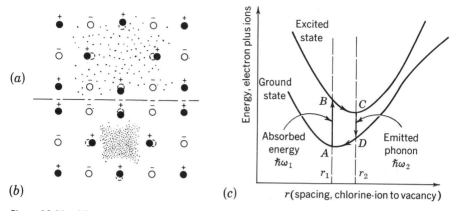

Figure 10.23 Electron associated with chlorine vacancy ("F center") in NaCl (a) in an excited state, (b) in the ground state. (c) Energy of electron plus surrounding ions.

electron to jump rapidly (vertically in Fig. 10.23c) up to the higher-energy state. The ions then relax to ion spacing r_2, giving up the energy difference in phonons. This process is much slower. Upon receiving radiative or phonon stimulation, the electron drops again into the lower state, releasing photon energy $\hbar\omega_2$ at a frequency ($\omega_2 < \omega_1$) *lower* than that originally absorbed. The system finally relaxes slowly to the initial state, releasing more phonon energy. Thus photon absorption must be at higher energies than the resulting emission. This energy difference is known as the *Stokes shift*, and may typically be of the order of an electron volt. Although our argument has been applied to an F center, it applies as well to electrons associated with other defects or impurity atoms.

The direct absorption-and-emission process described above is, however, only one way in which these materials may be made to luminesce. If it is desired to obtain output emission considerably lower in photon energy than the exciting radiation, an additional impurity, termed a *sensitizer*, may be added, which absorbs the primary (incident) radiation, emitting secondary radiation at a lower energy. This secondary radiation in turn excites other impurities which radiate the desired wavelengths. Emitted photons are reduced in energy by *two* successive Stokes shifts.

The distinction between ionic and semiconducting phosphors is not a sharp one. Certain impurities, even in materials normally thought of as semiconductors, may have several electronic states within the forbidden band of the host crystal. Completely localized transitions of the type described may certainly occur. Since recombination even in semiconductors is usually accompanied by phonon emission, which makes output energy less than input energy, presence of a Stokes shift is a characteristic of either mechanism. The manganese-doped phosphates, tungstates, and silicates used as phosphors in common "fluorescent" lamps, however, are more strongly ionic in nature, as compared with the II-VI compounds commonly used in cathode-ray-tube phosphors. The former materials presumably luminesce as a result of excited "centers" involving no electron transport.

Another application of luminescent solids is in the detection of high-energy radiation, e.g., x rays. A large detector volume is required because of large aperture areas and high penetrating power of high-energy radiation. Ionic crystals (such as sodium iodide, with a thallium activator) produce short intense flashes of light, upon excitation by such radiation. These crystals are transparent and easily grown and make an inexpensive solution to this detection problem. The light emitted can be sensed by vacuum-tube photodetectors. The rapid decay of fluorescence (0.3 μsec in NaI), together with the good high-frequency response of available phototubes, allows particles or x-ray photons arriving in rapid succession to be distinguished.

10.10   Electroluminescence

Electroluminescence, the production of light by direct application of electrical fields, is a composite of semiconductor charge transport plus luminescence phenomena. As might be expected, it is observed in wide-band-gap semiconductors such as ZnS. Although recombination radiation occurs in bulk semiconductors near well-defined forward-biased p-n junctions and in reverse-bias junction breakdown, single-crystal configurations are not practically suited to obtaining large-area luminous devices. An electroluminescent material should be a powder or film which can easily be applied to large-area surfaces. One reasonably practical solution has been found by imbedding individual phosphor crystallites into a plastic matrix. High fields are applied across a thin layer, using an a-c voltage. Ordinary phosphors dispersed in this way do not luminesce efficiently. More efficient electro-

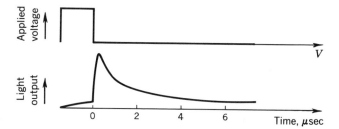

Figure 10.24   Response of an electroluminescent device constituting a layer of doped ZnS about 2 μ thick sandwiched between aluminum and a transparent but conductive coating of SnO.   Light output, with pulsed drive voltage, occurs mainly on the return-voltage step.   The light decay with time is found to have the power-law variation characteristic of two-particle recombination processes.   [*After W. J. Harper, J. Electrochem. Soc.*, **110**:41 (1963).]

luminescence may, however, be obtained in materials where an impurity agent (e.g., chlorine) has been diffused part way into the crystallites, from the crystallite surfaces.   Each crystallite might then be represented as containing a semi-conductor junction dividing it into an inner and an outer region.   The application of a high field to the layer induces fields across the crystallite junctions.   Internal current flow then produces carriers which are able to recombine and yield light output.   Because of the microcrystalline nature of the materials, it is difficult to determine exactly what basic processes occur.   An a-c supply voltage is essential, however, since in such a dielectric it is impossible for a steady current to flow.   Energy transfer to the phosphor is produced via *polarization* changes; accordingly, light output increases at higher drive frequencies.   Figure 10.24 illustrates response of an electroluminescent device to *pulsed* voltage.   Output is largest in the interval following the reduction of field, though there is some output during the pulse.   The response to a sinusoidal drive also reflects this same type of response.

Phosphor powders dispersed in dielectric layers are inexpensive and suitable for low-intensity illuminated surfaces, where surface luminosities up to several hundred foot-lamberts are obtainable (with sinusoidal drive at frequencies of several kilocycles and several hundred volts peak voltage).   Efficiency is ~5 lumens/watt at best, on the order of one-tenth that obtainable with conventional fluorescent lamps.

High efficiency is obtained *only* at low surface luminosity, however. Devices are not yet competitive as sources of illumination, but have advantages for some signal or display purposes where large-area illumination in a small source volume is desired. Electroluminescence is also obtained in thin metal-semiconductor-metal "sandwiches," as a result of the fields at the metal-semiconductor junction. Tunneling and avalanche processes probably play a part in the conduction. Because of the low mobility in the polycrystalline material, a-c voltages are again employed.

By placing a thin layer of electroluminescent material atop one of a photoconductive solid, it is possible to achieve "light amplification." An a-c voltage is applied across the two layers in series. Incident light impinging on the photoconductor permits current to flow through the electroluminescent layer, producing light output. A suitably opaque but electrically conductive layer must be placed between the two, to prevent direct excitation of the photoconductor by the luminescent material, if photons from the latter can excite the former. It is possible to intensify light images hundreds of times, using this scheme, although the slow time response typical of sensitive photoconductors (Sec. 4.7) is a practical limitation. Another valuable application is in amplifying images of x-ray fluoroscopes, permitting much lower x-ray intensities than are required for direct viewing of an x-ray-excited phosphor.

PROBLEMS

10.1(*a*) Consider a transition from a state with wave function of the form $\exp[-j(E_m t/\hbar) - jm\phi]$ to a state $\exp[-j(E_n t/\hbar) - jn\phi]$, where ϕ is the usual polar angle. (1) Show by evaluating the absolute square of a composite wave function such as exists during such a transition that the probability function "rotates" about the ϕ axis. (2) Show that the angular frequency of this rotation equals the transition frequency only by the selection rule $|m - n| = 1$.

10.1(*b*) At a time $t \approx \tau/2$ ($a_m = a_n = 0.707$) for the particular case $n = 1$, $m = 2$, plot $|\psi|^2$ from (10.1) and (10.4) at times when the $(E_m - E_n)t/h$ term in $|\psi|^2$ takes on maximum and minimum values. Show thereby that although $\langle z \rangle$ moves explicitly between limits, at these limits $|\psi|^2$ still extends over a large fraction of the potential well, so that z has appreciable uncertainty at all times.

10.1(*c*) In the limit of large m and n, what is the maximum excursion $\langle z \rangle$ can make, in the potential well of width a? Compare this coefficient with the lowest-frequency term in a Fourier series representing a *triangular wave z* versus t variation, of peak-to-peak amplitude a (i.e., the classical variation of z).

10.2(a) (1) Show that any classical model describing a radiating system must be represented in terms of currents and that *fixed* charges which are merely altered in strength do not produce radiation. (2) In terms of current flow, what is the equivalent of the acceleration of electrons?

10.2(b) (1) Show that *radial magnetic field* components (i.e., directed away from the radiator) are required to represent *angular momentum* in the photon.   (If the radiator is located at the center of a hollow sphere with nonreflective conducting walls, show that the current produced by the major field components, in the sphere walls, would interact with a small $\mathfrak{IC}_r$ to produce torque on the sphere.) (2) Using (10.13), describe how such a radial field component can be produced, and give an example of a (classical) electronic motion through which it occurs.

10.2(c) The simplest classical model of a magnetic dipole is a planar (e.g., circular) closed loop of current-carrying wire, having a current I and area (in its plane) A.   The current-area product, which in rationalized units equals the magnetic dipole moment, is kept constant as the area is decreased, to produce the infinitesimal dipole. (1) Show, by analogy if desired, that the retarded-potential description of (10.12) and (10.13) is not very suitable for magnetic dipole radiation (as, for example, with a precessing dipole).   (2) Outline, using electromagnetic theory, a formulation which is more suitable for describing radiation from time-varying magnetic dipoles.   (HINT: Cf. J. A. Stratton, "Electromagnetic Theory," McGraw-Hill Book Company, New York, 1941.)

10.3(a) In a circularly polarized electric field, the quantum number m, which measures the angular momentum about some selected axis, can change in a transition.   (1) By classical arguments show that changes of m in one direction or the other ($m \rightarrow m + 1$ or $m \rightarrow m - 1$) can occur only in a field of the proper sense of polarization.   (2) Set up, but do not evaluate, an integral of the form $\int \psi_m^* H_1 \psi_n \, dv$ describing such a perturbation, using wave functions containing factors $e^{im\phi}$ and $e^{in\phi}$ and noting also any requirements on the radial parts of the wave functions.

10.3(b) A hydrogen atom makes a transition in which power is radiated at a constant rate, from a $2p$ excited state to the $1s$ ground state ($-3.4 \rightarrow -13.6$ ev), in a time 10^{-8} sec.   (1) Using the classical orbit for angular momentum of $\hbar$, estimate the decelerating ($\mathcal{E}$) field required to produce the stated instantaneous radiation rate. (2) If we increase the applied field by a factor of 10 over this value, to assure that the applied field controls the transition, how much electromagnetic power density ($W = \epsilon_0 \mathcal{E}^2/2 + \mu_0 \mathfrak{IC}^2/2 \approx \epsilon_0 \mathcal{E}^2$) per cubic centimeter would be required in the vicinity of the atom? (3) If this energy moves at the velocity of light, what is the power flow in watts per centimeter squared?

10.4 Transition probabilities are defined in terms of the probability of atoms *beginning* a transition from one state to another during a given interval of time. With broad-band radiation present, however, the inverse of the transition probability $(1/S_{21})$ equals approximately the time interval during which a photon is emitted. (1) Using (10.51), with $Z_{12} \simeq 1$ A, at what photon energy is the spontaneous-emission time so short that the photons might be thought to consist of essentially a single half-cycle pulse, that is, $\pi/\omega_{12} \approx 1/A$? (2) What is the uncertainty in energy ΔE of such an emission?

10.5(a) As a comparison with solid-state spectra, determine approximately the line breadth due to doppler shift and to collisions in a *plasma* by (1) finding the doppler-frequency shift in a 2-ev photon, for example, when an emitting neon atom is moving toward or away from the observer at a velocity corresponding to energy $kT/2$ (at $T = 10^4 °$K); (2) determining the "bandwidth" $\Delta\omega$ of 2-ev photons disturbed by collisions, as $\Delta\omega/\omega \simeq (\omega \Delta t/2\pi)^{-1}$, where Δt is the time between collisions. Here assume the mean free path is 1 cm, with the velocity calculated in (1). Express results (1) and (2) in terms of wave numbers.

10.5(b) In gases one sees many spectral lines, with successively smaller spacings, toward a short-wavelength limit. For example, in hydrogen $E_j - E_i = -13.6(1/j^2 - 1/i^2)$. (1) Why are these narrowly spaced lines seldom observed in solids? (2) Calculate the approximate per cent of impurity ions in a solid (e.g., germanium) which would correspond in density to a gas of pressure 10^{-4} atm.

10.5(c) When two energy levels $(E_2 > E_1)$ in a solid or other atomic system are irradiated at $t \geqq 0$ by an intense source of radiation at their transition frequency ω_{12}, N_1 and N_2 approach equality. In such a case, let $E_2 = 1$ ev and $E_1 = 0$ ev; $T = 300°$K; $A_{21} = 10^4$; $P_{21} = 10^4$. Assume $N_1 + N_2 = 10^{23}$, distributed thermally at $t < 0$. Find N_1 and N_2 versus t if $S_{21} = S_{12} = 10^5$ for $t > 0$.

10.6(a) A quantum-electronic system containing 10^{18} active ions has a completely inverted population $(N_2 - N_1 = N_2)$ in its 1.0-ev transition. The dipole moment of the transition eZ_{12} is 10^{-30} coul-cm. If the system is immersed in a *lossless* cavity of 10 cm³ volume, with a line-width factor of $g(\omega_c) = 10^{-7}$, and electric field amplitude is related to cavity energy density through $W = \epsilon_0 \hat{\mathcal{E}}^2$: (1) Show that the increase of oscillation energy with time will be exponential, at least initially. (2) Calculate the time constant.

10.6(b) In the system of Prob. 10.6a, but with a lossy cavity having a Q of 10^4, what population inversion $(N_2 - N_1)$ is required for oscillation?

10.6(c) An electronic oscillator having a tuned circuit of low Q may still produce highly stable and constant-frequency output.

Can the frequency stability of a maser oscillator using a transition having a *broad* spectral absorption line be very high?   Explain.

10.7(a)   (1) Solve (10.66) explicitly to find the condition [i.e., the numerator of (10.68) in *complete* form] for $N_2 - N_1 \geq 0$.   (2) Reduce this in the manner of (10.70), letting $P_{12} = P_{23} = P_{13}$.

10.7(b)   In (10.66), if parameters $P_{12} \approx P_{13} \approx P_{23} = 10^3$ sec^{-1}, and assuming $S_{23} = 0$, $f_{12} = 10,000$ Mc/sec, $f_{23} = 15,000$ Mc/sec, at $T = 4°K$: (1) Find $N_2 - N_1$ as a function of S_{12} and S_{13}.   (2) Find $N_3 - N_1$ as a function of S_{12} and S_{13}.   (3) Determine the conversion efficiency from pump to output-frequency power $|\omega_{12}S_{12}(N_2 - N_1)/\omega_{13}S_{13}(N_3 - N_1)|$ as a function of S_{12} and S_{13}. Find maximum efficiency at high pump level and at combined high pump and signal levels.   (Use throughout the solution the approximation $e^x \cong 1 + x$, as in the text.)

10.7(c)   In a given microwave maser oscillator at start oscillation, $N_2 - N_1 \approx 10^{13}$.   Representing the cavity via the circuit of Fig. 10.14, at resonance $E_{\omega_c} = CV_c^2/2$, where V_c is the *peak* voltage across the terminals; $C = 2$ $\mu\mu$f, $V' = 10$ cm^3, $\omega_{12} = 2\pi \times 10,000$ Mc/sec, $Q = 2,000$, and $g(\omega_c) = 10^{-8}$.   When the operating value of $N_2 - N_1$ is *twice* the start-oscillation value, output is 10^{-5} watt. Find the corresponding value of R_m.

10.8(a)   Show the validity of (10.74), using equations of the form (10.56) and (10.57), with the assumptions that relaxation P_{21} is negligible and that $A_{32} + P_{32}$ is very large.

10.8(b)   Using the definition of $Q =$ (energy stored)/(energy loss/radian), find the Q of a cavity consisting of a pair of parallel mirrors, one perfect and the other reflecting 99 per cent of incident power, as a function of the mirror spacing in wavelengths.   Consider only the infinite-plane-wave mode.   (HINT: Half of the stored energy travels at the velocity of light in each direction.)

10.8(c)   Although it takes perhaps 500 μsec to develop a sufficient population inversion $N_2 - N_1$ for ruby-laser oscillation build-up, output pulses are short and may follow one another at ~ 0.5-μsec intervals.   Attempt to explain the differences in these time constants, in terms of (1) the limiting $N_2 - N_1$ at which oscillation dies vs. the thermal-equilibrium value of $N_2 - N_1$, and (2) the existence of different modes of oscillation in the crystal, which are partly coupled by using the same ions for operation.

10.8(d)   (1) In terms of majority- and minority-carrier densities in the p region of a GaAs diode, define the inversion density for laser action (i.e., the expression equivalent to $N_2 - N_1$).   (2) For a GaAs diode made of materials having the characteristics given in Table 4.1, with 10^{18} cm^{-3} donor and acceptor densities and $\tau = 100$ μsec, estimate this inversion density at the p side of the depletion layer, when $J = 10a$ cm^{-2}, at $T = 300°K$.

10.8(e)   Discuss influence of factors in the choice of material and geometry for a pulsed laser to produce megawatt peak powers:

(1) location of absorption and emission lines or bands, (2) thermal conductivity, (3) thermal-expansion coefficient, (4) diameter, (5) length, etc.

10.8(f) Describe in terms of the analog of Fig. 10.10 the operation of a laser when used to obtain a "giant pulse."

10.9(a) It is difficult to make phosphors suitable for efficient infrared emission. (1) State and discuss reasons for this. (2) What type of materials should be best for infrared emission, and why? (3) Would low-temperature operation improve performance, and if so, how?

10.9(b) Indicate ways in which the emission spectrum of a phosphor irradiated by high-energy electrons should differ from one excited by ultraviolet light.

10.9(c) An ionic phosphor with low defect density might be expected to have a very narrow emission band. Why is this not the case?

10.9(d) Under certain conditions (exposure to halogen vapor, high-temperature treatment) the visible coloration of an originally "crystal-clear" ionic crystal will change to blue or other colors. What is happening?

10.10(a) Represent an electroluminescent phosphor by a semiconductor diode in series with a capacitor. (1) Determine qualitatively the current flow vs. time and the diode voltage when a suitably polarized voltage pulse is applied across the combination; also power input to the diode vs. time. (2) If the emission is associated with the rapid recombination of minority carriers, sketch the expected variation of light output with time. Compare with Fig. 10.24.

10.10(b) The inconvenience of using high-frequency alternating current to obtain high light output from electroluminescent devices suggests the desirability of some sort of continuously conducting device formed of thin semiconductor and phosphor layers. What fundamental or practical problems are encountered in (1) a *large-area* diode device which would emit recombination radiation or (2) a multilayer device in which electrons could be accelerated in one layer to energies sufficient to cause ionization of impurities in an adjacent layer?

GENERAL REFERENCES

Excellent collections of articles have appeared in *Proceedings of the IRE*, special issue of January, 1963, on Quantum Electronics, and in a supplement (supplement 1, 1962) to *Applied Optics*, the latter containing many references.

Lengyel, B.: "Lasers," John Wiley & Sons, Inc., New York, 1962.
(The first book dealing with the subject.)

Leverenz, H. W.: "Luminescence of Solids," John Wiley & Sons, Inc., New York, 1950. (A physical chemist's point of view.)

Singer, J. R.: "Masers," John Wiley & Sons, Inc., 1959. (A readable treatise, including considerable information on device properties.)

——— (ed.): "Advances in Quantum Electronics," Columbia University Press, New York, 1961. (Proceedings of a symposium.)

Townes, C. H. (ed.): "Quantum Electronics," Columbia University Press, New York, 1960. (Proceedings of the first such symposium.)

Vuylsteke, A. A.: "Elements of Maser Theory," D. Van Nostrand Company, Inc., Princeton, N.J., 1960. (Deals mainly with the paramagnetic and statistical theory, also with radiation-matter interactions.)

Williams, F. E.: Solid-state Luminescence, *Advan. Electronics and Electron Phys.*, vol. 5, 1953. (Presented from an electronic-transition point of view.)

Appendix A: elastic properties of solids

A.1 Stresses, Strains, and Elastic Deformation in Solids

The mechanical vibrations of crystalline solids play an important role in all electronic processes. To a large degree, these may be understood in terms of classical analysis of a homogeneous material, as carried out here and in the following section. While a single variable, pressure, serves to define the mechanical force applied to a gaseous or liquid material, a more complicated representation is required for a solid. Likewise, the deformation is more complex. In this section we define appropriate measures of force and deformation in a solid, together with their linear relationships in elastic solids.

Stresses are the forces applied to a body, while *strains* are the deformations of the body. Mechanical stress applied to a body is developed across an *area*, like pressure. Unlike the situation in a liquid or gas, even static stresses may vary from point to point in a finite solid body. It is therefore convenient to define stress by imagining that one removes from the solid, at a point in question, a small cube of sides dx, dy, dz (Fig. A.1). We then apply to it the same stresses to which it was subjected in the solid. On *each face* of the cube, there will in general be forces in the three orthogonal directions. Thus, on the cube illustrated, a tensile force $T_{xx}\, dy\, dz$ is applied to the left-hand yz face. T_{xx} is the force per unit area of face applied, along the x axis (first subscript), to the face normal to the x axis (second subscript). In the usual convention, *tensile* forces are defined to be positive. The tensile force applied to the right-hand yz face must be $[T_{xx} + (\partial T_{xx}/\partial x)\, dx]\, dy\, dz$, allowing for some small change in T_{xx} across the small cube. On the left-hand yz face there will also be *shear* forces in the y and z directions as shown, represented by $T_{yx}\, dy\, dz$ and $T_{zx}\, dy\, dz$, respectively. The corre-

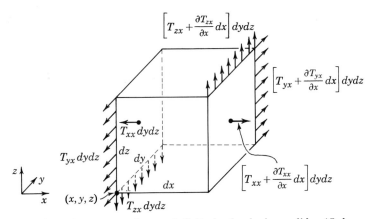

Figure A.1   Forces exerted on an infinitesimal cube in a solid.   (Only the forces on the faces normal to the x axis are shown.)

sponding shear forces applied to the right-hand face will accordingly be $[T_{yx} + (\partial T_{yx}/\partial x)\,dx]\,dy\,dz$ and $[T_{zx} + (\partial T_{zx}/\partial x)\,dx]\,dy\,dz$, respectively.   The sign convention is described in the figure; it is important to use a consistent convention,[1] obtained, as shown, by having the force T_{xy} produce a negative torque about the z axis, T_{yz} a negative torque about the x axis, and T_{zx} a negative torque about the y axis. The other three similar terms, T_{yx}, T_{zy}, T_{xz}, produce positive torques, in accordance with the *reversed order of their subscripts*.   On the pairs of $(dx\,dy)$ and $(dz\,dx)$ faces, there are also sets of forces in the x, y, and z directions, defined according to the same sign conventions.

The nine quantities T_{xx}, etc., represent the parts of the stresses which act to *deform* the solid.   Collected, they may be represented in the matrix form

$$\mathbf{T} = \begin{bmatrix} T_{xx} & T_{xy} & T_{xz} \\ T_{yx} & T_{yy} & T_{yz} \\ T_{zx} & T_{zy} & T_{zz} \end{bmatrix} \tag{A.1}$$

These nine quantities form a *second-rank tensor* (Sec. 1.4); the diagonal terms represent compressive-tensile forces, and the off-diagonal terms, shear forces.

We can also compute the *net accelerational forces* on the cube. The combination of forces on left-hand and right-hand faces leaves a force due to the T_{xx} component, $(\partial T_{xx}/\partial x)\,dx\,dy\,dz$.   The net x-directed force on the entire cube is, by combination of all three

---

[1] The reader will find sign inconsistencies in definitions in the various references.   This generally has no influence on the nature of results in device calculations.

terms of this type,

$$F_x = \left(\frac{\partial T_{xx}}{\partial x} + \frac{\partial T_{xy}}{\partial y} + \frac{\partial T_{xz}}{\partial z} \right) dx\, dy\, dz \qquad (A.2)$$

Similar considerations give the y and z forces on the cube:

$$F_y = \left(\frac{\partial T_{yx}}{\partial x} + \frac{\partial T_{yy}}{\partial y} + \frac{\partial T_{yz}}{\partial z} \right) dx\, dy\, dz$$

$$F_z + \left(\frac{\partial T_{zx}}{\partial x} + \frac{\partial T_{zy}}{\partial y} + \frac{\partial T_{zz}}{\partial z} \right) dx\, dy\, dz \qquad (A.3)$$

These are used in determining the *motion* of the body, as when we study vibrations, in the following section.

A net couple, or torque, is produced on the cube by the shear forces. The total couple about the z axis is due to T_{xy} and T_{yx} terms:

$$\frac{\left(2T_{yx} + \frac{\partial T_{yx}}{\partial x} \right) dx\, dy\, dz}{2} - \frac{\left(2T_{xy} + \frac{\partial T_{xy}}{\partial y}\, dy \right) dx\, dy\, dz}{2} = I_z \ddot{\phi} \qquad (A.4)$$

The couple may be equated to the moment of inertia I_z times an angular acceleration $\ddot{\phi}$ since the cube will rotate about the z axis when subjected to a couple of this type. The factor $\frac{1}{2}$ appears because the radius arm of the force is measured from the center of the cube. The derivative quantities are infinitesimal as compared with T_{xy} and T_{yx}. Since the couple varies as the *volume* of the cube ($dx\, dy\, dz$), while the moment of inertia of the cube, I_z, about the z axis varies as the *fifth power* of the cube edge, unless $T_{xy} \equiv T_{yx}$, the infinitesimal cube would by (A.4) perform infinitely rapid rotation about the axis. While it might seem that the forces T_{xy} and T_{yx} would directly oppose one another, together they produce a *distortion* of an elastic cube. Likewise, $T_{yz} = T_{zy}$ and $T_{xz} = T_{zx}$. There are thus only *six independent deformation stress components* (T_{xx}, T_{yy}, T_{zz}, T_{xy}, T_{yz}, and T_{zx}). These are conventionally given the notation ($T_1 \cdots T_6$) in the order given. The stress tensor (A.1) is thus expressible in the form

$$\mathbf{T} = \begin{bmatrix} T_1 & T_6 & T_5 \\ T_6 & T_2 & T_4 \\ T_5 & T_4 & T_3 \end{bmatrix} \qquad (A.5)$$

This brevity of notation is helpful when writing later expressions relating stress and strain.

Figure A.2 shows the nature of the stresses and the deformations they produce in a simple isotropic (e.g., rubber) cube. Application of a particular stress component to a crystalline solid produces, in general, a combination of several components of strain, *including* the one most closely associated with it. For example, even a rubber cube will contract somewhat in x and y axes with $T_1 = T_{xx}$ applied.

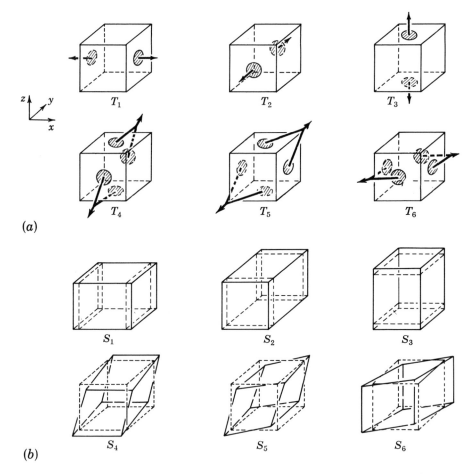

Figure A.2 (*a*) The indicated stress components will be produced in the cubes by application of forces in the manner shown (imagine the circles to be "suction cups" and the lines to be wires).   (*b*) Deformed cubes showing the form of the strain components $S_1 \cdots S_6$, each corresponding to simple deformation by application of the corresponding stress component $T_1 \cdots T_6$.

Defining *strain* in a solid also requires careful distinction between rotation, translation, and true deformation (which is the result of the stresses T_i).   Consider a point P in a solid (Fig. A.3), described by the radius vector **P** measured from some *fixed* origin O.   When the solid is deformed, the point **P** is shifted to a new position **P'**; that is to say, the atoms which we associated with P are now located at **P'**. The difference between **P** and **P'** is a measure of the distortion of the entire body, however.   That is, the effects of stresses are integrated from O to **P**.   If there are stresses on parts of the solid between **P** and

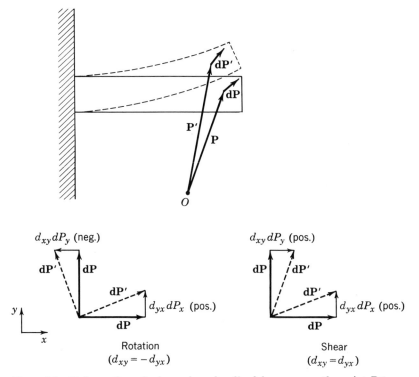

Figure A.3   Deformation of a beam by a localized force causes the point **P** to move to **P'**. *Local* deformation is indicated by change in length of $d\mathbf{P}$ to $d\mathbf{P'}$.

the origin, there could be a shift ($\mathbf{P'} \neq \mathbf{P}$), even if the vicinity of $\mathbf{P'}$ were under no *local* stress.

To find the local deformation we must accordingly describe not the gross distortion, but only that in the immediate vicinity of **P**. Imagine a second point very near P, having a radius vector $\mathbf{P} + d\mathbf{P}$. The distortion of this point is to a new point $\mathbf{P'} + d\mathbf{P'}$. The relationship *between* $d\mathbf{P}$ and $d\mathbf{P'}$ now describes local strain, but continues to define the *total rotation* of the local region, which we must separate from the pure deformation. For a given small $d\mathbf{P}$, each component of $d\mathbf{P'}$ may be expressed as a linear combination of the components of $d\mathbf{P}$. That is,

$$\begin{aligned}
\mathbf{1}_x \cdot d\mathbf{P'} = (dP')_x &= d_{xx}\,dP_x + d_{xy}\,dP_y + d_{xz}\,dP_z \\
(dP')_y &= d_{yx}\,dP_x + d_{yy}\,dP_y + d_{yz}\,dP_z \\
(dP')_z &= d_{zx}\,dP_x + d_{zy}\,dP_y + d_{zz}\,dP_z
\end{aligned} \qquad (A.6)$$

Note from the figure that if the deformation d_{xy} is the negative of d_{yx}, this pair of terms represents *only* a pure rotation about the

z axis. If, on the other hand, d_{xy} and d_{yx} are equal, only a pure deformation without rotation is indicated. We may therefore define two sets of coefficients, the *tensor quantities* **R** and **S**, which will represent the rotation and strain deformations, respectively:

$$\mathbf{R} = \begin{bmatrix} 0 & (d_{xy} - d_{yx})/2 & (d_{xz} - d_{zx})/2 \\ (d_{yx} - d_{xy})/2 & 0 & (d_{yz} - d_{zy})/2 \\ (d_{zx} - d_{xz})/2 & (d_{zy} - d_{yz})/2 & 0 \end{bmatrix} \tag{A.7}$$

$$\mathbf{S} = \begin{bmatrix} d_{xx} & (d_{xy} + d_{yx})/2 & (d_{xz} + d_{zx})/2 \\ (d_{yx} + d_{xy})/2 & d_{yy} & (d_{yz} + d_{zy})/2 \\ (d_{zx} + d_{xz})/2 & (d_{zy} + d_{yz})/2 & d_{zz} \end{bmatrix} \tag{A.8}$$

Each component of **R**, when added to the corresponding component of **S**, yields the corresponding component of d_{ij}. We are interested here only in the *strain tensor* **S**, since pure *rotation* of the body may be neglected in dealing with small-amplitude deformations, as, for example, in vibration problems. Note that the definition of the d_{xx}, etc., as *fractional* changes in the length of $d\mathbf{P}$, ensures that the strain **S** measures per-unit-length deformations; similarly, **T** has the dimensions of force per unit area (pressure).

By its definition the strain tensor is symmetrical ($S_{ij} = S_{ji}$); there are, accordingly, again only six independent components. In analogy to the convention for **T**, the strain components are defined:

$$\mathbf{S} = \begin{bmatrix} S_1 & S_6 & S_5 \\ S_6 & S_2 & S_4 \\ S_5 & S_4 & S_3 \end{bmatrix} \tag{A.9}$$

With this notation, in a simple elastic solid, S_i will be the major strain produced by the stress T_i, as illustrated in Fig. A.2.

The *elastic constants* of a solid relate linearly the stress and strain. These are applicable only where deformation is a strictly linear function of stress, completely relieved upon the removal of stress. Every solid has limits (the elastic limits) to the amount of strain it will accept without inelastic, or "permanent," deformation. Since the discussions here are directed toward understanding acoustical waves in solids and the small-amplitude vibrations of electromechanical transducers, linearity is an excellent assumption. As we show in Sec. 2.7, however, slight nonlinearities are required to explain acoustical distribution of thermal energy among the many vibrational modes of a body.

The stress **T** at each point in a body and the corresponding strain **S** are related completely by six linear equations:

$$\begin{aligned} T_1 &= c_{11}S_1 + c_{12}S_2 + c_{13}S_3 + c_{14}S_4 + c_{15}S_5 + c_{16}S_6 \\ T_2 &= c_{21}S_1 + c_{22}S_2 + c_{23}S_3 + c_{24}S_4 + c_{25}S_5 + c_{26}S_6 \\ T_3 &= \cdots \end{aligned} \tag{A.10}$$

Any such set of *inhomogeneous linear algebraic equations* has an inverse, which can be found by simultaneous solution of the first set:

$$S_1 = s_{11}T_1 + s_{12}T_2 + s_{13}T_3 + s_{14}T_4 + s_{15}T_5 + s_{16}T_6$$
$$S_2 = s_{21}T_1 + s_{22}T_2 + s_{23}T_3 + s_{24}T_4 + s_{25}T_5 + s_{26}T_6 \qquad \text{(A.11)}$$
$$S_3 = \cdots$$

While laborious, this inversion is straightforward.

The 36 components c_{ij} form what is called the *compliance tensor;* the terms s_{ij} form the *elastance tensor.* It may be shown that the sets of 36 components c_{ij} and s_{ij} in any material obey the symmetry conditions $s_{ij} = s_{ji}$ and $c_{ij} = c_{ji}$. The differential in the internal energy U of a small body of volume V, when stressed, may be written

$$dU = V \sum_i T_i \, dS_i \qquad \text{(A.12)}$$

These terms are equivalent to the differential work $F \, dx$, summed over all deformations. For example, a tensile stress T_1 applied to a cube of side l produces a force $T_1 l^2$ and a displacement $dS_1 \, l$, since S_1 is the deformation of the x length per unit x length. The product of force and displacement is therefore $l^3 T_1 \, dS_1$. From (A.12), we have $\partial U/\partial S_i = T_i$; from the definition of the compliance c_{ij} [Eq. (A.10)], we have $c_{ij} = \partial T_i/\partial S_j$. Therefore

$$c_{ij} = \frac{\partial^2 U}{\partial S_i \, \partial S_j} \qquad \text{(A.13)}$$

Since order of differentiation is unimportant, $c_{ij} \equiv c_{ji}$, and $[c]$ is symmetrical. The symmetry of $[s]$, $s_{ij} \equiv s_{ji}$, is a corollary.

There remain a maximum of 21 *independent* components of the elastance or compliance tensors. Only the least symmetrical of crystalline solids may have this maximum number of components, in which the compliance may be expressed:

$$[c_{ij}] = \begin{bmatrix} c_{11} & c_{12} & c_{13} & c_{14} & c_{15} & c_{16} \\ c_{12} & c_{22} & c_{23} & c_{24} & c_{25} & c_{26} \\ c_{13} & c_{23} & c_{33} & c_{34} & c_{35} & c_{36} \\ c_{14} & c_{24} & c_{34} & c_{44} & c_{45} & c_{46} \\ c_{15} & c_{25} & c_{35} & c_{45} & c_{55} & c_{56} \\ c_{16} & c_{26} & c_{36} & c_{46} & c_{56} & c_{66} \end{bmatrix} \qquad \text{(A.14)}$$

Such a completely filled-out compliance means that any stress component which is applied produces all possible strain components simultaneously. Fortunately, this complexity is seldom encountered in practice. An isotropic solid, as, for example, a material consisting of many crystallites of random orientation, or an amorphous (noncrystalline) material will have much less complex compliance and elastance, in the forms below:

$$[c_{ij}] = \begin{bmatrix} c_{11} & c_{12} & c_{12} & 0 & 0 & 0 \\ c_{12} & c_{11} & c_{12} & 0 & 0 & 0 \\ c_{12} & c_{12} & c_{11} & 0 & 0 & 0 \\ 0 & 0 & 0 & c_{44} & 0 & 0 \\ 0 & 0 & 0 & 0 & c_{44} & 0 \\ 0 & 0 & 0 & 0 & 0 & c_{44} \end{bmatrix}$$

$$[s_{ij}] = \begin{bmatrix} s_{11} & s_{12} & s_{12} & 0 & 0 & 0 \\ s_{12} & s_{11} & s_{12} & 0 & 0 & 0 \\ s_{12} & s_{12} & s_{11} & 0 & 0 & 0 \\ 0 & 0 & 0 & s_{44} & 0 & 0 \\ 0 & 0 & 0 & 0 & s_{44} & 0 \\ 0 & 0 & 0 & 0 & 0 & s_{44} \end{bmatrix}$$

(A.15)

The term s_{11} measures the amount of strain S_1 (i.e., tensile strain in the x axis) produced by an x-axis tensile stress. Clearly, since there is no distinction between x, y, and z axes in the actual material, the corresponding coefficients are equal: $s_{22} = s_{11}$, etc. Likewise, s_{12} measures the amount of y-axis strain which accompanies x-axis tensile stress. Imagine an isotropic elastic cube to be "squashed" by a compressive force along the x axis. It will expand equally as much in the y as the z directions; hence s_{21} and s_{31}, etc., must all be equal. There is, in such solids, no shear strain introduced by tensile stresses, or the converse, so the terms indicating such connection are all zero. Pure shear stress produces pure shear strain, whatever the shear axes; hence the shear coefficients are all equal ($s_{44} = s_{55} = s_{66}$).

Most solids used for *structural* purposes are polycrystalline and have elasticity constants defined as in (A.15). A simple test involves applying a tensile force to a bar and measuring the elastic elongation. The ratio of applied force per unit area to elongation per unit length is called the *Young's modulus*. Comparison with (A.11) shows that this quantity is completely equivalent to s_{11}^{-1}. In a similar measurement, the reduction of one edge of a bar of, for example, square cross section is measured. The ratio of per unit reduction in the side of the square to elongation per unit length of the bar is termed *Poisson's ratio* ($-s_{12}/s_{11}$). The *shear modulus* s_{44}^{-1} is measurable by applying a torque to twist a bar, generally of round cross section. In most metals, the Young's modulus (sometimes termed elastic modulus) lies in the range 1 to 5×10^7 psi. Poisson's ratio is usually in the vicinity of $\frac{1}{4}$ to $\frac{1}{3}$, and the shear modulus is somewhat lower than the elastic modulus. Measurement of elastic constants of single-crystal materials may require measurements in various stress configurations.

A.2   Acoustical Waves in Solids

The properties of small-amplitude acoustical (i.e., vibrational) waves in solids may be studied using newtonian mechanics. For small-amplitude theories to have validity, the total deformation must at all times be small compared with any overall dimension of the crystal. Fortunately, this requirement is satisfied with little error by the thermal vibrations of macroscopic crystals, and even by most electromechanical transducer crystals.

Equations (A.2) and (A.3) provide a relationship between *total forces* on the infinitesimal cube and the derivatives of stresses. Through (A.10) the forces may then be related to the strains S_i, then to the *total displacement* of the solid at each point. This elastic force-displacement relationship is finally combined with the accelerational force-displacement relation due to the cube's mass m:

$$\mathbf{F} = m\,\frac{d^2\mathbf{P}}{dt^2} = \rho_d\,\frac{d^2\mathbf{P}}{dt^2}\,dx\,dy\,dz \tag{A.16}$$

where ρ_d is the density of the material, and $\mathbf{P}$ is the radius vector to the point in question.

The missing link is the relationship between $\mathbf{P}$ and the S_i. If x, y, z represent the coordinates in the *stationary* crystal, then $\mathbf{P}$ is a *function* of x, y, z, t. In the earlier definition of strains, the total motion of $\mathbf{P}$ (to $\mathbf{P}'$) was permitted to be large. To obtain small-displacement solutions, we assume that the *total* motion of $\mathbf{P}$ is very small. If the displacement of point P defined by x, y, z is given by $\mathbf{P}(x,y,z,t)$, the displacement of a nearby point $(x + dx, y + dy, z + dz)$ will be given by $\mathbf{P} + d\mathbf{P}$, where

$$\begin{aligned}
dP_x &= d_{xx}\,dx + d_{xy}\,dy + d_{xz}\,dz \\
dP_y &= d_{yx}\,dx + d_{yy}\,dy + d_{yz}\,dz \\
dP_z &= d_{zx}\,dx + d_{zy}\,dy + d_{zz}\,dz
\end{aligned} \tag{A.17}$$

It follows that $\partial P_x/\partial x = d_{xx}$, $\partial P_y/\partial x = d_{yx}$, etc.; in general,

$$\frac{\partial P_i}{\partial x_j} = d_{ij} \qquad i, j = x, y, z \tag{A.18}$$

Substituting into (A.8),

$$\begin{aligned}
S_1 &= \frac{\partial P_x}{\partial x} \qquad S_2 = \frac{\partial P_y}{\partial y} \qquad S_3 = \frac{\partial P_z}{\partial z} \qquad S_4 = \frac{\partial P_y/\partial z + \partial P_z/\partial y}{2} \\
&\qquad S_5 = \frac{\partial P_x/\partial z + \partial P_z/\partial x}{2} \qquad S_6 = \frac{\partial P_x/\partial y + \partial P_y/\partial x}{2}
\end{aligned} \tag{A.19}$$

This is the desired (small-signal) relationship between displacement and strain.

The complexity of the controlling equations does not suggest the forms which possible vibrational waves may take in a simple body. This may be inferred, however, by considering waves traveling in a

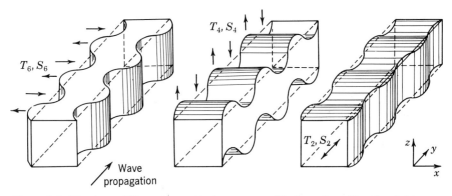

Figure A.4 The three different acoustical waves possible in a given direction (y) in an elastic solid. The two on the left are shear waves, that on the right a compressional wave.

given direction (Fig. A.4). Once the direction of propagation is determined, there can in fairly simple (e.g., isotropic) materials be three basic directions of the displacement of the material by the wave. When the displacement is along the axis of propagation, the wave is termed a *longitudinal* or *compression wave*. When motion is transverse to the axis, waves are termed *transverse* or *shear waves;* in isotropic material there may be two of these, with orthogonal displacements. In more complex crystalline material, several shear and tensile strains accompany one another in waves traveling in certain directions through the material, but by complicated analysis it is possible to isolate three noninteracting waves, all in general having different wave velocities.

Simple shear waves in isotropic materials are the simplest to analyze. Because of the absence of off-diagonal terms in the compliance and elastance, a single component of shear strain may exist, in the absence of other strains, as in Fig. A.4. Here we assume that the shear stress and strain T_6 and S_6 are involved and that the wave is a simple plane wave propagating in the y direction, so that x and z derivatives of all quantities are zero. Then, according to (A.2), there will be forces on an infinitesimal cube: $F_x = (dT_6/dy)\, dx\, dy\, dz$. In the isotropic material, $T_6 = c_{66}S_6 \equiv c_{44}S_6$, and thus $F_x = c_{44}(dS_6/dy)\, dx\, dy\, dz$. From Eqs. (A.19), $S_6 = (dP_x/dy)/2$; hence

$$F_x = c_{44}\frac{d^2 P_x}{dy^2}\, dx\, dy\, dv$$

The accelerational force on the cube is $\rho_d\, d^2P_x/dt^2$. Since the accelerational and restoring (elastic) forces must be equal,

$$\frac{c_{44}}{2\rho_d}\frac{d^2 P_x}{dy^2} = \frac{d^2 P_x}{dt^2} \tag{A.20}$$

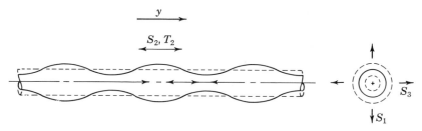

Figure A.5   Compressional waves in a thin round cylindrical rod.

This is a simple wave equation, having solutions $P_x = f(t \pm y/v_s)$, where the acoustical velocity v_s (for shear waves) is

$$v_s = \left(\frac{c_{44}}{2\rho_d}\right)^{\frac{1}{2}}$$
(A.21)

The solution predicts waves of constant propagation velocity v_s. The velocity is increased by raising the compliance or lowered by raising the density of the material, just as in the case of a mechanical transmission line consisting of masses connected by springs (Sec. 2.7).

The case of the compression wave is more complex, because the material tends to spread transversely if it can. We may consider two limiting cases of compressive waves, to illustrate methods of solution. First, let a uniform-plane compression wave be moving in the y direction through a body which extends to infinity in the x and z directions. Clearly, there can be no appreciable associated transverse movement, for this is restricted by the infinitude of the transverse dimension. We may therefore assume that S_1 and S_3 are zero, while S_2 forms the main strain in the propagation of the wave. Shear may be neglected, if the material has no shear-compression coupling terms in the compliance. We may then use (A.10) to show that $T_2 = c_{22}S_2 \equiv c_{11}S_2$. Although $T_1 = c_{12}S_2$, etc., the presence of transverse stress *without* transverse movement does not influence the wave motion. Following the same method as before, the wave may be shown to have a velocity

$$v_{c\infty} = \left(\frac{c_{11}}{\rho_d}\right)^{\frac{1}{2}}$$
(A.22)

In the opposite extreme, consider the same compression wave, in a rod of small cross section (Fig. A.5). Now, certainly, there will be *no constraint* to the transverse movement of the rod; i.e., there can be strains S_1 and S_3 in the x and z directions. If the rod is of small enough diameter, these strains cannot in turn produce any restoring stresses, since the surrounding air cannot provide these restoring forces. In this case, we may approximate the situation by the existence of strains S_1, S_2, and S_3, but *only* a stress T_2.   Equations (A.11) give

$$S_2 = s_{22}T_2 = s_{11}T_2 \tag{A.23}$$

Then, from (A.3) and (A.19), $F_y = dT_2/dy$, and $S_2 = dP_y/dy$.   The resulting wave equation, $d^2P_y/dy^2 = s_{11}\rho_d\, d^2P_y/dt^2$, has solutions with the constant wave velocity

$$v_c \text{ (thin rod)} = (s_{11}\rho_d)^{-\frac{1}{2}} \tag{A.24}$$

The definition of "thinness" has to do with the ratio of the rod diameter to the wavelength of the acoustical wave; this ratio must be small. In the case of a rod of large but not infinite cross section, a more detailed two-dimensional solution is called for.

GENERAL REFERENCES

Cady, W. G.: "Piezoelectricity," McGraw-Hill Book Company, New York, 1946.

Joos, G.: "Theoretical Physics," 2d ed., Hafner Publishing Company, Inc., New York, 1950.

Mason, W. P.: "Piezoelectric Crystals," D. Van Nostrand Company, Inc., Princeton, N.J., 1950.

Morse, P. M., and H. Feshbach: "Methods of Theoretical Physics," McGraw-Hill Book Company, New York, 1953.

Appendix B: quantum theory

B.1 Particle-wave Equations

The motion of systems on an atomic scale is not correctly described by application of Newton's laws. Processes such as electron diffraction (Sec. 2.9) suggest that particles often behave in a wavelike manner, while the discrete frequencies of energy absorption and emission of energy by matter suggest that atomic systems can exist in conditions of uniquely defined energy (unlike classical particle systems, which may have any energy).

Einstein observed in 1905 that electromagnetic energy occurs only in discrete units, or *quanta*, where the energy of one quantum, or *photon*, is related to its frequency f or angular frequency ω by

$$E = hf. \equiv \hbar\omega \tag{B.1}$$

The constant h is termed *Planck's constant* ($= 6.6253 \times 10^{-34}$ joule-sec). The quantity $\hbar$ (h-bar) equals $h/2\pi$, and is used universally as an abbreviation.

The simplest form of function often used to describe electromagnetic and other types of linear-wave phenomena is the uniform sinusoidal plane wave:

$$\cos(\omega t - \mathbf{k} \cdot \mathbf{r}) = \operatorname{Re} e^{-i(\omega t - \mathbf{k} \cdot \mathbf{r})} \tag{B.2}$$

Here $\mathbf{r}$ is a radius vector, and $\mathbf{k}$ a vector (which may be a function of frequency) known as the *wave vector*, or *propagation vector*. The condition $\mathbf{k} \cdot \mathbf{r} = \text{const}$ defines a plane ($k_x x + k_y y + k_z z = \text{const}$) over which the wave has a constant value at given time. The vector $\mathbf{k}$ is normal to the plane. The wave *travels* in the direction of $\mathbf{k}$, in that a given value of the wave function is found at a later time in a plane which is displaced in the direction of $\mathbf{k}$. The wavelength of the wave λ is defined as the perpendicular distance between planes for which the exponential changes by $2\pi j$:

$$\lambda = \frac{2\pi}{|k|} \tag{B.3}$$

Energy and momentum are meaningful in dealing with particles and waves of any kind and on any scale. An electromagnetic photon carries energy, in the associated electric and magnetic fields. It also carries momentum, which can be demonstrated by reflecting electromagnetic waves perpendicularly from a mirror surface. The magnetic field of the electromagnetic wave induces a current in the mirror, which interacts with the magnetic field to apply a force to the mirror (radiation pressure) in the direction of the incident radiation. This force can be thought of as the result of elastic "bouncing" of momentum-carrying photons from the surface. It can be shown from classical electromagnetic theory that an EM wave of fixed total energy carries a fixed momentum.

$$\frac{E}{p} = \frac{\text{energy}}{\text{momentum}} = c \text{ (velocity of light)} \tag{B.4}$$

A single photon having energy $E = \hbar\omega$ will thus have momentum $p = \hbar\omega/c$. For free-space electromagnetic waves, in one dimension the propagation constant k is simply ω/c, so that waves traveling in the positive z direction can be described by a wave function

$$e^{-j(\omega t - \omega z/c)} \tag{B.5}$$

If the parameters ω and ω/c are replaced by those describing a *single* photon, this may be reexpressed as

$$e^{-j(Et/\hbar - pz/\hbar)} \tag{B.6}$$

Since a particle or a photon moving in free space behaves in much the same way, (B.6) could also represent such a particle. In three dimensions, the equivalent form is

$$e^{-j(Et/\hbar - \mathbf{p}\cdot\mathbf{r}/\hbar)} \tag{B.7}$$

where $\mathbf{p}$ is the directed momentum of photon or particle.

The function (B.7) should be the solution of some wave equation. If (B.7) is substituted for ψ in a special wave equation,[1]

$$-\frac{\hbar^2}{2m}\nabla^2\psi = j\hbar\frac{\partial\psi}{\partial t} \tag{B.8}$$

[1] ∇^2 is the vector operator known as the laplacian; in cartesian coordinates

$$\nabla^2\psi = \frac{\partial^2\psi}{\partial x^2} + \frac{\partial^2\psi}{\partial y^2} + \frac{\partial^2\psi}{\partial z^2}$$

The result is the *classical* relation between energy and momentum of the free particle:

$$\frac{p^2}{2m} = E \tag{B.9}$$

The wave equation (B.8) is the simplest one having this property.

The principle is extendable to other problems, as discussed later (Sec. B.6). If, for example, a particle has potential energy $V(x,y,z)$ (as, for example, due to the interaction of its charge with an electric field), the appropriate wave equation is

$$-\frac{\hbar^2}{2m}\nabla^2\psi + V\psi = j\hbar\frac{\partial\psi}{\partial t} \tag{B.10}$$

This is the *time-dependent* form of the *Schrödinger wave equation.*

As a *linear partial differential equation*, (B.10) has solutions dependent on their boundary conditions. The wave-function solution ψ should not be confused with the particle itself, but as a representation of the particle it should presumably vanish when and where the particle does not exist. For example, the wave function representing a particle in a container with walls which completely confine the particle should vanish outside the container. (This is automatically satisfied if the potential V goes to infinity outside the container, since the equation cannot have a solution of finite ψ in such a region.)

Wherever a wave function represents a particle of *constant energy*, it contains only a time factor $e^{-jEt/\hbar}$ [a *positive* exponent here cannot be a solution of (B.10), but this has no physical significance]. The partial derivative with respect to time operates only on this time factor:

$$j\hbar\frac{\partial\psi}{\partial t} = j\hbar\frac{d}{dt}\,[(e^{-jEt/\hbar})\psi(x, y, z)] \equiv E\psi \tag{B.11}$$

The wave equation (B.10), in the case of constant-energy particles, can thus be written in the *time-independent* form

$$-\frac{\hbar^2}{2m}\nabla^2\psi + V\psi = E\psi \tag{B.12}$$

B.2   One-dimensional Particle-wave Solutions

Certain simple solutions to the one-dimensional form of the Schrödinger equation are highly instructive and useful in dealing with motion, as, for example, in electron devices whose dimensions transverse to direction of current flow are large. In its one-dimensional form, the time-independent Schrödinger equation

$$-\frac{\hbar^2}{2m}\frac{d^2\psi}{dz^2} + (E - V)\psi = 0 \tag{B.13}$$

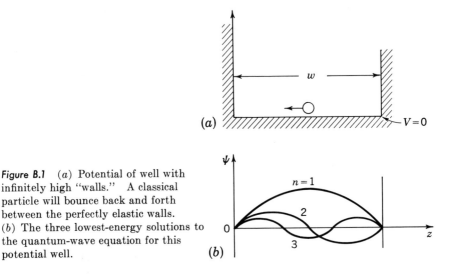

Figure B.1 (a) Potential of well with infinitely high "walls." A classical particle will bounce back and forth between the perfectly elastic walls. (b) The three lowest-energy solutions to the quantum-wave equation for this potential well.

has as general solutions either trigonometric or exponential functions. For constant V and $E > V$, the solution is[1]

$$\psi = Ae^{j[2m(E-V)]^{\frac{1}{2}}z/\hbar} + Be^{-j[2m(E-V)]^{\frac{1}{2}}z/\hbar} \tag{B.14}$$

A and B are complex constants whose ratio may be chosen to satisfy boundary conditions on the motion of the particle. So long as $E > V$, the solution will contain imaginary exponentials, but when $V > E$, solutions are the real exponentials:

$$\psi = A'e^{+[2m(V-E)]^{\frac{1}{2}}z/\hbar} + B'e^{-[2m(V-E)]^{\frac{1}{2}}z/\hbar} \tag{B.15}$$

In this situation, the energy which the particle must have to exist classically in the region *exceeds* the energy of the particle. Classically, the particle could not penetrate into the region. Quantum-mechanically, the solution does not vanish completely in the "forbidden" region, but is strongly attenuated.

A simple example of particle-wave solution for a *confined* particle is the one-dimensional *potential well* with infinite sides (Fig. B.1). The potential V is infinite beyond the walls, $x < 0$, $x > w$; hence ψ is nonzero only between 0 and w and zero at the boundaries. In the potential well we let $V = 0$. The solution in the well is (B.14); the boundary conditions require

At $z = w$: $\psi = Ae^{j(2mE)^{\frac{1}{2}}w/\hbar} + Be^{-j(2mE)^{\frac{1}{2}}w/\hbar} = 0$ (B.16)

At $z = 0$: $\psi = A + B = 0$ $A = -B$ (B.17)

[1] We omit the time factor $\exp[-j(Et/\hbar)]$ since it is not needed in the analysis of constant-energy systems.

The simultaneous solution of (B.16) and (B.17) yields

$$\sin \frac{(2mE)^{\frac{1}{2}}w}{\hbar} = 0 \tag{B.18}$$

This condition may be expressed as

$$\frac{(2mE)^{\frac{1}{2}}w}{\hbar} = n\pi \qquad n = 1, 2, 3, \ldots \tag{B.19}$$

The case $n = 0$ is not admitted, for a particle wave which is everywhere zero denies the presence of a particle. Typical solutions are sketched in Fig. B.1b. Condition (B.19) allows solutions only for certain characteristic values of particle energy E,

$$E_n = \frac{\pi^2 \hbar^2 n^2}{2mw^2} \tag{B.20}$$

The index n is termed the quantum index, or *quantum number*. Characteristically of quantum solutions, the lowest allowed energy (for $n = 1$) is *nonzero*. This *zero-point energy* suggests that there can be no state in which the particle is completely at rest. The allowed energy values for the particle in a potential well are termed the energy *eigenvalues* (loosely translated from the German, "characteristic values") of this particular problem. The associated solutions of the wave equation, termed *eigenfunctions*, are

$$\psi_n = \sin \left(\frac{n\pi}{w}\right) e^{-jE_n t/\hbar} \qquad 0 < x < w \tag{B.21}$$

So long as the energy of the particle is a constant, it must be described by one of the wave functions ψ_n. The wave solution may, however, be composed of a linear combination of terms like (B.21). This is the case, for example, when a particle is making a transition from one state to another, as discussed in Sec. 10.1.

Several important properties of particle wave become apparent:

1. Waves for a free particle can in principle extend to infinity, as (B.7), while waves for a particle which would *classically* be confined to a definite region of space are confined to (approximately) the same region of space.

2. Free particles may assume any of a range of values of energy, whereas particles confined to a limited volume have discrete energy values, the lowest one of which is usually *nonzero* (and termed the *zero-point energy*).

In a potential well whose sides are only finitely high, the solutions are not required to be zero at the boundaries, but rapidly decay outside the well because of a large negative exponential (the positive exponential applies for negative x), as shown in Fig. B.2. A particle may have only discrete energies for $E < V_0$, but any value for $E > V_0$.

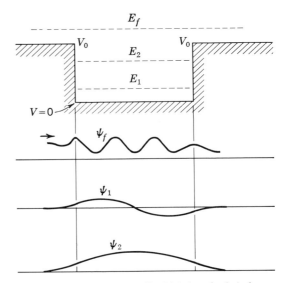

Figure B.2   A potential well which is only finitely deep. Solutions for energies E_1 and E_2, both less than V_0, extend beyond the well boundaries but not to infinity. Solutions for $E_f > V_0$ represent basically free particles, which are, however, impeded by the presence of the well. A particle wave coming from the left, represented by ψ_f, will be partially reflected, and only partially transmitted through the well region. (The solution ψ_f is only shown schematically, for it will be a complex function of position.)

A related problem is that of a potential *barrier* in the path of a moving particle (Fig. B.3). This type of potential appears (for electrons) in the tunnel diode (Chap. 5); it is also pertinent to *field emission* of electrons from unheated cathodes in very high electric fields. For the rectangular barrier illustrated, assuming a particle energy E, spatially dependent factors in the solutions to the wave equation in the region I are

$$\psi_{\mathrm{I}} = Ae^{-j(2mE)^{\frac{1}{2}}z/\hbar} + Be^{+j(2mE)^{\frac{1}{2}}z/\hbar} \qquad z < 0 \tag{B.22}$$

In region II, $V_0 > E$ and the solutions are

$$\psi_{\mathrm{II}} = Ce^{-[2m(V_0-E)]^{\frac{1}{2}}z/\hbar} + De^{+[2m(V_0-E)]^{\frac{1}{2}}z/\hbar} \qquad 0 \leqq z \leqq w \tag{B.23}$$

In region III, the potential is zero; the form of the solution is the same as that of region I. If the particle approaches from the left, it can be moving only to the right in region III, where the solution need include only a wave traveling in the positive z direction.

$$\psi_{\mathrm{III}} = Fe^{+j(2mE)^{\frac{1}{2}}z/\hbar} \qquad z > w \tag{B.24}$$

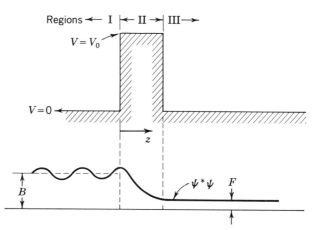

Figure B.3 A potential barrier in the path of a free particle causes reflection, and only a small fraction of the incident wave amplitude may appear on the far side, indicating a low transmission *probability* of the particle.

Since the wave equation is linear and second-order, the values of A, B, C, D, and F must permit the function ψ and its first derivative $d\psi/dt$ to be continuous across the boundaries. The term B represents particle-wave motion to the right in region I, and F the same in region III. We seek the attenuation of a particle wave in passing the barrier, that is, F/B. Equation of ψ_I and ψ_{II} and of $d\psi_I/dz$ and $d\psi_{II}/dz$ at $z = 0$ yields

$$A + B = C + D$$

$$j\frac{(2mE)^{\frac{1}{2}}}{\hbar}(A - B) = \frac{[2m(V_0 - E)]^{\frac{1}{2}}}{\hbar}(C - D)$$

From this,

$$2B = C\left[1 + j\left(\frac{V_0 - E}{E}\right)^{\frac{1}{2}}\right] + D\left[1 - j\left(\frac{V_0 - E}{E}\right)^{\frac{1}{2}}\right]$$

Equation of ψ_{II} and ψ_{III}, and of their derivatives, at $z = w$ yields C and D, in terms of F:

$$C = \frac{F}{2}\left[1 - j\left(\frac{E}{V_0 - E}\right)^{\frac{1}{2}}\right]e^{j(2mE)^{\frac{1}{2}}w/\hbar}\,e^{+[2m(V_0 - E)]^{\frac{1}{2}}w/\hbar}$$

$$D = \frac{F}{2}\left[1 + j\left(\frac{E}{V_0 - E}\right)^{\frac{1}{2}}\right]e^{j(2mE)^{\frac{1}{2}}w/\hbar}\,e^{-[2m(V_0 - E)]^{\frac{1}{2}}w/\hbar}$$

B can now be found, in terms of F, by substitution:

$$B = Fe^{+j(2mE)^{\frac{1}{2}}w/\hbar}\left[\cosh\frac{\eta w}{\hbar} + \frac{j}{2}\left(\frac{E}{V_0 - E}\right)^{\frac{1}{2}}\left(\frac{V_0 - E}{E}\right)^{\frac{1}{2}}\sinh\frac{\eta w}{\hbar}\right]$$

where $\eta = [2m(V_0 - E)]^{\frac{1}{2}}$.

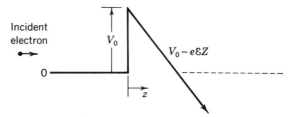

Figure B.4   Triangular-barrier potential-energy function used in approximate solution for field-emission and tunnel-diode problems.

In important practical situations, the sinh and cosh functions can be approximated by their positive exponential parts,

$$B \cong \frac{F}{2} \, e^{j(2mE)^{\frac{1}{2}}w/\hbar} \, e^{+\eta w/\hbar} \left\{ 1 + \frac{j}{2} \left[\left(\frac{E}{V_0 - E} \right)^{\frac{1}{2}} - \left(\frac{V_0 - E}{E} \right)^{\frac{1}{2}} \right] \right\} \tag{B.25}$$

As discussed in Sec. B.4, the probability of a particle passing from region I into region III is proportional to the *absolute square* of the amplitude of ψ in region III, for unit absolute square of the positively traveling wave in region I.   Accordingly, the probability of a particle passing the barrier is $|F|^2/|B|^2$, while $|A|^2/|B|^2$ represents the probability of a particle being reflected, from the barrier, back to the left.   Accordingly, for a large number of particles of energy E approaching the barrier from the left,

$$\frac{|F|^2}{|B|^2} = \text{fraction of particles passing barrier} \cong e^{-2\eta w/\hbar} \tag{B.26}$$

Thus, if a current of 1 amp (1.6×10^{18} electrons/sec) approached a barrier 1 volt high ($V_0 = 1.6 \times 10^{-19}$ joule) and ($w =$) 19 A wide, on the average about $1 \times e^{-20} = 2 \times 10^{-9}$ amp would "tunnel" through the barrier.   Whereas classical theory would predict no current flow, experiment confirms the correctness of the quantum-theory result.

When such a barrier is substantially wide, but not of constant V, a good approximation to the total wave attenuation is obtained by integrating the attenuation over each small dz element of the barrier. For the barrier shown in Fig. B.4, as might be produced by an electric field $\mathcal{E}_z$ applied at a conductor surface, the barrier height as a function of position z can be expressed as

$$V - E = V_0 - e\mathcal{E}_z z \tag{B.27}$$

The exponential term in the factor relating B to F can be approximated by

$$\left| \frac{F}{B} \right| \cong \exp \left\{ -\frac{1}{\hbar} \int_0^{V_0/e\mathcal{E}_z} [2m(V - E)]^{\frac{1}{2}} \, dz \right\} \tag{B.28}$$

This approximation amounts to assuming that the attenuation of each dz segment of the barrier may simply be multiplied by that of the other segments.[1] The limits are from $z = 0$ to the point at which $V - E$ is zero ($z = V_0/e\mathcal{E}_z$), beyond which there is no further attenuation of the particle waves. Evaluating the integral,

$$\left| \frac{F}{B} \right|^2 = \exp \left[\frac{4(2m)^{\frac{1}{2}}}{3e\mathcal{E}_z\hbar} V_0^{\frac{3}{2}} \right] \tag{B.29}$$

The exact solution, derived by Fowler and Nordheim,[2] deviates only slightly from this result.

The *simple harmonic oscillator* is another important one-dimensional quantum problem. The potential is of parabolic form as for a particle supported by a Hooke's-law spring.

$$V = \frac{kz^2}{2}$$

The corresponding wave equation is

$$-\frac{\hbar^2}{2m} \frac{d^2\psi}{dz^2} + \frac{kz^2}{2} \psi = E\psi \tag{B.30}$$

Since the potential $V(z)$ (Fig. B.5) somewhat resembles the square-sided well, the wave functions resemble sine and cosine functions. They do not become zero at some boundary, but decay toward large positive and negative z. Since the particle is "confined," only a discrete set of solutions exist (Fig. B.5). Successively higher energy solutions extend farther from $z = 0$. If we identify the nth solution as that having $n + 1$ maxima, or nodes, the energy level of the nth-order wave function $\psi_n(z)$ is found[3] to be

$$E_n = \hbar\omega_0(n + \tfrac{1}{2}) \qquad n = 0, 1, 2, \ldots \qquad \omega_0^2 = \frac{k}{m} \tag{B.31}$$

The energy of the lowest-energy wave function is again *nonzero*, but here the energy difference between any two adjacent levels is a constant, $\hbar\omega$. A particle or other system behaving as a harmonic oscillator may therefore accept any number of quanta of electromagnetic energy (photons) at a frequency corresponding to its classical oscillation frequency $\omega_0 = (k/m)^{\frac{1}{2}}$. While this may on the surface appear to be a trivial result, it applies to many systems other than particles. A lossless resonant circuit also has only the

[1] This is the Wentzel-Brillouin-Kramers approximation. Cf. D. H. Menzel, "Fundamental Formulas of Physics," p. 517, Prentice-Hall, Inc., Englewood Cliffs, N.J., 1955.

[2] R. H. Fowler and L. W. Nordheim, *Proc. Roy. Soc. (London)*, **A119**:173 (1928).

[3] In most quantum-theory texts. Cf. L. J. Schiff, "Quantum Mechanics," p. 60, McGraw-Hill Book Company, New York, 1949.

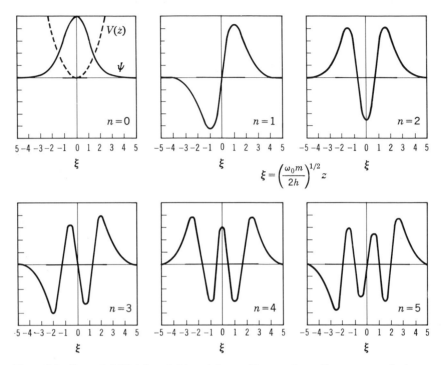

Figure B.5   Potential $V(z)$ (top left) and form of harmonic-oscillator wave solutions. Note the increased breadth of the function at higher values of energy n.   (*After L. Pauling and E. B. Wilson, Jr., "Introduction to Quantum Mechanics," pp. 74–75, McGraw-Hill Book Company, New York, 1935.*)

(electrical) energy levels as given by (B.31).   The relation applies separately to *each* resonance frequency of an electrical or an acoustical resonator.

B.3   Three-dimensional Solutions in a Confining Volume

The time-independent wave equation in more than a single dimension is a *partial* differential equation.   Solution is generally accomplished by *separation of variables*.   The following example for a particle confined in a rectangular-sided volume (a "box") is useful.

The confining volume (Fig. B.6) is enclosed by the planes $x = 0$, $x = a$, $y = 0$, $y = b$, $z = 0$, $z = c$.   The wave equation inside the box ($V = 0$) is

$$-\frac{\hbar^2}{2m}\left(\frac{\partial^2\psi}{\partial x^2} + \frac{\partial^2\psi}{\partial y^2} + \frac{\partial^2\psi}{\partial z^2}\right) = E \tag{B.32}$$

$V = \infty$, so that ψ vanishes, outside the box.

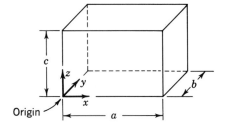

Figure B.6   A three-dimensional potential well, or "box," used in the example in the text.   Potential is infinite outside the boundaries shown.

In separation of variables, the solution is factored into functions containing only one of the variables: $\psi = X(x)Y(y)Z(z)$.   Substituting into (B.32),

$$-\frac{\hbar^2}{2m}\left(YZ\frac{\partial^2 X}{\partial x^2} + XZ\frac{\partial^2 Y}{\partial y^2} + XY\frac{\partial^2 Z}{\partial z^2}\right) = EXYZ$$

or

$$\frac{1}{X}\frac{\partial^2 X}{\partial x^2} + \frac{1}{Y}\frac{\partial^2 Y}{\partial y^2} + \frac{1}{Z}\frac{\partial^2 Z}{\partial z^2} = -\frac{2mE}{\hbar^2}$$

The energy E is a constant, while each of the terms in the parentheses is a function of at most one variable.   Each of the terms in the parentheses must be constant; therefore

$$\frac{\partial^2 X}{\partial x^2} = C_1 X \qquad \frac{\partial^2 Y}{\partial y^2} = C^2 Y \qquad \frac{\partial^2 Z}{\partial z^2} = C_3 Z$$

where $C_1 + C_2 + C_3 = \dfrac{-2mE}{\hbar^2}$

Boundary conditions on the wave function require it to be zero at the enclosing planes.   Solutions satisfying these conditions are the eigenfunctions

$$\psi_{ijk} = \sin\frac{\pi i x}{a}\sin\frac{\pi j y}{b}\sin\frac{\pi k z}{c} \tag{B.33}$$

Substituting into the original wave equation, the corresponding energy eigenvalues are

$$E_{ijk} = \frac{\hbar^2}{2m}\left[\left(\frac{\pi i}{a}\right)^2 + \left(\frac{\pi j}{b}\right)^2 + \left(\frac{\pi k}{c}\right)^2\right] \tag{B.34}$$

B.4   Expectation Values; Representation by Expansion over Constant-momentum Wave Functions

The wave solution representing particle motion contains many details not observed experimentally, for example, the "frequency" $E/\hbar$. We can often, however, carry out experiments to measure properties such as position, energy, momentum, etc.   When the observed property is one for which the quantum solution indicates a constant value (e.g., the energy, in the case of constant-energy solutions such as that of the potential well and harmonic oscillator), the results of a measurement will always be that constant. When the property measured is not a constant, however, the results of a series of measurements will not be identical. It is still possible to determine an average value, or *expectation value*, for many observable quantities, i.e., the average of a large number of measurements.

The amplitude of the wave function ψ clearly must have some relation to the location of the particle, for its vanishing in a region strongly suggests that the particle is not there. In fact, the *absolute square* of ψ has been demonstrated to serve as a *probability density function* for the position of the particle. That is, the probability of finding the particle in a region $x \rightarrow x + dx$, $y \rightarrow y + dy$, $z \rightarrow z + dz$ is proportional to

$$\psi^*(x,y,z)\psi(x,y,z) \; dx \, dy \, dz \tag{B.35}$$

The expectation value of the coordinate x (written $\langle x \rangle$) is, from probability theory,

$$\langle x \rangle = \frac{\displaystyle\iiint_{-\infty}^{\infty} \psi^*(x,y,z)x\psi(x,y,z) \; dx \, dy \, dz}{\displaystyle\iiint_{-\infty}^{\infty} \psi^*(x,y,z)\psi(x,y,z) \; dx \, dy \, dz} \tag{B.36}$$

The denominator may be eliminated if the wave function is *normalized*,[1] i.e., if multiplied by a constant such that the denominator is unity. The integrals need be taken only over the region in which ψ is nonzero. Similarly, expectation values for y, z or any powers of x, y, or z may be found by replacing the factor x in the numerator by the desired function of coordinates.

To complete a description of the expected motion of the particle one must be able to determine expected values of momentum and functions of momentum. Unfortunately, momentum cannot be expressed explicitly as a function of the coordinates, so the method of

---

[1] Normalization is convenient in manipulating combinations of wave functions. Another important property of eigenfunctions of the Schrödinger equation, occurring naturally because of the form of the equation, is *orthogonality*. That is, eigenfunctions of different energy have spatial variations satisfying

$$\iiint_{-\infty}^{\infty} \psi_i{}^*(x,y,z)\psi_j(x,y,z) \; dx \, dy \, dz \; = \; 0 \qquad i \neq j \tag{B.37}$$

The functions are said to form an *orthogonal set*. According to Fourier theory, *any* function extending over the same range of coordinates may be expanded as a linear combination of such functions, if the set is *complete*, a property also of solutions to Schrödinger's equation.

(B.36) cannot be applied. It is, however, possible to expand any wave function $\psi(z)$ as a Fourier integral over the set of functions $e^{ip_z z/\hbar}$. That is, there is some function $\phi(p_z)$ such that $\psi(z)$ can be written

$$\psi(z) = h^{-\frac{1}{2}} \int_{-\infty}^{+\infty} e^{+ip_z z/\hbar} \phi(p_z)\, dz \tag{B.38}$$

For any wave function $\psi(z)$, a unique Fourier transform $\phi(p_z)$ is obtained by the inverse transformation

$$\phi(p_z) = h^{-\frac{1}{2}} \int_{-\infty}^{+\infty} e^{-ip_z z/\hbar} \psi(z)\, dz \tag{B.39}$$

The function $\phi(p_z)$ is a *representation* of the original wave function $\psi(z)$ in momentum space p_z. Since the original wave function is in effect subdivided into parts each of which has a constant momentum, the quantity $\phi^*(p_z)\phi(p_z)\, dp_z$ is a measure of the probability that a measurement of p_z yields a value in the range $p_z \to p_z + dp_z$. The expectation value $\langle p_z \rangle$ is, accordingly, found in a manner analogous to (B.36):

$$\langle p_z \rangle = \frac{\displaystyle\int_{-\infty}^{\infty} \phi^*(p_z)\phi(p_z)p_z\, dp_z}{\displaystyle\int_{-\infty}^{\infty} \phi^*(p_z)\phi(p_z)\, dp_z} \tag{B.40}$$

The integrals in (B.40) may be expressed in terms of the $\psi(z)$ using the Fourier transform; the numerator N of (B.40) can be written

$$N = h^{-1} \int_{-\infty}^{\infty} \left[\int_{-\infty}^{\infty} e^{+ip_z z/\hbar} \psi(z)\, dz \right] \left[\int_{-\infty}^{\infty} e^{-ip_z u/\hbar} \psi(u)\, du \right] p_z\, dp_z$$

The "dummy variable" z in one integration has been changed to u so that it can be distinguished. The order of integration may be changed, and the terms rearranged:

$$N = h^{-1} \int_{-\infty}^{\infty} \left[\int_{-\infty}^{\infty} \left(\int_{-\infty}^{\infty} p_z e^{+ip_z(z-u)/\hbar}\, dp_z \right) \psi(u)\, du \right] \psi^*(z)\, dz$$

But

$$p_z e^{+ip_z(z-u)/\hbar} = -j\hbar \frac{\partial}{\partial z} \left(e^{ip_z z/\hbar} e^{-ip_z u/\hbar} \right)$$

Then

$$N = \frac{-j}{2\pi} \int_{-\infty}^{\infty} \frac{\partial}{\partial z} \left\{ \int_{-\infty}^{\infty} \left[\int_{-\infty}^{\infty} e^{-ip_z u/\hbar} \psi(u)\, du \right] \right.$$
$$\left. \times\, e^{+ip_z z/\hbar}\, dp_z \right\} \psi^*(z)\, dz$$

The braced quantity contains a transform (B.39); hence

$$N = \frac{-j}{2\pi} \int_{-\infty}^{\infty} \frac{\partial}{\partial z} \left[\int_{-\infty}^{\infty} h^{\frac{1}{2}} \phi(p_z) e^{-jp_z z/\hbar} \, dp_z \right] \psi^*(z) \, dz$$

$$= -j\hbar \int_{-\infty}^{\infty} \psi^*(z) \frac{\partial \psi(z)}{\partial z} \, dz \qquad (B.41)$$

The denominator is found to be unity, and therefore

$$\langle p_z \rangle = \int_{-\infty}^{\infty} \psi^*(z) \left\{ -j\hbar \frac{\partial}{\partial z} [\psi(z)] \right\} dz \qquad (B.42)$$

It can be shown, similarly, that

$$\langle p_z{}^n \rangle = \int_{-\infty}^{\infty} \psi^*(z) \left\{ (-j\hbar)^n \frac{\partial^n}{\partial z^n} [\psi(z)] \right\} dz \qquad (B.43)$$

The expectation value of a function $f(p_z)$ of p_z is found by writing the function as a power series in p_z:

$$f(p_z) = a_0 + a_1 p_z + a_2 p_z{}^2 + \cdots$$

The *operator* F is then formed by substituting $-j\hbar \, \partial/\partial z$ for each p_z and applied in the integral; accordingly,

$$\langle f(p_z) \rangle = \int_{-\infty}^{\infty} \psi^* F(\psi) \, dz$$

$$= \int_{-\infty}^{\infty} \psi^* \left(a_0 \psi - j\hbar \frac{\partial \psi}{\partial z} - \hbar^2 \frac{\partial^2 \psi}{\partial z^2} + \cdots \right) dz \qquad (B.44)$$

The extension to three dimensions involves expansion in a momentum space of three components (p_x, p_y, p_z), i.e., an expansion of the given wave function in terms of constant-momentum *plane-wave solutions* like (B.7).

B.5   "Uncertainty" in Wave Functions

The particle wave corresponding to the motion of a free particle at a precisely known momentum is of the form (B.7). Such a wave function has uniquely defined energy E, exists for all time, and extends over all space. In practical problems, the dimensions of vacuum tubes, conductors, semiconductors, etc., in which electron waves move and can be observed are always finite. On a particle wave traveling in the z direction, we might impress the condition that it be restricted to a path of limited transverse dimension. The wave amplitude across the conductor may appear as shown in Fig. B.7. Here we limit only the transverse x dimension. With this boundary condition ($\psi = 0$, $x < 0$ or $x > a$) the x dependency of the wave

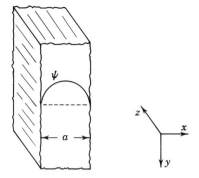

Figure B.7   Possible quantum wave-amplitude function describing a particle passing through a conductor of finite transverse dimensions.

may be expanded in a series of terms of different p_x values:

$$\psi = \sum_{n=-\infty}^{+\infty} B_n e^{-i(Et/\hbar - p_z z/\hbar - n\pi x/a)} \tag{B.45}$$

The B_n are undetermined coefficients (but boundary conditions require $B_n = B_{-n}$). The least complicated form which the transverse variation may assume is

$$
\begin{aligned}
\psi &= e^{-i(Et/\hbar - p_z z/\hbar)} \sin\frac{\pi x}{a} \\
&= \tfrac{1}{2}\left(e^{-i(Et/\hbar - p_z z/\hbar - \pi x/a)} - e^{-i(Et/\hbar - p_z z/\hbar + \pi x/a)}\right)
\end{aligned} \tag{B.46}
$$

This wave consists of *two* partial waves, having components of x momentum $p_x = \pm\hbar\pi/a$. Using the probability interpretation of the wave function, measurements of p_x would yield values $\hbar\pi/a$ and $-\hbar\pi/a$ with equal probability. There may thus be said to be an uncertainty of $2\pi\hbar/a$ in the results of measuring p_x. The particle might be located anywhere within the width a. The uncertainty $\Delta x = a$, multiplied by the uncertainty in the x momentum ($\Delta p_x = h/a$), equals in this case the constant h. Heisenberg's *uncertainty principle* states this more generally: The product of the spatial extent of a particle wave times the extent in the corresponding dimension of momentum space is at least of the order of h:

$$\Delta x \, \Delta p_x \cong h \tag{B.47}$$

One might also restrict the y motion and z motion of the particle, obtaining like results. In the more general case, where the wave is not zero outside certain boundaries, a Fourier integral may be used to express it as an *integral* over p_x, p_y, p_z. It is a general property of Fourier integrals and their inverses that the spatial extent of the wave function $\psi^*\psi$ is inversely proportional to the extent of the transform $\phi^*\phi$ in momentum space. (Analogous relations apply for a time-pulse length and the associated frequency spectrum.) Relation (B.47) cannot be expressed as a definite *equality* because of the wide range of possible spatial forms which a wave may assume, any more than we can establish a universal relation between pulse length and frequency spectrum.

There is also a similar uncertainty relationship between energy and time. Suppose a particle to be moving in the z direction. A planar shutter covering the $z = 0$ plane is opened and, after a time τ, is again closed. Should the particle be known to pass through $z = 0$ in this interval, its time dependence at $z = 0$ must be zero before $t = 0$ and after $t = \tau$. The time-dependent part of the wave function may therefore be of the form

$$f(t)e^{-iEt/\hbar}$$

where $f(t)$ is zero except in the interval $0 \leq t \leq \tau$. Taking a simple possibility, that $f(t)$ is of the form $\sin(\pi t/\tau)$ in the interval, the time-dependent factor in the wave function can be written

$$e^{-iEt/\hbar} \sin \frac{\pi t}{\tau} = \tfrac{1}{2}(e^{-i(E/\hbar - \pi/\tau)t} - e^{-i(E/\hbar + \pi/\tau)t}) \tag{B.48}$$

Although there is still only one particle, its original precisely known energy E now has uncertainty $\Delta E = 2(\pi\hbar/\tau) = h/\tau$. This may be expressed by the uncertainty relation

$$\Delta E \, \Delta t (= \tau \, \Delta E) \cong h \tag{B.49}$$

B.6   Correspondence between Classical and Quantum Theories

The mere development of a wave equation for free particles, and solutions to that equation, do not demonstrate useful means of solving more general problems, such as those of many-particle systems. Fortunately, a *correspondence* has been found to exist between classical variables and their equivalents in quantum theory. To any classical *observable* variable which can at least in principle be measured, there *corresponds* in quantum theory a *linear operator*. The operator corresponding to a coordinate of classical mechanics is simply the coordinate itself. The quantum-mechanical operator corresponding to linear momentum (for example, p_x) in classical mechanics is $-j\hbar \, \partial/\partial x$. (This operator appeared in the analysis for $\langle p_x \rangle$ of Sec. B.4.) If we know the operators corresponding to coordinates x, y, z and the corresponding coordinates of linear momentum (p_x, p_y, p_z), it is possible by coordinate transformation to derive those for angular momentum, kinetic energy, potential energy, etc. One can expand the method of Sec. B.4 to calculate expectation values for any observable quantity.

To draw equivalence between quantum and classical mechanics, it is important to observe that in quantum mechanics it is *momentum*, and not velocity, which plays the significant role as a kinetic variable.

Even in simple classical mechanics, energy and momentum are the basic properties which are conserved, for example, in collisions of bodies. The original newtonian formulation of classical mechanics does not put coordinates and momenta on the equal footing which they must have in quantum theory. The *hamiltonian formulation* of classical mechanics does so, however.[1] In this formulation, one derives equations of motion from derivatives of a function H termed the *hamiltonian;* this function is in most instances just the total energy of the system *expressed in terms of the system coordinates and momenta.* For a particle of mass m in potential $V(x,y,z)$,

$$H = \overbrace{\frac{p_x{}^2}{2m} + \frac{p_y{}^2}{2m} + \frac{p_z{}^2}{2m}}^{\text{kinetic energy}} + \overbrace{V(x,y,z)}^{\text{potential energy}} \tag{B.50}$$

where p_x, etc., are the components of linear momentum. (A somewhat more complicated expression is necessary in the presence of magnetic fields.) To obtain the Schrödinger equation (B.10), we replace each linear-momentum component by its corresponding operator and replace $V(x,y,z)$ by itself (because it is a function only of the coordinates and they represent themselves, as operators). If we let H be represented by the *hamiltonian operator* $j\hbar\,\partial/\partial t$, the resultant operator equation *operating on the wave function* ψ is completely equivalent to the Schrödinger wave equation. This principle can be extended to any system for which one can write the hamiltonian. In the case of electron spin (Sec. B.8), one can even find a quantum operator for which there exists *no classically definable variable.*

B.7 The Hydrogen Atom; Angular Momentum in Quantum Theory

Solution for the energy levels of the hydrogen atom represents convincing demonstration of the value of quantum theory. This is the simplest atomic system and at the same time the only one for which an almost exact solution can be obtained readily in analytical form. The solution has usefulness not only for the hydrogen-atom problem, but also as a first approximation for that of heavier atoms.

The hydrogen atom must be represented by six coordinates, for example, the cartesian position coordinates of the proton and the electron. It is more convenient, however, to use *center-of-mass coordinates.* The motion is composed of the motion of the center of mass of the atom, on which is superimposed the relative motion of electron and proton, i.e., the *orbital motion.* The motion of the center of mass is precisely that of a free particle; hence the wave function

---

[1] Cf. H. Goldstein, "Classical Mechanics," chap. 7, Addison-Wesley Publishing Company, Inc., Reading, Mass., 1959.

for the atom contains a factor like (B.7) representing the motion of the center of mass. We are interested only in the relative orbital motion. This may be described classically[1] in terms of the spacing of electron and proton r and the angular position of the electron (in polar coordinates, the angles θ and ϕ) with respect to the center of mass. The motion of the electron-proton pair is classically reducible to the motion of an electron of *reduced* mass $[m' = m_e m_p/(m_e + m_p)]$ at a radial distance r from a *stationary* nucleus. The classical hamiltonian for the orbital motion is

$$H = \frac{p^2}{2m'} - \frac{e^2}{4\pi\epsilon_0 r} \tag{B.51}$$

The second term is the potential energy of the electron in the presence of the electric field of the proton, as found from simple electrostatic theory. Converting to a wave equation of the time-independent form by the rules described in Sec. B.6,

$$\frac{-\hbar^2}{2m'} \nabla^2 \psi - \frac{e^2}{4\pi\epsilon_0 r} \psi = E\psi \tag{B.52}$$

The laplacian operator ∇^2 may be expressed in cartesian coordinates, in which case $r = (x^2 + y^2 + z^2)^{\frac{1}{2}}$. The equation is more readily solved, however, if ∇^2 is represented in polar coordinates, in which (B.52) becomes

$$\frac{-\hbar^2}{2m'} \left\{ \frac{1}{r^2} \frac{\partial}{\partial r} \left[r^2 \frac{\partial \psi}{\partial r} + \frac{1}{r^2 \sin\theta} \frac{\partial}{\partial \theta} \left(\sin\theta \frac{\partial \psi}{\partial \theta} \right) + \frac{1}{r^2 \sin^2\theta} \frac{\partial^2 \psi}{\partial \phi^2} \right] \right\}$$
$$- \frac{e^2}{4\pi\epsilon_0 r} = E\psi \tag{B.53}$$

The laplacian operator permits solution by separation of variables in many coordinate systems, including this one. The solution is written

$$\psi = R(r)\Theta(\theta)\Phi(\phi) \tag{B.54}$$

The solution is obtained most readily by beginning with the ϕ function. The mechanics of solution are detailed in most quantum-theory texts and will not be repeated here. One finds the ϕ function to have the form

$$\Phi = e^{im\phi} \qquad m = 0, \pm 1, \pm 2, \ldots \tag{B.55}$$

When this solution is substituted into the original equation, an equation for the θ function can be separated:

$$\frac{1}{\Theta \sin\theta} \frac{d}{d\theta} \left(\sin\theta \frac{d\Theta}{d\theta} \right) - \frac{m^2}{\sin^2\theta} = -C \tag{B.56}$$

[1] *Ibid.*, p. 58.

where C is an undetermined constant. Making the substitution $u = \cos\theta$, the equation takes the classical form of a Legendre equation, in which it is appropriate to give C the value $l(l + 1)$:

$$(1 - u^2)\frac{d^2\Theta}{d\theta^2} - 2u\frac{d\Theta}{d\theta} + \left[l(l + 1) - \frac{m}{1 - u^2}\right]\Theta = 0 \tag{B.57}$$

The solutions to (B.57) which are finite at $\theta = 0$, π and may therefore correspond to reasonable wave functions are termed *Legendre polynomials*. The index l may have only the values zero or a positive integer. These functions are tabulated in most differential-equations texts.[1] They are usually written $P_l{}^m(\cos\theta)$ and are nonzero only for values of $|m| \leqq l$. For a given value of l, then, m may take on only the values $l, l - 1, l - 2, \ldots, 0, -1, -2, \ldots, -l$ for a total of $2l + 1$ different values.

Figure B.8 shows the θ variation of the $P_l{}^m$ function (plotted in the graphical manner used in plotting antenna or loudspeaker radiation patterns). The functions for $m = 0$ contain $l + 1$ nodes between $\theta = 0$ and $\theta = \pi$. In $P_l{}^m$, this number is reduced by m, and near the poles is reduced so that the function is "flattened" toward $\theta = \pi/2$. The function $P_l{}^m$ has $(l + 1 - m)$ nodes from $\theta = 0$ to π.

When the angle-dependent terms are replaced by the constant $c = -l(l + 1)$, there remains only the radial equation

$$-\frac{\hbar^2}{2m'}\left[\frac{1}{R}\frac{d}{dr}\left(r^2\frac{dR}{dr}\right) - l(l + 1)\right] - \frac{e^2 r}{4\pi\epsilon_0} = Er^2 \tag{B.58}$$

This equation has a set of solutions which have finite values for all r. These take the form of the product of an exponential and a polynomial in r. An additional index n is introduced, and these radial functions are dependent on both n and the index l introduced in the θ functions. The functions are usually expressed as $R_{nl}(r)$; for example,

$$\begin{aligned}
R_{10}(r) &= (2r_0)^{-\frac{3}{2}}e^{-r/r_0}\\
R_{20}(r) &= 2(2r_0)^{-\frac{3}{2}}(1 - r/2r_0)e^{-r/2r_0}\\
R_{21}(r) &= 3^{-\frac{1}{2}}(2r_0)^{-\frac{3}{2}}\frac{r}{r_0}e^{-r/2r_0}
\end{aligned} \tag{B.59}$$

where the radius $r_0 = 4\pi\epsilon_0\hbar^2/me^2 = 0.529$ A equals the circular orbit radius for a *classical* hydrogen atom with angular momentum $\hbar$. Some of these functions $(r^2R_{nl}{}^2)$ are plotted in Fig. B.9. The radial function for $n = 2$, $l = 0$ is positive for small r and negative for large r, that is, has $n = 2$ nodes. For $n = 2$, $l = 1$, the function R_{21} has only a single node; the number of nodes of the general function $R_{nl}(r)$ is $n - l$. The functions are nonzero only if the integer l is *smaller than* the integer n.

[1] Cf. L. A. Pipes, "Applied Mathematics for Engineers and Physicists," p. 322, McGraw-Hill Book Company, New York, 1946.

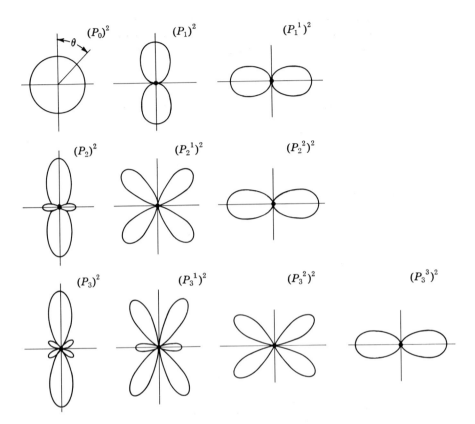

Figure B.8 The form of the polar-angle θ variation of the hydrogen-atom wave functions vs. quantum indices l and m. Note the flattening of the function toward the equator for large m, particularly noticeable at large l.

The functions take this form only for integral values of n, for which the energy E must have the values

$$E_n = -\frac{m'e^4}{(4\pi\epsilon_0 \hbar n)^2} = -\frac{13.603}{n^2} \quad \text{ev} \tag{B.60}$$

(The reference $E_\infty = 0$ corresponds to an independent electron and proton.)

The quantum states of the orbital motion of the hydrogen atom are therefore characterized by three quantum indices, or *quantum numbers: n, l,* and *m.* The index n is termed the *principal quantum number,* and may take on any positive integral value. This index measures the radial extent of the function. The index l may take on positive values less than n, and is termed the *angular-momentum quantum number,* as will be explained shortly. The index m is termed the *magnetic quantum number,* also to be explained, and may

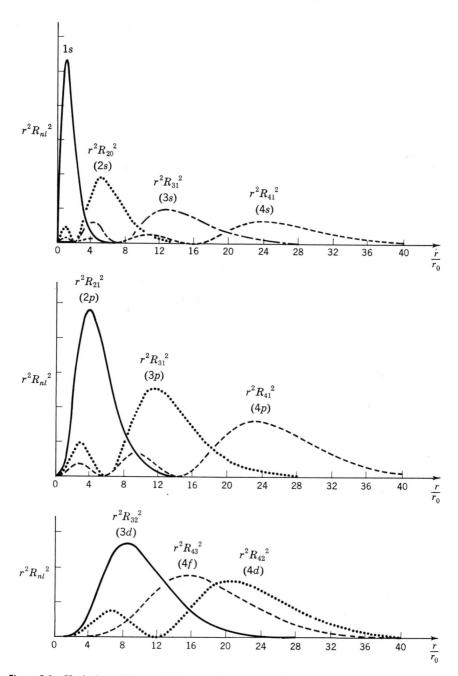

Figure B.9 Variation of the radial factors R_{nl} of the hydrogen-atom wave functions ($r^2 R_{nl}^2$ is plotted). The symbols (1s, 2s, etc.) are explained in Sec. B.11. (*After E. U. Condon and G. H. Shortley, "The Theory of Atomic Spectra," Cambridge University Press, New York, 1953.*)

take on positive or negative integer values not to exceed $\pm l$. In this approximation, only the principal quantum number n determines the energy of the atom, according to (B.60). All wave functions for a given n have the same energies, and are said to be *degenerate*. This degeneracy is partly removed when the spinning motion of the electron and proton is also taken into account (Sec. B.8).

The three factors in the hydrogen-atom wave function are multiplied to form the complete three-dimensional orbital wave function. A number of features of these functions are suggestive of classical orbital motion. Using the probability interpretation of $\psi^*\psi$, the absolute square of the wave function may be thought of as an *electron density* about the center of mass, a sort of "smeared-out" electron. For higher n, and therefore higher energy, the radial extent of the electron orbit becomes greater. With $l = 0$, the complete wave function is *spherically symmetrical*.

Combining the azimuthal (ϕ-dependent) factor $e^{jm\phi}$ with the time factor in the wave function, we have $\exp{[-j(Et/\hbar - m\phi)]}$, a wave rotating about the polar axis. A negative value of m corresponds to a wave rotating in the opposite direction; m is thus somehow related to orbital motion about the polar axis. The classical angular momentum $\mathbf{L}$ of a particle about an origin is defined, in terms of the particle's linear momentum $\mathbf{p}$ and the radius vector to the particle $\mathbf{r}$, as a vector

$$\mathbf{L} = \mathbf{r} \times \mathbf{p} \tag{B.61}$$

For example, a particle in a classical circular orbit has its angular momentum directed normal to the orbital plane. The cartesian components of the angular momentum vector can be found directly from (B.61); e.g.,

$$L_z = xp_y - yp_x \tag{B.62}$$

The quantum-mechanical *operator* corresponding to the classical variable L_z may be found directly by substitution of $-j\hbar\,\partial/\partial x$ for p_x, etc. This operator has much simpler form, however, in polar coordinates. Letting the z axis be the polar axis, cartesian coordinates can be transformed directly to polar coordinates through the transformation $z = r \cos\theta$, $x = r \sin\theta \cos\phi$, $y = r \sin\theta \sin\phi$. The transformed operator corresponding to L_z is then simply

$$\text{Op } L_z = -j\hbar \frac{\partial}{\partial\phi} \tag{B.63}$$

Similarly, the operator corresponding to the square of the total angular momentum $\mathbf{L}^2$ is found to be

$$\text{Op } \mathbf{L}^2 = -\frac{\hbar^2}{\sin\theta}\frac{\partial}{\partial\theta}\left(\sin\theta\frac{\partial}{\partial\theta}\right) - \frac{\hbar^2}{\sin 2\theta}\frac{\partial^2}{\partial\phi^2} \tag{B.64}$$

It is a rule in quantum theory that whenever an operator, operating on a particular wave function, gives as a result a real constant multiplying the wave function, the observable quantity corresponding to the operator has that constant value. (The wave function is said to be *an eigenfunction of that operator*, with the constant value its *eigenvalue*.) In the present case, consider the operator (B.63) corresponding to L_z. Operating on the hydrogen-atom wave function requires differentiation only of the ϕ-dependent part:

$$-j\hbar \frac{\partial \psi}{\partial \phi} = -j\hbar R\Theta \frac{\partial \Phi}{\partial \phi} = -j\hbar R\Theta (jm)\phi = m\hbar\psi \tag{B.65}$$

The component of orbital angular momentum in the polar axis is just $m\hbar$. The same result would of course have been obtained by taking the expectation $\langle L_z \rangle$. The value $m\hbar$ is an eigenvalue, i.e., a constant, just as is the energy E_n.

The operator corresponding to the square of the total angular momentum $\mathbf{L}^2$ can be applied most simply by substituting into (B.56). One finds that, for the function $P_1{}^m(\cos \theta)$, the square of the total angular momentum has the eigenvalues

$$\mathbf{L}^2 = \hbar^2 l(l + 1) \tag{B.66}$$

Any system of atoms, no matter how complex, has similar restrictions on angular momentum. The component along some axis may have only values which are measured in units of $\hbar$, while the square of the total angular momentum has magnitude $l(l + 1)\hbar^2$. When electron spin (Sec. B.8) is taken into account, m may take on half-integral ($\frac{1}{2}$, $\frac{3}{2}$, etc.) values, as may l. In any case, the largest positive and negative values of m are equal in magnitude to l. Thus, $\mathbf{L}^2$ is always *greater* than $(L_z)^2$. This means that L_x and L_y cannot both be zero. It is a fundamental point in quantum theory, however, that one cannot measure simultaneously and precisely all three cartesian components of an angular momentum $\mathbf{L}$. One can measure with precision only the square of the total angular momentum and a *single* cartesian component. The quantities L_z and L_x, L_z and L_y, L_x and L_y (in pairs) are said not to *commute*. Likewise, a cartesian coordinate and its associated momentum (x and p_x, etc.) do not commute, for the uncertainty relation (B.47) indicates that both cannot be specified simultaneously with precision. An uncertainty principle can likewise be applied to the angle ϕ and the corresponding momentum L_z:

$$\Delta\phi\,\Delta L_z \simeq h \tag{B.67}$$

The distinction of $\theta = 0$ as a special axis deserves comment. If the atom is isolated and free of externally applied fields, there is indeed no way to identify the $\theta = 0$ axis. (The same problem arises in describing resonances in a spherical electromagnetic or acoustical cavity.) Since we can in no way distinguish states of different m, but only states of different n and l, the problem is somewhat academic. If, however, an electric or magnetic field is applied to the atom, states of different m are slightly perturbed so that their energies are different; the assignment of the direction of the field along the special axis ($\theta = 0, \pi$) is then appropriate. The index m is termed the magnetic quantum number because it is observable in this manner.

B.8 Particle Spin; Spin-orbit Coupling

The classical hamiltonian for the hydrogen atom describes the electron and proton as infinitesimal particles having no integral degrees of freedom. This description is incomplete, for both electrons and protons (as well as neutrons) have *internal* angular momentum, which is termed *spin*. If electrons and protons were actually rigid rotating bodies, the wave equation would contain the spin-orientation angle and angular motion specifically and the solutions would contain spin quantum indices akin to l and m. We should expect infinitely many spin states (all l and $|m| \leq l$) for a *free* electron or proton in a magnetic field. There are found to be *only two* spin states; the internal angular-momentum component parallel to a magnetic field can have *only the two values* $\pm\hbar/2$. *There is no correct classical analogy* as there is with orbital motion. This spin is truly quantum-mechanical in nature. Dirac has shown that the two spin states of an electron result when the Schrödinger equation is set up in a form applicable at relativistic velocities.

Since electron spin is inseparably connected with the magnetic properties of the electron, we should consider the fields produced by spinning and orbiting electrons. For our purposes, orbital motion of the electron may be represented by a *current loop* (Fig. B.10) and produces magnetic flux in the same way. *Magnetic moment* $\mathbf{p}_m$ is the basic measure of the magnetic influence of a current loop, and is defined in rationalized units as the product of the current and the loop area (for a planar loop): $p_m = IA$. It is a vector quantity, directed in the direction of the magnetic flux produced

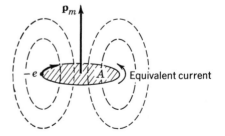

Figure B.10 An electron in orbit simulates an electric current flowing in a loop of the same dimensions. The direction of the magnetic moment is that in which the loop produces magnetic flux, as shown.

on the axis. An electron moving in a circular orbit of radius r, at angular frequency ω, is equivalent to $\omega/2\pi$ electrons/sec flowing steadily in a current loop of area πr^2. The magnetic moment p_m produced by this motion is therefore $IA = \omega e r^2/2$. The orbital angular momentum of the electron is $mr^2\omega$. The ratio of the magnetic moment to the angular momentum is, accordingly,

$$\left(\frac{p_m}{L}\right)_{\text{orbit}} = \frac{-e}{2m_e} \tag{B.68}$$

Because of its negative charge, the electron's magnetic moment $\mathbf{p}_m$ is directed just opposite to its angular momentum $\mathbf{L}_{\text{orbit}}$.

Since (B.68) contains only the *ratio* of charge to mass, we should expect that the same ratio might apply to the spinning motion of the electron, if the electron's charge and mass are similarly distributed. However, the measured ratio of magnetic moment to angular momentum, for spin, is found to be *twice as large* as the classical ratio; i.e.,

$$\left(\frac{p_m}{L}\right)_{\text{spin}} = \frac{-e}{m_e} \tag{B.69}$$

This could be explained if it were assumed that the charge of the electron was located on the surface of a sphere and the mass distributed uniformly through the sphere. Since a classical analog is inadequate, such a model is of no further value. The difference in the magnetic properties must be attributed to fundamental differences in the orbital and spin motions.

The magnetic moment $\mathbf{p}_m$ of the spinning electron will have an interaction energy with a field $\mathfrak{IC}$, the energy being a function of the orientation of the dipole in the field:

$$E_{\text{interaction}} = -\mu_0 \mathbf{p}_m \cdot \mathfrak{IC} \tag{B.70}$$

This is the classical form of interaction, as would apply also to a macroscopic "permanent magnet" in a field.

Quantum-mechanically, we cannot measure the precise orientation of the angular momentum $\mathbf{L}$ or of $\mathbf{p}_m$, but we can measure the components L_z and $\mathbf{p}_m \cdot \mathbf{1}_z$ parallel to a field (whose direction is assumed to be along the z axis). For spin motion alone, the spin quantum number s defines L_z:

$$L_z(\text{spin}) = \hbar s \qquad s = \pm\tfrac{1}{2} \tag{B.71}$$

It follows that the component of magnetic moment parallel to the field is $\mathbf{p}_m \cdot \mathbf{1}_z = -(\hbar e/me)s = \pm\hbar e/2m_e$. The interaction energy is thus

$$E_s = \frac{\mu_0 e\hbar}{m_e} \mathfrak{IC}s \qquad s = \pm\tfrac{1}{2} \tag{B.72}$$

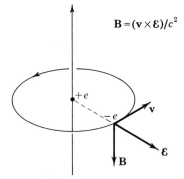

Figure B.11 In orbit around a charged nucleus, the electric field of the nucleus transforms via the electron's motion into an effective magnetic field **B**.

While (B.72) is of classical origin, it is found to apply in quantum theory as well. The equivalent interaction energy for a *proton* involves the same charge but a mass 1,836 times as great. The magnetic fields produced by the nuclear dipole moment are proportionately weaker than those of electrons.

The existence of spin must be taken into account in an accurate quantum theory of the hydrogen atom. In the ground state ($n = 1$, $l = m = 0$), the spin of the electron makes itself apparent only when a magnetic field is applied, by separating the ground state into two distinct energy levels ($s = \pm\frac{1}{2}$) separated by very nearly the energy difference (B.72).

When the hydrogen electron is in a state of *nonzero* orbital angular momentum ($l > 0$), the *orbital* angular momentum produces a magnetic field which interacts with the spin (Fig. B.11). This interaction, which occurs even in the absence of *applied* magnetic fields, is termed *spin-orbit coupling*. The component of spin angular momentum parallel to the field established by the orbital motion may have values $\pm\hbar/2$. Using the relation from Fig. B.11, with classical electron velocity of the order of 10^6 m/sec, the field experienced by the electron due to orbital motion should be of the order of 10^4 oe. The two hydrogen energy levels for $n = 2$, $l = 1$, and $s = \pm\frac{1}{2}$ actually differ by 4.5×10^{-5} ev, in crude agreement with the result obtained using a field of 10^4 oe in (B.72).

We observed in Sec. B.7 that in the absence of an aligning magnetic field the orientation m of the hydrogen atom could not be determined. This is still true when spin is taken into account, but the *internal* coupling between spin and orbital motion requires that the *total* electronic angular momentum be a *combination* of the orbital and spin values. Because of spin-orbit coupling, the total electronic angular momentum **j** (represented by a quantum number j) can have values corresponding to $j = l + \frac{1}{2}$ or $l - \frac{1}{2}$, depending on the relative directions of spin and orbital motion. The square of the total angular momentum $\mathbf{j}^2$ is, as before, given by $\hbar^2 j(j + 1)$. When a modest magnetic field is applied, the angular-momentum component parallel

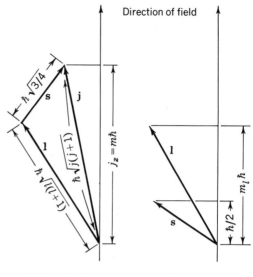

(a) Low fields   (b) High fields

Figure B.12 Vector diagrams describing the combination of spin and orbital angular momenta (a) at low fields where spin-orbit interaction is stronger than magnetic interaction of either motion with applied field, and (b) at high fields.

to the field may assume any of the values $\hbar j$, $\hbar(j - 1)$, $\hbar(j - 2)$, . . . , $\hbar(-j)$. This is to say that the *composite angular momentum* $\mathbf{j}$ of the electron, *not* the individual spin and orbital momenta, is quantized according to the usual quantum-angular-momentum rules. With external fields $\gg 10^4$ oe, however, the magnetic interaction between the spin and the field and between the orbital motion and the field will each be much larger than the spin-orbit coupling. In this case, the spin and orbital motion are quantized separately.

The combination of spin and orbital angular momenta may be shown conveniently by use of a *vector diagram*. The total angular momentum $\mathbf{j}$ of an isolated atom may be conserved. For the weak-field case we may represent it by a vector of length $\hbar[j(j + 1)]^{\frac{1}{2}}$, that is, the square root of its (known) square. The direction of the vector, while in fact fixed, is not known accurately; we may measure only one cartesian component, say, j_z. We therefore construct a vector diagram in which the component of the vector along a given axis is j_z (some multiple of $\hbar$) (Fig. B.12a). The $\mathbf{j}$ vector is composed of an $\mathbf{s}$ vector of length $\hbar(\frac{3}{4})^{\frac{1}{2}}$ added (vectorially) to an $\mathbf{l}$ vector of length $\hbar[l(l + 1)]^{\frac{1}{2}}$. While $\mathbf{j}$ is fixed, $\mathbf{s}$ and $\mathbf{l}$ may be imagined to be precessing around $\mathbf{j}$ in a random fashion with time, so that the length of $\mathbf{j}$ is $\hbar[j(j+1)]^{\frac{1}{2}}$. The $\mathbf{j}$ vector in turn precesses about the field axis. When the external magnetic field is large enough, the spin and orbital angular momentum vectors each precess about the field axis, as shown in Fig. B.12b.

B.9 Perturbation of Degenerate States

In dealing with atomic and crystalline systems containing large numbers of particles and with the influence of electric and magnetic fields on these systems, quantum mechanics becomes almost hopelessly difficult unless simplifying assumptions are made. We may have interest in determining the influence of a small change in potential, for example, the effect of a small electric field $\mathbf{\varepsilon}$ which alters the potential energy of a system, for instance, changing (B.10) into

$$-\frac{\hbar^2}{2m}\nabla^2\psi + V(\mathbf{r})\psi - (e\mathbf{\varepsilon}\cdot\mathbf{r})\psi = j\hbar\frac{\partial\psi}{\partial t} \tag{B.73}$$

Instead of solving the equation entirely afresh, if the term $-e(\mathbf{\varepsilon}\cdot\mathbf{r})$ is fairly small with respect to the original potential $V(\mathbf{r})$, it is possible to approximate the solution more easily by resort to a *perturbation theory*, which approaches the correct answer through successive approximations. Several forms of perturbation theory are commonly used; the one here is addressed to the particular problem of determining the effect of perturbations on two states of the same energy (degenerate states). Other perturbation theories are used in Chaps. 7 and 10 to illustrate special phenomena.

It is assumed, in a perturbation theory, that the unperturbed system is described by a hamiltonian (energy) function H_0. The unperturbed energy eigenfunctions may be denoted as ψ_{0k} ($k = 1, 2, 3, \ldots$ includes all relevant indices) and have energy E_{0k}. The unperturbed wave equation is, with H_0 interpreted *as an operator*,

$$H_0\psi_0 = E_0\psi_0 \tag{B.74}$$

The perturbed wave functions will be ψ_k', with energies E_k', the result of a perturbed equation

$$(H_0 + H_1)\psi_k' = E_k'\psi_k' \tag{B.75}$$

The operator H_1 is the perturbation (for example, $-e\mathbf{\varepsilon}\cdot\mathbf{r}$ in the example above). Since the unperturbed wave functions may be assumed to form an orthogonal set of functions, ψ_k' may be expanded directly as a series in the ψ_{0k}, with as yet undetermined coefficients c_{jk}:

$$\psi_k' = \sum_j c_{jk}\psi_{0j} \tag{B.76}$$

Substituting in Eq. (B.75),

$$\sum_j (H_0 + H_1)c_{jk}\psi_{0j} = \sum_j E'_k c_{jk}\psi_{0j} \tag{B.77}$$

Transposing, multiplying by ψ_{0l}^*, and integrating over the space of ψ_0,

$$\sum_j c_{jk}(E'_k - E_{0j}) \int \psi_{0j}^* \psi_{0l}\, dv = \sum_j c_{jk} \int \psi_{0l}^*(H_1\psi_{0j})\, dv \tag{B.78}$$

We shall presume that the wave functions ψ_{0l} have been properly normalized and shall represent by the symbol J_{lj} the integral

$\int \psi_{0l}^*(H_1\psi_{0j})\, dv$

Then (B.78) can be expressed as

$$\sum_j c_{jk}[(E'_k - E_{0j})\delta_{jl} - J_{lj}] = 0 \tag{B.79}$$

where $\delta_{mn} = 1$ if $m = n$, 0 if $m \neq n$.

For each perturbed wave function ψ'_k, (B.79) represents a *set of linear algebraic equations*, one for each value of l ($= 1, 2, \ldots$). The unknowns are the c_{jk}. The equations are homogeneous; for the c_{jk} to be nonzero, therefore, the determinant of the set of equations must vanish. The energy values E'_k are found by solving the polynomial obtained by setting the determinant to zero. If the perturbations J_{lj} are small, the only coefficients c_{jk} which can be large are those associated with original wave functions ψ_{0k} of energy E_{0j} near that of the perturbed function E'_k.

Let us consider the case where an unperturbed system has two *degenerate* eigenfunctions ψ_{01} and ψ_{02}, having the same energy E_0, with no other functions having comparable energies. Of the c_{jk}, only c_{11}, c_{22}, c_{12}, and c_{21} will be significant. We write the two simultaneous equations (B.79) for the two values of index l.

$$\begin{aligned} l = 1: &\quad c_{1k}(E'_k - E_0 - J_{11}) + c_{2k}(-J_{12}) = 0 \\ l = 2: &\quad c_{2k}(-J_{21}) + c_{2k}(E'_k - E_0 - J_{22}) = 0 \end{aligned} \tag{B.80}$$

Since, for c_{1k}, $c_{2k} \neq 0$, the determinant must vanish,

$$(E'_k - E_0 - J_{11})(E'_k - E_0 - J_{22}) - J_{12}J_{21} = 0 \tag{B.81}$$

We shall simplify further by assuming $J_{11} = J_{22}$ and $J_{12} = J_{21}$ (the loss of generality is offset by the greater clarity of the results). Equation (B.81) has the two solutions

$$E'_k = E_0 + J_{11} \pm J_{12} \tag{B.82}$$

The energies of the perturbed wave functions depend on the perturbation integrals J_{11} and J_{12}. The coupling term $J_{12} = J_{21}$ appears with opposite sign in the two solutions. (A very similar expression is found when determining the resonant frequencies of two electrical resonators which are coupled by a lossless element.)

The perturbed wave functions may be found using (B.80). With one value of E_k', $c_{1k} = c_{2k}$, with the other, $c_{1k} = -c_{2k}$. This leads to

$$\psi_k' = c_{1k}(\psi_{01} \pm \psi_{02}) \tag{B.83}$$

The coefficient c_{lk} may be chosen to normalize ψ_k'.

$$\int \psi_k'^* \psi_k' \, dv = 1 = c_{1k}^2 \int (\psi_{01}^* \psi_{01} + \psi_{02}^* \psi_{02} \pm \psi_{01}^* \psi_{02} \pm \psi_{02}^* \psi_{01}) \, dv$$

If the original functions are normalized and orthogonal, this equals

$$1 = c_{1k}^2(1 + 1 \pm 0 \pm 0) \qquad c_{1k} = 2^{-\frac{1}{2}}$$

The perturbed wave functions, therefore, are

$$\begin{aligned} \psi_+ &= \frac{\psi_{01} + \psi_{02}}{2^{\frac{1}{2}}} \qquad \text{with energy } E_+ = E_0 + J_{11} + J_{12} \\ \psi_- &= \frac{\psi_{01} - \psi_{02}}{2^{\frac{1}{2}}} \qquad \text{with energy } E_- = E_0 + J_{11} - J_{12} \end{aligned} \tag{B.84}$$

B.10 Identical Particles and the Exclusion Principle

While problems involving many electrons in a single heavy atom cannot in general be solved exactly, some aspects of their solution can be appreciated from a perturbation approach. Consider the classical hamiltonian of the helium atom; assuming the nucleus is stationary,

$$H = \frac{p_A{}^2}{2m} + \frac{p_B{}^2}{2m} - \frac{2e^2}{4\pi\epsilon_0 r_A} - \frac{2e^2}{4\pi\epsilon_0 r_B} + \frac{e^2}{4\pi\epsilon_0 |r_B - r_A|} \tag{B.85}$$

The coordinates of the two electrons are r_A and r_B. In the *absence* of the final term, which represents the electrostatic interaction of the two electrons, the solutions of the wave equation formed from this hamiltonian factor into two hydrogenlike wave functions multiplied together:

$$\psi_1 = \psi_A(n_1, l_1, m_1, s_1)\psi_B(n_2, l_2, m_2, s_2) \tag{B.86}$$

In this wave function, the factor representing electron A has the quantum indices $n_1 l_1 m_1 s_1$. But interchange of the electrons must yield a second wave function, of the same energy:

$$\psi_2 = \psi_A(n_2, l_2, m_2, s_2)\psi_B(n_1, l_t, m_1, s_1) \tag{B.87}$$

If we now treat the interaction energy as a perturbation of these two degenerate states, according to the results of the previous section we have the two perturbed wave functions

$$\psi_\pm = \psi_A(1)\psi_B(2) \pm \psi_B(1)\psi_A(2) \tag{B.88}$$

The abbreviation (1) implies (n_1, l_1, m_1, s_1); similarly (2) implies (n_2, l_2, m_2, s_2).

While (B.88) suggests the existence of two states in which one electron has one set of quantum numbers and the other electron another set, the fundamental *indistinguishability* of the electrons means that only one state actually exists. It is an experimental fact, furthermore, that *an atom can have no more than a single electron occupant for each set of quantum numbers* (n, l, m, s). This is one way of stating the so-called *exclusion principle*. W. Pauli found that this situation is realized only in wave functions of such a form that the entire wave function *reverses sign if the coordinates of any two electrons are interchanged*. Such wave functions are said to be *antisymmetrical*. Thus, of the two functions (B.88) which we proposed, to describe the two-electron atom, only the one with the *negative* sign is physically meaningful. For, if we set $(n_1, l_1, m_1, s_1) = (n_2, l_2, m_2, s_2)$, this wave function vanishes, automatically excluding the possibility of both electrons having identical quantum indices, in a single atom.

The extension of the exclusion principle to heavier atoms or to any system containing interacting electrons is straightforward; it involves forming wave functions which are, as a whole, antisymmetric to exchange of coordinates of *any* pair of electrons. The major significance of the hydrogen-atom wave solution derives from the possibility of approximating the wave functions of electrons in more complex atoms by functions such as (B.88), incorporating products of hydrogenlike wave functions to form composite functions of the proper antisymmetry.

B.11   Structure of the Atom; The Periodic Chart

The wave solution for the hydrogen atom also applies, in the same degree of approximation, to a single electron orbiting a heavier nucleus of charge strength $+Ze$. The electron has a wave function similar in form to that of hydrogen, but a given density $\psi^*\psi$ extends radially only $1/Z$ as far from the nucleus. The corresponding energy is also Z^2 times larger than that of hydrogen. A single electron orbiting an argon nucleus ($+18e$ charge) in the lowest-energy state has an orbital radius (expectation value) of only about 0.03 A. An energy of about 4,400 ev is required to remove (ionize) it.

In atoms having more than one electron, if the coupling between electrons is much smaller than that between each electron and the nucleus, the wave function of the many-electron system can be approximated by a properly antisymmetrical sum of products of one-electron wave functions. That is, the electrons are to first order independent of one another. Consider the "construction" of an electrically neutral argon atom, beginning with a nucleus (charge $+18e$) and adding electrons one by one. The first electron, as already pointed out, behaves similarly to the hydrogen electron. At low temperatures, it will assume a state with $n = 1$, $l = m = 0$. Unless a field is applied, we do not know (or care) what s is. Successively added electrons will fall into states of lowest energy; by the exclusion principle, they may not have exactly the same set of quantum numbers as the first electron. The second electron will assume an s value negative to that of the first electron, as in helium. It is convenient to introduce a numbering system for the electrons. The most common system derives from early spectrographic notation. A particular electron is described by a number n, prefixing a letter indicating the value of l, as tabulated:

Value of l	0	1	2	3	4	5	6	$\cdots$
Symbol for state	s	p	d	f	g	h	i	$\cdots$

The first two electrons on the argon nucleus are both $1s$ electrons. The system A^{16+} is said to be in a $1s^2$ state; i.e., it has two $1s$ electrons. The next electron *must* occupy an $n = 2$ state, since both states for $n = 1$ are occupied. The state $n = 2$ will be of substantially higher energy than that of the first electrons; removing an electron in this state from the nucleus will require less energy than removing one of the earlier arrivals. As seen in Fig. B.9, the $n = 2$ radial wave functions are small near the origin (nucleus), where the $n = 1$ functions are largest. The third electron is frequently *outside* the radius of the first two and experiences a central force due to a charge as small as $18e - 2e = 16e$. It is said to be "shielded," or "screened," by the $1s$ electrons. If this shielding were complete, the energy level of the third electron would be approximately $-13.6(16)^2/(2)^2$.

For $n = 2$ a hydrogenlike electron wave has eight possible electronic states (two $2s$ states: $l = 0$, $s = \pm\frac{1}{2}$; and six $2p$ states: $l = 1$, $m = 1$, $s = \pm\frac{1}{2}$; $l = 1$, $m = 0$, $s = \pm\frac{1}{2}$; and $l = 1$, $m = -1$, $s = \pm\frac{1}{2}$). In the hydrogen atom, these states have the same energy except for small spin-orbit and relativistic effects. In the argon atom, the two $1s$ electrons provide part of the charge distribution in which the outer electrons must move. The states $2s$, as can be discerned from the radial function $R_{20}(r)$ (Fig. B.12), have a *higher* probability ($\psi^*\psi$) of being close to the nucleus than the $2p$ states, with $R_{21}(r)$. Since $2s$ electrons are more often nearer the nucleus than $2p$ electrons, they are more often under the influence of a stronger net charge. Their energy levels will accordingly be *more* negative than those of $2p$ electrons. The third and fourth electrons on the argon nucleus should therefore occupy $2s$ states. The fifth electron must then occupy a $2p$ state, bringing the entire system to a state described as $1s^2 2s^2 2p$. A value of m for this electron cannot be determined unless a magnetic field is present, for all states of different m are degenerate except in the presence of a magnetic field. If a field is applied, m may assume the value for lowest energy; that is, $m = -1$. (Because the $2p$ electron has spin, the ion's actual component of angular momentum parallel to the field will be $-\frac{3}{2}\hbar$, by the arguments of Sec. B.8. The angular momentum and magnetic moment of the filled $1s$ and $2s$ "electronic shells" will be zero.)

The six $2p$ states are all completely filled in the argon atom; hence the order of filling the states is of no concern. Likewise, the two $3s$ states, higher in energy than the $2p$ states, are filled by the next two electrons, and the six $3p$ states by the following six, to complete the electrically neutral argon atom. The final state may be written $1s^2 2s^2 2p^6 3s^2 3p^6$. All electrons in the atom are paired with others of opposite spin and opposing orbital angular momentum; hence the atom is not only electrically neutral, but magnetically neutral, as well. It is, as a result, chemically inactive.

All elements from hydrogen to argon behave regularly, in that electrons added to balance an additional nuclear proton fill an incomplete set of electronic states before entering states of higher quantum indices (n, l). Logically, in potassium $(+19e$ nucleus) one might expect the next electron to occupy a $3d$ state. The additional electron in potassium is in fact known to occupy a $4s$ state, however. For given n, states of lower l have lower energy because their wave functions extend toward the nucleus and are to a lesser degree shielded from it by the intervening electrons. In addition, successive states of higher n have higher energy levels, just as in hydrogen. In potassium and the heavier elements following it in the *periodic chart* (Table B.1), the $4s$ electronic states are so decreased in energy by the strong nuclear charge that they are of *lower* energy than $3d$ states. Beyond potassium, however, the $3d$ states begin to fill in until, with *copper*, these states are all full. The intervening atoms may have one or two $4s$ electrons. Some of these, however, exhibit several values of chemical valency; this suggests that one of the $3d$ electrons lies near enough to the $4s$ levels so that it can be removed, for the formation of a chemical band. Beyond copper a similar process takes place in the next row of the chart, until finally, at *krypton*, we again have a chemically inactive atom. Elements with two partially filled electronic shells are called *transition elements*. Many of these are important in solid-state electronics; for example, all magnetically important elements must have incomplete inner shells.

In solids, the atomic descriptions in the periodic chart lose some of their significance, for the orbital motion of the outer electrons is strongly perturbed by the presence of neighboring atoms. Since the concept of constant angular momentum is based on *central force fields* (i.e., fields having spherical symmetry, as that due to the nucleus of the hydrogen atom), the outermost electrons of atoms in solids are not accurately described as having constant-angular-momentum orbits. Electrons deep within the atoms, however, experience substantially the same forces as in free atoms and behave similarly.

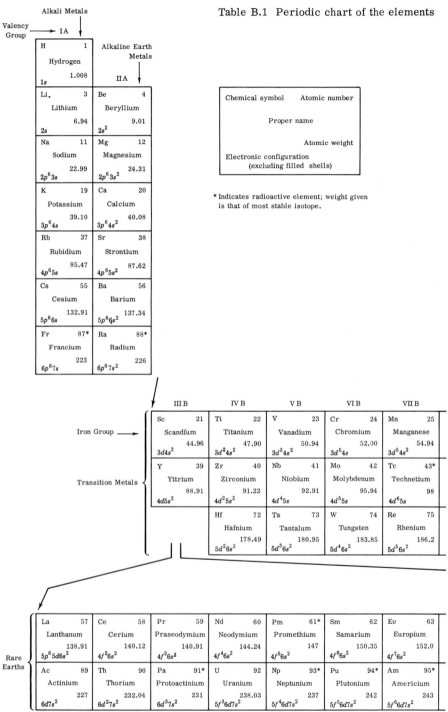

Table B.1 Periodic chart of the elements

598

				Halogens	He 2
					Helium
					4.00
IIIA	IVA	VA	VIA	VIIA	$1s^2$
B 5	C 6	N 7	O 8	F 9	Ne 10
Boron	Carbon	Nitrogen	Oxygen	Fluorine	Neon
10.81	12.01	14.01	16.0	19.00	20.18
$2s^2 2p$	$2s^2 2p^2$	$2s^2 2p^3$	$2s^2 2p^4$	$2s^2 2p^5$	$2s^2 2p^6$
Al 13	Si 14	P 15	S 16	Cl 17	A 18
Aluminum	Silicon	Phosphorus	Sulfur	Chlorine	Argon
26.98	28.09	30.97	32.06	35.45	39.95
$3s^2 3p$	$3s^2 3p^2$	$3s^2 3p^3$	$3s^2 3p^4$	$3s^2 3p^5$	$3s^2 3p^6$
Ga 31	Ge 32	As 33	Se 34	Br 35	Kr 36
Gallium	Germanium	Arsensic	Selenium	Bromine	Krypton
69.72	72.59	. 74.92	78.96	79.91	83.80
$4s^2 4p$	$4s^2 4p^2$	$4s^2 4p^3$	$4s^2 4p^4$	$4s^2 4p^5$	$4s^2 4p^6$
In 49	Sn 50	Sb 51	Te 52	I 53	Xe 54
Indium	Tin	Antimony	Tellurium	Iodine	Xenon
114.82	118.69	121.75	127.60	126.90	131.30
$5s^2 5p$	$5s^2 5p^2$	$5s^2 5p^3$	$5s^2 5p^4$	$5s^2 5p^5$	$5s^2 5p^6$
Tl 81	Pb 82	Bi 83	Po 84*	At 85*	Rn 86*
Thallium	Lead	Bismuth	Polonium	Astatine	Radon
204.37	207.19	208.98	210	210	222.
$6s^2 6p$	$6s^2 6p^2$	$6s^2 6p^3$	$6s^2 6p^4$	$6s^2 6p^5$	$6s^2 6p^6$

VIIIB			IB	IIB
Fe 26	Co 27	Ni 28	Cu 29	Zn 30
Iron	Cobalt	Nickel	Copper	Zinc
55.85	58.93	58.71	63.54	65.37
$3d^6 4s^2$	$3d^7 4s^2$	$3d^8 4s^2$	$3d^{10} 4s$	$3d^{10} 4s^2$
Ru 44	Rh 45	Pd 46	Ag 47	Cd 48
Ruthenium	Rhodium	Palladium	Silver	Cadmium
101.1	102.91	106.4	107.87	112.40
$4d^7 5s$	$4d^8 5s$	$4d^{10}$	$4d^{10} 5s$	$4d^{10} 5s^2$
Os 76	Ir 77	Pt 78	Au 79	Hg 80
Osmium	Iridium	Platinum	Gold	Mercury
190.2	192.2	195.09	196.97	200.59
$5d^6 6s^2$	$5d^9$	$5d^9 6s$	$5d^{10} 6s$	$5d^{10} 6s^2$

Gd 64	Tb 65	Dy 66	Ho 67	Er 68	Tm 69	Yb 70	Lu 71
Gadolinium	Terbium	Dysprosium	Holmium	Erbium	Thulium	Ytterbium	Lutecium
157.25	158.92	162.50	164.93	167.26	168.93	173.04	174.97
$4f^7 5d6s^2$	$4f^8 5d6s^2$	$4f^{10} 6s^2$	$4f^{11} 6s^2$	$4f^{12} 6s^2$	$4f^{13} 6s^2$	$4f^{14} 6s^2$	$4f^{14} 5d6s$
Cm 96*	Bk 97*	Cf 98*	Es 99*	Fm 100*	Md 101*	No 102*	Lw 103*
Curium	Berkelium	Californium	Einsteinium	Fermium	Mendelevium	Nobelium	Lawrencium
247	247	251	254	253	256	254	257
$5f^7 6d7s^2$	$5f^8 6d7s^2$	$5f^9 6d7s^2$					

GENERAL REFERENCES

Bohm, D.: "Quantum Theory," Prentice-Hall, Inc., Englewood Cliffs, N.J., 1951.   (A thorough, somewhat rambling treatment.)

Dicke, R. H., and J. P. Wittke: "Introduction to Quantum Mechanics," Addison-Wesley Publishing Company, Inc., Reading, Mass., 1960.   (An excellent modern treatment which includes operational methods.)

Dirac, P. A. M.: "The Principles of Quantum Mechanics," 4th ed., Oxford University Press, Fair Lawn, N.J., 1958.   (One of the classics, using Dirac's special notation; not recommended as an introductory reference, but philosophically challenging.)

Persico, E.: "Fundamentals of Quantum Mechanics" (transl. and ed. by G. M. Temmer), Prentice-Hall, Inc., Englewood Cliffs, N.J., 1950.   (Contains a patient treatment of matrix methods.)

Schiff, L.: "Quantum Mechanics," 2d ed., McGraw-Hill Book Company, New York, 1955.   (Based on the wave-equation approach; contains all the important elementary principles.)

Sherwin, C. W.: "Introduction to Quantum Mechanics," Holt, Rinehart and Winston, Inc., New York, 1959.   (A very readable elementary treatment.)

Sproull, H. L.: "Modern Physics," John Wiley & Sons, Inc., New York, 1956.   (At a good introductory level, written for engineers.)

Appendix C: statistical physics

C.1 Thermodynamic Energy Functions; Thermal Equilibrium

The classical science of thermodynamics deals with the time-average properties of systems containing large numbers of particles. It thus avoids description of the individual motions of the particles. By manipulation of thermodynamic variables, many thermodynamic relations can be developed, enabling one to calculate many of the thermal, electrical, and mechanical properties of matter from a relatively limited set of measurements.

Any thermodynamic system may be described by a total energy U, sometimes termed the *internal energy*. Since it is not really possible to define absolute zero-energy conditions, energy is generally measured with respect to some arbitrary reference conditions (such as zero temperature). It is, however, possible to define, precisely, *changes* in energy. These changes can come about from a number of external sources, as a result of these energy sources making a change of some internal property. For example, if a change in volume dV of a system occurs while a pressure p is applied, the change in internal energy must be $dU = -p\,dV$. Other sources of energy are electric fields, magnetic fields, stresses, and sources of heat energy. Each means of altering the system energy involves some external force function whose magnitude is independent of the size of the system (electric field $\mathcal{E}$, magnetic field $\mathcal{3C}$, stress $\mathbf{T}$, and temperature T). These variables are termed *intensive variables*. The changes in the system are proportional to the number of particles in the system, and are termed *extensive variables*: volume V, electric polarization $\mathbf{P}$, magnetic polarization $\mathbf{M}$, and strain $\mathbf{S}$ (although, as usually defined, the strain is independent of the system size; it is defined as elongation or shear per unit length). A differential change of system energy may be expressed as

$$dU = dQ + \boldsymbol{\mathcal{E}} \cdot d\mathbf{P} + \mu_0 \boldsymbol{\mathcal{H}} \cdot d\mathbf{M} + \mathbf{T} \cdot d\mathbf{S} - p \, dV \tag{C.1}$$

This is expressed as for a system of unit volume, since the quantities $\mathbf{P}$, $\mathbf{M}$, $\mathbf{T}$, and $\mathbf{S}$ are so defined. It implies that these quantities are uniform throughout the system.[1] The quantity dQ represents *heat input* to the system. We should expect that this is also the product of an intensive variable with the differential of an extensive variable, like the rest. This is indeed the case when the heat input takes place slowly so that the system remains always at *thermal equilibrium*. A system in thermal equilibrium need not be at rest, for this is impossible even at absolute zero temperature. At equilibrium, however, there must exist no thermal (temperature) gradients in the system. Nor can there be electrical conduction currents moving steadily through the material, for such currents imply conversion of externally supplied energy into heat (except in superconductors).

When there is heat input to a system maintained at thermal equilibrium, the differential dQ equals $T \, dS$, where T is the temperature and S a complementary extensive variable termed *entropy*. Suppose that a system is composed of two parts, A and B, each of which is at thermal equilibrium but having different temperatures T_A and T_B. If a quantity of heat energy dQ passes out of part A into part B, the change in entropy of part A must be $-dQ/T_A$ ($= dS_A$). The change in entropy of part B is dQ/T_B ($= dS_B$). The change in entropy of the entire system is $dQ \left(\dfrac{1}{T_B} - \dfrac{1}{T_A} \right)$. The heat flow will be from the hotter part to the colder part; hence, if $T_A > T_B$, the system will experience a net *increase* in entropy *without* the addition of heat energy from an external source. The entropy of the overall system will continue to increase until the temperatures of the two parts become equal. This type of change is termed an *irreversible* change, for there is nothing we can do to the entire system from outside to reestablish the temperature difference which existed initially. Only when heat is added to the system slowly, while equilibrium is maintained constantly, is the change in entropy given by dQ/T. Accordingly, we can write, in general,

$$dQ \leqq T \, dS \tag{C.2}$$

where the equality applies for reversible changes in the system, and the inequality for irreversible changes. Accordingly, (C.1) should be stated

$$dU \leqq T \, dS + \boldsymbol{\mathcal{E}} \cdot d\mathbf{P} + \mu_0 \boldsymbol{\mathcal{H}} \cdot d\mathbf{M} + \mathbf{T} \cdot d\mathbf{S} - p \, dV \tag{C.3}$$

[1] This need not be true in a real system. Any such system can usually be divided into subsystems for which (C.1) is true.

This differential relation can be interpreted as a criterion for thermal equilibrium; i.e., if the entropy, polarizations, strains, and volume are kept constant, $dU \leq 0$. The energy will seek a *minimum* value in keeping with the constraints on the system. These constraints, however, are difficult ones to maintain (for example, it is very difficult to maintain constant the volume of a solid). One can form new *energy functions*, sometimes termed thermodynamic potentials, which are more readily handled. For example, form the function

$$G = U - TS - \boldsymbol{\varepsilon} \cdot \mathbf{P} - \mu_0 \mathbf{3C} \cdot \mathbf{M} - \mathbf{T} \cdot \mathbf{S} + pV \tag{C.4}$$

the differential of which is $dU - T\,dS - S\,dT - \mu_0 \mathbf{3C} \cdot d\mathbf{M} - \mu_0 \mathbf{M} \cdot d\mathbf{3C} - T \cdot dS - \mathbf{S} \cdot d\mathbf{T} + p\,dV + V\,dp$. We shall call this the *free energy*. Substituting into (C.3), we have

$$dG \leqq -S\,dT - \mathbf{P} \cdot d\boldsymbol{\varepsilon} - \mu_0 \mathbf{M} \cdot d\mathbf{3C} - \mathbf{S} \cdot d\mathbf{T} + V\,dp \tag{C.5}$$

Since the parameters U, T, S, P, etc., involved in the definition of G, are all uniquely definable functions of the system, G is unambiguous. If, however, all *intensive* variables are held constant—and these are the ones we generally have control of—the condition on dG is

$$dG \leqq 0$$

As equilibrium is approached in a system under these conditions, therefore, G seeks a minimum value. It is therefore a very valuable function to use in equilibrium calculations (as in Chap. 9).

Many other thermodynamic energy functions can be defined. The more useful ones are the *enthalpy* H and the *Helmholtz free energy* F, defined by

$$\begin{aligned} H &= U + pV \\ F &= U - TS \end{aligned} \tag{C.6}$$

These functions are more generally used in thermodynamic descriptions of gaseous systems. Particular functions are most valuable in dealing with particular thermal processes. For example, when heat ΔQ is added to a system at constant pressure to raise temperature by an amount ΔT, we do not directly obtain a measure of the change of energy U. However, since

$$dH = dQ + V\,dp \tag{C.7}$$

we have at constant pressure $(dp = 0)$

$$\left(\frac{\partial H}{\partial T}\right)_p \left(= \frac{\Delta Q}{\Delta T}\right) = c_p \tag{C.8}$$

This particular parameter is termed the *specific heat at constant pressure*. It is presumed here that no fields, stresses, or strains are involved.   Likewise, the *specific heat at constant volume* c_v is defined as

$$c_v = \left(\frac{\partial U}{\partial T}\right)_V \tag{C.9}$$

While c_v is useful in dealing with gaseous systems, the specific-heat values for solids are generally taken at constant pressure.

By the definitions of the various energy functions, it is possible to define a number of thermodynamic relationships enabling one to find one function from another.[1]

C.2   Inhomogeneous Systems

Most macroscopic systems of practical interest (e.g., electronic devices) are composed of several parts.   The *separable* parts of a thermodynamic system are termed *phases*.[2]   For example, an iced drink contains two phases, the liquid phase and the solid phase (the ice).   Undissolved sugar in the drink would constitute a second solid phase, a stirring spoon another phase.   The dissolved sugar molecules and the H_2O molecules, however, are intimately mixed and constitute only a single phase.   This phase, however, has two *chemical constituents*, or *species*.   While the phases of a system must be distinguishable, this does not preclude the transfer of atoms or molecules of the constituents from phase to phase; for example, the ice melts; sugar dissolves or recrystallizes.   Often each phase will contain some quantity of all chemical constituents present, but some of these may be small (e.g., the stirring spoon should not dissolve into the liquid!).

In a system of several phases the extensive parameters of the entire system are the *sums* of the extensive parameters of the separate phases.   For example, the volume of the liquid plus the volume of the solid phases equals the total volume, in the iced drink.   Likewise, the energy U is the sum of the energies of the two parts.   The same applies for S, F, G, etc.   In one phase, however, we cannot measure extensive parameters for each of the chemical constituents present.   (Dissolution of sugar in coffee does not increase the volume of the sweetened coffee by an amount equal to the volume of the dissolved sugar.)

At equilibrium, temperature is the same in all phases, as generally is pressure.   In addition to changes of the entropy, dS_α,

---

[1] The reader who finds it necessary to make use of such relationships will find valuable the book by P. W. Bridgman, "The Thermodynamics of Electrical Phenomena in Metals and a Condensed Collection of Thermodynamic Formulas," Dover Publications, Inc., New York, 1961.

[2] It may in practice be difficult to separate phases in a crystalline material having small crystallites of two (or more) structural forms.

and volume, dV_α, of a phase α, there may also be changes in composition. The addition of an atom or molecule (or even an electron) to one phase will generally raise its internal energy by a small amount. In the absence of field- and stress-dependent terms, we have for the system of several phases

$$dU = \sum_\alpha T\, dS_\alpha - \sum_\alpha p\, dV_\alpha + \sum_\alpha \sum_i \mu_{i\alpha}\, \Delta m_{i\alpha} \qquad (C.10)$$

The variable $m_{i\alpha}$ is the total number of "molecules" of chemical constituent i in phase α, and $\Delta m_{i\alpha}$ the change in this number. The parameter $\mu_{i\alpha}$ is known as the *chemical potential* for constituent i in phase α. It has the dimensions of energy per molecule and is the energy which must be given to one molecule of i to move it *into* a particular phase α. Equation (C.10) permits description of an *open* system, for we can add molecules from an *external* supply as well as exchanging them between phases.

Other energy functions may be found as before. Substituting in (C.10) the definition of G, again in the absence of fields and stresses,

$$dG = -\sum_\alpha S_\alpha\, dT + \sum_\alpha V_\alpha\, dp + \sum_\alpha \sum_i \mu_{i\alpha}\, \Delta m_{i\alpha} \qquad (C.11)$$

In a *one-constituent, one-phase* system (again dispensing with fields and stresses) at equilibrium, temperature and pressure are the only variables. In a more complex system, however, molecules or atoms move from one phase to another, or chemical reactions may take place to minimize the free energy G. At equilibrium (constant T and p), passage of a molecule from one phase to another, or of an atom from one chemical compound to another, should *not* further lower the value of G. Thus, if one "molecule" of constituent i goes from phase α to phase β, the increase of G in phase β must exactly equal the decrease of G in phase α. Here $\Delta m_{i\alpha} = -1$, $\Delta m_{i\beta} = +1$, and

$$\begin{aligned} dG = 0 &= -\mu_{i\alpha} + \mu_{i\beta} \qquad \text{(equilibrium)} \\ \therefore\ \mu_{i\alpha} &= \mu_{i\beta} \qquad\qquad \text{(all } i \text{ and all } \alpha, \beta\text{)} \end{aligned} \qquad (C.12)$$

The chemical potential, at equilibrium, is therefore *the same in all phases*, for each constituent i.

An important principle which may be inferred from (C.11) is the so-called *Gibbs phase rule*, which states the number of degrees of freedom (variables) available in a system. Description of the thermodynamic state of a system of P phases ($\alpha = 1, 2, \ldots, P$) and C chemical constituents ($i = 1, 2, \ldots, C$) includes the pressure and temperature of the system and the *composition* of each phase. The latter requires in general $C - 1$ variables; we need specify only the fraction of $C - 1$ of the constituents, the final one being given

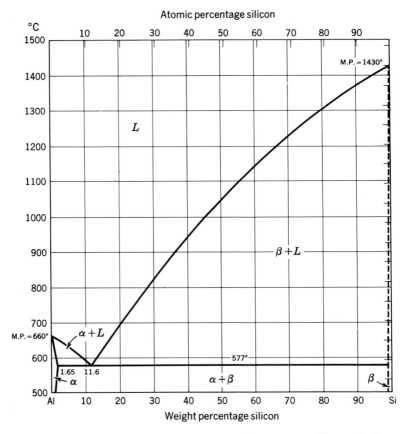

Figure C.1 Phase diagram for the aluminum-silicon system. Phase α is the face-centered cubic crystal structure, characteristic of aluminum. Phase β is the silicon (diamond) crystal structure. L represents the liquid phase. Diagram is for atmospheric pressure. (*From American Society for Metals,* "*Metals Handbook*," *p. 1166, 1948.*)

automatically (e.g., the composition of a 75–25 per cent copper-gold alloy is defined by *either* fraction). In P phases, allowing the possibility that each phase contains at least a small quantity of each constituent, one requires $P(C-1)$ composition measures; with T and p, the total number of variables is $PC - P + 2$. All are not independent, however; there are constraints in the form $\mu_{i\alpha} = \mu_{i\beta}$, for each of the C constituents in each of the P phases; there are $C(P-1)$ of these constraints. Three phases have two such constraint relations for *each* constituent. Each constraint reduces the number of independent system variables required by *one*. The total number of independent variables required to describe the system is

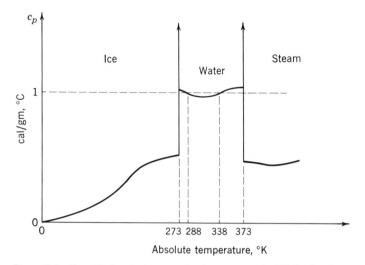

Figure C.2   Specific heat at atmospheric pressure, for H_2O, showing *heat of fusion* (273°K) and *heat of vaporization* (373°K).   (The variations in c_p in the liquid phase are somewhat exaggerated.)

therefore

$$P(C - 1) + 2 - C(P - 1) = C - P + 2 = \text{degrees of freedom} \qquad \text{(C.13)}$$

The phase rule helps to explain *phase diagrams*. The most common phase diagrams represent equilibrium states of metal mixtures which form *alloys* over certain ranges of temperature and composition. An alloy is an intimately mixed solid solution of one metal in the other. Atoms of different metals form solutions over wide ranges of composition when of comparable size and valence. A small percentage of atoms of a disparate size or valency can be accommodated in another metal, but when the foreign atoms become too numerous, they tend to precipitate out into crystals of their own. Figure C.1 is a phase diagram for the aluminum-silicon system. The temperature is plotted as ordinate, the *overall* composition as abscissa. The various crystalline forms the material may assume are labeled with Greek letters (α, β, etc.). The presence of *two* Greek letters in a particular region of the diagram means that the system, in equilibrium, has two phases, with some crystallites of structure α and some of structure β. Since p is assumed fixed at the atmospheric value, *all* variables are fixed when three phases coexist ($C - P + 2 = 2 - 3 + 2 = 1$—pressure). Over a *range* of temperature at fixed overall composition, only two phases may coexist, but at a particular temperature, a boundary may exist between one pair of phases and another pair of phases. This is shown at the horizontal line (*eutectic line*). The lowest-melting alloy (11.6 per cent Si by weight), a

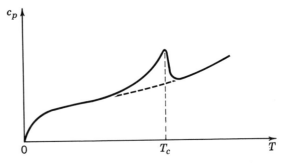

Figure C.3 Specific heat (c_p) for a metal such as nickel, having a second-order phase transition (magnetic transition) culminating at the Curie temperature T_c. The dashed line illustrates the behavior of non-ferromagnetic metal, having no such transition.

mixture of α and β crystallites, is termed the eutectic. The solubility of silicon in aluminum or aluminum in silicon is also indicated in the diagram; at 0°C only about 1 per cent silicon may be added to pure aluminum before two phases must be formed (move to the right from the left-hand side). The solubility of aluminum in silicon is slightly larger.

In *phase transitions*, the specific heat c_p changes characteristically when a system undergoes a transition from one phase to another. Where the phase change is abrupt (melting and boiling processes), finite heat (entropy) must be added or removed in order to move past the transition temperature (Fig. C.2). Such a transition is termed a *first-order phase* transition. Many transitions in solids are more subtle. Examples are the so-called order-disorder transition in alloys, where the special ordered atomic arrangements (Fig. 1.17) cannot exist above a critical temperature. Another example is the ferromagnetic-paramagnetic transition at the Curie temperature T_c in ferromagnetic materials (Chap. 8), where remanent magnetism cannot exist above T_c. In such second-order phase transitions, the transition begins taking place at lower temperatures (Fig. C.3), raising the specific heat because a part of the material begins the transition. At the critical temperature, c_p would ideally have a finite discontinuity, corresponding to the completion of the transition process.

C.3   Statistical Mechanics; Fermi-Dirac Systems

While thermodynamic relationships may be used to develop relations between properties of materials, *equations of state* defining a particular many-particle system as a function of temperature and pressure, etc., can be found only from a statistical analysis of the system. A complete solution for particle motions is beyond reason, but fortunately is not needed in statistical mechanics.

The general problem of statistical mechanics is the determination of the *distribution* of particle energies over the various values they may assume. The total system energy and other energy functions can then be found. To illustrate the method it is convenient to make use of the same "particle in a box" model used in Sec. B.3. Here we shall assume that there are not one but many particles, N, in the box. We shall assume, however, that the density is not so great that the particle-particle interaction greatly perturbs the motion of individual particles. This assumption is apparently satisfactory for electrons in conductors and semiconductors, but not in superconductors.

The state of the system can be described if the particles in the box have half-integer spin and therefore obey the exclusion principle, by stating the quantum numbers i, j, k, s for each particle. Since the particles are totally indistinguishable from one another, however, it is even more meaningful simply to list N sets of quantum numbers which the particles possess. Here the argument must branch, for with particles obeying the exclusion principle (*Fermi-Dirac particles*, or *fermions*, for example, electrons) the N sets of quantum numbers must all be different. If the particles do not obey the exclusion principle, there may be many particles having the same quantum indices. This is true of *photons*, for a given resonance of an electromagnetic cavity may have any number of photons. Photons and integral-spin particles (such as helium atoms) obey a different statistical description, termed *Bose-Einstein statistics* (Sec. C.7), and are called *bosons*.

While it is convenient to neglect the interaction of particles in our system, in order to achieve thermal equilibrium any system needs to have interaction between all the carriers of energy. With even the slightest probability of collision between particles or of particles hitting nonelastic walls of a container, equilibrium is eventually achieved. That is, if a single particle initially possessed all the energy of a system, the energy would eventually be distributed among all the particles in the system, as the system reached equilibrium.

Since there are an infinite number of states that any particle may assume, there are an infinite number of possible particle-energy distributions. At given temperature and pressure, an equilibrium system must have a particular distribution. In statistical mechanics, one finds a *most probable* distribution in a system of fixed energy (and a fixed number of particles). The basic premise of statistical mechanics is that, subject to these limitations on energy and particle count, any particular state which the system can assume is equally as probable as any other. We must therefore be prepared to enumerate *system states* of a given total energy (the sum of the energies of all

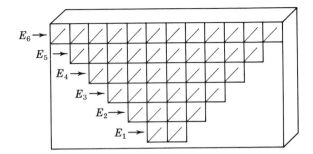

Figure C.4 Schematic of an array of compartments for determining distributions of particles among particle states. For Fermi-Dirac particles, each compartment can contain at most one particle. (Numbers of compartments do not correspond to the text example.) We show the lowest-energy particle states at the bottom, in analogy to most of the energy-level diagrams in the text (e.g., Fig. 8.1).

particles). We begin by enumerating all single-particle states and their associated energies. For example, for electrons in a box, i, j, k, may take on any integral values, and s the values $\pm\frac{1}{2}$. In the absence of a magnetic field which would make the value of s influence the energy, there are only two states of lowest energy ($i, j, k = 1$, $s = \pm\frac{1}{2}$) and *six* states of next-higher energy ($i, j, k = 1, 1, 2; 1, 2, 1$; $2, 1, 1$; with $s = \pm\frac{1}{2}$). Representing all possible values of particle energy by a single set of indices, we can tabulate the number of states having given energies; in the case mentioned for lowest energy E_1 [the value given in (B.34) when $i, j, k = 1$], $n_1 = 2$. Likewise, $n_2 = 6$ at energy E_2, etc. We could in principle enumerate all the states, tabulating the n_i for each E_i. This is not necessary for the general theory, only when applying it to a specific system (as in Sec. C.6).

In a Fermi-Dirac system containing a large number of particles, N, a distinguishable state of the system is defined when, for each of the n_i possible particle states of energy E_i, we specify whether the state is occupied by a particle. We can therefore imagine an analog consisting of a total of N balls and a set of compartments of which n_1 are numbered 1, n_2 are numbered 2, etc. (Fig. C.4). A compartment can contain at most one ball. A state of the system is defined by distributing the N balls into N of the compartments.

Let us now count how many system states there are in which a total of m_i of the n_i single-particle states of particle energy E_i are occupied, for each i. Here the total energy is $U = \sum_i m_i E_i$. We begin by placing m_1 balls, in all possible ways, in the n_1 compartments of energy E_1. The first ball can be placed in any of the n_1

compartments, the second in any of the $n_i - 1$, the third in any of $n_1 - 2$, etc. When placing the m_ith ball, there are $n_i - m_i + 1$ compartments remaining, so that there are in all a total of $n_1(n_1 - 1)(n_1 - 2) \cdots (n_1 - m_1 + 1) = n_1!/(n_1 - m_1)!$ different ways of distributing the m_1 particles, in sequence. However, the many rearrangements of the m_1 particles between specific m_1 filled compartments number $m_1(m_1 - 1)(m_1 - 2) \cdots (2)(1) \; (= m_1!)$. There are in fact only $1/m_1!$ as many *distinguishable* distributions.

Number of distinguishable distributions of m_i indistinguishable

$$\text{particles between } n_i \text{ distinguishable states} = \frac{n_i!}{m_i!(n_i - m_i)!} \tag{C.14}$$

Since the distributions of m_1 balls among n_1 compartments are independent of the distributions of m_2 balls among n_2 compartments, the number of possible distributions for all compartments is the product of terms (C.14):

$$D_{n_i, m_i} = \frac{n_1!}{m_1!(n_1 - m_1)!} \cdot \frac{n_2!}{m_2!(n_2 - m_2)!} \cdots = \prod_i \frac{n_i!}{m_i!(n_i - m_i)!} \tag{C.15}$$

Only those system states are possible, however, for which $\sum_i m_i E_i = U$ (energy conservation) and $\sum_i m_i = N$ (particle conservation). Subject only to these two limitations, there are still many possible distributions of m_i values. We might, for example, have $N - 1$ particles at the lowest available energy levels and one particle at a very high energy level. Alternatively, all particles might take on *exactly* the same energy. Intuition would suggest that neither situation would be highly probable. We must, accordingly, find that set of values m_i giving the greatest number of system states, D_{n_i, m_i}. This is equivalent to finding a maximum value of D_{n_i, m_i}. Then, if D is very large for a given set of m_i, this energy distribution will dominate. Our problem is to find for *each* (n_i, E_i) the proper m_i, to maximize D.

In working with typical systems having $\sim 10^{23}$ particles, the factorials appearing in D may be expressed by much simpler approximations. The *Stirling approximation* for the factorial $x!$ is

$$x! \cong (2\pi x)^{\frac{1}{2}} x^x e^{-x} \tag{C.16}$$

For our purposes even the $(2\pi)^{\frac{1}{2}}$ factor may be omitted. Substituting this into the continued product (C.15), we obtain as its logarithm the summation

$$\ln D \cong \sum_i [n_i \ln n_i - m_i \ln m_i - (n_i - m_i) \ln (n_i - m_i)] \tag{C.17}$$

Finding the maximum value of a function generally requires setting its derivative to zero, but here there are many variables m_i.

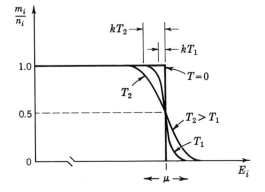

Figure C.5   The Fermi-Dirac distribution function, plotted for a given value of μ ($= -\alpha/\beta$) and for several different values of β ($1/kT$).   The fractional state occupancy m_i/n_i is always $\frac{1}{2}$ at $E_i = \mu$. If μ changes, the curve simply moves horizontally on the E_i scale.

The *method of undetermined multipliers*[1] provides a means to obtain the desired result.   One sets separately to zero *each* of the derivatives:

$$\frac{\partial}{\partial m_i}\left(\ln D - \alpha \sum_i m_i - \beta \sum_i E_i m_i\right) = 0 \tag{C.18}$$

where α and β are yet-undetermined parameters, which will later be shown to be related to the temperature T and the chemical potential μ.   For the present they are treated simply as constants.   Carrying out the indicated differentiation on (C.17),

$$\ln \frac{n_i - m_i}{m_i} = \alpha + \beta E_i$$
$$\frac{m_i}{n_i} = \frac{1}{1 + e^{\alpha+\beta E_i}} \tag{C.19}$$

The parameters α and β must be chosen so as to satisfy the constraints.   Therefore

$$N = \sum_i \frac{n_i}{1 + e^{\alpha+\beta E_1}} \tag{C.20}$$

$$U = \sum_i \frac{n_i E_i}{1 + e^{\alpha+\beta E_i}} \tag{C.21}$$

These two relations determine α and β in terms of the system energy and number of particles.   Plotting m_i/n_i versus E (Fig. C.5) for

[1] Cf. J. E. Mayer and M. G. Mayer, "Statistical Mechanics," p. 433, John Wiley & Sons, Inc., New York, 1940.

some positive value of β, this *most probable energy distribution* has a larger fraction of lower-energy states filled than higher-energy states. If a given system had equally many states of each possible energy ($n_i = n$ for all i) the actual energy distribution m_i versus E would be of the same form as the m_i/n_i. Usually, however, the n_i are not uniformly distributed over all energies. The *density-of-states function* (n_i versus E_i) takes a variety of forms for electrons in metals and semiconductors, which influences the electronic behavior of these materials in subtle ways.

C.4   Identification of the Parameters α, β, and ln D

The energy levels E_i are established by the volume and the number of particles in the system. By adding small amounts of heat we should not change the E_i or n_i, only the various m_i (but application of pressure could change the E_i, n_i). The heat added to the system is then

$$dQ = \sum_i E_i \, dm_i \tag{C.22}$$

where dm_i represents the change in m_i. While dm_i is actually an integer, it may be treated as a differential. Let us now calculate the change in ln D of the system *due only to changes in the m_i*. From (C.17),

$$d(\ln D)_{E_i, n_i=\text{const}} = \sum_i \ln \frac{n_i - m_i}{m_i} \, dm_i \tag{C.23}$$

Substituting the Fermi-Dirac distribution (C.19) for the m_i/n_i,

$$d(\ln D) = \sum_i (\beta E_i + \alpha) \, dm_i \tag{C.24}$$

Since α and β are constants and the total number of particles does not change,

$$\sum_i dm_i = dN = 0 \qquad \text{and} \qquad \sum_i E_i \, dm_i = dQ$$

where dQ is the total heat energy added. Therefore

$$dQ = \frac{d(\ln D)}{\beta} \tag{C.25}$$

From Sec. C.1, the relation defining T and S at equilibrium is $dQ = T \, dS$. Since the quantity D is dimensionless, the classical and statistical results agree if

$$S = k \ln D \tag{C.26}$$

$$\beta = \frac{1}{kT} \tag{C.27}$$

The universal constant k (Boltzmann's constant) makes the equations dimensionally correct. The entropy measures the number of possible system states available to the system. As U is made smaller (heat taken from the system) the number of system states will reduce to a very low value at zero temperature. Entropy measures system *disorder*, in the sense that it is proportional to the log of the number of system states available to the system.

We may likewise identify α by comparing the classical thermodynamics expression for the differential energy dU in a single-phase system of one component,

$$dU = -p\, dV + T\, dS + \mu\, dm \tag{C.28}$$

with the statistical expression

$$dU = d\left(\sum_i m_i E_i\right) = \sum_i m_i\, dE_i + \sum_i E_i\, dm_i \tag{C.29}$$

Combining (C.24) and (C.25),

$$dQ = T\, dS = \sum_i (E_i + kT\alpha)\, dm_i = \sum_i E_i\, dm_i + \sum_i kT\alpha\, dm_i \tag{C.30}$$

If the term in (C.29) containing dE_i is identified with the $-p\, dV$ term in the classical expression,

$$\alpha = \frac{-\mu}{kT} \tag{C.31}$$

The Fermi-Dirac distribution function may now be written

$$\frac{m_i}{n_i} = \frac{1}{1 + e^{(E_i - \mu)/kT}} \tag{C.32}$$

The variation of this function versus T, for constant μ, is shown in Fig. C.5. At $T = 0$, the probability of occupancy of all states of $E_i < \mu$ is unity, while no states above μ are occupied. At nonzero temperatures, μ marks the energy at which $m_i/n_i = \frac{1}{2}$. In this connection, μ is termed the *Fermi level*, or *Fermi energy*.

It is very desirable to get a "feel" for the use of this function. In Fig. C.6 a density-of-states function typical of conduction (valence) electrons in a metal is shown—the states are so close together that $n_i(E_i)$ can be expressed as a continuous density function $n(E)$, where $n(E)\, dE$ is the sum of n_i's from E to $E + dE$. The application of (C.20) requires that μ be adjusted so that the available number of particles be distributed according to (C.32) over the available states. In metals, where $n(E)$ is nearly constant over a broad energy range in the vicinity of μ, μ is essentially independent of temperature. In semiconductors, the variation of μ causes very interesting characteristics (Chap. 4).

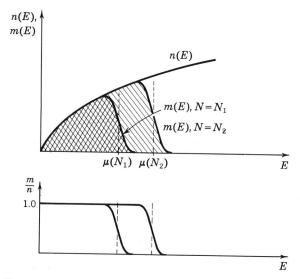

Figure C.6 $n(E)$ and $m(E)$ for valence electrons in idealized monovalent metal. The *Fermi factor* m/n is plotted below. The value of μ is set by the number of particles occupying the system; it is larger if the electron density N is greater, since the area under the $m(E)$ curve must equal the density of particles. [Two particle densities ($N_2 > N_1$) are shown.] μ is also a function of temperature, particularly so where $n(E)$ has rapid variation with E.

In the solution of problems of electronic-conduction theory, it is common to treat the electrons as if they formed an independent system and the remainder of the solid were merely equivalent to a heat bath. While this is not quite correct, it is a sufficiently good approximation for most purposes.

C.5   The Boltzmann Approximation; Ideal Gases

The Boltzmann approximation to quantum statistics was originally derived for classical systems in which particles may have any of a continuous range of energy values. This is equivalent, in quantum statistics, to having an n_i for each allowed energy level which is as large as we wish. The result is that, for any energy level, m_i/n_i is extremely small. Accordingly, in (C.32), the Fermi energy must lie well below the lowest allowed energy level, in which case the energy distribution takes on the Boltzmann form

$$\frac{m_i}{n_i} = e^{(\mu - E_i)/kT}$$

(C.33)

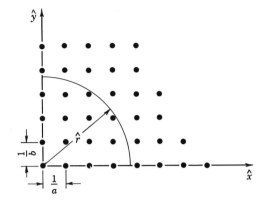

Figure C.7 Construction to estimate the number of states per
unit energy [$n(E)$], for particles
in a "box." (Only two dimensions are shown.)

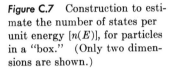

While actual systems always satisfy either Fermi-Dirac or Bose-
Einstein statistics (Sec. C.7), a system containing a small number of
particles and having a relatively large energy per particle can be
described quite well with the Boltzmann distribution. The most
common example is the *ideal gas* (or Boltzmann gas), to which real
gases at low pressure and high temperature are good approximations.

The energy levels of noninteracting particles in a simple rectangular container are given by (B.34):

$$E_{ijk} = \frac{\pi^2 \hbar^2}{2m} \left[\left(\frac{i}{a}\right)^2 + \left(\frac{j}{b}\right)^2 + \left(\frac{k}{c}\right)^2 \right] \qquad i, j, k = 1, 2, 3, \ldots$$

The tabulation of n_i versus E_i is greatly aided by an artifice:
We imagine plotted in a three-dimensional cartesian space the points
($\hat{x} = i/a$, $\hat{y} = j/b$, $\hat{z} = k/c$) for all the positive integer values of i,
j, and k. These points will form a rectilinear three-dimensional array
(Fig. C.7); each represents one particular particle state. Points
corresponding to energy E lie on a *spherical surface*

$$\hat{r}^2 = \hat{x}^2 + \hat{y}^2 + \hat{z}^2 = \frac{2mE}{\pi^2 \hbar^2}$$

Inside a spherical surface of radius $\hat{r} = (2mE/\pi^2\hbar^2)^{\frac{1}{2}}$ lie a total
number of points (i.e., states) determined by the *volume* of the sphere.
Since the points lie separated by distances $1/a$, $1/b$, $1/c$, the volume
in $\hat{x}\hat{y}\hat{z}$ space which is associated with *one* point is $1/abc$. Since the
points corresponding to distinct states occur only in one *octant*
($\hat{x}$, $\hat{y}$, $\hat{z} > 0$) of the sphere, the volume including all points out to a
certain energy E is given in terms of the usual formula

$$\frac{V_{\text{sphere}}}{8} = \frac{1}{8}\left(\frac{4\pi\hat{r}^3}{3}\right) = \frac{\pi}{6}\left(\frac{2mE}{\pi^2\hbar^2}\right)^{\frac{3}{2}}$$

The number of states within this volume is found by dividing by the state volume $(abc)^{-1}$:

$$\sum_{E=0}^{E} n_i = abc \frac{\pi}{6} \left(\frac{2m}{\pi^2 \hbar^2}\right)^{\frac{3}{2}} E^{\frac{3}{2}} \tag{C.34}$$

The degree of approximation is very good when $\hat{r} \gg 1/a, 1/b, 1/c$. If the particles represented are electrons, each of the states counted should really be a pair of states, for $s = \pm\frac{1}{2}$. When the system consists of particles having a spin of $\frac{3}{2}$, there are four possible spin conditions for each state considered here. This introduces a multiplicity, which we may write $2s + 1$. The number of states in a limited range $E \rightarrow E + dE$ is found by differentiation.

$$n(E)\, dE = (2s + 1)(abc) \frac{\pi}{4} \left(\frac{2m}{\pi^2 \hbar^2}\right)^{\frac{3}{2}} E^{\frac{1}{2}}\, dE \tag{C.35}$$

Formally, this equals $2s + 1$ times the number of $(1/abc)$ volumes in a thin spherical lamination, between radii corresponding to energy E and $E + dE$.

Instead of taking a sum over each possible value of E_i, we now make an integration of dn over E. The distribution function (C.33) is also modified, to the form

$$dm = e^{(\mu-E)/kT} n(E)\, dE \tag{C.36}$$

The summations whereby one obtains the values of μ and N (total number of particles) become integrals:

$$N = \int dm = \int_0^\infty e^{(\mu-E)/kT} n(E)\, dE$$

$$U = \int E\, dm \int_0^\infty e^{(\mu-E)/kT} E n(E)\, dE$$

The ideal-gas density of states [(C.35)], when substituted into these integrals, gives

$$N = (2s + 1) \frac{\pi}{4} \left(\frac{2m}{\pi^2 \hbar^2}\right)^{\frac{3}{2}} (abc) e^{\mu/kT} \frac{\pi^{\frac{1}{2}}}{2} (kt)^{\frac{3}{2}}$$

$$U = (2s + 1) \frac{\pi}{4} \left(\frac{2m}{\pi^2 \hbar^2}\right)^{\frac{3}{2}} (abc) e^{\mu/kT} \frac{3\pi^{\frac{1}{2}}}{4} (kT)^{\frac{5}{2}} \tag{C.37}$$

By division,

$$\frac{U}{N} = \tfrac{3}{2} kT \tag{C.38}$$

This is the *energy per particle* in a Boltzmann gas. *Specific heat* $c_v = 3k/2$.

We may compare (C.28) and (C.29) to obtain

$$\sum_i m_i\, dE_i = -p\, dV \tag{C.39}$$

The energy levels E_i are strictly dependent on volume, for in (B.34) each energy value (for a cubical box, $a = b = c$) is proportional to (volume)$^{-\frac{2}{3}}$ ($E = $ const $\times V^{-\frac{2}{3}}$). It follows by differentiation that

$$dE_i = -\frac{2}{3}\frac{E_i}{V}\,dV$$

Substituted into (C.39),

$$-p\,dV = -\frac{2}{3}\frac{1}{V}\left[\sum_i m_i E_i\right]dV$$

But the bracketed sum is simply the energy U; hence, by (C.38),

$$pV = \tfrac{2}{3}U = NkT \tag{C.40}$$

This is the familiar *equation of state of an ideal gas*, containing both Boyle's and Charles' laws.

One may use the same Boltzmann method to treat gas particles having a greater number of degrees of freedom than the three of an infinitesimal particle. For example, a diatomic (two-atom) molecule has six degrees of freedom, three coordinates to describe each atom. At sufficiently high temperatures so that molecular vibrational and rotational motion is strongly excited, the specific heat approaches $U/N = 3kT$. This equal contribution from each degree of freedom of the particle is termed *equipartition of energy*.

C.6 The Dense Fermi Gas

The Boltzmann approximation is applicable only to gases at low density. One *mole* (6.03×10^{23} molecules) of an ideal gas occupies 22,400 cm^3 at standard temperature and pressure, with a density $\approx$ 10^{19} molecules/cm^3. The valence electrons of a metal, being essentially free in their motion, may be regarded as a gas which is, always, nearly in equilibrium with the positive nuclei. For example, copper, with a density 8.9 g/cm^3 and atomic weight of 63.6, has one free valence electron per atom, and a density of $6.03 \times 10^{23}(8.9/63.3) = 8 \times 10^{22}$ electrons/cm^3. Boltzmann statistics do not well suit such a dense gas, as one may show by use of (C.37). While we can disregard the influence of electron interactions in altering the electronic wave functions of electrons in metals, we cannot disregard the exclusion principle. Simply stated, the electrons are so dense that at the lower energy levels they fill all the available electronic states, so that the approximation $m_i/n_i \ll 1$ is untenable.

The density-of-states distribution is the same as that for the ideal gas [(C.35)] with $2s + 1 = 2$ to account for the two spin states. The value of μ must now be derived from the exact Fermi distribution, using the integral

$$N = \int dm = \int_0^\infty \frac{n(E)\, dE}{1 + e^{(E-\mu)/kT}} \tag{C.41}$$

This integral is unwieldy, to say the least. Figure C.5 shows that if $\mu \gg kT$ (as we shall presume), the distribution $m(E)$ at zero temperature differs little from that at higher temperature. We can obtain $\mu(T = 0) = \mu_0$ very simply, for as the figure shows,

$$N = \int_0^{\mu_0} n(E)\, dE \tag{C.42}$$

Using (C.34), for unit volume ($abc = 1$) and doubling to account for the two spin states $s = \pm\frac{1}{2}$,

$$N = \frac{\pi}{3} \left(\frac{2m}{\pi^2 \hbar^2}\right)^{\frac{3}{2}} \mu_0^{\frac{3}{2}}$$
$$\mu_0 = \left(\frac{3N}{\pi}\right)^{\frac{2}{3}} \frac{\pi^2 \hbar^2}{2m} \tag{C.43}$$

Substituting $N = 8 \times 10^{22}$ cm^{-3} as appropriate for copper, we find μ_0 (copper) $\cong 10.7$ ev. The internal energy per electron can be found in the same way:

$$\frac{U(T = 0)}{N} = \frac{\int_0^{\mu_0} E^{\frac{3}{2}}\, dE}{\int_0^{\mu_0} E^{\frac{1}{2}}\, dE} = \frac{3\mu_0}{5} \tag{C.44}$$

The average energy per degree of freedom is $\mu_0/5$ even at $T = 0$, where classical equipartition predicts zero energy per particle. The *change* in Fermi energy μ as T increases will be very small, because of the small range of E where m_i/n_i [or $m(E)/n(E)$] is appreciably different from zero or one. Not only is the zero-point energy of the system extremely high, but specific heat c_v will be lower than predicted for a Boltzmann gas. The low electronic specific heat of metals is an important justification of Fermi-Dirac theory.

C.7   Bose-Einstein Statistics

Integral-spin or spinless entities satisfy *Bose-Einstein statistics*. In solid-state theory, the most important of these bosons are photons, phonons (vibrational waves), and magnons (waves of coupled-spin motion).

The derivation departs from the Fermi-Dirac treatment at the point at which one begins "putting balls into compartments" to find the number of distributions of m_i balls among the n_i different compartments, each belonging to a state of energy E_i. Each compartment (state) can accommodate *any* number of bosons. We must now count the number of distinguishable ways in which m_i indistinguishable balls may be placed in n_i compartments *without* restrictions on compartment occupancy. This count, according to permutation-combination theory,[1] is

$$\frac{(n_i + m_i - 1)!}{(n_i - 1)! m_i!} \tag{C.45}$$

The total number of distributions (system states) corresponding to sets of m_i bosons distributed among the n_i states of energy E_i is therefore

$$D = \prod_i \frac{(n_i + m_i - 1)!}{(n_i - 1)! m_i!} \tag{C.46}$$

The approximation for $\ln D$, using Stirling's approximation as in (C.17), leads to an undetermined-multiplier relation

$$\frac{\partial}{\partial m_i} \left[\sum_i (n_i + m_i - 1) \ln (n_i + m_i - 1) - (n_i - 1) \ln (n_i - 1) \right.$$
$$\left. - m_i \ln m_i - \alpha \sum_i m_i - \beta \sum_i E_i m_i \right]$$

Differentiating,

$$\ln (n_i + m_i - 1) - \ln m_i = \alpha + \beta E_i$$

Finally,

$$\frac{m_i}{n_i} = \frac{1}{e^{\alpha + \beta E_i} - 1 + 1/m_i} \cong \frac{1}{e^{\alpha + \beta E_i} - 1} \equiv \frac{1}{e^{(E_i - \mu)/kT} - 1} \tag{C.47}$$

The final approximation requires $m_i \gg 1$, a reasonable assumption in a large system.

The difference from the Fermi formula (C.32) is a negative sign in the denominator. This permits multiple occupancy of states for a range of energies $\mu < E_i < \mu + kT \ln 2$. Furthermore, μ must lie *below* all energies E_i, since negative m_i values are not physically meaningful. In the limit $\mu \ll -kT$, the Boltzmann approximation (C.33) is again valid.

For *particles* (such as helium atoms) obeying Bose statistics, the particle count in an isolated system must be constant; hence μ is derived from the limitation $\sum_i m_i = N$. The energy distributions of a Bose system at several temperatures are illustrated in Fig. C.8. As in the Fermi-Dirac system, the energy μ will be a function of temperature. At very low temperatures, it will approach asymptotically the lowest particle energy level E_1, so that all particles are found in this state. This might be described as a "condensation"

[1] *Ibid.*, p. 438.

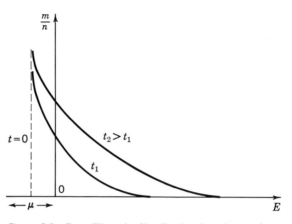

Figure C.8 Bose-Einstein distribution functions m/n for two temperatures, for a given value of μ. As in Fermi-Dirac systems, μ must be adjusted so that the area under the $m(E)$ curve equals the number of particles. If the bosons are not particles, but massless wave entities, μ will be zero.

of particles into the lowest-energy state. "Superfluid" phenomena such as superconductivity (exhibited by pairs of electrons coupled with spins canceling) are sometimes described thermodynamically in terms of such a condensation.

When the system consists of photons (as, for example, in an electromagnetic resonant cavity) or other massless waves, one may not apply a condition $\sum_i m_i = N$, for a single high-energy photon may be absorbed and reappear as a number of lower-energy photons or acoustical-wave quanta (phonons). Accordingly, for photons or phonons, the Bose statistics have the simpler form

$$\frac{m_i}{n_i} = \frac{1}{e^{E_i/kT} - 1} \tag{C.48}$$

A rectangular *electromagnetic cavity* will have resonant modes of the form

$$\mathcal{E} \propto \sin\frac{\pi i x}{a} \sin\frac{\pi j y}{b} \sin\frac{\pi k z}{c} \qquad i, j, k = 1, 2, 3, \ldots \tag{C.49}$$

(This is just the same form as the particle waves of Sec. B.3.) The solution of the wave equation $\nabla^2\mathcal{E} = -\omega^2\mathcal{E}/c^2$ requires

$$\left(\frac{i}{a}\right)^2 + \left(\frac{j}{b}\right)^2 + \left(\frac{k}{c}\right)^2 = \frac{\omega^2}{\pi^2 c^2} \tag{C.50}$$

By the same procedure as used in (C.34), the number of resonant modes in the frequency range $0 \rightarrow \omega$ is $(\pi/6)(\omega/\pi c)^3$. The two different polarizations of the $\mathcal{E}$ vector for each function (C.49) give distinguishable modes; hence the count should be doubled. The product of the Bose function (C.48), the density-of-states function $\frac{d}{d\omega}\left[\frac{\pi}{3}\left(\frac{\omega}{\pi c}\right)^3\right] = \frac{\omega^2}{\pi^2 c^3}$, and the energy per photon, $\hbar\omega$, gives the famous *Planck radiation formula*

$$W(\omega) = \frac{\hbar\omega^3}{\pi^2 c^3}\frac{1}{e^{\hbar\omega/kT}-1} \tag{C.51}$$

for the *radiation density* per unit volume, per unit (angular) frequency. This describes the thermal radiation density in any volume, regardless of boundary conditions, so long as the dimensions of the volume are substantially greater than the wavelength considered. For resonant modes whose wavelength is comparable with the dimensions, each mode is correctly described by (C.48), with $n_i = 1$.

GENERAL REFERENCES

A great many thermodynamics texts are available, of which the following represent but a small sampling. The interested reader may be wise to compare treatments in several texts. In general, only the more modern engineering-thermodynamics texts take a statistical-mechanics viewpoint.

Callen, H. B.: "Thermodynamics: An Introduction," John Wiley & Sons, Inc., New York, 1960. (A modern generalized treatment of the classical subject.)

Fast, J. D.: "Entropy," McGraw-Hill Book Company, New York, 1963. (Shows the application of thermodynamics to many physical processes.)

Landau, L. D., and E. M. Lifschitz: "Statistical Physics," Addison-Wesley Publishing Company, Inc., Reading, Mass., 1958.

Mayer, J. E., and M. G. Mayer: "Statistical Mechanics," John Wiley & Sons, Inc., New York, 1940.

Slater, J. C.: "Introduction to Chemical Physics," McGraw-Hill Book Company, New York, 1939. (Contains a brief introduction to statistical physics.)

Zemansky, M. W.: "Heat and Thermodynamics," 4th ed., McGraw-Hill Book Company, New York, 1957. (From a popular series of undergraduate texts.)

Index